A Private Life Of Henry James

Lyndall Gordon was born in Cape Town, South Africa and received her doctorate from Columbia University. Before becoming a full-time writer in 1995 she taught at St Hilda's College, Oxford. She is the author of a prize-winning two-part biography of T S Eliot, which has now been revised and published in one volume as *T.S. Eliot: An Imperfect Life*. Her other books include *Virginia Woolf: A Writer's Life* (winner of the James Tait Black Prize for Biography), *Shared Lives* – chosen by the *New York Times* as one of the most notable books of 1992 – and *Charlotte Brontë: A Passionate Life* which won the 1994 Cheltenham Prize. She lives in Oxford.

ALSO BY LYNDALL GORDON

Virginia Woolf: A Writer's Life
Shared Lives
Charlotte Brontë: A Passionate Life
T.S Eliot: An Imperfect Life

Lyndall Gordon

A PRIVATE LIFE OF HENRY JAMES

Two Women and His Art

VINTAGE

Published by Vintage 1999

2 4 6 8 10 9 7 5 3 1

First Published in Great Britain in 1998
by Chatto & Windus

Vintage
Random House, 20 Vauxhall Bridge Road,
London SW1V 2SA

Random House Australia (Pty) Limited
20 Alfred Street, Milsons Point, Sydney
New South Wales 2061, Australia

Random House New Zealand Limited
18 Poland Road, Glenfield,
Auckland 10, New Zealand

Random House South Africa (Pty) Limited
Endulini, 5A Jubilee Road, Parktown 2193, South Africa

Random House UK Limited Reg. No. 954009

A CIP catalogue record for this book
is available from the British Library

ISBN 0 09 938611 9

Papers used by Random House UK Ltd are natural, recyclable products made from wood grown in sustainable forests. The manufacturing processes conform to the environmental regulations of the country of origin

Typeset by Deltatype Ltd, Birkenhead, Merseyside
Printed and bound in Great Britain by

I think of her feverish earthly lot exchanged for this serene promotion into pure fellowship with our memories, thoughts and fancies.

Henry James (29 March 1870),
after Mary Temple's death

He cherishes for the silent . . . dead, a tenderness in which all his private need . . . finds a sacred, and almost secret, expression.

Henry James (29 September 1894),
after 'Fenimore's' death
(writing in her room)

For Linn Cary Mehta
in friendship

Contents

Illustrations

Between pages 180 and 181

28 Francis Boott as an old man, c. 1900. (By permission of the Houghton Library, Harvard University: f MS Am 1094 box 1)
29 Elizabeth Boott, friend of Minny, 'Fenimore', and Henry James. Portrait by Frank Duveneck. Cincinnati Art Gallery. (Photo by permission of the Houghton Library, Harvard University)
30 Palazzo Barbaro, Venice, owned by Daniel and Ariana Curtis, friends of Henry James. He used to write in the top-floor library looking this way.
31 Villa Castellani, Belloguardo, Florence. The Bootts lived there and, for a little while, 'Fenimore'.
32 Villa Brichieri, Bellosguardo, Florence. 'Fenimore' lived there from 1887–89, and James briefly in December 1886 and April–May 1887.
33 Constance Fenimore Woolson (from *Five Generations*, ed. Clare Benedict)
34 Casa Semitecolo, Venice, where Woolson died in 1994. (From *Five Generations* ed. Clare Benedict)
35 Woolson's grave in the Protestant Cemetery, Rome.
36 Clara and Clare Benedict. (Courtesy the Western Reserve Historical Society, Cleveland, Ohio)
37 James on the sands in Suffolk, 1897. (By permission of the Houghton Library, Harvard University: pf MS Am 1094)
38 Portrait of Henry James by Minny's niece Ellen Emmet Rand (1900). (Owned by Estate of Leon Edel and reproduced in the *Letters of Henry James and Edith Wharton*, ed. Lyall H. Powers)
39 John Chipman Gray at the time of his retirement as Professor of Law at Harvard. (Harvard Archives, Pusey Library)
40 Alice Howe James (Mrs William James) whose transcription of Minny Temple's letters survived their destruction by Henry James. (By permission of the Houghton Library, Harvard University: f MS Am 1092.9 (4598))

I
A Biographic Mystery

In April 1894, a middle-aged gentleman, bearing a load of dresses, was rowed to the deepest part of the Venetian lagoon. A strange scene followed: he began to drown the dresses, one by one. There were a good many, well-made, tasteful, and all dark, suggesting a lady of quiet habits and some reserve. The gondolier's pole would have been useful for pushing them under the still water. But the dresses refused to drown. One by one they rose to the surface, their busts and sleeves swelling like black balloons. Purposefully, the gentleman pushed them under, but silent, reproachful, they rose before his eyes.

The dresses belonged to a writer, widely read at that time, called Constance Fenimore Woolson. She was a great-niece of James Fenimore Cooper, author of *The Last of the Mohicans* (1826) and other frontier tales, and the first American writer to achieve world-wide fame. 'Fenimore', as she was known to choice friends, had combined Western vigour with the quiet manner of a patrician family strongly rooted in the New World. In 1879 she had settled in Europe, and a few months later met a fellow-expatriate, the distinguished but less popular novelist Henry James. The course of their long friendship was rudely broken when, on the night of 24 January 1894, Fenimore, aged fifty-three, had fallen to her death from her bedroom window in Venice.

A mystery has always surrounded this death, but James believed it was no accident. It was suicide. He, alone, was certain. What exactly it was that James knew of Fenimore which convinced him, remains obscure, blurred by his claims that Fenimore, contrary to appearance, had been mad – beyond help. The very urgency of his repeated denials of responsibility calls attention to their tie. So does his attempt to drown her clothes. Henry James was a bachelor of fifty-one at this time, with a high forehead, accentuated by receding hair and a high nose with the faintest bend to it. He had a mobile, sensitive mouth, with a fuller lower lip, firm, not petulant. It was exceptionally wide; parallel to the edge of his eyes. In repose, it would have shown a long line, slicing through the lower half of his face, had it not been hidden by a brown beard – a natural-looking growth, neither unruly nor too clipped. He dressed in English clothes with too much care to be an Englishman. Some thought he looked like a Russian count; others, a bishop. What friends noticed first were the eyes: light grey and extraordinarily keen (when they were not veiled by his lids), looking at them with complicit amusement or with scorching intensity as though he could see into their secret selves. He was known for explorations of the inward life: the unvoiced exchange and the drama of hidden motives. These were his skills, as well as a power, beyond that of any other man, to plumb the unknown potentialities of women. Two women, in particular, provoked his attention – a creative attention which claimed them through their untimely deaths.

Fenimore* was the second of these two women. The first was his cousin Mary Temple, known as Minny,† who had died in 1870 at the early age of twenty-four. Where Fenimore was part of his middle years in Europe, Minny had been the real-life 'heroine' of his youth in Newport, Rhode Island. James saw her as a free spirit, 'a plant of pure American growth', amongst the polished ladies of

* It is hard to know what to call a woman who was called different names by different people. Her family called her 'Connie'; acquaintances called her 'Miss Woolson'; her fiction and travel writings were signed 'Constance Fenimore Woolson'; academics nowadays call her 'Woolson'. Because she is an elusive character, I shall allow the name to shift as her situation changes. She will be called 'Fenimore' whenever this book treats her as a private person in relation to the people who called her by this name, and 'Woolson' whenever this book treats her as a writer. To use 'Fenimore' is not an endorsement of previous views of her. I share the view of those who call her 'Woolson', but it is inappropriate in a biography to call a child 'Woolson'; nor is it entirely appropriate to a well-bred nineteenth-century woman who would have expected to be called 'Miss Woolson'. The strongest argument for 'Fenimore' is that she liked it.

† Sometimes spelt 'Minnie'. Both 'Mary' and 'Minny' will be used as appropriate.

their time. The very air of Newport was 'vocal with her accents, alive with her movements'. Fenimore was free in a different way: a solitary, mature woman who pursued her ambitions with an intentness that matched his own. In her, James encountered the kind of writer with whom he might share, now and then, the privacy of the artist.

The freedoms of these two women went masked, as most nineteenth-century women were masked (whether they knew it or not) by the demands of social consensus: publicly, they fitted themselves to approved models of womanhood. Fenimore appeared to everyone as the needy gentlewoman she in fact was, and this helped to establish her in her career. Her need did her no harm with editors, who found they could combine profit with gallantry towards a lady with a widowed mother and broken-down brother. She disarmed editors and fellow-writers with modest, self-deprecating letters which go out of their way to stress how inferior was the fortune of a single woman who must write for her living to that of a cherished wife. It is uncertain to what extent she actually believed this in the loneliness she certainly endured, but her best stories subvert contemporary pieties about wifehood and womanly dependence. For herself, Fenimore was strong, serious, and determined to put her work first. She published fifty-eight stories (amongst them her best work), five novels, poems, and travel-writing.

Where the freedoms of Fenimore passed scrutiny in the guise of retiring gentlewoman, the freedoms of Mary Temple were acceptable in the guise of vivacious young girl. Intelligent men, all destined for public distinction, surround her in the woods of New Hampshire or on Newport verandahs. Their eyes follow her advance in her buttoned, high-necked dress. She holds her slight form erect as she hugs her arms. Her eagerness for ideas, her directness, and wide laugh showing all her teeth, seemed to Henry James the embodiment of innocence and untried youth. Yet, with others – his brother, the future psychologist William James, and a law graduate, John Chipman Gray – she was different: less playful, more troubled. Overwhelming questions about human possibility in the face of fate disturb her letters to these men. Why was she less serious towards Henry James? Why did she make fewer demands on her favourite, her 'dearest Harry', who was the fittest to gauge her depth?

Mary Temple left behind the mystery of those with promise who die young. An unfinished life cries out for form: this challenge took hold of James with Isabel Archer in *The Portrait of a Lady* (1881), Milly Theale in *The Wings of the Dove* (1902), and in a memoir he published in 1914. There was something uncategorisable in Minny. Like his brother William and other gifted men, he saw an uncommon spirit behind the girlish vivacity; but the uncommon was, of course, unwelcome to guardians of gender. Henry's mother – small-minded Mrs James, the ruling angel in the James house – deplored the expanse of Minny's laugh, while Henry's sister, Alice, seething with correct repression, scorned her eager response to every idea. Given the obscurity and brevity of her existence, it is hard to find the woman behind the fictions. Barring access is the safe label of girlish charm or the unsafe label of 'aggressive': one implies that Mary Temple knew her place as a woman; the other, that she did not. Yet her questions – a dying plea to James or query about the purpose of living – open up an order of existence not to be defined in reductive ways.

Fenimore began to publish in 1870, the year of Minny's death. Though she differed in many ways from Minny, she provided a second model of independence. Her looks displeased her, or so she said, but photographs reveal delicate features, curly hair, and a classic profile, set off by a narrow velvet band about her throat. As a 'local colorist' of the latter half of the nineteenth century, Constance Fenimore Woolson did participate in a genre going out of fashion at the time of her death, yet as a watcher of women's lives – the single woman, the exile, the artist – she now invites renewed attention. Her innovative fables of artists precede those of Henry James.

This biography will draw out these two women in their own terms, marking the points at which they intersect with the shaping consciousness of Henry James.* It is easy to see how he put his

* Both ties are long known. In a biography published in 1951, F. W. Dupee made a persuasive case for Minny's part in the fiction. Fenimore's friendship with James was known since her niece, Clare Benedict, published family memoirs in 1930. Further research in the 1960s by Leon Edel showed how some of James's

stamp on them, and made them 'Jamesian'. The mystery is why he kept them under wraps: his reasons for doing so, and for the weird behaviour which the circumstances of Fenimore's death provoked, remain to be uncovered. He did not forget them; on the contrary, they return obsessively in his works.

James is the most elusive and unwilling of subjects. He rejected the prospect of biography, not only to protect his privacy, but also, we might guess, because he was so much a biographer himself – he well knew the excitements and dangers of biographic power. He drew out others with intent curiosity. In his attaching way, he 'preyed ... upon living beings', as T. S. Eliot recognised. His experiments in human chemistry, 'those curious precipitates and explosive gases which are suddenly formed by the contact of mind with mind', have in them 'something terrible, as disconcerting as quicksand', which make the character he comes to know, 'uneasily the victim of a merciless clairvoyance'. His awareness of buried possibilities, the gifts of the obscure, and gaps between the facts, invites the infinite challenge of his own life.

To approach James at precisely the points he screened raises the issue of the biographer's right to know. Questionable as this is, it does grant access to a more compelling and dangerous character, as well as a new reading of the major novels and a host of puzzling tales. James was a man of secrets, sunk from sight a hundred years ago. Why did he lock away his photograph of Minny Temple? Why, when ten and a half thousand letters of Henry James were allowed to survive, did he make a pact with Fenimore to destroy their correspondence? No other such pact is known. And why, when Fenimore died, did he travel all the way to Venice to ensure secrecy in April 1894? Sinking her dresses at that time was not, I believe, a casual act, but sign of a strange bond which James guarded with discretion, and which suicide almost exposed. At the height of their relationship, in 1887, they shared a house on the hill of Bellosguardo near Florence. Few knew of this arrangement, and

greatest fictions grew out of this association. Edel's documentary research is valuable, but the view of Woolson has shifted away from a caricature of her as a 'plain' spinster hungry for romance, 'elderly' (though she was only three years older than James) and with an 'exalted notion of her own literary powers' (Edel, ii, 416–17).

it didn't last – one reason being the scope for scandal. Two other stays abroad were kept wholly secret, as were many short visits. And we might wonder, too, why James, as an old man, forty-four years after Mary Temple's death, destroyed a batch of her letters – philosophic letters, written with undimmed spirit in the face of death – after he had used what he wanted for his memoir.

Researchers are increasingly aware 'that interpretation has *already been built into* the documents allowed to survive'. Yet some residue of an alternative story does remain: amongst the leavings, four letters from Mary Temple to Henry James, and a large batch of her letters to John Chipman Gray, the ones James destroyed but Mrs William James had the forethought to copy before handing them over. Her copy is amongst the James papers at Harvard together with an unnoticed batch of letters from James to Minny's niece Bay Emmet, which bear on the closest fictional re-creation of Minny in *The Wings of the Dove*. In Ohio, there are two records of Fenimore's last days where facts fit with revealing clarity. Four letters from Fenimore to James in the early 1880s fell through the net, while many letters from Fenimore to others lie buried amongst the papers of various men of some importance in their day.

James's own letters are, for the most part, too public, too busy, too fulsome to give much away. Now and then, he cast off this social being with raging impatience. The crowded engagements, the comedies of manners in his letters and their effusions of fondness, were a façade for the private action of this most private of lives. His fables of a writer's life instruct us to start with the work. 'My dear sir, the best interviewer's the best reader' is the message of a literary lion for a pleading journalist. 'This last book . . . is full of revelations.'

'Revelations?' pants the journalist.

'The only kind that count. It tells you with a perfection that seems to me quite final all the author thinks . . .'

James tells us that he understood women almost better than we understood ourselves. 'You see what I am,' says the Jamesian woman to the Jamesian man who befriends her in one of the novels. Minny and Fenimore, and in a sicker way his brilliant sister, Alice, allowed James to 'see' their frustration, their fund of unused 'life', their alertness to the unspoken, and unanswered, passions – as though they had agreed to participate in the form he gave to the potent shadow in which women of the past lived; as though he understood, with them, that what is distinctive in women's lives is precisely what is hidden, not only from the glare of publicity, but from the daylight aspect which women present for their protection – or, it may be, for the protection of those who can't face what they are. James was irresistible to women because he met authenticity without fear, possessed himself of it, and put it out to play on the stage of his imagination. His knowing, supremely intelligent, ageless, and – yes – irresistible, is what makes James increasingly pertinent.

It was necessary to his purpose to engage certain women in ways which remain to be defined. The man who did so is not the socialite James who is exhaustively documented, nor the aesthete, nor the detached observer, nor the Anglicised expatriate – all faces of the legendary Master. Instead, we shall follow an inchoate, troubled man who remained in the making to the end of his life. As such he had two rules: art must have passion, and it must be hard as nails, 'hard as the heart of the writer'. This James is not passive; he is wilful, even ruthless, and stranger than he appeared respectably clothed under an umbrella of benevolence. The real James remained an American: a visionary moralist, he did not indulge in the European vogue for decadence. He was not a cynic. With him, virtue is seen to hold in a period when art-for-art's sake debunks Victorian morality, and Modernism with its array of ineffectual men – Prufrock, Petroushka, Chaplin's little tramp – takes the stage. The vision of James has outlived the disillusion of the twentieth century; as the Moderns move farther into the past, he is with us, more than ever our contemporary. Only now do we approach the kinds of manhood and womanhood he proposed, not viable in his own age, but possible – essential – in ours. A reinvention of manhood began with Civil War tales where wounded, dying men discover a higher form of manhood than may be found on the battlefield or in the drawing-room. He marked the capacity of men and women to transcend themselves in the face of mortality. The otherness of women made them a focus for an alternative to the pressure of wartime ideals of masculinity: this alternative manhood could take on qualities traditionally assigned to women.

James looked beyond the Woman Question, as it was framed in his time, the question of the vote and education in the nineteenth century, the question of professional advance in the twentieth century. When Isabel Archer 'affronts her destiny', she approaches the evolutionary frontier with the question of woman's nature, yet to be addressed. The depths of her nature are 'a very out-of-the-way place, between which and the surface, communication was interrupted'. James wished to promote the power of innocence, a conscious innocence without ignorance or naïvety. The twentieth century favoured *The Turn of the Screw* which toys with perversions of innocence, but his extraordinary women, Isabel Archer and Milly Theale, await a farther future – Milly's wings bear her beyond her lifetime.

The women who adored James and whom he came to know in his special way were not submissive, not the helpless muse. Minny and Fenimore had the strength not to relinquish their sense of being. Minny was freer, more familiar with James than anyone would be again. And Fenimore undertook a dialogue with him in stories that re-create him as a beguiling authority who proves a destroyer. Their friction fed on gender reinforced by the antagonisms of popular and high art.

Alone, it seems, Mary Temple and Constance Fenimore Woolson were bold enough to cross the uncrossable boundary of that private life. Somewhere lies the clue to what they gave him. Henry James was not shielding some form of love; he was fading out the ghostly companions of his art. And this may have been necessary because he did *not* acknowledge them, openly and visibly, as they perhaps wished and certainly deserved. If there was love, it was not the usual love of men and women but an intuitive closeness that remained unspoken.

We approach, here, ties more intimate than sex, closer than those of family and friends. Genius appears to soar above such ties, a lone phenomenon, but this is romantic myth, perpetuated by James himself in the rarefied solitude of a writer in 'The Private Life'. Genius, though, cannot emerge in a void. Here is a starting point: to challenge the myth of the artist with a truer story of what we might call, for want of a better word, collaboration. To some extent, of course, James invented himself, but he could not have written as he did without partners – female partners, posthumous partners – in that unseen space in which life is transformed into art.

2

To the Frontier

Stories of the James and Cooper families have often been told. Their descendants were to gain worldwide distinction, outstripping that of father or grandfather as the case might be. But less is known about the parts played by Constance Fenimore Woolson, born in 1840, and Mary Temple, born in 1845. Henry James spoke of Mary Temple in terms of 'noble flights', by which he meant a spontaneous freedom like the promise written into the American Declaration of Independence – something, he could not quite say, of that high order. Fenimore was also indefinable in ordinary terms. In photographs she averts her head. In what remains of her history, her back recedes through the woods, leaving no message where she is going.

All three were born within five years of each other in the early 1840s, but their stories go back to the end of the eighteenth century when two families established themselves in upstate New York. With the end of the Revolutionary War in 1783, the possibilities for expansion and enterprise were so favourable in the area of Albany, stretching westward, that the leading figures of these families became legends in their own lifetime. William Cooper, a wheelwright without money or property but with a taste for reading and a sense of adventure, became 'Judge Cooper of Cooperstown', the settlement he blocked out on the southern shore of Lake Otsego, the frontier, in 1786. William James, an Irish emigrant from Bailieborough in County Cavan, some fifty miles north-west of Dublin, who sailed to America in 1789, became 'Billy James of Albany'. By 1832 – the end of his life – he was one of the richest men in the state, leaving a net amount of $1,300,000, and vast tracts of the new state of Illinois as well as western New York stretching to Buffalo. He literally bought Syracuse, then a poisonous swamp, with a shrewd eye to its salt springs. The spoils of Syracuse were to aid his grandson Henry James through much of his writing career.

The wilderness of western New York, in the last years of the eighteenth century, was rather different from the popular image of the frontier at other times. In the seventeenth century, when colonists were carried off by native Americans, they internalised the wilderness in allegorical terms of trial, punishment, and salvation; in the nineteenth century, the frontier took its character from the loner, the scrambler, or trickster. But William Cooper went to the frontier with an eighteenth-century ideal of fraternity. He meant to bring together a close-clustering society based on responsible bonds of interdependence, commerce, and shared prosperity. It was part of his masterplan, in fact, to resist any impulse to self-reliance, by refusing to sell larger lots to townsmen: in his view, the blacksmith should get on with his trade and not waste time trying to grow his own vegetables. He does not own this in his record, but his theory nearly wrecked a precarious settlement in the winter of 1788–9 when famine set in. There came a point when 'not a morsel of bread' was left, and settlers resorted to living off wild leeks and maple syrup. His story has the plot of a Western: two hundred families are saved by a huge shoal of herrings which arrives miraculously in the Susquehanna River.

American myth took off in this place. There was the myth of an uninhabited wilderness, though in actual fact the land had been wrested from Iroquois peoples displaced from hilltop settlements where women had conducted a flourishing agriculture – women's work did not impress the invaders as a claim to land. The diminishing Iroquois were then devastated during the war by American raids in 1779, and abandoned by their British allies in 1783. At the heart of the myth of the untrammelled wilderness stalked a mythical character whom Constance Fenimore Woolson was to call 'the most original creation in American literature': the wandering backwoodsman who precedes the settlers. James Fenimore Cooper, the Judge's son, created this figure as Natty Bumppo, bonded in spirit and the dignity of nature to his red brother, Chingachgook or Great 'Sarpent'. Chingachgook has the virtues 'of a man', these virtues being the alacrity with which he 'did lay about him like a man!' in fights with enemy tribes. 'I met him', Natty recalls admiringly, 'with eleven Mingo scalps on his pole.' The westward footsteps of the shifting woodsman move 'far towards the setting sun – the foremost in that band of pioneers who are opening the way for the march of the nation across the continent'.

On the heels of the lone woodsman comes the practical man with ready fists in the cause of civilisation – the image the Judge projects in his own story. *A Guide in the Wilderness* (1810), written in his fifties, tells the primordial frontier story with the unfussed brevity of a man of action:

> In 1785 I visited the rough and hilly country of Otsego, where there existed not an inhabitant nor any trace of a road; I was alone three hundred miles from home, without bread, meat, or food of any kind; fire and fishing tackle were my only means of subsistence. I caught trout in the brook, and roasted them on the ashes. . . . I laid me down to sleep in my watch-coat, nothing but the melancholy Wilderness around me. In this way I explored the country, formed my plans of future settlement and meditated upon the spot where a place of trade or a village should afterwards be established.

Other land agents had failed, the Judge thought, because they rented land instead of selling it. By offering a poor man a hundred acres and an encouraging mortgage, he hoped to give him a permanent stake in the settlement's future: 'He then feels himself, if I may use the phrase, a man upon record. His views extend themselves to his posterity. . . . His spirit is enlivened; his industry quickened; every new object he attains brings a new ray of hope and courage . . .'

These are men's stories. Women are invisible or peripheral, locked in the dominant plot of enterprise and political battle. Beyond that plot, their lives and feelings are not on record, as though they had no meaning in their own right; there is not a word on the experience of women in William Cooper's account of his settlement, though without women such a community could not have existed. At the age of twenty, in 1774, he had eloped with Elizabeth Fenimore, a Quaker heiress from Burlington, New Jersey, because her father opposed the match. William's deep laugh as he 'lightened his way with his anecdotes and fun', his sweet voice, songs, and 'fine, rich eye', had the appeal of conviction. His impudence sat easily on a rather innocent face, round and pleasant; though tall, his manner was not overbearing, his purpose contained by an air of repose, reflecting the genial and eloquent confidence of the foremost revolutionary gentlemen. Like them, he acted on his ideas.

He believed that a frontier settlement could work only if he lived amongst his settlers – he did think of them as 'my' settlers on 'my' land, though legally they owned their holdings. By November 1790, he was ready to move his wife, seven children, two slaves, and five servants (including a man to run the store) from the long-settled Burlington to the remote Cooperstown whose main street was filled with tree stumps. At the last moment, so the story goes, when the wagon was piled high with household goods and the children had climbed aboard, Elizabeth could not bear to go. Seated on a remaining chair – a Queen Anne chair which had belonged to her father – she would not hear her husband's arguments. So, being the man he was, he lifted her, still in the chair, and carried her to the waiting wagon. A family wit interpreted this as a ploy to retain his father-in-law's library chair. There is no record of her helplessness (for was it not the duty of wives to accompany their husbands?). All we know for certain is that she was borne off along muddy, rain-soaked trails; that she carried a baby, the future James Fenimore Cooper, born in 1789; and that she had one more child in 1792. In the manner of wilful men who like to think well of themselves, her husband hoped to console her for the loss of civilisation with a dramatic gesture: he had the latest musical invention, an enormous early form of barrel organ (designed as a piece of domestic furniture), lugged through miles upon miles of woods to grace her drawing-room.

There is a glimpse of her ten years later in a letter written by her elder daughter, Hannah: 'It is very late at night – nobody in the house up, save myself and mama, who is playing upon the organ. The amusement engages her every night after the family have separated . . .'.

Did it cheer her? She did mind her husband's long absences in Albany, New York, and Washington when he went into politics.

She sent messages (she could not write) begging him to return: she was 'weakly & very low-spirited'; she was 'desirous that you should engage a House at Burlington before your return as it is her determination never to spend another winter in this Country'. In 1798 her husband did buy the house in Burlington; then, a month later, she returned to Otsego. James Fenimore Cooper believed this was a sacrifice for her children, who missed the landscape of the frontier; another notion is that it was a response to the death of her youngest child in Burlington. And there is yet another possibility: it is in the nature of exile to dream of a return and to find it impossible in reality, for the past is no longer there, and the exile no longer the person who left. The Judge tried to appease her with a grand brick Hall built to his own design between 1796 and 1799, but as the years passed she was increasingly reclusive.

The sole residual fact, coming down to us from their son James, is that his mother was the last of the Fenimores, and when she came to die, eventually, in 1816 or 1817 (even the date of her death is obscure), she cared enough to beg him to exchange the name of Cooper for Fenimore. By the time he attempted to do so, in 1826 when he was departing for an extended stay in Europe, he had already published *The Spy*, *The Pioneers*, and *The Last of the Mohicans* under the name of Cooper. The legislature at Albany therefore refused to allow him to abandon his name, but ruled that 'Fenimore' might be added.

Constance Fenimore Woolson, a great-granddaughter of Elizabeth Fenimore, also remains obscure – in her case, deliberately so. She was as determinedly private as Henry James: a pact with her sister to destroy their letters suggests that her pact with James to do the same would have pleased her, for it freed her writing to a distinguished man whose papers would pass to posterity. Though she was widely known to readers of her time, her name faded. In February 1995, when I visited a restored boarding house in St Augustine, Florida, where she stayed in the mid-1870s, the guides had not heard of her. This blank was repeated in nearly every archive. And yet, back in 1884, James wrote to his friend and fellow-novelist William Dean Howells, 'You are the only English novelist I read (except Miss Woolson) . . .'. To see this woman, to enter the fogs and labyrinths of her fiction, and hear its soundless pain, we must open up a space between the facts.

There is, on the other hand, the physical fact of the American frontier moving inexorably westward, from Albany on the Hudson River, to Cooperstown in 1786, and onwards to Cleveland on Lake Erie in 1796. There, in Fenimore's childhood in the 1840s, she saw the frontier stretch to the remoter waterways of the Great Lakes, with their island outposts and terrifying winters, as the Western Reserve became the industrialised states of Ohio and Michigan. And then there is the apparently disconnected fact that Henry James, at one point in his irreproachable existence, risked scandal by living alone with an unmarried woman. Though he was too sophisticated to be secretive – after all, they were within easy reach of Florence with its large expatriate community of literary lion-hunters – James did not see any reason to mention this arrangement in letters to his family except once as a matter of convenience. What, if anything, connects the American frontier and the Europeanised convergence of Fenimore and James on the hill of Bellosguardo in 1887?

When Fenimore began writing for publication she often chose frontier settings, under the aegis of 'Uncle Fenimore'; later, she took up the Jamesian drama of Americans in Europe. She was, then, a mediator between these traditions, linking James with native grit. She embodied the independent, endlessly shifting America of the frontier – the real America, some would say – otherwise beyond his reach. Wandering, adventurous, she offered James an imaginative gain of this kind. His father, Henry James Sr, churned out unreadable philosophical tomes, overblown with verbosity; for all his ambitious high-mindedness, he simply could not compare as a predecessor with Fenimore Cooper. So Fenimore, as James persisted in calling her, had an importance for him that extended beyond simple regard; she mattered as a frontiering extension to his far-reaching self.

The vital edge of Fenimore's America was not primarily that of men; she rewrote the edge of existence in terms of women. In Cooper's novels women are beauties clinging to men as they are carried through war-torn woods; fifty years later, his great-niece parodies Cooper in 'St Clair Flats' (1873), where all the men are ineffectual in the wilderness and dependent on Roxana, a sturdy woman from Maine who has created a domestic refuge there. She supports her husband, an idle, self-absorbed visionary who, long ago, had been an object of senseless instinct – she had thrown herself at him ('a-crying with my hair down, and my face all red and swollen'). This is reality, not Cooper romance: Roxana now seems 'commonplace' – her dress limp, her hands roughened, and her small, dull eyes, as she thinks of her buried child, struggling 'to express the grief that lies within, like a prisoner behind the bars of his small dull window'. The 'commonplace' fits the findings of de Tocqueville: 'In the utmost confines of the wilderness I have often met young wives, brought up in all the refinement of life in the towns of New England, who have passed almost without transition from their parents' prosperous houses to leaky cabins in the depths of the forest. Fever, solitude, and boredom had not broken the resilience of their courage. Their features were changed and faded, but their looks were firm. They seemed both sad and resolute.'

Where Cooper fixed on the physical dangers of the wilderness, Woolson turned to mental dangers: the vacancy of lives locked off from all contact with the outside world by months of ice; the emotional constrictions of self-reliance; the small-mindedness of those who entrench themselves in a conventionality which secures them from question, but leaves them warped; and, not least, the capitulation of almost all free-minded women to matrimony. Her view of this plot could not be bleaker, as it glides into place with ominous inevitability under cover of the blandness which was her sop to sentimental readers and magazine editors (on whom she depended for her living). Her almost unrelenting darkness can be traced to an extraordinary series of family tragedies.

Judge Cooper's two daughters, Hannah and Ann, were educated at New York schools, and with their intelligence and loveliness the two girls proved a blessing to him, unlike his eldest son, William, expelled from Princeton, or his youngest son, James, withdrawn from Yale (at the request of the College) and sent to sea. Hannah, brilliant, yellow-haired, evoked verses in her honour from the urbane French emissary Talleyrand. She was her father's favourite companion when he travelled to New York. In September 1800, aged eighteen, she was riding to visit a young neighbour called Morris, when she was thrown by her horse: her head was flung against a tree; her neck broken. The Judge wrote a verse for her grave which calls her 'Thou more than daughter of my fondest care'; she was his 'kindred soul'.

Her younger sister, Ann, named her second daughter Hannah. The name pleased the Judge, who designated the child his future comfort, but as it happened he died the following year. Hannah, the namesake, was born in 1808 in the two-storey stone house, Pomeroy Place, which the Judge had built for Ann and her husband, George Pomeroy, on the corner of River Street and Main Street in Cooperstown, after their marriage in 1803. Some years earlier he had built a stone wall on the west side of River Street, which never held firm. James Fenimore Cooper told his children – Hannah's generation – that behind this wall sat an Indian who resented it. A new owner of the plot decided to replace the bulging wall, but when it came down, the story goes, there sat an Indian skeleton, gaunt and hollow-eyed, with his chin on his knees, and about him his pots and weapons. He was left in place, but the new masonry wall, a stay against his anger, duly cracked for all to see. In Hannah's lifetime, the town was thick with ghosts, especially River Street with its overhanging trees, favoured by the dead when the unlit village was wrapped in silence – the only sound the croak of frogs.

The Historical Society in Cooperstown owns an old notebook with a mottled brown cover and leather spine. Its original owner, one Mary Morris Cooper, has dated it May 24th 1826. This book passed to Hannah Pomeroy, who was eighteen in 1826. She cut the used pages, tried out various signatures on the flyleaf, and at the back copied out the inscription from Hannah Cooper's tomb. The notebook is filled with death, as if the owner felt fated by her name. She opens with a poem by William Cullen Bryant whose message is to approach the grave deliberately so that it does not snatch one like a runaway slave.

Hannah was not morbid by nature: humour pervades a journal written after her marriage in 1830 to Charles Jarvis Woolson. Their first years were spent with his family in Claremont, in the hill country of western New Hampshire. The journal spoofs her New

England in-laws: the grim father, Thomas Woolson, who sat in silence at meals, and her first Thanksgiving, broken up by the abruptness with which every single member of the family (including her new husband) escaped, each to his own pursuit, leaving her, a stranger amongst them, to shed a few tears in her room. Though she complied with custom out of courtesy, she was not submissive, nor spare of flesh or words, nor given to moral pulse-taking. She remained unabashed by her lack of interest in the minutiae of domesticity.

A portrait of Hannah shows a handsome, dark-haired woman, the strong column of her neck rising from the narrow square of her dress edged with a narrow film of white lace. The simplicity of dress and hair offsets her statuesque features: the shapely, almost tactile substance of her lips, the sheen of her warm cheek, her darkly luminous gaze. This woman had a bodily presence, a rounded physical ease, glowing, dignified. In the summer of 1839, at the age of thirty-one and pregnant with the child who was to become Constance Fenimore Woolson, she took this portrait to Cooperstown, as she records in her journal: 'I am pleased to find that my portrait is generally liked. Uncle Fenimore calls it an excellent likeness . . .'.

A journey from New Hampshire was not undertaken lightly when, as yet, the railroad stretched only seventeen miles from Albany to Schenectady. The Woolsons travelled for several days by coach via Bennington, Vermont, and Troy; a few miles beyond Schenectady, Hannah rejoicing to see the Mohawk Valley open out before them. Taking possession of her old room at Edgewater, a large house occupied by her elder sister, she greeted 'dear, dear Otsego lake, with its beautiful bays, its projecting points and wooded hills and mirror-like waters'. James Fenimore Cooper called it the Glimmerglass in *The Deerslayer* (1841) 'seeing that its whole basin is so often fringed with pines, cast upward from its face; as if it would throw back the hills that hang over it'. At her mother's, Hannah 'tried again the swing in the garret' and 'took tea from the same old fashioned blue china cups' with numbers of callers. She returned calls to houses called Woodside, Apple Hill, and Doughnut Hall, renowned for its baking. 'Cooperstown is the most hospitable place I know of,' she thought. Her welcome included a boating picnic to Three Mile Point, where they heard the echo of 'the Lady of the Rock' – to Hannah, a familiar and benign call, but frightening to her four-year-old daughter, Annie. On 8 August her father, George Pomeroy, celebrated his sixtieth birthday: Hannah records a feast of roast ducks, broiled chickens, boiled chickens, new potatoes, corn, succotash, squash, onions, bread pudding, raspberry pie, strawberry tarts, and champagne, which was followed by an evening tea at Uncle Fenimore's. Calling included a visit to the family burial ground 'to look at the last resting places of those we loved in life. I often think', she adds, 'how short a time it may be ere I too am laid under the shadow of the old stately pines.' Occasionally, Hannah kept to her room with the ills of early pregnancy.

Although childbirth had its perpetual hazards, she produced six girls without mishap between 1831 and 1840 – her only regret that she had no son. But six months after that happy summer and two days after she gave birth to her sixth child, the dread disease of scarlet fever hit the household.

Constance Fenimore Woolson was born on 5 March. Within a month, the three middle girls lay dead – Gertrude, aged four, and Julia, aged two, died on 22 and 24 March; then Annie, aged five, died on 3 April. The newborn was protected by her mother's immunity, and the two eldest, Georgiana and Emma, aged nine and seven, recovered. Hannah was in a state of collapse – almost demented. Her husband was advised to remove her from the scene of death.

In the fall of 1790, Elizabeth Fenimore had been lifted bodily on to the wagon heading for the frontier of western New York. Fifty years later, in the fall of 1840, her granddaughter Hannah was helped into a coach, bound for the Great Lakes. Where Elizabeth had left home in a state of protest, her granddaughter left in stricken inertia – en route for the unknown. Her furniture followed in the spring: a mahogany bed; a sewing table with twisted legs and a deep, rounded drawer which had been a wedding present; a wardrobe which was once a bookcase from Cooperstown. So it was that the Woolsons took their path to the West where there were no associations. They took off into the unstoried distance, the coach rolling away from a row of three identical graves in Claremont, New Hampshire. Behind them they left, also, all the props of family and the familiar faces of Claremont and Cooperstown. And with them went that baby who grew up to be a loner who would turn her back on familiar people again and again.

Cleveland, where they settled, was a 'Forest-City' (as Hannah called it) with a population of six thousand in 1840, not yet industrialised but no longer the frontier. Charles Jarvis Woolson established an iron foundry and manufactured stoves. The family's first home was on Rockwell Street, opposite the post office; then on the corner of Prospect and Perry Streets, known as 'Cheerful Corner'; and afterwards they lived in the Kelley house on Euclid Avenue, a large stone house with a porch, the setting for Woolson's prizewinning story for children, *The Old Stone House* (1873).

In Cleveland, three more children were born to Charles and Hannah: first Clara in December 1841, then Alida, who died aged one in 1843. Alida's 'lovely, caressing ways' was the only characterisation of a dead child that ever came from Hannah's tight lips. Her journal laments 'a year of grief and anguish ... in our sorely smitten household'. Those who had known Hannah before her children died said that she was never the same. At last, after eight girls, the longed-for son, Charley, was born in 1846. Congratulations poured in with verses in his honour and predictions of wonderful things a boy would accomplish. Years later, when Charley was always in trouble, Hannah recalled his birth in early September as a time 'when flies buzzed and mosquitoes stung'. The boy cried loudly, refused to be petted, and wanted toys that made a noise.

Hannah sang Scottish ballads to her more receptive girls: 'I used to sit on one arm of the old rocking chair,' Clara recalled, 'Connie on the other arm, Mother's arms holding us on, and the toe of her slipper just touching the floor to keep the chair rocking in time ...' There is a photograph of the sisters, aged nine and seven, facing the camera solemnly in 1849 in dresses with scooped necks, gathered from shoulder to waist. Their long ringlets fall from their centre partings – Connie's pushed back behind her ears. She sits rather stiffly, with her hand closed upon her lap, her mouth tight, and her rather fey, slanted eyes facing the camera with a gravity beyond her years. She was called 'And Why' because she asked so many questions. Clara is fair, more languid as she leans against her sister. She has her mother's shapely lips, rounded eyes, and tactile presence with exposed shoulders – the unconsciously nubile little-angel of so many nineteenth-century photographers. Clara has the flat prettiness of a child who is content to be looked at; Connie is already a person – but what that person may be is elusive. She is more than self-contained; in order to face the camera, she has locked herself away.

Their father encouraged their powers of observation. He would interrogate his daughters, and when he would say to Clara, 'is that all you saw?' she felt shamed. Both daughters were to be keen note-takers abroad; their avidity for 'Europe', a sign of superiority amongst Americans of that time, was also implanted by their father. By the age of eleven, Connie had 'a very strong desire to see the old world'. She wrote to a schoolfriend who was taken abroad: 'I wish I could be in "exile" too, if I could visit the most beautiful and famous places the world can show!' She did not 'care to be forced into quiescence yet awhile. But whether we will or no, we *are* quiet to the depths of stagnation . . . I am Rhine-mad . . .'. In her copy of Hawthorne's Italian novel, *The Marble Faun*, she read of a wish gradually absorbing all of one's life: 'Yes; for instance, Europe!' she scribbled in the margin.

She flared up, backed by Clara, when her father remarked, 'Only one woman in a thousand is logical.'

He conceded with mocking lameness: 'both Connie and you, Clara, are logical.'

In contrast to the Coopers, Mr Woolson was as unremarkable as his forebears. The Woolsons were proud to go back to seventeenth-century New England. But though nothing unworthy appears in their records, there is nothing of interest either beyond the fact that Eleanor H. Porter, the creator of Pollyanna, was a third cousin, and that in about 1818 Connie's grandfather, Thomas Woolson, invented the first iron cooking stove that had any success. In 1828 he was elected state senator, supporting the Eastern patrician John Quincy Adams against the frontier democrat Andrew Jackson. There was a vein of gloom in the Woolsons as well as a rigorous work ethic which Connie inherited, and which may have bound her to her father. Both were depressed by cold, and Mr Woolson used to warn his daughters that occupation was the way to fight it. 'Now you are just beginning life', he said, 'and I can tell you that wherever you live there will be rain, snow, fog, and cold; *don't* let it cloud you, have things to do when it does rain, and don't grumble.'

He seems to have been more didactic than inspiring – an instigator of worthy goals. Nowhere is there a suggestion that he encouraged his daughter's writing. It was Hannah who passed on the verbal facility, and when Connie selected the pen-name of 'Fenimore', briefly at the outset of her career, she aligned herself with her maternal inheritance. It is telling what she recalled of her father many years later: not his mind, nor his influence, but his extraordinary capacity to love her despite her conviction that she was unlovable – this memory filled her with intense and almost pathetic gratitude.

Childhood summers were marked by returns to Cooperstown, a family base that was to remain for Connie a place to which she might, one day, return. Her favourite aunts, unmarried daughters of Fenimore Cooper, lived at Byberry Cottage on River Street. They were called 'the girls' (until they protested in their sixties). In 1850, Aunt Susan, who was Cooper's assistant and a great raconteur, published her own work, *Rural Hours*, a chronicle of village life during 1848. There was an encompassing domesticity to those summers in Cooperstown where women, rooted in extended families, exchanged daily calls, recipes for raspberry vinegar and indelible ink, and advice on how to cure skins with the wool on or keep a gun from rusting. At Pomeroy Place there was a cellar with bunks for runaway slaves, part of the underground railroad, a network of safe houses in the 1840s and 1850s for slaves trying to reach Canada where the British Act of Emancipation became the law from 1833. (It remained part of family lore that the Judge had freed his slave, Joseph Stewart, who as a 'faithful free servant' was eventually buried in the family plot.)

A few blocks away, the focal point of Cooperstown, lived famous Uncle Fenimore and his wife, Susan De Lancey, who came from a Tory family which had been pro-British during the Revolutionary War. (Her sister, who had been in England during the war, had refused to return to an independent America, and had married McAdam, the road-maker.) The couple lived at Otsego Hall, now oddly renovated with Gothic crenellations in imitation of Abbotsford, the seat of Cooper's friend and model Sir Walter Scott. For Connie, Otsego was haunted by Cooper's scenes; she saw, 'at dusk, the campfires of the Iroquois gleam from the gravelly points of the eastern shore', and Natty 'gliding in his canoe'. She learnt to row, and as she grew stronger it was her habit to row for miles – first, Otsego; later, inlets in Florida, infested with snakes and alligators, where no human had ever been. She went alone, part of her wandering, intrepid existence – a female Natty.

At school, the Cleveland Female Seminary, she was singled out by her teacher, Linda Guilford, an early graduate of Mount Holyoke, the first women's college in America. Miss Guilford read out weekly essays during her Wednesday composition class, and a fellow-pupil recalled the flush of pleasure on Connie's face when the circle of listeners broke into applause. As an advocate of Temperance, Miss Guilford's style was excessively fervent, but she served as a model for the new breed of professional woman. Her pupils read *Corinne, ou l'Italie* (1807), a novel about a woman writer who finds glory in an Italy of dreamland. Her genius is manifest more in her impetuous ardour than in her craft. Corinne's talk is brilliant, as was that of her creator, Mme Anne-Louise-Germaine de Staël (1766–1817), identified with Corinne and visited by the foremost men of the age: Jefferson, Goethe, Talleyrand, and Napoleon (who found her sufficiently dangerous to exile her from Paris). Most gifted girls in the nineteenth century had that dream of independence called Corinne – including Margaret Fuller in the early 1840s, whom Emerson called the 'Yankee Corinna', Kate Chopin 'the Corinne of St Louis', and the actress Fanny Kemble (who wished to write more than act) – and none wanted this more than quiet Connie Woolson of Cleveland, whose great-grand-father, Judge Cooper, had corresponded with Mme de Staël after the death of her father, Jacques Necker (banker of Geneva and finance minister to Louis XVI), with whom the Judge had a partnership in Canadian land.

Adolescence was marked by another bout of tragedy. In

September 1850, when Connie was ten, her eldest sister, Georgiana (often called Georgie), married Samuel Livingstone Mather, who founded an Iron Mining Company in 1847. He came from a distinguished line of Puritan divines, and his grandfather Samuel Mather (1745–1809) had been a director of the Connecticut Land Company which first surveyed the Western Reserve. Soon after this marriage, the second Woolson sister, Emma, became obsessed with a handsome, sick minister, the Revd Timothy Jarvis Carter. At the age of eighteen, she was determined to marry him. Her parents sent Emma off to school. There, she pined so badly that her parents gave way, and she was married in May 1851. The next we hear of her, in August 1851, is that she had not slept for twelve weeks, nursing her husband; he died of tuberculosis and Emma caught the disease. A widow of nineteen, she returned to her parents' home, much changed – even her voice had changed – and when she was dying in 1852, she asked for her sisters: Connie, aged twelve, and Clara, aged ten, were brought to her bedside, where their stricken mother sat.

Georgie had been a lively child, a favourite with Cooper, who had called her 'Romping Granite'. As a young woman she tossed off cheerful, rather clumsy rhymes. Suddenly, in the middle of her second pregnancy, in July 1853, a rhyme for her husband on his thirty-fifth birthday sounds a different note: in the mirror, she looks 'forlorn' and 'changed', so much so he might well disown her. She cannot summon strength, coughs, and pants when she climbs a hill. Georgie died of tuberculosis on 3 November 1853, four months after the birth of Katherine (known as Kate). Connie was then thirteen. The Mathers were to be her only tie to Cleveland, largely because Georgie's children remained there.

The teenage Connie walked for miles, with more affinity for rocks, precipices, and the dense undergrowth of the woods than for society. She lived from the winter of 1840–1 until the early 1870s in Cleveland – more than thirty years – and no attachment beyond the family remained from that time and, apart from one teacher, nothing much in the way of friendship. Instead, her lasting bond was with Mackinac Island in Upper Michigan in the straits between Lake Huron and Lake Michigan, near the Canadian border, where the Woolsons began to summer from the time she was fifteen. At this age she still wore her hair falling in long ringlets from a centre parting: the dark curls falling over a wide lace collar and the delicate features – a small nose, wide eyes, and perfectly even mouth – present an image of romantic purity. During her second summer at Mackinac, when she was sixteen, she was gripped by Thomas Moore's ballad 'The Lake of the Dismal Swamp' about a posthumous love affair. The forlorn hero follows a 'death-cold maid' to the Dismal Lake where he hears her paddling her 'white canoe'. After his death they paddle together.

Within the family, the bond was strongest with her father. She accompanied him on business to the shores of Lake Superior, through the farming districts of the Western Reserve, and up and down the Ohio Valley. Cleveland was within reach of the thinly populated islands of the Lakes, stretching to the wilds of the Northwest Territory. These were settings for her early stories of people fighting their way through winters – storm, fog, ice, appalling cold – calling forth ingenuity or bare endurance. In one story, the roughs lose their respect for a female preacher when she falls in love. The men feel betrayed by her desire: if she's not above it – 'our Lady' in her dove-coloured dress and hair-concealing cap, who is 'dropped from heaven' – then she's nothing, 'only a woman like any other'.

In accordance with family tradition, Connie was sent to a finishing school in New York. Mme Chegaray's was a French school dominated by Southern girls, daughters of Old Virginia and Carolina families who ruled their neighbourhoods. They introduced themselves grandly as 'The Daughters of Carolina', to the astonishment of the new pupil, one of only three Northerners, '(who had never thought of styling herself "The Daughter of Ohio")'. Connie observed the languor of her schoolmates with the amusement of her mother observing the rigidity of New England. Once, a Southerner called to a cleaner two floors below to come up and shut her bedroom door rather than shut it herself. In winter, to each of these girls there came, by express, great boxes containing four large black plum cakes, thickly iced, made by slave cooks. The girls thought nothing of eating solid wedges, weighing a pound or two, every day. They were proud of their feet and boasted that water could run under their insteps. The experiment was tried in the dormitory to the discomfiture of Connie, who took her revenge by pointing to her wide forehead and remarking that Northerners were 'not in the habit of carrying their brains in their heels!'

At Mme Chegaray's she became proficient in French, her first step towards a life in Europe. She graduated in 1858 at the top of her class in languages, music, and botany.

As a young woman, she carried out her father's plan for an extended tour of the eastern seaboard. Clara's memory of her sister as a social winner does not ring true, but it does tell us about the marriage market. Connie seems to have shielded herself with a sheaf of paper and a bottle of ink; carrying these about one morning, she spilled ink over a fine new dress. With outward politeness and inward determination, she wrote every morning during this expensive tour. There is no suggestion that any man singled her out; no proposals. She was reserved but not cold: she owned to a passionate nature, coexisting with an absolute and perhaps withering conviction that no man could match her idea of love.

When, exactly, did she decide not to marry? Did the deaths of her older sisters when she passed through puberty bear on this decision? In so far as she took a position, it was the standard line that marriage provided the only happiness for women. When a Cleveland friend became engaged, she wrote: 'A man's true, earnest love is a great gift. If you do not accept it and enjoy it, I shall – shake you! . . . Everything else is trivial compared to it. You and he are really alone in the world together. Two souls in love always are.' Her most eligible years, from twenty-one to twenty-five, coincided with the Civil War: men of her own age marched off and died. After Clara's marriage to George Stone Benedict when Connie was twenty-eight, she saw herself 'a desolate spinster', adding, 'I have drawn myself into my shell . . .'.

What she said, though, is not to be taken at face value. She was a devotee of Browning's impersonations. A persistent enigma lurks behind her performance of unlovability. It was enacted so repeatedly that she came to believe in her lack of appeal, an image contradicted by all her photographs. One, with hair drawn back, shows a tilted chin, a shy hint of a smile, and those mysterious slanted eyes. The sculptor Horatio Greenough, who modelled a bust of her after an illness when her hair had fallen out and then regrown in curls all over her shapely head, called her 'my lovely boy'. Why, then, call herself 'an ugly woman'? Later photographs show a womanly bloom; she was, if anything, even more lovely in her mature blend of softness and strength. With any other woman, it might be argued that self-deprecation invited reassurance, but she spoke explosively with the bitterness of suppressed feeling. The implication, as in her stories, is that men prefer a frail empty-head of transient prettiness.

Gradually, family ties became her stronghold against the whole outer world with its social distractions and impossible norms of womanhood. She might be said to have been a native of her family – more so, in fact, than Henry James was a native of the James family (in his brother's well-known phrase). James always embedded himself in a wider social network that provided a context for his fiction; Constance Fenimore Woolson was more exclusive and excluding, and more rigorous about her rules. As far as other writers were concerned, she preferred letters to meetings. Until she met Henry James, she admitted no one to the privacy of her writer's life.

The writer who emerges from this story was a child of tragedy. Her birthday, each year, began a month-long anniversary of three sisters' deaths. Given her unfortunate place in the sequence of children, she had been at the centre, though not the focus, of a mother's nightmare. Twelve to thirteen years later, at the outset of adolescence, she had witnessed the deaths of her eldest sisters as they ventured on marriage. In her early twenties, from 1861 to 1865, men of her generation were cut down in close-fought battles. These cruelties of fate (as she would have seen them, for she was not religious) shaped a stoic and solitary. Nothing is known of her activities during the war; there is an odd blank in her twenties – at a guess, she was writing early versions of the stories she was to publish rapidly in her thirties. She may also have resented her mother's preference for the wastrel Charley. As her father's companion, sharing his bookishness, she enjoyed an attachment she was never to experience again. Years later, in one of her bursts of confidence to sensitive men, she said that her father had petted her as no one else would, and that his death in 1869, when she was twenty-nine, had hit her the hardest.

Yet the pathos of this story was only half the truth. It was the disarming partial truth of an able woman who could not exist without the cover of conventional womanhood. She was constructing a vulnerable image, inviting chivalry in almost literal terms when she told a friendly doctor that she feared horses, 'having been run away with and terribly injured when a child'. It is through that cover of helplessness that we approach the enigma she presents: the child of tragedy who became a sealed tower of resolution.

3
'A Fighting Man'

In July 1862, Minny Temple, aged seventeen, went on holiday to Vermont, 'and *then* for Newport!' she promised her friend, Helena de Kay, '– and for seeing you barefoot in Uncle Henry's breakfast-room! – I have an old pair of boots and some stockings *with holes in the toes*, which I will have ready for you . . .'. Helena, whose brother George had died that June in the Civil War, was drooping. It would be a consolation to parade their toes and tatters round the properly clothed propriety of the James table.

The previous year, Minny had cut her hair shorter than a boy's in an age when women's hair was regarded as a crowning glory. Hers was no more than half an inch long. She sent a photograph to her cousin William James at college. He was shocked at her 'insanity' and excited by the bared contour of her head and extended neck. 'Was she alone when she did it?' he pressed her sister Kitty. 'Could no one wrest the shears from her vandal hand?'

There were no parents to control her. Both had died when she was nine: Colonel Robert Emmet Temple, a graduate of West Point, died of tuberculosis in July 1854, and his wife, Catherine, daughter to Billy James of Albany and younger sister to Henry James Sr, died three months later of the same disease. To Henry James Jr, as a small boy, his family offered 'a chronicle of early deaths' and 'orphaned children'. Yet the mood was not entirely grim. In contrast with the distancing and isolation of the Woolsons, the Temples were gathered into an extended family under Catherine Barber James, their widowed grandmother in Albany. The memoir Henry James wrote towards the end of his life, elides her burden and sees her sighs as rather quaint: in his eyes, the Dutch house at 43 North Pearl Street was 'so much and so sociably a nurseried and playroomed orphanage'. His bereft cousins seemed to him romantic, 'somehow more thrilling than parentally provided ones'.

The Temples left six children: Robert, who was fourteen (sent off to school in Scotland where he went to the bad); William, who at twelve took on the dignity of responsible manhood, good-natured, smiling, light of foot; and four girls down to Henrietta, who was only a year old. It was the second daughter, Mary ('Minny'), who stood out for James. Her eagerness, her unformed longing for fullness of life, was to be diffused into various of his heroines who are either orphaned, like Isabel Archer or Milly Theale, or lack parental care, like Daisy Miller, and although none is an exact portrait of Minny Temple, all suggest that lack freed them to be spontaneous – not finished like other girls, but always in the making.

Minny's resilience held up in a more fraught situation than James owned, for the household included the unfortunate offspring of a widowed Albany uncle, John James, who was destroying himself with drink and gambling. In 1856, when Minny was eleven, he committed suicide, leaving a daughter, Helen, aged sixteen, and a son, John Vanderburgh James, who died two years later, aged twenty-three, in an asylum.

Neither this nor the ruin of Minny's eldest brother dented the dream. James set Minny apart as a soaring spirit with no place in a warped society. He vowed in his twenties to become the medium through which she would persist. This was one of a set of prophecies which propelled his work: he would outdo the master of 'the deeper psychology', Nathaniel Hawthorne, who died in 1864, the year James published his first tale; he would promote Minny Temple beyond her lifetime; and beyond his own time, his prose would 'kick off' the tombstones of critics, and rise from the dead.

The ferocity of his ambition, always '*couvé*' beneath his calm manner, took shape in the course of the 1860s at the same time as the Woman Question rose to prominence as a public issue. James never concerned himself with political rights, but no man was more alert to the pressure of unused endowment. 'My Bible . . . is the female mind', declares a diarist in an early tale, 'A Landscape-Painter' (1866), a man disillusioned by the inanimate lady of the marriage market. The remark is addressed to a sassy woman called Miriam who has some attributes of Minny Temple: she is 'natural' and outspoken, and she is also 'careless' in the best sense, unconcerned with proprieties.

Minny's rarity came home to James in their late teens when their paths converged in 1861 in Newport, Rhode Island, on the New England shore. 'Shining Newport, all silver and blue,' was then a haven for Europeanised Americans who lived with opera-glasses trained across the Atlantic and read the *Revue des deux mondes* with rapture. Henry James Sr was a new recruit to this intellectual élite, which was not unlike the Darwins, Stephens, and Trevelyans in Victorian England, but had its own character of moneyed leisure, and the self-conscious, rather deliberate and careful manners of a society committed to the democratic fiction that class does not exist.

Henry James Sr had rebelled against his mercenary father. In 1829–30, as a student with unpaid debts and a reputation for drink, he ran away from Union College in Schenectady, a college his father virtually owned. 'Distinctly Irish', Billy James remained an outsider until the last years of his life when, in the manner of the rich, he bought acceptance by highly visible schemes of public benefit. In 1825 at the opening of the Erie Canal, linking the Hudson River on the eastern seaboard with the Great Lakes of the Midwest, his windy speech puffs importantly from 'enterprise' to 'resources' to 'revenue' to a great gust of 'grandeur' and 'honour'. He was a ruddy man of middle height. Expressionless black eyes under heavy brows stared from a broad block of a face: a husband who replaced wives smartly after they died and, being preoccupied with business, glanced impatiently at a woman approaching his front door. 'Mrs James is not at home,' he told her curtly. She was a little put out, for (so it is said) she *was* Mrs James – the third.

Their son, Henry James Sr, abandoned raw power for a life of the mind, disconnecting himself and his children from the taint of trade – the tobacco, snuff, cigars, shoes, hats, coffee, molasses, and soap which his father had sold. Quantity of money was to be transformed instantly into quality of mind and character. He went at this headlong; we can't hope to grasp the phenomenon of the James family without marking this ferment that composed its gentility. Oliver Wendell Holmes (1841–1935), a proper Bostonian who distinguished himself as a judge in the Supreme Court, said you would have to 'invent a word' for the odd atmosphere of the James household. He recalled 'its keen personal intuitions, the optimistic anarchising of the old man (a spiritual, unpractical anarchism), its general go-as-you-please but demand-nothing, apotheotic Irishry'. Emerson, too, saw the anarchy. He was amused to hear that his friend's daughter, Alice, was highly moral. 'How in the world does her father get on with her?' he wanted to know.

When, in his youth, Henry had run away, he had landed in the Boston office of the *Christian Examiner*. It was as though, with that dash across country on his peg leg, he exchanged the undeflected force of his father's material drive for an equally undeflected urge for spiritual gain. He seized on inward divinity, the message of Emerson's heretical 'Divinity School Address'. Henry senior spoke in similar terms of 'the actual life of God himself in human nature'. He disliked the institutional aspect of religion, which interfered with spiritual freedom; he thought all ceremonials to do with birth, marriage, and death were damned nonsense; and he came to believe in a radical equality of the soul ('no difference between the most virtuous lady and the vilest prostitute'), a godlike position unencouraging to moral codes. No doctrine, until he came upon Swedenborg, could fit his wafting thoughts. His talk rolled out as if there was no end to it, and he wrote books with long, solemn titles and woolly content (which he published himself). His son Henry praised the fervid energy of these unrewarded efforts. Another son, William, designed a title page with a woodcut of a man flogging a dead horse.

A strongly built man, with a grey beard, and keen eyes above wire-rimmed glasses, Henry senior was a variety of failed prophet, and not the harmless kind, though he may have appeared so when he flung about rather precariously on one leg with the aid of an ivory-tipped cane. He was harmless enough when he ranted to another radical, Bronson Alcott, about the subserviency of priests, pedants, and fine folks – even Emerson did not come up to his mark. He was on very easy terms with God. 'My dear Madame,' he remarked to the Boston Brahmin Julia Ward Howe, 'God is working all the time in his shirt-sleeves with all his might.' But Henry senior was not harmless as the scourge of sin – then, he was mad. In 1844 he experienced a fit of demoniacal possession – evil seemed to be supreme and irresistible in the universe – and he was drawn to men with similar obsessions, like Dr Joseph T. Curtis, a New York physician who heard voices from the spirit world commanding him, amongst other things, to kill his children. Curtis was twice committed to an insane asylum, and committed suicide in 1857, but Henry senior continued to assert that Curtis had been 'no more insane that I am at this moment'. A dubious assertion for a father who would say to God incessantly, 'take these dear children away before they know the evil of sin'. In *Substance and Shadow* (1863) Henry senior said: 'If by any one act I could fully express, *i.e.* satisfy, the affection I bear my wife, child, my friend ... my next act towards them would logically be one of extermination.'

When he found his brother John James in the clutches of Pat Hearne, barracuda of New York gamblers, he tried to be a scourge of gambling: in February 1855 he wrote anti-gambling pieces for the New York *Tribune*. His biographer, Alfred Habegger, wonders if fear of retaliation was the real reason Henry senior left town in 1855. He took his family to Europe. At this time the eldest son, William ('Willy'), was fourteen; Henry ('Harry'), twelve; Garth Wilkinson ('Wilky'), ten; Robertson ('Bob'), nine; and the only girl, Alice, seven. The restless journeyings abroad, where the Jameses lived for years at a stretch without close companions, locked the children in the family unit as their sole home.

On their return to America in 1858, they gravitated to Newport; but after a year, the children were jerked abroad once more. The reason, this time, was to bring William 'into contact with books and teachers' (as though these were unavailable in American colleges), and to keep his children pure and obedient by removing them from the free social mingling of boys and girls in America. The real reason was the father's own sense of failure. In the autumn of 1858 he visited Emerson in Concord and insisted on dominating a gathering which included Bronson Alcott and Thoreau. 'He charges society with all the crime committed,' noted Thoreau, 'and praises the criminal for committing it. But I think that all the remedies he suggests out of his head ... would leave us about where we are now.' Emerson's aunt, Mary Moody Emerson, who suffered no fools, became so irritated by James senior that she scolded him for his 'lax notions': the visit was not a success. Later, his son Henry complained of his 'scant and miserable education and educative opportunity'. William was to be the star. Henry spoke of himself in the third person: 'No one took any interest whatever in *his* development, except to neglect or snub it ...'. He was a voracious reader of novels, his father noted with some unease, and as a corrective to a 'loose' imagination, and also because his Latin was not up to European standards, in the autumn of 1859 he was tossed into a technical school in Geneva, with a pure science curriculum, mainly mathematics, for boys going on to careers in engineering. In a cancelled fragment from his memoirs, he said that his abhorrence of mathematics had made the Institution Rochette entirely 'waste and anguish'. From eight in the morning to five in the afternoon, with only one hour's break, he sat blank and helpless, while his classmates prepared for 'dreadful ordeals', those of mining and the higher mechanics. Except for a part-time English boy, none of his classmates spoke to him. The Institution Rochette was a dilapidated old stone house opposite the Cathedral of St Peter, where Calvin had preached. It was now a run-down quarter of Geneva, abandoned it seemed except for a prison next door. From his seat, James could watch the prisoners, who looked the meekest of men; he had no eye for abstractions on the blackboard.

He was a solid enough failure to be allowed to leave in 1860. Instead, he attended literature classes for a few months at what is now the University of Geneva.

In Geneva in the spring of 1860 his younger brother Wilky became intrigued by the persistently locked door of Harry's room. One day he managed to peek inside and saw, as he put it, poetical-looking manuscripts on the table and his brother with an author-like air – it was the start of 'the private life', the novelist's phrase for the invisible space in which an artist sheds his public character. Officially, the family's return to Newport the following September was intended to further William's knack for drawing. In that light, it appears an odd move but, in truth, Henry senior was at last tired of Europe, and inclined to think America would suit them all. In no time he had floated back to the easy optimism of his generation of New England Transcendentalists, and placed Wilky and Bob under Franklin B. Sanborn, of sweeping cheer, who had recently founded an abolitionist school in Concord. Fellow-pupils were the children of Concord residents Emerson and Hawthorne, and Louisa May Alcott, daughter of Bronson Alcott, attended a few classes.

Henry senior was blithely unaware that his second son remained incapable of the 'long jump' of adaptation. Henry junior felt they had broken 'all but catastrophically' with Europe: 'we had landed somewhere in quite another world or at least on the sharp edge of one . . .'. He saved the sharp edge of America amidst a hoard of 'impressions'. Though he took up art with William in the Hunt studio in Newport, he soon recognised the inferiority of his talent, and went on writing – a long and secret apprenticeship (for he showed nothing to his family, and there is no evidence that he submitted tales for publication before the latter half of 1863). It was this apparently mild but secretly directed and intransigently alien youth of seventeen who went out walking on 13 January 1861 with his cousins, the Misses Temple, when they arrived in Newport.

By this time, the four Temple sisters, Katherine ('Kitty'), Minny, Ellen ('Elly'), and Henrietta, had outgrown the nursery in Albany. Their grandmother had died in 1859. As wards of their father's sister Mary Tweedy, they now spent school holidays with her – perhaps some consolation for the three children she had lost. In 1848 she had married wealthy Edmund Tweedy, a friend of Henry senior. The James and Tweedy families were therefore doubly tied by friendship and Uncle Henry's attentions to the orphaned daughters of his favourite sister. The Tweedys, like the Jameses, defined themselves in relation to Europe; immediately after their marriage they had spent the requisite few years in Italy that gave such Americans their gloss of detachment from their own country. Newport, alone in America, provided some ground for reattachment. It was looked on as a watering place, comparable in England to eighteenth-century Bath or Regency Brighton, where the well-to-do might repair their health, know one another, and take their ease. Henry senior suggested that Mr Tweedy take a house there too. So, in the New Year of 1861, the Tweedys settled on the fashionable Bellevue Avenue, with the James household nearby on an offshoot of this avenue, 13 Kay Street, a modest clapboard house conveniently near to the Redwood library, a toy-sized Palladian building tucked in a quiet corner.

All shingle and clapboard, rustic lanes and stables, with barouches clattering up and down an unpaved drive along the sea, Newport of the 1860s had as yet none of the opulence of the later nineteenth century when Edith Wharton lived there. The westward expanse of beach and salt-brown meadow – later covered with palaces – was a solitary place for a walker, as Henry junior described it: 'For miles and miles you see at your feet, in mingled shades of yellow and gray, a desolate waste of moss-clad rock and sand-starved grass. At your left is nothing but the shine and surge of the ocean . . .'. Beyond the wharves of the harbour was the old residential quarter, the Point, built by people of 'severe simplicity': the houses were bare, shingled boxes, with homely notches and splinters, steep grey roofs, barnacled with lichens, like barges left on the beach to dry. For James, the low, uninhabited headlands, densely shrubbed, had a hidden beauty that 'triumphs in impalpable purity'. This landscape, with its 'precarious tracks' that led him across country and returned him 'through the darkling voids', a space guarded by 'a sense of margin and of mystery', was imprinted on his mind and work.

In the newer part of town, centred on the Avenue, each snug villa with its shutters and flower-beds was enclosed in its own variety of wooden palings. Newport as yet retained the unspoilt atmosphere of small-town America with a mid-century influx of serious, unshowy Bostonians: some were summer inhabitants like Charles Eliot Norton, William Greenough (the sculptor), Julia Ward Howe (soon to write the famous 'Battle Hymn of the Republic'), and the historian George Bancroft, sleekly angular with a jutting white-tipped chin, long legs beautifully pointed, and high sharp elbows, as he bowled along the drive against a sunset sky. Others, like the Jameses and Tweedys, lived in Newport all the year round. There was Henry junior's first real friend, Thomas Sergeant Perry (1845–1928), a descendant of Commodore Perry, the hero of the battle of Lake Erie in the War of 1812. The two took long walks every afternoon to the Point or along the cliffs to Spouting Rock and Lily Pond. Once, at Lily Pond, they discussed Fourier's plan for regenerating the world. Henry junior tried to back his father's discipleship but failed to convince Perry, who was already a sophisticated reader. Then there was the artist John La Farge (who married Perry's sister Margaret) and, not least, the four Temple sisters, in narrow-buttoned, wide-gathered dresses, who now made Newport their home.

Here, the settled circle welcomed the return to America of a supremely cultured father and daughter who were to enter James's fiction (and, later, through him, to befriend Fenimore). Francis Boott (1813–1904), an heir to New England textile mills who had graduated from Harvard in 1831, was a musician and composer, and dabbled also in book reviews, letters to editors, and light verse. His daughter, Elizabeth ('Lizzie'), born in 1846, was a painter. She had a patient air, slightly drooping lips and the luxuriant hair sometimes rather surprisingly attached to pale young women, as though much of their animation had been channelled into that heavy growth. It was immaculately plaited and wound like an abstract sculpture of polished knobs attached, as it were, to the whole back of her head and balancing, in profile, her long, elegant nose. She painted with a professionalism unusual in a girl, encouraged by her exquisitely tasteful father with his soft beard and crossed knee. The Bootts were the ultimate in Europeanised America, outdoing the Jameses, having lived all Lizzie's life in Italy.

Lizzie and Minny made friends, though they were altogether different. Lizzie, for all her polish, struck Henry junior as too limp, too passive, too '*produced*' in the manner of European girls. She was admired by everyone else, including Mrs James, as a model of her sex. By such standards, Minny appeared unchecked, uncultivated, even lazy. In the eyes of Mrs James, nursing her emotionally dependent husband and doting children, Minny, with her careless, laughing ways, had a long way to go.

To less conventional eyes, what was special about Minny was her ease, unlike her cousin Alice, born in 1848, a proper product of her limited mother. Mrs James's limitations were never acknowledged by her family, but they pervade her letters. She was boring.

She and her sister giggled together when they visited the Carlyles in London. Of the husband, Carlyle might remark, 'Not a *bad* man nor altogether a fool,' but of his wife, as Jane Carlyle put it, 'what could anybody say?' The truth was Mary James had not a thought in her head beyond maternal nursing. In his memoirs, her son recalled 'her complete availability', accomplished with 'a smoothness of surrender' so complete that she '*was* each of us'. Her children found it hard to grow up; three of the five, Willy, Henry, and Alice, became long-term invalids. This, in turn, allowed Mrs James to extend her sway as an angel who gave herself so entirely to others that there was (her menfolk told themselves, admiring and humbled) nothing else. In this way, her abnegation was absorbed into family myth: a service to great men, rewarded by their uncritical love. Not surprisingly, the most damaged was the daughter.

Photographs of Alice as a young woman show a round, uncommunicative face, like an empty plate, and lips firmly closed in a downward curve. She was immaculately dressed and smoothed in the tidy-doll fashion of the day. With a dull mother as her model, yet seething with the intellectual gifts of her eldest brothers, Alice was in a straitjacket; and intense rivalry, combined with the rectitude of her domestic training, led her to tighten that straitjacket to maximal pressure. The James family practised the self-conscious refinement of those new to it. If ladies were constricted, then Alice James had to be the most constricted of all. There followed a succession of breakdowns – attacks of nervous 'hysteria' in the jargon of the day – fuelled by suppressed rage which surfaced only in cutting judgements: she was particularly hard on her cousin Minny for allowing herself what Alice chose to see as shallow freedoms. She deplored Minny's flares of thought as mental promiscuity, erratic, light-weight. Alice had judgements like iron, reinforced by unusual strength of mind, and into these bars she locked herself: imprisoned as much by her own mental powers as by gentility. It is possible that her resentment of Minny, as later her resentment of Fenimore, arose from the different alternatives they presented to constriction – alternatives intriguing to Henry James, but shut off in Alice.

Did Alice set herself to be too perfect a daughter to her parents?

Was Mrs James the type of 'maternal paralysis' James called 'Mrs Morte'? He was alert to 'the obscure heroine her daughter (so the reverse of the maternal paralysis!)': a lively girl caught in the coils of a deadening mother. Alice proposed to kill herself, she told her father at the age of fifteen. Instead of enquiring into this, he told her she was at liberty to do so whenever she pleased; all he asked was that she choose a humane method to spare others' feelings. Alice sat 'immovable reading in the library', where violent impulses filled her (she later recalled) 'such as throwing myself out of the window, or knocking off the head of the benignant pater as he sat with his silver locks, writing at his table'. An imitative effacement compelled by her mother was reinforced continually by William, her eldest brother, with all the force of the family's star, dark, sardonic, with a dazzling vivacity of mind.

William's admonitions to Alice, at fifteen, about how a girl should present herself, show his conventionality. 'Chérie charmante', William addresses Alice in 1863 in the flirtatious tone of a busy man in a museum, surrounded by fearsome skeletons and mastodons, taking the trouble to teach his sister a few necessary lessons. Lesson number one is to efface herself like 'timid little girls' in the museum '(reminding me of thee, my love, only they are less fashionably dressed), who whisper "Is folks allowed here?" It pains me to remark, however, that not all the little girls are of this pleasing type, many being bold-faced jades.' Pleasing girls, ignorant of grammar, don't presume to speak; at most they 'whisper'. And here is William again in 1868, once more dictating the finer nuances of the angelic code, this time to their parents as agents of his sister's construction: 'Let Alice cultivate a manner clinging yet self sustained, reserved yet confidential, let her face beam with serious beauty, & glow with quiet delight at having you speak to her; let her exhibit short glimpses of a soul with *wings* . . .'. Quiet. Short. These adjectives police the limits of his sister's existence.

Invalidism dominated his own undirected existence – he was slower than Henry to settle to a career, and slower than all his brothers to think of supporting himself. In the meantime he exercised his mastery within the family, transforming the carping tone of family exchanges into flashing wit. Like his father, he craved attention, and there was an element of performance in his readiness to engage others. He combined the emotional energy of his father with a clearer head. His warmth, the informal freshness of his intelligence, and comfortable, not too glossy, good looks made him, as a man, extremely attractive. His letters play on others with seductive hilarity. 'The loveress of W.J' is his teasing caption to a drawing of Alice in 1860 as a girl-child with down-cast eyes. For his sister, aged twelve, her entrancingly jocular brother had a repertoire of gallantries. 'I lay entranced & dreaming / My Alice, sweet, of thee', he warbles. The song goes on:

Upon the Sea-shore lying
Upon the yellow sand
The foaming waves replying
I vowed to ask thy hand
I swore to ask thy hand, my love
I vowed to ask thy hand
I wished to join myself to thee
By matrimonial band.

Despairing of her 'childlike form', he prepares to drown himself: 'Since I may not have thee / My Alice sweet, to be my wife.'

'Alice took it very coolly', William reassured their father. When she became visibly disturbed, William passed it off as idle fret: 'I hope your neuralgia, or whatever you believe the thing was, has gone and that you are back at school instead of languishing and lolling about the house.' He was extraordinarily blind to his effect on Alice. Her helplessness served to build up his agency, granting him the delicious exercise of authority. She was 'the lovely babe' with a temper that left something to be desired; she was 'my apricot-nosed sister' whose letters were so precocious she must think herself a little Mme de Sévigné. Alice had the quirky force that can be crushed when it comes into conflict with puberty and its overwhelming pressure to conform to what men say.

Minny's vivacity was the opposite of expressionless Alice in her Parisian-doll dress – to the annoyance of Mrs James. She was a girl 'with whom everyone was desperately in love' (according to Perry, gratified to get a valentine from Minny with an adroit rhyme: 'his form . . . alone is / In beauty the match of Adonis'). Girls vied for her friendship. Miss Paige, who accompanied her on a visit to Albany, lost her ladylike control, Minny observed to her friend, Helena de Kay: 'It is the most amusing thing to see her "get on the rampage" when I speak of you. The other night, after we had *retired*, she informed me in great wrath, that "she would, without doubt, *kick* me out of bed," if I mentioned your name again.'

This was no impeccable Alice, no mousy miss in a corner like Emerson's daughters, bent over their sewing, 'saying never a word nor looking a look'. Minny did more than participate; she lit up conversation, posing questions with an alacrity that made James call her the 'amateur priestess of rash speculation'. In old age, William remarked that he never again met anyone like her. Compared with Fenimore's dainty and regular features, Minny's were large, especially her teeth, but their mobility gave an impression of lightness.

Well-bred women in that period adopted a frozen manner. It was a sign you were a lady, a creature of low vitality and virtuous reserve. Henry senior took the view that the virtue of woman 'disqualifies her for all didactic dignity. Learning and wisdom do not become her.' The solemnity of this pronouncement recalls Jane Austen's advice to women: 'Where people wish to attach, they should always be ignorant. To come with a well-informed mind is to come with an inability of administering to the vanity of others which a sensible person would always wish to avoid. A woman especially, if she have the misfortune of knowing anything should conceal it as well as she can. . . . I will only add in justice to men, that though to the larger and more trifling part of the sex, imbecility in females is a great enhancement of their personal charms, there is a portion of them too reasonable and too well informed themselves to desire anything more in woman than ignorance.' Jane Austen herself had the encouragement of an enlightened father. It is easy to see why less fortunate young women of active intellect, like Alice James, felt monstrous. Florence Nightingale reports that when middle-class mid-Victorian women went to bed at night they felt they were going mad and were obliged to lie down by day in an effort to subdue themselves to modish icons of domestic devotion or frail femininity.

Though tumults of emotion – was it hate? – surged through

Alice James, she never rebelled. In her diary, Alice looked back to the winter of 1862–3 when she wandered along the cliffs under 'the low grey Newport sky' and felt her 'young soul struggling out of its swaddling-clothes' as she saw how she was to be: destined 'to clothe myself in neutral tints, walk by still waters, and possess one's soul in silence'. Charlotte Brontë, who had no mother to tell her what not to say, could utter the inward speech of women with a vehemence that shocked many in the nineteenth century who called her 'coarse'. To be 'coarse' was above all what ladies feared, like Alice and Fenimore, who caged themselves with relentless severity, Alice's hair neatly netted, Fenimore's dresses subdued, tailored to be inconspicuous, both muted by their guard on correctness and bringing their vast reserves of strength to that vigilance. Thoughts, bold and fearful, lurked in the secret space of their minds; it was rare for anyone to reach them.

Unlike them, Minny was 'absolutely afraid of nothing', as James recalled, one who advanced over a horizon unimagined by others. Her hunger was not for learning, but for people and scenes. It appealed to James as a prospective novelist, hungry for 'impressions' and impatient with formal study. Minny, though, was higher-spirited and more outspoken than her cousin, who was slow of speech and halting in his choice of words. She also had grand connections, always interesting to him. When she visited Canada she stayed with Sir John Rose (1820–88), a statesman and financier, known as 'Rose of Montreal'. He had married Minny's aunt Charlotte Temple Rose, sister to Minny's father and to her guardian, Mary Temple Tweedy. The Temple history was a matter of both pride and shame.

Minny's grandfather was a man the family wished to forget. Robert Temple the elder (1783–1834) was 'a *bastard* son of Sir John Temple, the "founder" of the family in America, & he hanged himself after burning the public office of which he was in charge, to cover the tracks of his peculations', Henry James relayed the history to his brother William. Robert Temple the elder was a lawyer who collected pensions in the name of veterans of the Revolutionary War, and failed to hand over the money. He shot (not hanged) himself after burning his papers. His children, Minny's father, Aunt Mary, and Lady Rose, naturally preferred to associate themselves with remoter and more respectable branches of the family.

The English Temples were a noble family whose pedigree is sometimes said to go back to Lady Godiva. The most distinguished was Sir William Temple (1628–99), a statesman and writer who in about 1680 built Moor Park with a canal and Dutch garden, near Farnham in Surrey. It became famous through Jonathan Swift, who, as Temple's secretary, lived there for many years. The founder of the family in America, John Temple (1731–98), was not a descendant of the famous Sir William, and the relation of the British Temples to their American namesakes remains unclear. John Temple's descendants, Henry James thought, tended to make too much of their great name 'under circumstances which would, had they been wiser, made them keep silent or even drop it. They came about it through illegitimacy & through an individual who was horribly dishonoured.'

He spoke with distaste of '*THAT* strain' in the Temple blood. It reappeared in Minny's eldest brother, Robert Temple III, a charming rogue, leaning to the wrong side of the law. Years later, in England, James felt ashamed when a son of the Roses eventually bought Moor Park in 1891. He felt that all the family should present themselves as 'solid burgess' class, not ask for sneers from the genuine nobility (with whom he mingled). The unusual heat of this opinion suggests the complexity of his attitude to the Temples. James would dearly have liked an English forebear – anyone, let alone the ruling class. He fantasised that Catherine Barber James came from English stock but, alas, his grandmother was as Irish as the Jameses. The 'aristocratic' pretensions of the Temples (James used inverted commas) could have put them above their cousins, a source of friction in a family full of disturbance and failure, of one kind or another, in the early sixties.

Henry junior's failure at mathematics in Geneva, then in the art studio in Newport, was followed by a misguided enrolment in Harvard's Law School for 1862–3. He attended lectures with obedient regularity but, listening to the quavering accents of Dr Theophilus Parsons, not one ray of the subject entered his mind. Professor Joel Parker had a head in the shape of an oblong dome, edged with a fringe of ringlets, and his dry, hard prose was 'prose unrelieved'. From a 'meanly retentive' mouth, 'ignorant of style', issued what seemed to the student the deadliest language he had ever heard – all the more deadly when Parker demonstrated his mastery of law. Then, on 10 March 1863, James failed to defend a case before a 'moot court', a confirmation of his incompetence in a profession for which he had never had the slightest leaning. Yet law school offered an acceptable substitute for a more unthinkable activity: fighting in the Civil War. Obviously, what he wished to do was write, but his father had warned of possible 'damage to what might be best in a man by the professional pursuit of "art"'.

At the very time James lost face at law school, Minny was in trouble in her school for young ladies at Farmington, Connecticut. In February–March 1863, she and her friend, Helena, were 'inattentive and disobedient'. They complained of bigotry and narrowness in a teacher called Miss Fanny and in the school's clergyman.

Mrs de Kay, Helena's mother, tried in vain to invoke 'Christian duty' and sympathy for Miss Fanny, who had to work for a living. Helena was not disposed to bow her head when her mother, conceding that 'bigots and narrow-minded people are very unlovable', appealed to the two girls to set an example by not being intolerant themselves.

'... We must forgive [bigots] as we would forgive our enemies – they almost seem to be such to those whose views are truly liberal – '.

Mrs de Kay, who had written in this temperate way, was astonished by Helena's reply, accusing her mother of taking the school's side. 'I did not think you would have answered my letter with so much vehemence dear daughter. You could not have taken time to consider, I am sure.' She advised Helena to calm herself, or she would 'use up' her life all too soon.

It was the familiar struggle of girls who want to think for themselves. Helena had lived aboard in Dresden from 1859 to 1861, and was unaccustomed to the small world of a girls' school. Nor, as her mother reminded her gently, was her nature submissive: from her mother's point of view, this made regulation all the more desirable.

So, Mrs de Kay was not quite pleased that Helena had discovered a twin spirit. She and Minny developed a cult of friendship, and the school's head, Miss Margaret, confronted with such fervour, was unable to cope. In a 'sad, grieved' tone, she sent out two formal complaints: one to Mrs de Kay; the other to Minny's uncle, Henry James Sr. The complaint gave Mrs de Kay 'more pain than anything I have known for a long while', and she begged Helena to 'go to Miss M and tell her you are sorry to have caused her so much ... trouble'. Assuming Minny, two years older, was behind this trouble, Mrs de Kay issued a warning.

'You are doing a wrong and dangerous thing in allowing your fondness for Minnie to become an engrossing passion. Do not surrender your *self* your convictions of *Truth – justice – piety* & *honour* to any one – much less to a young and undeveloped perhaps, mistaken person of your own age – '

But the two were closer than ever. Helena was in her own way as compelling as Minny. She had the social ease of an old family: Willem de Kay, born in London in 1589, grew up in Haarlem, where his Huguenot family had settled after fleeing from France. In 1640 he migrated to New Amsterdam (later New York). Helena's mother, Janet Halleck Drake (1814–90), had married Commodore de Kay when she was fourteen and he much older: their eldest daughter, Katharine, comes into this story at a later stage, as a friend of Henry James and Fenimore. Thirteen years older than Helena, Katharine recalled a tomboy childhood on their father's estate on Staten Island, New York. He believed children should be close to nature and not over-tutored. In 1855, Katharine, whose scholarly bent had been encouraged by a convent school in Washington, married a cultured, sickly man called Arthur Bronson. Helena thought him 'coarse' – for this reason, she later declined to accompany the Bronsons to Paris in 1869. The Bronsons had one child, Edith, born in Newport in 1861, and it was for the sake of Katharine and the baby that Mrs de Kay took a house in Clay Street, Newport. During school vacations, the proximity of Clay Street to Bellevue Avenue reinforced the bond Helena and Minny had formed at school.

Two little dents of concentration above Helena's dark eyes and the tender curves of her upper lip invited intimacy as she talked in a low voice with a vibration of feeling. John La Farge, who was to be her mentor as an artist, called her a 'good counsellor'. The writer Mary Hallock Foote, who was to meet her at art school and remain a lifelong friend, recalled how people 'said things to her with absolute recklessness'. Her colouring was warm: a crest of brown hair with a deep wave as it turned off her forehead and a soft, peachy cheek, set off by the dark browns she tended to wear, with glints of gold or pale yellow and sometimes a flash of pure red. One of her appealing ways was to share a poem with a friend, half-sounding the words as though too deep for utterance – two voices murmuring 'Let me not to the marriage of true minds / Admit impediments . . .'. That shaded, beneath-the-surface quality was there in her drawing, which felt its way towards form, avoiding hard, precise lines. The opposite of cocksure, she lent herself to her subject as to people. Minny was 'a passion', Helena said in after years, '– lasting forever as my passions do I think – So was I to her . . .'.

As Minny saw it, Helena gave her 'dear, *motherly* care'; as Mrs de Kay saw it, Minny was stirring rebellion in a way that challenged the controlled passionlessness of good little women. Minny had the spontaneity and verve of Jo March, without any 'Marmee' to admonish her. Mrs de Kay warned her daughter that a girl who resisted the social code lost her 'honour'.

Minny was not inclined to bend to the social code when she encountered her cousin William James in Newport in the first week of March 1863. Instead of propping a clever young man, Minny went on about Montreal the previous summer. On a cloudless day, 5 March, they took a walk which William reports in a letter to Alice: 'I have just returned from a walk with Min to Spouting Rock. The foam lathered the coast all round with its suds. Minny sped along in front of me, digging her heels into the ground, and kept me so out of breath that I couldn't talk.' He felt that he never wanted to come again.

There were hidden causes of friction. One was Minny's brother Will Temple, a captain in the Civil War, who had been sent home to Newport with fever in December 1862. While his sisters had nursed him over the winter, he had been impatient to resume his part in the action. A strapping soldier, ambitious to turn his men into a 'crack regiment', Will Temple scorned contemporaries who did not enlist. The nearest man who did not enlist was his cousin Willy James, exactly Temple's age (both born in 1842), a nervy scholar shielded by doting parents. On 1 February, Temple had waved his last goodbye, and returned to the field in his brushed blue uniform, polished boots, and white gloves. Minny adored her brother and, at this time, must have feared for his health and safety on the long marches that characterised the Civil War. And here was Willy James, unable to keep pace on a walk.

There was, however, another and stronger reason for Minny to dig in her heels and walk fast: Willy James had done something of which there's no record except one letter from Minny to Helena: 'And now my dear, I am going to tell you the result of that *Counterfeit* bill', she wrote. 'It *was* a Counterfeit. You were right and *I* was utterly *wrong*. I got a long and *lively* letter from Willy on Christmas Day, telling me all about it. You may imagine how I felt! – I *cannot* describe my emotions! If it had been anyone but Willy, anyone less manly less entirely generous than he I should have felt *horribly* and never wanted to see him again, but he wrote me such a dear kind letter, just like himself that it made it all as right as it could possibly be under the circumstances.' Though Minny held to her belief in his fundamental goodness, William had been called into question. He did not forgive Minny for a long time.

She returned to Newport, with Elly, a month after her walk with William, and recounts a visit from 'Harry', all the way from Harvard, as soon as she arrived. Within a day, he asked her to analyse Helena, '*body and mind*'. Minny responded with a torrent of information, as she owned to Helena with her easy candour in an unpublished letter which bears the breath of this moment like a scene in a drama:

Newport
April 3rd, 1863
Friday evening
Uncle Henry's table

(Harry sitting by me reading)

. . . We got to Newport safely, and found Willy James waiting for

> us. We came directly to Uncle Henry's, because Aunt Mary Tweedy is very ill, and we could not go there now, on account of the noise. ... I found dear old Harry here, he had come from Cambridge for a day or two *expressly* to see *me*, which renders me quite happy.
>
> Willy James is the same strange youth as ever, stranger if possible, but good as ever. He is not *cross* to me, but I think he has rather *renounced* me, in the depths of his heart, as a *bad* thing. Harry is as *lovely* as ever, verily the *goodness* of that boy passeth human comprehension. I found Kitty and Henriette delighted to see us. Small Henriette is to sleep with me tonight, and I expect to be *mauled* within an inch of my life. I have been *tearing* up the Avenue and over the beach to Spouting Rock today with Kitty. ... Harry requested a short description of you, *body and mind*, and I told him *loads* about you. Now don't *go* and *pretend* you're angry, for you're *not*. How could I help talking about *you* to any one so *dear* as Harry? Willy is perambulating this room like an uneasy spirit.

There is tension in the air, the brothers opposed in their view of Minny. The younger's bond with the '*bad* thing', and his interest in the '*loads*' she could tell him, came from a prospective novelist at a critical moment when he realised he was no use at law and would drop out soon with the end of the academic year. Minny, for her part, dismissed 'weak-minded' boys and welcomed the '*lovely*' alternative 'Harry' presented. She had a feeling for what he called 'verity of character': you were expected to fulfil the character she discerned; if you did not, she withdrew her attention. She was to remain for James 'the supreme case of a taste for life as life'. They shared a taste for the inward life – Minny as searching 'as her splendid shifting sensibility, moral, personal, nervous ... might at any moment determine'. She was 'psychologic' in her approach, he noticed, with little interest in society.

During Minny's stay in the James house in April 1863, she was shown Miss Margaret's accusation. She laughed it off as 'a marvellous production'. Miss Margaret had written: 'those *two* ... do each other a great deal of good, and *also* a *great deal* of harm.' The harm, as Minny reported it to Helena, was 'in our forgetting the rest of the *Human race*, etc. etc. Ha! ha! ha! – I don't agree with her. Do *you* think we love each other too much? For my part, I know that it is just this one thought of *you* and *your love* that makes me feel myself *blessed* beyond the *common* lot; for I do not think dearie, that people often have so much happiness in each other.'

This comes at the end of the letter that singles out 'Harry' as her friend. The rest of those who mattered in the James family – her uncle, aunt, Alice, and William, all holding to the model of passive refinement – would not have taken kindly to ha-ha's and impenitence. A boy could be packed off to war (the oncoming answer for Bob James, who loathed school), but what might be done with an uncontrolled girl?

The '*bad* thing' and the law school failure: when Minny Temple and Henry junior met in the spring break of 1863 neither was fitting in. The following autumn both stayed on in Newport: Henry, ostensibly, with nothing to do and no plans; Minny reading Dante, together with Helena, under a schoolmaster, George Bradford, a classmate and friend of Emerson, whom Alice recalled in her diary as '*the* flower of New England maidenly bachelorhood, the very last ... of his very special kind'. The schoolmaster, aged fifty-six, bookish but ineffective, and inclined to be sentimental about the charmers in his advanced group, found himself 'hassled', as he put it, by Minny and Helena, whose 'obstinate questionings' he was unable to satisfy.

There is no surviving fact about Henry junior in the autumn of 1863, except that he stayed at home and had not yet found a voice. William noticed 'Harry's stoic visage' – it must have been hard. Yet Minny was there, obstinate as ever. Readers familiar with Henry James will think of *Daisy Miller*, his portrait of an American girl who denies social rules, and brings on her own death as a result of persistent defiance. One of the many ways in which the fiction of Daisy is different from actual life is that Daisy acts alone in her defiance; she dies unknown, unmatched. In actuality, James was as determined as Minny, if less openly so, and if we are to understand the making of the novelist, we must explore the progress and outcome of this unconventional bond. We must go far back to the early 1860s when Minny was ordinarily and flagrantly alive, and not yet the material of art. In what James would remember ever after as 'the pure Newport time' – 'the so considerably prolonged formative, tentative, imaginative Newport time' which, he said, 'I have reasons for thinking sacred' – they backed each other. We must enter into a time when the outcome was in question – the question, in play throughout the 1860s, how James would act as a man. This issue of manliness was opened up by the pressing test of the Civil War.

One after another of his companions – brothers, cousins, classmates – marched into battle, and not all returned. Some were wounded repeatedly, like Oliver Wendell Holmes, who shared the Harvard and abolitionist background. Wendell, as they called him, was not a natural solider but stuck it out. In 1863, young men in the James family were flinging themselves at death; and for Henry junior to turn aside to cultivate the aesthetic aims of a writer would have appeared, in the patriotic heat of that year, too unmanly and also, at that point, too improbable, to voice. In the course of 1863, he had to face the truth that he was no fighter – or not in the usual sense. He could not join the battles of his generation, like his younger brothers, nor could he succeed in one of the professions, like his older brother, who appeared to be pressing on with science at Harvard. For proper men, at that time, there were only two plots, and neither would do.

The American Civil War was not at the periphery of his life: he was drafted for the Union Army, and not at once released. There is no mention of this fact in his memoirs, though he may have referred to it obliquely when he declared that the early 1860s were 'more coercive to the imagination' than anything Americans of his generation were ever again to know. Three million fought, and two per cent of the total population gave their lives. 'In our youth our hearts were touched with fire', Wendell Holmes recalled, and Henry junior was not exempt from the impact of the war and the challenge it presented. In Paris in 1856, American newspapers had brought the report of a Southerner's assault on Charles Sumner when he made a speech against slavery in the House of Representatives. To thirteen-year-old Henry, who had just read *Uncle Tom's Cabin*, it had been 'like a welt raised by the lash itself across the face of the North'. War was inevitable, the boy felt, 'for what but fighting had for its sign great men lying prone in their blood?' He was 'drenched' in feeling for Lincoln as suffering giant, and heard the 'insuperable' anti-slavery eloquence of the preacher Wendell Phillips. He said that external appearances were 'never to hold out for me as they held during those four years [1861–5]. Wondrous this force in them . . .'. This external force reached its peak for him in the course of 1863.

The war opened when Confederate troops (from slave-owning Southern states which had seceded from the Union) fired on the Federal arsenal at Fort Sumter, in Charleston Bay, on 12 April 1861. On 18 April, twelve hours after the first soldiers left Newport, a fire broke out in the town. In the effort to extinguish it, James claimed an 'obscure hurt' which he never explained but which was to exclude him from physical action for the duration of the war (as he seemed to know at once). The fact that a Boston specialist (probably Thomas Bigelow, who attended Henry senior) pooh-poohed the injury suggests it was minor – no more than back strain while James manoeuvred at an awkward angle between two fences, bending and pulling at Newport's ancient pump in the effort to synchronise with other firefighters. His hurt was an odd parallel to his father's boyhood injury in an Albany fire, resulting in long illness and amputation.

William James, aged twenty, enlisted in the Rhode Island Artillery Company on 26 April. There is no further record beyond the silent fact that his name gets obliterated during the period when the term of recruitment lengthened from ninety days to three years or the duration of the war. Henry senior supported his two eldest sons as they backed out of war. These two were his spiritual heirs with the nervous energy to carry forward his own self-transforming leap. He taught them to find a promise of transfiguration in the least likely situations. As Henry junior understood this, it was not to be achieved through 'blood and fire' but 'in the quietest of all quiet ways' through *enjoyed* contact. Meanwhile, Henry senior swung noisily from one position to its opposite in the course of the war. In the first phase, while his younger sons were schoolboys and only the two eldest eligible to fight, he took the line that the war was not worth one 'clean' life. On 4 July 1861, he denounced Lincoln for failing to take a stand on slavery. Here was another reason not to fight: it was not a just cause. In his Independence

Day oration, Henry senior stated that he would prefer to see the United States fall to pieces than see it corrupted by slavery.

Protected by this position, William entered the Lawrence Scientific School at Harvard in the autumn, and Henry remained at home another year, participating in the family's move to a larger house, covered in ivy, on the corner of Spring Street and Lee Avenue. It had a lawn with several large willows; an added third storey allowed the family to invite Emerson's daughters to stay in the summer of 1862. They were amused by adversarial talk at the James table. When, that August, Minny declared herself 'highly disgusted' with Lincoln, she was voicing the current abolitionist position in the James household.

Late in August, following Minny's example, Henry junior and Perry visited wounded soldiers at Portsmouth Grove, a newly improvised hospital of tents and shanties along the Rhode Island shore. There, he decided that his own lingering pains gave him some sort of 'share' in the national experience. Exalted by his notion, he went round the wards, inviting soldiers' stories, and offering them money from his 'poor pocket'. He was grateful not one coin was refused. It was not conscience money but an offer and acceptance of his notion that he and the wounded were as one: emblems of their suffering country. Going home on the steamer, his hurt began to ache as he sat on a deck stool and leant against the bulwark, a not unwelcome vindication of his fancy that he had measured 'wounds against wounds' in a common fact of endurance. That late summer afternoon, in the second year of the war, it seemed to him he shed at last his Europeanised self in a recognition, wonderfully fresh and strange, of 'our common Americanism', as he reached out across 'gulfs of dissociation' to other hurt men whose stoic reserve could melt in communicative confidence.

'I drew from each his troubled tale . . .' This was the heart of it: a prospective writer in touch, at last, with real material. During that long sail home – long in thought – down the mouth of the Sakonnet though the slow summer dusk, James saw that he might participate, after all, through an alternative form of action, the imaginative response that would create a national bond, a real Union of '*consecrated* association'. In after years, he aligned this experience with Whitman's visits to Civil War hospitals, and those communions of 'dear old Walt' which issued in lasting poems. In James, it was perhaps the first flicker of a power to lend himself imaginatively to sick soldiers in his Civil War tales, 'The Story of a Year' (1865) and 'A Most Extraordinary Case' (1867). In each, a soldier's recovery turns on whether a woman can respond to him as a man, and, in each case, she cannot. She pities him, but does not want him. So, the soldier's life fades without the marital union which Henry senior urged on his sons as the vital experience in life. One of his arguments against their enlistment was that neither should risk his life until he had known this fulfilment. Henry junior's 'obscure hurt' and the declining soldiers of his Civil War fiction underlie a recurrent figure in the great works of his maturity: a sensitive man who is all the more compelling for his unused powers, from the acutely aware invalid, Ralph Touchett, in *The Portrait of a Lady* (1881) to the waiting John Marcher in 'The Beast in the Jungle' (1902).

His identification with the troops continued when James entered Harvard on 3 September 1862. He saw himself as a 'recruit' while, as he put it, 'the bristling horde of my Law School comrades fairly produced the illusion of a mustered army. The Cambridge campus was tented field enough for a conscript . . .'. In fact, he found a reassuring abundance of 'fine fierce young men', the forty per cent who, like himself, 'hadn't flown to arms'. Yet before the month was out, the anti-war position of the New England élite changed utterly.

On 22 September, following a limited victory at Antietam, Maryland, Lincoln made a Preliminary Proclamation that all slaves in the Rebel states – fourteen million out of the country's population of thirty-one million – would be formally emancipated on 1 January 1863, and be 'thenceforward, and forever free'.

This changed the war from what had been primarily a political struggle to preserve the Union into a crusade for human freedom – as Lincoln put it in his Gettysburg Address, a little over a year later, a test whether a new nation, conceived in Liberty, and dedicated to the proposition that all men are created equal, could sustain itself. Abolitionist opinion in New England now swung behind the war, and Henry James Sr went with it – or, more accurately, preceded it. For, with sudden enthusiasm, ten days *before* the Proclamation, he took his third son to the recruiting station on 12 September when Wilky enlisted in the 44th Massachusetts Infantry. At seventeen, a product of Sanborn's school, he was the most idealistic of the James children and eager for war. His father encouraged Wilky's enlistment at the same time as he continued to assure William it was wrong for a young man to throw away his life before he had lived. The apparent contradiction might be explained by the father's claim to encourage each son to develop by his own lights, but it was not to prove the case with his youngest son, Bob, as events will show, and Wilky himself was increasingly pained at the thought of his father's alacrity. And well he might be, for Wilky lacked William's intellectual promise, even though he had his quota of James sensitivity. Wilky, who had once been warm and genial, tucking an arm under that of a prospective friend and walking him off, became, in time, a broken man and carried his bitterness to the grave.

From Harvard, Henry junior visited Wilky at Readville, a training camp near Boston, where he saw his 'soft companion' of childhood, his particular partner in the domestic schoolroom, metamorphosed as a soldier amidst other blue-togged, sunburnt, laughing young men who seemed 'to bristle ... with Boston genealogies'. His own apartness lurks in the interstices of these observations, as he tries out a posture he was to make his own: the gaping observer. Here he 'gapes' at the sudden superiority of his junior brother, as he draws out the element of fiction in facts: 'such a fairy-tale'. Battles and bodies remained remote; nothing as yet jarred the dreaming mood of his return journey from Portsmouth Grove or the consoling fantasy of Harvard as tented field. It delighted his eye to watch his agile, red-headed cousin Gus Barker receding across Harvard Square, on his last leave, in the dashing uniform of the 5th New York Cavalry.

William and Henry James devised a plan to salve their conscience. In January 1863 the legal emancipation of slaves opened up a new role for abolitionists: William and Henry now applied to go south to help contrabands (a term for freed slaves, deriving from the fact that during the Civil War many escaping slaves took refuge with the Union Army; in 1862, General Butler argued that they were no longer the property of Southern owners but 'contraband of war'). It was an unlikely plan for two undergraduates with no experience of law, medicine, or education, an attempt to sidestep their youth which was the only qualification required to face the sword and the newly invented machine-gun. The threat of these came closer in February 1863 when Lincoln pushed a draft law through Congress. He was desperate to replace the nine thousand troops killed at Fredericksburg and to counteract a substantial anti-war movement of 'Copperheads', Northern men who had been prepared to fight for the Union but were not prepared to fight for slaves. The main purpose of the draft was to encourage voluntary enlistment.

The brothers' withdrawal from the battleground of their generation continued to cast their manhood into question. In March–April 1863, William's 'renunciation' of Minny immediately preceded Henry's approach to her: the one a fretful visit, provoking indifference; the other a fruitful one with intimate talk. In the context of war with its inflated images of manliness, the brothers took up opposed positions towards this heroine of their scene – investing her with alternative meaning – at the very time their younger and, till then, less promising brother Wilky prepared to sail south to the arena of the war, crowned with their father's pride.

At this very point, a new demand appeared: the state home guard. All men of Rhode Island between the ages of eighteen and forty-five, 'liable to perform military duty', were to register by 20 April. William's name appeared on the enrolment list; Henry's did not.

Unlike them, Will Temple was restless for action. 'I hope that we will have a battle soon', he wrote in a letter at that time. 'We have been getting lazy this winter, and want something to stir us up. If we do meet the enemy, I will get a brevet or go under.' In another letter he said, 'I would give a leg for a brevet.' His thoughts were all of glories to be won, and he talked in this vein to the comrade who shared his blankets the night before the battle of Chancellorsville, Virginia, where the Union Army suffered a humiliating defeat on 1 May 1863, trapped by the unexpected tactics of the Southern commander General Robert E. Lee. Disdaining to take cover,

Temple stood within range of snipers, considering his next move. He was struck fatally by a musket-ball which entered his lung and passed through his back. Two of his men carried him to a farmhouse, his beautiful face hanging back towards the ground. Seventeen thousand Northerners died that day under one of their bungling leaders, General Hooker. 'My God, my God!' groaned Lincoln when he heard the frightful news. All Minny could see was her brother's '*sweet heavenly* smile' which made her think of Mama.

It took three weeks for his body to be recovered; he was buried in the family vault in Albany. In the meantime Minny, at home in Newport, wrote to Helena at school.

Newport
May 12th, 1863

... I have found out, I believe it now, that Willy is dead. Yes he is dead, and I am never going to see my boy again in this world. I see it now plainly, what at first seemed too terrible to think of, or believe. At first it was only the terrible blow that I felt, the awakening to the feeling he had been taken away from me by a strong and irresistible hand, and that I could not keep him, that it was possible to *live on* without my darling, that all my life I had loved and leaned on and trusted in. I could not *breathe* when I thought of it; it seemed as if everything had been *torn* out of life and yet I lived. But *you* know the feeling my child, the first fearful feeling; which thank God, Helena has not lasted. ... Our Home is very desolate without him. He was *all*, *everything* – and it has left a great *void*, a vacancy that makes me feel like *dying* when I think of it. ... Oh, Helena, he was so full of life, and hope and beauty, that I almost thought he could not die, and the feeling that I have of him now is not as of *Death*. I cannot think of death in connection with him. ... Dearie, our friends are never so truly ours as when we seem to have lost them in death. *Nothing* can take them from us *then*. ... I feel a peaceful feeling that I am not separated really from my boy, that he is *always* with me. ...

Henriette is standing by me, and sends her love to you and thanks you for the doll. Goodnight my dear one, my own Helena – Love to Miss M. Miss C. and the girls. I have you in my heart, my precious one.

God keep you and bless you.
Yr aff. *M. Temple*

Henry senior tried to persuade her that her brother's death was for the best: 'Uncle Henry says that no human-being can stand for a life time without almost superhuman strength the spontaneous *worship* almost that every one gave him.'

Privately, she rejected her uncle and aunt's advice: 'Uncle Henry and Aunt Mary think I ought to go back to school again – At first I could not make up my mind to go – Kitty needed me, and I could not summon up enough courage to go back to my old course of study, my old everyday life, with only *this terrible* blank in my life, but Uncle Henry told me it was my *duty* to go, and urged me to overcome my *feeling* by my sense of *Right*'. She obeyed, not 'from any *real* feeling that it was right in itself', but because grief drained her power of resistance: 'I could not bear *controversy* or *opposition* just now . . .'.

At this time of Union defeat, Wilky switched from the 44th Massachusetts to the first black regiment, the 54th Massachusetts, under Colonel Robert Gould Shaw. It had been formed in response to Lincoln's announcement (in the Emancipation Proclamation of 1 January) that blacks 'will be received into the armed services of the United States'. The blacks' spokesman Frederick Douglass had argued that it was absurd not to use their offer to fight in a cause so close to their hearts. But there was also a pragmatic reason to use them: the resistance to the draft law, with riots in cities by the poor who resented the ease with which the rich could buy themselves out. To join the blacks was a brave gesture on Wilky's part, for the South vowed to put to death any officer from this regiment whom they captured. On another visit to Readville, Henry junior detected 'an air of sacrifice' – prophetic, as it turned out. 'Two months after marching through Boston, / half the regiment was dead', Robert Lowell commemorated them with nostalgic piety in 'For the Union Dead' a century later. It was not a survivor but the non-combatant William James who was to unveil St Gaudens's relief in their honour in 1897, more than thirty years after the Civil War: 'at the dedication, / William James could almost hear the bronze negroes breathe', Lowell went on. At the head of the doomed, on 28 May 1863, Wilky marched through Boston, with banners, benedictions, and the driving thump of bands, cheered by some crowds, booed by others. What did he know about the barbarism of war? He was little more than a schoolboy, pumped full of his father's airy verbiage, and as unprepared as his commander for the uncontrollable violence of their men, whose first achievement was to pillage and burn Darien, Georgia – no better than white troops elsewhere. Which fact Boston, Lowell, and William James chose not to remember, but witnessed by Wilky.

In Charleston Bay, he was interviewed by the *Tribune* for an article syndicated in the Boston *Journal.* It pictured Wilky sitting against the flagstaff at Fort Sumter, gazing in a melancholy way at Fort Wagner. His brother William gave out that Wilky was behaving 'in a very theatrical way', and sent Wilky a cartoon of himself swollen with self-importance, brandishing a fat foot at Fort Wagner. From his foot drip three drops of blood, his measly badge of courage.

The defeat at Chancellorsville opened the way into Northern territory via the Shenandoah Valley. To halt the Southern advance, a major battle was in the offing. Gus Barker, the athlete of the family whose head wagged with energy, was at the ready with a dashing record: he had enlisted in October 1861 as a second lieutenant, and had been promoted first lieutenant in May 1862. He made the same heroic declarations as his Temple cousin: 'To-day or to-morrow I would gladly go to fight, either to distinguish myself or *die*. . . . I will be in a battle . . . or never go home.' In August he took three prisoners single-handed, came down with typhoid, was fetched home by his father, recovered, and rejoined his regiment as a captain in November 1862. In March 1863 he was outwitted by a woman, Miss Antonia J. Ford, 'Honorary Aide-de-Camp' to the Rebels, who led him into a trap. Taken prisoner, and in the midst of his captors, he tried to escape, wheeling round and galloping off through the mud in the thick pine woods of Virginia. In the end he was caught and cast into Libby Prison. There, amidst the gloom, he retained his bounce, and in May was exchanged for a Southern prisoner. As ever, he was eager for action.

The James family, aware Gus was to fight, held its breath as the battle began at Gettysburg on 1 July. Henry junior never forgot that long, hot day, when he and New York cousins stood about in the garden at Newport, daring neither to move nor rest, as they *listened* together for 'the boom of faraway guns' in southern Pennsylvania. One hundred and fifty thousand men fought muzzle to muzzle, at lethal range, over three days. Gus went into battle with thirty-two men and came out with three; his horse was killed; and a round-shot struck the ground near him, almost burying him with earth, but he escaped without a scratch. For the first time, Lee was defeated. He lost twenty-eight thousand; the North, twenty-three thousand, which was called a victory. A soldier from Massachusetts called it, more truly, 'a perfect hell on earth' – and photographs and telegraphs proved this with a promptness never known before in the reporting of war.

Suddenly, for Henry junior, war was no longer a distant dream of bristling hordes and tented field; it was there, in his garden; he felt the heat of its menace. And then, soon after, the hot breath of war was upon him: on 11 July, the *Newport Mercury* named him as one of eighty-six drafted by lot, under federal law, out of 287 men of eligible age in Newport's fifth ward.

His draft notice arrived on 16 July. Two days later, Wilky was wounded in his side, back, and foot at the battle of Fort Wagner, South Carolina, which is where half the regiment was killed, including Robert Gould Shaw and Wilky's friend Cabot Russell. One of the two men who tried to drag Wilky to the rear had his head shot off; the other fell too. A danger, at this moment, was to be captured: as an officer in the black regiment, Wilky could not expect to be saved as a prisoner. He would be executed or punished by a military tribunal infuriated by Darien. Passing out and coming to, Wilky crawled feebly towards the ambulance and found himself next day in a field hospital.

He was carried back to Newport by the sad father of Cabot Russell, arriving at the front door of his home on 31 July, so near death that the doctor ordered his stretcher to remain just inside the door. The wound in his side had to be cut open to remove gathering pus. His foot had to be sliced through at the sole to remove a bullet. In his delirium, Wilky would cry out for Shaw, Russell, and the rest of the Union dead. Louisa May Alcott, who had nursed soldiers in Washington until she succumbed to fever, made Wilky an afghan. Kitty Temple, depressed by her brother's death, spent two or three hours a day in the James house, tending her wounded cousin.

These events may explain the otherwise puzzling fact that, unlike other rich men – the father of Theodore Roosevelt or Andrew Carnegie or J. P. Morgan – Henry junior did not buy his release from the draft by paying a $300 commutation fee. Another common solution would have been to pay a substitute to go in his place. The ideological seriousness of the James home, reinforced by Wilky's heroism and present agony, precluded any such dodge. It is understandable, in the circumstances, that Henry junior preferred to appeal for release on the basis of a 'hurt' now two years old.

While Wilky suffered and Henry appealed against the draft, their youngest brother, Bob, sailed for the South on 21 July with a second black regiment, the 55th Massachusetts under Colonel Hallowell. The enlistment age was seventeen and Bob was, at this date, only sixteen, which means that his parents allowed him to lie. There is a gap here: what did Henry junior think and feel during the following weeks, as one younger brother hovered at the brink of death and another brother, no more than a boy, replaced him in the field? He did own to feeling 'ignobly safe' during the battle of Gettysburg and that Wilky's heroism was 'humiliating' to him. In the high-minded abolitionist circle to which the Jameses belonged, not to wear the blue (the uniform of war) was worse than unmanly; it was unconscionable. Facts suggest the mounting pressure of a moment of truth in which he could no longer play out a fantasy of shared endurance: the lacerated bodies and the 'arrested expression' of Will Temple, Cabot Russell, and Wilky seemed to look, he said, 'through us or straight over us at something they partake of together but that we mayn't pretend to know'. Eventually, he was able to convert the 'stress of life' into a form of 'work . . . to do by one's self and, in the last resort, deep within one's breast'.

At length, he came before the Rhode Island Board of Enrolment in Providence on 29 August, and was exempted from military service, along with several others, on the grounds of 'various complaints' (as reported in the local paper on 5 September). Two days later, Bob fought in the recapture of Fort Wagner. Ten days after that, Gus Barker was picketing the Rappahannock with three hundred men when he was shot by a sniper behind the lines near Kelly's Ford, Virginia. He died the next day, 18 September, at the age of twenty-two. His body was taken to Albany, and buried with military honours on 10 October.

As Wilky regained consciousness, he asked his father to preach a sermon. Henry senior began to hold forth on the Lord's protection, taking the Twenty-Third Psalm as his text, when Wilky broke in with a gory picture of his abandonment on the battlefield. Lying 'apparently forgotten by all the world', sick and faint with loss of blood, and wondering if he would ever see his home again, he had heard a groan beside him and, turning his head, saw an Ohio man with his jaw shot away – 'who finding that I was unable to move, crept over me and deluged me with his blood. At that moment I felt – '. Wilky could speak no more.

His father's account of this to the Boston reformer Elizabeth Peabody claims to have grasped 'the horrors of this dreadful war' but, in fact, he continued to pressure his youngest son to remain in the field.

Looking back afterwards, Wilky saw himself 'given' as a 'mite' to the cause dear to his father's heart: 'a sacrifice worth any cost'. He had been brought up, he said, to the 'stern duty' of the war; if necessary, to lay down his life: 'the North was smiting her children into line'. Though he avoids any direct accusation, a sense of paternal betrayal breathes through every sentence. By the time Henry senior's sons went off to war, its bungling conduct, the ineffectiveness of Northern generals, and their careless sacrifice of lives were all abundantly clear. For this was a war fought on home ground. Unlike foreign wars, slaughters could not be obscured: there were close-ups of corpses.

Henry junior records that his parents shed no tears at Bob's departure: 'we smiled as over the interest of childhood at its highest bloom, and that my parents, with their consistent tenderness, should have found their surrender of their latest born so workable is doubtless a proof that we were all lifted together as on a wave that might bear us where it would.' We? Us? It was Bob who was borne away on that wave of war fever, but the rhetoric swept past him, inflating the family with participatory fervour.

'I cannot but adore the Great Providence which is thus lifting our young men out of indolence and vanity', Henry senior told Miss Peabody the day after Bob's departure. '. . . I still had the courage, spiritually, to bid him put all his heart in his living or dying, that so whether he lived or died he might be fully adopted of that Divine spirit of liberty which is at last renewing all things in its own image.'

Henry senior loses sight of a sixteen-year-old in the importance of his own sermon, and though he gives a nod to heartbreak, it is literally in the subordinate clause, a foil to his own soaring. Bob had been bored by Sanborn's school, and soon left. His surliness was offset by a Jamesian gift for words – his talk 'charged with natural life', as Henry junior put it; William thought him the best letter-writer in the family, a formidable distinction given the conscious brilliance of William, Henry, and Alice when they addressed themselves to others. After a few months in the army, Bob regretted his enlistment and missed home. He confessed this to his father after he participated in Seymour's raid into Florida and a night-long battle at Ostulee with two thousand casualties in February 1864. Henry senior sent a stern reply, warning against the sins of idleness, and urging the boy to be a man. The discourse of manliness, investing it with a spiritual sanction, seems coercive, even sinister, from this sweet-voiced philosopher of secular transfiguration. Wilky, he boasted everywhere, had been educated 'up to manhood', and bore his wound 'like a man', while, in similar terms, he appealed to Bob's 'manhood' to resist the temptation to leave the army (though a discharge was recommended on the grounds of sunstroke and dysentery bad enough to make him unfit for service). It would be 'effeminacy', his father urged, 'an unmanly project'. 'I conjure you to be a man', he said, 'and force yourself like a man to do your whole duty'.

Wilky had returned to the field as soon as he was fit. Wrenched to fit this model, Bob, a sensitive James who worshipped his father, was forced to become a seasoned warrior – though, like Wilky, he was to fail at everything else for the rest of his life. He saw black soldiers die from dysentery and neglect, unpaid by the government; and he was amongst the first troops to enter Charleston in the spring of 1865. There, at the end of the war, he and Wilky met. Charleston, Wilky wrote home, was full of negroes who 'fall about you & cling to you fairly with delight'. He visited Fort Sumter with men cheering the old flag while a band played 'The Star-Spangled Banner' and 'Yankee Doodle'. Few soldiers would have said, as Wilky did at this point, 'There is nothing I want so much as literature.' He had read a book on Waterloo and Shakespeare's *Henry VIII*: both were 'marvellously good'.

Wilky still missed his family and asked: 'Can't H[enry]. come down and pay us a visit of 2 or 3 weeks? I can get him a War Dept pass'.

Henry James recorded his 'inability to accept this invitation'. He gave no reason, but in truth was preoccupied with his 'reserved but quite unabashed' design to be a writer. It seemed to him that the years from the spring of 1864 to the autumn of 1866 were strewn with garlands. His connections ensured he was not overlooked when he approached James T. Fields of the prestigious *Atlantic Monthly*, Edwin L. Godkin of the *Nation*, and Charles Eliot Norton, the 'apostle of culture' to America as the influential editor of the *North American Review*. February 1864 was the starting point, when he published his first tale, about a woman who murders her husband. An uncle, Smith Van Buren, forbade Elly Temple to read it. Mrs de Kay noticed that this 'brought a smile of quiet contempt to Harry's lips but anger and indignation to those of Miss Minnie Temple'. Young girls must be shielded from the unpleasantness of murder, while men must fight and die – all 620,000 of their generation killed in the war.

Henry senior, who changed his views in the course of the war, made and broke his sons. He made the two eldest in so far as he excused their non-participation; he broke his two youngest in so far as he waved them off at the earliest possible age to an arena of mass slaughter in the first mechanised war, from which neither, in mental terms, ever recovered. The friendly, demonstrative Wilky and the pathetically young Bob, annoying his father with teenage surliness, were his sacrifice to the abolitionist ideals of his society.

In a letter of 1861 Henry senior pretends he held back his two 'scamps' (William and Henry) by their coat-tails as they tried to rush off to war. This rueful posture of himself as wise old man whose eldest sons were dashing braves reveals how much he cared for public opinion, despite his reputation for unworldliness. With his elder sons, Henry senior was the protective father – that part of the image was accurate. William and Henry had clear instructions: they were not to throw their lives away. They were granted a parental endorsement of invalidism: the 'horror' expressed by Henry junior over his 'obscure hurt' was a matter of perception. A good number of men who fought were no more robust than he and William. The sense in which their parents made them is therefore ambiguous: they were saved from brutalities to better purpose; at the same time they sank into invalidism.

Thirty years later, in 'Owen Wingrave', Henry James fictionalised the moral trauma of a youth who refused a military career in the face of maximum pressure. Owen Wingrave belongs to a family of soldiers who have gone manfully to early graves. Scorned for cowardice, he is seen only through the distorting opinions of people who back the institution of war, but what does echo through to us is that this young man despises war as 'crass barbarism', provoked by those with too little imagination for fear. It is, in any case, a stupid way of resolving issues; society must find a better. Given the 'immeasurable misery' of wars, the youth asks why nations don't tear to pieces the governments that go in for them. He refuses to waste his young life ('*he* wasn't so dull a brute') despite the shame of being thought unmanly – underlined by the contempt of an attractive young woman ('damsels doubtless always had their ideals of manhood – in the type of belted warrior').

The tale is set in England – at a fictional remove from the author's own past – but it takes the view of James himself in the most convincing phrase in his autobiography: 'still so young and so meant for better things'. This plain reason not to fight is wrapped in a paragraph three pages long about the 'honour' his 'obscure hurt' conferred upon him as a 'sort of tragic fellowship'. James took this line fifty years after the Civil War; whether he deluded himself at the time is impossible to know. It might be argued that truth in its humdrum sense doesn't apply to the fecundities of a developed imagination. Yeats dreams of a sublime death for an Irish hero in the First World War, while the poet sits safe at home in his artist's tower. For the space of a poem, we lend ourselves to delirious heroism. Are we to respond in such a way to James as a 'recruit' amidst the bristling hordes? A bombardment of military metaphor strains our assent to the point of incredulity. This is reinforced by another, less obvious distortion: his fragmentary record of a turning point in his youth.

It is an undated typescript answer to a query that came to James late in life, about its turning point. His answer is to look at his student self in 1862–3 in the 'shade of queer old Dane Hall', the Law School. He asks the reader to contemplate his wrongness in that place, and the inevitability of his turn away. This would appear plausible were it not for the fact that James claims not to remember, and closes off the question. To block reflection was out of character; anyway, it is simply not credible that he should have forgotten the mounting pressure of the war as family opinion swung, in the course of 1862–3, towards enlistment. No, the real trial was to go home to Newport at the end of his academic year, to go home with no apparent plan – and not budge. To do so in the face of the pro-war feeling that was running high by this time gave pre eminence, from now on, to the perils of the inner life. There was an alternative drama, an alternative manhood that had to wait in the wings.

The turning point, then, did not take place in the shade of Dane Hall but in the doorway of the family home, where Wilky lay on an army stretcher, his face gaunt with agony, his mouth open, near to death – while through the second half of July and all through August of 1863 his elder brother held out against the draft. The view of military action in 'Owen Wingrave' is unambiguous. It is stupid, and to refuse it, in the face of public and family pressure, is a form of action reserved for the enlightened: a supreme act of moral courage in which a haunted mind does battle with reproachful kin who have given their lives in battle. To front these ghosts proves that 'he *is* in a high sense of the term, a fighting man'.

Throughout the writer's own trial, Minny's moral courage to defy opinion drew them together. 'Few spirits were as free as hers,' William said in old age, repeated in a memoir by his brother

Henry, who absorbed her spirit. His heroines who 'affront' their destiny look back to Minny improvising a course of her own, which made Newport itself 'insistently romantic, romantic out of all proportion', to her attentive cousin. He never forgot the toss of her head; her quick speech; her long, looping step; her large, postponing, renouncing laugh as though some part of it were held back to protect her company – or even herself – from the full impact of her response. Outfacing the old drama of damsel and belted warrior, their closeness began in acts of defiance – Minny's outspoken, his silent. This set them apart, the start of an understanding that was to outlast Minny's life.

4
A Girl of the Future

A spate of happiness for James coincided with the end of the Civil War in the spring of 1865. His 'invalidism' seemed to vanish. His fiction appeared in print, and that summer he took a holiday with the Temples in northern New Hampshire, remembered as the high point of youth. On the face of it nothing happened there; the drama was inward, 'unspeakable' (as James always said when emotion came into play). His memoir of Minny, written in old age, puts her centre-stage, 'the heroine of the scene', as though the focus she had provided for defiance through the war years now shifted, with a lift of ardour, to the focus of art.

As he shed the shame of the non-combatant for the elation of the writer, a certainty of genius expanded in an emptied space around him. His younger brothers remained in the army: Wilky would leave the service only in August, Bob a month later. In March, William departed for Brazil on a scientific expedition with Louis Agassiz of Harvard – he was to be away almost a year. There was mild rivalry between the two eldest brothers, but they were particularly close, expressed constant concern and affection, and had more in common than most brothers, with their ear to mental and spiritual states. It is possible, though, that William's more dramatic invalidism, reinforced by his authority as a medical student, infected Henry, as it did Alice, and that however much they looked up to William, both were compelled, at length, to detach themselves from his fascination for their ills. Such moves lay far in the future; at this point, simply a quickening in William's absence and a renewed strength with the publication, in March 1865, of 'The Story of a Year', the first fiction to bear the name of Henry James and, in itself, a triumphant alternative to the insensibility of fighters.

Ostensibly a Civil War story in the course of 1862–3, the narrator declines to record John Ford's letters from the battlefields of Virginia: 'My own taste has always been for unwritten history . . . the reverse of the picture.' He shows the reverse of the picture to be a different kind of heroism: Ford, wounded and near to death, resigns his fiancée, Lizzie Crowe, to a non-combatant she has come to prefer in his absence. His mother, filled with vindictive hatred of Lizzie, breaks the news of her defection, and this blow, given in the name of maternal care, in effect kills her son – kills him more surely than shot. His secret engagement proves fatal: his mother and Lizzie vie for possession; the surname, Crowe, an augury of death in *Macbeth* when 'the crow / Makes wing to th' rooky wood'. From the first, names in Henry James point to the emblematic element in character. Like Hawthorne, James wished to bring out 'the interest *behind* the interest' of a situation. Outwardly, there is the common tug between two women. Behind that lies the impact of the mind on physical illness, and behind that – and more indefinable – is a rare approach to death, one James would explore repeatedly in the course of his writings. What Ford feels for Lizzie Crowe in his last hours is not less love, but love expanded beyond its object. In the foreground is the wavering attachment of a popular girl, but recessed behind this is the exceptional consciousness of John Ford – a private ordeal that internalised a national trauma. James was to date America's loss of innocence from the Civil War. In this tale, he explores the unwritten history of the war whose unhealed wounds compel a new form of manhood. By shunning war himself, and the 'manliness' of his father's inflated babble, James could imagine a man who loses illusions and is not warped.

'Now I am immortal', he told Perry after he completed the first draft. The terms of their correspondence about this story verged on the religious: Perry was struck by some resemblance to the Book of Job, and James thanked him for a 'heaven-inspired letter. . . . Y[ou]r letter touches upon great questions . . .'. It is an easy step to Eliot's retrospective remark in 1923 that Henry James 'pulsates with the agony of the spiritual life'.

At once, and with extraordinary assurance, he laid down the central matter of his work: selfless love, often in the face of death –

love that is the reverse of war, that survives on its own, that outlasts the gender game.

Ford's transcendent love shames Lizzie into renewed loyalty but we are left with questions: can it hold against the possessive love of Mrs Ford and the sleigh-ride love of her second suitor? Mr Bruce seems destined to conquer, given his name – that of the conqueror in the only novel Lizzie has read, the *Scottish Chiefs* (1810). Both men embrace her shallowness. Ford defends it as engaging simplicity. Her weakness inflates him with 'a sudden rush of manhood' when she assumes the body language of dependence. His shoulders seem to expand and become stalwart with 'a silent desire for the whole fair burden'. As protector, he shoulders her parasol as though it were a musket. His own musket and blue uniform, the props of war, construct manhood in a reciprocal way. Bruce wants prettiness and a kind heart, to him the essence of womanhood, as he explains his suit to Lizzie. A woman of character is conspicuous by her absence.

Minny embodied that alternative for James. In the spring and summer of 1865, he moved between Boston, where the James family had settled a year before, and Newport, where Minny still lived and which remained, for James, the landscape of their tie. She was, he said, 'the very genius of the place', and something of her may be expressed, indirectly, in his memory of 'a thousand delicate, secret places', dear to the rambler; faraway, lonely coves; 'rock-set, lily-sheeted ponds, almost hidden'; and the expanse of the sea 'just over some stony shoulder'.

There never was such a coming and going, James recalled of the spring of '65. The previous year he had nursed his back as he sat writing his first reviews in his third-floor room in the red-brick house which looked out on Ashburton Place at the summit of Beacon Hill. Now, at the age of twenty-two, having survived his wartime trial and hung with the garlands of publication, he returned to Newport. Little record remains beyond this 'coming and going', but a formative postwar 'scene' was coming into being with Minny at the centre – a girl of the future who posed the purpose of existence to the 'endlessly conversing group' of clever men – 'our circle' – now turning to the 'high art of peace'. She delighted in playing the piano where, as James recalled, 'slim and straight, her shoulders and head constantly, sympathetically swaying, she discoursed with an admirable touch and a long surrender . . .'. He noticed how 'ardently' she worked at her music which, she said, brought out 'the absolute value of the individual – the absolute necessity of uncompromising & unfaltering truth, the way in which we like our own likes, & our *unlikes* . . .'. Music was 'a revelation of completeness'. She declared that 'some of the most direct revelations of spiritual things that I have ever got, have been through music.'

James remembered, too, afternoon walks by the sea. Minny had 'a grace of free mobility and activity, as original and "unconventional" as it was carelessly natural'. She was part of the laughter on wide verandahs of the newer 'cottages' along the Avenue, whose doors and windows stood open. On Saturday nights there were dances in the hotel, the wooden Ocean House, its vast terrace filled with rocking chairs and girls swaying in cool, white dresses. The shrubbery stirred as they fanned themselves. Song, 'the high brilliant notes of women's art', came through an open window to those outside, including the young James sitting on the steps 'where the shade of the evening was thickest'.

In July, when Minny left Newport for North Conway, New Hampshire, it was agreed that James would follow her for the month of August. He commanded her to keep her 'eyes peeled' for simple lodgings for himself and Wendell Holmes, who was to join the party. After 'superhuman efforts' Minny could find only a single room with only one bed. In high spirits, James promised Wendell they would pull the bed of the 'wretch' who owned the room from under him. The room was cheap – $2.50 per week – with no food. Minny arranged for the men to dine at a neighbouring house – it was 'the very best' she could do.

'If you don't mind it, *I* don't', James assured Holmes, 'as the lady said when the puppy-dog licked her face.'

In the interval, he 'ate of the lotus, to repletion', rising at nine-thirty, relishing his distance from Boston. It was a homecoming, in so far as any place could be called home, and pleasing to be in demand; old friends like La Farge seemed to 'snatch' him from one another. When he looked up from his writing he saw a sea and sky 'of cobalt'. Here, a man could 'ripen into absolute perfection'.

Part of his happiness was anticipation: 'I pant for the 1st of August', he told Holmes. 'I will keep Minny Temple on the look out.'

Holmes, who had left the army a year before, brought along a fellow-officer, Major John Chipman Gray, another lawyer, who had risen to the position of judge-advocate in the course of the war. Gray came on the scene a bit later. So it was that 'three quite exceptional young men', as James was not too modest to say, 'travelled up from Boston with their disposition to admire inevitably quickened' to join the Temple sisters, aged twenty-two (Kitty), twenty (Minny), fifteen (Elly), and twelve (Henrietta). They were found at the Blue Blinds under the eye of their great-aunt, Miss Charlotte Perkins, who looked, James thought, exactly like benign portraits of General Washington. If he was father to the nation, Aunt Charlotte, erect and genial, had the air of its mother.

As the two ex-soldiers went through their paces, Minny was less than spellbound. Their 'fine' military experiences, designed to draw her, were 'common', as James perceived with veiled satisfaction. Gray bored her as he held forth on Trollope. She struggled to stay awake in his company, marvelling at the stamina of her sisters. Cool, unsentimental, Gray was 'hard-hearted', she thought. Though, in time, she came to depend on him, and though she respected his sense and rectitude, she never enjoyed his stiffly handsome presence quite as much as her sisters, who thought him 'lovely'.

Wendell Holmes was long and lean, upright as befitted a soldier, with craggy features and flourishing moustache. Enlisting early in the war, after he graduated from Harvard, he was wounded in his first action. Letters from his commanding officer and doctor to his father are tributes to masculinity: 'so full of manly spirit', wrote one officer on 25 October 1861; 'passed all ordeals manfully' and 'never flinched from duty', wrote others. They picture Holmes in the field hospital, smoking and full of easy cheer as he contemplates photographs of 'certain young ladies. He declared that to look at the portrait of Miss Agassiz was like having an angel in the tent.'

The unspoken was scrawled on a scrap after three years of war: Holmes's self-disgust with the corrupting insensibility of men required to 'kill – kill – kill'.

After years of killing, after the mud, dysentery, and boredom, as well as two life-threatening wounds, he still found it hard to explain to his abolitionist parents why he had to muster out of the army nine months before the end of the war. For Holmes left the battlefields of the Civil War having lost all faith in abolitionism and other causes based on morality. He had become a Darwinian who saw only a struggle for survival against forces of annihilation. When he met Minny in the summer of 1865, he had completed the first year of an LL B degree at Harvard, with a starry future ahead as the greatest legal mind America has produced. His combination of birth, boyish charm, and piercing blue eyes encouraged a parallel career as womaniser – a desperate flirt, according to Alice James. The best that can be said is that in these early years he flirted with unusual women like Minny Temple, Clover Hooper, and Fanny Dixwell, all three restless with intelligence: Minny with her questions about the meaning of existence; witty Clover, ('a perfect Voltaire in petticoats', James thought); and dark-eyed Fanny, whose embroideries were works of art – rarely exhibited and, later, largely destroyed.

Part of Holmes's charm, for some, was his vein of romantic lyricism. He would go on about bees toiling in sticky buds, and sigh over 'passionate breezes' and 'rejoicing hills', all piercing the heart 'with an ecstasy I cannot utter'. To this day, respectful legal commentators relay what they call the Wordsworthian in him, though it is posturing tosh, unfelt and tedious. Years later, when he sent Henry James a copy of his address on 'The Soldier's Faith', James obliged with effusive praise for 'romantic eloquence' and 'chastened nobleness', and played to perfection the unworthy worshipper of manliness. 'I envy you the right . . . to so gallant a thesis', he said, 'so few & far between are the men that have it – among the men who can use it.' Privately, he remarked to William that he found Wendell unreal.

Though in the summer of 1865 the scene was 'swamped' by a 'monster tide' of 'masculinity', though James could smell it in discarded uniforms – army-cloth 'saturated' with men who had served – and see it in 'bronzed, matured faces' and hear it in soldiers' stories, and though his own masculinity continued to be called into question, he also defied this.

Silently, at North Conway, he applauded Minny's refusal to defer to the heroes of the hour. Devoid, himself, of the verbal 'luxury' of military exploits, ceding this ground to men of action, he took the measure of an alternative 'heroine', a counterpart to himself. Even as he seemed to defer to the kind of masculinity represented by men who had worn the blue, he felt a superior power to draw Minny as kinsman and 'painter'. The apparently peripheral position of James in relation to two veterans was, in fact, reversed; they were invited players in a Jamesian drama in which he placed them in a situation that circled Minny, there, in the shade of the rustling pines as the summer stretched itself out to its fullness. Letting the veterans trumpet their 'common' experience, he paid her the rarer compliment of silent knowing. There were, of course, the bit-players – elderly Aunt Charlotte; Kitty and Elly with the dew still upon them of the old Albany naturalness; and the juvenile Henrietta – but 'essentially, we of the true connection made up the drama'. He rejoiced in having 'such a heroine that everything else inevitably came. Mary Temple was beautifully and indescribably *that* . . .'.

The very absence of defining terms provoked the portraits that were to follow. They 'came', as it were, from the indescribable quality of her being, as though she, not James, were their author. He perceived 'a divinely restless spirit', awake, like himself, to invisible drama and unresolvable questions, but readier to expose herself publicly as 'one of the "irreconcilables"', like her friend, Helena, who hurrahed 'the new man and woman, *with* a soul'. Only 'a great spirit', James thought, would be equal to 'her exquisite energy of wonder, conjecture and unrest'. His feeling appears contradictory: 'I loved her', he told his mother; 'I never was [in love with her]', he told William, though 'everyone else was'. He may have wished to know her, more than he wished to love her (though the two are not mutually exclusive). The extent to which his knowing blends with the spectatorial discipline of the artist is impossible to determine, but the artist in James can never be overestimated.

James calls himself a 'painter' as opposed to veterans of the war. In the autumn of 1865, he completed a tale called 'A Landscape-Painter', about 'a woman of character' untouched by spurious norms. In the backwater where she lives, a sophisticated artist-cum-diarist – an arch-observer – takes lodgings. Miriam is 'a woman of some originality' who teaches the piano, reads novels, and takes walks with a dog 'like one of Miss Brontë's heroines'. She has Minny's round chin, graceful movements, and unhesitating laugh; she speaks her mind with no concessions to 'sentiment and sweetness', and shows herself as far as possible from the ornament of society, Miss Leary, to whom the diarist was once engaged. Direct as she is, Miriam has an air of having something to say but not saying it which the diarist perceives as a 'natural' mystery, not the artifice of acquired femininity. He is increasingly obsessed with the character she secretes. It may surface for a moment but remains inscrutable; her fresh, proper dress covers a nature she may not reveal; her future is unfinished. Her eyes defer the diarist's desire; he calls it 'this little secret of ours'. We see, through his desire, the raindrops and mud that cling to Miriam when she comes home from work; her hands red with cold, which the diarist would like to kiss; her dress that sits well on her without whalebone; the easy way she folds her arms when she sits on the doorstep as evening falls. Her physical presence seems all the closer for the absence of touch, a voluptuous awareness expanding to the fullest attention.

Like James, the diarist is a spectator who finds himself involved with his subject; unlike James, he does take on marriage – though not for long. He dies, we are told, five years later. Can this be a cautionary tale about the fatality of marriage?

'I have only to let myself *go*!' James told himself in what he called his 'fermenting and passionate youth'. The sense of this – the need for it – rolled over him, at times, 'with commanding force'. But he never did let himself go.

An undisguised attraction to young men declared itself later in James's life. How early he felt this is not known; nor is there proof of commitment. The ease of his expressiveness to men in an age when deviance (as it was seen) was punishable by law, suggests that, for James, there was a significant difference between imaginative desire – extending to hugs and kisses – and consummation. He was a complex person who could be extravagantly open in his feelings for both sexes, and at the same time intensely, even enjoyably, secretive. To label him would be reductive; suffice to say he aimed to use the full human endowment, displacing the distorted manhood his father had imposed on his fighter sons.* In the aftermath of the Civil War, he began to imagine a new form of human being, consistent with the new idea of evolution (laid down in *The Origin of Species* in 1859). Neither a new manhood nor a complementary womanhood would fit the social institutions of the day, nineteenth-century marriage for a start. This was the basis for his affinities with Minny and, after her, Fenimore. Whatever Minny was in actuality, what was important about her, from his point of view, was that he foresaw no place for her in social terms. But since the question of manhood had its source, for James, in his experience of war, its implications were wider than the Woman Question and the covert issue of the love that had no name.

James would dream and re-dream his youth, but the notion of having had one was a fiction of old age. In his late teens and early twenties, he was in thrall to physical ills and, from 1864, to a full-fledged professionalism from which he never looked back. These two occupations may seem contradictory, but for at least three of the most ambitious people in the nineteenth century – Florence Nightingale, Charles Darwin, and Henry James in the earliest phase of his career – invalidism provided a socially acceptable solitude in which the greatest feats might be achieved: reorganising the hospital system, transforming the view of our place in the universe and, in the case of James, revolutionising gender and fiction. This is not to say that these famous invalids did not

* The Civil War brought about a marked narrowing of the idea of manhood, with an emphasis less on character than on strenuous public deeds. The pressure to be masculine in a tougher sense gave the word new meaning, and 'masculinity' made its way into the language. By 1890 it was in the *Century Dictionary*, the equivalent of the *Oxford English Dictionary* in America, and talk of manliness continued until about 1910. It was promoted by William James, amongst other leading educators who looked on a writer's life as inferior. See Kim Townsend, *Manhood at Harvard: William James and Others* (NY: Norton, 1996).

actually suffer the ills they claimed, but that these ills proved remarkably convenient and did not prevent prodigious efforts. The retirement required by James's back, and at least two prolonged cures for his unyielding bowels, promoted his chosen pursuit: the tales and reviews pouring swiftly from his pen.

Invalidism, then, was the visible occupation of his early career. Uninteresting in itself, it had repercussions for others – his younger brothers and Mary Temple – and so needs a brief account. Dr Denniston's water-cure at Northampton, Massachusetts, from August to November 1864, had marked the start of the bowel trouble that was to dominate the next six years. This developed in a family context that backed it to the hilt: the unfailing indulgence of Mrs James towards this, her favourite and most obedient son, and her contrasting hardness towards her fighting, commercial sons. She gave out, and no doubt believed, the individualistic cant that each son was free to cultivate what she chose to call his 'genius'. In practice, she glued the younger two, as well as her daughter, to the most commonplace outlines of manhood and womanhood. She was too dull, and her husband too dizzily preoccupied, to understand why complex organisms like Wilky, Bob, and Alice, could never fit the cut-outs she designed. She saw their torment, but in her manipulative way thought it must do them good. 'Alice is busy trying to idle,' she once told Henry junior, 'and it is always very hard and depressing work, this to her; but I think it will tell in the end.'

Mrs James, that ordinary woman, may be an important clue to mental disturbance in the household: it was not genius, alone, that caused the trouble, but rather genius in thrall to dullness. To be small-minded and busy is a recipe for maximum damage. The icon of domestic angel gave Mrs James a licence to twist her children to her will. Henry had to get away from his mother if he was not to be invalided for life. Before him was the warning figure of his father – a man of large ideas reduced to an infant clinging to the hand of his nanny-wife.

Henry senior did not lack for ideas, but they had no human application, and he was as capricious and baffling (in his captivating way) as a guru playing god. In Europe in 1859–60, he had toyed with a notion that his youngest son, Bob, had the most vigour. Then, in the course of that year, he decided abruptly that Bob would never earn a living in one of the professions. The boy was then only thirteen. Curiously, the pattern of indulgence was already in place, for if any son was a failure in the course of that year it was Henry, who dropped out of school. Again, three years later, Henry dropped out of law, and was allowed to remain at home – as 'the Angel' – with no overt work nor income in the winter of 1863–4, while Wilky returned to the field, and Bob was forced by his father to remain there.

This underlying wrong in the James family persisted after Bob's discharge from the army in 1865. That autumn, while Henry was tucked up at home on Beacon Hill writing 'A Landscape-Painter', Bob was working for the railroad far off in Iowa; lonely and utterly miserable, he wrote to ask if he might be allowed to come home and study architecture. Like William, he had a taste for art, and hoped his chance would come to try out an artistic career. Mrs James replied that though Bob might have a certain talent, he tended to exaggerate it. She did not trust him to stick three years of study – this, despite the fact that Bob had recently stuck three years of war. She told her homesick son that since they were leaving Boston for six months, they could not offer him a home. (In the event, they moved no farther than the North Shore of Massachusetts Bay where Wilky was urged to visit.) Mrs James then drove the knife deeper when she expressed a doubt that, even if Bob did persevere with professional training, he would ever make money – though such an argument was not held against Henry. A writer who aimed at the 'reverse of the picture' could hardly hope for wealth.

The divide between favoured and unfavoured sons meant, once again, that Bob, a sensitive and potentially talented James, was aligned with the quixotic Wilky, and forced to join him in Florida. Mrs James said it would fulfil his 'genius'; the real motive (as though Bob didn't know it) was a Bob-free home. Wilky's idea was to start a plantation. It would provide jobs for free slaves who knew how to raise cotton. In February 1866 Henry senior bought three thousand acres in Gordon, Florida, at huge expense. Part of the land was for cultivation; part for speculation: to sell to Northerners who wished to try planting on a smaller scale. There was a naïve plan to form a settlement of Northern men with a view to doing the country 'a great deal of good'. The reality was they had no experience as farmers, and freed slaves did not provide grateful or reliable labour. It was also dangerous for Northerners with the rise of the vengeful postwar society of the Ku Klux Klan, who pounced at night and murdered their like as well as pesky blacks. The brothers struggled on for two or three years, and then had to admit massive failure. The crops were ruined by rains and caterpillars. Wilky fell ill with fever in 1867, and came home for a spell with Bob.

At a James dinner party in October, a visitor teased another for sleeping so soundly that a servant had feared him dead. Henry senior remarked, 'She'd have no such fear if Bob had been under her care for he makes such a noise in his sleep.'

'But she would have been afraid he was *drunk*,' said Henry junior. Alice saw Bob squirm.

As soon as Wilky was out of danger he went back, in November, and ploughed on alone. 'It will be a severe discipline to Wilk that dreary life there,' Mrs James acknowledged to William (funded by his parents to cure a collapse with nineteen months in Berlin), 'but it will make more of a man of him than the life here would.' She owned that Wilky looked 'much altered', thin and sallow, with 'his mind evidently much shaken'.

'I am pretty lonely & secluded & often think of you & mother & all the family with intense longing', Wilky wrote to his father on 8 April 1868, '& wonder whether the day will soon come when I can with honor & satisfaction to myself & with profit to the family, live once more in your midst free from all the many smallnesses & wretchednesses arising out of this chaotic condition of southern society.' He longed for 'sympathy & instruction'. He had not heard from home for two weeks, he said, '& am getting pretty mad'.

A further series of failed ventures out west led to crashing morale. Later, in Milwaukee, Wisconsin, Wilky confided to Gray that 'every year of this western life becomes more & more intolerable to me . . . The West commercially is to be admired, and will continue to grow in that way, but the dreary commonplaceness of its social life is unspeakably demoralising.' When Henry grew impatient with Cambridge, he reminded himself that he '*might* be lodged in one of the innermost circles of the inferno – in Wisconsin' where his brother toiled in hopeless exile. To the end of his life Wilky dreamt of returning to live in Boston or New York. Bob, too, tried to endure his banishments; then collapsed into rage, drink, and lust, losing self-respect and inviting further reproof. This was to become the pattern of his existence while, for decades, the favoured ones, none too stable themselves, shook grave heads over 'Bob's fits of madness' and what William termed his 'nervous degeneracy'. Alice did concede it was effect not cause, but a sting follows: 'The poor creature seems to have no inner existence of any kind, he has always made upon my mind the impression of a human bladder.'

Bob's writings give a different impression. He struggled to subdue his sensibilities in order to become the enterprising man his parents ordained. Squaring his shoulders, he hoped repeatedly to hold out, though he, too, loathed the West – his next destination. He tried to work in mundane jobs, thwarted by assaults of lowness and the James knack for self-absorption. Hating himself and his failures, he made an array of new starts, but when he fell in love with a cousin, Kitty Van Buren, and become secretly engaged to her in 1869, he was crushed by William's ruling that cousins must not marry. William was convinced he and his siblings carried a taint of 'infirm health', an inborn 'evil', which it would be a 'crime against humanity' to propagate.

February 1866 was a critical month for all the family: firstly, the ill-fated purchase of land made an irretrievable dent in the James fortune: none of the sons would be able to live as gentlemen of leisure like their father; secondly, William returned from Brazil and, at this time, Alice's 'attacks' became manifest as an unnamed condition. William noticed that, beside their blithe parents, he, Henry junior, and Alice seemed 'aged solemn owls'. Then, too, in February 1866, Minny Temple and her sisters arrived in Boston to discuss their own problem. Their brother, Robert, had been wheedling money from anyone who would oblige. Now he was convicted of forging a cheque and sentenced to a year's hard labour on Bedlow's Island.

In the midst of family troubles, Henry junior pursued his future with 'silent pluck'. The portrait of Miriam, the first of his remarkable women, was published that February. But it was to be a long time before he could support himself.

With so many dependants, together with the outlay on a Southern plantation, Henry senior had to economise. In the spring of 1866, the family gave up their fashionable address in Ashburton Place and took a cottage at Swampscott, a quiet settlement of clapboard houses on the North Shore, en route to Salem and Beverly. They found themselves on a wind-scoured plain with low hills, grey rocks, stone walls, scrubby fir trees and apple orchards. The sky was so clear, William said, you could see every blade of grass on the horizon and the distant rocks almost scratched your eyeball. He was encouraged by the wholesomeness of a 'popping' climate and 'oceans of milk and cream'; Henry, though, languished from the start of July when he came back 'from a bad little "sick" visit' to Minny in New Hampshire – this one remark is all that remains.

For the rest of the summer, he lay on his back, nursing its aches, as he read through George Eliot for two reviews. 'Thrilled' as he was in private, in public he sneered at the exemplary preacher, Dinah Morris, a stand-in for the sympathies of the woman writer in *Adam Bede.* It is as though James, at the age of twenty-three, cannot afford to own the huge influence of George Eliot (1819–1880). His early reviews affect the annihilating manner of the James dinner table, as he ridicules Whitman, carps at George Eliot, or savages Dickens for shallow characterisations. These reviews are skewed by a patent agenda: if Henry James is to make his mark as a novel phenomenon, then the shadow of great predecessors must be eliminated. The power play of the young critic was the obverse of his inability to let himself go which he justified by extravagant helplessness: 'miserably stricken by my poor, broken, all but unbearable, and unsurvivable *back*'. After the visit to Minny, he felt 'dismally alone'. It was too hot to walk, and impossible to read *all* day. He was forced, he said, 'to feed upon my own soul – a specie[s] of diet wh[ich] gives me bad dreams'.

Minny, he thought, knew him at his 'worst' yet never realised quite how 'sick & disordered' he was. He hoped the time would come when he would recover enough to become 'more active and masculine'. She never knew, he thought, the man who could take the 'lead', waiting to emerge in the later 1860s.

Meanwhile, Minny befriended Holmes. While Holmes was in Europe in the spring and summer of 1866, his mother wrote to say that 'One of your fair friends ... called here this forenoon – Miss Minnie Temple. ... She is at Cambridge – &, I dare say she will come again'. His adventures in the Alps and London drawing-rooms tempted Henry James and Minny to go abroad. For an unknown reason, Minny abandoned the idea by the end of the year when she and her sisters came to stay with the Jameses over New Year. She seemed, James thought, 'rather glad to have done so'.

During this visit he was 'decidedly brighter'. He recounted the visit, in high spirits, to Alice, who had left in November 1866 to undergo a six-month cure in New York – against her wish. The cure involved filling her with butter on the principle that butter (or any other fat) was good for the nerves. She was a live-in patient with a Broadway doctor, Charles Fayette Taylor (1827–1899), who specialised in women's disorders as well as orthopaedics. He believed that unnatural intellect in women would curve their spines. His theory was that if books were removed, their spines would straighten into proper, upright, unthinking womanhood. Henry senior concurred in so far as he never changed his view that woman was inferior to man in passion, intellect, and strength. He thought it did not become a woman to be too educated, and Mrs James sent Alice fancy-work to fill her days. Henry junior, who perceived that 'in our family group, girls seemed scarcely to have had a chance', tried to console Alice with lamentations at her absence. He told her the Temples never stopped talking about her. 'A hundred times a day they cry out how they miss you & then our tears break out afresh & we all sob & tear our hair together.'

The week of New Year saw 'the heroine of the scene' once more in action: the regrouping of 'Harry', 'Willy', Holmes, and Gray around the Temples in the James family parlour at 20 Quincy Street, Cambridge, opposite the Harvard campus; Gray, at a family 'banquet' in the girls' honour, voted 'as nice as ever' by Mrs James and 'more "lovely" than ever' by Minny's sisters. If we can believe Mrs James, Minny was less pretty and 'quiet disenchanted' with

Holmes: 'She talks of his thinness and ugliness and pinchedness, as well as his beautiful eyes – and seems to see his egotism.'

As Minny came to know Holmes better, she can't have missed their fundamental difference. Minny believed in and strove to practise an ideal of generosity, aware that in worldly terms this 'paid not at all'. Holmes, who told a friend, 'I lost my humanity . . . in the army', wished 'every word of moral significance could be banished form the law altogether'. Eventually, he adapted the nation's law to the growing power of its manufacturing corporations and technology, so that economy, with its hardness and selfishness, replaced morality as the basis for law. There was, at the time, an alternative response to the challenges of biblical authority by the German Higher Critics, geologists, and Darwin, in the new Humanism advanced by George Eliot, who spoke of an ideal of goodness entirely human. Henry James was amongst her admirers who devised a secular faith, drawing a happier lesson from evolution: a trust in humanity without divine sanction. The 'scene' around Minny had these ideological divides: her idealism and that of her cousin were aligned; Holmes, though he remained a friend to both, stood poles apart. Unlike Henry James and Gray, who were to see Minny as formative, the girl of the future was irrelevant to Holmes.

Holmes looked on women as light relief. There are times, he said, when a man sets aside his 'high aims' to take his ease for a few hours in female company. He stressed the difference between his jolly self and Henry James: 'Harry never lets up on his high aims – sometimes it connects itself with the absence of humor in him . . .'. Holmes goes on at length about his own 'not infrequent times when a bottle of wine a good dinner a girl of some trivial sort can fill the hour for me'.

Henry James took the opposite view in his first extended portrait of a lady who is anything but trivial. In one of his finest early tales, 'Poor Richard' (serialised through the summer of 1867), Gertrude, an heiress, is the kind of articulate, generous woman James would later call heiress of all the ages. She attracts, simultaneously, three different types of men: one is a cynical major in the Civil War; another is Richard, a drunken ruffian in Gertrude's family; and the third is a sensitive man, called Severn, on sick leave. The last, the Jamesian suitor, is a shadowy figure whose health and initiative have suffered from the Civil War. Though this is the man Gertrude likes, he is unable to put himself forward. None of these suitors succeeds or makes any serious attempt to know her. And none liberates her passions or even perceives they exist.

James visited Minny twice in the spring of 1867, while he completed this story or awaited publication. In April, Kitty and Elly came to Cambridge to discuss two problems with the Jameses. The first was their brother, whose term of enlistment in the army was due to expire in July. It was put in this bland way, but presumably, given his criminal record, an extension of his service was not on offer. The second problem was a recent blow: the Tweedys who had taken over from their grandmother no longer wished to provide for them.

Mr Tweedy said he had recently lost a lot of money. What was unspoken was the fact that for eight years he had sheltered the four girls, and now thought others might take a turn. Their natural protector should have been their brother, but he was a liability. They did, though, have another potential protector in their mother's brother, Henry James Sr. Mrs James pressed her thin lips together when Kitty suggested they might fend for themselves. Henrietta was only fourteen, and it was not done for unmarried girls to live alone. Kitty, at twenty-four, was prepared to find a house in Newport 'for the winter', and thought Aunt Charlotte Perkins might live with them. A drawback was Aunt Charlotte's failing health: she had recently had a stroke.

Mrs James thought it 'a crazy scheme' but had nothing better to suggest. She did *not* offer to take in any one or all of them. She said rather grimly that if the Tweedys wished to 'break up', the girls would '*have* to make two ends meet'.

There may be a hint here that there was not a lot of money. The first task, then, was to find a reasonable house, and it may have been with help in mind that Henry junior, sporting a new-grown beard, returned with 'the girls' to Newport. A house was taken in Bull Street, away from the wide, fashionable Avenue where they had lived and closer to the old part of town and harbour.

As in the spring of 1865, when William left for Brazil and Henry bestirred himself to come and go, so once more, no sooner did William leave for Germany in April 1867 than Henry revived ('I have felt quite strong since you sailed', he wrote on 10 May). He went again to Newport, this time with John Gray. Later, he said that he had enjoyed pleasing Minny almost as much as if he had been a suitor: 'I cared more to please her perhaps than she cared to be pleased.' James's manner was, in fact, no different from that of the other gifted men in his circle. 'We are all of us so cultivated intellectually, & yet practically so lifeless and ineffectual . . .', James owned in an unpublished letter. All enjoyed long friendships with the intelligent young women who were part of their circle – Clover Hooper, Fanny Dixwell, Eleanor Shattuck, and Minny – and for years they went on visiting, talking, walking, while their contemporaries married. The women – belonging to conservative families who did not send daughters to college or think in terms of a career – felt their stagnation, to judge by a caustic letter that Clover wrote to Eleanor in January 1870: 'A pleasant little dinner at Brooks' [Adams'] with soup, fish Sayles, & Gray – ditto at James' on New Years, with the variation Boston affords of raw oysters, then soup Gray & Holmes that was quite different you see if only one thought so.'

On 6 August 1867, while 'Poor Richard' was still running, Minny came to stay with the Jameses in Cambridge, en route to North Conway after a visit to her cousins the Emmets in New Rochelle, New York. The Emmets were descended from Anglo-Irish Protestants in Dublin. Their great-grandfather Dr Robert Emmet had been State Physician of Ireland. His sons were courageous idealists involved in the Irish uprisings of 1798 and 1803. One son Robert was hanged at the age of twenty-three for treason; another son Thomas, a barrister, was imprisoned, and then emigrated to New York as a political exile in 1804. His grandsons were too placid for Minny. She preferred her James cousins, but Alice did not make it an easy visit.

Gray and Holmes were due to follow Minny to North Conway, and Alice did not disguise her jealousy. 'She is not nearly as interesting as she used to be,' Alice gave out, 'she is so much influenced by the last person she has been with and taken a fancy to that one never knows where to find her. She was looking very pretty and her manner is certainly perfectly fascinating . . .'

Alice wondered if an engagement was in the air. Her cousin Elly Van Buren (sister of Kitty Van Buren) had recently become engaged to a doctor and was writing 'the most rapturous effusions' about him, Alice rather down in the mouth informed William. 'I only hope as it is going to be a long engagement that he will not become weary of her before it's over.'

One of the strangest aspects of the James family is its fiction about Alice, even to one another, as though they willed her to be as other girls. She accompanied her mother to buy a sewing machine, taught sewing to 'the dirtiest of little dirty children' (since this is what good girls did), and learnt to prattle with the best of them – shrilling with delight over an invitation to tea and shaking her head over a schoolfellow's plan to study medicine. Alice expressed her fervent hope that so unladylike a prospect might be deferred indefinitely. 'What pleases me most in the female of my own country', William encouraged Alice, 'is . . . a total absence of that worldly wisdom, or rather that muscular ability and joy to cope with all the commercial and material details of life which characterizes her European sister.' Henry did collude in the construction of Alice, casting her as domestic angel when he wrote to William: 'She is a great blessing to all of us' (10 May 1867) and 'Alice is extraordinarily sweet' (21 May). William duly rejoiced in 'the gentle Babe' (26 September). Sweet and gentle was just what Alice was not. She was cutting in the manner of clever people who score off others, and in this she had the backing of a family who functioned as a unit.

How did Henry junior act within a closed unit that questioned Minny? Given his devotion to Alice, his loyalty to the family, his obedience at home and, not least, his invalidism and dependence at the outset of an uncertain career, it's unlikely he could stand by Minny, at least openly.

In 'Poor Richard', determined rivals contrive to turn the invalid back at the only moment when his initiative takes hold. Although Severn is recessed behind more familiar types of masculinity, James conveys the stifled desire of the sick man with convincing delicacy: he understands the precariousness of initiative, and how tragically that moment can pass – destroying another's happiness as well as his own. Severn's diffidence and delay, exploited by his conqueror-rivals, leave Gertrude ultimately alone. As he recedes into the further distance until we hear of his death in the Civil War, her 'duty was to fold her arms resignedly, to sit quietly on the sofa, and watch a great happiness sink below the horizon'. The author's feeling for her containment, sealed by the code of passivity, did not go unnoticed. Alice heard from Wilky of 'a perfect *furore*' of young women in Lenox who wished to meet the author; but, she went on, 'Harry with his high calm alabaster brow maintains his usual indifference.'

This was his first attempt to explore an able woman's states of mind. Gertrude has 'a certain latent suggestion of heroic possibilities' which diffuses itself about her like a delicious fragrance, inviting detection. The tale, the narrator declares, is based on the 'actual existence' in certain men's minds of a 'mystifying' sense of this perfume. A contemporary reviewer picked this up: 'the physical influence of sex is very perceptible; but . . . in Mr. James's stories it is not only refined but subtle – an aroma, as it were'.

When James called Minny Temple 'the heroine of our scene' he emphasised the fact that she embodied a '*question*'. She suggested an unrealised alternative to the traditional lady, a parallel to the shadowed man who 'reversed the picture' of traditional heroism which a war fought on home ground had exposed in all its horror: the marauding soldiery, the burning towns, the wounds sent home, the operations to cut out festering shot, the spread of fever in filthy hospitals, and young lives laid waste.

James entered a long period of retreat following his contacts with Minny in the spring and summer of 1867. He wrote to William in November 1867: 'Life here in Cambridge – or in this house, at least, is about as lively as the inner sepulchre.' Lilla Cabot, who knew the family over a long period, recalled 'the poky banality of the James house, ruled by Mrs James, where Henry James's father used to limp in and out and never seemed really to "belong" to his wife or Miss Walsh [her sister, Aunt Kate], large florid stupid-seeming ladies, or to his clever but coldly self-absorbed daughter. . . . Henry James's mother (even to my own perception as a child) was the very incarnation of *banality*, and his aunt, Miss Walsh, who lived with them, not much better. His father always ... seemed to me out of place in that stiff stupid house in Cambridge.'

Outside the house, too, James complained, there was no society in Cambridge, 'only a ghastly simulacrum of it'. There were Sedgwicks, Nortons, and Dixwells who could not be called on more than three times in six months, and they seemed to him the best there was. Much has been made of ties in the literary marketplace, but though James sustained a lifelong friendship with William Dean Howells, rising editor of the *Atlantic Monthly*, this did not assuage his alienation. Howells (1837–1920) was quick to recognise James as 'extremely gifted – gifted enough to do better than any one has yet done toward making us a real American novel', yet Howells was too close to the market not to note the difficulty James would have in gaining a large readership. After 'Poor Richard', Howells remarked to Charles Eliot Norton, 'I suspect that he must in a great degree create his audience.'

For a year following Minny's visit in August 1867 there is no record of any contact between her and Henry James. The only fact that survives is that she was writing letters to William in Berlin. William's response to this overture was suspicious: 'Would I c[oul]d think her sincere! Heigh-ho!' He remembered 'the strange levity of Henrietta & the ill-disguised indifference of the elder girls – on the eve of bidding adieu to me, – it might be, forever'.

William was being obtuse. For years he had romanced Kitty Temple. In 1861 he had painted her portrait; in 1864 he had joined her on holiday in Montreal, after which he had sent her an extravagant letter; at New Year 1867, when she stayed in the James home and Mrs James fancied a love affair with John Gray, it may have been William she liked. While there, she had worked him a pair of slippers. He owned in February, 'I find Kitty growing upon me very much.' Yet he took off to Europe for an indefinite time, leaving Kitty – beautiful, caring Kitty, well into marriageable age but still unattached – to bear the responsibility for three younger sisters discarded by their guardians. What William saw as indifference on the part of the girls could have been bravado.

Meanwhile, Henry junior was preoccupied once more with his

health. He was not worse, but had 'ceased to improve so steadily' as during the past summer.

'It is plain that I shall have a very long row to hoe before I am fit for anything', he said.

His drawn-out condition was an obvious source for his study of an invalid in 'A Most Extraordinary Case' (published in April 1868). Ferdinand Mason is languishing after the Civil War. The question of recovery turns, as before, on a woman. James explores the attraction of an original but ill young man for a young woman who is able to enter into his mental life. The feeling is presexual – illness defers expression – but that does not mean it is not a consuming desire. The invalid, balancing on a blade edge between recovery and collapse, becomes obsessed with the otherness of his aunt's ward, the orphaned but resilient Miss Hofmann. Her health and appetite for life have a voluptuous appeal: 'Mason's eyes rested awhile on the vague white folds of her dress, on the heavy convolutions of her hair' as she sits at the piano.

Miss Hofmann's life 'is quite in her hands', her aunt tells Mason. 'My attitude is little more than an affectionate curiosity as to what she will do with it. Of course she will marry, sooner or later; but I'm curious to see the man of her choice.' This forecasts the similar situation of Isabel Archer in *The Portrait of a Lady*, her aunt's detachment, and her cousin's spectatorial fascination – his vicarious life as an invalid.

Though Mason is warned against falling in love, it is unavoidable – and fatal. An invalid may not take that heady step into life, any more than the artist of 'A Landscape-Painter'. A second warning takes place during a walk to the Hudson River. Mason longs to act, and is so infuriated by his weakness, that he makes the abrupt gesture of a frustrated man:

> 'You *have* torn your dress,' said Mason.
>
> Miss Hofmann surveyed her drapery. 'Where if you please?'
>
> 'There, in front.' And Mason extended his walking-stick, and inserted it into the injured fold of muslin. There was a certain graceless *brusquerie* in the movement. . . .

James emphasised the crudity of the gesture in his revision: Mason 'poked out' his walking-stick, and inserts it with 'unexpected violence'.

When William read the tale, he remarked on the autobiographical element. Some 'expressions of feeling from the sick one', he told his brother, 'had to me the mark of being drawn from experience'. In the early tales of James, a promising woman often prefers a hearty specimen of manhood to one ill, wounded, or on the margins of society. To James, who felt unfit all through the 1860s, women – however intelligent – were prone to fall into the biological trap which might be summarised as the survival of the fittest. Their choice of partner will not serve their latent possibilities, and in this way they co-operate in their limitation. Miss Hofmann is biting a cake as she owns to Mason that she will marry solid Dr Knight (who has selected her as a robust specimen). The cake marks her instinctual turn to the stupefying senses, away from an alternative bond, 'extraordinary', undefined, which dies with the invalid.

Alternative manhood without an exceptional woman is simply not viable. The assumptions are heterosexual and, as such, painful: a man's losing struggle to wrench himself apart from his generation of fighting men. The struggle manifests as invalidism – in this 'case', an exemplary trauma.

In the summer of 1868, Kitty surprised the family when she announced her engagement to Richard Stockton Emmet (1821–1902), one of three wealthy grandsons of Thomas Emmet. Kitty was twenty-five; Richard ('Dick') Emmet was forty-seven, with a large house in the country, at Pelham, outside New York. The marriage would enable Kitty to provide a home for her sisters.

William was 'outraged', he wrote to Kitty from Montreux on 17 August 1868: '. . . I must say that considering the relation we have been in for so many years past I little thought it would come to this as soon as my back was turned.' When Henry James heard the news he was alone on holiday in a 'racketing roadside tavern' in Jefferson, New Hampshire, on the farther side of the White Mountains from North Conway. His letter of congratulation to Kitty distances himself from marriage as such. His father had found marriage 'disillusioning' because women could not fulfil the ideal they held out. Ideally, there should be a 'union of souls' with no regret for the 'lower & transient delights' and 'lapsed endearments of the body'. Henry senior felt that 'the only lovely person is one who will never permit himself to be loved'. His son feared, he told Kitty, that marriage turned you into someone else.

'If I had any advice in my poor inexperienced head you would be welcome to it', he added, 'but the married state being to my perception a most dim and untravelled region, I feel loth to risk any directions for your guidance. I take it to be much like the New Hampshire mountains on such a day as this – all enclosed in smoke and mist ... so that you can only see a transparent circle around your footsteps ...'

He asks no enlightenment from Kitty herself, but begs Minny's opinion in terms which suggest the real nature of his interest in her. 'I wonder about many things ... how Minny in that deep inscrutable soul of hers, contemplates your promotion. It is a rare chance for Minny's cogitations – heaven bless her! If she could drop me a line I should be very glad to have her views. ... I sigh when I think of Conway. ...'

James planned to go on from Boston to Newport in early September. Did he intend to see Minny with a view to two projects? At this time, he was writing an unusually heated and fulfilling romance between a footloose scribbler and a woman forbidden him (for reasons of birth). Gabrielle's situation reflects that of Minny: an intelligent young woman who laughs 'with extraordinary freedom' is stagnating under the roof of a mindless brother. She marries the scribbler in the face of family opposition. Minny pronounced the tale 'charming' when it was serialised the following summer.

The second project in September 1868 was a pro-feminist article James published the following month on 'Modern Women'. In this piece, a few sharp blows demolish the marriage market. Sympathy for women's plight as victims of a set plot came easily to a man who had experienced the pressure of the war-plot of his generation. James commends women for their patient adaptation to male dreams and, on a fiercer note, declares the Thackeray era of misogyny at an end. A new age has begun in which laughing at women is crude. Their plight, he announces, is to be taken seriously. And here, for the first time, he conceives 'the American girl' as a distinct phenomenon – a hope for the future. Later, he acknowledged that Mary Temple had epitomised, for him, her sex and nation: the free American girl of his fiction.

At the end of 1868 Minny fell ill. It was consumption, the disease that had killed her parents. In mid-November, William James returned home, after a year and a half abroad, and spread the news to one of Minny's admirers:

> My dear Wendel
> T'were well you spake not of the 'deposit' in Mary Temple's lung to any-one. Some people have a morbid modesty about letting such things be known to any one. I told you because I knew that within the family circle so to speak she would not care to keep it concealed. But I'd rather that if even Gray were to learn of it, he should learn it from her directly.
> Dost twig?
> Trusting that your lurid & suspicious imagination will read nought personal in this, no reflections on the native delicacy of your complexion &c &c &c
> I remain
> Ever til deth
> W.J.

Apart from its flippant tone, this note carries a poisonous message: a girl known to have consumption would be dropped from the marriage market. William James is letting a potential suitor know that Minny is damaged goods. In social terms, if no other, she was of this moment doomed – the moment her condition leaked beyond the family (what William was doing here, while pretending to protect her wishes). He projects false modesty on to Minny, and excessive morbidity, for though there were times she gazed at the grave, she declared herself to be 'not easily frightened'. Malice lurks in William's careless wave at 'deth'. For William and Holmes, death is, happily, a long way off; not so for this annoying young woman.

Until this moment, William's rejection of Minny as a '*bad* thing' had been ineffective: she had ignored his opinion and continued what she called, defiantly, her 'evil courses'. But, once she was vulnerable, William could move against this 'coquette'. During this winter, he 'abused' Minny to Henry. The sole report of this is William's admission, a year later, that he had wronged Minny. We can't know what he said at this moment, but William's capacity for virulence might be measured by his comment at this time on Jews who practised 'Christian graces': they 'revolted' him more than those who did not, and later he described Jews in Rome 'squatting all along the sides of houses just like maggots in a piece of flesh'.

Henry James collapsed that winter so badly that he was unable to read. When he had been immobilised by backache in the summer of 1866, he had read copiously – most of George Eliot to date. Now, he was immobilised mentally as well as physically. Afterwards, he spoke of 'those stupid months', and ascribed this to his bowels. To retreat from action so far as not to read, so that inaction no longer protected the private life but undermined it, suggests depression. The fact that his condition, in its acute phase, continued over 'months' suggests, further, that it was not passing lowness but something intractable. And if constipation were linked with depression, and provided a label for it, this would explain his moans over the following year which otherwise sound absurdly abject. What caused his collapse that winter?

In the absence of proof, the best we can do is assemble what facts exist: Henry James completes a historical romance between a scribbler and a young woman like Minny. He declares himself 'particularly & abundantly – I might indeed say, repulsively –well' on 18 November 1868, and adds that William is due back from abroad any day. William, whose presence seems to coincide with outbreaks of disturbance in the James home, duly returns; Mary Temple coughs blood; Henry who was '*lovely*' in her eyes is prostrated, too inert to lift a book, yet a plan goes forward for him to wander three thousand miles away for an indefinite period. And during these months came that exchange with William when Henry did not save Minny from abuse.

The man who came forward to stand by Minny in her trial was John Chipman Gray. At twenty-nine, he was six years older than Minny, a partner in a Boston law firm, and about to start his lifelong career at Harvard Law School. On 7 January she sent the first surviving letter of a correspondence that had begun while Gray was abroad the previous summer. Immured under the Emmet roof, dependent on the favours of a dull brother-in-law, Minny craved some exchange of ideas. Her passionate friendship with Helena de Kay had cooled. '. . . Someone came between us', Helena said, 'and it seemed to me as if death were better.' Helena, now an art student at the Cooper Union in New York, believed that person was Kitty Emmet, but it could as well have been Kitty's conventional husband. Richard Emmet would not hear of Minny leaving his house for grander relations in Canada. He gave the nod to shopping in New York and Gracie King's ball at Delmonico's. It was two years since Minny had been to a ball. She danced mainly with a travelled man of leisure, one Mr Lee, whose sisters, he proudly told her, had married German princes. Yet such pleasures could not satisfy her longing for experience – for truth.

'You must . . . tell me something that you are *sure* is true', she asked Gray, 'I don't care much that it is, & I will take your word for it.'

Only a man of intellect could answer this need. She thought men in New York society that winter were 'principally a lot of feeble-minded boys'. Pelham was no more satisfactory. When Minny explored shadowy connections, her sisters thought her 'queer'. This, she confided to Gray, put 'an end to anything but conversation of the most superficial kind'. If she voiced her 'usual mental question of why I was born', her sisters grew impatient.

'I wouldn't be you for anything,' Kitty or Elly might say, and now, in her weakness, she could not stand up to reproach.

Neither her sisters, nor the ballroom, nor her present refuge with the Emmet tribe were her rightful settings, and this setting she had not yet found. Fixed in Pelham as in a mental prison, she turned to Gray. There was no one else. Stiffer than her James cousins, and minus their vivacity of mind, Gray was readier with his attentions. And at the end of a visit that winter, he did indicate, in his dry way, an awareness of her buried treasure.

'Pyramid', he said, 'goodbye.'

Afterwards she reminded him of the '*name*'. It expressed, she teased him, 'your greatest disapprobation' of 'a cold, hard, unsympathetic, uninteresting body'. But he'd shown unexpected perception. Long letters began to race between Minny's sickroom in Pelham, New York, and the scrupulous lawyer with his Boston gravity in Pemberton Square. They resolved not to look for answers from Henry James Sr.

'I agree with you perfectly about Uncle Henry', Minny said, 'I should think he would be very irritating to the legal mind; he is not at all satisfactory even to mine.'

Gray's letters became her chief support during attacks of the 'enemy' – haemorrhage – an enemy, she tried to convince herself, that did not gain on her. During one week from 20 to 27 January, she had seven major and several smaller bleeds. 'I can't stop them', she told Gray, 'but, as I said, I mean to try and beat them yet.'

Confined to bed, she read *The Mill on the Floss* (1860). Its heroine, Maggie Tulliver, reflects the restless intelligence of nineteenth-century women bound by ties of duty and emotion to conventional, small-minded families who jarred them at every movement. Maggie is 'a creature full of eager, passionate longings for all that was beautiful and glad: thirsty for all knowledge ... with a blind, unconscious yearning for something that would link together the wonderful impressions of this mysterious life and give her soul a sense of home in it.' The book left Minny with an 'overpowering admiration and affection for George Eliot. I don't know why it has so suddenly come over me,' she mused, 'but everything I see of hers now-a-days makes me feel a deeper interest in her.' 'I see that she understands the character of a *generous* woman, that is, of a woman who believes in generosity, & who must be that or nothing, & who feels keenly, notwithstanding, how hard it is practically to follow it out.'

Forbidden to speak, even whisper, she wrote secretly to Gray 'as a pleasant break from the monotony of gruel and of thinking of the grave'. She was not deceived by her doctor's cheer, holding instead to her own courage. '... If the choice were given to me, I would a good deal rather stay up here, on the solid earth, in the air and sunshine, with an occasional sympathetic glimpse of another person's soul, than to be put down, under the earth, and say goodbye forever to humanity – with all its laughter and its sadness. ... The Dr. tells me I am not in any danger, even if the hemorrhages should keep on – "but you can't fool a regular boarder" as Mr Holmes would say, & I can't see why there is any reason to think they will heal, a week later, when I shall be weaker than now, if they can't heal now – however *I* think they *are* going to stop *now*. I haven't had one since yesterday at *four*, & now it is three o'clock, nearly twenty four hours. I am of a hopeful temperament, & not easily frightened, which is in my favor. If this *should* prove to be the last letter you get from me, why take it for a good-bye. I'll keep on the look-out for you in the spirit-world . . .'.

Her hope, sustained through these attacks, dropped early in February, when she heard that Henry James would leave for Europe, alone, at the end of the month. Longing filled her: a dream to go too. It was her unhappy lot to remain in an adverse climate, she thought, 'but such as it is I've got to take my chance in it, as there is no one I care enough for, or who cares enough for me, to take charge of me to Italy, or to the south anywhere. I don't believe any climate, however good, would be of the least use to me with people I don't care for.'

Soon after her brush with death, so soon that she must have defied caution, she dashed to Boston (accompanied by Elly), and had another haemorrhage. The only record of this visit is an unnoted letter from George Bradford, the schoolmaster, to Helena de Kay, dated 14 February 1869. It tells us nothing beyond the fact that Minny was in Cambridge. James put her outburst in his memoir as though it were wholly a medical problem. He implies that it was simply not in his power – in no one's power – to fulfil her dream. This, though true, obscures a subtler problem: Minny's wish for experience, a wish he shared, beating in her with extreme urgency. What can't be determined is whether he felt an impulse to aid this 'heroine' who cared for him. Thirty years later, a mature James understood the life-and-death need of commitment for the orphaned, ill Milly Theale; in 1869, it was a live issue. As blood gushed from a girl's mouth into her bedroom basin, she begged to live on her own terms before it was too late.

5
Minny's Dream

At the end of the month Minny saw her cousin for the last time. He had two days in New York before he sailed. She came towards him, straight and thin, with her long, almost sliding step, in the old-fashioned Pelham parlour, quiet in the daytime when he called. He thought her transparency 'becoming', a modish ideal of ethereal womanhood.

Concerned, all the same, he asked her about sleep.

'Sleep,' she said with her light, renouncing laugh that made her mouth fill up her face. 'Oh, I don't sleep. *I've given it up.*'

His pockets were crammed with introductions, one of them to George Eliot. Minny longed to know more of her life: 'how far her lofty moral sentiments have served her practically – for instance in her dealings with [George Henry] Lewes.' She was curious about a woman who, without denying her independence, had managed to find a partner who answered passion as well as intellect. Minny asked James to 'give my love to her'. Her enthusiasm made him feel that his main satisfaction in meeting the great novelist would be for Minny's sake.

It was wholly detestable, they agreed, that he should voyage off without her. But there was comfort, for Minny, in plans for the following winter. An excitement emanates from the sick girl that hovers somewhere between the figure of her departing cousin and the romance of Europe, an infectious eagerness – fixing on Rome where, as they part, they plan to 'romantically meet'. Their parting was far from sad: they laughed continually, heartened by the prospect of this meeting. The dream took hold, even as Minny realised how unlikely it was. 'Harry came to see me before he sailed for Europe', she told Gray in more realistic mood on 4 March. 'I am very glad that he has gone, although I don't expect to see him again in a good many years. I do not think he will come back for a long time. I hope it will do him good, & that he will enjoy himself, which he hasn't done for several years, I think.'

The good Gray continued to write to her, and gratitude led her to hold back her side of the correspondence in order to give him 'a little holiday'. She owned that she had needed him during her haemorrhage in the middle of February, but had thought 'illness even was hardly a good enough excuse for behaving like a baby, when one had reached the advanced age of twenty-three – and at all events, I could not quite reconcile it to my conscience that you, an unprotected man, having done nothing to deserve such treatment at my hands, should be the victim – fine sentiment, wasn't it? Please give me the credit for it.'

Her tone is light as she frees Gray from obligation, even as she asks for continued support. Her lightness sounds what James called her 'woodnote wild': 'Goodbye. I wish that conventionality would invent some other way of ending a letter than "yours truly". I am so tired of it, & as one says it to one's shoemaker it is rather more complimentary to one's friend to dispense with it altogether & sign one's name abruptly, after the manner of Ellen Emerson & other free Boston citizens.'

It was easier to ask favours of a man to whom she was not drawn. The distance between the cool Gray and her expressive ideal is measured by their disagreement over David in the Old Testament. Gray disparaged David; Minny declared a 'weakness' for him: 'Think how charming and loveable a person he must have been – poet, musician & so much else combined – with however their attendant imperfections.' She conceded: 'I don't think I should care to have been Mrs D. exactly'.

Tiring of seclusion, Minny now planned 'a wild excitement', 'the mad career upon which I proposed to rush headlong': a week of music, by day and night, starting with *Faust*, in New York. But no sooner did she arrive, bundled up against the cold, at the home of her hostess, Mrs Griswold, than a lung specialist, Dr Bassett, came to listen to her chest. He seemed 'irresistibly ludicrous' as he solemnly laid his head under one of her shoulders and then under the other, for ten minutes at a time, but the result curbed her smile, for he ordered her home on the instant. She left before she could unpack. His further orders, as she put it, were 'not to get excited, nor to listen to music, nor to speak to anybody I care about, nor to do anything in short that the unregenerate nature longs for.'

She clung to the doctor's assurance that her lungs were sound – he told her the blood came from the lining only or that of her throat – though reason led her to protest: 'either sound lungs are a very dangerous thing to possess, or there is a foul conspiracy on foot to oppress me.'

She may have seen through the lie, but the hope it opened to her of a future in Europe was vital to her continued resilience in the face of weakness when she ventured no farther than Philadelphia that spring. There for the benefit of an inland climate, she found it trying to be with strangers, however kind. Men who were ornaments of Philadelphia society impressed her no more than the 'boys' of New York. This stay confirmed the impossibility of travel without the company of someone who loved her: 'It may be that the mental atmosphere is more important than any other', she saw. One reason for going to Philadelphia was to hear a celebrated preacher, Phillips Brooks (1835–93), who she had hoped would 'banish doubt' in Christianity.

'. . . He did not touch upon the real difficulties at all,' she found. She had most wished to know 'any good reason' for her sense of spiritual power. How was she to interpret a '*feeling*' that came from her freest spirit, in terms of meekness and obedience? What could she believe when her spirit deserted her? 'I feel sadly run down tonight,' she admitted to Gray, 'as if I should like to see some honest old pagan & shake him by the hand.'

Gray wrote from Boston to say that Mr Brooks never did touch 'the main point', and expressed a pious hope Minny might find an answer elsewhere.

She replied almost curtly: '. . . That satisfaction that you so kindly wish me is, I am afraid, not to be got from any man.' Henry James shared her scepticism. 'The explanations of such as him [Phillips Brooks]', he said, 'require more explanation than anything else in the world.'

The mystery of the world, she thought, 'grows and grows, & sticks out of every apparently trivial thing, instead of lessening'. To others, she feared, her thoughts might be 'the incipient stages of insanity!'

Discouraged by her failure to penetrate the 'mystery', she returned to her dream. Backed by the doctor's promise of 'matchless lungs', she now formed a plan more adventurous than she had so far 'dared to hope'. She meant to take wing from the constraints of her present life, and stay abroad – the flight was to be 'permanent'. The only person to whom she confided this plan was Henry James: her letters to him expose it to his attention again and again, with the lightest tread back and forth across the limits of their tie as she groped her way towards some basis for a future in Europe. Since marriage would have been an obvious solution, she took conspicuous care not to propose it, and even joked about saving herself the stress of a refusal.

'If you were not my cousin', she told him, 'I would write & ask you to marry me & take me with you – but as it is, it wouldn't do. I will console myself, however, with the thought, that in that case you might not accept my offer, which would be much worse than it is now.'

She prods him with teasing affection, inviting a masculine response as well as a cousinly one. 'My darling Harry –', she addresses him on 3 June, '(You don't mind if I am a little affectionate, now that you are so far way, do you?)' The tone of her non-proposal might seem flirtatious were it not for the fact that her need of a protector in Europe – someone who could be relied on to provide the 'mental atmosphere' vital to her well-being – sustained her precarious existence.

His letter had arrived, she went on, 'while I was in the very act of having the third hemorrhage of that day, & it quite consoled me, for them – .' There had been one more slight attack during the past week, in Newport, where she had come to see an ailing aunt, Miss Clarke, and Lizzie Boott. Lizzie found in Minny a new kind of friendship, 'quick affinity', while Minny hoped to know for herself what it was like to be Lizzie, steeped in the rich old medium of Italy. Though the 'admirable John Gray' had given them 'his pleasant society' for a couple of days, Minny informed James, she would rather be in Europe with her 'dear'.

One particular point of envy was his proximity to George Eliot:

'Have you seen Mrs. Lewes yet? Kiss her for me – But, from all accounts, I don't believe that is exactly what one wish[es] to do to her. If I were, by hook or by crook, to spend next winter, with friends, in Rome, should I see you, at all? – '. Commas register her hesitation, each short breath as she sets out that all-important question.

She understood that survival depended on her will to live, which depended, in turn, on the response of others. It was therefore essential to woo them to her cause. Remember, she urged James, 'that of all the princes & princesses (so to speak) who now seek your society, none of them love you half so well as I do'.

She reassured him that she felt 'all right again now, for the present'. Without denying her condition, she took a brave line, encouraging James to do the same:

> Do you feel strong again? – I hope so – God bless you, dear – Don't forget me – or that I am
>
> Always your loving cousin
>
> Mary Temple

She was not happy in Newport in the absence of anyone to care for her. Mr Tweedy had escorted her from Pelham to Newport, but there is no sign of other attentions, nor, though the Tweedys travelled incessantly to Europe, an offer to take Minny there. The Jameses did invite Minny to join them in Pomfret, Connecticut, during July; but Minny remained in Pelham throughout the summer, her place taken by Lizzie Boott (who, Minny heard, fell in love with Uncle Henry and Willy).* Mrs James, who saw Lizzie as suitably 'unconscious', told herself complacently there was 'no danger of her exciting any personal fascination' over Willy as he lounged in the hammock with a volume of Browning while Lizzie sketched under the pines. Lizzie, she decided, was to save Harry from the wrong sort of girl.

'You know Father used to say to you, that if you could only fall

* Though Lizzie was more congenial than Minny to the James family, there may well have been an ordinary explanation for the substitution of Lizzie at Pomfret: Minny may not have felt well enough to go, or she may have decided to remain with Kitty, who was then in her last month of pregnancy.

in love it would be the making of you', Mrs James wrote to him on 24 July. Lizzie was a striking instance of what 'thorough education can accomplish'. In America, she could never have achieved such polish. 'Minny has all her tastes and capabilities naturally in a higher degree, and look at the difference.'

James reversed this judgement: his fictional re-creation of Minny as 'a great swell, psychologically' would dominate his re-creation of Lizzie as the well-schooled Pansy in *The Portrait of a Lady*. The American nurture of the 'swell' was crucial to her native self-reliance. The Europeanised Pansy is what others have willed her to be: in so far as she lacks self-reliance, she is without character. This is exactly what appealed to Mrs James in her ladylike guest: Lizzie, she told her son, put so little of *herself* in her drawing 'that it seems something quite celestial'. So, Mrs James co-opted Lizzie on the side of the angels, and placed Minny beyond the pale.

In fact, just then, Minny was planning a 'sudden' descent on 'darling Harry'. She was about to take a 'strange step', she broke it to him on 15 August. A Mr and Mrs Jones had agreed to take her to Rome next winter, and she meant to stay for a year at least: 'Think, my dear of the pleasure we would have together in Rome – I am crazy at the mere thought.'

A new reason to leave her present situation was a 'startling event'. Elly, aged nineteen, was engaged to another Emmet, aged forty-seven, brother to Kitty's husband. Christopher Temple Emmet (1822–84) had made a fortune from railroads. For the last few months he had been living in Pelham, in the same house as Elly. Excited by her wildness – as a teenager Elly had kicked and scratched Willy James, who said he 'dreaded' her – Temple Emmet began to ply her with gifts and say in jest what he could do if she became his 'little wife'. Mrs James believed his bounty had 'seduced' the girl, but security was the obvious motive for these orphans who had shifted from one home to another, whom Mr Tweedy had cast out and Uncle Henry did not take in. Elly claimed to be in love, and Minny tried to believe it. To Gray, Minny contrived to hope that Emmet might prove 'a kind & devoted husband', but to James, as a member of family, she wrote more frankly.

'. . . I must confess my imagination had taken higher flights in the way of a spouse for Elly', she said. 'Kitty's little venture in the way of marrying one's grandfather has turned out so well that I ought to feel quite safe about Elly. But I have quite determined that the line must be drawn *here*.' Her sisters, she told James, were doing 'queer things', marrying grandfathers, and the presssure was on: 'why should I be behind-hand?' In the absence of appropriate suitors, she could lose her nerve. 'I must flee this spot, unless I wish to become the prey of a bald-headed Emmet – There seems to be a fatality about it, which I would fain escape.'

This is an appeal to chivalry. James, who had evidently offered no response to her plan in the reply she had received on 6 July, and whom she pictures roaming the Alps 'without a link or a tie to bind you', was alerted to her need for rescue. Stubbornly, she repeated, 'I want to go abroad, & I mean to think deeply about it, & try to get there.'

The third and strongest basis of her appeal was fear of death: if Europe might be expected to cure her 'dearest Harry', might it not save her? Rome, with its dry winter and cloudless skies, was the common hope of consumptives. Freezing temperatures at home, she argued, could kill her: 'I am not very strong now-a-days, altho' it is summer, & I am afraid that another winter might go far toward finishing me up. & I would give anything to have a winter in Italy.'

Whatever the counter-pressures of family opinion and invalidism, James would have found it hard to ignore this cry for help. He might have ignored humorous pleas for pleasure and escape, but her plea to be saved from death was naked, grim, unavoidable. As he read this, did James feel any impulse, however transient, to encourage Minny – to take on, that is, primary responsibility for her? If he did, he would have had to risk what he cared about more than anything: writing. That future required the income his mother had recently confirmed with a fount of maternal tenderness for her 'dearly beloved child': 'throw away prudence', she had said, 'and think only of your comfort and pleasure, for our sakes as well as your own. . . . Take the fullest liberty and enjoyment your tastes and inclinations crave, and we will promise heartily to foot the bill.' The liberty of taking on Minny was not the kind of pleasure his mother had in mind – though she could hardly object if Minny travelled with others. But the whole idea could have been dispelled by Minny's further letter of two pages, written a week later and sent at the same time.

Here, on 22 August, Minny told him that nothing of importance had happened, but what she went on to say was, in fact, of crucial importance to her. The 'nothing' that had happened was that Minny had done nothing about the journey. Now had been the moment to act, and it is this withdrawal from action that James would eliminate from the fictional ventures of the dauntless American girls he based on Minny. In actual life, this girl could *not*, in his famous phrase, 'affront her destiny'.

'I have taken no steps about the European trip,' she admitted, '& truth to tell, dear, I have not the heart for it. The evening I wrote to you I was enchanted with the project, but by the next morning I was disenchanted – I am really not strong enough to go abroad with even the kindest of friends, since they be not relatives. . . . I have been ill nearly all week with a kind of pleurisy, which makes me clearly perceive that it would never do for me to be ill away from home, on the bounty of strangers for my nursing – See'st thou?'

The message is stark in its apparent simplicity; it seems to reverse the situation. Yet James was too astute a reader to ignore the resonance of a subordinate cause, that a member of family who required no social effort would be different from the Joneses: 'since they be not relatives, or people upon whom I have some special claim'. He, alone, a relative already there, might help her. Her plea was all the more powerful for its modesty. She was not asking for formal protection; this the Joneses would provide. But she had to have a companion. Since she could not marry a cousin, or marry at all, given her condition, kinship would be the welcome alternative. To be with him would effectively free her from the unwanted company of 'the kindest' of friends.

From the other side, all we know is that James did reply and that he promised himself he would redeem her dream when he brought Europe home to her. An hour on a Sunday afternoon with George Eliot, hearing what seemed to him an angelic voice of counselling sagacity – the 'one marvel' of his weeks in England (from March till May 1869), where letters of introduction from Charles Eliot Norton gave him an entrée to the leading writers of the time: the simple benignity of Darwin at Down House in Kent; the medievalism of William Morris in Queen Square, London, with Jane Morris on the sofa in an aura of aesthetic hair and 'medieval toothache'; and Dante Gabriel Rossetti, sinister, bristling, perverse in the Chelsea dusk. These impressions, James thought, 'would serve for Minnie's curiosity'. She would be there, always, taking 'noble flights', with an occasional 'drop', but rising again, and yet again.

Flights and drops: what is significant in the signals between them is that she did not replace the 'flight' letter of 15 August with the 'drop' letter of 22 August. She sent both because, even though the 'drop' letter appeared to cancel the projected flight, the two continued to coexist – as late as February 1870 when hope, for Minny, was finally destroyed. It is possible to know that a course of action will not be feasible, and yet to hope that by some miracle it will, just as Minny recognised the danger of death, and at the same time sustained hope with remarkable buoyancy – she drank in the comfort of doctors while deriding it.

So, she set before James her dream in all its possibility and fragility, and her capacity to rise and fly made him wonder if, against all the odds, she would still come. 'What of Minny Temple's coming to Italy?' he asked his mother in September. 'Is Minny coming abroad?' he asked again from Venice later that month. There was a wilful blindness in the way he would not grasp the gravity of her illness and the urgency of her pleas to him to take her on.

Minny's tenderness for 'dearest Harry' was deepened by the insufficiency of John Gray – not as a correspondent, but in person. So long as they wrote she opened her mind to him, but when in June he had come to see her in Newport she had recoiled from a lawyer with a 'priestly' face. Loftiness in a man of nearly thirty held no more appeal than the soldier of twenty-six who had talked too much, four years earlier, at North Conway. It occurred to her to offer Gray a chance to know himself. Few men of her time – Henry James was the rarest exception – would have understood the purity of her impulse to speak without bounds as one soul to another. Her directness came as a shock to a mannered man like

Gray, and the letter she wrote him explains to some extent why Mary Temple evoked hostility in those who saw her as 'queer' or 'insane', and why she appealed to Henry James, who chose to print this unflattering letter in his memoir (to him, a 'delightful' sample of her 'pitch of lucidity'):

Pelham
June 27th. 1869

Dear Mr Gray.

How can I write to you, when I have forgotten all about you? But how can one forget what one has never known – but then I am not quite sure whether I know you too little or too much to be able to write to you. Do you comprehend the difficulty? Of course you don't, so I will explain. The trouble is, I think, that to me you have no distinct personality – I don't feel sure to whom I am writing. When I say to myself that I will write to Mr Gray, I mentally see three men, all answering to that name, & each liable to read the letter I write, & yet differing so much from each other that the letter which I might with all propriety write to one of them, would be quite unsuitable to send to the other. Do you see? If you can once settle for me the question 'who gets my letters?' I shall know better what to say to them – Is it the middle-aged man I used to see at Conway, (I cannot say know,) with a beard, I think, smoking and gravely discussing Trollope's novels with Elly or Kitty, good, perhaps, but not interesting (to me) to whom I never felt disposed to speak, & in whose society I used to get sleepy at eight o'clock, & wonder how the other girls could stay awake till eleven. Is it that man that reads my letters? Or is it the young man I saw recently at Newport – with a priestly countenance, calm and critical, with whom I have certainly no fault to find, as a chance companion for three or four days, but whom I should never dream of writing to, or bothering with my affairs one way or the other, happinesses or unhappinesses, as he would doubtless despise me for my nonsense & wonder at me for my seriousness. Does that man get my letters? Or is it finally the same man who has from time to time written me letters, signed by the name that the other two gentlemen appropriate? If it is the last man, I know where I stand, & please Heaven, I mean to stand there some time longer. This last one I won't describe – but he is the only one of the three that I care anything about, and it is altogether a pleasure & sometimes a comfort to write to him & hear from him. He is very different to the other two. I hope he is the one that gets my letters, but I have my fears because I always address them to Mr Gray's office & I think *my* friend is the least likely of the three to go every day to the office. I hope you appreciate, dear Mr Gray, how perplexing a position I am in. Won't you solve the mystery for me *very* soon? Do write & tell me those other two men don't see my letters, & then I'll write to you – as of old & tell you what I am about. In the mean time good-bye whatever you are. If the first or the second man should open this I beg leave to sign myself his very truly –

Mary Temple

(But if it should happen to be the third man he may read instead of truly, *affectionately*)

As it happened, it was the second John Gray, the lofty Gray of the law office, who received this challenge. He was offended, even (as Minny detected) angry. 'Verily', he replied stiffly, 'you are a plain-spoken young woman' limited by 'narrow sympathies'.

Discouraged, she wrote again on 7 July of 'this weary world, where it is so hard for one soul to know another, under all the necessary & unnecessary disguises that keep them apart'. She added: 'when I saw you, I realized all the hindrances that exist to a friendship between you & me.'

It was easy to misunderstand Minny – easy for the first or second Mr Gray to feel discomfited. In her reply, she took care to emphasise her attachment to the third Mr Gray, though from now on she felt this wall of incomprehension. They continued to correspond, but he became rather a joke – one she could share with Henry James. When Gray visited Pelham in October, she bounced his stiffness along country lanes as she drove the pony-wagon, 'shook him up & splashed his clothes', and then compelled him to kiss Kitty's baby, William (named for their dead brother): 'he kissed the baby, at parting, as it had never been kissed before – that is with none of that lingering & caressing fondness that one is apt to indulge in in kissing babies . . . – but you will readily imagine how he did it.'

She mocked Gray's armour when she relayed facts about the infant: 'I don't suppose you care to hear that he weighs $8\frac{1}{2}$ pounds, or that his hair is dark brown & curly, . . . but these are very interesting details to his doting aunt. . . . I part his hair in the middle & brush it up each side, in a very becoming manner – & as he has no clients to conciliate, he lets me arrange his hair as I like without a murmur.'

Gray declined to be amused and, a few months later, took his revenge. He told Minny that she stood 'far-off' from him and, when she asked why, told her bluntly that she was 'intellectually' unsympathetic. Yet he did want her liking. Her failed attempt to reach the third John Gray provoked a confession: his fear that as people got to know him they liked him less. Minny reassured him that this was not so for her; she had grown to like him 'slowly but surely' since she had first come to 'know' him during their second summer at Conway in 1867. As a measure of this, she signed her letters from now on 'affectionately'.

A truce, then, disguised the divide between them: Minny backed Gray's virtues ('You are a sensible man, & I like you') and undertook to adapt to his rules of conduct: 'It is all right – and I'll be good, and try never to bother you any more.'

Minny was actually inviting an original response – an acceptance of her help from three of the most intelligent men of her time. With Henry James, who revered her as 'the priestess of rash speculation', Minny exposed her hunger for natural life. With the matter-of-fact John Gray, she played the priestess. With William James, she tried to melt his hostility towards a woman who upset the gender game. It was as though she wished each to extend his limits to cover her range. '. . . Let us fearlessly trust our whole nature,' she urged. She refused to allow 'a bit of compromise'. The meaning of existence, she believed, was not to be found through formal religion or the willed performance of good works, but 'through no other means surely than by our being *true*'.

Neither Gray nor, still less, the Emmets were equal to such ideas, and in late August she declared the impossibility of marriage on her own terms. Since no man was offering to marry her, this was a theoretical position, but one that evidently gave her moral satisfaction. In a letter of 29 August, Minny declared to Gray that she could not condone anything less than a marriage of true minds. '. . . This marrying is a very solemn thing,' she said. '. . . I am aware that if all other women felt the eternal significance of matrimony to the extent that I do, that hardly any of them would get married at all, & the human race would come to a stand-still.' She asked Gray whether her position were 'simply fanatical and impracticable', then defended it, aligning the married with Browning's monster of worldliness and hypocrisy: 'the other side has, with Bishop Blougram, the best of it, from one point of view – but I can't help that, can I. We must be true to ourselves mustn't we, though all the rest of humanity be of a contrary opinion. . . . Do you remember', she demanded, 'my old hobby of the "remote possibility" of the best thing, being better than a clear certainty of the second best? Well, I believe it more than ever, every day I live. Indeed I don't believe anything else – but is not that everything?'

When James quoted this more than forty years later, he eliminated 'eternal significance' and put in a more commonplace phrase about the 'seriousness' of marriage: this blurred the distinction she was making between herself and the mass of women who compromise for the sake of safety. Such a woman was her sister Elly, whose marriage to another dull Emmet appalled her.

The family gathered for Elly's wedding on 16 September 1869. The lawless brother, Robert Temple, turned up, tall, wiry, and ready as ever to extract whatever he could from pained relatives. He hoped his new brother-in-law would employ him on the railroads or fund a grocery store in Texas. Grey and grave, the image of his father, he claimed perfect self-control in drinking, and deplored as always the wickedness of the world. 'The wages of sin is death,' he would declare. He felt this more and more every day, he would add sincerely. He then proceeded to Florida to sponge on Wilky, and when Wilky rebuffed him, applied to Henry senior for $50, also refused. Unabashed, Temple wrote again to beg his uncle to retrieve a chest held back by his landlord for debt. In exchange, he offered to keep silent for five years (backing this ploy with a flourish of Pope: 'The world forgetting, by the world forgot'). He was amused to find his sisters in the similar business of selling themselves.

'. . . Our little gentle, girlish Elly was yesterday married to a *Railroad* King!' he wrote to Henry James on 17 September. 'He is [a] large, fat, old bald-headed, grey-whiskered, red-faced, substantial, solid, portly, *opulent*, not to say *affluent*, person. . . . Kitty is happily married to a prosy man, & has a fat Baby.' With Elly 'a Railroad Queen', eyes turned now to the last of the Temple sisters, Henrietta, who was 'very lively' and popularly supposed to be waiting for 'another elderly unmarried Emmet'. Temple assured James that Minny was exempt from these aspersions. 'Minny looks & talks older: she is the best one of the family, & at any rate will never sell herself for gold.'

'I have written to Minny about her sisters', Henry James told William on 25 September. 'Elly's marriage strikes me as absolutely *sad*. I care not how good a fellow T. Emmet may be: Elly deserved a younger man.'

His September letter to Minny was his reply to her 'drop' letter of 22 August. Here is the crucial gap in their story: his response to the blood-soaked fact of the third haemorrhage of the day, to Minny's need to escape the Emmets, and her craving for Rome whose winter climate might prolong her life. All we know for certain of his reply to Minny's letters of August 1869 was that he said, 'I have written to Minny about her sisters'. Her *sisters*, not herself. Evidently, James did not answer Minny's plea in any real sense, as her subsequent silence made clear. What she does not say is as telling as what she does, and she does *not* say that his letters support her (as she says often, gratefully, to Gray). Those who offered her material and moral support, the Emmets and Gray, were men she could not greatly like; while her 'dear', her 'darling', preserved the immunity of distance.

His inability to respond to her pleas for help or tentative offers of attachment, as well as a deeper block that reached beyond Minny herself, may be associated with another period of disturbance, projected on to his rectum which refused to 'open'. For his family he had 'none but the worst news with regard to my old enemy no. 2 – by which of course I mean *my* unhappy bowels. . . . I suffer so perpetually & so keenly from this hideous repletion of my belly . . . My condition affects alike my mind & my body: it tells upon my spirits . . .'. From October, he collapsed into an invalidism so intractable and absorbing that it must, of necessity, exclude any need but his own.

When William had complained from Germany, his mother had

urged him to come home and be 'nursed'; when Henry complained, in the same family vein of swelling groans, there was no invitation to return. This son was supposed to get himself well at a distance.

William encouraged the groans with avid attention – 'I blush to say that detailed bulletins of your bowels, stomach & as well as back are of the most enthralling interest to me' – and bombarded Henry with letters of advice. (One suggestion was to insert an electrode in his rectum, and give it a shock.*) In the course of the summer he had offered his brother a diagnosis of 'dorsal insanity'. During the autumn, he assured Henry that his life was 'blighted' by a 'hideous affliction.'

So loud, so insistent, were the groans across the Atlantic that they reached even Minny's ears. Her letter to James, on 17 November, expressed her pity, and silenced her dream – though it never left her. It was a letter of one invalid to another, a surrender to his drama. A man who had a 'condition' that told on his spirits could not contemplate the kind of action that would invite dependence. Only in retrospect was he to realise that her dependence would not have lasted for long (a realisation built into the plot of *The Wings of the Dove*, where the Jamesian hero, Densher, contemplates a brief marriage with a dying girl whose generous spirit wins him *after* her death.) Venice had appeared to him like a voluptuous woman to whom he could not surrender, he said, as if 'I had been born in Boston'. The glide of the gondola made him think of Minny.

'My dear,' she returned in her November letter, 'I hope you may henceforth *live* in gondolas, since gondolas sometimes make you think of me – So "keep a doin' of it" if it comes "natural". I "guess" it is all right, & even expedient, once in a while.'

Minny had recently been on a visit to the James family in Cambridge. She had gone to say goodbye before embarking on a

* 'Electricity *some*times has a wonderful effect, applied not in the piddling way you recollect last winter but by a strong *galvanic* current from the spine to the abdominal muscles, or if the rectum be paralysed one pole put inside the rectum. If I were you I wd. resort to it.' WJ in Cambridge, Mass., to HJ in Florence (25 Oct 1869), *CWJ*, i. 113. At this time, it was becoming a widespread practice to use electricity for all kinds of ailments.

three-week voyage to join Elly and Emmet, who preceded her overland to California. It was, she said, an expedition arranged by her 'friends' – presumably the Emmets. An escort on the voyage was to be yet another all-too-willing Emmet. It was not her choice, but she resigned herself to a warm climate out west, since another winter at Pelham, as she had put it to James, 'might go far toward finishing me up'. The plan was to stay three years: it seemed interminable, and she feared she would never return. This would mean the end of her preferred plan. Her distress at going west, rather than east to Europe, she expressed to James in her November letter:

> 'When shall we meet again,
> Dearest & best,
> Thou going Easterly
> I, to the West?' as the song saith.

There is the slightest edge to this letter, a quiet reminder to James that he was not the only suffering creature in existence: 'To think that you should be ill & depressed so far away, just when I was congratulating myself that you, at all events, were well & happy, if nobody else was – Well, my dearest Harry, we all have our troubles in this world –'

An answer, to herself as much as to him, was to hold even blindly 'to some conviction, never mind what, that God has put deepest into our souls, and the comforting love of a few chosen friends . . .'. She felt an 'eternal right' to love, 'not a mere arbitrary desire for it', and asked James if he didn't see this.

As always, she turned abruptly to lighter matters, as though to cheer him with her vivacity. Silent about her illness, she laid on the kind of social report that fills thousands of James letters: Arthur Sedgwick (soon to be appointed instructor in Constitutional Law at Harvard) did not, she said, 'thrill my soul – but why should he?'; she had lunched with steady, good Lizzie Boott, and there met Gray's sister, Miss Bessie Gray, who was handsome and cordial. Gray himself had gone to New York to be a groomsman. Various engagements in their milieu had taken place; one couple was willing to wait for years. 'Sich is life' was the phrase both she and

James used when happiness could not be had. In the meantime, he might think of her 'once in a while' in his gondolas, and she would send him her photograph taken before Elly's wedding – 'a very good photograph', she told James, though to Gray she called it melancholy. It shows no sign of illness, but no sign either of her vivacity. Her wide mouth is closed; her eyes stilled. The motionlessness demanded by studio photography lost the vibrant Minny who was in her element when she spoke and moved. She is posed as though she were an item of memorabilia in the making. Her curled hand emerges from a ruched sleeve; her dark hair is drawn back and pinned above her ears; her round strong chin rests on her palm, her elbow on the arm of the fringed chair in which she is seated.

Minny was amazed to see from a photo James had sent his parents that George Eliot's partner, George Henry Lewes, was a 'pretty thing' in his way: 'To think that my adored George Eliot should have found among all human creatures she knew, the most comfort & sympathy from that one.'

A great deal of living went into her spell in Cambridge – an 'epoch', she called it. She saw Fanny Dixwell, who touched her 'deeply – as few people do – as hardly any other woman does'. Fanny was the daughter of a classicist, a Harvard graduate and teacher at the Boston Latin School who had then opened his own school in Cambridge. Amongst his ex-pupils was Wendell Holmes, who had known Fanny from childhood and continued a special friend. The Dixwell house in Garden Street was an intellectual rather than social centre, and Fanny managed to resist the usual social fashioning. She was reserved, and embroidered in seclusion. In the late autumn of 1869, Minny, too, had been secluded for a year, and recognised a quality in Fanny that seemed to reflect herself: 'To analyze it – I think she impresses me with a possibility in her of abandonment, devotion to an idea, a conviction, more than most people. She has what people call *self*-reliance very strongly, which seems to my mind to be reliance upon God – trusting her own soul. . . . She gave me one of her embroideries – an extraordinary production for a young lady of the 19th century – very beautiful in the workmanship & in design.'

Central to this 'epoch' was a reversal in her relations with the

James family. She managed to stand up to Alice, dissipate William's hostility, and forbid her uncle to meddle with her soul. She wrote triumphantly to Elly ('My darling little Elephant') in San Francisco that Holmes had been 'as nice as ever', Willy 'nicer', and Alice had not snubbed her 'as much as usual. She began by doing it but I asked her to stop, wh. she consented to do.'

These may have been concessions to illness, but a swing in Minny's favour was also connected with a recent disruption in the James family. In 1868, Henry senior's half-brother, the Revd William James, had died. He had practised a tolerant Calvinism, under the aegis of Presbyterianism, the family faith going back to Ireland. In their youth, he had guided Henry senior, but when the latter broke with the Presbyterian Church he began to write abusive letters to his brother, and never made up. In 1869 his brother's admirers had published a memorial volume of his writings, and Henry senior, jealous perhaps (since his own self-published works had no success), now resolved to attack his brother publicly. Alice declared it would be a 'great indelicacy', but her father insisted he would then have his say anonymously, and sat down to ask his disciple, Julia Kellog, to copy and submit the attack.

According to Henry senior, Alice 'grew furious & cried out for help' from William, who retorted, 'Why of course he will do it. He is so little restrained by conventional considerations that if you or I or Mama were to die tonight he would send off a contribution to the Daily Advertiser tomorrow tearing us to pieces.' His father, charmed by repartee, switched moods suddenly. He 'thought this very good'.

It may be that Henry senior's reckless conduct disrupted the household on more occasions than can now be recorded, for his papers were destroyed selectively, over three generations. Quantities of his letters were burnt by his sister-in-law, Aunt Kate, because she 'thought it better that "the children" should not see them'. With his caprice, his godlike pretensions, disciples, and unreadable scriptures of his own concoction, he was somewhat absurd. Worse, he had not scrupled to publicise a Fourierist theory of free love. 'I presume', he had announced, 'a day will come when the sexual relations will be regulated in every case by the private will of the parties; when the reciprocal affection of a man and a woman will furnish the sole and sufficient sanction of their material converse.'

It was hard for Alice to bear this. She and her mother kept an ultra-respectable home to counteract her father's scandal. He was wildly erratic, talking free love one second, selflessness the next. In terms of social conduct, Henry James stood with his mother and Alice; far more intelligent than his mother and stabler than Alice, he cultivated a calm manner crossed with the moral scrupulousness of his adoptive Boston. At the same time he harboured a horror of publicity. Where he based his morality on private assessment, his father was exhibitionistic and confessional (as when he confided to Bob that he'd been tempted by 'lascivious memories, unchaste nay unclean desires').

During the visit of his niece, Henry senior, never diffident about the soul, took it into his head to lecture her on Christian humility – this, after his assault on his brother's Christianity. Minny refused to listen. She found her uncle 'neither reasonable nor consoling'. He so 'disgusted' her that she told him plainly that she found his talk of humility 'not only highly impractical, but ignoble & shirking'.

Her uncle accused her of '*pride*' and '*conceit*'.

Minny was not cowed by this judgement. His views, she asserted, 'didn't touch my case a bit – didn't give me the least comfort or practical help and seemed to me wanting in earnestness & strength'. She refused to be led like a weak-minded woman. During 1869 Henry senior had been pronouncing on Woman in an illogical manner that shamed William. On this score there had been a 'discordance' between himself and his father due to the latter's 'absence of *intellectual* sympathies of any sort'. Henry senior had been arguing that morality, the sphere of strict duty, should not be confounded with spirituality, whose 'law' is 'freedom'. This was the exclusive preserve of the male. Woman's prime duty was to 'vindicate' and empower men; she should not lend herself too keenly to conjugal and maternal delights. He saw no contradiction between the glorious amoral freedom and his breast-beating over Man's fallen nature.

William had to try hard to sustain the family myth that their father was a genius. 'Father has been writing a couple of articles on "woman" & marriage in the Atlantic', William commented to Henry. 'I can't think he shows himself to most advantage in this kind of speculation.'

Henry disagreed with William's judgement: he shared with his father a reverence for the inspiring woman. Minny's existence meant most to him as 'a life of the spirit'. But, that spirit, conceived in freedom, was, in practice, the antithesis of the passionless retirement his father had in mind. William was, in fact, closer to their father in his retrogressive position on domestic dependence. In his review of John Stuart Mill's *The Subjection of Women* (1869), William argued that, for American men at least, women must remain as they are because men cannot do without the emotional haven of their uncritical dependence. 'However he might shrink from expressing it in naked words, the wife his heart craves is at bottom a dependent being.' His argument is no less emotive than that of his father. The difference is that William James puts his case clearly and without pretence that women's interest is to be considered in any way.

Minny showed a generous impulse to reach out to the better William she had always admired. 'M. Temple was here for a week a fortnight since', William reported to his brother Henry on 5 December. 'She was delightful in all respects, and although very thin, very cheerful. I am conscious of having done her a good deal of injustice for some years past, in nourishing a sort of unsympathetic hostility to her. She is after all a most honest little phenomenon, and there is a true respectability in the courage with which she keeps "true to her own instincts" – I mean it has a certain religious side with her. Moreover she is more devoid of "meanness," of anything petty in her character than any one I know, perhaps either male or female. *Je tiens à* telling you this, as I recollect last winter abusing her to you rather virulently.' He ends with the news that, at the last moment, the Emmets had telegraphed Minny not to join them. As business had called the Railroad King to the West, so business ruled again and called him east. The grand plan for Minny's recovery was incidental.

'I rejoice in the felicity of M. Temple's visit', Henry James replied from Rome on 27 December, '– & deplore her disappointment with regard to Cal[i]f[orni]a. But I mean to write to her.'

Though she heard from him a month later, in the interim a new bond sprang up between Minny and William which allowed her to speak her mind at full stretch. Two letters have survived, the first only a fragment, but they show Minny in her most searching mood and suggest that William recognised himself as one of those few with whom Minny claimed an 'eternal' bond. All the same, Minny held him off, with an aversion to 'sickening introspection ... exhausting & nauseating subjectivity'. She had to explain to William that much as she loved him, she couldn't tolerate his company. William was in the middle of what he called in his diary a 'great' collapse, while Minny was in need of 'rest'.

Christianity beckoned as a comfort, for she longed to resign her struggles, physical and mental. This seemed, briefly, a blessed alternative to self-reliance in her precarious effort to get through the winter. She reconsidered her uncle's lecture on humility: 'what if the good gentleman had all along got hold of the higher truth, the purer spirituality?' Eventually, after much self-examination, she rejected this. Willed moral effort always seemed to her less effective than spontaneous acts of generosity. Here is the surviving fragment of a letter Minny posted to William James on 15 January 1870:

> ... this Christianity would seem to be the only comfort – & the more I live the more I feel that there *must* be some comfort somewhere for the mass of people, suffering & sad, outside that which stoicism gives – a thousand times when I see a poor person in trouble, it almost breaks my heart that I can't say something to them to comfort them. It is on the tip of my tongue to say it – & I can't – for I have always felt myself the unutterable sadness & mystery that envelops us all – I shall take some of your chloral tonight, if I don't sleep – Don't let my letter of yesterday make you feel that we are not very near to each other – friends at heart – altho' practically being much with you or even writing to you much would not be good for me. Too much strain on one key will make it snap – & there is an *attitude of mind*, (not a strength of Intellect by any means) in which we are much alike – Goodbye –
>
> Your aff. cousin
>
> Mary Temple –

To William, this letter – possibly the destroyed section – had a special importance: he placed it behind his photograph of Minny with her hair cropped in 1861, and so it remained for the rest of his life. His diary shows that in the winter of 1869–70 he recognised his inability to relate to others. He bore her no grudge for protecting herself against him at this time, and sent her a new drug, chloral, to put her to sleep. He also arranged for her to be sent an English translation of Wilhelm von Humboldt's *Letters to a Female Friend*, in which the eighteenth-century philosopher upholds the 'strength and courage' of Charlotte Diede, whom he met once and never saw again. William offered Minny the Harvard code of manly endeavour, promoted by its new president, Charles William Eliot, a chemist with whom William had worked. 'Willy James sometimes tells me to behave likea man & a gentleman, if I wish to outwit fate', Minny informed Gray without resentment. She was touched by his concern: 'What a *real* person he is', she thought. 'He is to me, in nearly all respects, head and shoulders above other people.'

To keep up her courage, Minny revived the dream of Europe. Her new plan is first mentioned at the end of November as a 'proposal that has been made to me, not of matrimony, but better'. A cousin called Mary Ann Post now offered to take Minny, along with her own four children, on a journey abroad the following summer. They intended to stay in Europe for fifteen months. As Minny's dream took shape over the next two weeks, her health improved beyond recognition.

'I don't remember ever feeling so well & in such good spirits in my life', she declared. 'Not that I am not generally pretty cheerful, if there is the slightest excuse for such a frame of mind.'

She began to get up at six and read German, in preparation for Europe (she spoke of her progress with the language in the same breath as she spoke of a secret 'plan'). Most of the days were spent driving herself about the countryside in a sleigh with her 'dear little pony'; and on 11 December she was able to attend a matinée of *William Tell*. It delighted her, and she slept all night afterwards.

Her 'plan' was Minny's lifeline through the winter in Pelham, but it held only if she could rely on her cousin to take up the farther end. On 26 January, she received a long letter from Florence in which Henry James spoke of homesickness. Since it was Minny's habit to mention any form of encouragement, and since for once she had nothing hopeful to say, it is possible that, unintentionally, this letter made her 'drop' when he broke it to her that he would not wait in Europe until she arrived. She never replied.

There followed a night that was 'rather the most unpleasant' she had ever spent when she despaired of recovering 'the gift of sleep'. She took morphine at two in the morning, and when it had no effect took a double dose which left her feeling as ill the next day 'as one would desire'. On that day, 27 January, she wrote her only distraught letter to Gray in which she confessed a temptation to end her life – with her usual cover of colloquial humour: 'the strain is a "leetle" bit too hard, & I am sometimes tempted to take a little "pison" to put me to sleep in earnest'. She did have her supply of chloral.

For a while, she wondered again if the Christian vision of Redemption could rest her questing spirit. The life and death of Christ was 'the brightest spot in history', a model for all to follow, but it was her nature to walk alone. She was too self-reliant to accept 'vicarious' suffering. 'I didn't want it, & I didn't understand, even intellectually, the standpoint of people who did.'

She liked to test ideas 'practically', and what healed her in practice was human not divine love: natural, spontaneous love for Kitty's child. 'The one bright spot in my existence now is the baby – he is indeed a small bit of Paradise.'

With something of her young defiance, she swung back to 'the old place – Paganism', her word for Emerson's faith in the spiritual power of the individual. This did bring a measure of comfort: 'One at least feels that here one breathes one's native air – welcome back to the old *human* feeling, with its beautiful pride, and its striving – its despair, its mystery, and its faith.' Two weeks later, on 10 February, she explored this with William James in a twelve-page letter questioning Christian aims of humility and perfection, as she seeks, still, her 'true life':

Dearest Willy –

I can't write you much of a letter, for I have been awake nearly all night, & feel very seedy – but there are one or two things I want to say to you – First, thank you most heartily for your letter – which was so much to the point, & so kind & sympathetic. Then, you ask why the feeling toward & subsequently the reaction against Christianity ... – in short, I saw that I simply couldn't practically live a holy life – that even if I succeeded in doing a given act, it was done with weariness & grudgingly – & the *rest* that Christ had promised his disciples was certainly not in that ceaseless striving after the impossible Ideal – Do you call that feeling 'separated from God', which you ask if I felt? I don't – I call it feeling that I must have mistaken the mission of Christ, or else that Christianity was not the whole of life – or else finally, the third alternative that I was, indeed, hopelessly trifling. Then came the sleepless night that I told you of, when casting about in my mind for something or other to lay hold of, I thought of what Uncle Henry said that Christ didn't come that we might be unselfish & pure like him, but to show us once for all that we were selfish & impure – there followed the thought that I wrote to you about – what if there should be truth in the old Orthodox Atonement after all – a mysterious intervention of God to save us & make us happy by the *vicarious* suffering of Christ ... which gave us every blessing simply by accepting Christ's meditation with humility – As I tell you, I was tired out physically & mentally then, & I saw in this idea a delusive *Rest* which was grateful to me, but which subsequently was distasteful & seemed ignominious to me. So, dear Willy, that doesn't at all satisfy me – I am, after all, a good deal of a pagan – certain noble acts of bygone stoics & philosophers call out a quick and sympathetic response in my heart. If I had lived before Christ, music would have come like a divine voice to tell me to be true to my whole nature – to stick by my keynote & have faith that my life would, in some way or other, if faithfully lived, swell the entire harmony – This is a grander music than the music of the spheres. Of course the question will always remain, what is one's true life – & one must each try & solve it for ourselves. I confess that I am ... [the end is missing.]

Minny's craving for '*Rest*' and her turn to the stoic solution of suicide are marks of her losing battle with tuberculosis. On 13 February, Henry James revealed how out of touch he was when he asked William to verify if 'Mrs. Post has asked Minny to go abroad with her. Is it even so?'

Just about this time, Minny, feeling 'a good deal knocked up', resolved to see a doctor called Metcalfe with a reputation in New York. He was to visit her at Mrs Post's, where she stayed, on a Sunday, but in the meantime Mrs Post urged her to consult her own physician, Dr Taylor, who came on Saturday as Minny was going to bed. Until this night, Minny had clung to a belief that her disease lay in the lining of her lungs – not in the lungs themselves. In other words, she had been telling herself all through 1869 that however bad she felt, there was no systemic damage, and she could hope to get well.

After sounding her lungs, Dr Taylor spoke solemnly. 'My dear young lady, your right lung is diseased – all your haemorrhages have come from there. It must have been diseased for at least a year before they began.'

Feeling she had been an 'idiot' to believe anything different, Minny assured Dr Taylor that she was not a bit nervous of hearing the truth. 'If there are no tubercles, am I curable,' she asked, 'and if there *are*, am I hopeless?' She asked for the most unfavourable view he could take of her case, though she did not mean to ask exactly how long she would live, so was unprepared for his reply, 'Two or three years.'

'Well Doctor,' Minny said, not wanting to make him repent his frankness, 'if my right lung were all gone, I should still make a stand for my left.' Then, as she described the scene later, 'by way of showing how valiant a stand I proposed to make, I fainted'.

When she came round, Dr Taylor tried to assure her that her condition was not dire after all. She found him 'objectionable' with his bad grammar, and was relieved when he went away. She 'slept very little that night'.

The following night, the paternal Dr Metcalfe arrived, a man who had known her father at West Point. He told her that her right lung was decidedly weaker than the left, which was sound, and assured her that if she could keep up her general health she might get well. He had known a case that was ten times worse recover completely. Then he urged her to go to Europe. So the plan to sail with Mrs Post was renewed, as she put it to Gray, 'if I am not dead before June'. She declared: 'my spirits are good, & I don't propose to lose them if I can help it, for I know it all depends upon myself whether I get thro' or not. That is, if I begin to be indifferent to the result I shall go down hill quickly.'

By this time, James had returned to Great Malvern in England to take a cure for his bowels. He was comparatively 'open', and now in that settled state in which chronic 'invalidism' combined so conveniently with immortal longings. William had been reading *The House of the Seven Gables*, and was struck by the similarity of his brother's style. 'I'm glad you've been liking Hawthorne', Henry replied on 13 February. 'But I mean to write as good a novel one of these days (perhaps) as the H. of the 7 G.s.' At this 'thrilling prophecy' he laid down his pen. His query about Minny and Europe was only an afterthought. But he held her in mind – always expressive. 'Goodbye, dear Harry', she had ended her last letter in November. '"Words is wanting" to tell you all the affection & sympathy I feel for you.' At Malvern, Mrs Ray, the young wife of a Scottish laird, carried her arms a bit like Minny but was 'to Minny as water unto wine'.

'I have been very sorry to hear of Minny's fresh haemorrhages', he told Alice, but as further news reached him of Minny's sufferings he continued to hold by his image of her vitality. 'I was of course deeply interested in your news about poor Minny', he wrote to his father. 'It is a wondrous thing to think of the possible extinction of that immense little spirit. But what a wretched business too that her nerves should be trifled with by the false information of unwise physicians. Mother says that she asks for letters – which I'm glad to know of. Writing a dozen pages is easy term for lightening such a miserable sorrow. But something tells me that there is somehow too much Minny to disappear for some time yet – more life than she has lived out.'

In late February he wrote her a long letter which should have reached its destination early in March. He expected some response because, later, he urged his mother to pass on whatever Minny said at this time: 'If you remember any talk of hers about me – any kind of reference or message – pray let me know of it.' There was no message. Uncharacteristic silence followed the letters he wrote her over the winter of 1869–70, though she replied – at length – to others.

As James endured the bleating of Englishwomen (Florence, they said, was 'so very nice'; George Eliot, they said, was 'so very clever'), it pleased him to recall exemplars of American womanhood. To find such freedom in England, he mused, you'd have to look amongst duchesses. Thinking of Minny, he filled with pride, averting his eyes from women in dowdy beads, dirty collars, and linsey-woolsey trains.

'I revolt from their dreary deathly want of – what shall I call it? – Clover Hooper has it – intellectual grace – Minny Temple has it – moral spontaneity.'

On the day he wrote these words, 8 March 1870, Minny Temple died three thousand miles away in Pelham, New York.

6
'Pure Fellowship'

In the decade that followed Minny's death, James achieved international fame. Between the ages of twenty-seven and thirty-seven he settled in Europe, and embarked on what is known as the international theme: fictions of Americans in Europe, or Europeans in America. His expatriate's fascination with the uncrossable Atlantic led him to explorations of national character with ambitious titles like *The American* (1877) and *The Europeans* (1878). James published nothing that was not accomplished, but we might distinguish between the uninspired professionalism of his early novels, *Watch and Ward* (1871), *Roderick Hudson* (1875), and *Confidence* (1879), and the first great wave of genius, taking its rise from Mary Temple: the high destinies of Bessie Alden and Isabel Archer, American girls who go abroad.

His mother broke the news of Minny's death with regrets for 'dear bright little Minny', and James grovelled over this morsel of praise: 'God bless you dear Mother for the words. What a pregnant reference in future years'. This young man, who had savaged Dickens and Whitman, could contemplate his mother's banality as a marvel of insight – a measure of her power over him at the age of twenty-seven. James always carried filial reverence to extravagant lengths, but here his mother's words were crucial in that her sanction of Minny (now she was dead) helped to unblock a deluge of feeling. A tide of recollections flowed into his mind: Minny's need to know and do; her leading him on to understanding; her 'absolute defiant' and 'breathing immortal reality'.

On that day, 26 March 1870, his first act was to 'promote' Minny to partnership in the private life: 'I could shed tears of joy far more copious than any tears of sorrow when I think of her feverish earthly lot exchanged for this serene promotion into pure fellowship with our memories, thoughts and fancies.' Their 'fellowship' had a purity not to be realised in any living tie, for Minny would now be 'locked away, incorruptibly, within the crystal walls of the past'. James tried to impress on his conscience the fact of loss, but what he actually felt was all gain. Minny, he told his mother, was '*dead* – silent – absent forever – she the very heroine of our common scene.' He told William: 'While I sit spinning my sentences she is *dead*'. In some way her death and his act of writing were linked, as though her vitality had passed to him. This came at once 'with irresistible power' and 'the sense of how much I knew her and how much I loved her'. It was no longer a romantic feeling but something 'deep' as the 'foundations' of his being, he realised on a long walk, near Malvern, that first afternoon.

He dismissed her disappointment ('but one little dream the more in a life which was so eminently a life of the spirit'), and transfigured her sleeplessness as a process of 'waking wider & wider, until she awaked absolutely!' His distance across the Atlantic, which had prevented his seeing her physical end, pleased him: that event would not break the continuity of fellowship. 'Twenty years hence what a pure eloquent vision she will be,' he foresaw with a conviction that prompted him to offer his vow to Minny herself: 'Twenty years hence we shall be living with your love and longing with your eagerness and suffering with your patience.'

It was William who felt the loss. He spoke to Minny of 'that big part of me that's in the tomb with you', leaving a page of his diary blank for a drawing of her tombstone. 'Minny,' he cried, 'your death makes me feel the nothingness of all our egoistic fury.'

William felt diminished, Henry enlarged. Across the sea, words poured from him like breakers rolling towards the distant shore of future works. There, Minny would take her way. The advance on Europe of this most intransigently American of girls, the meeting of the New World and the Old, the imaginative resonance of their reunion, had been a shared dream. Now, when it was too late, it returned to James in a night dream, as though meeting were still possible.

'In exchange for you, dearest Minny, we'll all keep your

future . . .' So he spoke to her as he trudged the Malvern Hills. She was to fill, not empty, his life: 'what a secret from those who never knew her!' To experience Europe for her sake, to tell her his tales of the England and Italy she had longed in vain to see, had been a dream of his return; now, he saw the act of speech shift to her. 'I shall have her forever talking to me. Amen, Amen to all she may say!'

No silence, then, no absence, but a future directed by a soundless voice – a continuation of a living voice. It echoes through the letters Mary Temple wrote over the last year of her life: the quick, ready breath of a 'communicative spirit', defying the divides between them to rouse her 'darling Harry' as he 'looked forward with a certain eagerness' to taking the lead in a 'masculine' way: 'I had worked away from the old ground of my relations with her, without having quite taken possession of the new: but I had it constantly in my eyes.' A fundamental (though nameless) understanding had persisted, and her death brought home what she had meant to him – meant still – a feeling so intense, in letter after letter in the spring of 1870, that it verged on a sort of ecstasy, strange and extraordinarily sustained.

James reread Minny's letters at the end of March and, back home, in his old room in Quincy Street, he invented an alternative scenario with a happy outcome. In 'Travelling Companions', written in May–June 1870, he imagined a meeting in Italy of a Europeanised American called Brooke and Charlotte Evans, a newly arrived American, aged twenty-two, who walks with a light, rapid grace, full of decision and dignity, and whose ungloved hands support her folded arms. The experience of Charlotte Evans is remarkably close to Minny's dream, and provides a clue to the process by which James transformed her as the material of art, leading to his great portraits at the end of the decade.

Brooke favours American women for their 'frankness and freedom', but this one manifested, he observes, 'a different quality of womanhood from any I had recently known; a keenness, a maturity, a conscience, which deeply stirred my curiosity'. Charlotte is accompanied by a flagging father who provides formal protection, but Brooke becomes her true companion in the glories of Italy: 'We stared, we laughed, we wept almost, we raved with a decent delight'. The emotions wrung by Rome, by Leonardo's *Last Supper* in Milan, and the rhythmic slide of a gondola bind them. 'We had infinite talk', Brooke relates, 'she was worthy to know Venice.' She is not eclipsed by the voluptuous women of Titian – 'as deeply a woman as they, and yet so much more of a person' – as fit to be loved, yet also a friend. It is a tale of parallel awakening: Miss Evans discovers the wonders of Europe, Brooke his masculinity.

To link work with life is plausible only in the knowledge that a writer will transmute actuality into something else. 'Travelling Companions' cannot tell us what James felt for Minny Temple; all we may infer is the fact of this fantasy at this particular moment in his development: it was not beyond his power to imagine that a man as unformed as himself might come to be more to a woman than a 'companion'. But this fantasy followed Minny's death. It was her death, not her life, that opened up for him the possibility – or certainty – of a love as intense as 'faith', passing though the senses into 'mystery'.

James made two lingering journeys, in 1869–70 and in 1872–74, before he settled in Europe at the end of 1875. Europe meant art and refined Americans who had little or no contact with the natives. Though the foremost intellects in England – George Eliot, Ruskin, Darwin – had received him, James was not satisfied. He saw that, in England, intellectuals, even celebrities, were not the élite (as they would have been in Boston), and he feared that society would remain closed to him: 'To have any but really *Good* Society there ... would be rather more intolerable than to have none at all.'

American travellers clung, for the most part, to their copies of Hawthorne and Washington Irving, and associated only with other travellers or expatriates. There was a certain pride in this, somewhere between the robust independence of James Fenimore Cooper, who had refused to fawn for favours during his travels from 1826 to 1833, and the rigid conformities of Old New York – people like Edith Wharton's parents – who took care to be more exclusive than Europeans. As Wharton recalled, the 'Americans who forced their way into good society in Europe were said to be those who were shut out from it at home'. So, Americans of that class, many of them more European than Europeans, looked down on fraternisation with accessible natives. This is central to the plot of *Daisy Miller*, where a democratic innocent falls foul of her compatriots when she befriends the charming Giovanelli in Rome. James befriended Mrs Wister, daughter of the actress, Fanny Kemble, who in certain lights showed 'a startling likeness to Minny Temple,' but the likeness, it turned out, was 'all in the face'. By 1874 James had wearied of Rome's 'American village': it was no longer the romantic dream he had shared with Minny, nor the place through which he had reeled and moaned with pleasure in the autumn of 1869.

In this period of transition, his work was often slight as he exercised his skills on travel-tales, mixing the two genres, stirring in local colour, and squeezing the orange, as he put it, before he lost the edge of his first responses to Europe. He thought of impressions as 'property': 'I helped myself to it . . . and tucked it away.' During 1869–70, when impressions were keenest, 'invalidism' had stopped his writing. Now he worked rapidly. The demand for travel-writing from American magazines helped James to become economically independent of his father from about 1874.

Unfortunately, the men in these travel-tales, the type of Passionate Pilgrim, are not as interesting as the invalids in his best home tales of the 1860s, while the foreigners are faintly ludicrous, like the Neapolitan matron who (somehow, by singing in a boat) makes a man of Brooke. There was no short cut to 'Europe'. He had to investigate his fictional ground, participate in the lives of the natives, and find ways to speak to them as closely as to Americans. How measured his career was; how deliberately and patiently he kept the '*Americana*' (the American girl) in the wings until he learnt what she might do.

In 1873, James was enthralled by the 'nobly strenuous' Dorothea in George Eliot's masterpiece, *Middlemarch*: 'To render the expression of a soul requires a cunning hand; but we seem to look straight into the unfathomable eyes of the beautiful spirit of Dorothea Brooke. . . . We believe in her as in a woman we might providentially meet some fine day when we should find ourselves doubting of the immortality of the soul.'

The elation is unmistakable. He insists that the subject of *Middlemarch* is not Middlemarch, a provincial town, but 'an ardent young girl ... framed for a larger moral life than circumstance often affords, yearning for a motive for sustained spiritual effort and only wasting her ardor and soiling her wings against the meanness of opportunity'. He reads into *Middlemarch* his own waiting subject: a woman of untested distinction whose destiny would dominate the novel. Dorothea, he argued, was 'altogether too superb a heroine to be wasted; yet she plays a narrower part than the imagination of the reader demands'. Certainly, it is what James demands. This is no ordinary reader; it is the heir apparent to George Eliot's pre-eminence in the genre. *Middlemarch*, he announced, 'sets a limit ... to the development of the old-fashioned English novel'. He would invent a new kind of novel that would limit social detail in favour of interior space. George Eliot was too diffuse, he thought, too concerned with the social web. James did not deny its use – he made a case for Eton, Ascot, and political breakfasts – but his ambition was to co-opt the social medium for a drama of ideas. American literature is not literature in the English sense of the word; it is a form of sermon or moral debate with a character of its own, what James would call its 'little secret'. With cool effrontery, he declared that English readers may think they enjoy *Middlemarch*, but to relish its 'inner essence' one must be an American.

By the mid-seventies James wished to settle. From the time of his visit in 1869 he was attracted to London, but because he feared to take it on he tried New York and then Paris in swift succession in 1875–6. Neither would do: New York was too shadowless and too expensive; Paris too much 'a city of shop-fronts, a great fancy bazaar', denying access to what lay behind. He had the impression that the French did not like strangers nor wish to know them.

During the year in Paris, from the end of 1875 to the end of 1876, James was happiest with the Russian expatriate Turgenev. Honest, unpretentious, Turgenev owned that portraits in his fiction came directly from life. The master advised James to trust what was there – to draw it out, not invent – and accordingly,

James turned from an invented American called Newman to a more personal portrait of an '*Americana*'. She would be to *The American* as 'wine unto water'. As national figures, both are innocents plunged in the corruption of the Old World, but the Americana is more than an allegorical construct: ready to break the mould, she is alive in a way Newman is not.

An eager young girl would come to Europe, of course, but what was she to *do*? Marital tyranny in George Eliot's final novel, *Daniel Deronda* (1876), offered an idea for a plot to which James might give an American twist. His venturesome Americana was to marry a tyrant of a type she would not recognise: masked by the refinement of a Europeanised American, but more snobbish, more self-consciously aesthetic in his tastes than any Englishman or European, a type James knew intimately. In George Eliot, the proud Gwendolen is chastened, almost broken by her marriage. The question was whether the freer character of an Americana could hold her own when she finds herself caught in an alien net.

Deronda may have offered more than a plot. Although, publicly, James criticised this novel (putting forward the common view that Deronda, an exemplary Jew, was too perfect to be true), privately he told Alice that he did not expect her to have had one-tenth his pleasure in reading a work so incomparably superior to French ingenuities. Flaubert's problem, Turgenev remarked to James, was that he had 'never known a decent woman', only prostitutes and light-weights. It may be that George Eliot's portraits of deep-souled women drew James to England as an environment congenial to future work. He had *Deronda* in mind on arrival, for one of his first contacts was a Jewish journalist called Child, an Oxford man whom James had met and liked in France. Theodore Child was handsome and intelligent, very like Deronda, James observed.

He arrived in London on 10 December 1876. Though it was winter, the crossing was smooth. His letters stressed the contrast between the amenities of Paris – its vivacity, salons, restaurants – and the wretched restaurant food, woolly smell, smutty dirt, and thick fog of London. But if London was less convenient 'for a lonely celibate', it was 'more inspiring' than Paris, even though he spent Christmas Eve in his rooms in Bolton Street, Piccadilly, writing to his mother for contact. He dined alone again on

Christmas Day, but felt sure that soon he would establish himself. So it proved.

James was now thirty-three, an eligible bachelor who had filled out to advantage, as an American acquaintance, William H. Huntington, noted: 'He has mildly swelled, not to fatness, not to stoutness, but well nigh to the brink of plumpness, also hath whiskers, full but close trimmed. By reason of these fulfillments . . . he has much more waxed in good lookingness, and is in his actual presentment (specially *qua* head) a notably finer person than one in the next 10,000 of handsome men.' His hair was brushed straight back from his great forehead, and his dense beard set off long, full lips. His brows came together in a frown of concentration, overhanging his attentive eyes in a straight line. He was ready with conversation and, as his mother's son, had a fair tolerance for the prosaic. He did note the pervasiveness of the prosaic in London and in the country houses he began to frequent: the number of even eminent men who offered no more than practical advice. Tennyson astonished him with his bluffness. Yes, a socialite confirmed, you can't get Tennyson to discuss anything more elevated than 'the best way to roast a buttock of beef'. That James was surprised shows how little he understood English manners: the matter-of-factness that is not humility, rather an unwillingness to show off intellectually, out of consideration for others. The very foreignness had its attractions: 'I positively *suck* the atmosphere of its intimations & edifications,' he noted a little over two months after his arrival.

Smoothing his way were letters of introduction from Henry Adams, a descendant of two American Presidents, John Adams and John Quincy Adams. Leslie Stephen (editor of the foremost literary magazine, the *Cornhill*; later, father to Virginia Woolf) made James welcome and introduced him to English readers; and Motley, the American historian, arranged for him to have temporary membership of a writer's club, the Athenaeum (membership normally took sixteen years). Rescued from the wretched restaurants, James now fed contentedly at the club, and observed the rituals of teatime. Gentlemen lolled on couches, magazines in their laps or books from Mudie's library (James took out six at a time and read sixty per cent), while minions in knee-breeches offered buttered toast. Soon he was elected to the Reform Club, an anchor for life where he found the best conditions for a bachelor. James had made up his mind not to marry by the time he settled in London, and though he appeared to be charmed by attractive women he met at dinners, he did reserve his warmest praise for the elderly or safely married. He was not at this stage encouraging to men: when he found himself amidst male lovers in a pension near Naples, he rejected 'the fantastic immoralities and aesthetics of the circle'. A fear of a sexual or emotional claim is the simplest explanation for the shutting off of response – shutting off; not absence. James was far from cold; his imagination and prose are suffused 'with open-eyed desire'. It was strongest in Italy, where what William called a 'sensualism' in his brother emerged more easily than in Boston.

While James embarked on his adventure in expatriation, the friends of his youth were, at last, settling in pairs. In 1872, Wendell Holmes married Fanny Dixwell (whose originality had struck Minny on her last visit to Boston): he was thirty, she thirty-one. Holmes did not let the wedding interrupt his career: his diary records the event with one curt word, followed by several words about his new position as sole editor of the *Law Review*. For a creative woman like Fanny, marriage to a public man like Holmes was a disaster. Bored and intimidated by society, ill, wasted, increasingly unhappy with her husband's philandering, she sat out her life in her darkened room talking to pets and imaginary companions. Her embroideries vanished.

One by one the old circle broke up: the two youngest James brothers married in 1872 and 1873, and soon became fathers; Clover Hooper married the clever but supercilious Henry Adams in 1872, and (it seemed to James) had her wit clipped a little. 'She is very open to instruction. *We* shall improve her,' Adams wrote to an Englishman, Charles Milnes Gaskell. 'It is rather droll to examine women's minds. They are a queer mixture of odds and ends, poorly mastered and utterly unconnected. . . . My young female has a very active and quick mind and has run over many things, but she really knows nothing well . . .'. The next year, Sargy Perry, who now taught literature at Harvard, became engaged to Lilla Cabot, and John Gray married Anna Mason – rumour had it that she was too like Rosamond Vincy, the spoilt beauty in *Middlemarch*.

In 1874 Minny's friend Helena de Kay illustrated *The New Day*, a collection of love-sonnets by Richard Watson Gilder, a poet on the staff of *Scribner's Monthly* and soon to be the influential editor of the *Century* magazine. Helena married Gilder, who had a 'young' soul to match her 'old' one. The pair entertained James during his spell in New York in 1875, most likely at Helena's 'Friday evenings' where the artistic, literary, dramatic, and musical world of New York met for the next thirty years.

In 1876, Minny's last sister, Henrietta, married a Newport man, Leslie Pell-Clarke, the younger son of the Pell family, known to the James brothers from the time of their arrival in Newport in 1858. James found Henrietta informed and 'superb' when she breakfasted with him in Bolton Street on her wedding tour in 1878.

The last of all to settle was William, who in 1878, at the age of thirty-six, married a schoolmistress, Alice Howe Gibbens, aged twenty-nine, chosen by William's father for her mature sense of duty. A photograph taken before her marriage shows her reading with grave calm; in all photographs after her marriage, the calm is crossed with care. She was an intelligent woman who took a long time to think over the prospect – as well she might, given William's history of invalidism. His sister, Alice, who turned thirty in 1878, had a massive breakdown, the worst of her life, at the time of this wedding, which she did not attend. The James family did not connect her breakdown with William's marriage. His wife was the only daughter-in-law to be welcomed by his parents as a daughter – displacing his sister as the only one – but more trying was the fact that she no longer came first with her brother. She was saved by a burgeoning friendship with Katharine Loring (1849–1943), a practical feminist who had taught, together with Alice, for the Society to Encourage Studies at Home, an organisation founded in 1873 to promote women's education without overstepping men's prerogative of college education. William found Miss Loring more like an official than a woman. The family worried over the possible irregularity of the attachment but felt unable to interfere, and could only hope they might tire of each other. It seems that Miss Loring managed to calm Alice with larger doses of opium than doctors advised. She nursed Alice on and off (mostly on) for the rest of her life.

While his two needy siblings found nursing partners, the letters of Henry James between 1877 and 1880 show how little he enjoyed any real friendship or intimacy, despite his increasing immersion in English society. Even if he hobnobbed with the great, dined out 107 times in his peak social year of 1879, and dropped innumerable grand names in letters home, we can't assume his integration. 'I am still completely an outsider here,' Henry wrote to William after a year and a half, 'and my only chance of becoming a little of an insider (in that limited sense in which an American can ever do so) is to remain here for the present.'

From now on James cultivated the high-life image which has stuck ever since. His letters don't just drop names; they bombard you with society gossip and the image of the writer in the thick of it. Like all effective façades, it was in part accurate: James was, undeniably, a snob and, like others of his set, an anti-Semite. There has been massive attention to his social contacts on the assumption that society was James's subject. But was it, really? What he called the 'mere twaddle of graciousness' fills thousands of surviving letters. It is a presentation so calculated, so deliberately unrevealing and so insistently substitute that it invites question even as it tempts us with deceptive fullness.

George Eliot, Flaubert, and Turgenev believed, as did Fielding, Jane Austen, and Dickens before them, that there is no existence outside society. This is not an American belief. The heady promise of Emerson is an access of power if we kick free from society and transcend it on wings of individual integrity. The most influential philosopher of nineteenth-century America, Emerson frequented the James household. As late as 1872, Henry junior, aged twenty-nine, had visited Emerson, aged seventy, to read a paper. Whether he read or liked Emerson doesn't matter. For Emerson shaped him, as his father shaped him. Their radical fervour was what the James household lived and breathed. In Henry James the 'medium' is what an individual pits herself against, in order to test not society, plainly corrupt, but the power of individualism. This was at the core of the James plot, together with an attitude to society that is neither European nor colonial. For James, society serves as a test-ground; it's not important in itself. The settings and manners he absorbed over his years in England were the rind, only, of introspective works in the American tradition. These works invite acceptance as studies in manners, but remain allegorical trials, like Hawthorne's, turning enigmatically on their moral axis.

The social Henry James is a good fellow who enjoys company and goes out of his way for other people. This blocks from our sight a stranger character, extremely private and fiercely ambitious, who had scruples but could be ruthless when privacy or ambition was thwarted. In the same way as his father and William, he made a calculated distinction between a performing self and the underlying spiritual self, what William would define in his *Principles of Psychology* as 'the most enduring and intimate part of the self' containing conscience and 'our indomitable will'. His involvement in high life was 'a pious fiction': he had to force himself to 'keep on the social harness'. William affirmed that his brother lived 'hidden' in the midst of his alien manners – assumed as 'protective resemblances' – like a marine crustacean draped in 'rich sea weeds and rigid barnacles'. His asides to his Boston milieu mark the inferiority of the English élite to the seriousness of New England. At the end of April 1878 he walked on the downs of the Isle of Wight with Miss Mary Peabody, a descendant of New England divines, with whom he conversed 'quite in the Boston manner'. He was not cut off, he reflected: 'I know what I am about, and I have always my eyes on my native land.'

James wasn't idling in great houses. He was inspecting his material. ('London dinners were all material and London ladies were fruitful toil' sums up the social effort of a literary lion in a tale James wrote years later.) It is in this sense that we may understand his repeated comment to other Americans in the late 1870s that such a London dinner or such a house-party was 'not of first-class interest'. He was not entirely a voyeur. He had 'a real tenderness' for 'the personal character of the people', and told Norton that his dream was 'to arrive at the ability to be, in some degree, its moral portrait painter!' Again, George Eliot lurks behind his words, and in the spring of 1878 he visited her once more: 'The great G.E. herself is both sweet and superior, & has a delightful expression in her large, long, pale equine face. I had my turn at sitting beside her

& being conversed with in a low, but most harmonious tone.' He liked a modest, matronly confidence in Englishwomen in contrast with Italian and Frenchwomen and Americans, too, who adopted the fashion for helplessness, 'like a species of feverish highly-developed invalids'.

He developed a special attachment to the 'crepuscular' midwinter with its greasy fogs and eternal candlelight. He did not explain why this habitat was more congenial to him than the white glare of Boston, but after his death Virginia Woolf observed that James had shaped his art in 'the shadow in which the detail of so many things can be discerned which the glare of day flattens out'.* The works James began to write in the late 1870s enter this shadow. He leads us to see that, with certain subjects, the glare-of-day facts, the outer arena, is a kind of blind – not untrue exactly, but eclipsing another truth that forms behind it.

As James felt his way into the shade of his own life, a new figure appears in his fiction who was to reappear many times. The apparent harmlessness and marginality of this man goes with an extraordinary power of involvement, revealed and concealed with the utmost calculation. He appears for the first time in *The Europeans* (1878). Mr Acton is a New Englander who is well-travelled without appearing the least active. Acton's name seems ironic, for a characteristic posture has him lying on his back. His strongest feeling is attachment to his ethereal mother, though for a space he visits a full-blooded woman, experienced and a little damaged, in retreat from a European marriage.

Acton does, in fact, act on this woman. He is scrupulous, with decent reserve, which might point to the Boston gentleman were he not more than that. For he has a connoisseur's taste for the

* A similar shadow was to haunt the crepuscular habitats of T. S. Eliot; and it was to haunt Virginia Woolf herself, who, at the time of her comment, was setting up the antinomy of Night and Day (in *Night and Day*, 1919). She wanted to crack through the paving stone and be enveloped in a mist. Eliot, in a late interview, noted the influence of James in about 1910 when he began to write. From this point of view, James is a precursor of Modernism. The shadow in Henry James is a portent also of the Modernist shadow in Conrad: it falls upon the Thames, reflecting on the centre of civilisation an obscurity at the heart of *Heart of Darkness*.

unusual, which draws him out. Then, at the brink of intimacy, he draws back. It is this act, silent or insufficiently explained, that is unnerving to a woman who has come to trust such a man. It is impossible not to doubt herself: the more devious she may be, the more dependent on this man's insight, the more she is undermined. She has no basis for protest because the understanding (for want of an exact word) is unspoken.

A more dangerous incarnation of Acton is Winterbourne, who blights the springtime of Daisy in *Daisy Miller* (1878). Looking at Daisy's jaunts and death through his eyes, the tale tells us more about his kind of Europeanised American than about its apparent subject, a rich American girl on tour in Vevey and Rome. Daisy forms an attachment to Winterbourne, who seems oblivious to the fact that he has shown an interest in her that has awakened her feelings. 'No young lady had as yet done him the honour to be so agitated by the announcement of his movements.' For him, she provides absorbing material, as does Aurora for the American student in 'The Pension Beaurepas' (1879).

Winterbourne thinks he offends convention but really blights a girl's trust when he takes Daisy, alone with him, to the Château de Chillon and then withdraws, telling her carelessly, on the return journey, that he's about to move on. With a similar carelessness, ever laughing and exercising his wit, the student draws Aurora literally to him where he stands at a gate, keeping the red tip of his cigar towards her as she emerges from the Pension on her last night there. Blighted by her mother, Mrs Church, a maternal monster of soft-spoken will, misguided in her schemes (like Mrs James or 'Mrs Morte'), Aurora is drawn to the student's sympathetic awareness, and quickly, in the manner of Daisy, confides in him. Here, enacted, is the subtle form of involvement, calling out desire and, with it, a secret self. But this young man is too 'reasonable' to involve himself seriously in a girl's bid for freedom. As a future writer, the height of his desire is to observe the romantic extremity of her need to escape through that gate where he had placed himself so invitingly.

Both Winterbourne and the student are confident that nothing is owing to Daisy or Aurora because they are wiped out by European classifications – Daisy as 'the little American flirt', 'indelicate', a 'coquette'; Aurora as 'sly' or 'hypocritical'. There is something unexplained in both tales which has nothing to do with contradictions in the girls, the effect of foreign contexts which distort them. What is unexplained is the conduct of Winterbourne and the student: their blend of sensitive involvement and withholding. This is seemingly explained by their reasonableness in the face of unreasonable and headstrong girls. We see these girls through the controlling eyes of men who appear to themselves, and to us, pained to hear innocents reviled. So concerned do they seem that we almost forget that they are not only observers or narrators of girls' destruction, but might be seen to have been implicated in that destruction, had we access to the victims' point of view.

This work brought James fame, inflated by controversy on both sides of the Atlantic. 'Harry James waked up all the women with his *Daisy Miller*,' William Dean Howells remarked to the Boston man of letters James Russell Lowell. 'The thing went so far that society almost divided itself in Daisy Millerites and anti Daisy Millerites.'

Winterbourne shifts uneasily between these positions, rather in the way James had shifted between Minny's blithe naturalness and the force of his mother's disapproval – projected here as Winterbourne's aunt, an arbiter of acceptability. But this shift, with an eye to the reader, masks the depth of his involvement with the *subject*, Daisy. The reader is drawn into complicity with Winterbourne's spectatorial concern, forgetting that he is the prime actor in Daisy's story. He wields an internal guard so that his flair for intimacy backs off at its height. Daisy cannot crack his guard, and the price of failure is her death.

In a preface to this novella, written as an old man in 1909, James spoke of the 'brooding tenderness' with which he had approached this heroine. Daisy derives from a defiant young Minny, vulnerable, though she may not appear so, to loss of esteem. Daisy remains cheery towards Winterbourne, yet her last words show, to us if not at once to him, the injury he inflicted when he cut her in the shadowed arena of the Colosseum: '"I don't care," said Daisy in a little strange tone, "whether I have Roman fever nor not!"' We may well wonder if there were limits to the inexhaustible humour with which Minny bore slights from the James family.

'You don't mind if I am a little affectionate, now that you are so far away, do you?' Minny had written to James nine months before she died. Her death was as unexpected for him, as Daisy's for Winterbourne, who stares 'at the raw protuberance among the April daisies' in the small Protestant cemetery in Rome. Only afterwards is he confronted by the possibility that Daisy would have reciprocated his affection: 'She sent me a message before her death which I didn't understand at the time. But I have understood it since.'

When he heard of Minny's death, James had glanced at the oblivious countryside: would England have lived up to her dreams? The Temples stood on their English origins, and Minny's 'sense for what was English in life', James remembered, 'was an intimate part of her, little chance as it enjoyed for happy verifications'. In 'An International Episode' (1878), a woman like Minny is launched on a future that might have been hers. An English visitor to Newport, Lord Lambeth, asks eager, questioning Bessie Alden if she has been to England. 'Never – except in imagination,' says Bessie. 'But I daresay you'll go soon, won't you?' the Englishman persists. 'It's the dream of my life!' Bessie declares.

Bessie's fate when she gets there treads a fine line between the fulfilment of expectations and their disillusion. She continues to dream of a finer England than Lambeth presents, an England which lives through its writers, the 'clever' sort his lordship would not care to know. 'You mustn't mind what you read,' he tells Bessie.

> 'Oh, I *shall* mind what I read!' Bessie Alden rejoined. 'When I read Thackeray and George Eliot, how can I help minding them?'
>
> 'Ah, well, Thackeray – and George Eliot,' said the young nobleman; 'I haven't read much of them.'

Bessie must encounter the philistinism of the ruling class, and its irresponsibility. 'But why don't you address the House?' Bessie asks Lambeth. 'Because I have nothing to say,' he replies with disarming candour.

Modest and good-natured as Lambeth is, he is unfit for the possibilities Bessie represents. Where Daisy projects Minny's defiance, Bessie projects the seriousness of Minny's enquiring mind as well as her openness in the style of Newport. Bessie is approached through doors opening out to rocks and sea, 'apertures' with 'such an accessible, hospitable air, such a breezy flutter, within, of light curtains, such expansive thresholds and reassuring interiors'. There is a comic clash between the stir of Newport where Bessie 'says things out' and the constraint of Lambeth's mother and sister when they call on her in London, confirming the clash between the 'irritable' intelligence of Bessie and the placidity of Lambeth. 'Irritable', and the unexpected adjectives that hover round Minny – 'reckless', 'defiant', 'strenuous', 'divinely restless' – try to define the indefinable: a reach upwards in the scale of evolution. Bessie regrets nothing in refusing the lord's offer. It is a triumph James designed for his American girl.

It may seem that James imposed this outcome on his memory of Minny, but it was consistent with her idea of a marriage of true minds: the 'best' or nothing. Lambeth is a trial-run for Lord Warburton in *The Portrait of a Lady*. The test, in both cases, is whether an Americana of the finest character and intelligence could resist a romance plot.

To refuse this plot is to come to an abrupt end which is, for Bessie, no ending: it is only an 'episode' in the story of a 'lady' affronting her fate. 'An International Episode' is a preliminary to a novel which would test the farthest reach of an unconventional American girl. Bessie remains on the edge of a human frontier she may, or not, cross.

James conceived *The Portrait of a Lady* in 1876, put it aside as 'an aching fragment', and then took it up in Florence in April 1880.

'I had [Minny Temple] in mind', he said as he wrote the novel, 'and there is in the heroine a considerable infusion of my impression of her remarkable nature.'

This statement circulated from Grace Norton, sister of Charles Eliot Norton, to Helena de Kay Gilder. Thirty-four years later, at the time James published his memoir of Minny, Helena passed it on with the following note: 'I am enclosing the copy of a wonderful letter from Henry James. . . . M.T. is Mary Temple – my great great friend a very remarkable person. He used her personality in "The Portrait of a Lady," tho' her circumstances were in every way different.'

The germ for the novel, according to James, had been a long-term grasp of a single character, 'a *grande nature*'. Writing at 'that exquisite Bellosguardo [and] at the Hotel de l'Arno, in a room in that deep recess, in the front,' he was deeply happy. It had taken ten years for his gift to equal his ambition. Now, at last, at the age of thirty-seven, he was ready to engage fully with an unusual young woman who emerges from the New World (in fact, from what is patently the Dutch House, in Albany, where Minny had lived with their grandmother). Minny's longing for other forms of life across the sea is projected into Isabel Archer landing in England with 'the determination to see, to try, to know'.

It is not yet clear what she will '*do*', but her search for some 'independent' form of action whets our expectation. As an unmarried girl from America, Isabel is free of the social net – at least at first. Her natural companion is her Europeanised cousin, Ralph Touchett, whom she meets at a country house, Gardencourt, owned by his father, old Mr Touchett. Her cousin at once marks Isabel's distinction: 'He wondered whether he were falling in love with this spontaneous young woman from Albany . . . "A character like that", he said to himself, ". . . is finer than the finest work of art. . . . His cousin was a very brilliant girl, who would take, as he said, a good deal of knowing; but she needed the knowing, and his attitude with regard to her, though it was contemplative and critical, was not judicial.' Ralph perceives his cousin's nature as a sealed building. He has glimpses of a promising interior, but 'the door was fastened, and though he had keys in his pocket he had a conviction that none of them would fit'.

Isabel's novelty comes straight from Emerson. When we are told that 'she had a desire to leave the past behind her, and, as she said to herself, to begin afresh', she is speaking the language of Emerson's essay on 'Self-Reliance': 'Whence then this worship of the past?' and 'This one fact the world hates; that the soul *becomes.*' Emerson's quintessential America is located on a self-made frontier, a venturesomeness that can go anywhere so long as it sheds the past – in the case of a 'lady', the past of her sex. Isabel's field of action is to be Europe, and her venture is fuelled, at the outset, by rejections of two eligible men: the New England knight of the cotton mill, Caspar Goodwood, and the English lord, Warburton. In refusing them, she refuses the clichés of romance, for either suitor would have been the plum of the novel that ends happily ever after. Isabel throws out the plums in quick succession: first, the oblivious force of Goodwood, whose letter reads, 'I . . . I . . . I . . .'. He persistently announces his presence but is incapable of an act of attention. Isabel likes his command, but his figure is too stiff (like John Gray's in Minny's jokes to James), suggesting his inability to lend himself 'to some of the occasions of life'.

The nobleman presents a worse trap. Isabel's instinct to escape the future Warburton offers deepens in the revised version: as Isabel listens to his proposal, 'she managed to move back into the deepest shade of [her opportunity], even as some wild, caught creature in a vast cage'. Her instinct is confirmed by a telling, unconscious gesture in one sister, Miss Molyneux, who 'ladylike and patient' awaits her brother's pleasure. The point is emphasised, again, in revision: 'Miss Molyneux – as if he had been Royalty – stood like a lady in waiting.' To veer from this opportunity is to take an uncharted course. Isabel thinks, 'Who was she, what was she, that she should hold herself superior? What view of life, what design upon fate, what conception of happiness, had she that pretended to be larger than this large occasion? If she would not do this, then she must do great things, she must do something greater.'

Ralph is the Jamesian invalid. 'The liberty of falling in love' has a place on Ralph's programme, but it is a liberty to be 'very temperately used'; he can enjoy it only in the 'safest form', in silence, for he is forbidden any demonstration. Isabel is aware that Ralph's illness had 'a sort of comfort in it', absolving him from official emotions. This frees both to break through the artifice of manliness and femininity: 'he made her feel what might have been.' She would have liked to enter his locked chambers to sweep them, but he guards his safety with a belief that he was not destined to fall in love with her, re-enacting the author's ambiguities in relation to Minny. If Ralph does not fall 'in' love in the usual way, he does make it clear to Isabel that she has 'been loved', emphasised in the revision: '– Ah but Isabel – adored!'

Ralph liberates his cousin. He invites her to take risks with him, and she responds with spontaneous ease: 'her conversation was of a sort that gave a large licence to violent statements'. Marriage, Ralph sees, would end Isabel's licence; he concurs with her instinct. To marry Warburton would be, from a social standpoint, a brilliant career, but Ralph understands 'it would be prosaic. It would be definitely marked out in advance, it would be wanting in the unexpected.' He has a motive of his own that fits Isabel more closely than sexual union: her fulfilment, in the largest sense, is to be the experience of his life – his life itself. It is in Touchett's terms what most excites him. His name denies detachment; he fronts, as no other man, a woman yet to be, and has 'a sort of vision' of her soaring above the heads of men. At the end of this discussion on the frontier of possibilities, the cousins exchange 'a gaze, full on either side, but especially Ralph's, of utterances too vague for words'.

Greatness in a novelist is a power to see people not only as they are but as they might be, on the outposts of consciousness. James asked himself what would be a woman's 'adventure'? He rejected the standard adventure of being an event in a man's life: that was women's fate according to an arbitrary social plan. If a woman were freed from that plan, economically by making her independent, and psychologically by freeing her imagination, what would this creature do? This question matches an observation James made about Mary Temple in March 1870: she had been nothing less than an 'experiment of nature'.

Ralph Touchett sets up an experiment by imposing on Isabel's life a test of his own devising when he persuades his dying father to leave Isabel a large part of the fortune that would have come to him. The fortune is to free her imagination to act at its maximum potential. His motive is not generosity; he is curious, and, in this, Ralph Touchett is a fictional counterpart of the novelist who deploys the empiricism inherent in the genre.

The flaw in the experiment is the untried innocence of the American girl which exposes Isabel to the most predictable of predators: a fortune-hunter. She is taken up by the sinister Mme

Merle, who hands her over to the even more sinister Gilbert Osmond, the impoverished father of Mme Merle's daughter, Pansy. Since Pansy is illegitimate, the world has been told that she is motherless. She lives on a hill outside Florence with her father (superficially, in the way Lizzie Boott devoted herself to her refined father on Bellosguardo). An exacting connoisseur, impressive to a young woman eager for art and knowledge, Osmond is, in fact, nebulous, as Isabel comes to realise after their marriage. His soul has atrophied, and in its smallness conceives a hatred for his wife's 'larger qualities'. The outcome of the experiment is that the freest woman, who was to devise a new destiny, finds herself imprisoned in the lightless dungeon of a marriage that would never have happened without a fortune. One night in Rome, Isabel sits motionless before a dying fire, taking the measure of her prison. Osmond is evil: his egotism lies hidden like a serpent in a bank of flowers and poisons what he touches, a touch of exquisite refinement that withers any fertile outcome of Touchett largesse. Osmond exercises his skill in mental torment to demean Isabel's idea of herself. It is only after she has experienced the full force of this negation that she can bring herself to acknowledge the failure of Ralph's experiment. 'You wanted to look at life for yourself,' he tells her on his deathbed, 'but you were not allowed; you were punished for your wish. You were ground in the very mill of the conventional!'

At that moment, they discover something other than death and failure: their mutual endurance. 'For me you will always be here,' Isabel tells him. Their dialogue is an aria of the unsaid – or barely suggested. 'We needn't speak to understand each other,' Isabel says, and Ralph replies, '. . . if you have been hated, you have also been loved.'

'"Ah, my brother!" she cried.'

That night, he dies, but his spirit visits her: 'she saw his white face – his kind eyes; then she saw there was nothing. She was not afraid; she was only sure.'

Sure of what? James injects a silence that weighs on the reader. It is impossible for this articulate woman to say what she means because words fail before a rapport beyond the actions of this world, beyond death. The ghostly visitation confirms their hold on a rare and absolute love. It is a possibility that can exist only in the recess of consciousness where, in James, all real action takes place. And it is by this absolute that the final scene between Isabel and Goodwood must be judged.

Goodwood arrives at Gardencourt to save Isabel from the grip of corruption. He would carry the strayed Americana back to America. Will Isabel bolt with Goodwood at the touch of a kiss like 'white lightning': will she let the American knight of the cotton mill rescue her from the dungeon of her marriage? She breaks away, it seems instinctively, and the revised version marks her recoil: 'she felt each thing in his hard manhood that had least pleased her, each aggressive fact of his face, his figure, his presence ... made one with this act of possession.' When Isabel breaks away, she makes for the 'very straight path' to Rome. The ambiguities are not resolved: will Isabel really go on with her blighted marriage, or does Goodwood do well to persist, as he always has and, it seems, always will, in the hope of a weak moment when Isabel will finally succumb?

James is testing romance, and denying his reader a fictive escape. We cannot gorge ourselves on the usual dessert course of plums. Nor are we allowed the moral certainties of allegory: a girl who begins her adventure in a place called Gardencourt was bound to meet a snake in a bank of flowers, but we are left uncertain of her future relation to that snake. Goodwood too, the old-fashioned hero, is open to question. His kiss obliterates the past as sweepingly as Emerson's philosophy, yet Isabel holds to her commitments, including her vulnerable stepdaughter, locked in a convent and awaiting her return. For Isabel is no longer the Americana who set out from Albany. She has taken on Europe; she is now a composite of two remote worlds. This is quite different from joining an expatriate community abroad, that exclusive 'American village' in Rome or Florence, which James ridiculed (while enjoying its attentions). Isabel is enmeshed in a foreign society whose values are alien, particularly for girls, as Pansy's obedience to her father demonstrates. But is her spirit destroyed, as Pansy's seems to be?

The unresolved ending compels us to grasp the complexity of the whole truth, and resist the reductive answers (yes or no; sad or happy; guilty or not guilty) of the 'judicial' mind. Is Isabel's return to Rome a flight from one trap to another? It is clear that Isabel is too strong to remain a victim, and that the cousins' bonding across the divide of death – their deathbed aria and the ghostly visitation – empowers her in a way unknown to others. The resolve to pursue her marriage is no rash act; it goes back to an early exchange between her and her aunt:

> 'You are too fond of your liberty,' [says Mrs Touchett].
>
> 'Yes, I think I am very fond of it. But I always want to know the things one shouldn't do.'
>
> 'So as to do them? asked her aunt.
>
> 'So as to choose,' said Isabel.

Not until the final scene does Isabel choose for the first time. She had thought she exercised choice in marrying Osmond but had been manoeuvred into it, 'made use of' by Mme Merle. A choice that will finally determine her destiny is seen, now, in the light of what it is to be a 'lady'. The shadow of this being moves through darkness towards a door, challenged by Goodwood, and by Isabel's friend Miss Stackpole, a feminist who models herself on men. Her cousin alone promotes the unseen Isabel who goes forward 'sure' into her unknown future.

Early in the novel, Isabel underlines the need for a shift in definition when she argues with Mme Merle about appearances. To the Europeanised Mme Merle, a 'lady' is identified by the 'envelope of appurtenances': her clothes, manners, house, and friends. Isabel answers in the American language of self-reliance: 'I don't know whether I succeed in expressing myself, but I know that nothing else expresses me.'

James completes the portrait in so far as her act of choosing does, at last, express that self with the true freedom of knowledge as opposed to the illusory freedom of ignorance. And we ask again the implied question of the whole novel: what will she '*do*'? One aspect of her choice to return to Rome is certain: she will keep her promise to Pansy, who, without Isabel, must bend to her father's will. To be a 'lady' is not to reflect a set of proper attitudes, as Osmond and Mme Merle would have it, but to hold one's own with the certainty conferred by the ghost of Gardencourt. To go with Goodwood, to make that adulterous break with convention, would have been convention itself: to be a mistress, an event in the life of a strong man. It would lock her in one of the slots in the social system, exchanging one prison for another. Freedom was to find agency, however constraining the given conditions may be. This was the ethos of the James family, evident also in William and Alice: to live fully – strenuously – is to discover thc freedom to act within the limitations of circumstance. Alice was to discover it through a remarkable diary written on a daybed from which she never moved; Minny Temple had discovered it between bouts of haemorrhage beyond her control; Isabel Archer, within an imprisoning marriage. All exhibit the ethic of transcendence, what Emerson called 'the integrity of the private mind'.

In this great work, James tested the American promise of infinite potential, laid out by Emerson in the previous generation. He tested it through a 'lady' who, as a woman, was in a weak position; later, in *What Maisie Knew* (1897), he was to test it again, through a rejected female child – the weakest of all positions. He projects the idea beyond America as a promise that looks to the future – our future. On the one hand there is a nature of infinite possibility; on the other, the social net, constraining, often corrupt. Isabel cannot live, as Emerson imagined, in a delirious void. She must eat of the tree of knowledge: she cannot escape the conditions of a social existence. Her triumph – like that of Bessie Alden, Catherine Sloper in *Washington Square*, the child Maisie, Milly Theale, and Maggie Verver in *The Golden Bowl* – is to know and not be corrupted. All retain their verity; some, like Isabel and Milly, rise to altruism. Through these qualities they take on a new image of a saviour. For the ultimate test is to have the charity to take on those, like Osmond, who manipulate others for base ends. Isabel Archer, and later Milly and Maggie, have the strength not to abandon men, but to try to redeem them. As such, they embody a new kind of 'lady'. 'The ladies will save us,' said old Mr Touchett, 'that is, the best of them will – for I make a difference between them.'

When Grace Norton read the first two numbers of the serial, in November and December 1880, she recognised Minny Temple.

When she questioned James, he said it was not a portrait but a 'completion', because Minny had been *'incomplete'*, as all living people are incomplete.

This answer is peculiarly tight-lipped compared with the expansive picture of Minny he gave to Grace a month after Minny's death. What James now said played down what Minny contributed as a guide to the hidden nature of women: her demand for 'verity of being'. Subsequent works will show that James did not surrender his commitment to the collaborative art of 'pure fellowship', but he closed a door against the public gaze – even so friendly and knowing a gaze as that of Grace Norton – in order to construct his image as solitary artist. His motive was not necessarily egotism as opposed to fellowship; it could well have been the subtler motive of secrecy: the preservation of the private life and its continued fellowship ('what a secret from all . . .') with an eye to that 'vision' he had marked in the far future.

There was another reason for secrecy. James made it public that Osmond derived from Boott (taking care to absolve Boott of Osmond's manipulative side). This uncharacteristic explicitness about Boott (who was unlike Osmond in many other ways, supportive of his daughter and, later, her suitor), together with a fade-out of a stronger source in Minny, raises the question whether James might have projected a little of himself in the connoisseur who would appropriate the Americana as art object: a silver plate, as it were, to display the ornaments of his mind. Here is an aesthetic marriage devised by the aesthete, not the woman. Was there some guilt in the portrait of Osmond that led James to distract attention from an element of self-portraiture by proclaiming another source? It is obvious that James did project himself in the cousin who has the Americana act beyond the range of other women. The husband's wish to use her, and the cousin's wish to activate her by conferring on her a drama of fortune, are similar in their will to shape the phenomenon she presents. It is suggestive that it is her cousin to whom the Americana is bound in spirit, and the aesthete with whom she agrees to live: a man who will use her as far as she allows. Her part is to be a new kind of 'lady' who will continue, in the afterlife of the book, to choose what she does.

7
Meeting Miss Grief

A storm hit the *Gallia* as it plunged through winter seas en route to Liverpool. Every wave swept over the steamer; in her cabin, Miss Woolson watched the sea rush across the small, thick glass let into the deck for light. A train carried her from Liverpool to London past hedges sheeted in ice. Under her feet was a flat tin box filled with hot water, renewed at stops on the journey. Constance Fenimore Woolson had long contemplated the possibilities of a tie between an ambitious woman writer and a sophisticated mentor. She was now on her way to find Henry James.

Providentially, for James, she arrived finally on the Italian scene of *The Portrait of a Lady* just as it was taking shape in the spring of 1880. In Florence, Osmond strolled with Isabel in the Cascine gardens 'in its quietest part' during 'the early hours' when it was 'void of all intruders', and here, in the mornings over seven weeks in April and May, 'Mr James' was conversing with venturesome 'Miss Woolson' on a bench at 'the end of the pretty little Cascine', as his 'completion' of Minny Temple came to life. These meetings established a second strange bond.

Ever since the death of her father in 1869, Miss Woolson had felt 'desolate and oppressed with care'. There was not enough money, and she inherited instead a depression that came, she said, 'unexpectedly' and made all things 'black': '. . . My father battled against it all his life, and again and again warned me about it; but I was young then, and only half believed in it. Now, he is gone, and it has come to me. I tried to conquer it and sometimes I succeed, sometimes I – do'nt.'*

In order to support herself and her mother, she was given a start

* CFW's habitual punctuation.

at the age of twenty-nine by her sister's father-in-law, a newspaperman called George A. Benedict, and a Cleveland journalist called Bone who took her to New York and introduced her to editors. Her Cooper connection ensured interest, and she began to publish articles and stories in the foremost magazines, *Harper's*, *Appleton's*, *Lippincott's*, and the *Atlantic*.

No other facts whatever remain of her twenties, when she must have transformed herself from reading girl into woman of purpose. One remark, in her thirties, does allude retrospectively to a soldier she had fancied during the war: somehow, it doesn't carry conviction, as though she merely wished to legitimise her femininity with a gentleman-correspondent. (It occurred to her, now and then, to offer gentlemen reassurances about her true womanliness, her weakness, and envy of their wives.)

The war itself was quite another matter. Looking back years later, from the age of fifty, she said that anyone who had been young in the early sixties was marked for ever. As she moved through the South in 1873, she chronicled the bloody events of 1863–4 in meticulous detail on the flyleaves of a newly published biography of the Southern commander Robert E. Lee: 'the creek ran blood,' she noted of the two-day battle of Chickamauga on 19 September 1863. 'U.S. forces defeated. Terrible losses on both sides, U.S. 15,000. Confederates, 12,000.' (This was twenty-one days after twenty-year-old Henry James had come before the draft board in Providence to plead his release, and exactly the time his daring, red-haired cousin Gus was killed.) She notes the fate of men from her own state when they took the pass of Ringgold on 27 November 1863: 'Here it was that the 74th Ohio was cut to pieces on the hillsides . . .'. Eleven years after the end of the war she said, 'I cannot even now hear the old war-tunes, or pass these soldiers' cemeteries at the south, or see an old flag, without choking up and turning away my head.'

The most significant surviving document of her thirties, apart from her work, is a long letter written at the age of thirty-four, which describes the battlefields she visited in 1874. She departed from Asheville, North Carolina, with six trunks and a placid mother in a red, covered wagon called a 'palmetto', and travelled south via Atlanta, heading for St Augustine, the oldest settlement in the United States. (Established by Spain on the north-east coast of Florida in the sixteenth century, it was ceded to the U.S. in 1821, entered the Union in 1845, and now in the 1870s was gaining favour as a winter resort.) Woolson always hauled about quantities of memorabilia, books, and other possessions, partly because she was a hoarder, partly because she was a wanderer trying (in vain) to feel at home. The driver of the wagon, a mulatto, 'rode in a crook-back position all the way, whistling and singing to himself'. For two days, their route took them along the margin of the French Broad River with great cliffs on one side and foaming water on the other. The few others on this road were 'tall mountaineers in their blue jean suits' who, with 'native politeness', turned their big, clumsy wagons half over or into the river to make way for two women.

At this point the letter takes on the Cooper mood of adventure, with dangers that delight the writer. With five miles to go, at four on a winter afternoon, rain came down in torrents, 'and it grew dark rapidly down in our gorge with the great cliffs on each side'. Soon it was entirely dark, with rain continuing to blind their sight. She joined the driver on the front seat, aware that the river 'was rushing and roaring within ten feet of us, and the rocky road just wide enough for our wheels'.

The next day they reached the Great Smoky Mountains: 'the great peaks were purple and misty', she recorded, and there were 'terrible battlefields in every direction [from Lookout Mountain]. Up those very heights where we were standing had swarmed the ranks of the blue and the gray, down in that beautiful valley below us, they had died, poor fellows, by thousands . . .'. From the long blue line of Missionary Ridge opposite all the way down to Chickamauga, ten miles distant, every step had been fought. 'Was it at Chickamauga that Horace Burnham [from Ohio] was killed? As if to give emphasis to these thoughts, there on a green slope below us gleamed the low headstones of fourteen thousand of our soldiers, gathered from the hillsides around. And now all was calm and peaceful, the river curving around the little town, the blue distant peaks visible in seven different states; the only sign of the past were those graves, and the old earth-works and rifle pits in every direction. The [train] ride to Atlanta along the identical track fought over by Sherman and Johnson, was almost startling from the names called in at our door; Dalton, Resaca, Ringgold, Allatoona, Kenesaw, &c, all names of the most terrible battles our western troops took part in. How they brought back the war!'

When they reached Atlanta, it was the graveyard she went to see: there, too, the low stones, 'thousands upon thousands. . . . So many of them were young, all died painful deaths, and almost all left broken hearts behind them . . . – so we went "marching through Georgia".'

Woolson was one of those vulnerable people who are stubborn enough to carry through an unconventional course of action. In the 1870s it was odd to be a Northern woman living by choice in the ruined South. From 1873 to 1879 – from the age of thirty-three to thirty-nine – she made a base in St Augustine. For the first two winters, she had the one large room on the upper floor of the Ximénes-Fatio House built from coquina (shell-stone) by a Spanish merchant in 1798. It had been a boarding house since 1830, with slaves working large punkah fans over the dining table, and freed slaves tended to stay on. It was customary to have straw matting on the floor, and rope beds with a mattress of Spanish moss. Woolson wrote in her bedroom or possibly on the sunny end of the inside balcony reserved for single ladies (men lodged downstairs). It overlooked a garden with the long, fringed leaves of a banana tree and a dancing crane (who appears in one of her novels). In the afternoons, she thrived on her 'wild freedom' to walk for miles 'through the hummocks, where it looks as though no one had ever walked before, gathering wild flowers . . . or sitting down under the pine trees to rest in the shade'. She went on in the matter-of-fact style of her great-grandfather William Cooper, entering the wilderness of western New York: '. . . On other days I take a row boat and go prowling down the inlet into all sorts of creeks that go no one knows where; I wind through dense forest where the trees meet overhead, and the long grey moss brushes my solitary boat as I pass. I go up the Sebastian River as utterly alone as Robinson Crusoe. I meet alligators, porpoises, cranes, and even deer, but not a human soul.' She liked to look at snakes, and rowed up certain creeks especially to find them.

For Northerners, the country below St Augustine was unexplored frontier in the 1870s, an eerie landscape of river-swamp where trees are rooted in water, holding themselves erect by twining their roots with those of other trees – a hidden thicket under the water where alligators lie in wait. The trees depend on 'knees', spikes of bark, jutting from the water and treacherous to boats. A labyrinth of stagnant channels opens into narrower channels with dense undergrowth, hanging moss, and snakes dripping from branches overhead. To be alone in that wilderness is to feel a mote in creation, and the proximity of an inward swamp which society keeps off.

Society in St Augustine consisted of US Army officers who manned the great fort, the Castillo de San Marcos, and about thirty winter visitors who mingled along the sea wall on moonlit nights. No one made up to Miss Woolson as a woman. 'I am truly out of that kind of talk as a nun,' she said. 'I go about a great deal, but always as an "observer," "a very superior person," and that sort of thing.' At her sister's insistence, she ordered a navy silk suit from New York, 'colour very dark and everything in the latest', at a cost of $150 which she could ill afford. She wore it resignedly with hat, gloves, and parasol to match – and still failed to disguise her oddity as adventuring lady-authoress. Her mother did not permit her to wear her glasses since they would give 'the finishing touch' to her ineligibility.

She took no comfort in her own sex, who appeared to patrol the bounds of a respectable artifice she tried to simulate but could not meet. 'If women would ever say what they mean I should like them better,' she said. 'As it is I am afraid of them; afraid of their "ridicule-behind-one's-back," I mean.' When she met up with Southern schoolmates from Mme Chegaray's, she found 'the same old grandiloquence had survived through all their sorrows and sufferings'. One of her letters mimics a stilted exchange in the winter of 1875–6 with a regular in St Augustine, a fashionable guardian of East Coast snobbery who was unaware the Woolsons hailed from Ohio.

'Do you not think we have a very different class of person here this season than ever before?'

'I have not observed it especially,' Miss Woolson replied.

'Haven't you? O, I have. There seem to be a great many people here this winter who wear green merinos and come from the West.'

During these years, she used to say that she lived here for the sake of her mother's health, but her own susceptibility to depression improved in a warm climate. She never returned to the Midwest with its long, harsh winters. Then, too, there was the matter of money. It was easier to be straitened gentlewomen in the impoverished South than to try and support her mother in New York, where they had moved for a spell after they left Cleveland.

Some of her stories were collected on the local-colour basis then in vogue. These were the first real picturings of the South to the North after the Civil War. The regionalist identity which brought swift fame – and swift extinction when that vogue faded – can now be seen to have been somewhat misleading. Her true subject was the self-reliant woman, like Honor Dooris in an uncowed outpost of the South (in 'Up in the Blue Ridge', 1878), who succumbs at last to the force of instinct and backward ties. It is this subject that speaks to us now: works written under the influence of Charlotte Brontë and George Eliot who, she insisted, meant more to her than Bret Harte and other minor writers in the 'local' slot where critics consigned her.

Her able women come to nothing but loneliness or marriage: Roxana, the pioneer wife of the useless visionary, lost to sight in labyrinthine waterways; Miss Marion Manning, an amateur mathematician in a Southern backwater; and Miss 'Jonah', a lighthouse keeper, aged forty-two, who sits out icebound winters as the sole inhabitant of Ballast Island in Lake Erie, walks by night like a 'wild creature' on the beach, and plans an unrecognised suicide. Her reason cannot be explained, she tells a young couple – 'the heart knoweth its own bitterness' – but she does reveal something of her depression: 'It isn't easy to be dead before you've died. If I were really dead I shouldn't be hungering after what can't be. At least I hope not. Else what's the use of death?' She extracts a promise from the couple to bury her invisibly. In this way, 'she made herself ready beforehand'. As long as she lived, a 'stony endurance' had been her 'armor against suffering'.

Another variety of able woman, Miss Vedder, supports all forms of life about her, including the cousin, Dwight, who takes her for granted. 'Miss Vedder', published by *Harper's* in March 1879, a month after the author's mother died, is an unmarried daughter, a Northerner living in the South with an aged mother who, at the end of the tale, dies. The final paragraph is the single line 'Miss Vedder was left alone.' Loneliness goes with unrequited passion, the result of Dwight's oblivion to the fact that companionable Miss Vedder is right for him. Instead, his fancy lights on a girl-bride who doesn't love him. There's a telling complaint from the girl to the effect that he imposed a fantasy on what she was. In reality, she's frail, indolent, and none too bright; her appeal comes from her capacity to mimic the passionate insights of mature women: her German music teacher and Miss Vedder. We come to see that Dwight is defying the laws of nature, those of natural selection, conditioned as he is by a culture that has taught him to select a weak, helpless, and ignorant creature whom he mythologises. As such, the story is a study in the warped fancies of the intelligent adult male, with the result that his natural counterpart must go through life alone.

A companion story to 'Miss Vedder', and the first of Woolson's three great stories of woman artists, is 'Miss Grief'. Here, a woman writer of untutored genius seeks out a sophisticated mentor, an author who studied manners. She has come, she explains, because of a sketch he has written, ignored by critics. Inwardly he agrees: it was 'incandescent'; its climax, an enigmatic exchange between a man and a woman which ventures into the gaps of communication. Miss Grief recites this by heart in a way that shows the author she understands him almost better than he understands himself. She is his perfect reader.

Miss Grief is not the visitor's real name, which is Moncrief. Her pen name is Crief: the author's manservant mishears her, and the author, who is a bachelor, adopts the misnomer because it suits the faded, black-clad figure of his visitor. Her age is forty-three, but she appears ten years older – the result of poverty and emaciation.

'Miss Grief' is less about Miss Grief than about the narrator, the unnamed mentor she is determined to meet: in the lap of society, he cultivates stylistic graces at the expense of content. He is astute enough to perceive the genius of Miss Grief, but is shocked by a philosophy that contradicts the progressive optimism of the nineteenth century: in Miss Grief's work of fiction, the saviour is a doctor who helps patients to die when life becomes unendurable. A 'murderer', thinks the mentor. He tampers with her fiction, but in vain. For it proves as impossible to eliminate that doctor as to take out a 'figure in a carpet' without unravelling the whole.

The frail, starved aspect of Miss Grief contrasts with Miss Woolson, who was healthy, active, and the opposite of dingy: she dressed as the professional she was, neatly buttoned and braided with no skimping on cut and material. The sobriety of her colours was a regard for decorum: a Jane Eyre look. Yet, for all these differences, 'Miss Grief' was autobiographical in a concealed way: there was old grief for her sisters and father, fresh grief for her mother, a huge accumulation of loss; there was the inward exile of a woman starved of mental companionship; and, lastly, the proximity of death. Miss Grief shocks the mentor when she owns that had he dismissed her play, she would have 'destroyed' herself. The play is called 'Armor', and since work is all that keeps Miss Grief alive, the title suggests work as armour against fortune's arrows. The mentor, who regards suicide as a sign of weakness, deplores the vulgarity of 'sensationalism'. Miss Grief retorts that the body is mere 'clay'; all that matters is that her work should survive.

Women writers who were ladies held off from the mire of the marketplace. Those without protection, Miss Grief, and more so Woolson, who published under her own name, were exposed to painful venom, as when the *Nation*, in December 1874, accused Woolson of 'infesting the magazines'. Woolson, who had no one to act for her, was politely compliant when *Harper's* asked her to write for them exclusively. The magazine had a circulation of 200,000 and a policy of reconcilation with the South. Though punctual and productive, with a growing readership, she feared her publishers, Joseph W. Harper and Henry Mills Alden. She did try to tell them that she thought of 'Miss Grief' and 'Miss Vedder' in a separate category from 'Local Color' but, given the market value of the latter, it's unlikely she was encouraged. She slid these stories into the marketplace on the back of her growing reputation. Once, after *Harper's* published her probing story of Miss Gardis (a relic of the Old Guard in her decaying home who fights mentally as well as materially to hold out as mistress of her own space* and then succumbs to a Northern soldier), Woolson saw Mr Harper in New York for half an hour. As she sat quietly before him in her new black grenadine with long bones down the back (made at a 'swell' place for $100), Mr Harper ordered her to avoid 'the subject of the war in connection with the South'. She was 'abashed', fearful he might cross her off his list – and furious. 'I should think it would be a very comfortable lot to be a Harper,' she burst out, longing for enlightened support.

From 1874 she had developed connections with Clarence Stedman, a rich broker who was also an influential man of letters in New York, and Paul Hamilton Hayne, a South Carolina poet and the kind of gentleman she respected: the elderly Southerner, gentle, civil, not brutalised by war. Woolson had little face-to-face contact with these early mentors: she wanted letters, not visits, partly because her increasing deafness made conversation difficult, and because they did not perhaps interest her very much – despite her flattery of them (obligatory, she may have judged). She scoured what they wrote for indications of what editors wanted to publish, and awaited, though too polite to say so, their opinion of her work. She was a little put out when Stedman warned her off love-making: 'Why did you find fault with the love-making [of Miss Gardis] in "Old Gardiston," I wonder; such a small bit of it as there was too: I always steer clear of it if possible; I am afraid of betraying my ignorance. . . . My idea of love is, unfortunately, so high, that . . . nothing or nobody ever comes up to it.'

She was more than put out when a friend of Stedman's, called Bowker, tried to put her in her place. When she felt ready to attempt a long poem, as well as a first novel, Bowker told her she would not be up to major genres. He advised her to put the poem, *Two Women: 1862*, aside. Though she made the expected gestures of submission, she published it in 1877, and her dialogue of two women on opposite sides in the Civil War, caught on with a spate of dramatic readings across the country.

Stedman and Hayne, still less Bowker, were not adequate

* Perry, reviewing the story for the *Atlantic*, dismissed Miss Gardis as a 'little chit'.

advisers for a woman in Miss Grief's league. What Woolson wanted was someone to affirm her focus on alternative women and their need for alternatives to the 'iron-men and manufacturers' surrounding her youth. In the late seventies, she recognised such a man in Henry James. Her first response to James had been critical, and she resented the unconditional support he enjoyed from the powerful Howells, who, as a realist, had disparaged an element of fantasy in her own title story, 'Castle Nowhere', when her first collection was published in 1875. A fantastical boat floating nowhere and serving no purpose beyond the stultification of Silver, the owner's daughter, is, in fact, a parody of Cooper's ark, a bastion for the Hutter girls against wild Indians in *The Deerslayer.* Woolson always retained a residue of rage with Howells, simmering under a forced politeness. He made much of James, while she 'was very much disappointed in Henry James "Roderick Hudson"'. A change of attitude to James came about in the later 1870s: she thought *Daisy Miller* a 'masterpiece', and published a discerning review of *The Europeans* in the *Atlantic Monthly* in January 1879.

She concurred with James in his ridicule of the hotheads, 'the Brands', who had marched off to the Civil War in a now-fading era. '... During the war, the Brands had their chance,' she wrote, 'nobody minded their big feet on the plain of battle. ... Their strong conviction fired the assault; they headed the colored regiments. ... But now they ... are a good deal like mastodons, living by mistake in a later age, objects of amusement to the lighter-footed modern animals'. Such a light-foot was Benvolio, a sought-after poet in a James tale of 1875, whom Woolson associated with its author.*

Benvolio mirrors James in his alternation between public and private life. This is partially explained by his need for refreshment, but the truth is more complex: 'there was many a hiatus in the logic of his conduct'. This 'hiatus' remains obscure; it is clear, though,

*Miss Woolson later gave James an ancient coin she had set as a tiepin, a memento of Benvolio, who wears a Syracusan coin, by way of a pin, in his cravat. She assured James of complete secrecy: 'Nobody knows of my coins – the ones destined for you.' He chose one with a picture of Bacchus, and there is a photo of him wearing it.

that Benvolio will never take responsibility. All the same, he does involve himself, first in public with a worldly countess, then in private with a learned woman called Scholastica. Benvolio lives on the threshold of commitment, stirring passions of expectancy, and turning away at the very moment he lifts his hand, as it were, to open the door. He can't be dismissed as a flirt because he rather innocently wishes his victims well (as his name implies). Nor are they exactly victims, for they lend themselves to him of their own volition, drawn by their attunement to his interior murmur, 'the voice of the infinite – which lurks in the involutions of a sea-shell'.

Scholastica with her perfect attunement as reader and listener attracts Benvolio, despite the fact that the very authenticity of her learning makes her appear at first 'almost grotesquely wise. She was an anomaly, a prodigy, a charming monstrosity'. An erotic fantasy precedes his first glimpse of Scholastica: he remembers a Venetian painting of Andromeda, 'the beautiful naked maiden chained to a rock, on which, with picturesque incongruity, a wild fig-tree was growing; the green Adriatic tumbling at her feet, and a splendid brown-limbed youth ... hovering near her on a winged horse'. Scholastica, locked in seclusion, is superimposed on this image, her charm and 'subtle' prettiness showing forth only slowly and dimly, as if 'covered with a series of film-like veils, which had to be successively drawn aside'.

Miss Woolson looked into the mirror of Scholastica, took in the 'indefinite black-dressed figure', and wished to meet the man who conceived her. Later, when she gave him a memento of Benvolio, she said it was 'destined' for him, as though she, like her gift, had been destined to enter the life of the great writer. Her stories spoke of 'the sanctuary where each soul waits for its interpreter' and of 'those deep shadowed waters of feeling' ignored by society: 'It is but seldom that souls see each other face to face in this world of masks and armor.' In her deepening solitude after her mother's death at Green Cove Springs, Florida, on 13 February 1879, when Woolson was thirty-eight, an impulse to shed the stern endurance that had been an 'armor against suffering' sent her in search of Henry James.

Minny's sister Henrietta was the intermediary. After her marriage to Leslie Pell-Clarke, the pair went to live at Swanswick, a large estate at the head of Lake Otsego near Cooperstown, where Henrietta came to know the Cooper family. Most likely, she met 'Connie' Woolson in 1879 when she returned to her ancestral town, depressed, unsure what to do with herself. After her mother's death she felt there was 'nothing left to live for'. She was homeless and unlikely to marry. Her sister Clara suggested a journey to Europe, something she had craved during an earlier depression in Cooperstown in the summer of 1876. At that time, it had been impossible to leave her mother. Now, at last, in November 1879, she, the widowed Clara, and Clara's only child, Clare, left for England. Miss Woolson carried with her an introduction to Henry James from his cousin Henrietta, but when she reached London he had gone to Paris.

A cold coming they had. London was dark and icy, and Paris, when they reached it in December, lay under deep snow. Many shops and some theatres were closed. By then, James had returned to London. The sisters made their way south to Mentone, and in March moved on to Florence. There, Miss Woolson found James. She saw 'a picture of blooming composure': a gentleman of thirty-seven with an aquiline nose who appraised her with eyes 'from which he banishes all expression'. He owned to a reputation as 'censorious and cynical'. His receding brown hair was cut close to the head in the French fashion, which revealed a finely cut profile – she was partial to profiles – with the lower part concealed by a beard. Keen eyes could detect something shadowy in his aspect, countermanded by practised courtesies.

He was cold at first, but 'extremely unpretending' and very English 'in an unobtrusive way' – unlike many Americans she had known in the last ten years 'who were English obtrusively'. Behind this, she sensed the steel: '. . . I wouldn't like to be the person who should think from his unpretending quietness that he could not be incisive when he chose!' To her surprise, he chose to single her out, and despite many invitations to lunch and dinner he found time, she reported to Cleveland, 'to come in the mornings and take me out'. When he called for her at the Barbensi pension, an old Medici palazzo on the Arno, near the Carraia bridge, he saw a woman of forty, just above medium height with blue eyes and dark-brown, curly hair plaited into a low coil on her neck. She had shapely hands and a contralto voice, but her main beauty was her complexion. She had deep colour in her cheeks and lips, offset by a fair, almost transparent skin. Her greeting was gracefully impulsive, combining an air of independence with old-fashioned distinction – like old lace, Clarence Stedman had thought. Nothing old, though, in her beliefs.

'I cannot see the sense of the profession of "clergyman" in the new dispensation,' she declared. The evolutionary findings of Darwin, Huxley, and Tyndall had made her a humanist: she was not against worship; she wished to see it in the conduct of daily life, 'pure', as she put it, not systematised as religion. 'The truth is I am so "dreadfully modern"!'

James continued his attentions, despite initial difficulty with her deafness. He was amazingly 'kind', and soon proved a 'delightful companion', her letters repeat as though she can hardly believe it. He took her 'sometimes to galleries or churches, and sometimes just for a walk in the beautiful green Cascine'.* She was introduced to 'the beautiful narrow-mindedness of Fra Angelico' and Bronzino's *Portrait of a Lady*, but felt compelled to admit that Giotto was beyond her. 'Some day you will see it,' James said calmly.

The novelty of his opinions challenged her awakening eyes. 'He has been so much in Italy', she thought, 'that he knows the pictures as well as I know Florida.' When she quoted his published views, he replied almost contemptuously, 'O *that* was written when I was a boy.'

She found the interior of the Duomo 'too vast and cold'. On her first visit, she went alone on a rainy afternoon, and found herself the only person in 'the great, gloomy space. I went there again with H.J. who admires it, and tried to make me admire it too.'

Nudes were new to Miss Woolson: she was 'not sufficiently acquainted with torsos, flanks, and the lines of anatomy, to know when they are "supremely beautiful" and when not'. Michelangelo's statue of Lorenzo, in the Sacristy of San Lorenzo, was clothed, 'and therefore', she said, 'comes within my comprehension, and

* The gardens stretching along the River Arno in Florence.

oh! he is superb'. He conveyed to her 'the sadness of the strongest kind of human mind – almost the sadness of a God. . . . He seems to represent the whole human race; remembering all the past; conscious of all the future; and waiting.'

Two reclining figures at the base of the statue, representing 'Day' and 'Night', were once more 'beyond' her.

'Of course you admired those grand reclining figures?' James asked when he took her to Michelangelo's house.

'No,' she replied honestly. 'I did not. They looked so distracted.'

'Ah yes,' he said, '*distracted*. But *then!*' Words seemed to fail him as he walked over to look at a fresco and probably, she thought, 'to recover from my terrible ignorance'.

His face, now alive with talk and humour, now shrewdly, even coldly observant, was alert to what another listener called 'that underworld of destiny through which move the weaknesses of men and women'. Miss Woolson, he saw, was 'intense'. She was absorbed in the pictures, and receptive to learning in the way he conveyed it, not as a proud possession but something that made life more full of emotions and sensations which he was eager, without a touch of pedantry, to share. He did this by the adroitest of hints and indirection. He was politely certain, to begin with, that his listener knew it all; then he walked *with her* round the subject, turning it inside out, playing with it, making mock of it, and catching it again with a sudden grip, or flash of eloquence. He took a slow approach towards a point which in the end came through in a triumphant rush. Darts of fun and chaff banished any strain on the attention.

Talk alone, he believed, could deal with Florence, 'talk as light and delicate and many shaded as its own inestimable genius'. He saw Florence as a woman: 'It's the most feminine of cities. It speaks to you with that same soft low voice which is such an excellent thing in women. Other cities beside it, are great swearing shuffling rowdies. . . . Florence has an immortal soul. You look into her deep grey eyes . . . – so studious, so sensitive, so human.'

The spring of 1880 was 'particularly radiant'. At the Hôtel de l'Arno, looking down at the yellow-green Arno with the little overhanging cabins of the Ponte Vecchio directly beneath him, he was, he said, charmed and completely possessed. James was conspicuously happy during these weeks in Florence. It was 'blissfully' better than London. To guide a newcomer through galleries and museums was to stimulate a renewed feeling which had dimmed a little since his first visit in 1869, ten years earlier. Miss Woolson responded with intent seriousness.

'I am very impressionable & go into it too deeply', is the way she described herself. She dissociated herself from tourists: 'I turn my head when I see them arriving & look in another direction.' Her avidity for 'Europe' matched his own 'as almost the sharpest American characteristic' at a time when women, he thought, had begun 'to wander as they have never wandered'; her restlessness fitted his evolving idea of Isabel Archer, who travelled like a thirsty person draining cup after cup. Independent, new to Europe, full of impressions, Miss Woolson provided a complementary model for his Americana, one reason to see her. Osmond, who guides an avid Isabel through the Florentine galleries, invites her 'to make one's life a work of art'.

That May, Miss Woolson explored the Buonarroti gallery and the Riccardi palace (a Medici palace built in 1440), while her inspection of a Bacchus by Michelangelo (at the National Museum) was directed by an eye for 'a unique conception of Bacchus which expresses not the mirthfulness of the god of wine, but his sleepy seriousness, his capacity for profound dreaming'.

At the same time, a barrage of authorities in her Baedeker, all schooled in the same overbearing tone, Symonds, Taine, Musset, Pater, Ruskin, were dinning in her ear. Mercifully, deafness came to her aid. She could block the din and judge for herself. A fresco by Filippino Lippi (1486) in Santa Maria Novella was 'grotesque, capricious; & exaggerated'. Ruskin, she said, could see nothing without a ladder or a magnifying glass: 'the little details are all he can see. The general effect of the whole, from a distance – this escapes him entirely.' She hated Ruskin, and hate was enlivening.

Every afternoon she took a long walk outside the city into its surrounding hills. '. . . One I had this afternoon from Bellosguardo, was so exquisitely lovely', she wrote to her brother-in-law Samuel Livingstone Mather on 10 April. 'The Apennines were snow-capped, while in the valley of the Arno below me, all the leaves were out, and everything in the freshest, lightest green. Fifty years ago at this season, the Coopers were here with their father [the novelist]. They remained ten months, living first in an old palace in the city and then in a villa outside of the walls, which I have been trying to find. ... We have been much interested in finding at a library here a book of Uncle Fenimore's which we have never seen – "Excursions in Italy".' Cooper had written: 'We left our palazzo within the walls and went to a villa called St Illario [between Bellosguardo and the Boboli Gardens] just without them. All the eminences around Florence are dotted with these retreats.'

For his great-niece, Florence fulfilled her dream of the Old World, a compound of Uncle Fenimore's years of travel, pictures, opera, *Childe Harold*, *The Marble Faun*, and George Eliot's Florentine novel, *Romola*. Florence had swept her, she said to a friend, 'pretty well off my feet! Perhaps I ought to add Henry James. He has been perfectly charming to me for the last three weeks.'

James made little mention of Miss Woolson in his letters, beyond a disclaimer to Alice designed to give the impression that she was only a devotee, requiring no more than passing courtesy: 'I see no one else [beside the Bootts] of importance here ... ; I have to call, for instance, on Constance Fenimore Woolson, who has been pursuing me through Europe with a letter of introduction from (of all people in the world!) Henrietta Pell-Clarke. Constance is amiable, but deaf, and asks me questions about my works to which she can't hear the answers.'

When she turned her head to hear, she revealed the classic proportions of her profile, set off by a black velvet ribbon about her throat and thick, wavy hair drawn back simply behind her ears. Soft curls escaped at her forehead. Her cheeks and body had a healthy roundness. Despising the invalidism of idle wives, she rose early, worked long hours, and walked several miles each day. Her energy went with a self-reliance that scorned the social favours James cultivated. (William, visiting his brother two months later, noticed that though he resented society, he did work at it exhaustively.) Miss Woolson commanded a finer reserve: reclusive, independent, she required no company but his own.

It had long been her custom to promote professional ties with men who mattered in American publishing. And James, for his part, was not, as it proved, averse to meeting the great-niece of Fenimore Cooper who was, he saw, a 'perfect lady'. Once, in his youth, on a visit to Schenectady, he had gazed to the west, dreaming himself into the 'glamour . . . of that big brave region of the great State over which the shade of Fenimore Cooper's Mohawks and Mohicans . . . might still have been felt to hang'. Later, he marked the 'secret connections' of one writer with another 'much as Fenimore Cooper's Leatherstocking . . . comes in the forest on the subtle tracks of Indian braves'. Miss Woolson was a link with this 'glamour'. His eventual decision to call her 'Fenimore' (between themselves) – not 'Miss Woolson' (which he called her at first), nor 'Constance' (when he spoke of her to Alice), nor 'Connie' (as she was called by her family) – shows his awareness of the fame she trailed, a mass appeal to which James aspired and ever beyond his grasp.

The speed with which they became friends suggests that Miss Woolson met a want. Despite the thirst for the Old World, she remained incurably American, and reminded him of the James who had always an eye on his native land. 'We shall make a George Washington of you yet,' she assured him. His foreign air amused her. If she spoke of her past in Cleveland, he would correct her, 'Cleveland, *Ohio*', as though they were not two Americans on their own.

After six years in Florida, she clung to her memory of 'beautiful' swamps, pine barrens, and an ' "inspirational" headland' which she told James, provokingly, was beyond his grasp – unaware how sharply he had envied Wilky and Bob their exposure to Florida in the aftermath of the Civil War, as viewed from Serenola, their plantation in the cottonlands. He later spoke of 'the single sense of what I missed': the 'defiant distance' of 'southern fields basking in a light we didn't know, of scented sub-tropic nights, of a situation suffused with economic and social drama of the strangest and sharpest'. Florida came to represent 'material wasted, my material not being in the least the crops unproduced or unsold, but the precious store of images ungathered'. Constance Fenimore Woolson turned out to be the writer who had gathered them, and James absorbed the fruits in her second volume of stories, *Rodman the Keeper*, published the year they met. She had seized the South through the eyes of a solitary Northern woman coming upon an abandoned plantation in the Cotton Country, who meets there a woman who has lost everyone in the Civil War: she had gazed into another's 'dry, still eyes of immovable, helpless grief'. If James had wandered in Europe, Miss Woolson had wandered in remote parts of their native land. She teased him with an offhand reference to the Maumee River: 'I suppose you have no idea where the Maumee is.'* The want she met in James was not just access to native material; it was intimacy, the lack left by expatriation.

He met a writer absorbed in writing even more completely than himself. Her withdrawal from society might be explained by her deafness, but this can't be the whole truth. Other women whose gifts transgressed the current bounds of femininity, Emily Dickinson and Fanny Dixwell, were reclusive by choice. James adjusted to her deafness, and Miss Woolson shifted her sacrosanct hours to fit his habit of writing from noon. He kept their meetings out of sight – society in Florence did not stir in the morning – and when he did refer to them, belittled her: she was an 'old maid'; she was 'amiable', 'a good little woman'; and so very diligent.

He used this as a cover for a tie that developed swiftly over a few weeks and, from the start, was secret. On 9 May he wrote to William about the rain and uneventful visits to the Bootts. On 14 May and 16 June, he informed his parents that Florence was rainy but delightful all the same, that the Bootts had gone to Perugia, and that he had 'nothing' to tell them – 'nothing', he repeated in an unpublished letter after he and Miss Woolson parted ways: she to Venice, he to London:

> You will have wondered what has become of me in all these days since I last wrote from Florence. Nothing amiss, I am happy to say – nothing but my journey back here. . . . Italy was lovely to the last, & all the while that I was coming away, I kept asking myself when I should go back. . . . There is nothing to tell of myself; I am back in London as if I had never left it, & my seven weeks in Italy seem an insubstantial, though enchanting, dream.

So, 'nothing' obliterates Miss Woolson. Only the letters she

* It runs into Lake Erie, near Toledo, Ohio.

wrote to him over the next three years give any idea why he saw so much of her, and even then this eludes definition. All that can be said for sure is that it had to do with writing: 'perfection' was one of the words that resonate between them. 'Miss Grief', published in May 1880 at the time they met, may provide a clue to an initial motive on her side. It is not marriage (the bachelor's first question of his servant is whether Miss Grief is eligible). Nor has their convergence anything to do with the external markers of status, age, or fame. Miss Grief has come to offer the understanding of a fellow-writer and to find the same. This is confirmed by the four surviving letters Miss Woolson wrote to James, which centre on an art that could 'divine' a woman's buried life. 'Divination' is another word that resonates between them.

It was plain to her that James was dangerous to a woman like herself: it was his habit to 'divine' – and forget. She in turn, divined in his future a need of forgiveness. She would be willing to forgive him, she said, for the sake of his *Hawthorne*, published the year before. Hawthorne was his predecessor not only in 'the deeper psychology' but also as master of 'the Unpardonable Sin', men who withhold themselves from others with a deliberation that confounds those who care for them. For Hawthorne, the ultimate fiendishness was to make a woman 'the subject of a psychological experiment' which 'wasted, absorbed, and perhaps annihilated her soul, in the process', while the man, secretly obsessed with himself, cultivates his powers of penetration 'to the highest point of which they were susceptible'. The 'Mr. James' of Woolson's letters resembles his own shadowed characters, like Winterbourne, who offer women an awareness that charms them but, at the very moment of mutual rapport, remove themselves. Such men are not cold, not cads – not recognisable dangers. On the contrary, they appear benign, with a genuine liking for women and an easy delicacy in their treatment of them. Gilbert Osmond mimics this delicacy that invites Isabel Archer to be herself, so that she carries away from her visit to Bellosguardo an image of 'a quiet, clever, sensitive, distinguished man' who has chosen a lonely life devoted to art.

'. . . How perfectly one understands the effect', Miss Woolson told James when he sent her the novel, ' – sees what she saw, feels what she felt. . . . And it seemed to me as if you were the only man who has ever divined it.'

Under cover of legitimate criticism, she confessed to a nature which, it seemed to her, he knew already. She had approached him in search of her interpreter; he had proceeded to examine her for a novelistic purpose of his own; and now she merged with Isabel in her response:

> With no character of yours have I ever felt myself so much in sympathy. . . . I found myself judging her and thinking of her with perfect . . . comprehension, and a complete acquaintance as it were; everything she did and said I judged from a personal standpoint. . . . I always knew exactly all about Isabel. . . .
>
> Poor Isabel! poor idealizing imaginative girls the world over – sure, absolutely sure to be terribly unhappy. And the worst of it is that it cannot be prevented.

This fits James's conviction that there could be no happy outcome for a woman of that calibre. 'How you know her!' Miss Woolson granted. 'Most men are so stupid about some women – if you know what that means! I will restate. Most men, although clear-sighted enough about many women, remain dense about the women of Isabel's temperament.' She praised his 'perfect divination' of a temperament in which 'there is no end to the visions, the imaginations' that grow of themselves and fill the whole sky. All the same, she alerted him to a further challenge if he wished to complete such a woman. He had elided her capacity for passion: it is rare, she told him, but it exists.

Though James was used to adulation, Miss Woolson was not afraid to tell him when he went wrong, as when Isabel says, 'Poor Lord Warburton!'

'. . . A girl of Isabel's age and of her delicate feeling would not say "Poor Lord Warburton!"' Miss Woolson went on. 'A woman of the world might; but even a woman of the world would feel it to be dangerous, or at least a false note – unless she intended to yield to him sometimes. Women do'nt pity men (who amount to anything) to their faces! They often do it behind their backs.'

So, she opened up a woman's mind to Henry James, as Minny

had done at the outset of his career. She steered him from too simplistic a view of self-reliance, and put it to him that a woman like Isabel Archer, affronting a new kind of future, would not automatically relinquish her past: 'it seems to me', she said, 'that the past is always safely stored in her memory. The lower floors of her tower are firm and well filled, although she enjoys life in an upper storey.' This is less true of Isabel than of Woolson herself. More deeply secured in her American past than Jamesian heroines, she was to draw on her store of memories for years to come.

She also alerted James to the untreated possibility of 'killing griefs' when Isabel finds out what Osmond 'really is', which James evades or leaves for the reader to supply. 'Personally, you know, I would rather not have it "left".'

The mutual 'divination' that drew Woolson and James together included scrutiny of each other as future material, and did not exclude rivalry. One morning on a bench in the Cascine when they were surrounded by Italian children, Miss Woolson had remarked on the strain of making a fair copy: she used to get a cramp in her hand and her arm would ache to the shoulder.

'Oh, *I* never copy', James claimed.

She made a mute gesture of amazement that 'perfection' in a first draft should come so easily.

'Do you think, then, that my work has the air of having been copied, and perhaps more than once?' James pressed his advantage.

Again, she made no reply, unable to stem a rush of 'despair'.

As it happened, James was not telling the truth, for his notebook reveals that he wrote every bit of the *Portrait* twice. But to Woolson, who started work at dawn, he made writing seem effortless, too completely the 'master of situations' for the weariness of those who struggle. Did he ever feel 'cross' in the midst of a working day? She herself had to fight against loneliness and depression. She felt depleted, not content, when she finished a novel, and admitted to James an edge of envy: 'I do'nt think you appreciated, over there among the chimney-pots, the laudation your books received in America, as they came out one by one.' She added ruefully, 'We little fish did! We little fish became worn to skeletons owing to the constant admonitions we received to regard the beauty, the grace, the incomparable perfections of all sorts and kinds of the proud salmon of the pond; we ended by hating that salmon.'

What appears to be adulation is really a challenge to the complacency of the literary lion – less majestic as a salmon, and certainly less awesome as ruler of a pond. Sarcastically, she holds up a mirror to a 'spoiled' author, as in 'Miss Grief'.

'Be as determinedly good ... as though you were a "failure",' she urged. 'Failures often fall back on their "goodness"; let us see a man of genius who is "good" as well.'

If Miss Woolson satisfied herself at any stage of her career, she didn't admit to it. She never mentioned her achievements while she questioned James about work-in-progress, and offered him 'the atmosphere of a very perfect kindness'.

Once, she slipped up. *Harper's* surprised her by doubling the sum already paid for her first novel, *Anne* (completed in 1878; serialised from 1880). It was the most popular serial in *Harper's* history (surpassed only by George du Maurier's *Trilby* ten years later). *Harper's* proposed, further, to give her royalties which had been excluded from her contract for the book. Inadvertently, she mentioned this to James, and at once regretted it. 'I am sorry that I said anything to you of my small success in *Anne*, at home,' she apologised. 'Even if a story of mine should have a large "popular" sale ... that could not alter the fact that the utmost best of my work cannot touch the hem of your first or poorest. My work is coarse beside yours. Of entirely another grade. The two should not be mentioned on the same day. Do pray believe how acutely I know this.'

This she meant. For she had the sense to discriminate between the marketplace and permanent value; she did recognise – more than critics, she claimed – his greatness. The public, she predicted, would recognise him eventually as the supreme novelist of the age. If, by chance, she mentioned herself, it was, she said, 'because I live so alone, as regards to my writing, that sometimes when writing to you, or speaking to you – out it comes before I know it'.

Her other excuse was liking. 'You see, – I like so few people! Though I pass for a constantly smiling, ever-pleased person! My smile is the basest hypocrisy.' She liked his keen criticism of his own novels, and his concern for his sister which confirmed, as she put it, 'that you are, really, the kindest hearted man I know, – though that is not, perhaps, the outside opinion about you'. She assessed his character from all sides, critically but granting, as she told him, 'your incorruptible, and dignified, and reasonable modesty; and your perfectly balanced common sense. It is a comfort that you have them!'

All the same, she knew her man, and guessed (rightly) his hostility to literary ladies who flooded the market he hoped to claim for himself. In his heaven of the immortals, there were 'no women', he had declared in his youth, as he walked off arm-in-arm with Shakespeare. 'Women aren't literary in any substantial sense of the term,' he ruled on another occasion. He worked himself into 'demoniac' fury when an American – 'sweet Miss Hilliard', according to William – asked him to meet her in London. How dared she ask him to call in so 'remote' a region as Paddington? He even complained of the three shillings for the cab. '. . . The literary spinster, sailing into-your-intimacy-American-hotel piazza type', he fumed, 'a maid I had never seen!' He blamed reviewers of 'the hen-sex' for Americans' dislike of *Hawthorne*. And he hated having to take into dinner a 'third rate female novelist', Miss Spedding, who wrote under the name of Susan Morley. 'If ever one meets a particularly pinched and prosaic British female', he said, 'she is sure to be a Virgin novelist.'

This prejudice Miss Woolson predicted before they met, when Miss Grief suggests she might be called 'aunt' by the celebrity to whom she makes her unwanted advance. Miss Grief hopes to defuse rivalry, as did Miss Woolson when she wrote to James, 'I do not come in as a literary woman at all, but as a sort of – of admiring aunt'. She was only three years older than James, but pretended to be aged, fat, and unapproachable, like a woman in a picture, walking away with her back turned.

'And the back view of me as I depart from you is like that of a Veronese woman! One of the elderly ones,' she joked, 'not very clearly seen.'

As she alternately concealed and revealed herself, she teased out what was elusive in his character. In this next phase, in the letters and stories that followed their meeting, they enter on a drama of character which two novelists conduct with amused expertise. Of one thing she was certain: his rivalry with women writers whose ground he had colonised with such success. Starting with a savage review of Louisa May Alcott's *Moods* in the mid-sixties, where he sneered at her 'precocious' girl (a precursor of his own American girl), James continued to disparage women writers. In her first surviving letter, written in February 1882, Miss Woolson brought out the rivalry, and served it into his court: a 'woman, after all, can never be a complete artist', she stated. '... You do not want to know the little literary women. Only the great ones – like George Eliot.' (In fact, James could condescend even to George Eliot: after her death in 1880, he remarked to Alice that her intellectual powers and energy had never been equalled in 'any woman. If, with these powers, she had only been able to see and know more of life, she would have done greater things.') To avoid disparagement, Woolson disclaimed her calling, as Dickinson had done when she challenged her reader: 'I'm Nobody! Who are you?' Nobody, in Miss Woolson's terms, was a doting elder a celebrity like James could take for granted.

As a 'perfect lady', Miss Woolson did shun publicity: she called it a 'sacrifice' when Howells forced her to allow Mrs Howells' brother Mead to make a medallion of her profile. Mrs Howells failed to soothe her when she said, 'think how nice it will be! When the Harpers want your portrait, to put in the magazine – as of course they *will* – it will be *all* ready.'

'In the magazine!' Miss Woolson shrank. 'The whole thing has become to me a sort of nightmare.'

Yet impeccable reserve and genuine modesty coexisted with a wish to make her work known. The newly identifiable lady novelist, published under her own name, was expected to be as professional as a man but, to avoid censure, hold off from the dusty struggles of the marketplace. Miss Woolson was doing just this when she claimed not to 'count' as a writer.

Earlier, in Cambridge, James had cultivated friendships with daughters of the foremost academic or intellectual families like Theodora Sedgwick, Frances Morse, Jane and especially Grace Norton. These friendship set the style – affectionate, mildly confiding, but not intimate – of future relations with women, old, married, or otherwise ineligible. He was resolved not to marry, he told Grace flatly in 1880. Miss Woolson exaggerated her age to signal ineligibility, and predicted, with the faintest shade of sarcasm, 'the sweet young American wife that I want you to have'.

'Only as a last resort', he countered.

Such 'horrible' resistance contented her. It matched her own.

In the exchanges of James and Woolson, the friction of two determined wills was contained by humour. The full force of their friction was unleashed in their works, which debate the issue of dominance with a fury that was a counterpoint to mutual graciousness. Fiction, it goes without saying, can't be read as record; it contains an imaginative truth that coexists with documentary truth, not always easy to detect, and especially so with writers as inventive as James and Woolson. If we align their works in chronological order, what seems to come into focus is a debate of the sexes, high-powered on both sides.

Erudite women, James said privately, were the only ones who interested him. It was Scholastica, with learned notes in her Baedeker, whom James encountered in 1880, and Scholastica to whom, like Benvolio, he lent his full and compelling attention so long as it fertilised his creativity. Woolson, too, was fertilised by their encounter: she may have presented herself as listener and note-taker but, of course, was creative as well. In 'A Florentine Experiment' (1880), drawing directly on their first meetings, Woolson devised a plot in which Scholastica wins. Brainy Margaret Stowe, newly arrived in Florence, meets a blasé gentleman called Trafford Morgan. His manner is so languid, with eyes not fully open, that Miss Stowe is surprised to learn he is an American like herself. She concludes that he must have lived much abroad. His hair is close-cut, as James's, and he is of like age: thirty-eight. 'He looks fatigued; he looks cynical', Miss Stowe comments to her aunt and benefactor, Miss Harrison. 'I should not be surprised if he were selfish.'

Miss Stowe is plain but has repartee and individual taste in literature, art, and music, together with a winning eagerness to expose her mind to what she does not know or like. Woolson draws an obvious self-portrait in her heroine, who wears simple dresses of the finest materials. Her dark hair is 'closely braided in a low knot behind', and when she turns away shows a well-poised head. She carries herself with unobtrusive distinction and a reserve born not of snobbery but indifference veiled by courtesy. Morgan, 'a man of observation', discerns the indifference like white sand under a shallow river. She surfaces, though, when she discovers Morgan can write, turns on him a 'quiet scrutiny', and invites him to expand on his tastes. Such are her skills as a listener that he is mildly conscious of 'talking better than the contrary'. To test her, he flirts, but she draws back. Flirtation is not what she wants, yet the intentness continues: 'his companion gave him an attention which was almost devout. Its seriousness, indeed, compelled him to be serious likewise . . .'. As he talks of Giotto and Botticelli, she encourages him with denigration of her sex, a common practice of Woolson herself: 'we are quick; but we are superficial.'

Margaret's full intellect is out of sight: we glimpse, behind her comments, a glare of *contemptus mundi*, but Morgan does not pursue what does not reflect himself. As she performs for Morgan a song she has composed, she breaks off before she gets to a particular phrase, 'the silent gift': ostensibly, it is unrequited love, but implies at the same time the gift of expression. Like Miss Grief, Margaret combines creativity with extreme self-suppression; and she, too, lives with an elderly, protective aunt who can't do much for her but is not afraid to manoeuvre on her behalf.

The coolings and comings together of Morgan and Margaret mark some more enigmatic exchange, recalling the 'incandescent' exchange Miss Grief recites from her mentor's *œuvre* which is her real meeting with him. What emerges in 'A Florentine Experiment' is a recognition of the other as a mirror image.

Margaret and Morgan meet all over Florence. They enact a scene that includes red guide books along the streets and small places of preserved wildness in the Cascine, 'so pretty and amusing to American eyes, accustomed to the stretch of real forests'. They are visible to others in the Boboli Gardens, but their final convergence is largely invisible. Both are expatriate wanderers, and their minds meet as they wander in and out of the shadows in the dim Duomo – dimmer in this fiction 'with dusky shadows, like great winged formless ghosts'. To come to know each other within this darkness is the result of a reciprocal flair for experiment.

Woolson's next story revived a disillusioned view of what might be called the Scholastica affair. In the autumn of 1880, as she wandered on to Lake Geneva, she came upon Coppet, the château where the French exile Mme de Staël had lived during the reign of Napoleon, and written her novel *Corinne*, about a woman of genius who dies of love. At Coppet, Woolson stared at the portraits, and sat some time in the room where de Staël's friend Mme Récamier had danced the gavotte. Woolson had recently read forty books on the literature of the region, 'such a mass about all that society', she said, 'that I could imagine it all!'

'At the Château of Corinne', one of her finest stories, was written at this time.* It is about an American Corinne, a young widow called Katharine Winthrop, who is an expatriate poet amongst a circle of admirers near Coppet. She is visited by a quietly derisive American, John Ford, who cannot believe that a woman can be a genuine poet. This belief is the more forceful because he is no philistine; he has read Winthrop's anonymously published volume before they meet, and when she demands his opinion tells her bluntly that her emotional colour is too high and her training inadequate, but what makes her poems worse than worthless is that her daring is out of place. In a climactic confrontation at Coppet, under a flamboyant portrait of Mme de Staël in a yellow turban, he argues that daring in a woman is absurd, and shames her modesty. He would close the sibyl's lips and lead her back to true womanhood. Though Winthrop makes a spirited retort, she is not immune to Ford's accusation of immodesty; her face flames with shock and anger. Ford's judgement of her calling and the sexual tension rising in their repartee overcome her: she will never write again. This is the price she must pay to satisfy instinct.

Woolson's 'Corinne' ends with a coda in New York where Katharine is now married to Ford. The vehemence of her voice

* There is a mystery about the fate of this story. *Harper's* accepted it in 1880, and then did not publish it for seven years. In no other case in Woolson's publishing career was there a delay of this length. This might suggest that for some reason she put the story aside.

echoing through the rooms of Coppet has given way to silence: the climax of her story is her absolute silence, as if she were not there, while her husband shows off the volumes of *Corinne* in his bookcase. Nothing could be more annihilating than his possession of them as a memento of conquest.

The greatness of this story turns on the confrontation of art and instinct. A related issue was the mire of the marketplace where, as Ford pictures it, a lady is unsexed and exposed to derision. In *The Portrait of a Lady*, Osmond takes the same derogatory view as Ford when he contemplates the American journalist Henrietta Stackpole: she is, he remarks, 'no woman'. Her absurd surname and her comic treatment as misguided intruder cuts her down. A 'literary lady' of an earlier generation is even more absurd: we are told that Osmond's mother, who 'had pretensions to "culture," wrote descriptive poems, and corresponded on Italian subjects with the English weekly journals', had styled herself 'the American Corinne', yet was only a poseur with a Roman scarf thrown over a pair of bare shoulders, a gold laurel wreath on her ringlets, and a sighing vague speech delivered in 'a kind of Southern accent'. In their convergence on Corinne, James and Woolson were totally at odds over the expatriate image of a woman writer.

Following the excitement of her first phase in 'Europe', Miss Woolson was displaced during 1881–2. No longer a tourist, not yet a resident, she drifted between Italy, France, Switzerland, and Germany, without contacts or social ties. Abjuring high life with the republican integrity of 'Uncle Fenimore', she felt homeless.

James returned to Italy for the first six months of 1881 in order to finish his novel. But instead of spending the bulk of his time in Rome (the setting for the second half of the *Portrait*), he switched to Venice. There he stayed from late March to the end of June, with no more than a fortnight in Rome at the end of April. He avoided Rome, he said, because it was 'infested with acquaintances, all ready to pour into one's existence the element I especially wish to avoid'. One of these acquaintances was Miss Woolson, who was settled in Rome since 15 January, an instance of the way James could switch from insight to absence when privacy was at stake. It was a year since their first meeting when, finally, in late April or early May 1881, he visited her 'sky-parlor' on the fourth floor of an old Roman house where she had '3 bright rooms & a loggia above, covered with vines'. She was living there alone after her sister and niece had returned to America, 'obstinately refusing to leave Rome'. It was teatime when James paid his call: she later recalled a 'sputtering kettle'. They discussed his work.

Though in the course of his professional career he offered outlines to various editors, there is no evidence, so far, that he discussed work with anyone else in the questioning way he did with Miss Woolson. He told her that he saw Osmond distinctly, but doubted he would be distinct to readers. 'Rest easy (only you are always easy); he is', she replied when she read the result. 'He is a more finished creation even than Grandcourt [the disastrous husband in *Deronda*][;] as distinct; more finely detestable; and haunting, and suffocating than George Eliot's Englishman, and overtopping him by not being emphasized by a violent death. It is real life in all its unavenging cold monotony that Osmond should go on living; and that point shows by how much you are the finer artist.'

One of Osmond's specialities was Vittoria Colonna, a poet who lived from 1492 till 1547. Widowed at thirty-six, Colonna entered a convent where she wrote her sonnets. It was now, in Rome, that Woolson took up this woman who combined retreat with writing.

James confided, further, plans for three novels, a dramatisation of *Daisy*, and future tales: all in all, his work for the next decade. Then, to the sputter of her kettle, he relayed the secret of his *œuvre*. 'I have often thought of the motif you told me about, in Rome,' she reminded him later, but tantalisingly does not say what it is.

The true reader, for James, discerns a motif which is the clue to the message of a great writer. This runs like a repeated figure through the whole *œuvre*, everywhere apparent – but only this reader can see it. Art, like a mystery no one seems to be able to solve, calls for a reader with the intelligence to break the code. James was to spell this out in 'The Figure in the Carpet', his parable of art that turns on this phrase appropriated from 'Miss Grief'. In this tale, written after Woolson's death, the elect reader is a woman who has died with lips sealed. All she would say of the secret was

'It's my *life!*' This sounds enigmatic but, if read literally, is very simple: art enters the life of the reader who responds to its transforming power. It shapes her, makes her, *is* her. In this sense, the tale may be a private tribute to Woolson, as well as a public statement about the challenge of art. For he singled out Miss Woolson – that quiet afternoon in Rome in the spring of 1881, an afternoon unmentioned amongst abundant records of his activities – as his true reader. She said afterwards: 'I wonder if you will understand me if I should tell you that . . . your writings . . . voice for me – as nothing else ever has – my own feelings; those that are so deep – so a part of me, that I cannot express them, and do not try to; never think of trying to.'

In Rome, at this time, James was dancing attendance on a worldly patrician, like the countess in 'Benvolio', a plump, bouncing widow, Mrs Philip Livingstone Van Rensselaer, who had pursued him in Venice. Socially, this was gratifying, for she was connected with the old Patroons in Albany, who would not have associated with a local shopkeeper known as Billy James. But Mrs Van Rensselaer was interesting to Henry James less for reasons of snobbery than for something more workaday, and the clue lies in an odd word in his notebook: she was a 'resource'.

To dramatise *Daisy Miller*, it was necessary to fill out Winterbourne's affair with a worldly-wise woman. At thirty-eight, at the height of her sexual powers, she provides a counterpoise to the innocence of Daisy. It was no accident that James chose to visit Rome in the Daisy season. 'I saw a great deal of Mrs. V[an]. R[ensselaer].; had (with her) several beautiful drives,' he recorded in his notebook. One Sunday they went beyond the Ponte Nomentano, left the carriage, and wandered in the Campagna. Afterwards, Mrs V.R. faded from the scene: 'resource' she may have been, but the flirtation had no future.

Deaf as Woolson was, she did pick up the resonance of 'resource' in the James vocabulary. In a story published in 1882, she attempted her closest portrait of Henry James in the figure of an idolised writer and dilettante called Raymond Noel. A favourite wherever he goes, he shifts from place to place on the strength of an inherited income, and in the course of his coming and going accumulates a stock of people who might at any time serve as a 'resource'. Another telling word was 'subterfuge': the James method of distracting attention from the quiet pools of the private life with a deluge of social trivia; other James words were 'unimportant' (Miss Woolson pretended to be frightened by that 'terrible word') and 'limited': Margaret Stowe disowns her philosophy because, as a woman, she is too 'limited' to have one. The single women who venture abroad in Woolson's stories of this period have in common a form of speech that blends American directness with unvoiced irony. This is clearest in the case of Ettie Macks, a self-taught artist from the West who comes to Europe to seek out Raymond Noel in 'The Street of the Hyacinth'.

She rents rooms on the fourth floor of a Roman building, similar to those of the author, and is the most confident of her women-artists. Ettie Macks is Woolson's answer to Daisy Miller: a talkative, straight American girl who cannot be called unconventional because she has no idea that convention exists. Like Daisy, Ettie is accompanied by an invalidish, self-centred mother who allows her daughter maximum independence. There's a brother too, but off the scene: a ne'er-do-well in the Far West, like Charley Woolson in California. Woolson built into the story her own resentment at a mother who loves her troublesome son more than the daughter who supports and cares for her. Woolson was usually impersonal in her work, like Ettie, but in this particular story she does fuse certain elements of herself – her black dresses; her musical voice; her exact memory for others' words; her determined ambition; and the encouragement of Miss Guilford at her Midwest school – with the youth and eagerness of Daisy Miller. As an artist-to-be, Ettie is original and unashamed of it – Daisy with a dash of Miss Grief. She comes to Noel, ready to quote his writings by heart. He combines a condescending interest with habitual detachment, a man who always has an engagement elsewhere and who, like Winterbourne, is caught up with a worldly woman.

Noel reminds us of the James whom Woolson rebuked in her letters for persistent elusiveness. 'He was an excellent evader when he chose to exert himself, and he finally got away from the little high-up apartment . . . without any positive promise as to the exact date of his next visit.' Woolson mimics the smooth evasions as she demonstrates his manoeuvre: 'My plans are uncertain,' he tells the girl he calls 'Faith'. 'But probably I shall come back. One always comes back to Rome.' He is someone who can disappear for two years and expect a welcome on his return. Woolson discerns, beneath the vagaries of the favourite, a system:

> It may be said with truth that Noel had not thought of Miss Macks for months. This was because he had other things to think of. . . . But as he never entirely forgot anything that had once interested him, even although but slightly (this was in reality a system of his; it gave him many holds on life, and kept stored up a large supply of resources ready for use when wanted), he came, after a while, on the canvas of his Roman impressions, to the figure of Miss Macks.

He 'might have done more' for her than he did, Noel admits to 'Faith': 'I have a habit of not assuming responsibility, I suppose I have grown selfish', and she retorts, 'you have been completely spoiled, and will always remain so.' He is blind to originality in a woman. With his Europeanised gloss, he cannot condone Ettie's Western art which, in Roman terms, appears brash. At first, Ettie refuses to imitate the masters, but her confidence cracks when she feels the force of criticism – Noel is as annihilating as Winterbourne with Daisy. Ettie dies as an artist: new forms, bold and vigorous, cannot sprout in the stony beds of Noel's strictures, any more than Ettie can survive as a new kind of woman. Stripped of the 'armor' of art, she is consumed by treacherous emotion: she falls in love with her destroyer. The story does not minimise the force of instinct; nor does it offer the consolations of romance. What is a satisfying conquest for Noel, is 'a great downfall' for the woman he continues to call 'Faith'*. Her consent to marry him coincides with the demolition of the Street of the Hyacinth. In the myth, Hyacinth was killed by a god lover: translated into the nineteenth-century terms of this story, a woman's space is eliminated by sexual surrender. In other terms – those of James's plan for his new version of *Daisy Miller*, outlined to Miss Woolson during his visit to Rome – a cool Winterbourne condescends to

* 'Faith' is named in the conqueror's tradition of naming, as 'Our Lady' is named in 'The Lady of Little Fishing', Silver in 'Castle Nowhere', and 'Miss Grief'. Also, 'Roxana' in 'St Clair Flats' is a name given by her husband.

marry a demolished and Europeanised American girl. Once more, at the end, the victor speaks and the wife is silent. Love and art are again at odds.

After the Roman jaunt, James returned to Venice where an acquaintance with Katharine de Kay Bronson of Newport, sister of Helena de Kay Gilder, deepened into friendship. They had met in the Accademia in Venice in autumn 1869. Six years later, they had migrated at the same time, in the autumn of 1875, on the same ship from New York to Liverpool, when she had rather miffed James with her friendliness to Trollope, who also made that crossing. Generous, hospitable, in her home at the mouth of the Grand Canal, Mrs Bronson opened the Casa Alvisi to distinguished guests, among them Browning. James dined there two or three times a week, and smoked on her balcony, under the awning, as gondolas slid past below. It was like a box at the opera: he would rake the outer scene, then turn to converse with Mrs Bronson in the drawing-room, peppermint chocolates and a volume of German poems to hand and, behind, a framed piece of tapestry, an icon, and a collection of gilded glass – it was said that she would turn down a Tintoretto for a dinner service of the right old silver.

He had rooms a few steps from the Alvisi, on the fourth floor of 4146 Riva degli Schiavoni. They were 'meagrely & hideously furnished', but the rent was low and the view from his desk 'divine': all four windows looked out on the far-shining lagoon towards Palladio's church, San Giorgio Maggiore. The pale whitish-green of the lagoon seemed 'to drink it in'. When he left at the end of June, friends from Boston, Daniel and Ariana Curtis, were settling into the Palazzo Barbaro, on the same light-drenched side of the Grand Canal.

After neglecting Miss Woolson for eighteen months, James made a sudden about-face and wrote to her repeatedly after his return to his parents' house in Cambridge, Massachusetts, in October 1881. He wrote on 6 and 12 November, followed by a third letter from Washington in January 1882. Surprised by these overtures, she was wary. He was homesick for Europe, she decided, and sending off letters in hopes of envelopes with foreign stamps. Determined not to be drawn by such caprice, she did not rush to answer, and when the third letter came she was not grateful for condescension.

Henry James Senior.
A variety of failed prophet,
and not the harmless kind.

Mrs James.
'Mrs Morte' was Henry
James's term for the kind
of mother who destroys
the life of her daughter.

Alice James, seething with intellectual gifts.

'Could no one wrest the shears from her vandal hand'? At sixteen, in 1861, Minny Temple cropped her hair.

Catherine James Temple,
Minny's mother, died in 1854.

Mary Temple Tweedy,
aunt to the orphaned Temple sisters,
who gave them a home in Newport.

Kitty Temple,
the eldest sister, oil portrait
by William James, 1861.

Henrietta Temple,
the youngest sister, met Fenimore
when she settled near Cooperstown.

Minny's friend, Helena de Kay. She welcomed 'the new man and woman, *with* a soul.'

Helena in her 15th Street studio in New York after her marriage to Richard Watson Gilder. Henry James confided his plan for a portrait of Minny, which 'you will be in a position to appreciate better than almost anyone else'.

Henry James at the age of twenty (1863–4). He was drafted
during the Civil War, and backed out on the basis of an 'obscure hurt'.

John Chipman Gray,
Minny's faithful correspondent.

Oliver Wendell Holmes, Jr,
part of the James-Temple circle in
the 1860s.

William James.
He 'abused' Minny Temple to his brother in winter of 1868-9.

Spouting Rock, Newport. 'I have been *tearing* ...over the beach to Spouting Rock today', Minny wrote on 3 April 1863.

James would always remember a 'lichened cathedral' and 'pulpit rock' in the woods of North Conway, NH, in the idyllic summer of 1865.

James secreted and brooded over this photograph of Minny
(September 1869, six months before her death).
'I prize the ghostly image all the more for the lapse of time',
he wrote in 1914, forty-four years later.

'If you didn't say any very horrible things in Florence and Rome, you are mentioning a few from Washington – when you tell me my letter was full of "amiable elements"! I do'nt think a letter could be described in a more depressing way.'

James was summoned from Washington when his mother died unexpectedly on 29 January 1882. Miss Woolson wrote feelingly about the desolation following the death of a parent, and went on to say that if he heard of her own death, he should know she was content.

'Death is not terrible to me,' she told him. 'To me it is only a release; and if, at any time, you should hear that I had died, always be sure that I was quite willing, and even glad to go.'

Her tone was matter-of-fact, not morbid. She assured James this wish was balanced by 'a very strong belief, that, while we *are* here, we should do our very best, to be as courageous, and work as hard, as we possibly can'.

James was too astute to be wholly reassured. He became uneasy about her, concerned and protective.

He did not remain with his father and sister longer than it took to see them settled in Boston, at 101 Mount Vernon Street. Though his father was declining, and not expected to live, Alice was left alone to care for him, and the son returned to England, as planned, in May 1882.

With his usual efficiency, he managed to dramatise *Daisy Miller* during his time in Boston, from February to April. By May, he already had a privately printed volume, to secure copyright while he showed the play to theatre managers. Yet again, there is a convergence with Woolson, whose Roman story, 'The Street of the Hyacinth', with its resonances of *Daisy*, was published in the *Century* at exactly this time, May–June 1882. James sent her a copy of the play, with instructions to keep it secret, and she assured him of her confidentiality: 'It is under lock and key, and no one has seen it or heard of it; or shall ever see it, or hear of it. I am a very faithful sort of person in such respects. I want to read it more, and when I am not so tired. I will return it to you sometime during the winter. I am so desirous to know whether you are going on in this new field? And everything you are doing.'

He was less sure of himself at this time. No one wanted to put on the play, and eventually it appeared in the *Atlantic* and as a book in 1883, publication being, in this instance, a sign of failure.

When Miss Woolson had received the privately printed volume in the summer of 1882, she had been in Baden-Baden, trying to meet an unrealistic delivery date for her second novel. She was always obliging to editors, a thorough professional who could push herself beyond her strength if need be. In July–August she wrote non-stop for eight consecutive weeks, and during the last two, when she came to copy her text, was at it thirteen hours a day, from five in the morning until six in the evening. It was during this stint, when her strength began to ebb, that she read *Daisy*.

She was supportive, though sceptical of the box-office ending where Winterbourne is reconciled to Daisy, and marries her. Recovered from Roman fever, Daisy cries: 'It was all for you – it was all for you!' Miss Woolson, taking a dim view of Winterbourne, saw that Daisy would not have been his choice. Aligning him with James, she detected an authorial *frisson* for Mme de Katkoff (Winterbourne's mistress, filled out along the lines of Mrs Van Rensselaer: a widow of about thirty-eight). In the play she is sexually experienced, having had an adulterous affair. Winterbourne's sexuality is also filled out: Mme de Katkoff testifies to the fact that he is not as cold as he seems. She likens him to a German stove of 'smooth white porcelain, without the slightest symptom of fuel or of flame. Nothing at first could seem less glowing; but after you have been in the room with it for half an hour you feel that the temperature is rising . . .'.

Miss Woolson warned James she was going to be 'personal', even if he didn't like it: she had divined from the play that the person he wanted was an amalgam of Daisy's innocent adventurousness with the sexual adventurousness of Mme de Katkoff. 'You know I have found fault with you for not making it more evident that your heroes were in love with the heroines; really in love. There is no trouble about that here! Winterbourne is more in love with Mme de Katkoff – or has been – than any of your other men have been in love before. It has *the true ring*.'

This drama entered their peculiar repartee. Winterbourne's indifference to Daisy Miller, followed by their marriage, matched

Noel's indifference to Ettie Macks, followed by their marriage. It is as though they had shared a scenario. Winterbourne 'will be a good husband', Miss Woolson remarked. She meant that he would treat Daisy with deadly kindness, as Noel treats Ettie.

She confessed to James that she had been ill: 'the American "lung-fever" ', she called it, combining fever and a cough. In Dresden, where she went to recuperate at the end of August 1882, she read his sympathetic reply. He had known, he said, what it was to be ill, abroad and alone. 'Pray do me the favour not to recommence,' he wrote. The phrase reminded her of a suicidal woman in a French novel who, rescued by the police, is asked in just such delicate terms not to recommence – and is calmed. 'Not to recommence,' Miss Woolson echoed, as though to herself.

Her efforts had drained her; she was 'nervous' and homesick, hauling her memorabilia and the spoils of travel from place to place: her tear vase; her collection of ferns; a picture of yellow jessamine (her favourite flower); a weighing machine; a stiletto from Mentone; etchings of Bellosguardo and the Arno; a gilt-framed mirror from Rome and a red transparent screen used there; a 1760 edition of the poems of Vittoria Colonna; seven old prints bought by Cooper in Italy which a cousin had given her together with the original contract between Cooper and his publisher, G. P. Putnam Sons; an engraving of Cooper; a copper warming-pan from Otsego Hall given to her by one of Cooper's daughters, Mrs Phinney; and a photograph of her cherished niece, Clare, which she hung in every room she occupied. She confided to James, 'there never was a woman so ill fitted to do without a home as I am. I am constantly trying to make temporary homes out of impossible rooms at hotels and pensions. I never give up, though I know it cannot be done; I keep on trying. Like . . . the beaver I saw in the Zoological Gardens here [in Dresden], who had constructed a most pathetic little dam out of a few poor fragments of old boughs. I stood and looked at that beaver a long time. He is an American – as I am! But I suppose *you* know nothing of beavers but hats. You do'nt know beavers, or prairies; you only know – Mme de Katkoff.' She seems to spit the name in her anger and despair.

She nearly packed up and fled back to America at this point; as it turned out, the point when a traveller becomes an expatriate. Fifty-six years earlier, in June 1826, when the London packet had left New York harbour, an Englishman aboard a passing boat shouted a query to the departing Cooper: 'How long will you be gone?' To the novelist's reply, 'five years', the response was, 'You will never come back.' Cooper writes: 'These words "You will never come back" were literally the last I heard on quitting my country. . . . I thought of them often'. For the European experience revealed contradictions within himself which he could not ignore. To be a descendant of Judge Cooper meant to have the frontier in one's blood and yet to find in oneself a resistance to the crasser obtrusions of democracy. Constance Fenimore Woolson, with her taste for civilised seclusion, endorsed his idea of the frontier gentleman; she was its female counterpart.

Her path crossed that of James in Paris at the end of October 1882. Miss Woolson was there with John Hay (1838–1905), who had been an unofficial secretary to Lincoln and had written a Civil War poem, 'When the Boys Come Home' (which was to become a hit when it was set to music during the First World War). A Cleveland connection had brought him and Miss Woolson together: Hay's sister-in-law, Flora Stone, had married Miss Woolson's nephew, Sam Mather,* in October 1881. A functional blandness, to judge by his letters, was a carapace for bouts of depression soon revealed to Miss Woolson. He preferred sensitive company to the roughness of political life, and continued writing poems and novels. Hay's writing and depressions, combined with power, made for the sort of man Woolson liked to know. He returned her interest, so much so that in the autumn of 1882 he was matchmaking on her behalf. He arranged a theatre-party in Paris, to be attended by Miss Woolson and by his friend Clarence King, a field geologist with a taste for black women, barmaids, and prostitutes. Hay believed Miss Woolson, 'that very clever person, to whom men are a vain show', had fallen in love with King 'at sight'. Whatever the truth of this, nothing came of it.

James, on his 'little tour' of France, joined King at the Grand Hotel. Since Woolson's remarks on their talks invariably go back

* Samuel Mather, known as Sam, and called this here in order to distinguish him from his father Samuel Livingstone Mather, who married Georgiana Woolson, CFW's eldest sister.

to Florence and Rome, he must have held off in Paris, despite the serious letters they had exchanged over the last nine months and the generosity of her attention to his work in the midst of her own effort. His, always. There were times when she could wish him less 'spoiled'.

James recrossed the Atlantic when his father died in December 1882, arriving too late. This time, he stayed longer. He was his father's executor, and had to right a will which struck a blow at Wilky, who was to get less than the other children, said the old man from beyond the grave, because he had had too much. Henry senior seems to have forgotten what it had been like to be singled out for denial by his own father's will and to take legal action against that ill-will that can never be righted. Wilky had always tried to please his father. After repeated failures, he was now a sick man. Henry handled matters with exemplary consideration, persuading William to give Wilky a fair share, and making over his own portion of the Syracuse income to his sister.

For nine months, he stayed on with Alice in the high house on Mount Vernon Street. Alice was now entirely dependent for company on her unmarried brother and Miss Loring, who had to divide her time between Alice and her sickly sister, Louisa. James took the opportunity to observe Bostonians, especially feminists, whilst he gave Alice the satisfaction of keeping house for him. So long as he was there, sleeping in their father's room, Alice was less of an invalid. James almost felt married, but had no intention to remain with his sister. He made William's wife 'miserable in a fine, inexplicable fashion'.

Meanwhile, Miss Woolson was welcomed back by the expatriate community in Florence, and began to feel less displaced. James wrote to her on 17 April, asking for a verbal 'picture' of Bellosguardo to keep him 'going' in Boston. This letter, like all the rest, was duly destroyed, but her reply conveys some of its contents. She tells him on 7 May that his letter was forwarded to Venice, where she had moved on 20 April, and offers in place of Bellosguardo a picture of her two large, low-ceilinged rooms on the third (top) floor of the Palazzo Gritti-Swift, a thrillingly delapidated yellow palace where she lived directly above the

English aesthete Arthur Symonds. There were two arched windows with small balconies overlooking the Grand Canal. So small were these balconies that they served as sofas with freshly covered red cushions. There were also two side-windows, one facing east, commanding a view of the Riva with its masts; the other side window looked out on one of the darkest of 'emerald-green' canals, so narrow that gondolas could pass only by hugging the walls. The climax of this description, as she warms to it, is an inviting, even erotic picture of the way to her 'red cushions' and matching 'red ledges'.*

Miss Woolson fantasised his future arrival at a winding stairway, as in a lighthouse, leading to her top floor, guarded by an entrance door. It had a small loophole, and through this 'aperture', with a grating over it, a maid would 'inspect' him before she let him in. 'And when at last you are in, you can't imagine where to go, so involuted is the hall, with all sorts of inscrutable doors, and curtains, and even steps (though you know you are at the very top of the house) leading out of it.' Down below was a water-storey ('the lowest & darkest I have seen'), an empty hall, out of which there suddenly opened 'an ideal courtyard with a round well, armorial bearings set on the pink façade, a willow tree, & an *outside* stairway of ancient white marble . . .'. The outside stair led to Symonds' rooms on the second storey.

Now and then, as she strolled in her straw hat, exploring the byways, losing and finding her way, or forgot her 'troubles' as the swift boat slid through the sunset, she wondered if she might 'live here, and die here' in a scene she claimed to share with James. A further stage in their relations seems to emerge in the spring of 1883 as a new emotive note entered her voice, fusing her eroticism with her participation in his feeling for the Venice he had recently personified as a voluptuous, nervously changing woman in a piece he had sent her. 'She has high spirits or low, she is . . . cold or warm, fresh or wan, according to the weather or the hour. She is always interesting and almost always sad . . .' Miss Woolson claimed to know this by heart, as though it were her very self: 'I

* As erotic as George Eliot on the landscape of 'The Red Deeps' in *The Mill on the Floss*, or James himself in his nostalgia for Newport with its open doors and shaded interiors.

can't begin to tell you. And why should I try, when you know it all so much better than I do? In the same way; but better.'

Part of the new intimacy, on her part, was the freedom she felt to reproach him that it was now three 'long years' since they had talked of themselves. James, in his letter of 17 April, had held out the prospect of 'talking over' her impulse to return to America. He imagined, as a background to their future talk, an Italian church wall.

'Your letters are better than you are. You are never in Italy,' she put it to him. She went on rather defensively, 'I don't complain; for there is no reason in the world why I should expect to see you; only, do'nt put in those decorative sentences about "Italian church-walls."'

He, for his part, had felt free to ask for the kind of unconditional support his mother had given him. She agreed: '... you would find the atmosphere of a very perfect kindness. You say you "fall back" upon my "charity," feeling it is "infinite." You can safely fall back; for infinite it is.'

Two weeks later, on 24 May, she issued a challenge, necessitating an extra letter all to itself. She placed before him an experience he must master if he is to become the greatest of novelists: '... Why not give us a woman for whom we can feel a real love? ... I do not plead that she should be happy; or even fortunate; but let her be distinctly lovable; perhaps, let some one love her very much; but, at any rate, let *her* love, and let us see that she does; do not leave it merely implied. In brief, let us care for her, and even greatly. If you will only care for her yourself, as you describe her, the thing is done.'

As she warmed to this idea, she suddenly dropped her guard: the lagoons and still canals, she said, 'send their love to you. They wish you were here. And so do I. I could go by in a gondola and see you on Mrs B[ronson]'s balcony. That would – be something. Good-bye.'

Recently, she had met Mrs Bronson, who praised *Anne* and informed Miss Woolson that Henry James was one of her dearest friends. Mrs Bronson boasted that James would end his Venetian day on her balcony. Miss Woolson conceded her advantage. She was not overwhelmed by an invitation from Mrs Bronson. 'I don't know that I shall go – because I do not want to be making calls here,' she confided to James. Expatriate society struck her as a whirl of driven phantoms circling to no purpose – one of the torments of the *Inferno*. She and James agreed on their horror of wives: James observed to her that Mrs Hay occasionally expressed herself with a singular lack of cultivation; and Miss Woolson observed in return that Mrs Howells was given to feminine malice and petty jealousy, a discontented bore propped by a doting husband.

Miss Woolson was more adamant than James in her refusal to be appropriated, even by such respectable admirers as Mrs Bronson in Venice or Miss Greenough in Florence. Miss Greenough was an elderly American, related to the Bootts, who had the best accommodation on the hill of Bellosguardo. Miss Woolson had turned down Miss Greenough's offer of an apartment on Bellosguardo, much as she longed for an old garden with a parapet and the vista down the valley of the Arno towards the west. The drawback was that Miss Greenough promised excursions and drives. Woolson shrank from this prospect, not because she did not like Miss Greenough, but she felt trapped: if she were locked into an engagement for four o'clock, she could not write at ten or two. All the same, she still had her sights on Bellosguardo as a Jamesian scene, a likely destination for Isabel's second self. '. . . You have known, perhaps, how I have wished to live on Bellosguardo,' she reminded James. 'Osmond and you.'

'You could not possibly have pleased me more than by telling me – as you do in this letter – of your plans for work,' she went on. 'You have undertaken a good deal. But I am very glad you have undertaken it. You will do it all; and superbly.' Now that George Eliot and Turgenev were dead, he was, she assured him, the foremost living novelist.

At this time, spring 1883, James sent his publisher, Osgood, an outline for *The Bostonians*: For two years, well before he completed the *Portrait*, he had been turning away from Minny Temple: 'I mean to "quit" for awhile paying so much attention to the young unmarried American female – to stop, that is, making her the central figure: which is of necessity a limitation.' Beginning a 'new era' in his career, he would take up public issues, starting with Boston reformers and the platform aspect of the Woman

Question. His new ambition was to document society in the droll manner of Balzac. Boston, however, did not take to the droll approach, and was not amused by his caricature of Miss Birdseye when the novel appeared in 1885. Bostonians recognised Miss Peabody, who had fought for women's rights and in 1860 had founded the first kindergarten in the United States. She was widely respected for her high-mindedness, her old family, and as the sister-in-law of Hawthorne. James denied using Miss Peabody – for once, he lost his calm. He was not believed.

The novel enters into feminist agitation to search out the weaknesses of those who promote it. When, at the end of the novel, the pretty feminist, Verena Tarrant, gives up speeches for marriage, she seems to escape a same-sex tie. The Cause is aligned with a current fad for mesmerism, as though it were no more than a draw for the weak-minded.

Richard Watson Gilder of the *Century*, who serialised *The Bostonians* from February 1885 to February 1886, was alarmed to find readers falling away. All three long novels of the 1880s were commercial failures, and the great wave that had carried James from *Daisy Miller* to the *Portrait* subsided in the years that followed. Woolson, on the other hand, was now at her peak: the big sales of her first novel (57,000) were followed by more ambitious work: the innovative artist tales of the early 1880s, and two further novels, *For the Major* (1883) and *East Angels* (1886), published on both sides of the Atlantic and praised by critics, including James. The woman he had distanced as an 'old maid' now became his 'distinguished friend'.

A pact to destroy each other's letters freed Miss Woolson to write with a verve at odds with her usual demeanour of irreproachable quietness and reserve. With James, she plays with words in the style of Viola and Rosalind, who dress as men and find their tongues freed from silence. In short, there's some disguise in play. At one moment, she's the bold critic, exposing his limitation as a novelist. At another, this voice is veiled by the contortions of abashed femininity (before the 'proud salmon of the pond') or the archness which females adopted at that time to signal – and spoof – submission. She relayed to James a report from Washington that society had been quiet until he arrived. 'And now of course it will immediately become hilarious – he is such a turbulently gay, eager, excitable person', she joked. The joke comes awkwardly from the edge of society. That edge was not far from her sight; she never lost sight of society, but she was fearfully alone: floating by in her gondola, a Lady of Shalott, looking on from her lone distance. Her detachment, part chosen, part wistful, was suffused with some strong feeling she would not define. Would it solve 'the riddle' of her existence to live in Venice and be buried in its lagoon? She put this to James.

If she was to remain a 'riddle', James was one too. She challenged his composure by spelling it out, followed by a barely apprehensible but questioning pause before she moved on to other matters. There was a habit, manifest in all his letters: a declaration of devoted intention. What makes this suspect is its uniformity: James took this devoted tone with everyone; he sang arias to intention on the edge of action. Miss Woolson resisted this performance: she refused his beguiling but all too vague intention to discuss her future beneath a church wall. Her loneliness was not to be defused in the picturesque. She did not care to be 'amiable'. And James persisted because 'amiable' was exactly what he willed this intense woman to be.

Amenable as she appeared, Miss Woolson retained control of her invisibility: one moment she surfaced; the next turned away. She was not flirting but testing. A test, she hinted delicately – even humorously – lay in their future: his capacity to behave badly ('I do'nt know that you do. But you could!') or do better: 'And then I am always thinking that perhaps you will improve. I hope right in the face of facts.' Her archness masks a sudden glare as the friendly hand she extends opens on 'sin'. Nothing specific; no more than a possibility she foresees in his character. As a reader she had so much to gain that she willed herself to tolerate whatever might be there: 'You may be what you please, so long as you write as you do.' Homeless, almost by nature, she found in his writing, she owned, 'my true country, my real home. And nothing else ever is fully – try as I may to think so.'

As an evolving Americana, as Scholastica, she lived most fully in a portrait of womanhood devised by James, while he lived most fully in a genre she opened up in the early eighties: parables of art and artists, initiated by the 'figure in the carpet' of Miss Grief's story. Both had much to gain from a relationship that does not fit conventional terms. They were not lovers; not 'friends' (though they used this term for the few who saw them together); it could be said, they were co-creators of 'the private life'. But that life had its weird side, as Miss Woolson was drawn into a Jamesian scenario – a dangerous 'home' for a woman always wary of involvement.

8
Unmarried Lives

In mid-October 1883, two months after James returned to London, Woolson arrived there, and settled across the Park, at 116 Sloane Street, South Kensington. She had come for the winter, an odd decision for one who fought seasonal depression in northern climes. For ten years, she had gone south in the autumn. To change this habit, to risk the fogs of November, the long nights of December, and the sooty bleakness of January and February, required some strong motive, and the usual conclusion has been that this sad female pursued the eligible James.

This view goes back to James himself, who was greeted, at the age of forty, with a London consensus that the time had come to marry. He was put out when Lizzie Boott joined the chorus, and told her straight that he would never complicate the convenience of his bachelor arrangements. It was in this context that he referred to Woolson with code names – 'The Costanza' or 'The Littératrice' – treating her presence as a flattering joke which might be mistaken as a threat to his single state. However self-effacing, however constant 'The Costanza', he would not have even her: '*ma non prenderò neppure lei!*' he confided to Lizzie. At first, he lines Woolson up as the rival of 'The Rensellina' or 'The Realist', his code names for the socialite Mrs Van Rensselaer, she of the Roman excursions. In Italy The Rensellina had pressed him with notes; for the last few months she had swanned around London, and now appeared to advance on James, moving to Half Moon Street, close to his lodgings, until the day came when he found her moored beside him in Bolton Street. He held off single women – either because, for a space, they had appealed to him, or (like The Rensellina) served as a 'resource', or obliged him with 'infinite charity' – and if they presumed on further meetings, he would distance them as a joke: the dauntless Western maids coming to conquer or die – the trouble was that when they didn't conquer, they *didn't* die. Those who persisted became 'the devouring sex'. Twice in 1883–4 he pretended to sighs of relief that the rivals kept to their separate spheres – The Rensellina with the titled; The Littératrice alone with her pen – as though some fearful clash had been in the offing.

James, then, invited pity as 'the devoured'. It was a useful, if unsubtle, cover for his professional appropriation of women, and particularly misleading with Woolson. For, unlike his set ways in visible friendships – with the actress Mrs Kemble or, years later, Edith Wharton – James changed towards Woolson over the course of time, and, in any case, his statements about her were studied, as though doing duty for something else. Each time he tries to define her in the approved terms of the day – a 'perfect lady', a 'conservative' writer unwarped by women's rights – she eludes him, aware of his will to tame her and scale her down. If he calls her 'amiable', she protests at once; if he dares to call her 'worthy', she plans 'revenge'. In her, his formidable intelligence had met a match, and he found a growing satisfaction in her presence, owned privately to the very few in his circle who knew them both. 'Miss Fenimore Woolson is spending the winter [in London],' he remarked to Howells, 'I see her at discreet intervals. . . . She is a very intelligent woman, and understands when she is spoken to; a peculiarity I prize, as I find it more and more rare.'

What she offered him is suggested by a complaint he made later that year: 'There is almost no care for literary discussion here, – questions of form, of principle, the "serious" idea of the novel appeals apparently to no one, & they don't understand when you speak of them.' He was disappointed by lack of response to his innovative essay on the art of fiction: his contempt for sentimental endings with wedding-bells, husbands, babies, fortunes, and cheerful remarks; his defence of interior drama. In so far as Woolson had moved away from the action plot of her Cooper inheritance, and in her denial of its happy ending, she had taken up a position close to that of James, underlined by her comprehension of his achievement two years before when he had sent her a copy of the *Portrait*.

Soon after she settled in London, news came that her brother, Charley, had died in San Francisco. He was thirty-six. Nothing is known about the cause of his death except that he took to drink and morphine, and left a diary which, Woolson said, 'showed suffering so piteous that it broke my heart'. She was 'ill' for three months, her first in England, and ascribed it to grief for a brother she had not seen, and had not wished to see, for fifteen years. In 1878, her mother had thought to visit Charley in Chicago but, despite her attachment to her only son, Hannah had put her daughter first. Connie had been hard at work all winter, and needed the 'different air' of the sea. Now, five years on, his death made her suffer more, she said, 'than I have ever suffered in my life'. The state of mind she encountered in his diary matched her propensity to depression during the dark season. Yet, unlike Charley, she had self-control, evident in the fact that James, her sole contact in London, had no inkling in December 1883 that she was too ill to write. At that very time, he commended her diligence and self-sufficiency, calling her 'an angel of quiet virtue'.

Her silence is more remarkable in view of the simultaneous death of Wilky James in November. For some time he had suffered from heart disease, compounded by kidney failure. Since Henry made no secret of his brother's decline – so grim that Henry hoped from day to day for the end – Miss Woolson must have shared his distress at the death of a brother whose life had become a disappointment to himself and his family. Like Charley Woolson, Wilky James was played out by his thirties.

Woolson confirms the report that James was seeing her at discreet intervals: 'Henry James comes to see me now & then, & sends me books to read,' she told her nephew, Sam Mather. One of the many books he gave her over the years was a copy of Shelley's poems, in which he signed himself her 'confrère'. Bookish, starved of intellectual stimulus, she cared nothing for his dining-out and country-house existence, but pressed him about his professional milieu.

'. . . I have asked Henry James a thousand questions about that remarkable Mr. [Henry] Adams,' she reported to Sam's wife, Flora Mather, who had glimpsed Adams in Sorrento. 'And Henry James has done his best to complete the picture . . .'. Flora's father,

Amasa Stone, was a Cleveland industrialist who committed suicide in 1883. She inherited not only her father's vast fortune but also his sense of mission, and drew her husband into schemes for health and education, which they carried through, together, as a lifelong commitment. Alert, intelligent, Flora was small and thin with a strong forehead and receding chin, rather like Eleanor Roosevelt. Two results of this marriage were to be important to Woolson: firstly, although she always protested that she could not afford to return to America, and always lived modestly, she belonged to a secure class of Americans who have money, or access to money, but don't throw it about. There certainly was money in the Cooper–Mather–Stone background. Given Woolson's modern ideas of independence, she wished to support herself, but she would never have been destitute. In the late nineteenth century it was still customary for families to care for unmarried dependants, and Woolson was loved by an enlightened family who took pride in her career. Secondly, it was through Sam's marriage that Woolson came into contact with John Hay, who was married to Flora's sister, Clara, one of those bovine women – 'vaccine', James said – often paired with handsome, prominent men.

Woolson soon took up Hay, and began one of her intensive correspondences. Her letters were about loneliness and moods, and though only her side survives, her letters show that confidences were mutual. She invariably chose to write to distinguished men who fought mental blights, and liked an intelligent listener they could trust. James was not the sole beneficiary of her 'charity'. It came to be agreed between him, Hay, and Howells, that she was a good woman as well as a gifted one.

To Hay, Woolson spoke of the kind of illness 'that hangs on, & baffles effort, & takes the heart out of a man'. She had been ill in this way, and 'very unhappy besides'. Though alone in lodgings in a strange country through a long, northern winter, and unable to work, she showed determined resilience: resting her soul in England's 'soft still light' as she walked in the parks. They were 'beautiful and green' even in winter. She saw Turner's house near the river at Twickenham 'where he went to live in order to see the sunsets', and worked out a 'Thackeray' walk to Becky Sharp's house in Mayfair. She told herself to be thankful it was not cold, and passed the days with books from the Grosvenor Gallery Library, mainly French literature: 'so local, so "French" & nothing else! But how well they write!'

By the end of January 1884 she herself was able to write once more. 'The effort required for my first attempts at writing again, was something wh[ich] took every particle of will I possess,' she commented. 'And I've got a good deal – on a certain line.'

The result, two years later, was her best novel, *East Angels*, published in 1886, and this book, modelled in some ways on *The Portrait of a Lady*, provides a clue to her movements: a wish to be near the man whose writings were her 'real home'. James approved the 'transcendent' behaviour of Margaret Harold in her loyalty to a husband whose behaviour may 'be held to have absolved her'. (He has left her twice for another woman.) Margaret says: 'I must bear my life – the life I made for myself . . . I must bear it as well as I can.' This is the portrait of a woman more passionate and repressed than Isabel Archer. An onlooker perceives in her silence 'a fullness of intellect, a fullness at times almost throbbing . . .'. She fights her sexuality beyond the frontiers of society, deep in the swamps of Florida. The river, a temporary escape from society, and Margaret's sacrifice to moral duty recall the conflict of passion and duty when Maggie Tulliver sails off with her cousin's lover, then compels their return. Both Margaret and Maggie are doomed women, without the agency of Isabel Archer, but James might have been talking of Isabel when he approved Margaret's integrity as 'the larger sort of imagination' of a woman 'bent upon looking at life from a high point of view'. He approved, also, a 'perfectly free' mind 'watching life, waiting upon it and trying to catch it in the fact'. For a moment, it was a mentor speaking – the mentor Woolson craved. England remained her base just so long as she was writing this most Jamesian of her novels: in the event, three winters.

There were limits to what she could expect from James. She had access to this huge talent, but it was a law unto itself. James could lend himself to the glittering engagements of the literary lion and dash off effusions to an array of correspondents, but the real James was reserved for his art – as Woolson was too astute not to have known. She had no illusions about him nor, indeed, about anyone else. Her rejection of sexual partners was a rational cause of depression since, in the absence of close women friends, it meant a loneliness that often felt unbearable. She had long practised the containment of a nineteenth-century woman who sees, with clear-eyed endurance, that expression is impossible – except through writing, and even there it comes through silence or elision. In a travel-story, 'At Mentone' (1884), a young woman of twenty-eight, another Margaret, is drawn to an artist in the party, but like many able men in Woolson's stories he is blind to intelligence in a woman and prefers a shallow girl. Margaret is left like a statue she sees in a cemetery: her tears don't fall. 'Margaret had a great deal of self-control,' we are told, 'perhaps too much.' While Woolson tried to alert James to the presence of passion in women, he deplored its centrality in her work. It must be acknowledged that when she grants passion a happy ending, her work gets skewed and dated; it holds when passion is denied or when it terminates in a warping marriage.

Alone in London, she begged Hay to write to a woman who was 'not much entertained with the spectacle of daily life, as it exists for her'. She felt 'terribly alone' in her work. 'There seems to be no one for me to turn to,' she cried. 'It is true that there are only two or three to whom I wd. turn!'

Here was a related problem: she had Corinne's determination to mix with men of first-rate intelligence. 'You see that I have become exorbitant,' she admitted, 'I want to see the most agreeable people in the world, & only those! This is preposterous. I have nothing, absolutely nothing, to back it up with, alas! alas!'

Her plaints do not always reflect her actual situation, for within a few months she and James had established a sealed-off space in which their tie could flourish. He was a man of secrets, with little cubbyholes where certain friends were kept from other friends, and no friend was more self-contained than the 'angel of quiet virtue'. She did not trouble James, nor anyone else, to provide entrée to London society. None of his London circle knew of her presence in his life. On 28 February 1884, she went alone to see the Italian actor Salvini in *Othello*. There she encountered James with Mrs Kemble. He insisted that Miss Woolson take his better seat. The elderly actress, deprived of her escort, turned to Miss Woolson with comic rudeness. 'I am *sorry* Mr James has introduced you to me,' she announced. 'I shall be obliged to tell you, *now*, that I shall not *speak* to you, or *look* at you, or be conscious of your existence even, during the entire evening.'

In May, in the midst of the season, James dined with Lord Rosebery, the fifth Earl and future prime minister, in the company of dukes and other grandees. It was, he owned, 'a sort of festivity that I endure but don't enjoy'. He had a way of leaving a dinner party early with an air of preoccupation. The usual caricature of James has him holding forth at length to fervent admirers, but in earlier years he was more of a listener, and more displaced than he seemed, especially after the deaths of his parents detached him finally from Boston – to which, anyway, he had never entirely adapted. The English man of letters Edmund Gosse met a 'homeless man' who was still 'looked upon as a foreigner in London, while he seemed to have lost his citizenship in the United States'.

What Gosse recalled does not match other memoirs between the 1920s and 1950s which perpetuate the sociable image, nor does it match more recent biographies with their documentation of the vast façade of the writer's social life. We glimpse, here, another James, who mirrors the homelessness of Constance Fenimore Woolson. If anything, she was less rootless in so far as she never surrendered her nationality. Her identity as an Ameican writer was never in doubt, while James, though prolific and celebrated, was left out, alike, in surveys of English or American literature. Gosse saw that 'he endured in the world of letters, the singular fate of being a man without a country'. This displacement, combined with his contempt for society (despite his apparent immersion), drew him, now and then, to a solitary woman in whom he could find his other self.

'. . . The Costanza is handy, in Sloan[e] Street,' he conceded in the summer of 1884. She told him she would stay on till August: her plans, like his, were provisional; both conducted a life which left them free to move at will. Her determined freedom reassured James as much as her ladylike reserve, and his comments about her over the course of six months grew perceptibly warmer.

It was his custom to make gracious comments about others and then kill them with an apparently casual and spontaneous little afterthought that carried a lethal sting (as when he said that if Lizzie Boott had more initiative in her painting, she would go far '– as women go'). In one comment on Miss Woolson he stopped himself short: 'But she is a most excellent reasonable woman, absorbed in her work, upon whom I have not a single reflection to make. I like and esteem her exceedingly.'

The deliberation of this restraint demonstrates an impulse to resist his 'sin'. Woolson had challenged him to be better than he was, and now he made an effort to be loyal. 'But' alone suggests a reservation. For he retained a higher alternative to his professional and expatriate affinities with Miss Woolson: the pure fellowship with Minny Temple. In March 1884 there came to him a renewed image of Minny in the form of a dying invalid called Mildred Theory. She appears briefly in a slight tale, 'Georgina's Reasons', published that summer. Again, James drew on Minny's dream. 'There is no one I care enough for, or who cares enough for me, to take charge of me to Italy,' Minny had lamented on 3 February 1869. In 'Georgina's Reasons', a devoted younger sister takes the invalid abroad, as Elly Temple might conceivably have done had she looked to her sister instead of rushing into marriage with a railroad king. Mildred Theory, on her sofa in Italy, advising her sister against the time when she will be alone, is said to be 'as beautiful as a saint, and as delicate and refined as an angel'. With her elevation of spirit in the face of mortality, Mildred Theory is a precursor of Milly Theale, far still in the future, that 'vision' to which James had vowed to return.

In the winter Woolson had seen James now and then; by the summer she was seeing him 'quite often', but always out of sight. He began a custom of retiring to Dover in the summer in order to write in peace. In the summer of 1884 Miss Woolson had 'lodgings' in Dover. On a blustery day, 7 September, when she was staying for several weeks in Salisbury, she and James struggled to Stonehenge, as she reports in a letter: 'It was so cold that we could scarcely speak, and finally we became silent. On Salisbury Plain, the wind blew so that I thought the carriage would be overturned. The driver turned out of the road down into a gully where we waited half an hour with the wind roaring overhead. At last we reached Salisbury, dined on a Michaelmas goose in my lodgings in the [Cathedral] Close, and then we finished the day (and his visit) by going to see some strolling players in a hall not much better than a barn. They gave "A School for Scandal".'

'Miss Grief' was to appear with James in a volume of *Stories by American Authors*. He had given Woolson a photograph, and it occurred to her to request photographs of Hay and Howells to complete a trio of 'distinguished' and 'agreeable' men: she would display them as trophies. Friendship with first-rate men was a guarantee of her professional standing; a promise of support; a stay against her vulnerability as an unprotected woman in the market-place.

She had to see those faces as she wrote, and objected when Hay did not oblige: he neglected her, she accused him in April 1885. He must write, must send that photograph. By December, she had all three on her work table: Howells 'smiling and smiling'; Hay poetic; and James cynical. Their photos were unlike them, she observed: she had seen Hay 'cynical' and Howells 'furious' – when he had to attend too many tea parties in Florence during a stay in 1883. As James had silenced himself on Woolson, so, here, Woolson was silent on James.

A new claim on James began in November 1884 with the arrival of Alice, who never returned to America. Alone in the family house in Boston, she had felt like a person in solitary confinement: the minutes had opened caverns of emptiness; the walls had whispered 'alone! alone!' until she longed to fly to the firemen next door. She could not allow it was 'anything else than a cruel and unnatural fate for a woman to live alone, to have no one to care for and "do for" daily'. It was 'not only a sorrow, but a sterilizing process'.

When James went to Liverpool to meet her steamer, Woolson was in Vienna with her sister. When he went to Dover in the summer of 1885 to write 'in extreme retirement', Woolson herself retired to Leamington and from there made numerous excursions to Stratford, Coventry, and the gardens of Kenilworth Castle, where she walked on the 'red battlements' at sunset. She fell 'desperately in love' with Oxford. There is a doggedness about these plans, even about the pleasures she found in walks and excursions, as though she had to plan to keep depression at bay.

That winter found her living near James, in Seymour Street. Alice lived nearer him at 7 Bolton Row. In his study of the James family, R. W. B. Lewis noticed how when Alice moved closer, her brother moved away. In February–March 1886, James left Bolton Street and crossed the Park to an unfurnished flat at 34 De Vere Gardens, near the Royal Albert Hall and opposite Kensington Gardens. Alice later moved to this area.

In February, Woolson went to the Strand to buy a trunk; in March, she left England for Italy. There are parallels with Alice: both made it a point of pride not to burden others, though one was a chronic invalid and the other a chronic depressive; and both felt an affinity with Henry: Alice had the James intelligence; Woolson shared fictional aims. And yet, he was busy. He was writing two novels (*The Bostonians* and *The Princess Casamassima*), and planned a future on a prodigious scale. To do this, he had to guard his privacy. His sister and Woolson accepted this as a matter of course; both sought other answers to their need. Alice found her answer in Katharine Loring's combination of nursing, devotion, and feminism; Woolson tried to find an answer in moving on, but her instincts were domestic, and this was recognised as the crux of her 'troubles': she was a domestic creature without a home.

Even if these two women were self-sufficient, that does not entirely absolve James. His relation to Alice had its sharp edge, manifest in an unpublished exchange before she came to England. After he left her in Boston, he expressed his pity, and added uneasily that he didn't know what to do about it. Hopefully, she might get well enough to become her own Katharine 'or perhaps even the Katharine of another'. How oddly he misread his sister. Katharine, with her practical bent, was not an appropriate model. When Alice dismissed pity, Henry wheeled round and flicked his knife: he is delighted that she snubs him for daring to pity her, 'but I must tell you – so mind you – that you snubbed me still more for making some cheerful remarks to you on the occasion of Katharine's departure – saying that it was easy to be cheerful about the woes of others. . . . I held that this was a warning to lower my pitch – & sought to offend you less, by not assuming that . . . you were happier than you were. I give you notice now, once for all, that I shall hereafter take easy views of everything, at any price.'

Of course, this is all about his convenience. James was adept at avoiding inconvenience. When Alice resolved to come to England, and Grace Norton wrote to commiserate with James on the burden ahead, he replied blithely that his life would remain unchanged. Alice, he told himself, was coming to Europe, not to him. Anyway, she was too proud to impinge. This line allowed him to pit his sister's self-respect against her need of him. It was simply too much to take on Alice; it was easy to have Katharine look after her. When Katharine was unavailable and Alice very ill in Bournemouth in April 1885, he went there, he told people, to care for his 'poor sister'. In fact, he left his sister to the hired nurse he brought down with him, and spent only twenty minutes a day at her bedside. The crumb of attention improved her; even so, he spent every evening consolidating a friendship with Robert Louis Stevenson (1850–94). The Education Act of 1871, which introduced universal elementary education, had produced a new mass of readers who didn't want George Eliot or Henry James; they preferred adventure stories like *Treasure Island* (1883). Both Stevenson and Alice James were invalids whose company was brilliant – only, Stevenson was famous, and fun, and not his sister.

On another occasion, James could write easily to William, in the summer of 1886, that Alice had been six weeks in Leamington without a visit from him; nor did he expect to see her until the following winter when she would come to London. As it happened, he did visit her – once – in August. For a man who travelled to the ends of England and Scotland as a guest in great country houses, who wafted about the Continent at a moment's whim, and enjoyed total freedom as a bachelor, it is odd that a relatively short train ride to Leamington was so rare. His defence was that Alice did not wish to have him 'on her' for several hours. James is usually praised for attentions to his sister, but how much of this was family myth? Here was a woman, of like mind, who had come to live in England to be close to her unattached brother, but who was not important to him in the way Mary Lamb was important to Charles Lamb, or Dorothy to Wordsworth – other disturbed sisters whose writer-brothers loved them dearly, lived with them, and shared ideas. Miss Woolson had told him he was 'spoiled'; his own view of his 'spare' existence was that it was 'practically, about all I can manage, which shows how little nature constructed me for fringes & frills & ramifications'. He was not talking specifically about man or woman, sister, wife, child, or lover, but about his need to be 'horseless' and 'cowless', in short, free of inroads on his attention.

When Woolson departed for Florence, James planned to go there six months later. In the meantime, he asked Boott to take her up. He denied matchmaking, aware that her intelligence, good manners, delicate features, and fresh, quiet dress would appear eligible to a man of discrimination:

13 De Vere Mansions West W.
May 25*th* [1886]

> I wonder, my dear good Francis, whether you will do me rather a favour. My excellent and amiable friend Constance Fenimore Woolson is in Florence, and I want to pay her your compliment and administer to her some social comfort. The finest satisfaction I can confer upon her will be to ask you to go and see her, at Casa Molin; the old pensione Barbensi, on the Lung-Arno, which you will know. She appears to know few people there (i.e. in Florence), and though she has not made any sort of request of me touching this proposal (by which I don't mean that I want you to 'propose' to her, either for me or yourself), I am sure that the sight of you would give her joy. She is a deaf and *méticuleuse* old maid – but she is also an excellent and sympathetic being. If Lizzie could take a look at her and attract her to the villa I should be very glad. . . . When I think of what Bellosguardo must be at this superlative moment I grow quite limp and useless. . . . I shall come and see you soon. Ever dear Francis very affectionately yours
>
> Henry James

At this time, in the spring of 1886, Lizzie, aged forty, had unexpectedly married the son of a German immigrant to Cincinnati called Duveneck, who had been her art teacher for six years. It was a marriage between Bostonian refinement and a poor bohemian. Duveneck was large and stout, with a thick moustache and sleepy eyes, good-natured but (according to James) with nothing to say and unconcerned to promote himself. James saw it as reprehensible to be quite so careless of reputation. Lizzie's marriage had repercussions, of course, for her father, who had lived for her as she for him.

Here was a situation James would explore and transform in his last complete novel, *The Golden Bowl* (1904), where an American woman has to mediate between her old bond with her father and her new, and not fully discernible, bond with her husband, a man alien to her in a compelling way. In the fiction, James switched the husband's position in the social scale from poor bohemian to impoverished Italian prince, but they are alike in so far as both are at the farthest remove from the Boston proprieties of the Bootts – translated into the perfectionism of Adam Verver and his fine-tuned daughter, Maggie. As the Bootts had also inspired Osmond and Pansy in *The Portrait of a Lady*, they provided source material for two great international novels, which means that James had an eye to them that differed from ordinary social ties. They were interfused with his art, and this included Minny Temple, whom James discussed with Lizzie: 'with no one in the aftertime was I to find it more a blest and sacred rite ... to celebrate my cousin's memory.' It is conceivable that when James made his decision in May 1886 to introduce the Bootts and Miss Woolson, he was not merely granting Boott a measure of consolation and Miss Woolson a measure of social comfort, but bringing together two elements of his private life. He had no wish to promote a marriage between Boott and Miss Woolson; his interest lay in their capacities to generate an alternative world which could house his imagination.

Bellosguardo was an elevated rural retreat for the well-to-do (as it still is) within walking distance of Florence. When Fenimore Cooper had lived in the vicinity, he wrote *The Wept of Wish-ton-wish* (1829). He was so famous by this time that every novel he produced was published simultaneously in thirty-four countries including Italy, where he found his name known in country inns and post offices in small towns. He lingered in Italy for two years, and said 'it leaves behind a tender sensation allied to that of love.'

'Miss Fenimore Woolson' was one style James used in speaking of his friend. It was at this point that he shortened it to the more familiar 'Fenimore': the name coincided with her plan to live, like

'Uncle Fenimore', outside Florence. 'Fenimore', and a renewed promise James made in August to visit her when she was settled, mark the first hint, perhaps, of a tale: a classic American writer who had lived in Italy earlier in the century, and a middle-aged woman in the same place, living out her existence through a rather tenuous connection with that illustrious past. Perhaps the idea for *The Aspern Papers* had its earliest source in the August plan to visit 'Fenimore', rather than a later anecdote of Claire Clairmont and Byron which provided a plot.

Before Fenimore left Florence for the summer in Switzerland, Boott arranged for her to rent rooms in one of the wings of the fifty-roomed Villa Castellani, where he and the now-pregnant Lizzie lived with the addition of Duveneck. The Castellani dates back to the fifteenth century (in Vasari's *Lives* it is called Belvedere al Saracino and belonged to a family called Borgherini). It was now owned by Ellen Greenough Huntington, an expatriate American whose brother, Henry Greenough, was married to Boott's sister. Mrs Huntington had a daughter, Mary, who eventually inherited the Castellani in 1893. Nearby on Bellosguardo, and connected to the Castellani by a secret passage, was Villa Montanto with its battlemented watch-tower. Fenimore looked forward to evenings on the tower, with the vast landscape darkening slowly all around. The villa, once occupied by her adored Hawthorne – here he drafted his Italian novel, *The Marble Faun* – was now occupied by Lady Hobart and a dachshund, Pax, who endeared himself to Fenimore. (Later, Mary Huntington sent her a long letter in verse 'dictated' by this dog.)

With these prospects before her, including a friendship with the musical and amusing Boott, Fenimore felt 'wonderfully well – better than I have felt for many months', as she told her new doctor. William Wilberforce Baldwin (1850–1910) was an American in his late thirties, who treated the expatriate community in Florence, the poor in the region and, as his reputation spread, royalty all over Europe. He regaled Fenimore with descriptions of 'the wise, little, red-faced Queen [Victoria]', her daughter 'discontentedly representing her at Bazaars', and 'the tame cat of Battenberg'. Many American writers eventually came to consult him, including William James, Mark Twain, Edith Wharton, and

Howells. He had a grasp of the links between physical and mental health, and practised medicine as an art, reading his patients like books. It cannot have been incidental that this gifted diagnostician was a reader. He introduced Fenimore to Ibsen. (Later, in 1889, when James turned to drama, she returned to Ibsen, especially the feminist play, *A Doll's House*, where a child-wife, Nora, outgrows the 'doll's house' of nineteenth-century marriage.) Baldwin, like Boott, was another potential friend at this hopeful time. Fenimore trusted him, and all the more so because he too suffered from periodic depression. He was to become Fenimore's closest confidant in letters to him over the rest of her life.

The new-named 'Fenimore' was corresponding with James during her stay in Geneva in July–August. She read Rousseau's eighteenth-century novel about the chaste love of a mentor and pupil, *La Nouvelle Héloïse: Lettres de deux amants*, and in a letter to James pictured herself hanging over the balcony of the Hôtel National, looking down on the placid waters of the lake. When James relayed this picture to Boott, he imagined that, as Fenimore gazed at the lake, she was thinking 'of – you!' Boott was also in Switzerland that August, and James teased him: 'Perhaps you are not alone – I hope not; perhaps even you have met our friend Fenimore somewhere.' James was not blind to Fenimore's appeal for a cultivated old gentleman who might need companionship after his daughter's marriage.

On 1 September, Fenimore moved into the Castellani, 'a large ancient structure of pale yellow hue'. Its façade rose directly from the road, like many houses in Tuscany. The scale of the villa, in the shape of a parallelogram around an open court, was hidden by stone walls of massive thickness and by an entrance like the gate to a fortress. The courtyard was built in the quattrocento style with arched balconies on the first floor, and climbing plants covered the walls. There were five kitchens, serving five or six families. The Castellani was full of winding, dimly lit passages and mysterious staircases complete with a ghost who haunted Fenimore's bedroom. Miss Greenough,* in the apartment above, began to

* Related, presumably, to Ellen Greenough Huntington, the owner of the Castellani, as well as to the Bootts.

explain, but Fenimore stopped her: 'I adore "the Ghost" unexplained.'

In the Arno Valley below there were vineyards and olive groves. She delighted in her garden, contained enough to be intimate yet extending to a parapet. There were pomegranates, oleanders, laurel, and rose bushes, all half-wild amidst the long grass, and no flower beds. The grace of this old garden lay in its wildness and a vista that seemed to overhang half of Tuscany. From the vantage point of the parapet, Fenimore said, 'the vast landscape below rolls towards the sunset as wide and far-stretching as the hidden shelf, one's standing point, is private and small'. To enter this private place was to enter the charmed preserve of a James novel – a setting for the *Portrait*.

The last months of 1886 found Fenimore less isolated, entering into the lives of the Bootts, across the court. Lizzie invited Fenimore to be godmother to her child, and 'Mr Boott' became 'Francis'. And as the end of the year drew near, letters came from Henry James announcing his arrival. He planned to travel straight to Florence, impatient to be there, 'almost intolerably so; for long fasting, on the Italian question, has brought with it a positive ferocity of appetite'. His exchanges with Lizzie 'and the appreciative Fenimore' only made him 'more feverish to cross the Alps'. His awareness that the Bootts had taken to Fenimore quickened an interest of his own. Having ventured to admit her to his innermost circle, he felt free to refer to her or send messages in every letter (several unpublished). Boott should know that he and Fenimore were agreed in naming him 'the ornament of Bellosguardo'.

'Will you kindly mention to Fenimore when you see her,' he wrote, 'that I have also sent her one [copy of *The Princess Casamassima*] & that I have the same hope of its arrival. Please also impart to her that portion of the foregoing which applies to my departure for Italy – or any other part you may judge capable of interesting her. She is however very difficult to interest. It is, none the less, plain from her letters that you have achieved that result!'

His visit was to be a 'secret', he warned the Bootts. His idea in coming to Florence was to 'hide'. 'I don't intend to see *any one* there but you and Fenimore,' he warned yet again. 'Will you kindly ask *her* to observe an equal discretion?'

Mulling rather complacently over Fenimore's attachment to him, her 'power of devotion (to H.J.!)', he repeated to Lizzie that he would not marry her: Lizzie would not have to contribute towards a tea set* was the way he put it. Not 'for *me*!' he joked. Another man – her father – might want it.

Fenimore's rooms in the Castellani were available only until the end of the year. On 9 October, she went to inspect the two-hundred-year-old Casa Brichieri-Colombi, and leased an apartment for a year. She took nine of its fourteen rooms, with her bedroom and study on the floor above some spare rooms. It was a two-storey house on the brow of Bellosguardo, looking down on the towers and domes of Florence. Elizabeth Barrett Browning had visited the Brichieri, and Fenimore fancied it was Aurora Leigh's villa in the poem of that name. It had a rose terrace and, she noted, 'a cosy little "writing-room" where I hope to pass tranquil hours'.

Fenimore offered James her apartment in the Brichieri while she stayed on through December in the Castellani, a step across a small piazza at the top of that quiet hill. Even before he arrived, James was calling her 'my landlady'. She was concerned that he should have the comfort to which he was accustomed. There was to be a maid, Assunta, and a male cook, called Angelo, was to be his valet. Angelo was more than a cook – he had learnt his art in Paris, to which he added the Italian flair for sirops and ices. Declining an offer of wood from Boott, James said that Fenimore, 'whose devotion – like my appreciation of it – is *sans bornes*, has stacked me up a pile with her own hands. She is a gallant friend, but I am afraid she has bored you with me.' He was aware that he had freed Fenimore of discretion with the Bootts. In a sense, he had masterminded this group now bonding in readiness for him high up on Bellosguardo.

On 8 December, when James arrived and took up residence in the Brichieri, her found Fenimore next door – without the Bootts. They had moved into Florence for the birth of Lizzie's baby, due in two weeks. So, given the secrecy they had all preserved, James was alone with Fenimore and completely undisturbed on that

* A wedding gift.

hilltop for the next three weeks. There can be no doubt she had made it happen, as much as he. Given her frugal habits, Fenimore would not normally have undertaken to pay rental for two places at once. She could have moved into the Brichieri in December 1886, and James could have taken over the rooms she vacated. Her sole motive for staying on at the Castellani was to have him in her house. He enjoyed the yellow sun pouring into his window from the terrace, the towers of Florence at his feet, and beyond them the delicate purple of the Apennines, their summits tipped with snow. Indoors, he had great wood fires (London had coal fires) and, to warm his heart, Duveneck's sketch of Henry James Sr, like an aged prophet, hairless, with round eyes and long beard, stared from an easel in a room James called the 'salon'. In the 'sky-kitchen' (Fenimore's word), Angelo cooked delectable meals. This rather melancholy man-of-parts would get up at five in the morning and walk to Florence to secure the best produce. Fenimore supplied Ginori teacups, an after-dinner coffee service, and fruit plates.

For some reason, the Bootts were uneasy about these arrangements. Before James arrived, they expressed fear for his comfort. James waved their objections away. 'For what do you take me all – and for what do you take the divine Bellosguardo?' He was disposed to be pleased. The Bootts' fear that he would 'suffer' looks like coded language for some other concern: a worry about propriety or his effect on Fenimore. 'I see her every day or two,' James told Hay on 24 December, 'indeed often dine with her.'

The two were dining alone: the date is three days after Lizzie gave birth, and the Bootts were still in Florence. Despite the cold, twenty tea roses bloomed in the Brichieri garden – 'my' garden, Fenimore said with pride. During these last three weeks of December 1886, James came closer than he had ever been to a voluntary domestic tie, and Fenimore had the kind of intimacy she craved. Whatever we choose to call it – confrères, co-creators of the private life, romantic friendship (that emotional bond so prevalent in the eighteenth and nineteenth centuries) – their joint privacy now became intensive.

Before her, nightly, sat the subject of Sargent's sketch of September 1886, which caught, on the instant, his formidable presence. His beard, which had been rather wide and fluffy, obscuring his face, was now neatly trimmed: still a heavy beard, close and prickly, but not a cover. His bared faced appeared less 'cynical', more assured. This is the most determined, the least withdrawn, of all the images of James. He had a watchful, measured gaze, from a centre of mental command, less detached than the famous portrait Sargent was to paint of him at the age of seventy when he had become the supreme Master. In 1913, he was an observer with a huge space around him; at seventy, no one could approach that quintessence of consciousness. In 1886, at the age of forty-three, he was contemplative in a more connected way – the viewer can feel the vibration of his gaze, intent, engaged. His body does not lean far back, as in the later portrait; it's more upright, even forceful. This man had a look that held its subject in a vice.

Fenimore treasured his gift of the French translation of the complete works of Turgenev in nine volumes, and planned to exhibit them on a special shelf together with a photograph of the Russian author. She could not help a little boast about this gesture from 'Harry James', when she wrote to Cleveland. Only old intimates – Americans who had known him in his youth – called him 'Harry'. She was now on such terms. He brought her the three volumes of *The Bostonians* (inscribed 'To his padrona Constance Fenimore Woolson, her faithful tenant and friend, Henry James, Bellosguardo, December 1886,' and also gave her a reprint of *Roderick Hudson* (1886), with another photograph of himself.

Books, not people, Fenimore said, were her 'companions'. 'Where other people are talking, I must read.' In 1886–7, she bought some contemporary American classics, and it is likely that she continued her mission, evident in her surviving letters, to call out the American in James. Recently, she had acquired a volume of Emerson's poems, and followed these with Cabot's life of Emerson – the 'friend of my youth', she said, and now her 'god'. She had also bought a selection of Whitman (inscribed 'Florence, 1886'). On the flyleaf she listed her favourites, many of them Civil War poems: 'Vigil Strange I Kept on the Field One Night', 'A march in the ranks hard-prest', 'As Toilsome I Wander'd Virginia's Woods', 'The Wound-Dresser', 'Dirge for Two Veterans', 'Reconciliation', and the great elegy for Lincoln, 'When Lilacs Last in the Dooryard

Bloom'd'. As 'a warm patriot', she copied out another of Whitman's elegies for Lincoln:

> This dust was once the man,
> Gentle, plain, just and resolute, under whose cautious hand,
> Against the foulest crime in history known in any land or age,
> Was saved the Union of these States.

In November, Hay's *Lincoln: A History* had begun its four-year serialisation in *Century*. Fenimore hailed its celebration of 'the plainness of our American life', and hoped it would act as a corrective to the Europeanisation of Americans – and no one appeared more Europeanised than Henry James.

How pleasing, then, to find him deep in one item of Americana, her own works, in preparation for an essay he was to publish on 'Miss Woolson'. In the meantime, he praised 'the great merit and progress' of *East Angels*. He thought she had done 'a brave thing' in settling for two or three years in this rambling, somewhat mouldy old villa but foresaw a gain for her work – in which, he said, he now took an 'interest'. Here, at last, were signs of the professional reciprocity which Fenimore had willed for six years, ever since she had conceived – and to some extent acted out – 'Miss Grief'. The prospect of 'Miss Woolson' by the celebrated Henry James, whose other subjects were the likes of George Eliot and Turgenev, was disarming, like his attentions in Florence in 1880. Then, it had been the attentions of a writer to a newcomer to Europe whose impressions, as she changed her life's course, might serve for the *Portrait*. Then, she had been only one of a number of people who served James as a 'resource'. Now, he was preparing to recognise her publicly as a writer. The greatest living novelist was to give her a space in his *œuvre*.

As he dined each night with 'the gifted authoress', he saw her face to face – as few were permitted to see her. But the closer he got to a domestic bond, the more he denied it, first to Lizzie, then to Boott and Hay, then as the subject of a series of shorter fictions – *The Aspern Papers*, *A London Life*, and 'The Lesson of the Master', all troubled by the question of marriage and, associated with this question, by that surge that lifts his work to the level of masterpiece. A second great wave of creativity took its rise from the darkness of those winter evenings with his 'padrona' in December 1886, just before he outlined his next tale of an American lodger who inveigles his way into the house of a mysterious 'padrona' associated with a long-dead writer called Jeffrey Aspern. 'Jeffrey' sounds too close to the first two initials of J. F. Cooper to be entirely an accident; so too Miss Tita, the name (until the final draft) of the padrona's niece. The name comes from Tita Douglas, a passionate woman in Woolson's bestseller, *Anne*. The lodger plays up to Miss Tita with an eye to the immortal whose papers she guards. Like Cooper, the immortal has lived in Italy during the Romantic period, but 'his own country . . . had had most of his life' and he had been 'essentially American'. It was his native atmosphere that the narrator of *The Aspern Papers* prizes from the start: 'at a period when our native land was nude and crude and provincial, . . . when literature was lonely there and art and form almost impossible, he had found the means to live and write like one of the first; to be free . . . and not at all afraid'. It appears that Henry James did nothing that did not feed his art: this silent fact made him less ingenuous than he appeared.

So, at the end of 1886, a fantasy was rising – James was drawing 'Fenimore' into his form of involvement. A letter she dated 30 December is addressed from the Brichieri while James was still there. The Bootts' worry was not misplaced, but they were unaware of her complicity: her initiative in using James in the same fictional way he was now preparing to use her.

On New Year's Day 1887, James moved to the Hôtel du Sud, on the Piazza Goldoni, adjoining the Ponte alla Carraia, the bridge en route from Bellosguardo to the centre of Florence. With this move, secrecy vanished. Expatriate society mobbed James. Fenimore had never seen anyone so run after as this recluse of the private life. He graced the scene even while he hated the 'wretched little social smotherisation'. Amongst his new contacts were Dr Baldwin and a young Englishwoman, Violet Paget, who published under the name of Vernon Lee.

It was at Miss Paget's home, 5 Via Garibaldi, that James had a story from her half-brother, Lee-Hamilton, which gripped him at once. He recorded it in his notebook on 12 January. Less than ten years before, a man called Silsbee, a sea-captain from Boston, obsessed with Shelley, had discovered that Claire Clairmont, Shelley's sister-in-law and one-time mistress of Byron, was still living – in complete retirement – in the Via Romana in Florence. Silsbee had offered himself as a lodger, to gain access to a house where, he was sure, Shelley papers were secreted. When, at length, Miss Clairmont died in 1879, the papers came into the possession of a great-niece who lived with her and whose confidence Silsbee had contrived to gain. The climax came when the niece (an 'old maid of 50') proposed to the lodger as a condition for handing over the papers. The man fled.

In his notebook, James sympathised with 'poor Silsbee'. This has tempted some to construct a neat parallel, with James in flight from a feeble, ageing Miss Woolson bent on marriage. A truer and subtler point of sympathy between Silsbee and James is their susceptibility to conscience. Both draw out a woman for an ulterior purpose. Fenimore had a horror of publicity, much as James himself, yet 'Miss Woolson', due out in February 1887, exposed her life, using its lonely walks against her to hint of a depressive state of mind that draws her to 'dismal swamps' and 'brackish inlets'.* 'Miss Woolson' was a calculated betrayal; it carried an armoury of stings in its velvet glove.

It is a portrait of a lady writer flawed by the feminine weakness for love ('She likes the unmarried . . . but she likes marriages even better'), and flawed, too, by feminine isolation from the manly traffic of the great world. James regrets the sparse society of St Augustine (in implied contrast to the high society of his own chosen ground, a repeat of his regret for Hawthorne's 'thin soil' in 1879). Her characters who live outside society (notably, her gifted women) are said to have a 'shipwrecked' air, as though on a desert island. A tone of condescension spreads a pall of dullness over his friend's *œuvre*: her work is 'worthy' and 'pressed into service' such 'natural objects' as Negroes.

James approves the sacrificial wives in her two recent novels, but

* James cut this long paragraph on her life, possibly at her insistence, when he revised the essay for a collection of *Partial Portraits* (1888).

ignores the radicalism of *For the Major* (1883), where the collapse of a husband's sight signals his wife's release from the laborious falsities of femininity in the style favoured by the Old South: the pink tints and long, golden curls. Madam Carroll pins back her hair and bares the lined face of a woman who has grieved over the deaths of children; she extends to visitors a worn hand, no longer covered by muslin frills. This studied deconstruction of femininity counters the standard caricature of female artifice, like the painted hag Mrs Skewton (in *Dombey and Son*), who comes to pieces every night at her dressing-table. Far from demeaned by the loss of doll-hood, Madam Carroll gains in dignity and stature.

In the case of the unhappily married Margaret Harold in *East Angels* (1886), James ignored, too, the 'killing griefs', that element Woolson had warned was missing in his own disembodied portraits of ladies. Margaret, who has given up the man she wants, regrets it's 'not so easy to die', but the question is left open. '... It's this stifled love that's killing you,' another woman warns her. 'Women do die of such feelings, you are one of them.' There were critics, including Howells, who did not believe in Margaret. This roused the author to fury. Such women do exist, she insisted. James blocks out the heat of suppressed desire, and refers only to the 'high finish' of the erotic river journey where Margaret and the lover she has denied 'penetrated into the dim ... swamp' in the dark backwaters of the St John's River. 'Elms arose erect in the moss', and 'channels opened out on all sides. Only one was the right one. ... There came to her suddenly the memory of a little arena – an arena where the flowering vines hung straight down from the treetops to the water all round, like tapestry, and the perfumes were densely thick.'

James called this place 'unnatural'. He would have it that the author was a 'conservative' lady of the utmost propriety. 'Conservative' is not an aesthetic label James would apply to himself, suggesting as it does a want of initiative and imagination. His agenda is to inject his stings in the quietest way beneath the strokings of the velvet glove.

Both James and Woolson pursued the interior drama of renunciation, but James cannot hold back a sneer at the 'exaltations' of conscience in his friend's case. There seems to be a double standard. Woolson's advance on the terrain evokes extraordinary barbs: 'she cannot get on without a social atmosphere', he regrets; also her liking for the well-born who have 'a pleasant sense of a few warm generations behind them, screening them in . . . from vulgar draughts in the rear'. Is that James siding with the 'vulgar'? Or is he bristling a little that only one generation protects him from the Irish immigrant? 'I know not whether for the most part we are . . . so long-descended as in Miss Woolson's pages we strike ourselves as being . . .', he murmurs. Though he applauds the way she lends herself to the vanquished dumbness of the South, the barb does not fail to arrive: to feel sympathy is, after all, what women do.

His attack was so insidiously concealed in afterthoughts that many who read this essay, from William James (who called it 'happy') to Leon Edel (who saw a return for devotion), had the impression that James went out of his way for a friend. This was exactly the impression James meant to induce: the great writer doing his gallant best for a lady who had been wafted along by the publishing current of the day, to the degree that her proper reticence has 'not prevented her . . . from competing for the literary laurel'. There's the rub. The essay does not mention that Woolson's last two novels had been widely read compared with the poor reception of the last two novels by Henry James. The fact was, he had 'entered upon evil days'. He confided his dismay to Howells' 'most private ear': a double failure had 'reduced the desire, and the demand, for my productions to zero'. How galling to have to acknowledge that 'Miss Woolson' was flying higher than expected.

His rivalry, wrapped in yards of velvet, is plain enough. Yet we must avoid a temptation to dismiss his assessment entirely. James does make one fair warning about her novels. *Anne* falls off, and neither *For the Major* nor *East Angels* is on a par with the classics; he is right to urge a further leap. Where long fiction was concerned, she would fail this leap in *Jupiter Lights* (1889), where the exposé of a soak who batters his wife and breaks his baby's arm is eclipsed by the heroine's surrender to the strong-armed routine of a conventional hero;* and she was to fail again in her last novel,

* Woolson lacked the boldness of Anne Brontë's *The Tenant of Wildfell Hall* (1848), which foregrounds domestic violence with a clarity that made the author

Horace Chase (1894), a slow-starting soap about a self-made millionaire and his young wife, who falls for a charmer and is rescued by the paternalism of her husband.

The effect of 'Miss Woolson' is to emphasise limitations and the modest achievement of two novels. The real betrayal lies in what is left out. Ostensibly a tribute, 'Miss Woolson' damns its subject with faint praise and excludes any mention of her highest achievement: her stories of artists (1880–2), which precede his own triumphs in the genre. It is clear that James read 'Miss Grief' because, after Woolson's death, he was to appropriate the 'figure in the carpet' as the title of the most enigmatic of his artist tales. That phrase is now indissolubly linked with the name of Henry James, while 'Miss Grief' disappeared for almost a century. 'Miss Woolson' fulfilled a prediction in 'Miss Grief' where, after Miss Grief's death, her neglected work of genius is appropriated by her mentor, who literally buries her other works with her. In the essay, James allows an aside to the effect that Miss Woolson has written the odd European story, but he can hardly recall it. The offhand manner suggests those stories are negligible, though one kindly refrains from saying so. This influential misreading ensured Woolson's future obliteration.

The good mood she had enjoyed in Florence now deserted her. It cannot have lessened her mortification that James sent this piece to *Harper's*, her own magazine: his attack was directed at the heart of her readership.

Soon after 'Miss Woolson' came out, James went to Venice for a long stay, 'much troubled about many things'. He sent Fenimore an intriguing message via Boott, as though she had dared to reproach him: 'Tell Fenimore I forgive her – but only an angel would. She will understand.' He remained in Venice nearly eight weeks from mid-February to mid-April. This period was 'unsuccessful', and James felt unwell. His rooms were in the Palazzo Giustiani-Recanati, set back slightly from the Grand Canal and attached to the back of the Casa Alvisi, which Mrs Bronson rented for guests. Browning liked to be there, but James found it damp

notorious. No lady would open her lips on such a topic, said mid-century reviewers.

and gloomy. He thought he had jaundice – though Dr Baldwin, to whom James mailed bottles of urine labelled 'a.m.' and 'p.m.', was not convinced. The invalid, whose appetite remained hearty, stayed in bed for sixteen days. Digestive ills, in James, were not straightforward. In youth, they had been an indication of mental malaise.

Fenimore, too, was unwell in the winter of 1887. She knew it was 'owing to mental depression'. When she heard from James, she took pity on him and offered shelter, which he accepted. He arrived at the Brichieri between 12 and 14 April. Her generosity, combined with the loveliness and comfort of his surroundings, changed his mood at once. His rooms, on the lower floor of the Brichieri-Colombi, looked through a single door and three arches to the Duomo and towers of Florence. As strength returned, he took to walking into town for his dinner and then, crossing the yellow Arno to the south side, making the long climb back in the golden light of the late afternoon. Guarding the house were two great pine trees, one on the right near the gate, and one to the left of the house as he came up the curving road. For Fenimore, there was something blessed about this climb. Returning dull or tired from town, she would lift her head and see 'that house stand out like some of the bulwarks of the Celestial City, in Pilgrim's Progress. Its site, at exactly the top of the hill, gives it a look, sometimes, of being in the sky.' James shared this lift of the spirit.

'I sit here making love to Italy,' he wrote on 24 April, to Gosse in London. 'At this divine moment she is perfectly irresistible, & this delicious little Florence is not the least sovereign of her charms. I am fixed, till June 1st, in a villa which in England would be suburban, but here is supercelestial, whence the most beautiful view on earth hangs before me whenever I lift my head . . .'

Fenimore had an even better view from three windows opening out on to a balcony which runs the whole width of the house. Like her 'sky-parlor' in Rome in 1881, and her top floor in Venice in 1883, the rooms she chose were high for the sake of light and sun. In spring, before the hot weather, the shutters would have been open to the sound of birds in the thickets below the house where the hill falls away to the right. She said she was happier with a home of her own than she had been for years. James was to remember the Bellosguardo days as 'probably, on the whole, the most charmed and appeased, the most gratified and rewarded and beguiled days that she . . . ever passed'. 'Florence is at present quite enchanting – Bellosguardo is still more so – & I am completely restored,' he wrote to Mrs Curtis in Venice. 'I have a vast & vaulted apartment in this old villa . . .'. His letters make no mention of company but breathe a response so sustained, so compelling, he almost fears it: the view before him was 'as *personal* – and as talkative! – as a lovely woman. . . . As soon as I can stop making love to it I shall go back to England . . .'.

Two people in the same house would have seen a good deal of each other, but this remained invisible. William was told only that his brother had taken rooms on Bellosguardo, and James went to extraordinary lengths to hide the set-up from two visitors. One was a robust Englishwoman, Rhoda Broughton, the same age as Fenimore and the prolific author of romances with titles like *Alas!* in three volumes. She was a little too curious about Miss Woolson for comfort. James tried to persuade her that he just happened to be there, and would not normally go out of his way to see Miss Woolson. When he wrote to Mrs Bronson of her kinswoman's visit to the Brichieri, he referred to his housemate as a 'neighbour', as though they weren't living under one roof: the visitor 'appeared here yesterday punctually to call on my neighbour Miss Woolson, on whom I was also calling'. You don't call on someone with whom you are staying.

Working fast over five and a half weeks, from 14 April to 24 May, James drafted *The Aspern Papers*, transposing Florentine matter to a Venetian setting (with Mrs Bronson as the prime American resident, 'Mrs Prest'). Finding himself on the crest of a new great phase, he entered on his longest house-visit to date. 'There is nothing personal or literary in the air,' he lied to Gosse (recalling the 'nothings' of his letters from Florence in 1880). The secrecy, the closeness to Fenimore, and the misunderstanding that could arise from their situation supplied a useful tension. To say more, to equate James with a narrator who is called a 'publishing scoundrel', does not allow for fictional licence. It has been assumed that the narrator speaks for James when he resists a proposal from Miss Tina ('I could not pay the price'), but this has served to prop a biographic premise for which there is no evidence, that Fenimore hunted a husband. Certainly, she wanted James in her own way, but not marriage. Miss Tina is unintellectual, lean, dingy, naïve, and domestically incompetent; Fenimore was the opposite. The source is not Fenimore herself but her portrait of Miss Grief and her aunt, two faded expatriates in Italy. Miss Tina has all the pathos of a Miss Grief divested of her genius and, with it, her strength and self-reliance.

James left the Brichieri on 24 May. One purpose may have been to take in impressions of Venice for final touches to *The Aspern Papers.* He intended to return to Florence in ten days for three to four more weeks. In the event, he did not return, and remained in Venice for five weeks (one of his habitual switches of plan). This time, he stayed with the Curtises at the Palazzo Barbaro, 'a magnificent old palace – all marbles & frescoes & portraits of Doges – a delightful habitation for hot weather'. He wrote in the library on the top floor, 'one of the wonderful faded back rooms . . . with a pompous Tiepolo ceiling and walls of ancient pale-green damask, slightly shredded and patched, which, on warm mornings, looked into the shade of a court where a high outer staircase, strikingly bold, yet strikingly relaxed, held together one scarce knew how; where Gothic windows broke out, on discoloured blanks of wall, at quite arbitrary levels, and where above all the strong Venetian voice, full of history and humanity and waking perpetual echoes, seemed to say more in ten warm words . . . than any twenty pages of one's cold pale prose.' Eventually, the palazzo was to be the setting for a dying heroine, exploited by the man she loves, in *The Wings of the Dove*.

This was the culmination of a fertile period when he gathered impressions for several works. He dined with Katharine Bronson and her daughter, Edith, in a gondola on a glassy lagoon, in the pink sunset, with boats floating by like phantom ships. His eight weeks next door to Mrs Bronson in February–March had allowed him to observe her situation as a 'still-living' widow recently freed from a hopeless marriage. In the late seventies, Mr Bronson had become deranged, and he spent his last years in Paris, while his wife and Edith, now a young woman in her early twenties, lived on in Venice. Arthur Bronson was never mentioned in his wife's circle of expatriate artists, exiled royalty, and old Venetian families who intermarried with foreigners. Then, in 1885, Bronson died, raising the question what his wife would 'do' with her future. What to 'do' was a question in women's lives that opened, for James, if not always for women, a vista of possibility. In reality, Mrs Bronson took up the destitute of Venice. Many gondoliers lived precariously: when winter or illness came, their families starved. Mrs Bronson did more than hand out money to charities; she learnt the local dialect and invited poor families to live in the upper rooms of the Alvisi in winter (to James, 'incubi' who 'squeezed and cramped' the place). She established schools for rudimentary education and repaired shrines. In the evenings, gondolas jostled under her windows to serenade her – to the irritation of James, who called her a 'nursing mother' to four-fifths of Venice. As he preferred to see it, the vista that opened to Katharine Bronson was 'humilation'.

In his notes for the 'K.B. Case', she finds herself without the suitor she desperately wants. In actual fact, Mrs Bronson had a suitor of sorts in Browning. It was rumoured they were engaged; Browning himself called her 'more than friend'. It was another uncategorisable relationship between a man and a woman that was bound to intrigue James, but the way his notes shape it in terms of a widow's stifled need may tell us more about his own relation to a Jamesian woman of his imagination than about Browning and Katharine Bronson. His mental note of 'humilation' in 'The K.B. Case', and Tina's humiliation when her offer is spurned, precede a story James heard in Venice, on 20 June, about a young Mlle S. who, desperate to escape her home, proposed to a man. Shamed when he did no rush to accept her, she 'jumped out of the window of an hotel at Milan in her night-dress at 6 o'clk., in the a.m. while in the delirium of a fever'.

This act of humilation became the *donnée* for *A London Life*, a tale of a high-minded American, orphaned, exiled and unsettled in London, and revolted by the adulteries and scandals of its society (based on the Prince of Wales' set). 'In my opinion, English "Society" is dreadfully corrupt,' Fenimore had written to the Mathers just before she left London. In Paris and Rome, corruption would be unconcealed; in England 'there is *always* an outside surface of morality and respectability. . . . I am merely a "looker on"'. This aversion and other elements of Fenimore – the seriousness of her London excursions, her unsettled habits, and her apartness (a 'candid outsider', as James put it in his preface) – went into a portrait of Laura Wing, who finds that corruption has infected the married sister with whom she lives. Desperate to escape, Laura Wing turns to Mr Wendover, a 'decent', unthreatening American – sheathed in the clear blue innocence of his coat. With the easy-going alacrity of American custom, he takes it for granted that he can go about with 'Miss Wing' without the slightest sense of paying her special attention. There is no sexual murmur in his consciousness. He associates with her in the brotherly way James and his circle would see the Temple sisters, Clover Hooper, and Fanny Dixwell, for years on end. Wendover, who has '*liked*' Miss Wing as a London resource, hesitates to take her on when she asks to be 'saved'. Here he is questioned by Lady Davenant, pressing him on Laura's behalf:

> 'I'm very sorry for her,' said Mr. Wendover, who seemed to wince and who spoke with a gravity that committed him to nothing.

The fiasco of Laura's overture fills her with 'horror' at her 'grotesque' need for responsive passion – for nothing short of that could save her from humiliation: 'The one thing that could have . . . tempered the grotesqueness of her monstrous overture, would have been, on his side, the quick response of unmistakable passion. It hadn't come, and she had nothing left but to loathe herself. She did so, violently . . .'.

James follows her to the edge of suicide: a wish to 'escape from herself – an object of which her horror was not yet extinguished'. She threatens repeatedly to kill herself – though, in the end, she flees to America. James thought a death-leap too unlikely.

Back in Florence, Fenimore was again 'ill'. With her, this meant depression. She told Dr Baldwin: '. . . if I could have a house twenty miles from everybody, & on the line of the equator, I have no doubt but that I should attain the health, & age, of the Pharaohs.' Yet this was not seasonal depression: it was high summer. After James left and failed to return, she felt the renewed impact of loneliness. He heard enough from her to feel concern, for he wrote to her doctor that 'she ought to go away in order to flourish when she comes back. I take for granted she is overworking – but her power to keep that up has long mystified me. Everything beyond three hours a day (with *continuity*), in the *sort* of work she does, is a nail in her coffin – but she appears to desire that her coffin shall have many! Please don't repeat this to her – I have bored her half to death with my warnings . . .'. He offered a hope that he would return to Florence the following spring.

If 'Miss Woolson' continued to rankle, this might explain her decision to go ahead with the publication of 'At the Château of Corinne' in October 1887. And if the story is read as a reply to 'Miss Woolson', we look harder at the adverse effect of the compatriot, John Ford, as he blights the inner conviction of the independent woman who lives for her writing. Here was another round in the battles of James and Woolson, behind their 'infinite charity'. James always showed concern for 'Fenimore'; it was disconcerting, then, to find that a rival had struck her down – had done so, while he lodged in her house and dined with her *à deux*. He, in turn, did not care for his image in the 'Château of Corinne'.

'Fenimore appears to be really better of her dreary autumn illness,' he wrote to Boott in January 1888, '& to be driving her pen for the public benefit, as I judge – for she doesn't drive it for mine.'

As James delivered this barb, he was conceiving 'The Lesson of the Master', in which the Master annihilates women writers in the imperious vein of Ford. Woolson writes a feminist parable for her time; James retorts with a cynical 'lesson': stir intensity, and then leave it, the Master counsels a young man on the verge of greatness. Stir all the passion you need, but do not commit yourself. The disciple, Paul Overt, asks if there is not an exception to the rule: a permanent ally. Women haven't a conception of artistic work, the Master asserts. 'Surely they on occasion work themselves,' objects his disciple. 'Yes,' replies the Master, 'very badly indeed.'*

James and Woolson stand opposed also on the matter of unacted desire. Woolson regards it as a drain on a woman's creativity;

* It might be argued that 'very badly' comes from a fictional character, but it fits the author's own stabs at women writers, as well as a fictional attack on one in 'Greville Fane'.

James finds, to the contrary, that desire invigorates art. 'At the Château of Corinne' explores the mounting pressure of imaginative desire, more dangerous than sex with its power to invade the mind – especially that of a woman, fixed in her household, cut off from her country, and without the saving distractions of an active life. Her feelings prey upon her. In the 'Master', James explores the need for 'masculine' experience – 'personal' as distinct from 'intellectual passion'. A writer who divests himself of 'the common passions and affections of men' in the service of art can become a 'disfranchised monk'. The cover of fiction allowed James to confront the issue of celibacy. Without a 'masculine' response, does art lose vitality in pursuit of formal perfection?

As James put this question, there loomed out of the past the image of Mary Temple, transformed as a 'motherless girl' called Marian who has recently returned to England from India: she has the freedom and radiant promise of the young Minny, with an appetite for life so 'natural' that she is 'life' itself. Though there are obvious affinities with other portraits of Minny as Bessie Alden and Isabel Archer, Marian has more of a bodily presence: an inviting ease. Paul 'tumbles' into the 'crystal' well of her sympathy, a comic immersion rather than the rapt, spectatorial possession James had taken of Minny after her death, when he fixed her, for ever, in the 'crystal' walls of the past.

The Master, Henry St George, warns Paul against this. Henry's enemy has been a classy wife whose support – in circumstances to which she is accustomed – has required him to sacrifice art for the marketplace. In this way, 'The Lesson of the Master' combats the lessons of Woolson's stories where the enemy of the woman writer is the dominant male in her own art, the very one she chooses as mentor and husband. Although opposed as man and woman, Woolson and James both point to the way marriage blights art.

Henry and Paul, the middle-aged novelist and the young star, are both drawn to a 'rare' woman invested with those attributes of Minny that would seem to fit her to be the one exception to the Master's rule that women are the enemies of art. She is a 'provincial of genius' who takes her perspective, as it were, from the top of the Himalayas. For the tried Master, as for the Master to come, she spurs the imagination, and gives so freely of her spirit that both writers reach out for her as the material of art – such a woman could be 'the glory of the novel'.

In obedience to the Master, Paul locks himself away in the Alps, near the prison of Chillon, with the snowline creeping towards him – here, cut off from domestic ties (somewhat like Frankenstein), he gives birth to his creation, an extraordinary offspring of an unmatched brain. Through the dedicated Paul, James questioned the result of deferring 'life' until it is too late to retrieve it, as hc had done when he stayed abroad, alone, in 1869. It is as though James at forty-five addressed a young James set apart from other men who strove to engage 'the heroine of the scene'. Through the more robust and seasoned Henry, he posed the gains of an active engagement with a woman who is a natural mate. For in defiance of his own lesson, the widowed Henry marries Marian, and in the face of his 'lesson' enjoys, in his middle years, a new lease. For years, James had built himself into the fortress of solitary genius, but at this moment he allowed an alternative to come back into play for the older man – if only in imagination. At the same time, he leans to the young author who follows the lesson and loses the girl. He does not minimise that loss: 'He had renounced her, yes; but that was another affair – that was a closed but not a locked door. Now he seemed to see the door quite slammed in his face.' It's not just the woman he loses; it's the 'life' she confers and the virility she would have shaped.

This tale burst the bounds of the genre with timeless issues James would pursue for years to come: the ambiguous issue of the creative life as non-life, and a subtler issue of corruption. Marian assures Paul that the creative life is, indeed, 'life' itself. As much as she is Henry's potential wife, she belongs to Paul in a different way: a soulmate who, alone of her sex, sanctions the vitality of solitude. Their 'full interchange' about the 'valid' work of art 'will have lived for years in this memory . . .'. *Will.* The tense changes as it engenders the future, lone but fertile in its own way. Marian understands his commitment to 'perfection' – and with this word, and sustained talk with a woman as interested as he in 'the business', James draws on Fenimore and her attunement to his 'perfect' art.

The conflict of man and artist, of desire and withdrawal, seems reasonable, given the material demands of marriage with all the trappings of the privileged class to which James belonged. Yet James – with truly wonderful honesty – explores motives that lie beyond reason in the region of 'corruption'. If the artist is not a man – 'mostly not', Henry thinks – what then is he? If the artist is to 'live' in the future, if he is to realise the creative passion at its most intense ('a passion', Henry says, 'which includes all the rest'), he has to pursue a false relation to others who must die. He cannot allow temporal affections to take hold. When they threaten to do so – when Paul is gripped by Marian – he must take himself off. These people are supposedly English, but the drama of corruption is pure New England – pure Hawthorne. We are in the purview of the Unpardonable Sin: 'Happy the societies in which [art] hasn't made its appearance, for from the moment it comes they have a consuming ache, they have an incurable corruption in their breast. Most assuredly is the artist in a false position!'

Between conceiving and publishing 'The Lesson of the Master', James mulled over the 'immensity' of his ambition: 'Sunday, March 11th 1888. Here I sit: impatient to work: only wanting to concentrate myself, to keep at it: full of ideas, full of ambition, full of capacity – as I believe. . . . There is an immensity to be done. . . . But all one's manhood must be at one's side. xxxxx.' All 'manhood' was reserved for work – a lesson identical to the lesson of the Master.

Henry St George is known for a novel called 'Shadowmere'. With this tale, Henry James, king of the shades, enters a farther shadowland between the visible promontories of life and art, an area which Woolson had pioneered already in her stories of artists. Starting three months after she published the 'Château of Corinne', he proceeded to colonise this territory. It was a move that renewed his art, and to this day he remains the acknowledged master of the artist tale.

Given his gift, it seemed unfair – outrageous – that writers of the second rank, some of them women, had a place in the market which continued to elude him. Fenimore had foreseen envy and tried to forestall it when she played down the sales of *Anne*. The unqualified success of her next meeting with James suggests she forgave him for 'Miss Woolson', while he went out of his way to make amends.

People in touch with Henry James lost sight of his movements towards the end of 1888. In July and August the 'Master' came out, with its question of marriage brooding over Paul Overt as he writes in Switzerland. In September, James announced a plan to go to Paris. In October he vanished – he was not in Paris but with Fenimore in Geneva.

They stayed on either side of the lake, not far from Fenimore's setting for the 'Château of Corinne' and the Clarens–Chillon setting for 'Daisy Miller' and the 'Master'. Complicating further the nuances of this encounter was a gift from James: an inscribed copy of *The Aspern Papers*, the product of their previous stay together. It was a working holiday: James was writing a theatre novel, *The Tragic Muse* (1889–90), with an actress heroine in whom Minny's friend would recognise something of her young self: 'The girl in her crudeness and strength of purpose and conceit is so like Helena!' James envisaged a portrait 'of the odd animal, the artist who happened to be born a woman', with her 'impulses and shynesses, audacities and lapses'. Miriam Rooth is a quintessential James heroine: unconventional, articulate, assured, bypassing the four square demands of the women's movement with what James calls a 'nature'. Woolson was writing *Jupiter Lights*, in which Eve, a mature and resolute woman, fights her 'abjection' to the man instinct compels her to love. Her yielding will is 'so humilating that she must hurt something; that something should be herself.'

'That excellent and obliging woman', James told Boott, 'is plying her pen hard on the other side of this lake and I am doing the same on this one. Our hotels are a mile apart but we meet in the evening . . .'. For some time, Boott was the only one to know of Fenimore's presence, and all that was revealed to him amounted to reassurance that proprieties were being preserved.

James arranged a set of misleading screens about himself and Fenimore. In an unpublished letter of 30 September he told Aunt Kate, 'About October 10th I expect to go abroad for about a month – most of which I shall probably spend in Paris. I haven't mentioned this to Alice as yet, but she will be sure to urge me to it, as she has a dread of weighing on me . . .' After two weeks in Geneva, he told William that on 10 October he had had a sudden impulse to take a break from 'stale, dingy London' in a quiet place suitable for work. Stressing how busy he was, he made no mention of Fenimore, and went so far as to assure William, 'I have no time for wanton travelling.' To most others, he gave out that his main destination was Paris, and for this reason it occurred to him to excuse himself (in another unpublished letter) to his Parisian friend Henrietta Reubell for failing to contact her: he told her truthfully that he 'stole round' Paris, touching only at two stations, en route for Geneva; then he screens his actions with another misleading intention: 'my odd & perverse taste for Geneva', he claimed, was nostalgia for a place where he had stayed at sixteen (in part of the same apartment in the Hôtel de l'Écu). Yet James had been distinctly miserable here in the winter of 1859–60 when he had dropped out of the Institution Rochette, his mathematical school. Since then, he had never much liked Switzerland. Now, his feelings changed.

He said, 'I have enjoyed this familiar place, in extraordinarily beautiful autumn weather, with Mont Blanc, day after day, literally hanging over the blue lake, more than I almost believed I could ever again enjoy anything Swiss.' He was doing some quiet work, he told Miss Reubell, 'taking some quiet walks, looking at the admirable blue gush & rush of the Rhône and at the chaine des Alpes, which has been, every blessed day, fantastically near, clear & fair'. There is, again, no mention of a companion. A long letter to Mrs Curtis in Venice on 30 October talks of everything but Fenimore: the hotel, his boyhood, his travel plans. He gives the impression he is alone, for his 'only complications' are to look at Mont Blanc. In one of his tales of this time, discretion forbids some people from staying at the same hotel on a foreign lake, and they find the same solution as he and Fenimore – to stay a mile apart. 'Nothing', James writes, 'would be easier than to go and come between the two points, especially by water . . .'

His most recent publication was *A London Life*, serialised by Scribner's from June to September. It is likely that in Geneva, or some time later (Geneva would have been the first opportunity), James told Fenimore the story of Mlle S. who threw herself out of the window in her nightdress, that part of his *donnée* which he had rejected as unlikely. It would have addressed their debate on the 'killing griefs' which Fenimore put forward, and James excluded.

The books James gave her were another subject for discussion: Augustine Birrell's life of Charlotte Brontë (1887), his *Obiter Dicta* (1887), and *Underwoods* by Robert Louis Stevenson (1887). Most of his presents over the years were books, and she tended to talk back in the margins. Birrell's indulgence of Lamb's drinking particularly annoyed her (given her brother's Branwellian history): 'O "Obiter Dicta," what a man you are!' she burst out.

For Christmas in 1887 James had sent her a two-volume life of Shelley by Ernest Dowden (published in 1886). In the second volume, there is an engraving of Shelley's grave in the Protestant Cemetery in Rome. James never lost a romantic fancy for this cemetery where Minny might have ended, like other consumptives (Keats being the most famous), in that walled-off, transported world at the bottom of the Aventine Hill, where expatriates lie in tight rows, at random – Protestants, English and American, Greek Orthodox, even lapsed Jews, anyone who was not a Catholic – under the solid-blue canopy of the Roman sky. This was the setting for the tragic climax of *Daisy Miller*: 'Winterbourne stood there beside [Daisy's grave]. . . .' When James first visited the cemetery, in the seventies, Shelley's grave was 'buried in roses'. The stones told stories of 'passionate grief': the mother of Miss Bathurst confides to every passing gaze her fresh, unmitigated despair for her daughter, drowned in the Tiber in 1824. James had felt suffused with fine scriptural language, the 'echoes of massive Latinity with which the atmosphere is charged'. So compelling is this atmosphere, he said (thinking of Shelley at the grave of Keats), it makes one 'in love with death'.

Death was a topic close to Fenimore's heart. She marked the seventeenth-century treatise on death, *Religio Medici* (inscribed 'Florence, 1887'). Unusually, she has lines along both margins for the following words: 'He forgets that he can die, who complains of misery: we are in the power of no calamity while death is our own.' In 1888 she acquired a new edition of the Stoic philosopher, Epictetus. Her copy of his *Teachings* has double lines in both margins where he offers a way out through voluntary death, when basic needs, including gratification of the senses, cannot be met: 'the door is opened, and God saith to thee, Depart.' Three pages are missing, cut, probably, by Clare Benedict, who inherited her aunt's books. There was an obvious reason to destroy them, for these are the vital pages that expound the philosophy of the 'open door':

> What is death? A bugbear. . . . Now or later that which is body must be parted from that which is spirit. . . . Why, then, hast thou indignation if it be now? For if it be not now, it will be later. And wherefore? That the cycle of the world may be fulfilled; for it hath need of a present and of a future and of a past. What is pain? A bugbear. Turn it about and examine it. This poor body is moved harshly, then again softly. If thou hast no advantage thereof, the door is open; if thou hast, then bear it. For in all events it is right that the door should stand open, and so we have no distress.

The interlocutor asks, 'Shall I, then, exist no longer?'

The answer is simple and consoling: '. . . Thou shalt exist, but as something else.'

Someone, presumably the person who cut these pages, has tried and failed to rub out Fenimore's marginal line next to the editor's endnote that accompanies them:

> The phrase of the 'open door' occurs frequently in Epictetus, usually . . . when he is telling the average nonphilosophic man that it is unmanly to complain of a life which he can at any time relinquish. . . . The Stoics taught that the arrival of this time might be indicated by some . . . affliction which rendered a natural and wholesome life impossible.

Fenimore took in this rational justification for suicide. It can't be known if she discussed it with James, but we do know he had read Epictetus, having reviewed an American edition in some detail in 1865. James disagreed with Stoicism. He thought it simplified human troubles.

'It fosters apathy and paralyzes the sensibilities. It is through the sensibilities that we suffer,' he conceded, 'but it is through them, too, that we enjoy; and when, by a practical annihilation of the body, the soul is rendered inaccessible to pain, it is likewise rendered both inaccessible and incompetent to real pleasure.'

He argued that this philosophy denied hope and implied 'utter immobility'. His hopefulness provided a counterweight to Fenimore's darkness. If she did turn an eye to the 'open door', it would explain a constant anxiety about her James claimed to have had.

It had been a shock to them both when Lizzie Boott had died, of pneumonia, suddenly, in March 1888. She left a boy of fifteen months to her bohemian husband and gentlemanly father – an odd pair to be bound together, through that child, for the rest of their lives. The glorious days of Bellosguardo were over. After forty years, Boott packed up and returned permanently to Cambridge, Massachusetts. Fenimore, too, had became restless.

In Geneva she spoke 'of giving up her villa', and returning to Florida. 'I can't imagine why,' James protested, 'unless to mortify the spirit.'

They spoke constantly of Boott and Lizzie. 'Fenimore's mind and talk are indeed full of her last year or two at Bellosguardo,' James told Boott. 'I questioned her so much on all this that that is partly why she dwelt upon it. But she cherishes the mystical survival there of dear Lizzie.'

A few days stretched to weeks, the end of October was approaching, and still James did not leave Geneva. Alice now became restive. Two months before James came to stay on Bellosguardo in the winter of 1886–7, Fenimore had foreseen the possibility that Alice would resist her, and a letter addressing her in a sidelong way through Katharine Loring had tried to appease and disarm the sharp-tongued invalid, bolstering her social achievements with the curates of Leamington, and inviting her too to Bellosguardo. The bait Fenimore had offered was her own renewed health in the balmy air:

> I am grieved to hear that Miss James has been suffering. Tell her that an exclamation burst from me irresistibly night before last – namely – 'I wish she were here this minute!' ... The broad doors [of the Brichieri] stood wide open; the moonlight outside lighted up my old garden, & the dark, rugged outline of Hawthorne's tower; perfume from a thousand flowers filled the room; & I was so happy to be here

> that it was almost wickedness! It seemed to me, then, that if Miss James's couch could be drawn across that door, she would enjoy it so much. And she would not be wicked. (I hear her exclaiming, 'Yes, I should!')

This is a very careful letter. Its wary tone, its strained jocularity, its rather too fervent benevolence, suggest that one did not tangle with Alice if one could help it. The letter asks indirectly: can Miss James match this benevolence in order to defuse ill-will? Alice was devoid of sentiment, formidable, exacting. Once, when Henry said 'I must tell you something' (actually, a surprise visit from William), she shrieked, 'You're not going to be married!' That negative carried force. Her claim on her last unmarried brother precluded a competing attachment. Years before, when William had denied her priority, when he had married in 1878 (a saving move for him backed by their parents), Alice had collapsed with threats of suicide. Fenimore rightly feared that Alice might resent her, and tried to forestall it – as it proved, in vain. Early in November 1888 Alice detected the presence of Fenimore in her brother's vicinity.

'Henry is somewhere on the continent flirting with Constance,' Alice warned William, as though it were more reprehensible – furtive is the implication – to do so on the Continent. Certainly, Switzerland, out of season, where they knew no one and no one knew them, was quieter than Florence or London or even Paris, where James was known to a good number of inhabitants.

Alice, in a 'porcupine fit', accused her brother of 'galavanting on the continent with a *she*-novelist'.

He protested that it was a 'mild excess'.

If not exactly an excess, it was a secret that could not have continued without becoming a matter of scandal, and any hint of scandal would have appalled two writers who shunned bohemianism. This is not to suggest any basis for scandal. James probably told Alice a partial truth when he said it was 'mild': what he would have intended to convey in the veiled language of respectability was that he and Fenimore were not lovers. Yet in an emotional sense, whatever took place between them was not 'mild', certainly not for Fenimore, who was said to be 'stormy' however sternly she controlled herself. Mildness may have directed their speech and manners, but rivalry hurled its darts, and the charge of reconciliation – projected, as on Bellosguardo, through a radiant landscape – suggests the reverse of mildness. Though Alice demeaned them as 'flirting', theirs was not a shallow relationship. James was with a 'dear' and 'intimate' friend.

Early in November they parted, with James dreaming of a visit to Italy late in the spring. Fenimore returned to Bellosguardo; James went on to Genoa, and from there to Monte Carlo and Paris. Though he had refrained from any mention of Fenimore when he had explained his stay in Geneva to Miss Reubell, he stressed that he was alone when he wrote on 19 November from Monte Carlo: 'There is no one here . . .'.

From Genoa (not from Geneva), he answered a letter from Rhoda Broughton which had pressed him about Fenimore. How was she? Could he pass on her address? In answer to these questions (implied, if not asked) James set up another misleading screen. He took the precaution of telling no lie yet managed to suggest that he had not seen Miss Woolson nor had any intention of doing so. Miss Broughton received a statement to the effect that he and 'Miss Woolson' were on formal terms, and had communicated at this time by post alone. If Rhoda Broughton had once found him in Miss Woolson's house, she should not deduce any habit of intimacy. 'I came abroad a month ago,' he wrote on 6 November, referring to 'a foreign land' and Italy with no mention of Geneva. 'Miss Woolson's address is Villa Brichiere, *Bellosguardo*, Florence. She is well and flourishing I know – but I have – this time – no hope of getting to Florence. I *may* go to Rome for a fortnight, straight from here along the coast.'

It was true that Miss Woolson was flourishing. Used to depression with its train of illness as winter came on, the change struck her as worthy of record: 'I am quite scandalously well this winter,' she told the Mathers, with no mention of James or Geneva. 'Have'nt had an ill moment; & am stout as can be.'

9
A Message from Alice

During the second great wave of his career, James had to contend with failure. As he approached the age of fifty in 1893, he could no longer fend off the fact that he had lost the appeal of his late thirties. No publishers, he said, 'will have anything whatever to say to me'. He confided this to Stevenson at a safe distance in the South Seas: 'Tell it not in Samoa – or at least not in Tahiti; but I *don't* sell ten copies! . . . I never mention it – nearer home.'

James was not quite the victim of the marketplace that he liked to pretend. He addressed publishers with professional acumen, and did not succumb to poor offers. His works had dual publication, first in magazines, then as books, and they came out promptly on both sides of the Atlantic. The problem was not the loftiness that he projected but its opposite: he would not relinquish his ambition to reach a popular audience. Big venture after venture failed, including an attempt to establish himself as a playwright, which ended with humiliation: he was booed by the gallery on his opening night in January 1895 as he came forward on the stage to take a bow. And yet these middle years, from 1889 to 1896, saw a group of tales which are amongst his greatest works: 'The Lesson of the Master', 'The Private Life', 'The Middle Years', 'The Death of the Lion', and 'The Figure in the Carpet'. His subject is a writer who conquers despair with private triumphs in the face of an oblivious multitude, the James who said: 'I am working with patient subterraneity at a trade . . . supremely dangerous and heroically difficult'.

Here is the fighting man with all manhood at his side. What the tales don't show is a rage of depression revealed to intimates. At its height, in the first half of 1893, he was able to fall back on Fenimore.

For three years, from May 1890 to May 1893, she was back in England. After a year on Bellosguardo, she had begun to resent the intrusions of Florentine society. She had stayed for another two years, and during the season of 1889 had felt obliged to open the Brichieri for the first time: she held a tea, with dancing in bonnets and jackets downstairs, while she received upstairs in her drawing-room. All through that spring she continued to hold 'reception days' for people she loathed – 'loathed', James reported to Boott, a strong word to use to a gentleman of exquisite refinement, but passed on with the sympathy of a fellow-sufferer who was to write a tale about an author done to death by indefatigable celebrity hunters ('The Death of the Lion').

At forty-nine, Fenimore was still eligible, to judge from an item of gossip in May 1889 that intrigued James. One 'F.L.' seems to have assumed, mistakenly, that Boott was matchmaking on his behalf. 'Be polite – be merciful, to a Bore,' James wrote to Boott, '– to have it said you wish to lead him to the altar! What an example of the sapient idiocy of human judgments. I believe Fenimore *loathes* F.L.!'*

A consolation was her friendship with Dr Baldwin, whose 'kind visits', she told him, 'cheered me mentally'. He relieved the burden she carried wherever she went, a belief in her unlovability. An unaccustomed content with her appearance comes through a letter Fenimore wrote to him from Venice on 13 July 1889:

> I float; and float; and float. I wish you were here to float too! The warm salt air just suits me. I wear muslin dresses and a broad-brimmed hat, and shoes a size too large; and the result is cool tranquility. To-night, as the moon is full, I am going, alone, (with two gondoliers, so as to go fast) away out on the lagoon to an island called 'St George of the Seaweed'. There is nothing especial to see, I believe, but an old shrine; but it will be a voyage of three or four hours far out on this lovely moonlit water, away from the town. I go alone from choice. But I would take *you* – if you were here.

* There are various candidates for F.L. in HJ's notebooks and letters, for example Mr Frank Loring of Massachusetts, whose frosty manner was the model for Mr Wentworth in *The Europeans* (HJ to LB, 30 Oct 1878), but it is impossible to be certain.

For a space, 'tranquility' pushed back depression. Travel, walking, and now 'floating', were all, in a sense, remedies, and Baldwin, too, was a remedy. With him she felt easy, expansive, wanted – the best of cures. She ended, 'Your attached friend'. To Mrs Baldwin, she ended, 'Cordially'.

Her preference for men is always there. She did like Lizzie Boott and Ariana Curtis, encouraged by their links with James. She did undertake the odd letter to a female schoolfriend or relative, but no sustained correspondence of the kind that deepens ties. She saw herself as a professional, and sought out professionals, craving a support that never quite sufficed. Instead, she became plaintive or restless, with whims to go round the world. Her homelessness was a perpetual search for 'peace of mind'.

She moved from Venice to Richmond on the outskirts of London (for September–October 1889), to Paris (for the rest of October), back to the Brichieri to pack and move out (once more in the grip of depression), and then, from December to April 1890, took off with her sister for points east: Brindisi, Corfu, Athens, and finally Cairo – disappointed, at first, to find Cairo in January less warm – that is, less healing – than Florida.

'I saw Henry James in London,' she reported to Baldwin. 'He looks remarkably well, having lost flesh; he is writing hard; and seeing many people – as usual.' In much the same way as James reported on her to Boott, she reported on James to Baldwin: both did so with scrupulous respect for the other's privacy. These reports indicate reunions, at intervals, and between reunions a continuous correspondence of which not a word was to survive. On 11 January 1890, James reports to Boott on Fenimore's departure from Bellosguardo, stressing the extent of her hoardings:

> ... The rupture of our last tie with that consecrated spot has really taken place – in the unmitigated secession of our (apparently) so deeply-rooted Fenimore.... At the last she left Florence with (seemingly) a kind of loathing: loathing, I mean, for the crowd, the interruptions and invasions, ... and the conditions consequent upon her extravagant propensities for 'packing' – the most envious virtue that ever a woman was cursed with, and the blight of her whole existence. It appears to have taken her upwards of two months of

incessant personal labour, night and day, to get out of a Brichieri bed or two. But she is out now, evidently never to return....

While she lingered in Cairo, preferring its orientalism to Greek classicism ('Grecian things are too perfect for me. Perhaps if I had a classic nose myself, I should enjoy them more'), James planned a visit to 'the blessed Bellosguardo', 'the haunted Bellosguardo'. He was in his element in the act of recollection, hoarding memories as Fenimore hoarded old spoons and bits of tapestry. As he set out that April, he braced himself for 'the totality of the change' in their old place. 'I shan't even find our modern Fenimore there – our modern Fenimore having gone in for the hoary past & spent the winter ... in Egypt & the Holy Land. Where she may be now I know not', he continued to Boott on 23 April, 'she was at Cairo (alone, after the departure of her sister,) a month ago. She comes to England, I believe, for the summer – but spends it somewhere in the provinces – I believe she thinks of Bath.'

In the end she chose Cheltenham, and at the start of May settled in a terraced house behind a double row of trees with shops conveniently opposite. As usual, she chose the upper floors; below was a gentleman in a scarlet coat with splendid horses, who had come for the hunting season. Cheltenham was a spa with 55,000 inhabitants, mostly retired Indian officers and civil servants. Lonely as ever, she resolved to write to neglected contacts in America. Answers came, but they left her sad, for she saw they had been an effort. 'Of course', she thought, 'I can expect nothing else, as I have been away over ten years. To most people that seems half a lifetime! But, as I never change myself, it does not seem so to me.'

Meanwhile, James stood beside Lizzie's grave in the Allori Cemetery in Florence. Bellosguardo was now 'all ghosts and glorious views'. He wrote to Fenimore at her new address, 4 Promenade Terrace, and urged Boott to make the three-hour train journey to visit her '*without fail*' when he came to London that summer. Baldwin too came to London in August (staying with James), and Fenimore begged him to visit her 'dingy' dining-room in 'a provincial Promenade'. It proved 'a *great* refreshment' to see him. She suggested he make notes with a view to Reminiscences when he was seventy-five and all the actors were dead. The actors included, presumably, herself and Henry James. In this sidelong way Fenimore did license a posthumous disclosure of their tie by a man sympathetic to her.

After Baldwin returned to Florence, James reported on 29 September a most lovely Sunday with Miss Woolson, who seemed in very good case, while she reported on 5 October: 'Henry James came down here & stayed two days; & we went to Worcester. . . . I have been up to town for a little amusement also.' James teased Rhoda Broughton that 'Another' was beside him at the theatre to see Irving's *Ravenswood*. Fenimore had a *rapprochement* with Alice, helped by friendliness to Katharine Loring and an offer to explain her distance from women: 'Do not suppose . . . that I think the feminine mind inferior to the masculine. For I do not. But it has been kept back, & enfeebled, & limited, by ages of ignorance, & almost servitude.' She was aware that James would report on her, and asked Miss Loring if 'Mr. James has given a good account of me? If he mentions me as "worthy", let me know in private, that I may think of a revenge.'

His first concern, as winter came on, was his sister. Of her, there was 'nothing good to say'. He wrote to Boott 'from the midst of the black fog-life of London where we grope with glimmering lamps. I spend the winter & Alice spends the winter. . . . Our friend Fenimore hybernates [*sic*] at Cheltenham . . .'. During eight weeks of cold weather in December–January, Fenimore had twinges of 'the ache that stops my pen' (head- or earache), but Baldwin, she told him, had exorcised the 'big pains' of depression. James made a detour to see her on the night of Monday 5 January 1891, after a dramatisation of *The American* opened in Southport, near Liverpool, for its preliminary run in the provinces. We know he spent that night in Cheltenham because he told Alice to telegraph there as to her condition. To William he was more secretive: 'I paid a country visit after leaving Southport . . .'. No other hint remains of this visit save the fact that James showed Fenimore a draft of another play, *Mrs. Vibert*, his first original script. She thought it 'very striking'. He was physically well, she reported to Baldwin, 'but the feeble state of Miss James, who has seemed to be almost in a dying condition for months, is a great depression, of course, to the brother'.

Alice was now living near him in Kensington, first in the South Kensington Hotel, then from March 1891 in Argyll Road, in a house covered back and front in Virginia creeper, and opening to the sound of rooks in Holland Park. It was 'a blessing', he said, to have her near him, under the ceaseless care of her friend. It would be 'inhuman' to leave Alice, Katharine had told him. He understood that the family owed this woman a debt it could never repay: 'No one will fully know the long years of inestimable and disinterested devotion that she gave up to [Alice].'

Alice was more and more ill, though her powers of resistance, he observed, 'are as marvellous (in perpetual pain) as they are involuntary – for she only wants to have done with it, naturally'. Alice could joke, 'I am working away as hard as I can to get dead as soon as possible, so as to release Katharine.... The trouble seems to be there isn't anything to die of...'

In fact, there was a tumour in her breast which had spread to her liver. Dr Baldwin diagnosed it in the summer of 1891. His 'theory' about her, which he exuded from every pore, grasped her as a whole, not as an assortment of ills as did other doctors 'sicklied o'er with bed-side manner'. Baldwin was the only doctor Alice ever liked. She thought him 'inspiring', and discussed her impending death – including the use of morphine for the pain in her breast – as calmly as if she were talking of Queen Elizabeth. There would now be a fixed limit to endurance. She welcomed her end with relief and even exhilaration, eager to record in her diary the expansion of her consciousness as it approached its release from the 'grotesque obstructions supposed to be life'.

Her diary tells us that living, for Alice, ended in the chrysalis. Existence after adolescence, as she saw it, was the shrivelling of an empty pea pod. When William had paid her a swift visit in 1889, following a separation of nearly five years, she had recorded the 'illusion' of greening with restored life: 'What a strange experience it was, to have what had seemed so dead and gone all these years suddenly bloom before one, a flowing oasis in this alien desert.' Henry, it seems, could not do this for her – him, she loved for his intellect and virtue: 'At the risk of stirring Wm.'s evil passions I will state that Harry's virtues transcend as ever the natural.' But William of the evil passions, who could charm 'a treadmill', gave off a *family* perfume so 'exquisite' that life, dread life, seemed to stir in her again. When he came into her room, he found her lying in bed 'white as a sheet, with outstretched arms into which I threw myself . . .'. She seemed as witty as ever but the sarcasm which had jarred him in her letters struck him differently when '*uttered* in the softest most laughing way in the world.' The 'electric current', he felt, 'is closed between myself & sister . . .'. He seemed to her 'born afresh every morning'; she seemed to him like 'bottled lightning'. Yet she made herself 'a polished steel mirror' to William's 'manifestations of tenderness', compelling him to give up his courtly style for 'the major key' which, he told her, 'your invincible and amazonian spirit deserves'.

For decades she had wanted to die but found that to 'get dead' was 'the hardest job of all' – a feat to be measured against William's *Principles of Psychology* (1888) and Henry's *Tragic Muse* (1889–90). When she declared this on 16 June 1891 she had been keeping a diary for two years. 'Arm yourself against my dawn, wh[ich] may at any moment cast you & Harry into obscurity', she joked to William. Unknown to her brothers, who pitied her, she approached death as a creative act: her feat, recorded with Jamesian eloquence, was to intensify consciousness until she became 'a concentrated essence in this curtailment'.

To do this, she had to overcome a lifetime of 'moral discords and nervous horrors'. Alice had to search all day for the precise words to explain a lifelong fear of a state of mind that would 'sear the soul', a precondition for a feat of transcendence. Her diary of the last three years of her life (1889–92) proved her the purest native of the James family. For it followed a philosophy their father had devised to contain 'horrors' and, more, to make a virtue of them – the ultimate triumph, of course, was to make use of them as the material of psychology, philosophy, diary, and fiction. As Henry James explained, 'we had only to *be* with more intelligence and faith . . . in order to work off . . . the many-sided ugliness of life.' This was achieved not only by enjoyed contact and communication, but also by enjoyed pangs, 'since pangs and agitations, the very agitations of perception itself, are of the highest privilege of the soul'.

Alice, like Minny, 'shone' in the presence of mortality. They came into their own – as though, looking into the face of death, they could strip their natures and stand clear. Alice dismissed William's words of pity; she told him, 'Kath. & I roared over the "stifling in a quagmire of disgust, pain & impotence," for I consider myself one of the most potent creations of my time'. Henry was keener to meet potency with his alertness to where the evolution of the species might go – into consciousness and further powers of communication. It became, for him, an alternative mystery to that of faith, and he took to women who advanced with him into this mystery – provided always that they kept it secret.

Alice amazed her brothers. 'Your fortitude, good spirits and unsentimentality have been simply unexampled in the midst of your physical woes,' William wrote to her; 'and when you're relieved from your post, just *that* bright note will remain behind, together with the inscrutable and mysterious character of the doom of nervous weakness which has chained you down for all these years.'

Alice dictated to 'Kath' a brilliant reply:

41, Argyll Road
Kensington, W.
[London]
July 30 [1891]

My dearest William,

A thousand thanks for your beautiful & fraternal letter....

It is the most supremely interesting moment in life, the only one in fact, when living seems life, and I count it as the greatest good fortune to have these few months so full of interest & instruction in the knowledge of my approaching death. It is as simple in one's own person as any fact of nature, the fall of a leaf or the blooming of a rose, & I have a delicious consciousness, ever present, of wide spaces close at hand, & whisperings of release in the air.

Your philosophy of the transition [from life to another form of being] is entirely mine & at this remoteness I will venture upon the impertinence of congratulating you upon having arrived 'at nearly fifty' at the point at which I started at fifteen! – 'Twas always thus of old, but in time, you usually, as now, caught up.

But you must believe that you greatly exaggerate the tragic element in my commonplace little journey; .... notwithstanding the poverty of my outside experience I have always had a significance for myself, & every chance to stumble along my straight & narrow little path, & to worship at the feet of my Deity, & what more can a human soul ask for?

This year has been one of the happiest I have ever known, surrounded by such affection & devotion, but I won't enter into details, as I see the blush mantle the elderly cheek of my scribe. . . .

Your always loving & grateful sister
Alice James. . . .

Henry James was 'prostrated' by flu that summer, so he told Fenimore, and ordered to the coast. Though reluctant to leave Alice, he went to Ireland and remained away till August. During this time, Fenimore nearly abandoned England, when she happened to visit Oxford for a few days. It caught her fancy, and she moved there instead.

At this time of transition, she had one of her bouts of homesickness: 'I should like to go home for six months & re-dip myself in the old atmosphere. My relations came very near to buying back the sturdy, if rather ugly, old stone house in Cooperstown, which was built for my grandmother & given to her on her wedding day. It was in the market for a low price, & they thought of securing it & giving it to me. This may be my end yet. But I should like to get in some years of Venice, before I retire to Otsego county.'

James was in touch with her shifting plans. He thought Oxford 'a very right & good place for her. She believes she is then – after a year again going to Italy to spend the rest of her life,' he reported to Boott. 'I haven't either seen or heard of her "Bellosguardo story", but shall demand of her to send it to me. . . . She has been working for a year, hard, at Cheltenham & there will doubtless be soon, for a good while, a good deal to show. Her power of lonely industry is as remarkable & admirable as ever.' Six months before, Baldwin had revived her nostalgia for Bellosguardo when he told her he had seen her villa like 'a palace of pure gold, floating in the sunset sky', and there flashed before her a memory of the house waiting at the top of the hill like a bulwark of the Celestial City: 'Would that I could have stayed there!'

*

Her story 'Dorothy' is an elegy to Bellosguardo: it is haunted by a song of grief, 'Through the Long Days', with words by Hay and music by Boott, which Fenimore used to play and hum while she lived on Bellosguardo. In the story, Felicia, an unappealing single woman, plays the song, looking up at Mackenzie, a middle-aged bachelor who listens to women with a bend of his head. Felicia tries to work off her feelings with long walks through the Arno Valley, returning red-faced, unlovely – and still unsatisfied.

An expatriate tea party at the Dorio (a replica of the Castellani complete with view and parapet) sets the scene for what appears to be a comedy of manners: mainly, the manoeuvres of single women with an eye to Mackenzie, and suitors in love with Dorothy, a popular, cheery American girl. The vast Dorio, aligned with the girl's name, is largely unoccupied. It has been leased in its entirety by her aunt and stepmother, habitués of an American élite which manifests the same complacent oblivion we find, later, in Edith Wharton. Dorothy and Mackenzie marry, but when Mackenzie dies suddenly, Dorothy's aunt and stepmother assume that a rich widow of nineteen, who has made one advantageous marriage, will proceed to a second – after a suitable show of mourning. But Dorothy fades with the refrain of 'Through the Long Days' on her lips. None of the usual distractions – jolly visits from ex-suitors, a jaunt to the south of France – deflect her grief: she is on course for death.

So, a comedy of manners turns into a mystery: a question of death that starts, of course, with the character of the person who dies. The challenge is similar to the death of Daisy Miller: ostensibly, Daisy dies of Roman fever, Dorothy of inconsolable grief, both deaths unexpected in view of their vitality and apparent shallowness. What is not revealed is some part of consciousness that determines death – a space invisible to society and unknown to medical practice. The final words of the story negate the possibility of diagnosis: 'But the doctor did not know.' At nineteen, Dorothy becomes a shadow attached to a posthumous bond – like the author's sister Emma, who died at nineteen, a few months after the death of her husband. 'Dorothy' is more than a 'Bellosguardo story'; it is Woolson's distillation of the 'killing griefs'.

Dorothy's death is forecast by a scene at the outset. At the Dorio, a group of young women look at the view from the parapet, each characterised in terms of how they might negotiate 'its dizzy outer descent'. Since the wall is breast-high, it is clear that to fall would be no accident. Sturdy English girls would fall like rocks, but Dorothy would float: 'her supple figure conveyed the idea that she would fly – almost – so lightly was it poised upon her little feet; in any case, one felt sure that even if she should take the fancy to throw herself off, she would float to the lower slope as lightly as thistledown.' Some of 'Dorothy' was fiction, but its blood coursed through an autobiographical vein: the author's favourite song, her memory of her sister's death, and most of all that fancy about the parapet,* in line with her eye to 'sky'-rooms, promontories, cliffs, mountains, and ledges – going back to 1874 and her eye to the narrow cliff road, overhanging a river ten feet below, along which a younger, intrepid Connie drove through the darkening day, with her old mother in the wagon, on her way from Asheville to Atlanta.

She put down in Oxford on a Friday night, 23 July 1891, at 13 Beaumont Street. The rooms were small and the cooking 'of the most primitive, watery, British description'. For the rest of the summer she rented a place from Oriel College at 15 Oriel Street: a low-beamed house, five hundred years old, which seemed 'the essence of old Oxford'. It looked across a quiet square to Corpus Christi College, the back gate of Christ Church, and Oriel to the left. James visited her there, on 26 August, in the still of the long vacation; and she had the pleasure of another visit from Dr Baldwin, who stayed nearby, at the Mitre, an inn dating back to the twelfth century.

Part of her pleasure in Baldwin was talking of James, mainly, at this moment, *The American*. She had seen a provincial performance where the acting did not equal the writing. Now, she informed Baldwin, it was to be produced 'very brilliantly', with a young Kentucky actress, Elizabeth Robins (1865–1957), a champion of Ibsen and women's rights. Fenimore attended the opening night in London on 20 October 1891, seated amongst jewelled women in

* A standard volume on *Notable American Women* has it that in her late stories the settings are 'more decorative than integral' and the characters 'not strongly individualized'.

pink and blue satin. James, taking a bow at the end, was 'quiet and dignified'. On 14 November, she went up to London once more to be present at the fiftieth performance 'before a crowded and brilliant house'.

There was talk of their doing a play together, the only time James ever considered collaboration. It never happened, not surprisingly in view of 'The Private Life', a tale James conceived in July–August 1891 and published in April 1892: for the novelist and dramatist Clare Vawdrey, the creative life is a faceless life, a back turned behind a closed door. It cannot be shared.

The writer in this fable is a dual figure. There is the visible gentleman, the pink of propriety, who offers inoffensive banalities on a terrace in Switzerland, and there is the writer engaged in the creative act, who is invisible. An actress, Blanche Adney, is told he is writing a play for her, and sends the narrator to check Vawdrey's desk while he does his social turn. As the narrator enters, he is astonished to find someone there – a dim figure he cannot discern. It is the writer. He is never, in fact, *not* there, intent on work even as he idles outside on the terrace chatting to people who will fill hundreds of pages in biographic tomes.

'The Private Life' is a ghost story. For the dim outline glimpsed through the dark of Vawdrey's room is that part of him that will outlive his time. As he writes, he exists beyond time; while the Vawdrey outside on the terrace is a convenient stand-in who gets through with living as best he can: 'The world was vulgar and stupid, and the real man would have been a fool to come out for it when he could gossip and dine by deputy.'* The social façade fits reports of James in the nineties: he was 'very good-looking' but somehow unmemorable. The bared, monumental face of the James we recognise, was not 'delivered' until the last fifteen years of his life. In the 1890s, as long as James wore a beard, it was not as yet in evidence, 'so that for the greater part of his life he went about in disguise', as an acquaintance, Graham Robertson, observed. 'It was as though, when looking round for a face he had been able to find nothing to his taste and had been obliged to put up with a ready-made "stock" article.' Robertson's mother, a keen reader of James,

* Originally, James had Browning in mind, but Browning had none of Vawdrey's contempt for the vulgar and stupid.

used to complain, 'I always want so much to talk with him, yet when I meet him I never can remember who he is.' This is Vawdrey, for sure, who passes for . . . what he passes for. It is the ghostly figure who 'explained everything': the 'real man' is 'the other self', the 'alternate identity' – the rest is show.

The counterpoise to the private life is the public performer: Lord Mellifont is a vacant shell who cannot exist outside society. He has no 'private life', and his wife is as miserable as any wife can be. James gives the source for Lord Mellifont as 'F.L.', possibly the same 'F.L.' who presumed himself put forward as Fenimore's suitor and whom, James said, she 'loathed'.

In the autumn, with the start of term, Fenimore moved back to Beaumont Street, and settled for the rest of her time in Oxford at number 15: an elegant town house, looking towards the eighteenth-century vista of St John's Street. Her landlady, a former schoolmistress called Mrs Phillips, proved kind and 'devoted'. Her husband was the steward of Exeter College, so Fenimore had dishes from the college cook and, if needed, a college waiter.

Winter was always, for her, the risky time. Alice was in the final stages of cancer, and it is unlikely her brother could have spared concern for anyone else. Her *force d'âme*, he observed, was extraordinary. For Alice, death was not an end; it was 'going' or 'the moment of transition' – to what order of being, she was too rational to assume. It was a 'Mystery', the greatest. She craved death in the flesh, since what she had once felt herself to be was long dead: she spoke of 'killing' that self between the ages of twelve and twenty-four. Her diary sanctions suicide in humorous terms: 'I shall proclaim that any one who spends her life as an appendage to five cushions and three shawls is justified in committing the sloppiest kind of suicide at a moment's notice.' Secrecy, she deplored. 'What a pity to hide it, every educated person who kills himself does something towards lessening the superstition.' Far from shame, she thought it 'heroic to be able to suppress one's vanity to the extent of confessing that the game is too hard'. During February 1892, the dying Alice sent cheering messages to Fenimore, who had no prospect of release from a trouble which became, that winter, almost unendurable.

To improve her hearing, she had been persuaded to try a new invention: artificial eardrums. In January a flu epidemic had swept Oxford so severely that, for the first time in living memory, term was postponed. Fenimore was sure she hadn't had it, yet she was in pain, 'infernal' pain ('I can use no milder word'), first in her head, then successively in both ears. The local doctor thought her pain 'neurotic'. She believed it came from an infection of 'those artificial drums'. In increasing distress, she dosed herself with sleeping draughts.

'One night, I thought I should be mad, or dead, before morning,' she told Dr Baldwin on 5 February.

In intervals from pain, she tried to invent travel plans. She'd go to India. No, round the world. She'd return to America, and divide the summer between the Mathers' house on Lake Erie, Mackinac, and 'dear little Cooperstown'. Then Florida for the winter – perhaps she'd stay. 'If I do'nt,' she considered, 'I'll bring over my silver, linen, books . . . & settle in Venice forever.'

This was her fourth week of pain. England seemed like a continuous funeral with the ravages of 'the Plague' on all sides, cold, black fogs, and the death of Prince Eddie which put the whole country into black.

'Illness is so depressing to me, that it is only by constant reading – forced reading – and by sleeping draughts that I get on at all,' she continued the next day to Dr Baldwin. 'That sounds rather bad, does'nt it. And probably I do'nt really mean it. Very likely if the house should take fire, I should be the first to make a desperate effort to escape! . . . Alice lives, and even enjoys, for every now & then I get a witty message from her. If she had had any health, what a brilliant woman she would have been. Henry J. has not, so far, had a second attack of the Plague. But both of his servants have had one; and life in De V[ere]. Gardens has been a good deal mixed. – As I write, the pain has begun again – like a knife – in the left ear. . . . I cannot long stand this sort of pain.'

The 'intense, stabbing pain' went on for two more days. She doctored her ear with linseed poultices every fifteen minutes. In a 'low state of depression', she tried to convince herself the left ache would be over in a few days, as the right now was.

'The loss of time preys upon me most of all,' she told her

nephew. 'I try not to think of it. I read & read. And when I no longer do that, I even play solitaire!' She played 'drearily', with a tear-stained face, as she sat on the rug with an atlas propped on her knees and the poultice equipment on a tray at her side.

'I never play games you know,' she reminded Sam, 'so when I play solitaire, it is desperation indeed.'

Sam invited her to spend the summer in Newport. She refused because, she felt, every moment must go to completing *Horace Chase* in time for serialisation to begin in December. She had already postponed this a year, and feared *Harper's* would lose patience: 'I must keep my engagement fully & promptly this time.'

In this novel, she touches again on the impulse to fall from a height. Jared Franklin, who has gone mad, sways unsteadily on the steep incline of a rooftop. Death stares up at him: 'the cruel pavement below was stone'. Woolson told Kate Mather that this portrait was 'more or less from life'. Franklin is saved by Horace Chase, the millionaire, but dies soon after because he is 'played out'. His sister, Ruth, the millionaire's wife, falls for a man who cares nothing for her, and when she discovers this she, too, has the impulse to drop. Woolson imagines a despairing woman with 'just life enough left' to plan her end: 'Then she looked towards the verge; her hurrying steps took her thither. Sitting down on the edge, she let herself slip over, holding on by a little sapling. It broke and gave way. And then the figure in the dark riding-habit . . . disappeared.'

The next chapter reveals this was not a death-drop, more a slide into a dark hollow, as buried feelings possess her. In the end, Chase reappropriates his wife. Ruth returns to her idle, protected life as the 'little girl' of a man of action, his diversion and diamond-studded ornament, her womanliness not refined away by 'over-development' of the mental powers. For many readers this would seem a happy outcome; for the more discerning, it's a return to a doll's house.

On Friday 4 March 1892, Alice dictated the final entry in her diary: 'I had almost asked for K.'s lethal dose,' she said, 'but one steps hesitantly along such unaccustomed ways and endures from second to second.' Pain fell away like 'dry husks' from the mind, while hypnosis, conducted by Kath, held off the 'horrors'. Kath entered wholly into what Alice called her 'mortuary inclinations' and her welcome of 'the wonderful moment' on 4 March when she felt herself 'floated for the first time into the deep sea of divine cessation'. Kath notes that although she was very weak and it tired her much to dictate, she could not get her head quiet until she had it written: 'then she was relieved and I finished Miss Woolson's story of "Dorothy" to her.'

To read the death of Dorothy to the dying Alice was, of course, no idle choice. The two are linked by the fact that Dorothy wished to die, as did Alice; and by the associated fact that Dorothy's death remains a mystery. For these deaths had less to do with the flesh than with the creation of consciousness. Woolson provides the missing link between the dying Dorothy and the dying Alice: there was something Alice wished to say to Woolson. It became clear as she listened to the end of 'Dorothy', for it impelled her to send its author a last message. Alice died unconscious on Sunday 6 March 1892: the last two acts of her life were to hear the end of 'Dorothy' and to send her message to Fenimore. The message has not survived, but it was not trivial, because Fenimore kept it secret. There would have been no need for secrecy had Alice simply approved the story. The importance of the message may be gauged from the fact that, a year later, Fenimore forgot herself for once and blurted it out to her nephew and his half-brother, Will Mather, when they came to England the following spring. Afterwards, she excused herself as for a lapse. Her excuse, on 29 April 1893, is sole evidence of the message, and without the message itself the context of her excuse is telling. The context is Henry James.

By April 1893 Fenimore had resolved to return to Italy the following month. 'You will see in all this', she wrote to Sam Mather, 'that I am giving up being near my kind friend Mr. James.' She went on: 'I don't know what made me tell you and Will that last message of his sister to me, that touched me so much. But I suppose it was simply the relief of having some of my own family to talk to, after being so long alone. I felt that I could say anything to you, without having to think whether it was safe or not, wise or not, prudent or not. – But Mr. James will come to Italy every year. And perhaps we can write that play after all.'

The message was passed on by the faithful Kath. If there was a letter it has not, so far, come to light, and could have been destroyed along with other papers. Still, there are three possible clues to the content of the message. Separately, they are easy to overlook, and take on significance only together.

One clue is Fenimore's statement that her main concern in leaving England was leaving 'my kind friend, Mr. James'. The second clue is that what James missed most in the loss of his sister was a model for dealing effectively with 'the disappointment and depression' of his existence. No one was better adapted than Fenimore to replace Alice in this role. It cannot be proved but seems likely that Alice gave assent to a prime attachment which her own claim on James would have precluded so long as she lived.

The final clue must lie in 'Dorothy'. Imagine Alice, a riddle to doctors, longing all those years for death, and then, when she is thankful that release is near, she heard a story of a woman who defies life with an illness that baffles all about her. Her lips, like those of Alice, remain sealed: the depths of her nature remain a mystery except for the fact that she has no use for uncomprehending guardians: aunt, mother, doctor. Dorothy's author had grasped the buried power at the heart of trauma, and, as Alice listened, it came to her, I think, to resign her brother to Fenimore's care. Expert in grief, infinite in charity, Fenimore might take on the 'griefs, or aches or disappointments' of her brother's life. She would be, like Alice, a repository for the James malaise.

All bearers of the blood royal struggled with dark patches for longer or shorter periods, infecting those about them. William, the most captivating of the Jameses, had the most infective power, which may be the deep reason that Henry and Alice had to distance themselves if they weren't to go under in his proximity. His visits to them on the rare occasions he passed through England were oddly brief. William's wife could not avoid the infection, sturdy as she was: there is a statement by William James to the effect that Alice (his wife) had 'fits of morbid low spirits and depression about herself, which sometimes get very acute'. The creative energy in this family was closely interfused with what Alice (the sister) defined as 'moral discords and nervous horrors'.

Fenimore, a lifelong victim of depression, had, like Alice, the *force d'âme* to be a fighter in the dark gulf, and this may be one reason James visited her more often after his sister's death. He went to Oxford on 17 March (eight days after Alice's cremation), on 18 May, and on 5 June. That June, Fenimore retold the 'The Lesson of the Master' from the point of view of a woman in a warning story called 'In Sloane Street'.

An American author called Philip Moore, living in London, has a whining little wife who has dragged him down, and when they return to America her plan to enter Washington society will clearly be the end of him. With them in London is Moore's old friend and intelligent companion, Miss Remington, whom he takes for granted.* Amy, the wife, spells out the reason to Miss Remington: men are afraid of a spinster who reads deep books, wears tailor-made gowns, and pins back her hair plainly – that sensible look, adopted by Woolson, displacing the exaggerated femininities of curls and bustle. In a parody of the Jamesian Master, Moore lays it down that 'Women can't write. And they ought not to try.' He concedes that they might do children's stories, little sketches, and love stories. 'But the great questions of life, the important matters, they cannot render in the least.' He congratulates Gertrude Remington that she has never tried: 'It would be insupportable to me to have any of my personal friends among that band.' Miss Remington is reading a biography of Louisa May Alcott, who 'worked all her life as hard as she possibly could'. Earlier that day, she has taken Amy to Highgate to see the grave of George Eliot, and now reminds Moore that he once thought well of her, but even George Eliot is brushed aside. His spite against women writers derives, of course, from his sense of failure, but it can't be condoned. As he goes under, Moore will lose touch with his better self in the figure of Miss Remington: her truths, her agency, her very words seem to come from a freak.

The fear of being a freak daunts women. Their mettle is tested by the danger of surfacing. In the next century, Virginia Woolf spoke of the white monsters of the lower waters who would explode if brought to the surface. The difference between Henry and Alice

* As a 'spinster' story, 'In Sloane Street' reworks the subject of 'Miss Vedder' (1879).

James can be seen in this way: for the brother, a succession of waves, some greater, some smaller, but all making their way towards the shore; for the sister, incomprehensible explosions from the lower waters, then a seemingly ceaseless horror in 1878 'when I went down to the deep sea, its dark waters closed over me and I knew neither hope nor peace', and then, at the last, with 'Kath' at her side, the controlled rise of her remarkable diary.

Alice wished her diary to last. Kath printed four copies privately, one for herself and one for each of the surviving brothers. Though (between themselves) William and Henry recognised its genius, they resolved to suppress it, at the latter's insistence: 'I don't see what intrinsic impossibility there is for *us* in keeping . . . [the diary] *to* us an absolute & utter secret. It has only – the secret – to *be* really kept.' The two eldest brothers feared that Bob and his children would not join in what amounted to a resubmersion of Alice – and they feared, as it turned out, rightly, for in the next century it was Bob's children who interested themselves in the publication of the diary and who, alone in the James family, retained ties with old Miss Loring. William and Henry blamed Miss Loring for printing the diary – she never saw why. Henry, who destroyed his copy, professed to be horrified by casual remarks of his that Alice wrote down, but many of his letters were salted with similar gossip. Did the two brothers believe that a lady does not raise her voice in public?

This issue bears on Miss Remington, who we are led to suspect has a secret identity. Her surname is identical with the trade-name of the newly invented typewriter, which suggests that she is a professional writer. This makes Moore's slights all the more futile. In a tale published three months later, James vented his rage in a hatchet job on an ink-stained woman who turned out pot boilers under the name of 'Greville Fane'. She is despised as a creature of the market – as though James were not.

James had long entertained a notion he had fallen on 'evil days'. He gave out that editors kept back his tales as if they were ashamed of them. He told his brother that he found it hard to press on when his work was unwanted. None of this is strictly true, and the huge output did not flag. In truth, James was securely established: he saw ladies bend in graceful attitudes over his pages, even if they read no more than a few lines. Socially, he was much in demand, especially with women, as Elizabeth Robins recalled: 'There was a general impression that Mr. James was much beset by the attention of ladies. One story dates from the days when domestic electric lighting was not yet fully under control. The first of the great London establishments to install the new luxury was ... Grosvenor House. At the subsequent evening party when the scene was at its most brilliant, suddenly the lights went out. As suddenly they came on, to discover – so the story went – thirteen ladies clinging to Mr. James.'

The young actress witnessed for herself the sensation of his appearance at a tea party. He parried numbers of invitations and beseechments. Some that pressed too hard he treated with formidable irony.

The clamour, the unsatisfied ambition, and above all the fear that he would not fulfil his utmost potential, were concentrated in a tale of a celebrated but unfulfilled writer, which James called 'The Middle Years'. Its autobiographical basis is suggested by the author's eventual choice of 'The Middle Years' as the title for the final, unfinished volume of his memoirs. The tale explores an agony of self-doubt in the mind of Dencombe, the writer, who has been ill and turns out to be dying. Looking back on his unfinished *œuvre*, Dencombe's prime need is the support of a discerning reader, and it is this consolation, in the shape of a doctor, that enables him to confide his resonant last words: 'We work in the dark – we do what we can – we give what we have. Our doubt is our passion and our passion is our task. The rest is the madness of art.'

The madness of art: some may find this rather extravagant, but new evidence links it quite literally with the state of the author in the months prior to publication in May 1893. Fenimore told Dr Baldwin: Mr James 'has had grief this winter, & suffered a good deal'.

Baldwin's treatment was to prove to patients that he grasped their state by reflecting his own: this articulation encouraged patients to name the unnameable. A letter from Mrs William James to Baldwin late in 1892 thanks him for curing her husband of 'morbid depression' by talking of himself, as William had shrewdly noted, 'almost as if he knew how I was feeling'. Baldwin was genuinely ill. In April 1893, he told Fenimore how day by day he did his best, with a 'grim & desperate will to be resolute', waiting for the light that would surely come. It brought tears to her eyes. How strangely Baldwin, William, and Henry James converged in this nexus of depressive illness in the winter and spring of 1892–3.

In January James had an attack of gout, and the pain brought home an 'intense realisation of our common mortality'. In place of a shoe he had to wear 'a kind of huge luri-lumpish[?] golosh'. By February, he lost his facility, and found it more difficult every day to write. In this state, he was stung by acclaim for *Tess of the d'Urbervilles*. Tess is a variation on the familiar type of innocent sinner: her pink tongue appears like a snake when she yawns in her voluptuous way, exciting to men like Hardy whose response to women runs largely to voyeurism. '. . . She is vile,' James raged. 'The pretence of "sexuality" is only equalled by the absence of it.'

He tried to turn rage into submission, but it sounds rather forced: 'I am meek and ashamed where the public clatter is deafening – so I bowed my head . . .'. The seriousness of his 'grief' at this time is confirmed by the fact that Woolson assumed William (in his capacity as psychologist) would have conferred with Dr Baldwin. She wrote to the doctor: 'When we read the biographies of even the most successful (to the world's eye) men, we always find that behind the scenes there was a steady grind going on all the time, with any number of hard, very hard things to bear, & quantities of private discouragement.'

Fenimore had stayed on in England an extra winter, with a prospect of healing herself, eventually, in the warmth of Italy. James promised to come every year, and talked encouragingly of a pied-à-terre in Venice: a commitment of sorts to see her more often. It was, really, much the same as always: hopes, promises, loneliness and mutual care, friction and reunions.

She sent her array of trunks by sea. On 12 May she left Oxford for London to see a dentist before her departure, but there, in a hotel, she was 'prostrated'. A doctor was summoned at four in the morning. James intercepted her as she passed through Paris en route to Venice. No casual meeting this: he travelled expressly to meet her. Weak and low from flu, and in the midst of another migration, she accomplished their usual round of paintings. James was better, she told Dr Baldwin afterwards.

'I saw Henry James in Paris on my way down,' she reported in her guarded way. 'He came back from Switzerland to meet me, and for the four days I was there, he amiably took me out to the galleries, theatres, etc.' She chose 'amiably' with deliberation. It is written over 'as wont', slapping on James that tame image he had slapped on her and, at the same time, toning down the habitual in their tie. He himself kept Paris a secret in his next report to Boott, referring only to 'the *ingress* [to Italy] of our excellent friend C.F.W.'. His 'our' denies 'my' when he spoke of her to Boott or Hay, as though she belonged to all, but of course he did possess her in his special way. From the time she moved to London in 1883 there had been ten years of secrecy about meetings with Fenimore, in the course of which secrets became central to his art. It was an art in which the secret may not in itself amount to much – what grips us are characters as they manoeuvre around the secret.

10
The Death-House

'I should like to die without warning myself,' Fenimore said when she heard of the suicide of Clover Adams, 'but for those who are left it is very terrible.' Clover had killed herself unexpectedly in December 1885, seven months after her father's death. Like Fenimore, she had inherited her father's melancholia; but her death was more deeply connected to the loss of an expressive emotional bond, not replaceable by her husband, Henry Adams. Fenimore's response to Clover recalls her confidence to James, in 1882, that she'd be 'glad to go'. To Baldwin she said, 'Life is not worth living at all, without courage.' She was 'quite determined' never to outlive her own.

In the latter half of May 1893, Fenimore arrived in Venice 'depressed in spirits'. She could not shake this off, despite balmy air and afternoon swims at the Lido. The effort James made to come to Paris and take her about had not restored her. On 16 June she confided in Dr Baldwin. His condition had mirrored her own, especially his 'amazing wilderness of gloom', she said. 'For how often am I too lost in the same dark land.' Taking a measure of comfort in his proof that she was not alone, she tried to enact her doctor's resolution: 'I must take fresh courage from it.' Courage was her watchword; stoicism her philosophy. 'Nothing but sheer courage from day to day keeps *me* going,' she had told him two years earlier. 'But you have not the great drawback, & the lonely life, that are my lot.' As she points to this, she seals it off in the terms of her outcast character, Miss Jonah, who plans an unrecognised suicide: 'for the heart knows its own bitterness & cannot always explain it'.

With James due in the autumn, she began to search (together with Ariana Curtis) for the pied-à-terre he had wanted. She lodged, for the time being, at the Casa Biondetti, San Vio 715, not far from the great dome of the Salute which guards the entrance to the Grand Canal. The eighteenth-century painter Rosalba Carrera had lived here. It is a modest house, not a palazzo, with two floors above the water-storey. Fenimore's rooms were on the upper floor, with a sky-room perched on top of the building. The Casa is on the Grand Canal but reached from the back, down the narrowest of alleys, to the farthest, dark end, on the right. There, five well-bred Americans packed themselves into small rooms. Beneath Woolson, on the floor with the balcony, were Miss Felton, whose father had been President of Harvard, and Miss Lily Norton, the daughter of the Professor of Fine Arts, Charles Eliot Norton. Opposite were Miss Huntington and Mrs Quincy of Boston, whose son was Assistant Secretary of State. Fenimore would have lacked privacy, and her rooms on the canal, facing north, would not have had much sun – so, the sky-room, facing all ways, would have been the attraction.

Here, she became absorbed in a recent book, *The Law of Psychic Phenomena*, by Thomson Jay Hudson. He argues that a phantom is nothing but an 'embodied thought', a telepathic communication when feelings have been intense – the most intense being those that precede death by violence. Why are ghosts always well provided with apparel, the author asks, and suggests that the soul of the dead puts on, as it were, the soul of its clothes: 'We must therefore suppose clothes to have souls'. It is a commonplace that certain houses are pervaded by the mental atmosphere of the dead. No ghost may be seen, but 'the influence is felt, and cannot be thrown off'.

Fenimore echoed this idea, as she put it, 'that houses in which persons have lived, become, after a time, permeated with their thoughts –, in case these thoughts were powerful enough. . . . The book, by the way, is very remarkable as containing the only working hypothesis I have ever seen as regards the strange facts of telepathy, hypnosis, etc.' Since December 1890 she had entered into the current vogue for the extra-sensory. It may be significant that Katharine Loring had stayed with her in Cheltenham the month before. Miss Loring was adept at hypnosis and claimed to have seen a ghost, the topic of an earnest correspondence with William James.

The Biondetti was to be temporary; Fenimore planned to find a place of her own. 'I am so tired of changing,' she said, 'and sometimes so disheartened at the thought of all the labor that must be gone through, before a new place is any where near comfortable, – that it seems as if, after I am settled this time, I shall never have the strength or courage to move again. It is a curious fate that has made the most domestic woman in the world, the one most fond of a home, a fixed home, and all her things about her, – that has made such a woman a wanderer for nearly twenty years.'

By 14 July James had heard from her, because on that day he reports to Boott on her 'at last actual domestication (for which a permanent "flat" is indeed still needed) at Venice. She is looking at palaces. I hope to see her there in the autumn . . .'.

She went with Mr and Mr Curtis to look at an apartment in a 'beautiful' house which she decided would not do because it was not on the Grand Canal. (It has been assumed that she met the Curtises through James, but in fact Miss Greenough of the Castellani had introduced her in the summer of 1889.) James wrote to Ariana Curtis on the same day he wrote to Boott, but here he contradicts his intention to come in the autumn and, at the same time, corrects Miss Woolson's 'misconception' that he wanted a pied-à-terre in Venice. This letter, designed to stop their search, is directed at Fenimore through Mrs Curtis, and the reason for his roundaboutness is plain: it is, in effect, a blow which James lacks the courage to administer directly. For it tells his friend that a phase of withdrawal is about to begin. Following as it does her involvement in his depression, his withdrawal as he recovered while her own depression came to the fore was the reverse of the reciprocity to be expected from a friend. The chill of his caprice could not have come at a worse time. Here, unmistakably, is the Winterbourne voice of Henry James.

Speaking of Venice as a lover, he attempts to excuse what must appear 'criminal levity': 'I haven't been toying with its affections,' he defends himself, and blames rather the clumsiness of his *language*. Since James was a master of language, this statement assumes the formal air of a gentleman taking the blame for a lady's woolliness: 'I expressed myself clumsily to Miss Woolson in appearing to intimate that I was coming there to "live." ' He couldn't live anywhere but London 'for all sorts of practical reasons'. (This is prevarication: there had never been any notion that he should give up London.) He goes on to explain that when he is in Venice he feels 'the all but irresistible desire to put my hand on some modest pied-à-terre there', but this is a 'humble dream' which fades 'a little' when it is out of sight. In other words, what he says is not to be trusted because it may be a passing 'dream'. James grants, here, a glimpse of himself as he shifts ground and shuts the door. This is a man who shifts at will, to the confusion of friends who will have no alternative but to adjust to the latest 'dream': 'the next time I am there I shall probably act in harmony with it [the dream] – and then find myself unable (such are the tricks of fate) to occupy the place for a long time afterwards.'

The message is relentless: had he acquired a pied-à-terre, occupation could not be taken for granted. The deeper message is not to expect. Not to rely. He pleads for patience, and thanks Mrs Curtis (and, by implication, Fenimore) for their interest 'in the sordid little inquiry'. After their wasted effort on his behalf, he invites them to smile at the comic abasement of the 'sordid' and 'humble' adjectives in which he wraps himself. So he tries to disarm Fenimore before he delivers the next blow.

On the face of it, he merely shifts the date of his arrival from autumn to winter, but an apparent afterthought cancels any hope of commitment: 'I have the fondest hope of going to Italy next winter – but am learning by stern experience not to make hard and fast plans.' He invokes 'tricks of fate', admitting 'these things are vague'.

At this point, he turns to Fenimore as though she had not been the subtext of the whole letter: 'I am very sorry indeed Miss Woolson has trouble in finding a house, or a piano.' If 'Miss Woolson' has a problem, it is merely a practical matter, nothing whatever to do with him, and calls for no more than polite regrets.

James is a little disconcerted by his own manoeuvres, yet carries them through – the shuffling, the denials, the comic grovelling – with rueful ingenuity. So, he shut the door without locking it: no promises; no finality.

To attempt to settle in Venice without the prospect of intimacy had not been her plan – she knew Venice was not a good place to be emotionally alone. 'Venice is pre-eminently the place where one needs either an actual, tangible companionship of the dearest sort, or a memory like it,' says Morgan in 'A Florentine Experiment'. 'I, who have neither, keep well away from Venice!'

With a renewed sense of solitude, Fenimore moved on 10 September. This was an interim plan: since she had not, as yet, found a home of her own, she took an eight-month lease (till 10 May), at $40 a month, of the top two floors of the Casa Semitecolo. Niccolò Semitecolo had been the 'ablest Venetian artist of the 14th century', as she noted in her Baedeker. The present owner was an Englishman; a Cooper fan (he had made a pilgrimage to Cooperstown forty years before), Lieutenant-General de Horsey was delighted with his tenant. The Semitecolo is on the same side of the canal as the Biondetti; only a few steps away across the small bridge of San Gregorio in the direction of the looming Salute with its round dome. Fenimore noted that the Semitecolo was almost opposite the Casa di Desdemona; it looks across the canal to the yellow Gritti, where ten years earlier, in 1883, Fenimore had invited James to the red ledges of her top floor. The Gritti, like the Barbaro, and other palaces facing south, is bathed in glorious light: not so the Semitecolo. The entrance is gloomy, plunged between steep, eyeless walls through a gate off the narrow, dark Calle del Bastion. (At present, long fronds of dust-coloured creeper fall from each floor towards the stones below.)

Her thoughts at this time turned to Cooperstown, as always when she felt unsettled. To plan moves was a remedy for depression, and a plan to return to that ancestral home was, for her, a kind of safety-net. It was a fantasy, not a realistic solution; the communal bonds of small-town America would not have suited her need for privacy. Cheerful affection animating the family network had not relieved her over a prolonged stay in the summer of 1876 when her mother had taken her to Cooperstown, a kinswoman of thirty-six in a state of intractable depression. The rural contentment of her Cooper aunts had been an irritant; she had rowed away from them to the far reaches of Otsego. Late in 1893, she had news of old Miss Cooper, who had been her father's amanuensis and, briefly, an author herself: 'Aunt Sue says *she* is perfectly happy – I am very glad, but *I* am not.'

James was aware that all was not well. He told Ariana Curtis, 'I shall do my best to prove to Miss Woolson that Venice is better than Cooperstown . . .'.

Over the summer, he had written the first act of his doomed play *Guy Domville*. It concerns an eighteenth-century man about to take orders who is pulled back into the world when he inherits a fortune. He finds the world so repellent that, in the last act, he returns to the religious life. Coincidentally, Woolson, at just this time, wondered if the seclusion of a convent would provide the answer to her troubles. During her stay in England, she had acquired a book on Vittoria Colonna, who had intrigued her since her visit in 1881 to the Roman convent Colonna entered at the age of thirty-five. 'In this convent Vittoria Colonna came to reside in 1525 when widowed,' she had noted in her Baedeker, 'here she began to write her Sonnets.' She and James were religious extremists cut off by the *Zeitgeist* from traditional forms of faith. James whispers endless blessings and amens over his art. He seeks transcendence through plots that turn on renunciation. The renunciation at the end of *East Angels* pleased him, though Woolson confronts, as James does not, the torture of buried passion without transcendence.

At the end of October, Woolson completed a revision of *Horace Chase*, due to be published as a book in 1894. It left her, as usual, depleted. She warned *Harper's* that she was 'profoundly discouraged' and would 'do very little more'. She was now resigned to giving up her 'broken sword to Fate, the Conqueror'.

Alternatively, there was the model of Colonna: 'If I could go into a convent (where I didn't have to confess, nor rise before daylight for icy matins), I think I could write three or four novels better than any I have yet done. But there are no worldly convents. So I'll write my new effusions on another star, and send them back . . . by telepathy.' Some further existence seemed to her 'the only solution to the riddle of the present one, – this present one with its bitter disappointments.'

James confided to Boott a limited understanding of this state. He figured her 'as extremely exhausted (as she always is at such times), with her writing and rewriting of her last novel – a great success, I believe, in relation to the particular public (a very wide American one) that she addresses. She is to have, I trust, a winter of bookless peace.'

There's the slightest bristle at the idea of her success with a 'particular' public, as though this were not quite the readership he would wish for himself. Then, too, he expressed concern for her 'exhaustion' when he well knew it was depression. Later, he would acknowledge its seriousness, and say, at that later time, his anxiety for her had known no rest. In truth, he felt no obligation to support her in any immediate way. His arrival was now deferred, yet further, to the spring; and Venice, it now appeared, was no longer to be his destination. His friend was relegated to a stopover en route to Tuscany: 'I shall take Venetia by the way and pay a visit to our excellent friend Fenimore.'

Her detachment from James, from ambition, from society, widened even as she seemed to fulfil her 'domestication'. Gradually, in the autumn months of 1893, the 'rather bare' Semitecolo took on a 'cozy' aspect. At first she occupied the large rooms facing the canal, including a summer bedroom, but as winter came on she moved to the sunnier south side of the house, away from the canal, where she had her winter bedroom, a dressing-room, and a sitting-room with a large fireplace. Beside her bed she kept a small, silver-plated bell with her initials, 'C.F.W'. When her 'things' arrived from Florence, she welcomed in particular her stand-up desk and her special chair upholstered in yellow silk damask, alongside a carved Venetian writing-table bought for her by General de Horsey. She kept her unframed photographs and small pictures in the drawers of a Japanese cabinet of black lacquer. On every available surface were the spoils of her travels, including a piece of alabaster which she had picked up in the Temple of the Sphinx and an Arabian tile with a shameless label: 'stolen in April 1890 by C. F. Woolson, from the wall of the Mandarah (or reception room) of the ruined Palace of the Sheik el Moofti, at Cairo, Egypt. Date between A.D. 1200 and A.D. 1300.' She put up four etchings of Venice by Duveneck; 'How They Met Themselves' by Rossetti; and the small painting 'The Garden of Hesperides' by Meacci (after Rossetti), a favourite with James, which always had pride of place. There were the old framed photographs of James and of Turgenev, and her proudest keepsakes: a silver stamp box with the date engraved, given to her by James; silver spoons from Miss E. F. Poynter (an English author living in Florence); old embroidery in brown and gold from Frank Duveneck; coffee cups of glass with solid silver holders, given to her by the Khedive Tewfik of Egypt; and, not least, a scarab pin from Egypt with ancient, telepathic powers – or so she fancied. The last was a gift from Baldwin. All these 'things' represent a valiant effort to make a home. In her story 'Dorothy', accumulations of this sort can seem, at times, 'inhuman', and fail to console the 'old maid', Felicia, for her loneliness and unlovability: 'the plates and the plaques and the pots, the bits of silk and tapestry and embroidery, the old sketches and old busts and old shrines that adorned the wall, looked down upon her with their usual heterogeneous glimmer.'

To house 'things' proved costly. On 20 November, Fenimore asked Sam Mather to sell one of her bonds and send her a thousand dollars to cover the expenses of setting up house: '. . . I find I am beginning to be haunted by the fear that my reserve fund at the Bank here is not large enough to leave me free from immediate care.'

Ominous turns of phrase lurked behind the practical purpose of this letter. This sum of money was to relieve her mind like travelling in a low-slung carriage: 'with it, I feel that I can jump out . . . I never do jump & never want to.' She went on to argue against saving capital for the infirmities of age. '. . . My "infirmities" are upon me now,' she said, 'they will not grow worse. . . . I hope you will not be shocked if I add that for a long time my daily prayer has been that I may not live to be old.'

Unlike Florence, expatriate society in Venice did not run after newcomers. It was small and exclusive. Fenimore soon found – she expressed surprise – it did not exclude her. The Curtises, Mrs Bronson, and others with 'superb palaces', great fortunes, and priceless collections of art, 'called and called', toiled up her long stair, and 'established' themselves in her little sitting-room. She was touched by this welcome – never had she been so cordially received – but it was 'essentially a society of older persons, people who have retired from active life, and are taking their ease'. She preferred the company of Edith Bronson, now thirty-two. Like her mother (who made a study of Venetian naval architecture, and drafted an article on 'The Lost Islands of the Lagoon'), Edith had a scholarly bent, and busied herself collecting everything that had been written in Venice about Venice, which she hoped to publish in English and French. This sort of project would have appealed to Woolson. She tried to enjoy a visit from Edith's friend, twenty-eight-year-old Princess Olga, who stirred – momentarily – travel plans to her homeland, Montenegro.*

Yet despite these attentions, or rather because of them, most members of Venetian society presented a 'difficulty'. Woolson explained this to Sam Mather: 'though it sometimes *is* difficult for me to keep up my end of the tie when there are such big fortunes at the other, I do'nt mean that there is any difficulty *materially*; it is only spiritually that one feels the difference. Or perhaps "imaginatively" is the better word.' She refused all invitations except informal ones to tea.

It was easier to be with a dog. She bought a Pomeranian, two months old, for five francs from Dalmatian sailors. He was black and she called him Othello ('the Moor of Venice') – 'Tello' for short. He bit the buttons off her boots as she wrote, carried off a silk cushion James had given her, and slept in a basket beside her bed. It was a comfort that she never failed to hear his sharp bark – better, she said, than the loudest bell.

Towards Christmas she began to look for an unfurnished apartment, with the aid of Edith. Otherwise, she filled her days with further explorations of the lagoon. Soon after her arrival, she had visited San Francesco del Deserto, 'a far-away island'. In the autumn she had explored other far islands, looking to horizons and remote Alps. Ostensibly, this was material for a book, but her notes are sometimes elegiac, as though she were visiting the last places on earth. This fits the mood of certain letters which prepare friends for her death.

'I sometimes think that if I live, and live here, I may write a little

* 'Poor little ineffectual & impecunious princess,' James wrote when Olga Montenegro died not long after. 'I seem to see the poor little Olga's history, & setting etc, as a possible *subject* . . .'. (To Ariana Curtis (25 Sept [1896]). Dartmouth College, Hanover, NH.)

volume not about Venice, but on the islands of the lagoons,' she said. 'But I may neither live, nor live here.' New acquaintance could not assuage the expatriate void. And there was no return to her country of origin, for that was home no longer. As she set up house, she felt that 'herculean labors with strange rooms and temporary lodgings' could not be endured any further. Her repetition of this, despite habitual reserve, indicates how deep it went. 'The world has never produced a more home-loving woman than I am, yet by a strange fate I have been homeless for twenty years.' She thought up an epitaph for her tombstone, one of those jokes that aren't jokes: 'Gone to look for a home elsewhere.'

She wrote to another friend: 'I have taught myself to be philosophic, and I feel perfectly sure that the next existence will make clear all the mysteries and riddles of this. In the meantime, one can do one's duty or try to do it. But if at any time you should hear that I have gone, I want you to know beforehand that my end was peace, and joy at release . . .'.

Her 'duty' was the duty to live as though she might go on: she fulfilled this duty when she arranged her 'things', when she said she would start a book on 1 January, when she explored the Lido and the islands of the lagoon, and most of all in a growing collection of 'Mottoes, Maxims, & Reflections', some of her own, some copied out from other writers. Here, she still looks forward to future efforts. 'Nothing can be created from the outside,' she wrote. 'Nothing is true or effective which is not drawn from the heart or experience of the writer.' Her jottings include Horace, glossed, 'I shall be interested in your characters only to the same extent as you yourself, their creator, are interested in them' and Maupassant's injunction to 'describe what people *do*, not what they *think*'. She reminds herself that the 'most dramatic effects are those that indicate suppressed passion. . . . These are constantly utilized by Browning; they characterize the Puritan repression in Hawthorne.'

On one journey to the mainland at Campalto, on 17 December, her walk took her along a dyke surrounding the Laguna della Morte, 'where the tide does not come. Such a strange water-land, – into many channels, & wet meadows. . . . There was one old white horse wandering about these meadows near the house at the landing. He looked so desolate! I think there is nothing so lonely as the figure (in large field or waste, at evening) of a solitary old white horse. – On the way home there came up a dense white fog.' A trace of frontier blood stirs once more, recalling the fog of 'Castle Nowhere' and the labyrinthine waterways of 'St Clair Flats'. Waiting to pit herself against the elements, she almost hoped the gondoliers would lose their way. For a while it seemed they had, then they found the spiles, '& we crept along close to them, feeling our way over the lagoon from one to the next. We entered Venice by the Casa degli Spiriti, – an appropriate place for such a ghostly assay . . .'.

On Christmas Eve, starting at two in the afternoon, she took a gondola to the Lido, and walked with Othello for two hours on the beach. It was warm enough to wear only a light jacket – she left a fur cloak in the gondola. As she gazed across the blue Adriatic towards the great snow masses to the north, the peaks seemed to be riding along the rim of 'immeasurable space; they are the outer edge of our star; they cut the air as they fly. They are the rim of the world. I should *like* to turn into a peak when I die. . . . George Eliot wrote "O may I join the Choir Invisible" – But I should rather join the mountains . . .'.*

She sat for some time at the point of the Lido, on the grassy embankment of Fort St Niccolò, watching red sails. In the soldiers' cemetery she came upon a tombstone that suggests suicide, and copied out the inscription:

> *– dopo 45 anni di vita*
> *laboriosa ed onesta,*
> *affranto dalle avventure,*
> *per troppo delicato sentire*
> *finiva di vivere,*
> *Augusto – 1887.*

* The 'choir invisible' of George Eliot's poem (August 1867) is the 'immortal dead who live again / In minds made better by their presence'. The discords of 'rebellious flesh that would not be subdued' die into the 'life to come'. In 1876 CFW published a sonnet 'To George Eliot' which likened her to a mountain, and another poem of 1878, 'To Certain Biographers', pictures the great writer as a mountain whose distant peak may be admired but whose hidden places cannot be known to the biographer.

> I suppose this to mean – 'So & So, after 45 years
> of honest & hardworking life, worn out by misfortunes,
> & a too sensitive disposition, ceased to live in
> August – 1887.

On Christmas Day, she strolled in St Mark's Square, observing the crowds as they entered San Marco. Lady Layard, who owned a fine collection of paintings, had asked her to a party on Christmas Night. This invitation, like all others, she declined. Miss Grief preferred to sit alone by her fire 'and think of those who are gone'.

Meanwhile, James, in wintry London, was dreaming 'of a Venetian spring'. He asked Mrs Bronson to be kind to Fenimore, saying he was very fond of her. A recent letter told him, he reports to Curtis, 'that she hasn't yet found her house inadequately warm – & she rejoices in the virtuous Tito' (a gondolier who had served the Curtises for twelve years, and served Fenimore while they were in India). James adds: 'If she only didn't think it her bounden duty to "make plans" she might be happy yet. Speriamo that she will be . . .'.

With that hope, silence falls.

She did not answer his letter, nor did she answer one from Dr Baldwin. Nothing at all is known of the final days of 1893 and first two weeks of January 1894. Complete silence. What happened afterwards, after she fell ill on 14 January – what she said and did – comes at second hand through testimonies of others, chiefly an eyewitness account by an ex-teacher, Marie Holas, employed at the instigation of Edith Bronson to help her friend. Because the case is mysterious, its centre enveloped in silence, I shall set out in full the official testimony written down by Miss Holas eight days after the events, and then bring in certain points from an oral testimony which she gave a few days earlier – very close to the events – to a cousin, Grace Carter, who had been nursing her sister in Munich and rushed to Venice as the news broke.

Miss Holas will be familiar to readers of classic detective novels: the capable secretary. English was not her first language, but you would hardly have known it. She impressed everyone who came in contact with her over the next few weeks as supremely 'efficient'.

Her proficiency in Italian gave her an edge on Grace Carter, who was helpless without her when it came to a licence to transport a body by train from Venice to Rome. Grace Carter, large and soft, arrived wringing her hands, as it were, for failing to come as soon as she heard a relative was ill. She had feared to obtrude herself on her reclusive cousin (whom at times she called, deferentially, 'Aunt') without an unequivocal signal she was wanted. In essentials, the records are the same, but Miss Carter's is swollen with regrets and self-justification. Miss Holas was the rock to whom she clung. Her testimony, which remained (and still remains) in family hands, is convincing as far as it goes: clear, sure, coherent – but not excessively so, and uncoloured by emotion.

Venice. Jany 31st 1894

Dear Mr Mather

Miss Carter asked me to write & let you know all that has happened in the last days of the life of Miss Woolson. I had been introduced to her by her friend Miss Bronson, on the 15th of Jan. Miss Woolson was then in bed with influenza, but as on that same day, I wrote under her dictation to Mrs Benedict, the doctor said it was a mild case, & having spoken myself with him, he told me it was indeed a very mild one. Miss Woolson had no fever at all, & had only a little bronchial catarrh. Miss W. had been unwell since the beginning of the year, & had gone out in the 13th although the Dr had said she had better not, the weather being then very cold. She walked in the Public Gardens on the snow, & that was the cause. She was obliged to stay in bed again. She was quite alone & felt lonely, troubled by the cares of housekeeping & for that reason I was introduced to her, to relieve her from every care that might have troubled her in her present state of health. On the 15th, 16th & 17th she was in very good spirits, spoke to me, dictated many letters, & said she was much better than she looked. Now & then, she moaned & when I looked at her, thinking she felt bad, she smiled & said it was her habit of doing so – I was not to be frightened; that all her life she could not bear the slightest physical pain & as it did her good to moan or scream, why she felt a comfort in doing so – and the same she said to the doctor. During those three days, she ate a little more, without the feeling of nausea she had had before. I ordered her meals, & on the 17th at breakfast she told me that for the first time, for many days, she was looking in the dish, to see whether there was something more for her to eat. She spoke of death as one who does not fear it, & said one must be prepared for it. She wished to make her will, & told the Dr he must let her know when he thought she was growing worse & let her not die without one. She told the same to me, adding that for the first time in 20 years she was without a will, & wanted to make one as soon as possible. That she considered very wrong what people often did, to leave such an important matter to the last, & sometimes were too late. She mentioned even her dog, for which she wanted to provide. She told me also, that in case of her death I must not let her to be buried in the cemetery of Venice, as she hated the place, & the only place where she could rest in peace was the cemetery in Rome* – & she threatened me in case I did not tell her relatives what her wishes were to let me have no peace after her death. It was useless, she said to cable to her relatives in case she were worse as it would give them only pain, as they could not come at once; but if she were to die, then I should have to cable to you & to Mrs Benedict, to let you know, so that you might take your time & come here. As she had the house till the 10th of May, she wished everything to be kept as it was, the house closed & put under seals until you or Mrs Benedict came to look after her things & dispose of them, according to her will.

But, of course all these things were said half joking, & when I asked her why she spoke thus, she answered 'The Americans are fond of joking & we do so, even on our death bed – ' So I joined her in the joke, & asked her not to frighten me too much after death, & promised to do all she wished for –

When I left her on the 17th at night, she was in very good spirits, & told me, when I went to her on the following morning, she would be up, & waiting for me in her drawing-room. On the 18th instead of seeing her up, as I expected[,] I found she had great pains in her bowels & said she had suffered dreadfully in the night, & had taken laudanum to quiet the pains. I sent for the Dr who ordered morphia, with something else, & that soothed the pains. I left her in the evening later than usual. She was much better, sat in her bed, & read her letters & newspapers – When I went to her the next morning she had been worse in the night[,] had vomited very much & in showing the Dr the vomit, he wondered & said it was a bilious attack. He asked her if she had had anything that had troubled her more than usual. She answered there was not a person under the sun that had

* The Protestant Cemetery, known locally as the Testaccio Cemetery.

had more cares & troubles than herself for many years. She added, that every time she had finished writing a book, she felt for months afterwards a great nervous prostration. And that now, she was suffering from it, having finished her last novel Horace Chase – at the end of October, & that consequently, it required some time before she could be herself again. That same day she had fever – 39.3 – She gave me all her keys (she had given me all the money she had at home the second day I was with her) & said 'Do as you like, but please don't trouble me about anything.' She vomited still but the pains were almost gone & had no more fever. Although there was nothing alarming in her illness, the Dr said it was better a nurse should be called for the nights – Miss W. did not like it at first, therefore her maid was settled for one night in her dressing-room. That was on the 20th. But on the 21st a trained nurse was called. I gave her the instructions I got from the Dr & in the morning, took her place for the day – Since the 20th Miss W. spoke but little even to me, & when I was taking her [ear] trumpet to tell her something, she said she would rather not listen. Miss Carter had written she wished to come here, & when I asked her why she would not let her come, she said it was useless. But on the 22nd in the evening she told me to wire her to come – & in the meantime she gave me yours & Mrs Benedict's addresses[.] She told me to call the American Consul when she would tell me, to make her will – that there was a model[?] in a box where she kept some papers, I should have to look for it – (This paper was found after death, but has no importance[.]) On the morning of the 23rd she was much better, took some milk & did not vomit at all. But she was very weak. She asked the Dr to give her something strong to make her sleep & said 'If I sleep today, I shall be quite well tomorrow, but if I don't sleep, I shall be dead –' According to her wishes, the Dr gave her laudanum. Then she told me that if any telegram was coming, I was to open it[,] answer if necessary, but trouble her not with it. At 1 o'cl[ock] she asked me to send to the Dr & ask him to allow her to take some more laudanum. I got his answer & gave it to her. When I received Miss Carter[']s telegram I waited for a moment, when she wanted to speak to me, & told her – 'Good news, Miss Carter is coming.' 'Well, well,' she said[,] no more – In the evening when the Dr came, she asked him for some more laudanum, & begged him besides to make her an injection of morphia which he decidedly refused to do, for he said, she was so weak, she could not bear it, & never awake again. She would die in her sleep, & he would be responsible for her death. Then she asked me to change her position in the bed, to turn her & put her head on the other side, & so I did, with the help of the servants – I arranged her blankets, her pillows & cushions; she wished the door, windows, shutters, & curtains very well closed also that the slightest ray of light could not pass through – Then as I took the trumpet to speak to her she said 'I am so comfortable please let me alone.' I went out, after having prepared everything that might have been necessary for the night so that the nurse have all at hand, & had not to leave the patient for one moment. I went away at 9 o'cl[ock] having left Miss W. as quiet as possible. At 1 o'c[lock] in the night, her gondoliers came to fetch me, saying, she had jumped out of the window – Horror-struck, taking hardly time to dress, I ran to her house – but when I arrived, she had just died. The Dr told me she had lived three quarters of an hour unconscious, moaning slightly when they touched her. He said, she had died from internal commotion of the brains & bowels, & had lost all sensibility almost immediately in the fall. I asked the nurse, how it was she had left her, she said, Miss W. had been very quiet, & called her at a quarter past 12, wanting to know the time. Then asked for some milk, but refused to drink it in the cup she handed to her, & sent her to the diningroom to take another of pink china. She wanted that one & no other. The nurse went, & when she came back, she found the window opened, & the bed empty. This is the sad relation of the last days of Miss W's life – Nothing gave ever to suppose that she had such a sad purpose in her mind, nor can I think she had it, as she sent for Miss Carter, & was going to make her will, that same day. Many people speak of death when ill, & Miss W's illness was not such as to give any kind of anxiety. Had I had the slightest idea of what happened, on my own accord, I should have cabled to you, & wired much sooner to Miss Carter – I told Miss Carter every wish of Miss Woolson's & now her remains are at rest, in the cemetery in Rome.* I am at your & Mrs Benedict's orders for all that is in my power to do. If there is any other information you wish to ask from me, I shall do my best to satisfy you. I shall always be too glad to be of any use to you.

Believe me

Yours truly

Marie Holas.

There is an advantage, of course, in so reliable a witness, but

* She was buried that very day, 31 January.

there is a disadvantage too: she was an outsider, brought in at a late stage and treated as a functionary by her patient. Woolson kept her in her place. There is no sign of the bonds that often form around a sickbed. Woolson spoke to Miss Holas mainly to give instructions. We can learn a good deal from these instructions, and from what Marie Holas observed while on duty in the bedroom; and yet the very coolness of Miss Holas, the absence of empathy, the odd absence of any encounter between patient and helper, sustains the mystery of the last days and hours of this most hidden of lives. Woolson refused to allow Miss Holas to approach her with the ear trumpet: she had no wish to hear what she had to say. She wished to be obeyed – at once. If not, she was irritable, Miss Holas told Grace Carter in an oral report that is closest in time to the death.

'Aunt Constance seemed very nervous,' Miss Carter relayed to Cleveland, ' – very anxious to have everything on the instant, & at times excited, if things were not *instantly* brought.'

Miss Holas did not include this fact in her written testimony, because she did not think it noteworthy: the sick do get irritable. It seems a small fact, but it may be significant. What Miss Holas, as a latecomer, did not know is that Woolson was always polite – so considerate, so perfectly polite that no one (James said afterwards) could have guessed her mind any more than flowerpots in a window have anything to do with a figure lying on a bed. Her uncharacteristic irritability fits her determination, present in all that Marie Holas and Grace Carter have to say. It is clear from their reports that ideas of delirium, typhoid, and insanity came later.

These ideas prevailed as recently as 1983, when a conscientious scholar declared that the 'superficial details of that death are actually fairly well documented: how in January of 1894 Woolson – perhaps temporarily insane while suffering from a severe case of typhoid fever – either threw herself, or fell, from the window . . .'. Such statements derive from accretions of gossip. It was said at the time that 'no one who knew Constance, has ever for one moment dreamed that her fall from the window was intentional'. People said it was 'delirium'; it was a *second* 'acute' attack of the flu, people said, 'she couldn't have lived much longer'. They said: '. . . It is more than probable that this illness [the infection in her ears in 1892] predisposed her to the brain fever which formed a part of her last illness.'

Eyewitness reports, on the other hand, reveal that though Woolson was weak from a mysterious digestive upset, she was hardly ill – if ill at all, and never more lucid. Silent in that bed was an alert and planning mind. Her instructions were precise, and all except for the will were carried out as she foresaw: she specified a dress for her shroud; she forbade the morgue in Venice, with threats of haunting; she chose a cemetery at an awkward distance of hundreds of miles; she ordered that her papers be sealed – officially, by the American consul – until her sister should arrive; she charged Miss Holas to see to everything, and as a sign of trust (it effectively made its point to Grace Carter) handed over her household keys; she told Miss Holas where to find a model for her will, if a legal will was not made in time; she stressed care for her beloved Othello; and, finally, she arranged that Cousin Grace should arrive within hours of her death. Though Cousin Grace would wring her hands for not coming sooner, she acted exactly as Cousin Connie intended. Cousin Connie didn't want Cousin Grace at the bedside, but did foresee the red tape of Italian bureaucracy, and the need for a bona fide member of family to authorise her removal to Rome. Silent, as she lay, turned away, secured in her deafness, signing to Miss Holas to leave her alone, she planned her death and burial – and what came after – to the last detail.

There are, then, two testimonies of events that led up to that midnight leap on 24 January 1894 and that white form lying on the cold stones, stunned, not quite dead, moaning in the dark *calle*. These testimonies were given at different times over the next few days, so that different details emerge at closer or farther removes from the fatal leap. These are testimonies that would stand up in a court of law, but the plainness that makes them convincing from a factual point of view, makes them limited for biography, which requires insight as well as fact. Insight was not Miss Holas's forte. This is not simply the consequence of her position as latecomer: she was not hugely perceptive, but she was sensible and observant, and this will do if we explore certain details in the testimony of Grace Carter in relation to her own.

In the main, as stated, the testimonies are the same – not surprisingly, since that of Miss Carter derived in large part from Miss Holas – yet when Carter set down her impressions on 27 January, three days after the event and four days before the funeral, she was living with the body in the Semitecolo, and seeing with the eyes of a person attached to the deceased. She saw that the body was not mangled and no bones were broken. She reports on the face of the dead woman, who looked content to be dead. And it is Miss Carter who tells the family that Woolson's instructions had included a shroud, for Miss Carter herself clothed the body in the white dress her cousin had specified.

Miss Carter was also interested in the relation of doctor and patient – the supposed patient, we might say, reading between the lines. For respected Dr Chene states to all concerned that when he first saw Miss Woolson on 14 or 15 January, her flu was 'mild' with 'hardly any fever'. That word, 'mild', comes up again and again – the people on the scene deny emphatically any intimation of danger. What happened after that puzzled the doctor. Experience told him this was a robust woman who was nearly recovered. I have wondered if Woolson had in mind the dangerous illness that eludes diagnosis in 'A Florentine Experiment' ('No one could tell what was the matter with her') or Dorothy's decline (when 'the doctor did not know'). In actuality, Woolson was to find, as did Alice James, that it's not so easy to die. Dr Chene turned out to be not as conveniently obtuse as the doctor in 'Dorothy'. At once he asked Miss Holas, engaged to 'do writing' for 'a few hours' a day, to stay 'all the time', more (Carter explains) 'because he thought Aunt Connie would be lonely, than because he thought she needed nursing'.

Carter duly relates the sudden onset of 'terrible pains' and protracted vomiting ('green stuff') on Thursday and Friday, 18 and 19 January, accompanied by fever. On the Friday, her letter arrived in which she offered to come. Woolson said no. Over the weekend, the pains abated, leaving her weak, and at this point Woolson began to beg the doctor 'for doses of laudanum, saying she *must* have large doses as she was accustomed to take them & *must* sleep'.

There appear to be two plans here: under the cover of supposed flu, an unsuccessful attempt to kill herself, first, with an overdose of something that caused a violent reaction. The violent reaction recurs in the night, when Woolson is left alone; it abates during daylight hours when Miss Holas is on duty. The attempt leaves her handicapped by weakness, and in a moment of desperation she conceives plan number two: the sleeping-draught. The doctor explains to her, deliberately and carefully, that to give her the amount she requests will kill her. She won't wake up (as she intends). The doctor may guess this because he adds that he refuses to be responsible for her death.

So, a battle of wills took place: his patient demanded what she claimed was her customary dose. Evidently, she argued with vehemence (given the double underlining of Miss Carter's attempt to set down the tone of this exchange, as she heard it immediately from Miss Holas). The Holas testimony, four days later, left out the intensity, either because memory for emotional tones fades faster than fact, or because, to a stranger, it was not striking. Miss Carter, however, picked it up because it was unlike the woman she knew, who was perfectly restrained. Miss Carter was aware this would interest the family. The vehemence Woolson manifests at this point is because, naturally, she prefers a painless death.

This could all be mere supposition if it were not for one crucial clue: something that should have happened did not happen. (Sherlock Holmes finds his clue in a dog who didn't bark in the night.) What did *not* happen is that when Woolson is *in extremis* on Thursday and Friday, in paroxysms of pain and retching, she does not contact Dr Baldwin, if only for an opinion on her disorder. Her local doctor 'wondered' at her case; Baldwin, a brilliant diagnostician, was in Florence, not too far away, and in such a case would certainly have come. A telegram could have reached him at once; a letter within a day. When she had been *in extremis* in 1892, she had confessed a death-wish to Dr Baldwin, whose understanding, as always, brought relief. Not to advise her trusted doctor of her present condition was surprising (insane, said James), and suggests that her state of mind was somewhat different from the closely allied state of mind in the winter of 1892 when she had a combined assault of pain and depression. The difference, we can infer, was that in February 1892 she had wished for help; not so in January 1894. As her long-term doctor, Baldwin would have known exactly how much laudanum she was accustomed to take, and would have grasped at once her intention. So, he is not to know. No one is to stop her, even though Dr Chene forbade that she be left alone – not for a minute, said Dr Chene. He would send an experienced nurse, a nun, to watch through the night.

Woolson's maid watched out the night of Saturday 20 January and the night nurse began her duties on Sunday the twenty-first. Throughout the day Miss Holas remained in charge of the sickroom. She was in and out. It is now that Woolson turns to the windows. Miss Carter reports that she wanted them open. 'She would allow no one to stay in the room with her but it made her nervous, except Miss Holas, who[m] she would sometimes allow there – so the nurse sat in the little room just off, where she could come at an instant. The reason why Aunt Constance wanted them to sit in the little room was that she seemed to want a great deal of air, keeping the windows open, & said she hated to see them sitting in the cold.'

Miss Holas and Dr Chene proved formidable adversaries. Her sole chance was the nun – removed to a distance by Miss Woolson's concern lest she take cold in the winter air. Her silver bell beside the bed would summon the nun if necessary. The doctor, according to Miss Carter, remained uneasy.

'The last day [Tuesday 23 January] when the doctor came in the afternoon he told Miss Holas that Aunt Constance should not be left alone at all.'

Was she in danger, Miss Holas asked.

Not the least danger, replied the doctor. All the same, he remained puzzled by his patient's apparent weakness, and thought it might 'mean something'. Dr Chene was on the alert: he observed a woman who was 'very nervously excited'.

That day, Miss Holas stayed late. She wished to see Miss Woolson settled for the night. The patient requested that her curtains be closely drawn – not the least ray of light must penetrate her room, is the reason she gives. This ensures that her room will not be visible, during the night, from the street below. Her ruse is planned with precision: it is now or never. Miss Carter has been summoned, and in all probability is now on the night train from Munich hurtling through the Alps towards Venice. At nine, Miss

Holas at last ceases her attentions and goes away. At ten, Woolson takes the meagre dose of laudanum from the nun, and lies quiet. Then, just after midnight, the nun hears the bell. Her patient asks for a light and cold milk. When the nun brings it in the cup Miss Holas has left in readiness, her patient rejects it in a capricious way that would have surprised anyone who knew her. She grumbles this is not the cup she wanted. She must have her milk in the pink china cup in the dining-room – in that cup only. So it is that for a few seconds the nun goes off to the dining-room – and those few seconds are all that is needed. In two leaps, the patient is out of bed and out the window.

The sills overlooking the *calle* at the back of the Semitecolo are not low – not windows you topple out of with ease in a dizzy spell. It could only have been a deliberate act.

A second later, the nun returned with the pink cup. The bed was empty; the curtains flung wide. Rushing to the window, she saw a white heap on the stones below. She shouted for Angelo, a gondolier who was sleeping in the house, and as he dashed downstairs the front bell rang. It was two men carrying Woolson. She was not dead, and of course should not have been moved – she did moan when touched. The men heard her say 'some word which they thought was an Italian one for cold'. After that, she lived about three-quarters of an hour. A nearby doctor who was called and Dr Chene concluded that she died from shock to the head and spine.

What both testimonies clarify beyond doubt is that Constance Fenimore Woolson was perfectly rational in the days leading up to her death, and that, contrary to the stories that spread around the world, it was premeditated, not an impulse. The story of mad impulse was largely the creation of Henry James.

He made up this story in a state of 'shock', 'horror', and confusion in the face of the 'obscure' – these words echo and re-echo through his reaction. He felt 'ghastly amazement and distress', but not, at first, horror when he received a cable from Clara Benedict announcing her sister's death, and asking James to go to Venice. He decided against it when he heard Grace Carter was already at the scene. He wrote to her:

I am so utterly in the dark about everything that I am reduced to mere conjecture & supposition as to what has taken place & as to *how* Miss Woolson died. I had not ever heard a word of her being ill; Mrs Benedict's cable was a bolt out of the blue. It is all – I mean my fear that she was alone, *unfriended* at the last – too miserable to talk about. . . . I am waiting for some *knowledge* . . .'.

The horror hit him on Saturday the twenty-seventh when newspapers got wind of a drama:

MISS WOOLSON COMMITTED SUICIDE

THE NOVELIST JUMPED FROM A WINDOW OF
HER HOUSE IN VENICE AND WAS
KILLED ALMOST INSTANTLY

London, Jan. 27. – The Vienna correspondent of 'The Standard' says: 'Constance Fenimore Woolson committed suicide . . . by jumping from a window of a house in Venice where she had lived seven months. Death was almost immediate. Miss Woolson had suffered from influenza for four days, but she had been eccentric for a longer period.'

It was so. He saw it at once, and never budged from this conviction even though Sam Mather cabled a denial – to the effect that his aunt, dazed with 'severe influenza' and 'high fever', had fallen, not jumped – which the newspaper printed the following day. Ready as James stood to leave for the funeral in Rome, he cancelled his tickets at the last minute.

'. . . After Saturday I was too utterly sickened to move,' he explained to Miss Carter. 'But I shall stand there [at the grave] some day this spring.'

The funeral took place on 31 January. It was organised from the Roman end by John Hay, who happened to be there. The afternoon was 'exquisitely beautiful', he said, 'a real Roman day with sunshine as bright & sky as blue as summer, & yet with a lingering tang of winter in the air'. Hay and Dr Nevin, rector of St Paul's American Church in Rome, chose the spot for the grave. 'The ground is very crowded & eligible sites are rare,' Hay reported to the Mathers. 'But we were, I think, very fortunate in finding an unoccupied spot overlooking the cemetery, adjoining the graves of the Storys & very near to that of Shelley. I am sure it would have been a solace to her sensitive soul when living to have known that she was to repose forever in such a place & in such company.'

Her chosen company was expatriate and artistic, not religious. A cross is engraved on her tomb, but nothing in her life suggests faith. We can only guess why she came to lie here.

Woolson chose this cemetery with a fixed determination backed by threats. Its associations, for her, went back to her stay in Rome, when she visited the cemetery on 16 March 1881: 'Yesterday I went to the Protestant cemetery and stood for some moments beside the grave of Keats, which was blue with violets, and beside that of Shelley, with its inscription, "Cor cordium." The little burial ground is nestled in an angle of the old city wall, and the great gray pyramid of Caius Cestius looks down upon it, bringing the past very near us.' In the spring of 1881, a month and a half after she visited the cemetery, its association with *Daisy Miller* revived when James came to Rome at the end of April and outlined a dramatisation that would eliminate the tragic end: 'Daisy's grave was in the little Protestant cemetery, in an angle of the wall of imperial Rome, beneath the cypresses and the thick spring-flowers. Winterbourne stood there beside it . . .'. Woolson chose this place for all these associations. For James, who had visited the cemetery several times, the most touching aspect was expatriation, English inscriptions with 'their universal expression of that trouble within trouble, misfortune in a foreign land'.

Woolson had shared this feeling, and her wish to lie here was familiar to James. After her death, he spoke of 'the blest Roman cemetery that she positively *desired* – I mean in her extreme love of it – and of her intensely consenting and more than reconciled rest under the Roman sky. *Requiescat.*'

James hoped that the funeral of a writer with her 'extremely honourable literary position' would attract a few Americans '(having known her or not)' to stand with the Hays. Afterwards, Clara Hay listed the small group of mourners. They included the American Minister, Mr Potter; Richard Greenough, related to the sculptor of Woolson as a 'lovely boy'); and two unknown Englishwomen, 'one of whom came & begged a flower from the wreaths to send to Miss Poynter'. Several others were strangers to Clara. She added: 'Henry James had intended to come on to the funeral but finally gave it up at the last minute as he has not been at all well . . .'.

In fact, he had 'utterly collapsed'. He now 'let everything go', 'sickened' by the scene in his mind. The 'monstrous suddenness' of that leap by 'so close a friend of mine', who 'had been so for so many years', woke 'an intense nearness of participation in every circumstance of her tragic end'. Beside himself, vociferous, words pouring from his pen, he sent letters with his story in all directions.

He, naturally, had the imagination Miss Holas lacked: he saw – *saw* again and again – was 'haunted' by – the image of violence, an act that was the antithesis of his friend's nature as he had understood it, 'the gentlest and tenderest of women'. And worse than what he saw – for in time he would blot out that hideous scene – was his confusion. It remained 'impenetrably obscure to me', he owned to Gosse. 'But what an overwhelming, haunting horror – & intolerable obsession of the ghastly, pitiful *fact!*' He, the knower, the deep student of the female heart (as Hay had called him), was forced to acknowledge that he had not known a woman with whom he had been 'extremely intimate' for many years.

This confusion was so intolerable that he coped with it in three ways. First, he distanced her: no longer 'Fenimore', she was again 'Miss Woolson'. Then, he disseminated a story of madness – not depression, but '*dementia*' – and insisted on his story, at length, to two sophisticated men, William James and Francis Boott, to whom she had been sane and amusing. And then, three months later, he took himself to the scene of her death, 'Miss Woolson's sad death-house' in Venice.

James built up his version with all the power of professional eloquence, using his combined authority as 'intimate friend' and storyteller. Despite his claim that he let everything go, he wrote purposefully to everyone who knew of his tie with Fenimore: Baldwin, Boott, Clara Benedict, Grace Carter, John Hay, Rhoda Broughton, Mrs Bronson, William James, and, of all people, the Ranee of Sarawak (who had no connection whatever with the tragedy, but to whom James writes in the same terms: the shock, the deplorable circumstances, the whisper of insanity). The purpose is the same in all the letters: to fix on Fenimore the slur of uncontrollable *dementia*. The coded message is plain: no one, not the best of friends, could have prevented this death. He made his strongest attempt to exonerate himself in an unpublished letter to Miss Carter as official representative of his friend's family. She had informed him, as requested, of the last days. On 2 February, twenty minutes after Miss Carter's report arrived, he replied in eager haste, blending the truth of depression and deafness with prompt fictions of insanity and delirium:

> Your account of the circumstances and conditions *precedent* to the horrible event of last week interest me deeply, and give me to a certain extent the relief of seeing the matter with more clearness. Unquestionably she had become actively insane under the influence of her illness and her fever, but I seem to see now, in the light of the event, how far that depression of spirits to which she was at all times so tragically liable had progressed in her mind, and what a morbid obsession it had become. Other signs and symptoms came to me which I didn't fully read at the time. She was intensely unhappy, by her natural disposition (her deafness greatly increased it,) and unhappy in a way that no one, I think, however much fighting, as it were, on her side – I mean even in the closest sympathy with her – could effectually or permanently combat. But she had got much worse this winter – I now feel sure – and quite in spite of any external cause. The only external cause was – at last – her attack of influenza, which your letter shows to have been a much worse one than I at first supposed. (I mean that I supposed on first hearing of her death – getting the impression, then, that she had been ill only 3 or 4 days. . . .) It was this that aggravated a state of melancholy already existing – and then in a moment *determined* the delirious, irresponsible act.

All responsibility, according to James, must lie with 'Miss Woolson', who was 'intrinsically one of the saddest and least happy natures I have ever met'. When Boott begged to differ, and recalled their friend's 'joy in life', James denied it flatly, and whispered to William that only the unintelligent would take such a view. The delight in humour that does pervade her letters, including those to James himself, had no part in his story, for humour implies balance. The James story is all about latent and emergent mania.

He told Rhoda Broughton: 'The tragedy of Miss Woolson's death remains ... explicable only on the hypothesis of some sudden explosion of latent brain disease. ... I remember well our lovely May night at Bellosguardo.'

Two days later, on the day of the funeral, he had progressed to full-blown *dementia* in his more adamant version to Boott: 'The event seems to me absolutely to demand the hypothesis of sudden *dementia* and to admit of none other. Pitiful victim of chronic melancholy as she was ... nothing is more possible than that, in illness, this obsession should abruptly have deepened into suicidal mania. ... She was not, she was never, wholly sane – I mean her liability to suffering was the *doom* of mental disease.'

Then, two days after the funeral, on 2 February (the same day he defended himself to Grace Carter), rage surfaced in a letter to Baldwin: 'Miss Woolson's evident determination not to send for you seems to me insane – just as her silence to me does; in spite of letters which in a *normal* state she would infallibly have answered. She kept us both ignorant – with a perversity that was diseased.'

Perversity was the accusation at the heart of it, a sense of betrayal. She was not what he thought, this woman to whom he was 'greatly attached'. Her action had denied the role he had assigned to her: 'an angel of quiet virtue', renouncing the world and reserving for him, alone, her 'infinite charity'. He had liked to think of her as 'unspeakably touching' in her loneliness, multiplying the difficulty of her life in her 'ingenious, elaborate, passionate effort' to minimise his. Her 'perversity' was to deny this story with her own – a story she had not communicated to him beyond irrefutable proof of the poverty of his story from her point of view.

Angry at her silence, appalled by the reverberations of scandal, shuddering at newspapers in Venice, London, and across America reporting the mysterious death of a well-known writer, James did not spare sensational words when it became necessary to distance her from himself: her suicidal mania, her diseased brain, her perversity. She would '*insist* on suffering', while he had maintained an anxious guard. Half one's friendship for her was anxiety, he claimed. Boott, who had known her as a neighbour, must be persuaded that his enjoyment of her company had been mistaken; William must convey this to Boott. Hers had been a 'mechanical' cheer, James insisted, and anything genuine had been a tribute to Boott, and Boott alone: 'she put for him *all* the flowerpots in the window.'

If we compare the 'horror' of James, and two or three weeks of 'quite baffling indisposition', with the distress of Grace Carter, Clara, Clare, and the Hays, it is evident that James was much the most disturbed – 'sickened' while others, shocked though they were, felt a recognisable grief. What James felt after Woolson's death was no ordinary regret, nothing so simple. The 'horror' was bound up with publicity. He feared the reverberations of gossip that did surface, eventually, in the *New York Herald*:

> A floating newspaper paragraph states that Henry James, the novelist, does not marry because he thinks that the highest development of the intellectual life is incompatible with the petty frets and worries of domesticity. . . .
>
> The truth about Mr. James' bacherlorhood is known to very few people; that truth is his heart was buried nearly three years ago in the grave that covered all that was mortal of Constance Fenimore Woolson. For a long time he had been this other author's devoted slave, and, in spite of her deafness and increasing years, she possessed an attraction for him as intense as even the difference between their literary styles and methods. . . .
>
> It was one of the curious freaks of that mischievous imp, Cupid, that a feminine leader of romantic fiction should be so decidedly admired by an apostle of bald realism. Nothing more than an outward strong friendship was apparent betwixt the two, for Miss Woolson was not to be won. It was Mr. James, however, who cabled the news of her death to this country, . . . and who took upon himself the duties of the man of the family and principal mourner, as, indeed, he was.
>
> And so long as Miss Woolson's memory remains green in his heart it may well be said that he is too thoroughly celibate to ever think of wedlock.

Crude, inaccurate, this was the kind of public involvement from which he protected himself – he had, indeed, been guarding himself in the usual way when he withdrew from promises to 'Fenimore' during the last months of her life. To secure himself in this unprecedented situation, closer enquiry was necessary.

At the beginning of April 1894, James arrived in Venice. He usually stayed at the Barbaro, but this time chose to stay in Woolson's rooms in the Casa Biondetti. When he reached Genoa, late in March, he asked Mrs Bronson to secure these rooms, and took them for three to four months. It would cost him his privacy – he would live with other long-term lodgers, who would talk of Woolson.

When people are 'sickened' they crave knowledge, as James did. The Biondetti was not an idle choice: it was, in part, a practical one, close to the Semitecolo, but for a man alert to the extra-sensory it meant a chance to know Woolson through her rooms: would it be the polite 'Fenimore' with her 'dainty dignity', or the leaping woman who had shocked him? Woolson herself had believed in posthumous telepathy: she had said that the recently dead, whose acute feelings have pervaded their rooms, can make themselves felt there. This fits the finale to 'Owen Wingrave' (1892), where James imagines a ghostly encounter between the living and the dead: 'a fighting man' and an angered ancestor in the latter's room. Given the outcome – Wingrave dies behind the shut door – James understood that to confront the dead could be fatal, a word James invoked. Yet this was what he had to do in Venice, apart from the business of the 'death-house': he had, in some sense, to meet Woolson herself – meet her, shall we say, in the recess of consciousness.

To put himself in the way of the 'dreadful *image*' that had haunted him for three months, was an act few would have braved. Call it an act of imaginative truth. It was not only that he owed this to a woman who had been his 'intimate friend'; he owed it to himself – the master of consciousness – and he owed it to their lost future, an alternative life he had not pursued. Fenimore's death told him she did not believe in that unacted self – she refused, with utter finality, that phantom of possibility that had called out her own phantom of possibility, from time to time. These phantoms –

alternative selves, the mutual creation of two storytellers – had played together, unseen, on Bellosguardo, in Geneva, and, recently, Paris. Then, suddenly, without warning it seemed to him, the woman he had named 'Fenimore' – his creation whom he thought he controlled – took off, leaving behind an unnerving silence like a locked door.

The ghost of the Biondetti proved benign. For, soon after his arrival, James told Clare Benedict quite matter-of-factly, 'I found this pleasant little apartment [in the Biondetti] . . . appreciably full of the happy presence of your aunt.' He believed in continued communications from the dead who had a force of character that made them 'capable' of 'reaching us'. In the case of a life that went out 'in a single gust', with 'passions nipped in their flower', and 'waiting initiations' on the part of a recipient still vibrating at the mouth of experience, that expectant vibration could call forth the dead – 'to *something*'. There was more to apprehension than science could know: 'I reach' he said, 'beyond the laboratory-brain'. He would 'assault' the bounds of mortality; would 'seize' with 'aggression' what 'sources' he claimed for his own, even in the 'boundless' and 'beyond'. The core of the encounter lies in 'combinations'; the word 'share' ('one's share in it . . . and above all . . . its appeal to *be* shared') returns again and again: a dead person can sustain a 'being' that asks to be shared, and a man with the developed sensibility of an artist can find it in him to answer that 'intense desire of being to get itself . . . shared'. It is his 'privilege' to immerse in 'that fountain, to depths immeasurable'. This posthumous 'adventure' turns on desire – 'desire so confirmed, so thoroughly established and nourished, as to leave belief a comparatively irrelevant affair'.

James dramatised all this in a tale of a mature woman, unknown till her death, who finds a posthumous partner in 'The Way It Came' (1896). So long as she lived, she had been 'a private resource' for select friends, a resource cultivated 'more or less in secret, as a person whom one didn't meet in society, whom it was not for everyone – whom it was not for the vulgar – to approach, and with whom therefore acquaintance was particularly difficult and particularly precious'. The posthumous partner is a predestined friend she had somehow failed to meet. But after death she comes straight to him, offering an 'inconceivable communion' on the part of 'a being just engulfed in the infinite and still vibrating with human emotion' who appears to him through his open door until they stand 'face to face'. She comes with 'an impulse of reparation, of admonition, or even of curiosity'. It is a posthumous affair – an affair of passion – which 'makes up' for what is missed in the world. The man never marries, because the dead claim him. 'You love her as you've never loved,' a living woman accuses him, 'and, passion for passion, she gives it straight back! She rules you, she holds you, she has you all!' This is fiction, but it tells us what James could imagine.

The obverse of communion was deep silence: the unanswered letter, the locked door to her floor of the Semitecolo, the sealed papers. Was there silence – or would they discover a note, a manuscript, an explanation? Was there anything there in the Semitecolo that would involve him in her 'deplorable' publicity?

His letter of 2 February to Miss Carter sends out feelers about the sealed box. Miss Woolson would surely have left no unfinished manuscript, he puts it to Miss Carter, and then asks directly who was to sort the leavings. Would the family hire an agent to do this, or would the Benedicts come out to Venice? He was desperate to see Miss Carter, willing to go as far as her base in Munich. This was not his normal behaviour – James never concerned himself with the business affairs of people outside his immediate family. Though his tone affects lightness and charitable concern, these queries show, not surprisingly, that James was a worried man.

At this very time, the 'poor Benedicts' (as James called them from now on) had resolved on coming. At once, he had offered help. He had been on the pier when their steamer, *Kaiser Wilhelm II*, docked in Genoa on 29 March. And now, he was shoulder to shoulder with them when they broke the seal, waiting at the door when the Benedicts came on to Venice from their first trial, a visit to the grave in Rome. They were fragile in their grief. '. . . We are both in such a state that every little thing knocks us up,' Clara said. Together with Clara and Clare, he entered the death-house. He was there, full-time, every day for the first two weeks.

It must be borne in mind that this was not a domestic man, not one brought up to occupy himself with mundane tasks of sorting, cleaning, and clearing, but here he was, at it, over five weeks, deep in Woolson's 'immensely accumulated effects', turning over her papers (where he came upon the idea for what was to be, in the view of many, his greatest tale, 'The Beast in the Jungle')*, carrying off clothes, and laying hands on his favourite Meacci painting, 'The Garden of Hesperides', where three women are tending three trees in tubs raised high on plinths. The women draw water from a stream flowing across the base of the painting. Two of them lift up their arms to their work; the third bends to fill her bowl. They are like priests at their altars, robed in the purest white. James asked Clara to lend him this painting (and held on to it for fifteen years until she made an 'outcry'). As Clara put it, 'Henry James . . . never left us until all her precious things were packed and boxed and sent to America.' And all the while that James was at it, a fire was burning.

'Venice has been cold & wet & discouraging,' James told Miss Carter. 'The big fireplace at Casa Semitecolo was, day after day, a real source of life & faith.'

It has long been assumed that James burnt unwanted letters, but the practicality of this remained unclear. How did James manage it in the presence of the Benedicts? He could not have made a fire without their knowing. As it turned out, unseasonable weather worked in his favour: a fire was needed every day. Woolson found it hard to throw things away – so it is surprising that no letters to her from Katharine Loring and Baldwin survived. It is likely that these papers, including the deathbed message from Alice, as well as any remaining letters from Henry James, went into that convenient fire.

James found the Semitecolo a 'mad' place for his friend to have stayed, 'mad for *her*'. He may have projected his own mood, for though the entrance is gloomy, most entries in Venice are gloomier in their mouldering grandeur. The floor which Woolson had occupied is filled with light and the rooms, with high ceilings,

* Woolson's outline reads: 'To imagine a man spending his life looking for and waiting for his "splendid moment." "Is this my moment?" "Will this state of things bring it to me?" But the moment never comes. When he is old and infirm it comes to a neighbour who has never thought of it or cared for it.' (Benedict, ii, 144–5).

looking out on the rooftops of Venice, are charming. So, there was no reason to shudder at the Semitecolo but for the image it brought home to him. 'The sight of the scene of the horrible act is ... sufficient to establish her utter madness at the time.'

One of their activities was to search for the will. Though Woolson had told Miss Holas there was a 'model' for a will, and though at an earlier date she had told Boott of the existence of a will that contained a 'surprise', nothing that could be called a will came to light.

James exploded in fury when Boott brought up this will. He denied it. 'C.F.W. left *no* will, at all – & had evidently never made any – that "surprising" one she spoke to you of, nor any other. ... I think ... that that speech you quote of C.F.W.'s about the "surprise" of her will was just one of those numerous strange ruses that illustrated (as one looks back,) her latent insanity.' As he spoke he felt once more his 'horrible pain'.

It was a time of acute stress. The Benedicts proved retentive and obstinate. James complained to Miss Carter they '*opposed*' his advice to get rid of things: 'They took ... the whole situation in their own way & not as many people would have done – I mean those whose foremost wish wd. have been never to behold again any of the mere *things* that surrounded Miss Woolson in her last unhappy days. But on this point people feel in all sorts of directly *opposed* ways ...'.

On 16 April, at the end of two weeks, James owned, 'I have had, & still have, worries.' Three weeks later, the immediate stress was over. On 11 May, three days after the departure of the Benedicts, a letter to Miss Carter breathes relief: 'This dreary, dreary month is over & well over. ... I don't think there is the smallest loose end left to worry about ...'.

At last, we begin to see the nature of the twofold task James set himself during these five weeks in Venice: to meet the more familiar, benign spirit in the Casa Biondetti, and to destroy unsafe relics in the Casa Semitecolo. The danger was that the strange, untamed woman of the Semitecolo might prevail.

His task, he said later that May, had been 'an almost fatal job'. Fatal for James – or Woolson – or both? Central to his unwonted activity was the scene on the lagoon: a glimpse of James with a woman's dress in his arms – the balloon sleeves, full busts, and tight waists of the nineties – about to throw it overboard. In doing this, he opposed the general inclination of the Benedicts – though it is, of course, possible that he persuaded them in this instance to let him have his way. The Benedicts wished to preserve; James, to obliterate – to obliterate the 'dreadful *image*' and the dark dress in which the *image* was clothed. Its presence in the dress pressed upon him, and when he shoved it down he fought to free himself. *Terminations* was the word James chose as the title of his next book.*

It was not a luminous, pink and gold Venice that faded in the distance when James made that journey in a gondola piled with things from the Semitecolo. The city was grey; visibility was poor. The only record comes from an aged American, Mrs Huntington, to whom, as a listening girl, James had confided 'a strange story' – how much of it was true, how much a fantasy, no one will know. Mrs Huntington recalled it in 1956 for a BBC programme in memory of Henry James; an unedited transcript of the full interview remains. The voice of Mercede Huntington comes to us in thin, interrupted air-waves on a long-distance line from the Villa Mercede (once the Castellani) on Bellosguardo. 'Things', she said, 'things' belonging to 'some very famous person' who had died in Venice, were carried away. What exactly these 'things' were is, unfortunately, indistinct. All the same, the wording does not rule out the possibility that there could have been other 'things' besides dresses. There was also what Clara called 'the mask business' (the word is not very legible). There was one relic Clara wished to destroy, and the American consul – cautious, awkward Mr Johnson – did not consent. This caused Clara 'suffering' and sleepless nights. It was a serious issue, because the Benedicts and James were distinctly annoyed, and pulled strings to give Johnson 'his quietus'. Cables raced back and forth, and at length Clara Benedict had permission to destroy whatever it was – a death-mask, possibly – that upset her so much. 'The destroying of that awful mask[?], was another painful thing for *just me* to do, & nearly made me ill.' And if Clara was that upset – she and Clare

*This is the first time he used a new title, not that of a tale.

were on the edge of collapse, according to James – and if he was the support at hand, together with Tito, the trusty gondolier, it is just conceivable that this 'awful' thing was part of the haul on the gondola, gliding towards the centre of the lagoon, with Henry James waiting to perform his part.

This scene looks back curiously to a scene in *The Aspern Papers* where the lodger, shocked by his padrona's claim on him – 'poor deluded, infatuated, extravagant lady' – commands his gondolier to row him 'out into the lagoon!' He sits unseeing: 'I don't know where, on the lagoon, my gondolier took me.' His hat is pulled over his brow, his face is 'hidden', and he groans softly as he fails to convince himself that he is guilty of nothing. 'I had been as kind as possible because I really liked her', the lodger reassures himself, mulling over the question of 'fault' and denying it repeatedly: 'I hadn't given her cause – distinctly I hadn't.'

We might infer that James was inclined to blame himself. What if Fenimore had killed herself because of him? Avoiding her funeral had left her active – buried, not dead; dead for the world, not for him. He had to eradicate the '*image*' of violence in a woman whose feelings he had failed to measure.

Once only, he revealed it. In old age Mercede Huntington recalled how James had let it out 'in such an extraordinary sort of dribble' from the corner of his mouth, mumbling and funny. He told her he 'had to do certain things', as though he were following instructions or carrying out a will. Mercede did not know there was no surviving will. Young, entertained, she had listened as to a story: 'there were lots of clothes – you see – and a lot of these black dresses so he threw them in the water and they came up like balloons all around him and the more he tried to throw them down, the more they came up and he was surrounded by these horrible black balloons.' In 1956 – forty years after James's death – his listener, wandering at times, returned to this surreal scene: the black shapes on the *laguna*, the man beating them down, and the wide sleeves filling, the full fronts riding the surface of the water like wilful phantoms he could not dispel. And the dribbling voice telling her this with persistent hilarity, so many years ago.

At the end of May, James stood at the grave in Rome. It was

'beautiful', he saw, 'in a beautiful spot'. Hay had planted it with violets. On the way back to Venice, he stayed with Baldwin for a week in Florence – this would have been an opportunity to go over what James called the hole bored in his nerves by his 'horrid predicament in Venice': it had made him 'simply ferocious'. One day, he climbed to Bellosguardo and dined at the Villa Castellani.* It seemed now a 'cemetery of ghosts', he wrote to Boott; 'there is little joy in it left for me – or rather there would be little if I had not deep-seated dispositions to find myself secretly . . . fond of the company of the relics of the dead. Villa Brichieri seemed to stare down at one with unspeakably mournful eyes of windows.'

For the rest of June, he returned to the Biondetti, staying in the same rooms with the same Americans, Mary Felton and Lily Norton, below. He was in a strange state, 'both demoralized and dematerialized' and still ferocious. The Grand Canal seemed to be crawling with Americans whose voices made him sick. It was a '*vomitorium*' of the United States. He left Venice like 'Apollo fleeing the furies'. A year later he shrank from Italy with nervous horror – projecting it, still, on his countrymen: 'That way Boston lies, which is the deadliest form of madness.'

That summer James pored over his sister's diary with its taste for death. Alice James, who had contemplated suicide very seriously, made two remarks about its public aspect which bear on her brother's reaction. She thought it a courageous act. Alice deplored only the result: the spattering of relatives and friends with a secret they would rather not know. A suicide leaves behind a moral burden someone is compelled to assume: misery undiscerned or ignored. For six months following what James was convinced was suicide on Fenimore's part, his rejection of her mounted to a kind of madness of his own. But once his involvement was driven home by a rigorous conscience, he did not shirk the moral burden.

* This would have been the first opportunity for HJ to tell his black balloons story. There was another opportunity when he dined again at the Villa just before or just after his third visit to Fenimore's grave in 1907. He wrote on 23 June 1907 to Laura Wagnière-Huntington: 'I cherish the memory, please tell Mrs Henry, . . . of that delightful free-spoken dinner under the cool high noble loggia of the Villa. I greet affectionately . . . the exquisite gold haired maiden . . .'. (Houghton)

Slowly, over the next months and years, he was to awaken to missed truth: for a master of consciousness, the worst of failures. This cannot be seen externally, in feminist terms, but internally, in Jamesian terms, if we are to understand the full impact of Constance Fenimore Woolson on Henry James.

The death of Fenimore, like that of Minny, aroused intense and unaccustomed emotion – no ordinary emotion. The impact, in both cases, was supremely creative. Minny and Fenimore had powers of their own as emergent women, and James recognised in them a match of sorts, vital to his art. The women saw this match – Fenimore saw it before she met James – but for them it was harder, very hard in fact, because their own involvements were less resolved in higher purpose – and for this very reason they impress us with responsible sympathy. James did partake in the solace they offered, but his prime interest was creative: from his point of view, they were central to his life because it was wholly a creative life.

Restless, in August, he walked the 'purple & orange moors' at St Ives in Cornwall, grateful for the silence of his companion, Leslie Stephen: 'the dumbness of the English . . . has its merits.' His next host, the novelist W. E. Norris, pictured his 'aged legs' trotting feebly after James as he 'ran up and down' a verandah in Torquay 'like a caged lion'. What impressed James most in his sister's diary was her 'face-to-face' with life and death. Whatever he had faced at the Biondetti prepared him to try again at this point.

On 8 September 1894, James took a train to Oxford and knocked at 15 Beaumont Street. He had come to occupy certain rooms – the same rooms Fenimore had occupied from October 1891 till May 1893. The James who came to Oxford was different from the man confused by her death nine months before; different, too, from the man whose accusations of madness had set her apart from a nexus of depression in which he'd shared. This had been his punitive phase (continuous with stabs at her reputation in 'Miss Woolson'). Now, it was the writer who sought her out, and would find himself in finding her. Once, she had sought him out; now, he sought her. The fact that he lingered in her rooms, in her bed, for the rest of the month suggests his venture bore fruit. His notebook proves it. Psychic danger – braved by a Jamesian type of 'fighting man' – was rewarded with an idea for 'The Altar of the Dead', about a middle-aged bachelor who 'cherishes for the silent ... dead, a tenderness in which all his private need ... finds a sacred, and almost secret expression'. As this filled his mind, James, for once, closed off all other communication: no letters, no visits. He set down the outline in Fenimore's room on 29 September. It was followed a month later by a swell of purpose that marked the rise of the third and highest wave of his career: the earliest outline for *The Wings of the Dove.*

The tenderness brought Minny back, that 'vision' he had retained against the day he would be ready to meet it. Her image quickened with his resolve to meet Miss Grief, who had turned away without a word. 'It is now indeed that I may do the work of my life. And I will,' he told himself. 'I have only to *face* my problems.' For years to come, the gap between public and private widened while silently he closed with the dead.

11
Posthumous Affairs

Only after Fenimore died did James embark on portraits of mature women who love mutely and to the death. Unlike young girls, they don't die of shame:* in 'The Beast in the Jungle', May dies of waiting; in *The Wings of the Dove*, Milly dies of emotional betrayal when she discovers she has been put to use by the man she loves. These are not romantic deaths. And their impact takes time to make itself felt because, for the man who remains, in each case, death is tutelary – transforming.

Transformation can be traced back to an entry in his notebook a fortnight after Fenimore's funeral, on 17 February 1894: 'A man who has some secret sorrow, trouble, fault to *tell* and can't find a recipient.'† And then again, on 19 April 1894, in Fenimore's room in Venice, James imagines an older man with 'compunction' for some 'wrong' – he has 'disappointed' two women – and now wants 'tenderly and devoutly' to repair it. This repentance contrasts with the sexual bravado of another man. Real love – and the women will bear this out – is not swagger; it resides in the man who goes in 'silence and sanctity'. Sadly, it is the silent one, he of the real power, who '*uses*' women. James implies that to possess another's soul is more damaging than to use her body.

Two days later, on 21 April, still at the Biondetti, James returned to the issue of frustration: an 'ugly' burden that seeks relief. The

* In Laura Wing (1887), Vera Glanvil in 'The Wheel of Time' (1892), and Louisa Chantry in 'The Visits' (1892), he treats shame more than anything else. These girls expose their feelings with the urgency of youth. Unfortunately, the men in question lack the alacrity of a Mr Rochester, and abandon them to their deviations from the passive model of womanhood.

† The secrecy, the impossibility of relief, recalls the secret sin of the saintly Dimmesdale in *The Scarlet Letter*.

vain contacts and silent appeals of the burdened man, as he goes about in society, coincide with the alienation of James himself from the '*vomitorium*' of Venice. Wherever he goes, 'grief' seems a false note – 'grief', he repeats. Other words link this entry in his notebook with the letters James wrote at the time: 'shocks', 'horrors'. The notebook reflects a man in an incommunicable world of his own. A woman in whom he might safely confide has inexplicably gone away. He has been uncertain what he feels for her, but his need grants her new importance. She now returns with an 'ugly' trouble of her own – and when they are 'face to face', and between them 'the real sufferings of life', he finds peace of mind in lending himself to her with a pure pity that has in it none of his customary self-interest. 'Face to face' is the reverse of hollow contacts. It is by facing the authentic woman – her unsocialised self – that a man comes to face his wrong.

'The Altar of the Dead', the tale planned in Fenimore's other habitation, her room in Oxford, admits us to the transforming moments in the life of a man, well-to-do, outwardly active in society, but with another life, a very strange affair, unknown to his associates. The 'alternative associates' of his secret life are Mary Antrim who, like Mary Temple, died young, and a nameless woman writer who, like Fenimore, lives at the outermost rim of existence. This tale brings Minny and Fenimore together as strong spirits bared by death.

George Stransom, at fifty-five, is still in love with the memory of Mary, whom he was to marry. In her, Stransom has lost 'an affection that promised to fill his life to the brim' – yet his life is filled, not emptied, by his loss, in somewhat the way James claimed, after Minny's death: 'I shall have her forever talking to me.' Stransom is 'ruled by a pale ghost'. His life is ordered for him by this 'sovereign presence' and others who have died, as he puts it, 'possessed of me. They're mine in death because they were mine in life.' His peculiar possession of them is matched by their peculiar agency: 'They were there in their . . . intensified essence, their conscious absence and expressive patience.' 'Intensified', 'conscious', 'expressive': the adjectives deny the passivity of death. Stransom tends their flames, first in the privacy of his mind, later on an altar he sets up in a church with a perpetual candle for each of his dead. Once the dead have the locus of the altar – analogous to art – they hold their ground and make it immortal. It is the living, not the dead, who 'haunt' this ground – who come from the 'swarming void' of the world to find this interface between life and afterlife.

At the altar of his art, Stransom finds a Fenimore figure: an enigma 'whose back was all he could see of her', prostrate before her own dead. As Stransom comes to know her, he discovers that she is a writer who lives in genteel poverty with an aunt. As such, she appears another incarnation of Miss Grief. Like Fenimore, she makes light of her work and, like James, Stransom commends her quiet virtue. 'Her invisible industry was a convenience to him; it helped his contented thought of her.' Sad and solitary, she becomes an 'unfailing presence' in his life, sharing walks, visits to galleries and, above all, the 'spiritual spaces' of their altar. In 'Miss Grief', the woman writer and the worldly bachelor were at odds; here, minds meet: 'there was never a word he had said to her that she had not beautifully understood.' They don't care for things other people care for 'in the intercourse of the world'. They admit that they don't care for each other in the usual way of men and women, and with this, intimacy is born. Stransom has never felt so 'safe'. Their tie remains a secret from the rest of his acquaintance. When he disappears from public life, he is plunged 'into depths quieter than the deep sea-caves'. In this place, he is joined by the figure in black.

After long friendship, she takes Stransom to her home and, then, into her sanctum: '*my* room', she calls it. Here, 'he had at last real possession of her'. The sanctum, he finds, had 'the flush of life – it was expressive; its dark red walls were articulate with memories and relics'. Suddenly, he spies a photograph of a man called Acton, his best friend, who had done him an irreparable wrong. This is the Jamesian other – the potential lover in the line of Winterbourne and Acton in *The Europeans*. This Acton is dead, and it comes to Stransom that he is the one the woman mourns. Knowing Acton as a man who charms and acts on others, he infers that his companion has been 'used' and abandoned. Clearly, she has forgiven the wrong. It is obvious to Stransom that his companion is 'ineffaceably stamped' by Acton – he had more or less 'fashioned' her.

Stransom cannot conceive of adding Acton's candle to his altar; his companion cannot conceive of returning there without it. So, the two are estranged.

When the woman in black leaves him, one of the candles gains 'unprecedented lustre'. It seems 'to expand, to spread great wings of flame'. As he gazes, 'the source of that vast radiance burned clearer than the rest, it gathered itself into a form . . . – it was the far-off face of Mary Antrim'. At a breath of 'the passion immortal', his soul opens with 'a great compunctious throb' for the flawed Acton. With that, his estrangement from the writer ends: the moment he accepts Acton, she returns to resume her place as priest at the altar (as though, by accepting a wrong, the author could commune with Fenimore, and find forgiveness). As Stransom fades, it remains uncertain whether the last candle will be for him or Acton. Only one gap remains on the altar. So, two men, the attentive soul and the careless user, merge in that last light, soon to complete the array of the dead. Their final order, grouped about the winged figure of Mary Antrim, looms before us at the end.

James left Fenimore's room on 1 October and returned to London. Between that date and 24 October he wrote this tale, ending with the winged figure. Ten days later, on 3 November, he poured out a plan for the novel that became *The Wings of the Dove*. He added to it on 7 November, and when he went back to it the following February (a month after his failure in the theatre) he exulted: 'It's *full*.' Soon after, an unprecedented move, he sent Constable a 3,000-word synopsis.

The vision of Mary Antrim stirred the idea for a full-scale portrait of a dying girl. A young creature 'on the threshold of a life that has seemed boundless, is suddenly condemned to death', he jotted, 'by the voice of a physician'. Like Minny, the young woman 'is in love with life, her dreams of it have been immense, and she clings to it with a passion, with supplication'. Waiting all this time was the unused passion in Minny's dream. 'Ah, just to let one's self go – at last', he thought, 'to surrender one's self to what through all the years one has (quite heroically, I think) hoped for and waited for – '. The subject, he said later, 'represents to my memory a very old – if I shouldn't perhaps rather say a very young motive. I can scarce remember the time when the situation on which this long-drawn fiction mainly rests was not vividly present to me.'

To spell out biographical sources limits the leap James took in the autumn of 1894, so that, by the end of 'The Altar of the Dead', he stood on the brink of his 'major phase'. James insisted that it was by the treatment rather than the source that works of art should be judged. The aesthetic achievements that lay ahead came with his power to transform his subject. The writer's art removes the act of memory to a realm of its own which re-creates Mary Temple as winged angel and Constance Fenimore Woolson as a figure of grief. Their purity is distilled from the disturbing contexts of actual deaths; they are conjoined as tutelary forms, guides to transcendence, no longer women as we understand the word, more like the concentrated essence Alice felt herself to be as she approached death. The women are defiantly anti-natural: a radiant flame; a 'presence' wrapped in black. Faceless, fleshless, they are freed from matriarchal and patriarchal subjects of worship through all the centuries of religious art and iconography. The church might find this tale blasphemous, but it does effectively restore the priority of the soul to readers for whom the limitations of gender have had their day.

The failure of his play *Guy Domville* (in January 1895) was almost a relief: it released James from compromise with current taste – he loathed Wilde's comedies of manners – and turned him back to the interior drama of the novel, the genre best suited to his genius. This turn in his career was fortuitous, for it coincided with a need to approach his memories of Fenimore through the flawed self who had failed to know her. This fertile relation with Fenimore started nine months after her suicide. After the distancing, after the glib story of her madness, after his own madder attempt to drown her clothes, came a salutary creative response that was to keep her with him, in one guise or another, for years to come.

'I see ghosts everywhere,' James said in 1895. 'It's the woman who's the ghost – it's the woman who comes to the man,' he wrote in his notebook on 21 December 1895. He '*continues* to see the dead woman'. As always, his watching posts in society would yield him anecdotes that he turned into plots: a scandalous quarrel between a mother and son over inheritance became *The Spoils of*

Poynton (1896), and a report of children in the grip of evil, which James heard from the Archbishop of Canterbury, became one of the most terrifying tales of all time, *The Turn of the Screw* (1898). But his peculiar watching posts of 1894 – the vacated rooms of a dead woman, the 'death-house' itself, and the heaped gondola gliding to an unseen spot on the lagoon – yielded James a situation that was all his own.

He resolved, now, on subjects charged with emotion ('the passionate things'). Ideas came fast. 'I have my head, thank God, full of visions,' James exulted on 14 February 1895. 'One has never too many – one has never enough.' Everything of importance in the forthcoming phase goes back to 1895 – '*La Mourante*' (the Dying Girl, eventually *The Wings of the Dove*); the ageing bachelor in '*Les Vieux*' (The Old, eventually *The Ambassadors*), who confronts, '*too late*', 'the wasting of life', which was to be the source also for an ageing bachelor at a woman's grave in 'The Beast in the Jungle' – and we begin to see the shape to his career: two high waves of creativity, the first derived from Minny Temple, culminating in *The Portrait of a Lady*; the second derived from Fenimore, culminating in *The Ambassadors* and 'The Beast in the Jungle', and sweeping again round Minny Temple in *The Wings of the Dove.*

Having waited so long to write *The Wings of the Dove*, James delayed still longer. It was not the subject that had to ripen – that was '*full*' – but he had to be equal to it. In the meantime, he romanced an American girl who reminded him of Minny Temple: her niece Ellen Emmet, known as 'Bay'.

Minny's second sister, Elly, who at nineteen had married a 'grandfather' (as Minny had called him), had settled with the Railroad King in California. There, she had six children, five of them girls – the first, born after Minny's death and named after her. After Christopher Temple Emmet died in 1884 (fittingly, in a railroad car), Elly returned east in 1887 and settled – for spells – in Cambridge, Massachusetts. She now renewed contact with her cousin William James, who lived with his family in Irving Street, Cambridge. He responded with a burst of nostalgia, his thoughts so transported 'back into the twilight of the past – that mysterious and innocent time . . . that I forgot the last quarter of a century – it was as if it were not – and the world became filled with pure Temples again'. To his amazement, he found himself weeping, a man of fifty turning into 'a lachrymose ass'. But he refused to block it: 'dear old Elly,' he said, 'certain past things won't die, and I thank God for it.'

Elly then dismayed them all by another rash marriage. In January 1891, claiming she had 'never loved before', she embraced a Scot, George Hunter. What was a mistake for Elly turned out to be providential for Henry James since it brought Elly to England – and, in Elly's train, her grown-up daughters. He clasped them fervently, matching William's nostalgia but with the added incentive of a subject in the wings. On 28 December 1896, he pictures himself in the midst of three girls and their mother, who had lately made 'so inexplicable a second marriage'. From this date, his world, too, was filled with Temples again.

William's favourite was Elly's second daughter, Rosina, who lived at 95 Irving Street while she attended Radcliffe College. She had a blithe, outspoken way – 'the angel of Conversation', who reminded William of her aunt. 'She is so much the type of Minny with more practical ability and less charm,' he informed Henry, 'that I think it would do you good to see her, it would call up all sorts of buried things.' It occurred to William that he might have proposed to her if he were young, and he was chagrined when she would not play up to him. She was 'destitute of tenderness', he complained, 'and she doesn't give one any sentimental return for her board.' Henry, too, was drawn to Rosina, but irritated by her wish to publish, particularly as she leant to the 'barbarian' camp opposed to himself. His own favourite was the third daughter, Ellen Emmet (later Rand), who wished to paint and, in fact, had already worked as an illustrator in 1893–4 for the newly begun *Vogue* magazine and in 1894 for *Harper's* also. In England she met John Singer Sargent who influenced her portrait style. She was one of the first women in America to become a professional portraitist. 'Bay' (as she was called) was short and stocky with a square jaw and a mass of reddish hair. She would cram her hair under a felt hat while she painted, which made her look like a man – made her look, in fact, as she grew older, rather like James himself. He fancied her as wildly bohemian; entranced by her freedom, he called her 'my brave Bay' or 'Beloved'. Born in 1876, Bay was twenty when he met her, the same age as Minny in the charmed summer of 1865 when she had figured for her cousin as 'the heroine of the scene'.

In July–August 1897, he joined Elly, Bay, Rosina, and Elly's fourth daughter, Leslie, on the shore at Dunwich in Suffolk. Leslie photographed him on the sands, standing in profile in a peaked cap, one hand on his hip, his beard jutting as though he were about to deliver a ruling opinion. His young cousins were in fine feather, with the winning naturalness of the Temples – on the wild side, impulsive, freer than the Jameses. From the other side of the Atlantic, William James advised Rosina not to flaunt her 'excitement' and 'naked intelligence' so freely in England. Her 'high pitch' struck Henry as '*incurably* crude'. There was, it seems, some rivalry between the brothers in promoting their favourites, each matched in lyrical terms to the character of the aunt they never knew. William relived the past through Rosina: longed, he said, for her 'perceptions of truth' that would fall into his 'receptive soul'. He liked to imagine, he wrote, the 'changes wrought in you by all this experience' – much as his brother had 'completed' Minny in the *Portrait*.

With a second portrait on the horizon, Henry put himself in the way of Bay's 'bounding, glowing juvenility and girlish grace'. Between 1896 and 1915, he wrote twenty-two letters to Bay, many of them voluminous; also letters to her mother about Bay, recalling their times together. James was easy in his ardour, possibly because forbidden ties (including those with men) left him safe from the demands of marriage. With Bay, as with Minny, there was the old charm of consanguinity, similar to William's 'old-fashioned love' for Elly, his ardour for Rosina and, in the past, for his sister, Alice. Henry had his artistic purpose – though he hid its fierceness behind the urbanity of an *homme du monde*. He was able to cultivate exactly what he wished to feel, and the feeling he expressed for Bay between 1896 and 1900 revived his feeling for Minny in the run-up to *The Wings of the Dove*. In 1900, Bay was twenty-four (Minny's age when she died) and he fifty-seven.

His renewal went with increased abhorrence of society in the later 1890s and 1900s, the reclusive as opposed to the socialising James, a side revealed only to intimates. To Bay, who never disguised her scorn for art-lovers, he protests against 'time-stealing, blood-sucking company', 'the social vampire'. To his brother Bob's son Edward Holton James he condemns chatter and twaddle: 'Suspect them – detest them – despise them.' There was an abortive plan to cross the Channel in the spring of 1897 – three years after he had fled the 'furies'. He told Miss Carter: 'On April 1st I expect to return (for the first time in 3 years) to the haunted land of Italy – that is, to Rome & Florence. I shall probably go to Venice for a few days, because I *must* – having too urgent friends there. But for this I should never return to it, I think, again.'

Between 1894 and 1899, when he remained in England, he had a growing need to retreat from the social pressures of London. He began to stay in the country for increasing lengths of time. In 1896 he enjoyed a long stretch of complete isolation in Rye, on the south coast where East Sussex takes over from Kent. While there, he spotted Lamb House, built in 1723 by the mayor of Rye, James Lamb. It opened directly on to a quiet street in 'the little old, cobble-stoned, grass-grown, red-roofed town, on the summit of its mildly pyramidal hill'. The early Georgian house is small yet elegant, with a wide oak stair, brick walls (red bricks varied with black, giving a deep rose colour), and a nine-foot front door. It seemed the answer to his wish for a retreat between May and November. In September 1897 he signed a lease for Lamb House, and moved there permanently in June 1898. In 1900 he acquired the freehold for £2,000.

He hugged his 'hermitage', as he called it, 'letting the wave, after 20 years of London, carry me as far as it would & spend itself as slowly'. Not far off were Joseph Conrad, Ford Madox Hueffer (later, Ford Madox Ford*), and a young American, Stephen Crane, who provided the stimulus of other writers. When James recalled Fenimore, he thought 'how *she* (in spite of Venetian lures & spells or illusions) would have liked *this* particular little corner of England, & perhaps might have found peace in it' – as he had. 'Only Lamb House is mild; only Lamb House is sane; only Lamb House is true.' A tale, 'The Great Good Place', published in

* Hueffer got rid of his German surname during the First World War.

January 1900, evokes an idyllic retreat where inward life is restored.

Locked in a drawer in Lamb House, wrapped in silver paper, he kept a photograph of a young woman. Once, when Violet Hunt (a writer who lived with Hueffer) came to visit, James unlocked his treasure and carefully unwrapped it. He touched it as though it were sacred. Violet, not usually the most sensitive of creatures, had not liked to ask who it was. Probably it was the photograph of Minny Temple which James had asked his mother to send in 1870. 'I should like to have it', he had said, 'for the day when to think of her will be nothing but pure blessedness.'

Three months after James settled at Lamb House he invited Bay to stay: 'I'm impatient for Bay's advent,' he wrote to her mother, 'tell her please I'm in a fever for it'. He begged her to come again: '*Do*, do clutch *Saturday 30th* to come down to me, & release not your hold of it. I shall be enchanted to have you.' Like Minny, she was endowed with 'vision' of character, expressed in a flair for portraiture. James told her, 'the blessing of you is that *as* you see, you do; and as you see through the eye of a needle, so you go through the same – to the kingdom of heaven of art.'

To think of her was to 'dance a wild fandango about her easel'. He confided to her mother that 'Bay's immense campaign, & all its results & ramifications, down to the latest & bravest wipe of her palette-knife, have been as food & drink to me'. (Minny had been as 'wine'.) 'I applaud & acclaim & embrace you – I hug you all round.'

In Rye he was out of reach of most visitors, and better able to control his privacy. 'I stay in solitude. I don't see a creature. That . . . dreadful to relate, I like.' So he needled Gosse, who lived in the crowd, 'odorous with anecdote' – as though James had not himself filled many a letter with the tattle of the town. Fitted round his solitude were ties with young men: an American, Morton Fullerton, who was chief Paris correspondent for the London *Times*, and a Norwegian-American sculptor based in Rome, Hendrik Andersen, who rejoiced in gigantic, lifeless statues and hoped James would promote him. Later, there was Jocelyn Persse, nephew of the Irish writer Lady Gregory. James, who was conspicuously demonstrative, never thought of himself as deviant, for the simple reason that the Edwardians drew a sharper line between sexual activity and tender friendship. James felt free to express an alternative manhood: he liked a fond embrace, an arm on the shoulder, a kiss; but said 'I can't' to the young novelist Hugh Walpole. His increasing expressiveness on the verge of love, as well as an increasing tendency to hold forth in society, was, in part, a hunger for response in the wake of commercial failure. Lonely, now and then, in his fifties and sixties, he sent invitations to men who were mostly far away. They evoked sighs and self-pity, not great works.

Fullerton eroticised him (as he seems to have eroticised everyone he met). In response, James teased out a reply that strikes while the iron is hot: 'I could wish it were hotter, the iron of our thus fondly fancied or feigned (for the moment!) rapprochement; I could groan in fact that it is but tepid at the best; but I "strike", my dear Fullerton, as hard as my pen will whack, and withall as tenderly as my hand knows how to rest.' This is not a shy or stifled man; he flirts with ease. But it's hypothetical – he could wish, could groan, yet pleasure for him was, first and foremost, to wield his pen. It's as though he tries to convince himself an exchange of this kind can work – an exchange of words, not arousal. What roused James most was indignation when Fullerton was blackmailed by a mistress he had abandoned in the course of bisexual adventures – indignation excited in James by his own fear of publicity.

One enlightening letter to Fullerton, dated 26 September 1900, takes him through eroticism to some 'fire' beyond it. That 'fire' is what James wants – and for himself alone. His desire is 'insatiate', but nameless, not because it's 'the love that has no name' in an age that outlawed homosexuality, but because it has no name even now. In the exercise of this desire, James is the active party, and Fullerton his prey. Or, more accurately, it is Fullerton's resistance to this particular desire which led to a rare confession. James starts from the common ground of physical tenderness. The touch of a hand in a certain tender way, he says, 'finished' him. 'You are dazzling, my dear Fullerton; you are beautiful; you are tenderly, magically *tactile*, but you're not kind. There it is. You *are* not kind.' This is because Fullerton holds back what James wants – not sex, but 'self': 'you tell me . . . not a *piti*ful syllable about yourself.

That's your inhumanity.... "What," you might say, "you want, insatiate writer, *that* also?" Yes; I want that also. I want fire – you see there's a method in my madness – little common, kind, correct words that will hang somehow together as a Light on your Life. I can't help it if that's the way I'm made.'

In the end it's not much to do with gender: sensuality is merely a route to the appropriation of a 'Life'.* Women, too, were to provide a Light on their Lives. They were to surrender their Light, as Minny did when she told him '*loads*'. Bay was urged in pressing terms, but no ordinary drive gave what James called 'a fierce point to my desire to see you': 'Come for *3* days if you can't come for 13. Come for 2 days if can't for 3; but, dearest Bay, only *come*. I desire so your history – every fact and every triumph of it, since – so long ago – I had a snatch of you in London. You must have been through many things. Take *me* through them again with you.' When intimates obliged in this way, he would become 'possessed' of them – one of those words that resonate in the James vocabulary. He was not 'possessed' of Gaillard Lapsley, a young American don at Trinity College, Cambridge, and invited him to Lamb House to remedy this – to assume this was a sexual invitation would be to underrate the strange nature of the James desire. Its cover was playful benevolence, but behind it lay a terrifying will to possess the souls of certain people he had marked for 'use'. It's not surprising that some resisted him: Fullerton, for one, and Rosina Emmet.

Bay lit his fire with a glow of generosity. An extended visit began on 28 June 1900. She came to paint a portrait of her venerable cousin, who had recently shaved off the beard he had worn since 1867. His face looked rounder, softer, and so suddenly bared that it took on a rather helpless expression. There's an air of pathos in many of the later photographs at odds with the assurance

*James was in touch with a huge array of people whose 'light' he did not pursue. This may explain something odd about the bulk of letters – odd for a novelist especially – in that the element of character was often so thin. His letters were written at generous length; they were gossipy, amusing, and vastly benevolent; but they don't do what letters are supposed to do: reflect their correspondent. It may be that James was not greatly interested in the bulk of his correspondents, whom he constructs as creatures of goodwill to himself.

of the major phase. That assurance has full measure in the celebrated portrait by Sargent, painted later in 1913. Where Sargent promotes the cool observer, Bay brings out the ferment: her James is not the mannered Lion who courted society; nor is he the helpless babe; he is a figure otherwise invisible: the troubled, confiding writer of the books we read. Her James is continuous with the liquid look of La Farge's portrait of the Newport James of the sixties, dandified, inchoate, without the finish of 'Europe'. Bay took a bold decision to hide half the face: the portrait opens up a dark, indeterminate space belied by the mandarin detachment of the Master. It's a face in shadow: the seer of the ghosts, incomplete, in-the-making.

In mid-August, Bay departed for New York. James imagined her whirled into the native rapids, at the frontier of action, while he on his red hilltop watched with gasps. Emptied, Lamb House seemed haunted by Bay and others amongst Minny's nieces who brought her back to him – James speaks repeatedly of these ghosts who surround him. The following year, in the thick of his Minny-novel, he reminded Bay of 'our so genial, roasting, romantic summer-before-last here together, when we took grassy walks, at even-tide, & in the sunset'. He would give her a 'leg-up' over rickety stiles on Romney Marsh.

One day, in particular, when they had walked his dog, remained with him: 'Do you remember', he asked over two years later, 'our late afternoon stroke in the westward fields during the hot weeks when you were so (more or less vaguely) painting me? walks with which I associate the tiny Yorkshire Peter . . . & in which we sat on humps of grass in the sunset & watched him disport himself.' She had warmed his 'aged heart'; her 'rush of life' took away his 'senile breath'.

His delight had not been without purpose. James had commissioned the portrait – necessitating a period of protracted intimacy. The portrait, for which he paid, he thought, handsomely, was an opportunity to study the portraitist day by day with a view to his own portrait of Minny Temple gestating in his mind.

The following winter, he continued to brood over the far-off past. He wrote of this to Oliver Wendell Holmes, now Chief Justice of the Massachusetts Supreme Court – the next year,

Holmes would move to the Supreme Court of the United States. 'You remain a part of the palpable past, I mean one of the first portions of it I can fit, at all, into the present as depicted & projected for me.' He was not alone in his sense of the past: John Gray, now at the height of his career as Professor of Law at Harvard, read over Minny's letters to him, and decided to send one to William James, who likewise was at his peak as a founder of the field of psychology, an explorer of psychic phenomena, and more recently Professor of Philosophy at Harvard. His reply to Gray suggests how alive Minny remained for these eminent men:

> 95 Irving St. Cambridge
> March 17th
>
> Dear John,
>
> I am deeply grateful to you for sending me this letter, which revives all sorts of pregnant memories, and makes Minny live again in all her lightness and freedom. Few spirits have been *freer* than hers. I find myself wishing so that she could know me as I am now – as for knowing her as *she* is now – ??!!! –
>
> I find that she means as much, in the way of human character, for me now as ever she did, being unique, and with no analogue in all my subsequent experience of people. Thank you once more, dear John, for what you have done!
>
> Yours ever
> W.J.

Though William says 'no analogue', Minny's nieces did embody certain aspects of her: Rosina, her truth and indifference; Leslie, her 'lovability'; and Bay, her freedom and 'deep draughts of life'. This is why Henry's emotion could slide from one to another, as though he made 'long arms' to catch up as full a complement as possible of Minny's spirit.

None of the nieces was present when he began *The Wings of the Dove* in June 1901. In 1901–2 they were all back in the States. Elly was living in Salisbury, Connecticut. Rosina was teaching English literature, and Leslie, drawing, in New York City. There, too, Bay had more orders than she could meet for portraits at a thousand dollars each. She held a successful exhibition of forty oil portraits at the Durand-Ruel Galleries in New York in January 1902. The sisters lived on the edge of Washington Square in a fourth-storey apartment, furnished simply in bohemian fashion, with a studio for Bay on the ground floor. She was 'a pure *painter*, a real one, a good one', Henry remarked to William, 'with a large capacity, which will increase; & if *she* doesn't marry I think her future is safe. If she does, it will go – I mean as a painter.'* An eighteen-page letter to her on 2 October 1901, written until one in the morning after the day's dictation, shows once more the pattern of involvement and detachment that allowed the writer to combine knowledge of actual women with a retrospective possession of them. 'I feel your ghosts, all there, hovering tenderly & softly from room to room in poor little empty Lamb House now, & creaking gently on staircase & on old crooked floors.' Their 'romantic' summer hovered in the air of Lamb House and about the fields when he went out, taking his way past sketchers, 'the usual frumps & failures' on campstools. Ahead in the fields, ghosts sat on stiles, waiting.

Two fantasies in this letter to Bay reveal the shift from life to art. By October – about four months into the novel – James becomes aware that Rosina somehow eludes him. She has not allowed him to know her, and he spells out a fantasy in which she cannot escape. Sitting in his box, he has an opera-glass fixed on Rosina on a distant stage. James now takes action: 'if operaglasses could penetrate & hypnotise, [I] could drag her down over the front of the box & jerk her, through intervening space, into my arms. I feel somehow as if, for the time, I had lost her – but let her not too proudly believe she is really free, for I dedicate the remainder of my days . . . to winning her back.' The playful air does not disguise the force of his will.

The second fantasy is to spend a year with Bay in Italy: 'we could put it through together,' he assures her. Through Bay, he renewed the dream he had shared with Minny in 1869, played out

* This prediction was to prove untrue. After Bay married in 1911 she had three sons in quick succession, painting all the while. By her death (in 1941) she had done some 800 portraits, mainly of men. She had a number of distinguished sitters: Augustus Saint-Gaudens, William James, Pablo Casals and, later, Franklin D. Roosevelt. After the crash of 1929 she supported her family by painting businessmen (with less daring than her earlier portraits).

in various fictions: 'Travelling Companions', *Daisy Miller*, *The Portrait of a Lady*, 'Georgina's Reasons', and now in *The Wings of the Dove*. For Italy is where Milly comes in hope of a final chance to 'live'.

Milly Theale has everything in abundance but health. Her looks are too abundant for beauty: too much forehead, too much nose, too much mouth made her 'expressive, irregular, exquisite, both for speech and silence'. An orphan and heiress, like Isabel Archer, she can do what she wants. As an American of her class what she wants first of all, of course, is to go to Europe, and once she is there money smoothes her way, so that she travels through Switzerland as undisturbed as a princess.

Her companion is a mature writer called Susan Shepherd Stringham, who is at home in Europe and 'full of discrimination'. She understands the phenomenon Milly represents: 'She was alone, she was stricken, she was rich, and, in particular, she was strange' – strange to Susan Stringham, a proper Bostonian, who observes that her mourning is 'rebellious' in its gloom and 'frivolous' in its frills. The girl has a boundless freedom – 'the freedom of the wind in the desert' – which appears an 'unpacified state', but is actually 'one of the finest, one of the rarest . . . cases of American intensity'. It's a New York intensity, and New York does not see it as anything extraordinary. Yet, to the discriminating, Milly is a mystery (in the sense of miracle) not to be defined at once. Her peculiar beauty would take a good deal of explaining, for it is an inward beauty associated with her rarity and potential. Stringham sees 'the potential heiress of all the ages'.

James was obsessed with money – not money on an ordinary scale, but fairy-tale money, the fabulous fortune, American in its proportions. Like Fitzgerald later, he was intrigued by the transforming power of money: quantity changing into quality of character. In fact, quality of character in the James family was undermined, in many cases, by the fortune inherited from Billy James – his offspring were idle or dissipated, a 'lineage of squalor' William James called it, including John James, the gambler whose pecuniary embarrassments finished him off; Howard James, who died at forty-six 'destitute an in an inebriate asylum'; and Bob

Judge William Cooper,
painted by Gilbert Stuart (c.1797-8).
Frontispiece to his *Guide in the Wilderness*.

Hannah Pomeroy Woolson,
Cooper's niece and mother of Constance
Fenimore Woolson. Portrait painted
c. 1839-40 before her children's deaths.

James Cooper (1822), the year he wrote
The Pioneers. Woolson parodied the
masculine frontier of 'Uncle Fenimore'.

'Connie' as a young woman.

The Fatio House, St Augustine, Florida (1875), at the time Woolson boarded there.

In Florida, Woolson would go 'prowling' by row boat 'down the inlet into all sorts of creeks that go no one knows where'.

'Miss Woolson' met James in 1880.

John Hay, American diplomat, and writer. He holds a copy of *Democracy* by Henry Adams.

James (back, left) in America, visiting his Aunt Kate (centre, front) in the summer of 1883. He was preparing to write *The Bostonians*.

Alice James as an invalid in Leamington, with her companion, 'Kath' Loring. William James saw 'the same noble thoughtful face unchanged through the years'

Francis Boott, a source for Osmond in *The Portrait of a Lady*.

Right: 'Lizzie' Boott, artist, painted by her husband Frank Duveneck (1888)

Palazzo Barbaro, Venice, where James often stayed: the setting for *The Wings of the Dove*.

Villa Brichieri, Bellosguardo. James and 'Fenimore' lived there in 1887 while he wrote *The Aspern Papers*. 'Villa Brichieri seemed to stare down…with unspeakably mournful eyes of windows', James said after her death.

Villa Castellani, Bellosguardo, showing the parapet 'with its dizzy outer descent' which Woolson used in 'Dorothy'.

At the Brichieri, James called Fenimore 'the gifted authoress', but envied her popular sales.

Casa Semitecolo: 'Miss Woolson's sad death-house in Venice.'

Woolson's grave in the Protestant Cemetery in Rome. (Shelley's grave is behind the tree.)

Woolson's sister and niece, Clara and Clare Benedict, '*opposed*' James in wanting to preserve the dead woman's 'things', while he wished never to see them again.

James on holiday with Minny's sister and nieces at Dunwich, Suffolk in 1897. Photographed by Leslie Emmet.

Shaded portrait of the private Henry James by Minny's niece, Ellen Emmet Rand (1900).

Close to death in 1913, John Chipman Gray brought Mrs Henry James a packet of Minny Temple's letters that he had kept all his life.

'A gallant and haunting record', Mrs William James informed Henry James when she read the packet. 'You will know how to use it for some memorial of her.'

Temple, a convicted forger. All the same, Henry James retained his father's view of fortune as a means to liberty – a liberty to realise the highest flights of the imagination. He invests Milly Theale with this quality: she's not just rich; she has enough to forget money, bypass the struggles of existence, and develop her potentialities to the utmost. Granted unlimited liberty, she is at the outreach of evolution, a supreme 'experiment of nature'.

The experiment places her on an Alpine ledge that expounds her position alone on 'the dizzy edge', with a sheer drop below, threatening mortality. For a second, Stringham fears she is on the verge of a leap, then perceives that, on the contrary, this young woman is in 'a state of uplifted and unlimited possession. . . . She was looking down on the kingdoms of the earth'. It's a godlike posture, an Emersonian moment of infinite potential. From the start, Milly is a given quantity, emblematic of fullness of being, and this fullness seeks immediate – urgent – expression. This is the intimation on the dizzy edge: it is not yet articulated in her consciousness that she is to die, but from this moment she is propelled forward with a need to 'live' before it is too late. Experience, for her, means, in particular, one Englishman, a journalist called Merton Densher whom she had entertained in New York.

Densher, who has no money, is secretly engaged to Kate Croy, who is under an obligation to do better. She is the only hope of her shoddy father and plaintive, widowed sister, Mrs Condrip. If she marries Densher, her rich aunt, Mrs Lowder, will disinherit her. Kate is playing for time when Milly arrives in London, and they make friends.

Milly is innocent of the net into which she has walked – a network of aliens who prey on one another under cover of graceful manners. Mrs Lowder, who would like to marry Kate to Lord Mark, plans to co-opt Milly for her side; on the other side, Kate likewise has her plan to put Milly to 'use'. If Milly is indifferent to her fortune, others are not.

In the midst of the midsummer glow of Milly's success in English society, there comes a second intimation of mortality. During a visit to an English country house, Milly is taken to see a

Bronzino portrait because it resembles her.* Milly sees, as in a mirror, a 'pale sister' with a green complexion who is 'dead, dead, dead', and it seems to her at this moment that she will 'never be better than this'. What she means is that her summer must wane: 'everything will never be so right again', she tells a bemused Lord Mark.

An extraordinary surge of 'life' follows confirmation of her illness by a distinguished physician, Sir Luke Strett. A priestlike character, he converts Milly to a Jamesian faith that life is lived to its fullest when it is curtailed, and Milly responds with exhilaration. Gratefully, she receives the 'clean truth' that she is 'doomed'. The sentence of death is transfigured as a chance to know the nature of life. 'It's a great rare chance,' Sir Luke tells her, and she takes on the challenge. An onrush of excitement carries her through obscure London streets as she readies herself for an experiment in how to 'live' in the light of mortality. It is as though the doctor had opened a door to unprecedented advance.

This bravura scene demonstrates how James drew on the resilience of Minny Temple in the face of death, and how it was fictionalised: the setting is London, not New York; her sentence is not pronounced by crass Dr Taylor but by a doctor of superlative intelligence like Baldwin; and Milly's exhilaration derives in part from Alice, who had wanted to die, in part from red-haired Gus Barker, who had galloped so gallantly to his death in the Civil War, and in part from the author himself – his imaginative excitement at Minny's death. Minny had wanted to live, and James blends her fight for life with the 'vision' he had always hoped to attain: a young woman who transcends mortality in a way that comes from a posthumous union of his own frontiering mind with the 'noble flights' of his cousin.

Halfway through the novel, 'the season lay dead'. It is the end of one sort of life and the start of another. London and social success

* It's unmistakably Bronzino's portrait of Lucrezia Panciatichi painted in the 1540s: 'the face of a young woman . . . a face almost livid in hue', a figure of 'Michelangelesque squareness' with 'her eyes of other days, her full lips, her long neck', and her 'wasted reds'. See Adeline R. Tintner, *Henry James and the Lust of the Eye* (Baton Rouge: Lousiana Univ. Press, 1993) for a chapter-length discussion of HJ's adaptation of this portrait.

are left behind, and Milly shifts to her rightful place in a lasting domain: the Palazzo Leporelli on the Grand Canal in Venice. Like the Barbaro, it has a distinctive outside stair leading from the courtyard to the *piano nobile*. Milly takes possession as a natural heir. With her fortune, her black clothes, flaming hair and white face, she has a drama to match her setting. There, immured as in a chrysalis of all the ages, she transforms herself, and emerges to greet her money-minded guests – Kate, Mrs Lowder, and Merton Densher – as well as the watchful Sir Luke.

Backed by musicians, moving through her court, Milly has exchanged mourning for white, adorned from neck to knee with a double strand of pearls. Thin, pale, exquisitely awkward, Milly readies herself for the climax of her drama in which Densher alone will remain of the English party. Her braided red hair and white, jewelled presence, a centre of attention and yet somehow on the verge of our sight, has a rarity that seems here to eclipse showcase beauty in the form of Kate Croy. Croy shows to advantage in the overstuffed drawing-room of Mrs Lowder; Milly's 'form' is, by contrast, a palace that is a work of art. Mrs Stringham invites Densher to 'one of the courts of heaven'. Ironically, it is Croy, the one most given to the materialism of the marriage market, who first recognises Milly as the transforming dove of the Psalms: 'Though ye have lien among the pots, yet shall ye be as the wings of a dove covered with silver, and her feathers with yellow gold.'

At the time James was writing *The Wings of the Dove*, he devised a text to accompany murals of the Quest for the Holy Grail, designed in 1901 by Edwin A. Abbey for the Boston Public Library. Sexual purity in the James text for the tenth panel matches his insistence on sexual purity in his outline for the novel, and the whiteness of his evolving image of Milly: 'On the morning of his wedding with Blanchefleur, Galahad had a vision of the Grail, and knew that none but a virgin knight might achieve it. So he turns away. Blanchefleur, no less than Galahad, is alive to the lofty purport of the vision, and shows no deploring grief. Both Galahad and Blanchefleur know that the Quest, and what it will bring, can leave no room for earthly sorrows.' The purity of Milly in Venice is a challenge to the market morals of the Lowder set, whose plan to appropriate Milly and her money brings on a clash between two spheres of existence, one earthly, one sublime.

Milly is confident that she and Kate are 'tremendous friends', unaware of the 'dark home' from which Kate comes, the lair of Croys and Condrips with no scruples when it comes to feeding their troop. With Milly's fortune, Kate Croy could have everything – and nothing less than everything is what she wants. Croy has an appetite for 'life' that has seemed to align her with Milly, but the two women are as apart as different plots: one, the common novelistic plot of the marriage market; the other, the biblical plot of the new life. The different genres in which these plots belong come into conflict as soon as Milly appears on the scene: Croy fits the realistic European novel based on a certain number of roubles; Milly, the older genre of allegory or sermon which dominates American writing.

Croy's plot is to persuade Densher to make up to Milly, even marry her, with a view to inheriting her fortune when she dies. Her plot is set in motion in the shady corners of Milly's court. It turns on a bargain: Densher's demand that Croy sleep with him. So Croy sells Milly for one act – sex in the marketplace as a transaction. The base language of commerce, of bargain and profit, provides a counterpoint to the unknown quantity – quantity transformed as quality – of the heiress. Where Milly is a dove, Croy is identified by her family as an 'investment'; now, the price demanded by Densher is 'magnificently paid'.

An aftermath of sexual excitement lingers as he stays on in Venice into the autumn – 'a Venice of cold, lashing rain from a low black sky' – ostensibly to be with Milly. Densher has not looked forward to acting out a deception, but in practice finds it easier than ever to be with Milly, who has long owned to herself that she needs 'a healing and uplifting passion' in order 'not to have missed everything'. She would like a 'name' for her relations with Densher. 'She only wondered about the basis it would have for himself.' The basis, of course, is gain, and this makes Densher feel 'ugly'. As he looks into Milly's white face he sees she's 'divine' in her trust. Imperceptibly, the language of the soul supersedes the language of profit. Densher is aware of his proximity to 'transcendent motions, not less blessed for being obscure'. In his longing to undeceive her hope that he might love her, he pretends to be staying on in Venice in order to write a book. His 'crucifixion' is that Milly takes this with trustful seriousness. After this, he tries not to lie – what he fails to confront, entirely, is that his daily presence in Milly's palace is in itself a deception.

As the story unfolds, it has moved from one centre of consciousness to another: from Croy, to Stringham, to Milly, and now finally to Densher – at the last, it is Densher's story. He observes how Milly flies and drops as she contemplates 'a chance' he will give her to live; and he sees how she could drop 'almost with violence' when she fears he'll go away to 'escape' her need. The drop brings it home to Densher that anything he should do or not do 'would have reference, directly, to her life, which was thus absolutely in his hands. . . . It was on the cards for him that he might kill her.'

Densher well knows that he 'was mixed up in her fate, or her fate . . . was mixed up in *him*', but all he can think of is to be 'still' and 'kind'. It's a way of deluding himself that he means no harm; in fact, he kills with kindness. When Milly discovers his deception, it breaks her will to live. 'She has turned her face to the wall,' Stringham tells Densher. The dove of the Psalms is vulnerable as well as transcendent: 'My heart is sore pained within me; and the terrors of death are fallen upon me. Fearfulness and trembling are come upon me, and horror hath overwhelmed me. And I said, Oh that I had wings like a dove: for then I would fly away . . .'. The dove is dying, but consents to see Densher once more. With no word of reproach, she asks him to leave Venice, and, relieved more than shamed, he returns to London.

There, at a distance, he tries to imagine what it is like for Milly to die: grim now as she had never been, and never voicing her disappointment. Like Minny, Milly dies offstage; her illness is invisible – no marks of death, no chloral, no smell of drugs. James planned this in his outline: the physicality of death was not to get in the way. What he wished to bring out was the will to live and the mortal blow of its loss. Minny had declared (a few days before James had left for Europe), 'If I begin to be indifferent to what happens, I shall go down the hill fast.' Densher's sense of Milly's end is perfunctory, almost unfelt: 'Milly had held with passion to her dream of a future, and she was separated from it, not shrieking indeed, but grimly, awfully silent' like a victim in the French Revolution dragged to the scaffold. He makes do with the image of the Terror. This is a short cut, sheering away from the live Milly who is now lost to sight, and fixing her death as a historical event – something that will have happened by the time he hears of it – in the mind of a man who has not loved her in the natural way she had to be loved if she was to 'live'. It is as though the girl's death were an obligatory passage to a posthumous drama in which Densher is centre-stage.

In the days that follow Milly's end, feeling comes at last – comes in a rush. Densher is transformed, as though she had died that this might be. He lives with her dream; he hears her voice, 'something sentient and throbbing' like 'a faint, far wail'; he holds to a thought, increasingly precious, in the shadow of his rooms. It is not for the outside world; he secretes it, like Minny's photo: 'He kept it back like a favourite pang; left it behind him, so to say, when he went out, but came home again the sooner for the certainty of finding it there. Then he took it out of its sacred corner and its soft wrappings; he undid them one by one, handling them, handling *it*, as a father, baffled and tender, might handle a maimed child.' In this way, through posthumous acts of tenderness, Densher (who has needed to annex and possess life) takes to himself what otherwise he should 'never, never know'.

The focus of what he cannot know turns to a letter from Milly written in a firm hand well before her death but posted afterwards from Venice: it is to tell him that she has left him her fortune after all. Kate Croy throws the letter, unread, in the fire: she wants money, not its association with the language of altruism. She wants to hear the news from a business office in New York – she's finished with Milly. She sees that her friend was stupendous – a star, a dove – but this character does not concern her beyond its practical benefit. As far as Croy is concerned, her plot has worked. What she hasn't bargained for is the effect on Densher.

The unread letter spurs his imagination. In place of the letter there comes to Densher a voice audible to the spirit's ear in a still room – a voice of 'revelation'. So, he guards the 'sacred hush' that the voice of the dead might 'prevail there', a sound at one with an ache in his soul.

As *The Portrait of a Lady* closed with a choice, so too *The Wings of the Dove*. To redeem his exploitation of Milly, to separate himself from Croy's plot, Densher demands that she choose between him and the money. She can't have both. Croy asks him to swear that he's not in love with Milly's memory. Densher evades the question, saying he'd marry her at once, and they'd be as they were. Croy denies this possibility: 'Her memory's your love. You *want* no other.'

The notebook is more explicit than the novel that Densher will live 'single and faithful – faithful to the image of the dead'. Croy's final words are 'We shall never be again as we were!' With this, she confirms the transforming power of the dove when she stretched her wings to cover Densher after he had wronged her.

In this way James revived Minny Temple, whose model of conduct had been (in her own words) 'a woman who believes in generosity and who must have that or nothing'. Henry James always celebrated this element in Minny's character. 'She was a case of pure generosity – ', he wrote to William when Minny was no more. He had used this quality in Minny's lifetime in the bounty of Gertrude, the heiress in 'Poor Richard'. As far back as 1867, he had foreseen the problem of the future for a young woman of this calibre: death, or death-in-life, would seem to be the only course open to her.

In February 1901, a few months before James began the novel, Katharine Bronson died 'isolated' in her sixties. Her death was, for James, 'the end of so many things – so many delightful memories, histories, associations – some of the happiest elements of one's own past'. The Venetian setting for Milly's death derived most directly from Katharine Bronson, but at an earlier stage, in the notebook entry of 1894, Fenimore's death had been to the fore: James first imagined a death in Nice, Mentone, Cairo, or Corfu – the last two being the main scenes of Fenimore's eastern journey in 1890, places James had not seen, which she had described in her letters and pictured in magazines. Her travel book, *Mentone, Cairo, Corfu*, was published posthumously in 1896.

In his early works, *Washington Square*, 'An International

Episode', and *The Portrait of a Lady*, James demonstrated integrity as a triumph of human nature that, bullied by the interests of others, is an end in itself. In certain of his later works, integrity is more effective – even redeeming in the case of Densher. Milly's altruism is beyond what we expect of human nature; all the same, she is human in her hurt, and even unmannerly when she turns her face to the wall. Since it is hard to make good as compelling as evil, it was a feat of the first order to bring Milly to life and, through Densher, to keep her alive.

In the last scenes of the novel, Densher mulls over the wrong of leading Milly on with a view to her fortune. He does so at impressive length, and wins respect when he rejects her money. These gestures cover a crucial evasion. The Victorian novelist (and friend of James) Mrs Humphry Ward, who thought Milly the most exquisite of his heroines, remained uneasy about Densher. She questioned his version. Likewise, Leo Bersani, in 'The Jamesian Lie', observed how Densher underplays his annihilation of the sick girl. Everyone 'lets him off': Sir Luke, Milly, James himself. Densher is a killer, a passive kind, the most secret and dangerous because he appears, even to himself, so 'kind', so reassuringly concerned for others, so devoid of physical violence – so 'still'. Though James fingers this fact for a second, he does not exactly press the point. Understandably so, for Densher is close to the young author who did not grant the 'life' Minny begged, but used his 'Light on her Life' after her death. A 'love-story', he called it in November 1901, '– human, attracting, curious!'

In the winter of 1901–2, when James was deep in the novel, it happened that another Temple was drawn into Lamb House. Minny's youngest sister, Henrietta, came to Europe with her husband to celebrate their silver wedding. The Temple associations, in this case, were overlaid by Cooperstown. James welcomed them as figures in a Cooper romance on the shores of Lake Otsego: 'Your great shining frozen lake, your snow-crested forests, your jingling sleigh-bells and the blazing logs of your chimney-corner. You both, as the stately chief and the gentle squaw, are the Last of the Mohicans of my acquaintance – for, always, to my imagination, that sort of association, minus the tomahawk, hangs about you.

You may not trace the method of this madness, but, from one step to another, I do.' The steps may be traced to the frontier winter of *The Pioneers*, and the fictive name of its first citizen, Judge Temple, based on Judge Cooper; the marriage of Henrietta Temple which took her to the vicinity of Cooperstown, and her subsequent connection with Fenimore; and the letter of introduction to Henrietta's cousin Henry James.

The final act of his romance with the Temples took place in Rye at the time *The Wings of the Dove* was published in August 1902. Elly stayed at the Mermaid Inn with Bay and her son, Grenville, while her daughter Leslie and niece Eleanor stayed at Lamb House. Eleanor Emmet was the youngest of the six children of Minny's eldest sister, Kitty, in Pelham, New York, where Minny had spent the last stage of her life. Eleanor, in whom James saw an amazing likeness to her mother, was also an orphan: Kitty Temple had died in 1895, and her husband, Richard Stockton Emmet (this 'grandfather' outlived his wife), in 1902. Presumably, Eleanor, aged twenty-two, was sent to Europe to recover.

James revelled in what he called 'our romantic life together'. There was the old ease of consanguinity and, at the same time, the safety of the age barrier – this freed his emotions, and he wrote to Eleanor afterwards with the extravagance of a lover: 'My dear sweet Eleanor, Too long, too long have I sat pressing your last in silence to my heart.' He confided further to William: 'Eleanor is so solid & soothing & up to a certain point plastic . . . that I should almost like to attach her. But she has other attachments.' He felt 'possessed' of Eleanor, and didn't want her to marry because she would then cease to be of 'use' to him. There is an elegiac note in his words to Eleanor in the autumn of 1902, in the aftermath of his novel. He would go on to another, and the Temples would people his life no more – or not with the intensity of ties that served his work.

'My autumn is lonely', he wrote to Eleanor on 19 November, '& I think of . . . that time [the preceding summer] very much as a man put down off a ship on a desert island may think of the steward's pantry on the vessel & the band that played during dinner. *My* band has stopped playing now . . .'.

Bay, back in London, was no longer in evidence at Lamb House.

He thought she found 'a certain wild freedom in her bachelor life' – what Minny had dared before her, and Daisy Miller had flaunted: 'a rash young thing'.

From time to time in years to come, he turned back to Minny's kin. '... Your ghost seems to steal from behind a rose-bush and your presence to be with me again & pervade the scene', he told Eleanor on 30 June 1903, 'so it's become almost as if you hadn't been away.... Except for your ghost I should feel very much alone, since this is the 1st summer here, for several years, that I haven't had quite a choice of Emmets to keep me company. Tonight I am choosing you...'. He assured her he had not forgotten 'our romantic life together last summer – yes, it does hang about me here still...'. The following year he would meet her in New York. He warned, 'I have designs on you of the most violent character.'

In a long letter to Bay of 11 October 1903, he confides feelings for one cousin to another: how he longs to be involved with Rosina – so full of expressiveness towards her that 'a *touch* from her would shake this vessel so that she would be deluged with my words'. Words. It did have to be words that fountained from the touch of a man or woman. When Lapsley had to take a rest from tutoring, James fantasised on the 'perfections' of his recumbent form. 'Lie as flat as you possibly can,' he wrote. 'I am drenching you with my fond eloquence.' Words as the end of passion are common with writers. When Yeats declared that if Maud Gonne had turned her head, he might have thrown 'poor words' away 'and been content to live', we believe him only so long as the poem lasts. It's a glorious rhetorical gesture; it would not have happened. We believe Yeats rather when he says, 'Words alone are certain good.' So, too, for James – more so. Rosina had the sense to keep her distance. But James was far from finished with her. Half humorous, half fierce, he did not conceal from her mother that the main purpose of his plan to return to America in 1904 was to 'get *at*' Rosina: 'tell Rosina that I want to get at *her*. I can't get *at* her & she won't be got *at*. She shuns & avoids & ignores me, & I want to break it down.... I can't go on this way living without her. It's no use trying – it won't do. Tell her these things – as a mother *can* – with my love.'

Either he didn't trust Elly to convey such a message or he wished to confirm it directly, for he wrote to Rosina two weeks later in rather menacing terms: as yet, he says, he hadn't wholly got at her, but he was on the way to it, and intends to come over to achieve the rest of the road. The threat is wrapped in a comic fancy that he might attend one of her classes disguised as some fat, aged woman, the grandmother of one of her pupils, while Rosina taught one of his works. He longs to rat-tat on the door she shared with Bay and Leslie, entrée to a triple romance.

He called himself 'hopelessly celibate even though sexagenarian' in a 1904 letter to William, but he was neither tame nor passive. The unpublished Emmet letters reveal an amorous predator of the soul.

As a young man of twenty-six, James had met Minny's death with creative euphoria. His posthumous possession of her was thrilling – he rose again and again to verbal climax. Then, twenty-four years later, as a man of fifty, staggered by the 'bolt out of the blue' that was Fenimore's death and believing – shall we say, knowing – it was suicide, there came a more complex response. Again, the dead woman was appropriated as the material of art – an art of introspection and self-criticism. In two major works which reach back to Fenimore, a man's consciousness is shared by a woman whose relation to him defies name.

In *The Ambassadors* (written in 1900–1 and published in 1903), she is a Europeanised American who speaks in the divinatory manner Fenimore had used in letters to James. Miss Gostrey, at thirty-five, is younger and friendlier than Fenimore, but recognisable: the velvet band about her throat which sets off the poise of her head; her fine old sense of responsibility for 'our national consciousness, or ... our nation itself'; her independence and restlessness; her practised insights into people 'with a hand as free as that of a compositor scattering type'; and not least, her solicitude for a needy hero, recalling Miss Woolson's offer of 'infinite charity' to James in the spring of 1883 when she invited him to her rooms in Venice.

Lambert Strether, a fifty-five-year-old American on a mission to Paris, enters Miss Gostrey's room. It is crowded, almost dusky, with accumulations that testify to her appropriations of 'Europe': bits of old brocade, old ivory, glints of gold, and patches of purple, which catch the low light through her muslin curtains. He feels admitted to what he has not known before, 'the innermost nook of the shrine – as brown as a pirate's cave'. His entrée to a nook 'warm with life' revives the Miss Grief figure in 'The Altar of the Dead' whose sanctum had the 'flush of life' with its dark red walls filled with memories and relics, pressed flowers, photos, and scraps of manuscript. Miss Gostrey's 'things' point to the 'innermost' treasure of a woman who becomes at this moment Strether's 'blessing'. To have known it is 'to need it or miss it forever'.

Before he began the novel, James dictated a ninety-page outline (dated 1 September 1900) in which he describes Miss Gostrey as 'a study ... of a highly contemporary and quasi cosmopolite feminine type'. His idea of her as 'inordinately modern' recalls 'our modern Fenimore' (as James called her to Boott). If the plain, expensive propriety of her clothes hadn't declared her a lady of the first order, Strether might not have welcomed so readily a woman who takes the initiative when they meet. Strether (who, James said, had a 'vague resemblance' to himself) finds the courage of Miss Gostrey's curiosity entertaining, even exciting. He's unburdened, not alarmed, by her 'divination' because he trusts her as he trusts himself. Compatriots, spectators, relentless analysers of human nature, they meet as rare birds of the same species. The 'curious and interesting relation' between Strether and Miss Gostrey develops with a rapidity amusing to themselves, 'by the liveliest bounds, by a kind of mutual half-tender, half-ironic recognition'. James set all this down in the outline in terms which indicate the presence of Fenimore at an early stage:

> ... The congruity, the amusing affinity, that establishes itself for her, is altogether with Strether. They hit it off ... from the first; they strike up a comradeship which proves full of profit for future lucidity. An American spinster left by the accidents of life free to wander, and having wandered and re-wandered from an early time, Miss Gostrey, clever, independent, humorous, shrewd, a little battered, a little hard, both highly unshockable and highly incorruptible, and many other things besides, is above all full of initiations

> and familiarities, full of Europe, full of ways and means, full of everything and everywhere. Active and energetic, interested in the human predicament and full of divination of it and a semi-cynical helpfulness *about* it, she has no one directly dependent on her, and so finds a happy exercise of her temperament in cultivating a protective attitude when she sees a chance for one. . . . She takes an extraordinary fancy to Strether from the first; and the fancy that she takes to him is a secondary thread in the web, a little palpable gold thread that plays through all the pattern.

Strether is a type of innocent abroad, eager to lend himself to what is unknown. This includes women. He really does want to know, and this makes him attractive to very different kinds of women: the American, Maria, leaping from peak to peak in her confabs with Strether, and the Frenchwoman, Mme de Vionnet, a performer playing to him, scene upon scene of emotive manipulations. As James was to point out in his preface, Strether is close to a writer in his intelligence. Like James, he tests the set stories his culture has produced – in this case, a story of adultery (involving young Chad Newsome and mature Mme de Vionnet) – and comes to see, instead, a more indeterminate story that will elicit in the adulterous couple, in himself, in Maria, an uncategorised ferment of inward possibilities, which for Strether, as for James himself, constitutes 'life'. Whether that ferment should suffice for Maria is a question this novel will not answer. She offers herself to Strether as an alternative to a solitary old age, but though he hesitates for a moment at this opportunity, and allows Maria to see his hesitation, he turns her down.

'He *can't* accept or assent,' James says in the outline. 'He won't. He doesn't. It's too late.' These curt words put an end to the hopes of 'poor convenient, amusing, unforgettable, impossible Gostrey'.

Since the whole novel is contained within Strether's consciousness, it is left to the reader to ask questions he neglects to ask. Does he refuse 'life' in refusing Miss Gostrey? Though in Paris he congratulates himself on expanding his consciousness to an artistic height, which is 'life' in one sense, in another sense Strether remains a product of Woollett, Massachusetts, unable to change. Apropos Miss Gostrey, Strether admits he is 'great . . . at postponements'. He has only 'to get . . . afresh into the rhythm of one to feel its fine attraction'. As James put it in his outline, 'one's life takes a form and holds one'. The 'quiet lapse of life' has, for Strether, the charm of death. His insistence that 'life' has come to him 'too late' may perpetuate the deadness that wrapped him round before he came abroad. At fifty-five, he is not exactly on the edge of the grave – does he play the age card because, after all, he fears to 'live'?

It has long been apparent that Strether is a man who has much in common with James, and there is an identical pattern of involvement and withdrawal in relations with women. James re-explores this pattern obsessively: the guilt and obfuscation of guilt with what he calls 'expressive decency'. During the second half of his mission, Strether has less need of Maria Gostrey. He has always looked on her in the light of a 'convenience'; it has been convenient to have a 'receptacle for some of his overflow', and now and then he calls her back 'into requisition'. She yields with 'deep returns of indulgence'. There is the effect of a character seething with possibilities who is switched off and assigned a rudimentary function. Strether finds her resignation touching. As a sop to her silencing, she is given a little treat – a summer outing in Paris – during which she manifests 'occasional fatigues' and 'bewilderments', recalling Fenimore's last jaunt with James in Paris in May 1893 when she was en route to Venice, unsettled, and weak from flu.

Since we see events from Strether's point of view, it is easy to blind us to his use of Maria Gostrey. She is essential to his development, then marginalised as a 'convenience', and finally denied her share in his making, as though the author shuts the door on questions and ambiguities which the phenomenon of Maria has raised. Maria is recognisably a phenomenon. Other women are types: the strenuous widow of Woollett, Mrs Newsome, who plans to marry Strether if he carries out the mission (to rescue her son, Chad), and the adulteress, Mme de Vionnet. Maria Gostrey is quite another matter. She has the interest of the advanced women who allowed James to know them.

'. . . You've recognised me – which *is* rather beautiful and rare', Miss Gostrey says to him soon after they meet. 'You see what I am.'

Seeing is reciprocal. When he walks with her along the broad old wall of Chester in England – with dips, and gaps, 'queer twists, queer contacts' – he realises that she knows 'intimate things about him that he hadn't yet told her and perhaps never would'. He has told her a remarkable lot but not the real things. 'Some of the real ones, however, precisely, were what she knew.'

Five years after writing the novel, in a preface to a new edition, James played down Maria Gostrey in a curious sequel to the actions of his hero. Next to Strether himself, Maria is the memorable figure of the book. For present-day readers, she has a substance and a claim to attention that eclipse Mme de Vionnet and those Americans in the novel who act as ambassadors for puritanical values. James pumps Mme de Vionnet with mystery, but it is the spurious mystery of male fantasy; her devious femininity has dated beside the pistol point of Gostrey's talk. Why, after the fact, did James try to convince us that Gostrey is not really Strether's friend? The preface proposes 'to tear off her mask' and expose her as 'the most unmitigated and abandoned of *ficelles*' – the string by which the puppeteer manages his puppets. Some unacknowledged power-struggle between author and character would demote the gold thread in the pattern to a passive piece of string in the author's hands. This belies what the novel reveals: her stimulus, 'warm with life'. After the fact, James claimed that 'the subordinate party' (Miss Gostrey) was only 'pieced on'. The reader, he rules, must not take her 'ostensible connectedness' to Strether as 'real', nor must the reader grant her 'the dignity of a prime idea'. In this way, James unpicks the gold thread with relentless ingenuity.

To conceal the private element in the novel, James used the authority of the preface to kill off Gostrey as 'real'. This would seem to back the questionable assertion of Strether that he was 'right' to go on alone. 'The Beast in the Jungle', a tale close in conception to *The Ambassadors* and written soon after, comes to an opposite conclusion: Marcher, another Strether but a culpable character, comes to recognise that his denial of what a mature woman had to offer defines his failure to live. Where Maria will go on shifting around Europe so long as she lives, May dies, and it is the dead more than the living who have the power to transform.

'The Beast in the Jungle' is about a man who waits and watches for his 'splendid moment', which never comes. This was the idea James had appropriated from Fenimore's notes in the death-house. James adds a co-watcher he calls May. Early on in their vigil, she asks Marcher if the awaited experience could be love, and he dismisses this as too banal for his sense of importance. Over long years May serves at the altar of Marcher's ambition. Involved and sidelined, she is drained of the life she has offered, forced to become another *Mourante*. May blends the thinness and gallantry of the dying Minny (as James saw her for the last time in February 1869) with the turned back of Fenimore, who died in silence. May withers, like Daisy, in April: a May chilled by Marcher. A seasonal reverse cuts off the spring. It is in April that Marcher – a type of Winterbourne, a wintry character not incapable of life – comes 'face to face' for the last time with the woman who embodies spring. Seeing her in her extremity, he still can't meet her as she must be met and, depleted of hope, she dies. Years before, they had met at a place called, ominously, Weatherend. She had offered herself to Marcher saying, 'I'm your dull woman, a part of the daily bread.' Marcher is not attuned to the modest appeal of the prayer: give us this day our daily bread. A high-toned idea has led him to withhold himself from the common lot, and Marcher destroys his friend in its name. Marcher's unnatural blight of May repeats Winterbourne's blight of Daisy: both tales lead to a grave, but Marcher – unlike the shallow Winterbourne – is compelled to confront himself. Winterbourne's approach to Daisy's 'raw protuberance' in the Protestant Cemetery suggests the force of a recognition that almost brings him to life. By casting herself as a variety of Daisy, Fenimore turned James into a variety of Winterbourne who had not understood the fatality of his relation to her.

In 1899, when James had made his second and, from an artistic point of view, most important of three visits to Fenimore's grave, he saw a few yards away an Angel of Grief, created by the American sculptor William Wetmore Story in memory of his wife in the spring of 1894 (the time of James's first visit to Fenimore's grave). Story had wondered if his wife 'knows it and if she can see it'. So James records in his biography of Story (1903), as well as his own impression of an intensity of grief that seemed to mingle with a 'soundless voice' that 'nowhere hangs on the air with such a weight on the heart' as in that corner of the Protestant Cemetery. Grief throws herself with drooping wings and hidden face 'in utter abandonment' over a funeral altar. This image of grief inspired the finale to 'The Beast in the Jungle' when Marcher falls on May's grave. The story starts with the meeting of minds; it ends with separation: the woman stretched out beneath her slab, the man prone upon it, and between them an impassable wrong. Ironically, it is his wrong that proves to be his transforming experience – a savage end to complacency, like the lunge of a beast. Marcher, face down on the tomb, was face to face with a dead woman of absolute reserve. We cannot intrude on this encounter, only mark it there, on the edge of the unknown at the centre of lives.

Five years after Fenimore died, a successor, Katharine Fullerton, aged twenty, offered to make a home in his work. She had illustrious credentials as a descendant of William Bradford (the first American historian) and Nathaniel Morton of the Plymouth Colony. In 1900, as a senior at Radcliffe College, her story 'The Poppies in the Wheat' won the *Century*'s prize for the best story from an undergraduate. After taking a master's degree in 1901, she was appointed Reader at Bryn Mawr, Pennsylvania, another top college for women. Miss Fullerton was ambitious to be a writer, and approached Henry James through her cousin Morton Fullerton, in whose home she had grown up – James thought she was his sister.

From 1899, Morton Fullerton began sending on her letters to James, who welcomed them as 'documents' of 'the deeply feminine & the widely American order'. She confirmed what he, in a sense, created. Kate Fullerton was exactly the breed of eager, hopeful compatriot who evoked his 'intelligent emotion'. Her first two letters, sent in November 1899, 'spoke' to him 'in all sorts of ways, & above all with the unmistakable, unforgettable, indefinable New England voice. What an interesting, living creature – with what a natural, happy, delightful pen!' One of her most delightful allusions was to James himself as 'the Tourgenieff of our common country' and to 'the strange charm he exhales'. Like Fenimore,

Miss Fullerton was a writer who saw herself as a Jamesian woman, her letters so consciously Jamesian that she seemed to offer herself as his creation. This time, he resisted the temptation to draw her into the 'white light' of his art. He backed away via one of those rare letters which touch on his private life. Here is a glimpse of a James anxious not to create another wrong:

Lamb House.
Rye Sussex
October 18*th* 1902

My dear Fullerton.

I have liked keeping your letter *by* me, as it were, and eke your Sister's interesting perpetration: I seem to put them, comparatively speaking, a little *from* me. . . . And now I help the young lady, ever so gently, out & *down*: out, with every assistance through the narrow door of the vehicle in which she has been perched – even though the process be a little ruffling to her charming feathers & frills. . . . The pages you send me are beautiful in their good faith. . . . They *have*, probably, so close a relation to me that I seem not only to have written them, but to have written them many times over. . . . It *is*, but too sensitively, too insanely *me*, & I feel, over the case, quite painfully responsible. It is all beautifully done, *as* me; but I am not good enough, not right enough to do so well, & even not good & right enough to do at *all* with that intensity. Kindly tell her, with my anxious benediction, that at these rates I won't answer for her. She may see for a little where she's going, but I see where she's *coming* – & oh, the dangers scare me. . . . I want immense qualifying, & she presents me pure. Oh, so pathetically pure! She doesn't know what she is about. Hold her back. The great white light awaits – to engulf her. And she mustn't be engulfed. She must float & splash & scramble & remount the current; become distinct & distinguished, with the jolly reminiscence of having been fished from the whirlpool. . . .

Yours, my dear Fullerton, always & ever
Henry James. . . .

So, James spared Miss Fullerton. The white light of his imagination did not engulf her. By 1902, the year he completed *The Wings of the Dove* and 'The Beast in the Jungle', he could foretell the fate of women who validated his creations: they were not viable. On Thursday afternoon, 19 January 1905, Kate Fullerton entertained James to tea at Bryn Mawr, where he read a paper, and she made a laborious train journey from Oxford to Rye in order to visit him in 1908, but James did not allow her to lend herself to him in the manner of Minny and Fenimore. She went on to write nearly fifty stories between 1911 and 1929, admired by critics of the time for moral decency. Her protagonists were Puritans in different guises who stand firm against temptations of the flesh and the devil, holding to duty. In the end she married an academic, had two children, and stayed clear of Modernist circles who admired T. S. Eliot and Virginia Woolf. Her obsession with James brought out a strange fear: he was not afraid *of* her but *for* her. By the time she crossed his path, he was fully aware of 'the whirlpool' awaiting a Jamesian woman.

In Jamesian dramas of contrition, a man uses a single woman, May, Maria, or Milly, for his own ends; then recoils from usage of this kind. And yet, James himself continued to use two women as the material of art. It is consistent with the Lesson of the Master that art, of necessity, preys on others. This is the questionable point where James the man meets James the writer. He drew women out as no other man, exposing needs that lurk unexpressed on the evolutionary frontier; and then swerved from responsibility. Fenimore took a calculated risk when she made a 'home' in his work. His involvements were for readers, for posterity, and only in passing for subjects whose need for reciprocity remained active. For this reason, he was in his element with those who had died.

Jamesian heroes of the major phase often excoriate themselves more relentlessly than evidence against them might seem to justify. Their own sole detractors, they gape at their flaw: the oblivion of the sensitive gentleman. Of course, only a person of the calibre of James would have the moral courage to confront it.

Here is a fictional truth James offered in lieu of biography. He is right, of course, to urge the autonomy of art, were it not for one problem: a myth of solitary genius. That myth, it must now be apparent, is largely untrue. For James leant on the generosity of women who surrendered 'the Light of their Lives'. Feeling, breathing women who provided the original matter for Milly and Miss Gostrey were disappointed in untold ways not unconnected with their deaths. It is on behalf of these women that biography must redress the record James controlled.

12
The Figure in the Furnace

From a depression in 1893 to a breakdown in 1910–12 – from the age of fifty to sixty-nine – James was haunted by incompletion. His three last novels, great as they are, did not quiet his angst. There was the Master of the novel, and there was the Other: a man in the making, uncertain who he was in the end to be. Was he American or English, aloof Modern or popular Victorian, an angel (as his mother fondly believed) or the sinner Fenimore offered to 'forgive' (in the arch manner of her generation) for the sake of his work? 'I am that queer monster, the artist,' he told Henry Adams, as though he were joking. Were writers by nature monsters? Would posterity see? And what would biographers find – those unavoidable opponents (as he feared) far-off in the future?

Outwardly, in the final stage of his life, James presents a finished image, a Master with an imperious bearing and veiled eyes, looking through you with a view to the soul – 'the intolerable scrutiny', said Edmund Gosse. This made him appear overwhelming and massive, even though his height was no more than five foot eight. One friend, Ella Hepworth Dixon, remembered that 'his eyes were not only age-old and world-weary, as are those of cultured Jews, but they had vision – and one did not like to think of what they saw'. Here is James in authority, wielding the language with unapproachable control. When a Rye man, a golfing bore, goes on about how many strokes he'd taken to complete the course, James takes him by the lapel and says, 'My dear fellow, what a princely expenditure of time.' No remedy: that bore, whose name and face have vanished down the drain of the past, exists only because James deigns to shoot him down. It is the habit of the Master to hold forth to silenced listeners – silenced since they can't reach the back of his sentence where he turns and shifts. Nothing shows of the increasing urgency of his efforts until, in the blazing summer of 1911, James fell into a 'furnace' of unmaking. The figure in the furnace remained unseen. Its cover, the image of the Master, was reflected by a phalanx of admirers who transmitted that legend to future generations.

In August 1904, James sailed for America. It was exactly twenty-one years since he had left, in August 1883, following the death of his father. Arrangements for his voyage were made by Clara Benedict, who crossed with him, together with her daughter, Clare. He saw the new Manhattan skyline from New Jersey on his arrival, and within hours was exploring his childhood haunts of Washington Square. Neither his old home nor a church opposite remained in place. When he went on to Boston in the autumn, his family home on Ashburton Place, at the summit of Beacon Hill, was torn down, right then, between two visits. He felt violated by a rampant expansionism with no sense of the past; the ground of his being gave way beneath his feet, as though the bottom had fallen out of his biography. In place of old New York were massed towers like an upturned comb with teeth missing, and multiplied streets like a criss-crossed ledger. Their message was simple – money, not mind, made life; money made the American man, who seemed to care for nothing else. At first it seemed to James that a crass America was lost to art. This fear proved short-lived.

When he took off for northern New Hampshire (staying in William's house in Chocorua on the edge of the dense tracts of woods that surround the White Mountains), the ghosts were still there in 'the near ... the far country of youth' – he, Holmes, and John Chipman Gray with the Temple sisters in August 1865. There, as before, were the perpendicular rock-walls of the Ledges and, below, their 'sacred grove' in the Saco Valley.

Soon after he landed, in September 1904, he went to Salisbury in the north-west corner of Connecticut, to stay with Elly Temple at Barack Matiff Farm; then, in October, he made the first of several stays in the Berkshires of western Massachusetts, near Lenox, in the lavish country house, The Mount, belonging to the novelist Edith Wharton (1862–1937). She now became a friend – more to the man than to the work, which she found incomprehensible.

Once, when talk turned to Emily Brontë, Wharton owned that she had never read 'Remembrance'. Immediately, James found the poem and, his eyes filling, began to read aloud:

> Cold in the earth, and the deep snow piled above thee,
> Far, far removed, cold in the dreary grave,
> Have I forgot, my only Love, to love thee,
> Severed at last by Time's all-severing wave?

His stammer vanished, Wharton noticed, and his voice deepened with 'some far-away emotion', as the words 'swept him forward on great rollers of sound till the full weight of his voice fell on the last cadence'.

Another evening at The Mount, probably in the early summer of 1905, one of the party said to James, 'tell us about the Emmets' – 'the Emmetry', as he called his Temple–Emmet cousins.

For a moment he stood there brooding in the darkness of the terrace, murmuring to himself: 'Ah, my dear, the Emmets – ah, the Emmets!'

He forgot where he was, it seemed to his listeners, forgot 'everything but the vision of his lost youth that the question had evoked, the long train of ghosts flung . . . across the wide stage of the summer night. Ghostlike indeed at first, wavering and indistinct, they glimmered at us through a series of disconnected ejaculations, epithets, allusions, parenthetical rectifications and restatements, till not only our brains but the clear night itself seemed filled with an impalpable fog; and then, suddenly, by some miracle of shifted lights and accumulated strokes, there they stood before us as they lived . . .'.

Wharton was often to see the trick again – people he had known wavering then solidifying under the turn of his lens, 'but never perhaps anything so ample, so sustained, as that summoning to life of dead-and-gone Emmets and Temples, old lovelinesses, old follies, old failures, all long laid away and forgotten under old crumbling grave-stones'.

On 23 February 1905, James gave Henrietta a set of magazine instalments of *The Ambassadors*, inscribed 'To Henrietta Pell-Clarke / her tenderly affectionate old cousin and friend / Henry

James'. By this time Leslie Pell-Clarke had died, and when Henrietta sold the estate she burnt nearly all her James letters.

That winter he did a lecture tour (to cover expenses). At a distance, in California, he mused over the momentous spring and summer of 1865, and an 'inward passion' as he lay on his back on the North Shore in the summer of 1866. These memories are veiled; he could mean anyone or anything, even – conceivably – a passion for his own genius:

> Ah, the 'epoch-making' weeks of the spring of 1865! – from the 1st days of April or so on to the summer (partly spent in Newport, etc., partly at North Conway)! . . . Ah, that pathetic, heroic little *personal* prime of my own, which stretched over into the following summer at Swampscott – '66 – that of . . . unforgettable gropings and findings and sufferings and strivings and play of sensibility and of inward passion there. The hours, the moments, the days, come back to me – on into the early autumn before the move to Cambridge and with the sense still, after such a lifetime, of particular little thrills and throbs and daydreams there.

One of the dreams was 'Europe'. When, that summer, he heard of Holmes's success in England, he had '*vibrated* so with the wonder and romance and curiosity and dim weak tender (oh tender!) envy of it' as he had walked from his friend's house in Charles Street, up the slope of Mount Vernon Street – past the respectable mansions, towards the sobriety of the Boston Athenaeum – all the while humming with an excitement that was to determine, ten years later, his 'own vision-haunted migration'.

Could he recover his America thirty years after the romance of migration? *The American Scene* (1905–7) is less a travel book than a test of whether James can repossess his native land. It had never been securely his, given the early stints in Europe, the avoidance of the Civil War, and the loss of Fenimore, who embodied an older America which appeared to have vanished – Henrietta remained the last of these 'Mohicans'. There is an absence at the centre of this book, a strange kind of breathing silence, a beating pulse of a past of which there are only hints and guesses: the ghosts of the White Mountains; one of them (Gray), now in his sixties, unapproachable across the frail bridge of the past, bent over a book in the new Law

Library at Harvard; and ghostly inhabitants of Newport, men of leisure and girls in buttoned-up bodices and full skirts – modest, not shy – lazing beside the reeds of Lily Pond or clambering along the cliff walk with the sea pounding at outcrops of rock. No names; only place, and figures in outline. It's not autobiography; it's a formula for autobiography. Here is the landscape, it seems to say; can we fill that landscape with a life worthy to possess it? There is an eerie sense of a people poised on some frontier of the soul, facing a land unfilled or mis-filled.*

'There was a voice in the air, . . . a spiritual voice: "Oh, the *land's* all right!" . . . Thus it sounded, the blessed note . . .' Its plea to be loved, a womanly plea it seemed to James, was not so much a 'Live upon me . . .' as a 'Live *with* me, somehow, and let us make out together what we may do for each other.' See, the voice went on, how 'sympathetic' I am, 'and how I am therefore better than my fate; see how I lend myself . . . positively to aesthetic use: give me that consolation'.

In New Hampshire, the pulpit-stones and lichened cathedrals, seen through a drizzle of forest light, told a love-story in many volumes, 'the idyllic *type* in its purity'. The standard view of the *Scene* as an attack on what America had become (with the hypertrophy of the profit-motive), denies moments when James opens a door to a place of his past – not to explore, but to see *through* it 'the queer *other*'. This is the unsullied America of pure promise, reflected in the mild faces of lakes with wooded brims, like a breathing space in a large monotony, breathing a 'cult of the Indian canoe, of Fenimore Cooper, . . . of the immortalizable water-fowl'. Like Cooper in *Home As Found*, James did attack the violation of America by business interests, personified by Cooper as 'Dodge' and 'Bragg'.

James found, on his return, an exaggerated dimorphism of the sexes – nowhere had he seen men abdicate so much in order to pursue money. Society and the arts were left to women. De Tocqueville, in his monumental study of democracy-in-action, had remarked on the phenomenon already in the 1830s: 'And now that I come near the end of this book in which I have recorded so many

* Robert Frost recaptures this idea when he says: 'The land was ours before we were the land's.'

considerable achievements of the Americans,' he had concluded, 'if anyone asks me what I think the chief cause of the extraordinary prosperity and growing power of this nation, I should answer that it is due to the superiority of their women.' Seventy years later found men in a void. Their abdication to women, James felt, had been disastrous for women as well as themselves. For, he argued, though the American girl appeared free, and had an audacity not open to women elsewhere, she had to endure a vacant mate. Why did she not protest, he wondered, 'after watching the Man, the deep American man, retire into his tent and let down the flap?'

American manhood, its strain of ruthlessness – call it enterprise – haunts the hero of 'The Jolly Corner', a house Spencer Brydon has inherited in New York. As a Europeanised emigrant, Brydon embodies an alternative manhood. Returning (like James) to New York after thirty years abroad, Brydon hunts, and is hunted by, this rapacious Other, a self he might have been – might yet be – down a dark corridor of the family house, vacated, yet filled for him by a spectral presence to whom he is drawn obsessively under cover of night. Cornered one night on the bottom stair, the Other appears to expand as he mounts towards the civilised Brydon. Masked, at first, by spread gloved hands, he slowly opens the fingers – two of them stumps – to reveal a millionaire whose 'ravaged' face, 'ruined sight', and mutilated hands are emblems of inward disfigurement.*

James wrote in a letter on 15 August 1908, four months before the tale was published: '. . . I believe in feeling to the full all the

* It so happens that the gentleman-convict Robert Temple damaged two fingers while hunting in 1877. He wrote from Fort Townsend in Nashville, Tennessee, to his uncle Henry senior: '. . . I accidentally wounded myself in the right hand, tearing away 2 fingers. I have had to suffer amputation of one; the other I shall save, though disfigured.' Temple claims unflagging enterprise, and at the same time owns to '*intemperance*'. 'Were I a man like Harry's Christopher Newman [the innocent man of fortune in *The American* (1877)], it would be different – But I am not, & never can be now.' In 1885, when Temple was imprisoned out west, he penned disconcertingly graceful and amusing letters to members of his family (who, he well knew, would like to disown him). At this time he had appealed for help to his cousin Harry, the angel of the James family, who refused – 'Harry has deserted me, and the last prop has gone,' Temple declared in mock-despair.

pangs & pains' of our visitations. The wrongs in the James family lurked in shadow, there to confront through the medium of fiction: wills that docked errant sons, something we don't know that wrecked Alice at fourteen, and the relentlessness of Henry senior's injunctions to his boy Bob to be a 'man' at seventeen – to stay in the war – and then, when Bob was damaged by drink and whoring (being a 'man' with a vengeance), he was expelled from the family home and sent out west. Spencer Brydon, who stands for 'the triumphant life', is shocked by the hideousness of 'the bared identity' that claims him for its own. That warped man is both him and not him, he equivocates to his old friend Miss Staverton, a woman 'in the afternoon of life' who 'divines' him with mild irony.

She has divined the Other before Brydon encounters him, and faints on the floor of his house. Alice Staverton, who comes to his rescue, upholds the 'beast', the 'black stranger'. Her acceptance as he comes to, lying on the fur lining of her cloak with his head on her breast, recalls the forgiveness conferred by the woman who cradles Stransom in 'The Altar of the Dead' and the charity of May Bartram, who perceives the Beast intuitively, long before Marcher. To Miss Staverton, this beast promises an efflorescence of manhood when Brydon reveals to her a sense of 'a strange *alter ego* deep down somewhere within me, as the full-blown flower is in the small tight bud, and that I just took the course, transferred him to the climate, that blighted him for once and ever'.

'And you wonder about the flower,' Miss Staverton said. 'So do I, if you want to know. . . . I believe in the flower,' she continued, 'I feel it would have been quite splendid, quite huge and monstrous.'

She is certain the manhood of the Other – 'monstrous', 'quite hideous and offensive' as he fears it is – must be assimilated, not discarded. The Other has appeared to her as a death-mask that begins to breathe: an image of renewal.

It was rare for James to end with a hopeful union of man and woman. 'The Jolly Corner', as the home was called in the past, was derived from Fenimore's childhood home, 'Cheerful Corner'.

This tale was published in December 1908, after a third visit to her grave in May–June 1907. James had made his first pilgrimage there in May 1894; the second, in May 1899. He wrote to

Fenimore's niece Clare Benedict in the autumn of 1907: 'the most beautiful thing in Italy, almost, seemed to me in May and June last, the exquisite summer luxuriance . . . of the spot – I mean of course that very particular spot – below the great grey wall, the cypresses and the time-silvered Pyramid. It is tremendously, inexhaustibly touching – its effect never fails to overwhelm.'

The dual character of the expatriate reappeared in relation to Edith Wharton. With her, James tested his loyalty to the past versus the present: a conflict between the posthumous affairs of the private life and the support of a new friend, twenty years younger, with a lot to offer.

She met James first in the late eighties in Paris when she was about twenty-five, and again in Venice when she was twenty-eight, and though she tried to court his attention, on the first occasion with a tea-rose dress embroidered with iridescent beads and, on the second occasion, a dashing new hat, he retained no memory of her. When Wharton and James met a third time, for lunch in London, in December 1903, she now, at the age of forty-one, came forward as a writer. He found her 'conversable . . . and sympathetic in every way'.

At once, he used what she called 'his magic faculty of drawing out his interlocutor's inmost self'. She considered him 'perhaps the most intimate friend I ever had', though there was none of the secrecy of his tie with Fenimore. This was a conspicuous friendship. Wharton was the intelligent companion of an ageing man, who knew how to surround him with comforts and the right sort of admiring company. Like a society hostess, she hung on the talking Master who (she was too young to realise) was a belated exhibit born of failure. James became her tame celebrity, along with the French counts she managed to collect. She was a benefactress, bright-eyed, controlling. One Sunday afternoon at Lamb House another guest noted Wharton's trim dress (she was proud of her figure) and 'very determined' manner, 'full of metallic jangles'. Suddenly, 'she ordered James to walk with her about the garden, and set off with James behind. He must have made some protest . . . because across the garden came the clear voice of Mrs Wharton saying "Nonsense, Henry, it will do you good".'

Because Wharton was persuasive, and because she outlived James by more than twenty years, her version has prevailed. No doubt he did behave as she reported – a habitué of society, spinning the web of the higher gossip, fussy over the right hat in the midst of a motor tour through France, a little ridiculous in his wrapped-up, verbose old age – but this was not the James who wrote 'The Jolly Corner'.

Mistakenly, Wharton called him a novelist of manners, 'those of the little vanishing group of people among whom he had grown up', she said with pity. 'It was the only food his imagination could fully assimilate.' On the contrary, manners were merely a starting point, the outermost rind of hidden lives. The deep structure of the great works was still, as always, allegory: evil, renunciation, and the salvation of the soul. Isabel Archer of Gardencourt had to engage with a 'snake'. Like her, Maggie Verver, the American princess in *The Golden Bowl* (1904), eats of the tree of knowledge and is not corrupted. This was the James of the moral test whom Fenimore, with her feel for Hawthorne, resolved to meet. Wharton met a more public character, a novelist of high life, more distinguished but less read than herself. Theirs was not the kind of working tie James had enjoyed, now and then, with Fenimore. Similar as Wharton and James may be in their settings, he thought her too hard, too derisive, and their ends could not be farther apart. Where James advanced the higher possibilities of human nature, Wharton saw its futility. It was a view consistent with the misery of her marriage to a Boston socialite, Teddy Wharton. He was uninterested in her writing and increasingly depressed. They divorced in 1913, Teddy a ruin.

In Teddy, Edith Wharton picked a mouse – following other mouse-men like her lifelong friend Walter Berry. Her marriage to Teddy was not consummated for three weeks, and afterwards she had asthma attacks whenever they had to share a bed. A much-discussed fling with Morton Fullerton in 1909 was brief; recent evidence has suggested it lasted no more than a few weeks. At the time, Morton was engaged to his sister-cousin Katharine Fullerton. Encouraged by attentions that were more than brotherly, she had always worshipped him. In 1907, when Morton had visited her at Bryn Mawr, Katharine had accepted his proposal with a burst of passion – confined, it turned out, to epistolary passion, for Morton had promptly departed to visit Wharton at The Mount.

Wharton knew of the attachment, and used Katharine's unanswered letters in a story, 'The Letters'. Vincent Deering has an endearing manner bound to conquer women: he invites compassion, 'literary' talk, and tender kisses, but nothing holds. It is entirely in character that during three years of separation from a teacher he has courted, Deering does not answer ten desperately restrained letters – in fact, she learns later, he never even opened them.

Given Morton's promiscuity, what Wharton settled for was not exactly a relationship, more a passing fever. She was a voyeur: when she motored with James in France, she harped on the sexual escapades of George Sand – particularly the incident of Pagello, who came to doctor Sand's lover Alfred de Musset, and stayed to replace him – a subject which eroticised and, at length, wearied James. Wharton was fascinated by Sand's power as a woman of the world, and named her cars and even her chauffeur after Sand's lovers. There may be, again, a voyeuristic element to her assignation with Morton Fullerton at the Charing Cross Hotel, London, in 1909: that evening she had James dine with them *à trois*, as though inviting a reciprocal voyeurism on his part, for he was drawn in his own way to Fullerton's flair for feeling his way into another's soul, exciting affinity, then eluding it. Where Fullerton was only an accomplished flirt, James was sustained and serious in his purpose – which could make him more dangerous.

When Wharton touches on deeper love, it is doomed or distanced; she is more interested in disappointments. Her cynicism about the possibilities of happiness is not the prophetic disillusion of the Moderns, who had answers to propose; she was more a historian of manners. She 'did' Old New York like an anthropologist documenting a closed, exotic society which she understood better than anyone else. She understood its hierarchy and its strictures, as when Ellen Olenska, a refugee from a foreign marriage who threatens a local marriage, is cast out of the tribe in the course of a grand dinner. It is a bloodless ritual but no less savage than those of primitive societies.

While overtly James backed the gambols of Morton and

Wharton, and rejoiced with Edith when a defeated Katharine took herself off, his work rejects a worldly view of love. In 'Crapy Cornelia' (1909), James caricatured the advances of a fashionable, Wharton-type woman called Mrs Worthingham. A much-travelled New Yorker, White-Mason, prefers an old friend called Cornelia, who is the link with a dead, youthful love called Mary. 'Mary' and Mary Temple; 'Cornelia' and Connie (as Fenimore was called by her family throughout her life): these names, like their histories, cross and recross the history of Henry James, who aligned himself with White-Mason in one of his letters. The intrinsic value of two memorable women refutes the cash value of the present. Mrs Worthingham is very visibly rich as a result of her marriage to Mr Worthingham, now happily no more. With her rings and bangles, her pastel ruffles and puffed-out hair, she shows off an unshadowed opulence of the New York that James had hardly recognised as its skyline rose over the horizon: hard-edged, metallic. It's the side of Wharton that had the blanks of the super-rich, as when she wondered why James didn't acquire his own chauffeur and motor-car instead of using hers – to the last drop of petrol, she said, a little put out by what she took to be meanness.

Cornelia Rasch, who had disappeared some ten years earlier, now comes back into White-Mason's life. Like Woolson's Miss Grief, she appears 'dingy'. She wears black after successive deaths in her family. Single, with scant resources, Miss Rasch had gone to live in Europe, and to economise had settled in a provincial English town: Cheltenham, he seems to recall – or it may have been Bognor. She has an 'arch', bridling manner, the dated ways of women who came to maturity in the 1860s – women of his own generation – and he finds it rather touching because he understands the density of the shadow which archness concealed.* She has the rash pointedness of a shy woman, and he likes the directness of her 'good' little glare. Their old dialogues start up in their heads, and immediately, as 'survivors of a dead and buried society', they 'recreate' their 'lost world'. James worked in his grandfather's stint as a tobacco merchant two years after immigration: White-Mason

* The arch manner with its elisions had its acme in the great poet of the sixties, Emily Dickinson.

can recall a tobacconist's shop belonging to Cornelia's family, where, on the sidewalk, a large Indian had stood with cigars.* As a child, White-Mason had fancied the Indian as the last of the Mohicans.

Cornelia's modest lodgings are filled with memorabilia. Not smart objects like Mrs Worthinghams's, they have the warmth of the life they contain for those with the heart to remember. On a plain table are small carte-de-visite photographs of the sixties. White-Mason picks out a 'spectral' face, gives a stifled cry, and then holds it behind him. Now and then, he brings it forward and puts his eyes to it. This is Mary Cardew, who had loved him and died.

'You weren't fair' to Mary, Cornelia tells him straight. 'She didn't think so – to the very end.'

He had played on Mary, and then, when she was dead, inflated his feelings. Cornelia's knowledge that he has cherished all these years his own photograph of Mary makes him turn pale, as though a secret were exposed. Autumn 1868, they agree, is when things went wrong – in fact, this is the date when it began to be known that Mary Temple was spitting blood.

The final scene of 'crazy Cornelia' in her crapy dress adds a new turn to the Jamesian drama of posthumous affairs. What a man wants, White-Mason tells Cornelia, is a partner 'to know *for* one, to know *with* one', as she does. This prompts Cornelia to ask if he wants to marry her.

'No, Cornelia,' he says, shaking his head, ' – not to *marry* you.' Her service is to link him with Mary, and share their home in the past.

'But what – since you can't marry me! – can you do with me?' she asked.

'I can live with you,' is his answer, meaning the alternative of a pair who can '*make* together'. The exact nature of their bond can't be defined, but he can state explicitly, as he settles by her fire, 'I can't give you up. It's very curious.'

*

The late style of Henry James is laden with the unsaid – the

* Cigar-store Indians carved wooden ones advertising cigars. Probably, James meant one of those.

unsayable. Every subordinate clause adds its nuance to an expanded view of truth. He develops a sentence that searches for truth and grants its elusiveness, knocking at doors locked in silence.

The late manner directed a comprehensive revision of his novels, a massive task which James began on his return to England in July 1905. It initiated an even vaster task to doctor the life and intentions behind his works, everything he would leave to the delectation of posterity. The New York edition, encompassing all the works he wished to preserve, was the last firing of pots designed to last for all time. He planned, for instance, to bring out the 'poetic' aspect of *Daisy Miller*. He draws on the recent image of *The Wings of the Dove* to clarify the innocence of Daisy, whose first words to Winterbourne, in the new version, are 'winged with their accent, so that they fluttered and settled about him . . . like vague white doves. It was Miss Daisy Miller who had released them for flight.' In this version, Daisy appears more mysterious, less vulgar; Winterbourne's response to her, more complicated and knowing. Taking pains to bring out Winterbourne's loss or scrawling his balloons into the pages of the 1881 edition of the *Portrait*, James put his final stamp on his productions. The outcome was the image of the Master, a public construct haunted by the uncertain nature of an expatriate.

From 1906 to 1908, James toiled over his life's work, adding eighteen prefaces to the twenty-four volumes published between 1907 and 1909. The prefaces provided an opportunity to muse over the art of fiction, a genre (like biography today) in need of theory. James had reinvented the novel as a form of art, but the prefaces irritate us with their pretence to reveal how it was done. They don't. From this point of view they present a brilliant aesthetic blind to true sources and great predecessors. James, for instance, will not acknowledge what Fenimore saw at once, a source for Osmond in George Eliot's Grandcourt, a portrait of a tyrannical husband in the process of imprinting himself on his wife's mind. Then there's the humbug when the preface to the *Portrait* claims it is the first novel ever to make a woman central in her own right, as though James had never heard of *Clarissa* (1747–8), *Emma* (1816), and *Jane Eyre* (1847). He found it convenient, now, to point to his departure from George Eliot's 'frail vessels' – here, she is useful as a foil – since her heroines (unlike those of the Brontës) lack agency. This is the politics, not the substance, of art.

The prefaces skip past private sources. Politics again: the trick is to reduce to the level of idle gossip those stories and anecdotes others contributed to the James workshop. This promotes the legend of a solitary artist. Half a century later, the poet W. H. Auden wanted to give James 'a good shaking'. He saw how 'out of their monstrous vanity human creatures want to be their own cause'. Auden, otherwise an admirer of James, admitted that 'there are times [in the prefaces] when their tone of hushed reverence before the artistic mystery becomes insufferable'.

With their detached, theoretical pronouncements on the practice of fiction, the prefaces reflect the Master, while fictions like 'The Jolly Corner' and 'Crapy Cornelia' actually tell us more about James. The prefaces came after the fact; the notebooks before: as such they provide complementary entrées to the novelist's workshop – of enormous interest, of course, but not to be trusted if we wish to find a genuine source. In the notebooks the leaps into plotting are swift – and sometimes misleading. Though James says in the preface to *The Wings of the Dove* that it represents a 'young motive', his notebook does not identify the dying girl, and there is no sign that she is American – he makes a gesture of catching her out of the air. Similarly, we question the given source of 'Owen Wingrave' as a young Englishman sitting in a London park: the emotional impact of that tale goes back to his own resistance to fighting in the Civil War – war, says Wingrave, is not the way to solve problems. The moral position is absolute. I don't believe James thought up this position in 1892 for the sake of a peaceful young man in a park. It makes sense that much of what he wrote had its emotional and moral source in the fraught America of the 1860s.

As he put the finishing touches to his garden, James began to notice shoots of the next generation: the young writers and artists of the Bloomsbury set. At Trinity College, Cambridge, at the turn of the century, Leslie Stephen's son, Thoby, and his intellectual friends, including Leonard Woolf, Lytton Strachey, and Saxon Sydney-Turner, used to sit in pregnant silence in imitation of characters in Henry James. Every now and then, one of the party would murmur 'the Ultimate' in awed tones. In 1904, when these young men settled in the Bloomsbury district of London, they introduced their habits to Thoby's sisters, the future Vanessa Bell and Virginia Woolf (who reviewed *The Golden Bowl* in 1904, one of her earliest publications). When the Stephen sisters summered in Rye, James was appalled by the young men who visited them, the lank Strachey, the colourless Saxon, and the little poodle Clive Bell, whom he thought unworthy to marry the beautiful Vanessa. James was a trifle condescending about 'Virginia' going into print. He was surprised, and not altogether pleased, perhaps, by her modified rapture over the length of *The Golden Bowl*.

A suitor of Virginia, Sydney Waterlow, lived in Rye and befriended James. 'Tell her – tell her – ', James said to Waterlow, 'how sorry I am that the inevitabilities of life should have made it seem possible, even for a moment, that I could allow a child of her father's to seem to swim out of my ken!'

In the course of a walk with Waterlow, on Friday 31 January 1908, James confided views Bloomsbury would have shared: he thought Parliament an immense waste of talk and solemnity, and the Empire absurdly cumbrous – it was a mystery, James said, how it went on. Perhaps it was simply easier for it to go on than to stop. His next words prefigure his admirer T. S. Eliot, who in 1908 was an undergraduate at Harvard: the older he grew, James said, the more acutely and passionately he felt 'the huge absurdity and grotesqueness of things – the monstrous perversity of evil'.

Commercially, the New York edition was a colossal failure. The first royalty cheque was for $211. From 1909 James felt unwell, and consulted doctors about his heart. Then, on the last day of 1909, a new and hideous trial started.

It was, he realised, 'a sort of nervous breakdown'. In the early spring of 1910, he felt too 'undermined' to recover, and thought of suicide. A measure of relief came with the arrival of Alice Howe James, who crossed the Atlantic with William in order to nurse her brother-in-law.

'You can get better and you will with a whole new kingdom to reign over,' Alice assured him.

They all went to 'the drastic & dreadful' Bad-Nauheim for a 'humbugging' cure, then on to Zurich, Lucerne, and Geneva, where a cable announced that their brother Bob had died of a heart attack. With the worsening of William's own weak heart, Alice kept this news to herself for two days, then told Henry when they were alone on a steam-launch crossing the lake at Geneva. 'That moment made for me somehow a date', he told her later, 'determined my sense of my power, and above all of the intensity of my resolution, to get comparatively better.'

William, though, was failing. Henry sailed with him and Alice for America in August, and William died at Chocorua soon after their arrival.

'I sit here infinitely stricken & in deep darkness – but imperfectly recovered, myself, from a long illness of many months', Henry told Holmes on 14 September 1910. 'My beloved Brother & my sister came out, angelically to minister to me – he himself much menaced – & she & I returned with him, later on, but to see him horribly suffer & die. My privation is unutterable – he filled such a place in my personal & intellectual world.'

James realised he had been 'spoiling' for a breakdown for 'a couple of years'. Arguably, he had been spoiling for this since the early nineties, as the tide turned against him. His accounts for 1895–6 had shown that not one of his novels (and this must include *The Portrait of a Lady*) sold more than twenty copies. One publisher had sold sixteen books in all: 'Payable 3 months hence, so that I have that luxurious interval to gloat over the prospect, are £7. 0. 5.' In 1897 *Harper's* had taken him on to write 'London Letters', then dismissed him 'as you scarce would an incompetent housemaid'. He felt 'lost' as a writer, a 'silent, fatalistic, fantastic victim' of the book trade – 'the trade is brutal'.

He stayed on in America, officially to be with William's family but really because he was unfit to be alone. It was, he said, the illness of his life, like a long dark trail which is discovered to be 'truly the trail of the poisonous serpent'. Condemned to 'hell', he loved Bay more than ever and longed to clasp her to his soul. Bay was about to be married to Blanchard Rand, and James promised to come to the wedding, 'even in my pyjamas & a bandanna'. In New York for two months, cared for by Edith's sister-in-law, Mrs

Cadwalader Jones, he tried out Freudian analysis with a neurologist, Dr James Jackson Putnam. The illness, continuing through the summer of 1911, cracked open the Master. 'My accursed necessity of falling back into deep, dark holes is endless and unutterable,' he wrote to a law school classmate, a widower called George Abbot James,* in May 1911.

The letters of this time are not in the ornate hand of the Master of Lamb House; the writing is jagged and blotched whenever he went 'down in a deep black hole'. His 'helpless, hapless scrawl' had none of his usual affability, but is more compelling for its bared truth – to Elly, Bay, Ariana Curtis, Rhoda Broughton, and, of all people, Katharine Loring. All day he lay prone, 'speechless & graceless', an ordeal that seemed 'endless & unutterable', draining his confidence. To be in that hole is to believe one will never emerge; and yet he had the pluck to say, 'I shall come up again.' The real test was to tell himself – he did so by repeating the words to others – he would certainly 'emerge': 'I had to come back from very far,' he told Mrs Curtis in May, 'but in spite of everything . . . I *have* come – *almost* all the way . . .'. It was, though, far from over.

In the torrid heat of high summer, 'prostrate & helpless & ill', James felt his only hope was to escape from polished households (like The Mount) and go to George Abbot James at Lowland House, Nahant, '& not wear any clothes or do anything civil or decent'. He told Katharine Loring, 'I have such a terror of being "taken" in the fiery furnace again.'

To Bay he confided the worst of that 'appalling summer'. It could have been 'fatal'. The fusion of the outward and inward furnace, James tried to explain, 'simply demoralised me & flattened me out. Manners, memories, decencies, all alike fell from me, & I simply lay for long weeks a senseless, stricken, perspiring, inconsiderate, unclothed mass. I expected & desired nothing but to melt utterly away.' He saw himself become 'ungracious & uncommunicative': 'I lived from day to day, most of the time in my bath. . . . I was caught as in 2 or 3 firetraps – I mean places of great & special suffering [at the Merrimans' at Intervale, New

* No relation. He received his LLB degree from Harvard in July 1863.

Hampshire, from 30 June to 6 July, and after that, The Mount] . . . but I found a blest refuge with my kind friend George James . . . at the tip end of the Nahant promontory, quite out at sea, where, amid gardens & groves & on a vast breezy verandah, my life was most mercifully saved . . .'. He was to look back on this as 'Paradise': 'the blest time'. He took in 'the great restorative breath' of the sea; heard 'the soft boom of the surge' upon the rocks. There, on his couch, he exchanged 'the hot poison-cup for a long draught of the coolest and sweetest elixir!'

Thrust in the furnace, melting down to mere 'mass', with a 'blest' glimpse of 'Paradise', he came to the edge of existence. He walked naked at Nahant like an Ancient Mariner under the eye of the sun.

On 2 August he boarded the *Mauritania* for England. The ocean was so smooth that the ship seemed to make a mouthful of 'the waste of waters'.

He had hoped to cool down in Rye but found 'the same brassy sky & red-hot air' as in America. 'Everything is scorched & blighted,' he went on to Bay, ' – my garden a thing almost of cinders.' If it would only rain, he said, 'I should begin to find myself again. I can't do so yet & am waiting to see how & where I am.'

In this indeterminate state, the one identity he fell back on was a photograph of himself at sixteen which reminded him of Minny Temple. He enclosed a copy to Bay and Elly, claiming 'It looks a good deal like *her* about that time too – we were always thought to look a little alike.'

By the end of the year, he began to heal, helped by a suggestion from Alice: a memoir of William. At first, this was to be a 'family book' or notes to accompany a selection of William's letters; eventually, it became a memoir of Henry more than anyone else, in his own words, 'the history of a mind, . . . these movements of the spirit, these tides and currents of growth'. He, the subject, was not to be found on display: 'I had to draw him forth from within rather than meet him in the world.' The challenge was to centre the minutiae of the inward life – 'the poor dear inward life' – and 'translate' them 'into the terms of the outward': 'a tale of assimilations small and fine; out of which refuse, ... the most branching vegetations may be conceived as having sprung.'

His return to work in the winter of 1911–12, he told Elly, 'does me more good than anything else can do me harm'. So, at the age of sixty-eight and a half, he began to reconstruct himself through a form of autobiography: his first consciousness of the American scene when his parents returned with him at the age of two; the steamer up the Hudson, the night of strange paddling and creaking, and the excitement of docking at Albany in a dim, early dawn; his grandmother's Dutch house on North Pearl Street, in what was still a country town; and those new faces who were to people his life ever after: 'our cousins ... who pre-eminently figured for us; the various brood presided over by my father's second sister, Catherine James, who had married at a very early age, Captain Robert Temple, U.S.A.' And so to 'Mary Temple, radiant and rare, extinguished in her first youth, but after having made an impression on many persons, and on ourselves not least, which was to become..., for all time, matter of sacred legend ...'.

At the time he dictated these words, he wrote to Elly: 'My thoughts hang about you very tenderly & faithfully just now. They attach themselves particularly to beloved Bay – & once they get going they become almost as much of a pain as of a joy – by reason of the uncertain quantities amid which they move. ... My romantic little stay with you of last summer comes back to me. ... I affectionately press you to my heart – & then take Rosina & Leslie in turn for a similar demonstration. I hang devotedly over Bay, & almost aspire to participate in Blanchard's earnest attentions to her. Will you tell them this – with all my love? Perhaps, even, you will let Bay read my letter – & *then burn it straight up*, by reason of the above scurrility.'

Once more, attraction to Bay was blending with memories of her aunt: 'She is a magnificent creature & everything she does & is bears the stamp of her easy ... power & her noble nature.' He wished her to know 'how wide Lamb House only wants to open its arms' to her. To Eleanor, his other favourite, he pleaded: 'Love me the more as I lack you so dreadfully'.

Wharton secretly arranged to have Scribner's divert $8,000 from her royalties to James: ostensibly an advance for a new novel (*The*

Ivory Tower), never completed. The gesture was meant to restore his confidence, but though superficially he was pleased, the rejections from publishers, his failure in the theatre, and the loss of readers, had all left scars too deep to be healed in this way.

In October 1912, James began to suffer 'a new plague of Egypt'. It was diagnosed as shingles. He erupted into 'blisters & welts & *sores*' and 'accurst pain'. He described the pain as an 'indissoluble *knot* of long wicked needle-stabs & knife-edges'. Analgesics left him depressed, and worse was to follow. At the end of 1912, he had the misfortune to consult Sir Henry Head, a leading doctor with an impressive manner, whose remedies sent him 'down into hell'. He lay there 'sizzling'. (Following a consultation with Head the following year, Virginia Woolf attempted suicide. Her helplessness in controlling hands contrasts with the independence of James.) Wretched as he was, James resolved to close his mouth 'tight' to anything from Head's hand. The man's opinions were, James saw, 'vacuous'. Still, he did allow Head, who urged 'change' for the sake of change, to persuade him to move at once from Lamb House to London.

That same October he had taken a large flat overlooking the Thames, 21 Carlyle Mansions, in Cheyne Walk, Chelsea. The place was to grow on him, but at this moment he was unfit to move. He got up to London almost in his bedclothes and 'howling with pain', shortly before Christmas. To Alice, he confided that he was also 'full-blown' from 'utterly unbearable flatulent distension of the stomach, in the most obstinate and prolonged degree'. There was a further 'complication' which he does not name but which must have been depression, to judge from a confidence to his sister-in-law that it was a 'sequel' to his breakdown in 1910. Physical pain underlined mental hell in this second phase of the breakdown, yet in this phase James did not lose his eloquence. He sent his old friend Perry an amazing summation of his state of mind – it has the moral and visionary power of a work of literature:

> I have had blighted and ravaged weeks and weeks – been really, to the strangest degree, since about June last a victim of the harrying Fates or Furies, who don't seem able to keep their hands off me ever, now, for many days together; and have for the last two months, or

> more, suffered the last extremity from a visitation of 'shingles', infernal ailment ... which has dug for me a deep dark hole at the bottom of which, even in my ninth week, alas, I seem still to lie. I am during a brief morning lull of a couple of hours or so (11 to 1.30) mostly able to meet after this fashion the mild assault of my correspondence; then the waters too often close over me and I am disconnected from all things pleasant. Of those with which I *am* connected I will spare you the details; consisting as they do exclusively of the various, the shifting and bewildering but constantly confounding, shades of the damnable! One goes in short down into hell; and take it from me that I am thus writing you on the very edge of the pit.... I at any rate console myself with the thought that I have again and again risen to the surface ... after not having for real geologic periods stirred it by so much as a wavelet (as we used to say at the Berkeley Institute [their Newport school in 1858–9]....

He recalled a time when he had heard of this hell, presumably from his sister, Alice, his brother Bob, and, of course, Fenimore. Then, he'd understood it but vaguely. Now, he could not reconstruct his 'inhuman' detachment; his 'accursed' intimacy with the horror would dawn with its touch. 'This beastly thing is so bad ... that one is quite ashamed of ... having lived in a sphere where it *could* rage and of having brushed carelessly and detachedly by its victims.'

For the best part of four months he was unable to leave his bed, but he went on dictating his memoir for a few hours a day whenever he could. Too voluminous, by now, for one volume, it would have to be two, he advised Alice, not caring to mention that the 'small boy' of the first volume was not William but himself. In fact, in *A Small Boy and Others* (1913), William has little mention. Contemplating the second volume, James could not decide where to end the story of youth: given his own dominance in the text, neither William's return from Germany in 1868 nor the start of his attachment to Harvard would do.

One day John Chipman Gray called to see Alice in Irving Street. Retired from Harvard, he had been ill, and now walked with difficulty. It was rumoured he would never be well again. After he had rested awhile, Gray explained his purpose. He had a cache of letters from Minny Temple, and was uncertain how to dispose of them.

'Perhaps I ought to burn them but I shrink from doing it,' he said. Then he offered them to Alice, to keep or destroy. There was one proviso: he did not want them to go to Minny's family.

Alice at once asked if she might pass the letters to Henry James.

Gray only half assented. 'You must read them first, you must be responsible', he said. '*Here they are* – '. And he drew a packet from a pocket where Alice had seen no sign of it.

'I did read them – ah, so tenderly,' Alice reported to James. ' – Any one might read them.' Then she went to see Gray and told him how 'beautiful' she found them, and again asked Gray to let her send them to her brother-in-law.

This time Gray agreed. He said, 'I have been reading *A Small Boy* and I can trust his taste and judgment.'

'I think he is eager to have you use them,' Alice relayed to James. 'His slowness in assenting at first was simply caution & perhaps a touch of the indecision of illness. When I saw him next he said "*Did* you send them?" – as if he *had* agreed.'

The letters seemed to Alice 'a gallant and haunting record – almost too perfect to be broken up,' as she put it to James, 'but you will know how to use it for some memorial of her. The second time I saw him I promised to show him copies of your letters, the two written on hearing of Minnie's death – it seemed the only generous thing to do after he had given you the right to use his – and I felt as if you would say "Do it." He thought your letters most beautiful and just . . .'.

Gray added slowly, 'I too was never in love with her. I liked better to write to her than to see her. She was the only *just* woman I have ever known. Her friendship is one of the things in my life which I best like to remember.'

As Alice was going, Gray followed her heavily to the door. 'Anything you and Henry agree to may be done with the letters. I trust your judgment.'

She repeated this to James 'as a measure of his seriousness and to make clear that they must not, by any hazard revert to the Emmet relatives. It seems very graceless and impertinent of me to be cautioning you about your own cousin's letters, but unless I had promised[,] the letters would have been destroyed.'

When James received the packet, he was three-quarters through the second volume. His first opinion, 'what an infinitely pathetic faraway little ghostly voice it seems', changed as that voice took over. At first, he felt the distance of Minny's directness from the elaborate grandeur of his late style, and then the faraway Minny closed with him 'speaking of what she with a peculiar naturalness dreamt of and missed'. On 23 June 1913 James confided to Helena de Kay Gilder his plan to include 'dearest now – unspeakably – ghostly M.T.', a portrait 'you will be in a position to appreciate better than almost anyone else. I feel myself free to make use, after half a century, of a particular series of Letters of M.T.'s . . . which have come into my hands, and which . . . are extraordinarily interesting and touching. They have floated over to me across the wide gulf of time with the most wonderful opportuneness. *But kindly breathe not a word . . . in any quarter whatever before the book appears; I have a special reason for that.*' It was sustaining to think of Helena, with her 'faithful remembrance'. Minny's story, unfolding in her own words, was the climax of his memoir. Her death provided the needed finale. James completed *Notes of a Son and Brother* in October 1913. It was superior to the first volume, he told Alice, 'through superiority of substance'.

Never had he been so anxious about a book as he awaited the verdict. For his memoir contradicted his own stand in favour of privacy; then, too, there was a question of accuracy. When William's son Harry accused his uncle of altering documents (William's letters), his justification was that what he had done was no common memoir; it was a work of imaginative, not literal, truth. The ghosts of the dead had his ear, his spirit had communed with theirs, and the result was a biographic truth that was truer in its suggestiveness, its closeness to the 'unspeakable past', than figures nailed down by cast-iron facts. He argued that his changes were small and did no damage to his brother's identity.

The real issue, glossed over here, is the fictional presentation of the James family: as sole survivor of his generation, Henry James was free to invent a legend of unbroken harmony, even though his brother Bob had summed up his own life as 'a biography of broken fortunes' and Wilky had described himself as a 'mite' sacrificed on the wartime altar of his father's pieties. Henry had been reminded of these and other unpleasant facts when, in 1913, he had read Wilky's correspondence: he had expressed to Wilky's widow, Carrie, the torment of revisiting the 'far-away and yet so intimate ghostly past where everything and everyone lives again, and what seems to come forth are the old pains and suffering and mistakes'. His memoir of 'the happy working of all relations, in our family life' blots out the wreckage of three of the five childen. Another omission was their mother's exemption of her favourite, Henry, from the obligation to earn his living. Henry's refusal of the wartime draft, and even the home guard obligatory for others of his age, goes unmentioned; so does William's tussle with his father beyond the grave. For after Henry senior's death, William had edited a highly critical collection of his father's work, manifesting a recrudescence of Henry senior's impulse to score over an older brother through posthumous criticism – an impulse to which William, as a young man, had objected. The book, predictably, flopped. A huge cover-up is the question of what happened to Alice in her teens. James offered Katharine Loring implausible excuses about lack of material: the book closed 'when she was still in her teens – so it *had* to be that way – I mean her being out of it.' 'I daresay', Henry James owned to Harry, 'I did instinctively regard it at last as all *my* truth to do what I would with'.

He made no contact whatever with Minny's surviving sisters, Elly and Henrietta, who, as next-of-kin, were legal owners of the letters, as Gray would well have known – hence his unease about James. These two highly proper men did collude in this appropriation.

After James sent off the memoir to Alice, he wrote to her on 18 March 1914: 'I hope you will think that the use I have made of M.T.'s letters is as interesting as it *could* have been, & that J.G. will think so, poor dear man – if, ill & detached as he is, he still thinks or cares about anything. The whole working-in of Minnie was difficult & delicate – highly so; but I seem already to gather here that my evocation of her appears, by her touchingness & beauty, *the* "stroke," or success, of the book.' Ten days later, with more reviews, he added: 'What I have been able to do for *her* after all the long years – judged by this test of expressed admiration – strikes me as a wondrous stroke of fate. . . . I seem really to have . . . made her emerge and live on, endowed her with a kind of dim sweet immortality that places and keeps her'.

Notes of a Son and Brother was published to an acclaim in England such as he'd never had before. Praise was loudest for the last chapter, the memoir of Minny, dominated by her own voice. James has long extracts from her letters to Gray, and again took the liberty to reword some phrases. What he told his nephew of William's ghostly presence, charging him with a protective tenderness and directing his pen as partner in his own portrait, was the precedent for a final 'service' in his posthumous affair with Minny. He dictated with her 'ghostly image' before him, prized 'all the more for the lapse of time'. It was the small, faded photograph taken forty-four years back, in September 1869, at the time of Elly's wedding, which she had wished him to have. Unwrapped, it was now in the open. Here, in Newport, she sways at the piano, 'discoursing' through the bend of her body; here, at North Conway, a circle springs up about her as 'heroine of the scene'; and here, in one of the quiet old Pelham parlours, she glides forward, thin, laughing, to bid goodbye to 'Harry', whom she expects to see very soon in Rome.

At the back of his consciousness as he wrote was her intimacy with Helena and the '*loads*' on womanhood this had offered him. The young woman in the memoir is like those women in his fiction who suggest 'the reach and quality and capacity of human nature'. Now and then, he smooths out the jump in her voice, the young edge of her emphasis, drawing her towards the smooth, immense surges of his late style – a union beyond the fever of human lives, perfect, impossible, holding desire intact in the net of character.

Minny is unmistakably there: sure, sassy, saying 'Well, Doctor, even if my right lung were all gone I should make a stand with my left,' and reassuring others, 'I have fortunately, through my mother's father, enough Irish blood in me rather to enjoy a good fight. I feel the greatest longing for summer or spring; I should like it to be always spring for the rest of my life . . .'.

James let her speak for herself. He asserts this principle when he rebukes H. G. Wells for not sounding a woman's voice: to report it, James explained, 'strikes me as *not* the way to give the truth about the woman of our hour'. His portrait of Minny may not be accurate in every detail, but no man has done a truer portrait of a living woman, and it does, as he claimed, bring her back from the dead.

Alice perceived at once the power of the unstated. It was 'so *abounding* ... in what it so elusively tells us without saying it'. William, she said, would have rejoiced in this honour to Minny's memory. 'You may not understand in the least how I feel', she went on, 'but it almost seems as if I had had all that she deserved. Were you ever haunted by a "vicarious atonement" feeling? That some one else was going without that you might be blessed?'

Rosina Emmet, who was staying with Alice, reported that her mother was 'much upset by the letters and felt that they ought to have been given to *her*'.

James retorted that he couldn't communicate with Elly 'over such depths of illiteracy as surround her', brushing off the 'fatuity of her asking why the letters weren't sent to *her*'.

Alice did not tell Rosina that Gray would have sooner burnt the letters, nor did she wish Elly to know there were more letters than James had used. She reminded James of the agreement not to give the letters to Elly, even if she asked for them, 'for I gave John Gray my promise'. The fact that the memoir proved a revelation to Elly (who owned that she had no idea Minny was 'so much of a person') to some extent explains Gray's resistance. But there must have been a stronger reason – something Gray knew which James perhaps expressed when he deplored the poor management of tuberculosis in Minny's day. He expressed anger at Minny's family more openly to Helena, weeping as she read the memoir: Minny, he said, had probably been 'sacrificed', having had 'so tragically little real care' from 'people' without 'the presence of mind enough to do for her'. Helena, denied access, and he 'even further away', had been, he said, guiltless.

In the meantime, the ever-caring Alice went to see John Gray, who had been ill again and could no longer use his eyes, but she saw and communed with 'the third J.G.', as she put it to James, 'the man whom your cousin recognized and cared for'.

Gray said, 'When I thought I was dying those letters troubled me very much and I have felt anxious lest the family should be hurt or troubled by my action.'

Then he spoke of himself: 'All my life my work has been my joy and if anyone had told me that a time would come when I could work no more, use my eyes no more, not even able to walk from this chair to the door without aid I should have said on such terms life was intolerable. Instead of this I find in the quiet, in the *emptiness* all sorts of kind and lovely affections flow in and I can be happy for as long or as short a time as I have to stay.' He looked handsome as ever, serene, and unexpectedly gentle.

He did manage to send a 'word of appreciation' to James, who wrote back, acknowledging (privately) Gray's partnership in 'our vision':

21 Carlyle Mansions
Chelsea
[London] S.W.
April 20th 1914

My dear John.

I am . . . really relieved in particular to be able to feel that my so difficult & delicate & precarious last chapter does, to your sense, succeed in what it attempts. To read the letters you let me have was to *want*, exceedingly, to save them from the last obscurity – but I couldn't in the least be sure that our vision & value could get itself expressed so as to mean anything equivalent to this strange & remote generation. I had to *chance* it – at the risk of falling perhaps very short. Well, lo, what has happened is that in this country at least . . . the material & the picture have *told*; the image & the voice survive, & I can't be anything but glad that we have, so to speak, immortalized them. There have literally been intimations that we have, & it is all very wonderful & beautiful, & I want you to feel very much at ease & at peace, & above all that you have been very beneficent, about it. I commend myself to Mrs. John & to your daughter, & am yours all gratefully & faithfully

Henry James

He was exultant. After the blow of the New York edition, followed by his collapse, the two volumes of his memoir, he said, 'appear to have made me ... famous, & to be greeted as a new departure, a new form & manner struck out in my 70th year'. It 'moved' him 'much' that this should come about through his beloved cousin: the thing, he said, 'I had most uncertainty about & felt to be most experimental & most *chancy*, the use I made, in the last chapter, of the letters of Minnie Temple ... seems to have been almost *the* success of the volume.... I have received a very kind & generous letter from Willy Emmet [the baby who had given Minny a glimpse of Paradise and whom she'd held up to Gray to be kissed], which has given me great pleasure – but no other sign, of course, from any of that race.'

Elly kept silent until James was near to death, but Henrietta did signal assent, and James replied with a rush of relief, grasping this chance to justify himself to Minny's sisters. For all his charm, it is a strategic letter, silvering over the fount of Minny's spontaneity with conventional piety: 'our' Minny, he insists, as though his legendary Minny and the 'little' (unimportant) Minny her sisters had remembered were one and the same:

21 Carlyle Mansions
Cheyne Walk
[London] S.W.
May 5th, 1914

Dearest Henrietta,

It is a very great pleasure to me indeed to have got your letter and to find myself really talking to you again – to say nothing of you talking to me. It links together again the chain of association across all the long years and gives the flush of life and reality to memories that struggle against the tendency of all the objects of the unspeakable past to become fictitious and spectral.... But what I want mainly to tell you is how touched I am by ... your recognition of the devoted intention and the prompting tenderness and fidelity of that last chapter – so difficult as I found it to do.... My book was three quarters done when I received from J.G. through your cousin Alice at Cambridge, that packet of Minnie's letters of long ago, which, setting his affairs in order in those days of his own very impaired health and vitality, he asked Alice to read as preliminary to sending them to *me* (to do what I would with) rather than bring himself to destroy them. She read them with intense interest and emotion and said at once 'Do, *do* let me send them to Henry!' – They came, and when I had read them (with *such* irresistible tears!) I recognized my chance to do what I had always longed in some way to do without seeing quite how – rescue and preserve in some way from oblivion, commemorate and a little *enshrine* the image of our admirable and exquisite, our noble and unique little Minnie. It was not easy to do with all the right tact and taste – and there was danger that the long lapse of time would too much have bedimmed and weakened everything. But there at last was my material and my occasion and I embraced them with all the art and all the piety of which I was capable. I was uncertain as to how Elly and you would be affected by the fact of publicity – but it was out of my power to sound you in any way, and I felt that the immense beauty would make the publicity right. So it appears universally to have done – that last chapter of the book has been extraordinarily acclaimed . . . in this country – where I can best judge of the impression, and dear Minnie's name is *really* now, in the most touching way, I think, silvered over and set apart. I rejoice with all my heart that you feel nothing, so to speak, but the interest and the distinction of this. I haven't heard from Elly directly – though I have in a roundabout manner . . . but I gather that though her *first* impression, over my pages, was that of distress and wonder, she is now more than reconciled to what I have done. Do *you* remember that far-away old first summer at North Conway and the Blue Blinds, with J.G. and O.W.H. and Aunt Charlotte and H.J. in short all of us, or were you too juvenile a little shrimp?

Since the beginning of this I have had an interruption – I have to stop things very often, for general *health* reasons, and wait to go on with them; and in the interval have had a dear little letter from Eleanor [Emmet] Lapsley [now married to a relative of James's friend Gaillard Lapsley] . . . on the subject of the emotion that record of Minnie had caused her. But goodbye now, dearest Henrietta. Let me repeat that I delight in having had occasion, in your giving it to me, to spend this hour with you.

Yours all affectionately
Henry James

James replied tenderly to Eleanor, who had played her part in the run-up to *The Wings of the Dove*: 'Your gentle assurance – in the spirit of the ghost – give[s] me the greatest pleasure – I delight in having moved you to a sense of the reality & the beauty of some of those passages & persons of our general family history & feel myself particularly happy in having been able to do something for the exquisite memory of your Aunt Minny. I had often wished I might – it was so peculiarly interesting & inspiring & touching an image that she left with us, ineffaceably – .... My success has apparently been all I could have hoped, & there is no one, dear Eleanor, for whom I more rejoice to think I have made her live again a little for you.'

Here is a man who hears a voice faint and far away, who sees himself wrapping 'dim, sweet' Minny in the dignity of art, who appropriates 'my material' and 'my occasion' to confer immortality on her, and afterwards claims 'success'. This talk around the memoir is that of the Master who controls the matter of his art. On the other hand, there is the work itself: the return of Minny, the run of her voice up and down the scale of honesty. It is Minny, not James, who controls the memoir: her insistence on being 'true'; her dive for the depths of character in her attempt to rescue the third John Gray; and then, the desires she could not meet, aspiring as she did to knowledge and experience beyond her lot. Her distinction speaks for itself, finds its own immortality. Is it not she who confers the success – a sort James had not enjoyed since *Daisy Miller* and the *Portrait*? He fills out her voice with her mysterious 'indifference', something inviolable. When James, here and there, changed Minny's words, it was not tampering in his view; it was unison with the dead: *the* voice of the past, conjoined with his own in a finale of 'pure fellowship'.

We respond to an intensity that grips us slowly and completely: the heightened feeling of hands-off love. A current vogue for sexual labels and public confession flattens character and eliminates the secrecy that is part of attraction. The feeling James had for Minny – his enduring capacity to see her, hear her, and join his future to her deathless nature – renews the passion he said was vital to art.

James did not use Minny's letters to him. When he had reread her letters immediately after her death, he had decided 'they would say little to strangers'. At the same time, he may have wished to hide the fact that Minny's dream had pointed specifically towards himself. It is this living, breathing responsiveness to himself that

James omits from his memoir, together with his part in her story. But he kept his own letters safe while he burnt those to Gray on the grounds that 'there is little surely to add' to what he had made of them. Although he quotes heavily from her letters to Gray, he never once mentions his own correspondence with Minny, her repeated pleas to him, and the effect on her morale – her defeat appears wholly physical. He omits, too, whatever was superfluous to legend: her teasing interest in Gray's less-than-active love-life, her attentiveness to pairing in their milieu, and her comic appropriation of colloquial phrases which downplay her trials – 'sich is life' and 'keep a-doin' of it'. The effect of these omissions is a more solemn and tragic portrait, stressing Minny's 'indifferences' (not unlike his own), 'wrapping' her, as James says, in the 'dignity of art', and providing a plangent close to the 'youth' volume of an artist's life.

What James obliterated and what he created were interdependent. In burning the letters, he did carry out Gray's design to keep them from Minny's sisters, and this act can be seen, too, in the light of his repeated claim that the letters had been given him to use as he wished. And yet, one lingering shred of evidence gives us pause: it is that Alice, the go-between, was taken aback. On the transcript of the letters she and her daughter had made, deposited in time with the James Papers in the Houghton Library, there is a message: 'The originals of these letters were given by J.C.G. to A.H.J. – She sent them to H.J. who used them & afterwards destroyed them without saying a word to her.' He was high-handed; he was liberating: at the last, he defies our notation.

13
All Manhood at One's Side

'Huns', the warring English called the warring Germans: barbarians, unlike 'us'. 'We', 'us', 'our cause' are insistent words in the wartime letters and essays of Henry James. Long before, in an 1878 piece on Americans abroad, he had accepted their position as '*outsiders*'; now, in 1914–15, after thirty-eight years in England, he joined 'our' cause against the 'iron fist' of Germany.

Early in 1915, Harry James, hot from Germany (as part of Herbert Hoover's Commission for Relief in Belgium), informed his uncle about the new blight of shell-shock: a case of a young German soldier with staring eyes who counted over and over, *ein*, *zwei*, *drei*, and so on into the sixties, until he got to the number of the shell that had blown his mind. James, then, was not entirely ignorant of the Front, but his angina couldn't stand 'lurid' details. His pro-war essays are out of touch with bungling decisions by generals and the wanton sacrifice of young lives. James did not take in the horrors of trench warfare, as he did not take in the lethal proximity of the two sides at Gettysburg when he fancied Harvard Yard a tented field. Until 1915, when middle-class civilians were poured into the British Army to replace the regulars disappearing in the trenches of France and Flanders, soldiers had been mostly 'the scum of the earth' (in Wellington's phrase) led by dim aristocrats schooled in hunting. The literate recruits of 1915, like the poet Rupert Brooke, and other young men James had met on a visit to Cambridge University, recalled Harvard recruits fifty years back and 'the agitation of the New England air by Mr. Lincoln's call to arms'. He tried again and again to align this European war and the Civil War, but the link broke down, as though the ground of history gave way: 'one swung off into space, into history, into darkness, with every lamp extinguished and every abyss gaping.'

He did grasp that the world he knew had come to an end. A 'change in consciousness' overtook his world in a single night in August 1914, a 'sudden break with the past' – a breach in his reservoir of memories and, with them, his capacity for fiction: 'I find it too difficult to give verisimilitude to a world for which this huge bloody trap was all the while set and which childishly didn't know it!' It was as though a 'colossal convulsion' had hurled away everything that preceded it, far away into 'utter unreality, mere fond, dim, irrelevant fable'. From day to day, from hour to hour, he lived 'as in the face of an enormous series of interrogation points ?????? – the most formidable that could be thought of'.

His only course, as he saw it, was to throw in his lot with a people who had made him welcome. He accepted the chairmanship of the American Volunteer Motor Ambulance Corps in France, and visited the wounded in St Bartholomew's and other hospitals, thinking of Whitman's visits to hospitals during the Civil War. Naturally, he gravitated towards the classier soldiers, in one case a Grenadier guardsman brought back from Ypres in October 1914 where a battle still raged. The guardsman chatted agreeably to James about three bayonet charges. When James said how shaming it was, even as an old man, to leave fighting to others, the guardsman burst into a laugh. 'Oh but we can't *all* be there, you know!' he joked as if it were a kind of fun of which there wasn't enough to go round.

To make light of wounds – to say airily 'just a scratch'; to affect cheer; to be 'in the pink' – was the upper-class style of manliness, enforced on the rank and file, and part of the propaganda of the War Office. James was as deluded as the next civilian. It was to be another year or two – by which time some millions of young men had been killed to no purpose – before the poet Wilfred Owen countered false cheer with 'the pity of war, the pity war distilled'.

At his Thames-side window on 4 December 1914, James watched a march-past of Kitchener's army, with a multitude of London Scottish and a martial band, all in the freshest khaki. He heard that thirty thousand were enlisting every week. Men too old to fight hoped that the three million needed to 'push' the war would volunteer without resort to conscription – soon inevitable, given the toll of the trenches across the Channel. The model citizen was 'belligerent', and James observed how 'magnificently' the upper classes 'played up', aware as he was that 'society' always does so in wars because it is by them and for them that wars are mostly made. One flash of insight here; for the rest, James associated with 'the right people', who congratulated themselves when they took the trouble to send a motor-car to collect convalescent soldiers for gracious teas – soldiers suitably grateful for such attentions.

In 1915 James refused an invitation from Bay to take refuge from the war with her family at their farmhouse on a woodsy hilltop near Salisbury, Connecticut. 'Nothing', he replied, 'would induce me to be out of it for an hour, or to exchange its preoccupations and anxieties, intense as they are, for that comparative blankness of detachment in which the American scene ... strikes me as being still steeped'. His closest point of identification was the death of Rupert Brooke en route to Gallipoli – 'the stupid extinction of so exquisite an instrument', James exploded on 11 May 1915. It might have been himself extinguished in the Civil War – no *Portrait*, no *Wings*, no Middle Years. To Brooke's friend Eddie Marsh at the Admiralty, James refused consoling platitudes about Brooke's place in literature: the only 'place' was what they might imagine of 'the other being', the poet who had had it in him to 'wait, & grow with all confidence & power *while* waiting'. In June, the posthumous arrival of Brooke's last letter made him 'almost ready to howl'. This blank grief is wholly different from the elegiac flooding at the death of Minny Temple: to howl – without words, without an urge for art – was some sort of relief: 'I thank my strange stars that I can't *not* feel these things ...'.

Meanwhile, he continued to visit the wounded, lunched with the Prime Minister, Asquith, and met Winston Churchill and other war leaders. When he found he was classified an alien and had to report to the police before going to coastal Rye, he resolved to become a British citizen. Asquith was one of his sponsors; Sir Edmund Gosse, now the doyen of the literary scene (hopelessly outdated in the view of Eliot, its coming star), was another. The Home Secretary, John Simon, 'as an Englishman who cares for letters', himself welcomed the application: 'I am glad to think that "in spite of all temptations to belong to other nations" you are to be one of *us*.' James was awarded his certificate of naturalisation on 26 July. 'Civis Britannicus sum,'* he announced to his family two days later, admitting he felt as if nothing had happened except a release from a false position 'which Mr. [Woodrow] Wilson [the neutral American President] could so perfectly have prevented for me!' James felt alienated by a US note of 'amity' to 'the Enemy'. This writer who had denied himself the comfort of simplifications felt the 'glory' of coming down wholly on one side. 'You see how I talk of "we" and "our" ', he pointed out to American relations, 'which is so absolutely instinctive and irresistible with me that I should feel quite abject if I didn't!'

His war cries convey the comfort of closing ranks – a far cry from the moral courage of Owen Wingrave (who prefigured Wilfred Owen). This was a common misjudgement in a society of passive killers. To do James justice, he was at times torn between his rage to belong and the evolved mind he stood for which abhors a return to barbarism.

'. . . All one's manhood must be at one's side' was the lesson that ruled the fertility of Henry James. For most of his life, manhood meant endeavour, not war, not sex, and this explains why militarism could be demolished and why no category of sexual expression quite fits. Sex was not non-existent; it was transformed as desire of a different kind, a passion to possess and shape souls – James kisses, blesses, and prays to creativity in religious terms. His power to transcend himself recalls great monks, like St Augustine, who were not natural celibates yet managed to harness manhood to pure endeavour. Women were drawn to him – Minny and Fenimore were not alone. I feel this attraction a century on. For what he offers is what we at present want. A century on, it is easy to meet James, easy to enjoy his extraordinary intimacy with our far-out selves, but it was not easy for women of his own time who had to engage with the man.

When James called 'all' manhood to his side, he was not only

* Playing off the proud phrase '*civis Romanus sum*' (I am a Roman). According to Cicero, this phrase would sometimes save citizens in dangerous outposts of the Empire.

replacing the debased face of masculinity – swagger and violence – he was saying something ruthless of his own, something Minny, then Fenimore, had to grant when he leant their way. Not a gram of 'manhood' was wasted on women who did not fire his ambition. They had to participate in his ambition or fall away. Though perhaps he alone understood the claims they made on life, he could not meet them. Their own needs – Minny's dream of 'Europe'. Fenimore's dream of a mentor to share her privacy – did not address his ambition so long as they lived. Afterwards, the drama of thwarted women touched him. Nothing made James feel so alive as hearing of Minny's death. Where her death released pulsations of lyrical elegy, Fenimore's leap hit him with irruptions of shock. The sensation of life that came from death stirred the waves that carried him beyond the still pools of professional habitat into the giant breakers of the career.

Death, we might say, was the spur. It gave him the measure of women's silence, a hidden force which matched his own. This 'fighting man' who did not fight physically, who did not assent to a brute form of manhood, and sat apart from ex-soldiers in '65, was able to retain a side of himself that others were trained to deny: emotional expressiveness, vulnerability, compassion, alertness to the unspoken, and the rest of the vast endowment men share with women. James entered into women's needs because 'manhood' could extend that far. He did not fear women; he dissociates himself from the man who goes into his tent and lets down the flap. This was no weakling in retreat; he was strong, resolute, formidable when he drew women into his drama of unstated communion – and then withdrew at a telling moment to shut himself in the tower of art.

He had striking things to say about everyone but 'Miss Woolson'. Her, he called 'our excellent friend', a phrase like the shutters she closed at Bellosguardo. Only at night did she throw them open. The white heap on the stones of Venice; the 'loathing' for society who did not 'see'; the child of tragedy: facts group themselves; phrases fall with feet on the ground. Yet where is she, that young woman who called herself Fenimore? Did we unbury her, or did she vanish after all?

Minny and Fenimore were unlike as sun and shade: one radiant, the other melancholy; one outgoing, the other reclusive; one free, engaging, the other averted, finally unknowable. Yet they are linked as portents of womanhood meeting the 'manhood' of Henry James. His spectatorial posture obscured his involvements: his 'pure fellowship' with Minny, and the lost 'home' he shared with Fenimore. Was James innocent in the early years? Obscured in shadow is an angel's awakening to culpability. Fenimore's leap appalled him when he was fifty, but were there flickerings of culpability before then? Six years earlier, 'The Lesson of the Master' had confessed the 'corruption' of all art. One feat was to expose how people prey on one another in secret, a 'sin' many would not recognise but one an artist with scruples was fitted to face.

After almost a year and a half of silence, Elly wrote to James in August 1915 about her sister's letters. He was relieved, even though she reproached John Gray (who had died earlier that year) for exposing Minny to the public eye. She was surprised that Gray should have exposed himself together with Minny – and, by implication, she was reproaching James as Gray's partner in this action. But the fact that Elly had relented so far as to write, seemed to James a 'bridge' flung across a 'chasm' deepened by estrangement from his homeland.

'I snatch at it as at a kind of little ghost of a talk with you, & hang upon your voice & feast upon your charm.' So he replied in an immense letter on 3 September 1915 which ends with a defence of what he had done:

> I am so glad you speak to me of my transcript of those letters of Minny's by which I rejoice so that it was unexpectedly given me at the end of long years to preserve[,] to 'immortalize,' her exquisite memory. I jumped at the chance, ... & they have been incontestably the success of the book – they have made her live again for our unknowing generation & others still to come. But don't wonder, please, at J.G.'s having been willing to give them to the world; for they were all to Minny's honour & glory, & they reflect so extraordinarily little on *his* personality (he *had* almost none at all!) that he completely disappears in them. They don't lift so much as the

fringe of the curtain from his life; they are all Minny herself, & *that* he was willing the world shld. have – & well he might be!

Unspoken between them was Elly's outrage that her impulsive marriage to Temple Emmet, whom she had not loved, was exposed to view in the extracts from Minny's letters which James had published. The public might read of Minny's doubts, amounting to 'depression', when Elly became engaged; read that Minny could not talk of serious matters to her sisters, who thought her eccentric; and the public would know, too, of Minny's plaint to Gray (which James would seem to endorse since he chose to publish it) that no one in her family cared enough to take her to Italy or some other place in the south where, she believed, she had a chance of recovery. What James published made the caprice of Elly and Emmet clear: California was *not* the place of Minny's choice, but it was on offer for her better health only so long as it suited the Emmets – and it hadn't suited them long enough for Minny to get there.

In publishing all this, James had appropriated a batch of Temple papers as his property, justifying his action, repeatedly, by its 'success'. The Master took the high ground of aesthetic achievement, while Elly held to a moral position which he would have backed in her place: a right to privacy. In overriding this consideration, James infringed a principle he often expressed.

Throughout his career, James was hot on privacy. A formal defence of privacy came three years after Fenimore's fall landed within inches of his preserve. Shells of publicity exploded about him. 'Discreet' had been his word for his meetings with 'Miss Woolson'. James, who had thought her, like himself, a tower of discretion, was horrified, and not for her alone, when she threw herself out that tower: a violent public act. It contradicted his image of contained Miss Woolson whom he had labelled 'conservative'. For her death was a statement of sorts. James attempted to sink this statement when he gave out that she was mad, and when Boott questioned this James squashed him promptly. People who objected to his line were 'illiterate': Elly, questioning his right to Minny's papers; his nephew, questioning his alterations of family letters. Grace Norton was ridiculed for suggesting that Minny chose to die – even though James had published Minny's impulse to this effect ('. . . I am sometimes tempted to take a drop of "pison" to put me to sleep in earnest'). James would not allow Grace a possibility that seemed to conflict with his own image of Minny clinging to life to the last. Grace Norton's fault was to question a legend James had made his own.

'The figure that was to hover as the ghost has been of an extreme pertinence,' he said. Pertinence, yes: the ghost shaped the best of what he became. Yet he does not define his debt, except to hint how Minny ranged in her groping 'from end to end' of the human scale; how she turned from people who masked their 'veracity'; and how she refused 'the model life' in favour of 'spontaneity'. To inspect more closely the debts of fellowship would infringe his legend of the private life. Other fictions spell out the secrecy essential to perpetuate the mystique of legends.

In *The Aspern Papers*, when the aged lover of the great poet discovers her lodger snooping for secrets, she calls him a 'publishing scoundrel'. When Flaubert's correspondence was published, James felt he had been handed over to the Philistines 'with every weakness exposed, every mystery dispelled, every secret betrayed'. He wrote a series of tales in support of a writer's right to determine what his public should know, and what they should not: 'The Death of the Lion', 'Sir Dominick Ferrand' (where a researcher takes upon himself 'the *responsibility* of destruction – the destruction of papers, letters, records, etc., connected with the private and personal history of some great and honoured name and throwing some very different light on it from the light projected by the public career'), and 'The Real Right Thing' (where the ghost of a writer bars a biographer by the deadly name of Withermore). In 1915 James appealed to his nephew to preserve him from the 'post-mortem exploiter'. This plea seals a resolve, in his 1897 essay on George Sand (a life of sexual indiscretion), to outwit the future biographer:

> There are secrets for privacy and silence; let them only be cultivated on the part of the hunted creature with even half the method with which the love of sport – or call it the historic sense – is cultivated on the part of the investigator. They have been left too much to the natural, the instinctive man; but they will be twice as effective after it

begins to be observed that they may take their place among the triumphs of civilisation. Then at last the game will be fair and the two forces face to face.... Then the cunning of the inquirer, envenomed with resistance, will exceed in subtlety and ferocity anything we to-day conceive, and the pale forewarned victim, with every track covered, every paper burnt and every letter unanswered, will, in the tower of art, the invulnerable granite, stand, without a sally, the siege of all the years.

James left a trail of burnt ashes. His pact with Fenimore to burn their correspondence and the whiff of ashes in her death-house was still about him when he read his sister's diary in 1894 and longed to 'burn with fire' the four unexpurgated copies Miss Loring had printed. He had assumed his monumental tone in an attempt to persuade Katharine Loring that the diary was not worth keeping. Miss Loring, being no fool, held on to her copy* and, forty-two years later, defended the diary against suppression, speaking on behalf of Alice against her family in a statement to William's daughter, Margaret Mary James, now Mrs Porter. The letter is dated 6 June 1934:

Dear Mrs. Porter,

Mary Vaux† has sent me your letter, which I now answer to acquaint you with the facts of Alice James['] Journal. Neither your Uncle Henry nor your father knew anything about it before your Aunt died and before she died she gave it to me; of course I knew all about it because much of it I had written from dictation. The only thing I ever failed to do for her was that I did not have it typewritten while she lived as she wanted me to do; this was during the last month or six weeks of her life and I really could not manage it. Though she never said so I understood that she would like to have it published.

After I came home‡ I printed four (4) copies. I gave one to your

* This would eventually be the source for the expurgated edition of 1934. For no apparent reason (except, conceivably, a family fear that the relationship with Miss Loring had been irregular), an unexpurgated edition had to wait another thirty years. It was published in 1964, twenty years after Miss Loring's death.

† Bob James's daughter, who had authorised the expurgated edition.

‡ Katharine Loring lived for the remainder of her life in the area of Beverly and Pride's Crossing on the North Shore of Massachusetts Bay.

Uncle Henry which he tore up and said it was not worth while for anyone to read it; I gave one copy to your father which I believe you have. . . . When your brother [Harry James] gave the James papers to the Harvard Library, I sent him the third copy to deposit with the other papers. The fourth I have.

As far as I can remember, your father never thanked me for his copy, simply acknowledged the receipt of it and certainly never made any suggestion as to its being read or not. I respected your Uncle Henry's wish not to have it published because, knowing him so well, I appreciated his horror of having any responsibility about himself or his friends.

Mary Vaux and her brother Edward and his wife are the only grandchildren who have ever taken any interest in me or have asked me about my relations with the James family. . . .

I think your criticism of the impression that the diary would make is unjust, absurd and altogether unwarranted. . . .

Believe me

Sincerely yours,
Katharine P. Loring.

There are two interesting details here: first, Miss Loring's assertion of knowledge derived from her 'relations with the James family'. In her eighties, the last survivor of her generation and in full command of her memories, she has things to tell, and this, in fact, may be the reason for her exclusion from further contact with the family after an involvement of many years: she knew too much. (She knew, for instance, about sister Alice, since she discussed her disturbance with William James in letters which, in 1939, she asked to have destroyed.) Secondly, Miss Loring unleashes a sample of what she knew: the 'horror' of Henry James at the prospect of 'responsibility' for his ties.

Miss Loring was a Trustee of Wellesley College from 1927 and a contributor to the World Center for Women's Archives in New York (until it was closed down at the end of 1940, for lack of funds). She 'did not waste time', as she put it. At night, before sleep, she exercised her mind with calculations: the width of Solomon's Temple was exactly that of Beverly Public Library, though its length was far greater. She was practical, hardy, and thankful for coal in winter, the scents of her garden (she got in her potatoes in good time), and wild geese flying by. Alice had warned against bogus communications with the dead, like those delivered by William's pet medium, Mrs Piper. 'If anyone comes and tells you, I am talking through her, don't believe her,' Alice had said. In 1973 a great-nephew, Augustus P. Loring, remembered a certain Sunday in the 1930s when, as a young man, he had accompanied his father to lunch at Miss Loring's. She had announced 'in a very pleased manner' that she had 'burnt up all her correspondence of any personal nature. My father's face fell a mile and after he left, he commented, "My God, all of the Henry James letters up in smoke".'

James himself made a bonfire of his correspondence late in 1909 as he entered a black hole from which he might not emerge. On 2 January 1910 he confided to Annie Fields, a figure in Boston publishing: 'I kept almost all letters for years – till my receptacles would no longer hold them; then I made a gigantic bonfire & have been easier in mind since – safe as to a certain residuum which has to survive.'

There are many burnt letters in the works of Henry James. Aspern's papers go into the fire, one by one, a woman's denial of a man who would appropriate them (and their record of passion) without offering the reciprocity of real attachment. In *The Wings of the Dove*, Milly's post-mortem letter to Merton Densher is thrown in the fire before he can read it – and again an unread letter exerts a power stronger than fact. Everything in James – fictions, reviews, and memoirs – suggests that documentary truth is limited and needs the complement of imaginative truth.

James was himself an inveterate gossip who did not hold back from the intimate details of other's lives, as when he devoured the Carlyle letters: 'the whole Carlyle domestic and personal history is a thing I have an insatiable appetite for, as for some inexhaustible interminable *roman des moeurs*, that one has got in the habit of.' He reviewed over fifteen volumes of letters, and when he attempted a biography himself, the interest of boxfuls of old letters calling up ghosts, echoes, and reverberations was nothing less than 'exquisite'. Biography is here defined as an act of remembrance 'lively almost to indiscretion'. In 1895, James allowed Lord Lovelace, grandson of Byron, to show him the Lovelace Papers containing the much-discussed secret of Byron's incest with his half-sister, Augusta Leigh. Letters from Byron to Lady Melbourne during the three years before his marriage (in 1815) revealed, James said, 'the absolutely indubitable history of his relation to Mrs. Leigh, the sole *real* love, as he emphatically declares, of his life'. (Byron had confessed a connection that had an element of the terrible which made all other loves insipid.) In 1910, when the family asked James to sift Byron's letters, with the aid of John Buchan, in order to deposit an opinion in the British Museum, he did so with no hesitation, according to Buchan: '. . . Henry James and I waded through masses of ancient indecency. . . . The things nearly made me sick, but my colleague never turned a hair. His only words for some special vileness were "singular" – "most curious" – "nauseating, perhaps, but how quite inexpressibly significant".'

These words assume the connection of life and work. Then James swings round and assumes the opposite when he shuns biography as exposé: a sensationalist genre which smears art. The second stance sets up an antinomy of life and art, false to a biographer who sees art as the central event of an artist's life. Far from denying the latter, James demands it in 'The Private Life', 'The Figure in the Carpet', and 'The Death of the Lion'. Fenimore anticipates this position in her poem 'To Certain Biographers': she berates those who crawl with microscopes in barren places on a mountain, ignoring the peaks.

James left behind a 'granite' monument emptied of living matter. His guilt is there, locked in Marcher and Densher for all time, but no extraneous evidence was to impair the authority of art. From an aesthetic point of view, this is valid, but it is a view that discounts the validity of others. Biography is not a side issue: we lend ourselves to James as far as we can, then draw back to question the imperiousness of his appropriations. By the early years of the twentieth century, he had moved away from the Victorian sympathies of George Eliot towards the authoritarianism of the Moderns. As artist, he was so entirely in control – Napoleonic, in his deathbed ramblings – that he presented himself as the reverse: 'the hunted creature', the 'pale victim'. It is a blind that shuts off the source, the actual 'situation'. He feared a future beyond his control, so made this pre-emptive strike. It does strike home – shames biographic intrusion – yet is misconceived from our post-modern point of view. A biographer is not a single, supreme antagonist; merely one reader amongst many. An artist is not shut off, aloof, in the tower of art; he is a communicator dependent on a reader of his communication – something shaded, ever more unspoken. We hear the silence; we hear the Jamesian revelation that no life is without it. And the deeper the silence, the more intently it speaks.

Secrets plagued James as 1915 waned. Pain warned him his heart was failing; that winter he would die of two strokes followed by pneumonia. Immobile for months in a 'black cave', he emerged on 14 October and, panting for breath, 'pushed down' to Rye for a final visit to Lamb House – 'under absolute necessity'. As he went his dignified way, an ample figure in a high collar and waistcoat, memory raked the past for what the future was not to know. What these facts were we can infer from letters that should have vanished and elisions in his memoir: his draft notice at the height of the Civil War in July 1863 when he was twenty; his sparing, and that of William, offset by the sacrifice of younger brothers; Minny's pleas to join him abroad in 1869 when he was twenty-six; her wish for 'pison' when she 'dropped'; and Fenimore's strange question in 1883 when he was forty: would it solve the 'riddle' of her existence to live and die in Venice, and be buried in its lagoon? Then, eleven years on, himself advancing across that lagoon, a mature man of fifty-one, haunted by the horror of her death, with armfuls of her clothes, pushing them down, and down again, only to see them return.

Now, at seventy-two, he picked out the papers no one might see, and watched them burn. 'I stayed there a week', he reported to his nephew, 'and effected pretty well what I had to do.' He would leave behind ten thousand letters, the phantasmagoria of his memoir, and, towering above, his works of fiction, fortified with enduring theory, that stronghold of the New York edition in which he had sealed himself – alone. Now, at last, he was ready to hold out against the siege of all the years.

So he made a legend of the Master; so he shed the partners of the private life. But see, they return, and bring him with them.

Abbreviations

A	HJ, *Autobiography*, i–iii, ed. Frederick W. Dupee (1956; repr. Princeton University Press, 1983). i: *A Small Boy and Others* (1913); ii: *Notes of a Son and Brother* (1914); iii: *The Middle Years* (1917). Though I abbreviate the title of this edition, the only one at present available, HJ did not call it an autobiography and it might more appropriately be termed a memoir. It is not really categorisable.
AHJ	Alice Howe Gibbens James (wife of WJ).
AJ	Alice James (sister of HJ).
Benedict	*Five Generations*, i–iii (i: *Voices Out of the Past*; ii: *Constance Fenimore Woolson*; iii: *The Benedicts Abroad*, ed. Clare Benedict (niece of CFW) (London: Ellis, 1930). Copy in Bodleian Library, Oxford.
Berg	Berg Collection, New York Public Library.
CFW	Constance Fenimore Woolson (writer; friend of HJ).
CS	Henry James, *Complete Stories*, i–v (New York: The Library of America, 1996–).
CT	*The Tales of Henry James*, i–iii, ed. Maqbool Aziz (Oxford: Clarendon Press, 1973, 1978, 1984). First printed texts of the tales, mostly in periodicals.
CWJ	*The Correspondence of William James*, i–iii, ed. Ignas K. Skrupskelis and Elizabeth M. Berkeley (Charlottesville: University of Virginia, 1992–4). Contains a full and scrupulously edited compilation of HJ's letters to his elder brother. In the absence of a complete edition of HJ's letters, this is the preferred source for this particular correspondence.
Dupee	F. W. Dupee, *Henry James* (New York: Dell, 1951; repr. New York: Delta, 1965). Though for several decades this seemed to be superseded by full-scale biographies, it is worth retrieval for its graceful succinctness and perceptive readings of the fiction.
E(AE)	HJ, *Literary Criticism: Essays on Literature, American Writers, English Writers*, ed. Leon Edel, assisted by Mark Wilson (New York: The Library of America, 1984).
E(CP)	HJ, *Literary Criticism: French Writers, Other European Writers,*

	The Prefaces to the New York Edition, ed. Leon Edel, assisted by Mark Wilson (New York: The Library of America, 1984).
ECS	Edmund Clarence Stedman (friend of CFW).
Edel	Leon Edel, *The Life of Henry James*, i–v: *The Untried Years, 1843–1870* (1953); *The Conquest of London, 1870–1881* (1962); *The Middle Years, 1882–1895* (1962); *The Treacherous Years, 1895–1901* (1969); and *The Master, 1901–1916* (1972) (Philadelphia: J. B. Lippincott, 1953–72), followed by a condensed and revised edition (New York: Harper & Row, 1985; London, 1987).
EW	Edith Wharton.
FB	Francis Boott (Europeanised American; friend of the Jameses).
GWJ	Garth Wilkinson (Wilky) James.
HJ	Henry James (novelist).
HJSr	Henry James Sr (father of HJ).
Houghton	Houghton Library, Harvard University, the main repository of the James Papers.
JCG	John Chipman Gray (Professor of Law, Harvard; part of the James circle; chief correspondent of MT).
JFC	James Fenimore Cooper (novelist, great-uncle of CFW).
JH	John Hay (secretary to Lincoln, writer, friend of CFW).
Kaplan	Fred Kaplan, *Henry James: The Imagination of Genius: A Biography* (London: Hodder, 1992; New York: Morrow, 1992).
KL	Katharine Loring (companion of AJ; friend of CFW).
LB	Elizabeth (Lizzie) Boott (daughter of FB; friend of both MT and CFW, as well as of HJ).
L(E)	HJ, *Letters*, i–iv, ed. Leon Edel (Cambridge, Mass.: Harvard Univ. Belknap Press, 1974–87).
L(L)	*The Letters of Henry James*, i–ii, ed. Percy Lubbock (London: Macmillan, 1920).
Lewis	R. W. B. Lewis, *The Jameses: A Family Narrative* (London: Deutsch, 1991; New York: Farrar, Straus, 1991, repr. Doubleday Anchor, 1993).
MJ	Mary James (mother of HJ).
MT	Mary (Minny) Temple (cousin of HJ).
N	*The Complete Notebooks of Henry James*, ed. Leon Edel and Lyall H. Powers (Oxford University Press, 1987).
N(M)	*The Notebooks of Henry James*, ed. F. O. Matthiessen and Kenneth B. Murdoch (1947; repr. NY: Galaxy, 1961; repr. Univ. of Chicago Press, Phoenix paperback, 1981).
NYHA	New York State Historical Association, Cooperstown, New York.
OWH	Oliver Wendell Holmes, Jr, later Justice Holmes of the United States Supreme Court (friend of WJ, HJ, JCG, and MT).
PL	*The Portrait of a Lady* (New York: New American Library,

	1963). This reprint is based on the first British edition (London: Macmillan, 1881).
PML	Pierpont Morgan Library, New York.
RJ	Robertson (Bob) James.
Rollins	CFW Collection, Archives, Rollins College, Winter Park, Florida.
SM	Samuel Mather (nephew of CFW).
Strouse	Jean Strouse, *Alice James: A Biography* (Boston, 1980; London: Cape, 1981).
T(BA)	HJ, *Collected Travel Writings: Great Britain and America*, with notes by Richard Howard (New York: The Library of America, 1993).
T(C)	HJ, *Collected Travel Writings: The Continent*, with notes by Richard Howard (New York: The Library of America, 1993).
TSP	Thomas Sergeant Perry (Newport friend of HJ).
WAWE	*Women Artists, Women Exiles: 'Miss Grief' and Other Stories*, ed. Joan Myers Weimer (New Brunswick, NJ: Rutgers University Press, 1988).
WD	*The Wings of the Dove* (O.U.P.: World's Classics, 1984).
WDH	William Dean Howells.
WJ	William James.
WRHS	The Western Reserve Historical Society, Cleveland, Ohio.
WWB	W.W. Baldwin (American doctor in Florence; confidant of CFW).

Source Notes

Note: where no printed text is given, the matter quoted is unpublished.

Epigraphs

'... feverish earthly lot': HJ to WJ (29 Mar 1870), *CWJ*, i, 155.
'He cherishes ...': *N*, 98.

Chapter 1 A Biographic Mystery

1 *drowning dresses:* In 1956, Mercede Huntington of the Villa Mercede (once called the Villa Castellani), Bellosguardo, Florence, recalled a 'strange tale' told to her by HJ. The record appears in an unedited transcript of interviews recorded on tape for the BBC (Third Programme), 'Recollections of Henry James in His Later Years', transmitted on 14 June 1956. Originally owned by HJ's amanuensis Theodora Bosanquet. Now in Houghton: bMS Eng 1213.4 (20). Details published by Alide Cagidimetrio, 'Sceltadi Città: Venezia, Black Balloons and White Doves', in *Henry James e Venezia*, ed. Sergio Perosa (1987), 54–5. I am grateful to Victoria Press for finding the article and to Elena Ghiringelli for translating it during her first year at St Hilda's College, Oxford (1995).

2 *appearance of HJ:* Theodora Bosanquet and others in the above transcript; mainly his death mask. Houghton. (I do not recommend looking at it – an experience I should not like to repeat. To lift the lid of the tall box was like looking down into a grave. I saw a white face, rather shockingly lifelike, as though the eyes might open at any moment and look at you. I recalled Withermore, the biographer stopped by the ghost of his subject, and felt horribly intrusive.)

bishop: HJ to A. C. Benson (24 Feb 1895), HJ, *Letters to A. C. Benson and Auguste Monod*, ed. E. F. Benson (London: Elkin Mathews; NY: Scribner's 1930) copy in the Bodleian Library, Oxford.

'heroine': HJ to MJ (26 Mar 1870), *L(E)*, i, 221 ('the very heroine of our common scene'); *A*, ii, 508. 509 ('the heroine in the scene').

'a plant of pure American growth': HJ to WJ (29 Mar 1870), *CWJ*, i, 228.

3 *'vocal with her accents':* HJ to MJ (26 Mar 1870), *L(E)*, i, 222.

hugs her arms: HJ to AJ from Malvern, England (27 Feb 1870). Houghton. While there HJ had met the wife of a Scottish laird, Mr Ray, who carried her arms, he said, as Minny did.

4 *'aggressive':* Kaplan uses 'aggressive' three times, 77 (twice), 143–4. Alfred Habegger, *Henry James and the 'Woman Business'* (Cambridge University Press, 1989), uses the word in a way that affirms MT's subversiveness. His book contains fresh research on MT, modifying the views of critics in the mid- and later twentieth century.

CFW out of fashion: Rayburn S. Moore summarises largely disparaging critical opinion on CFW from 1923 to 1967 in his collection *For the Major and Selected Short Stories* (New Haven, Conn.: College and Univ. Press Services, 1967), 8. The most influential distortion in recent decades has been that in Edel, iii ('elderly', 'plain', p. 255). He did, however, do a lot of useful research for this volume (though we may not agree with its conclusions), and must have the credit for drawing forward into the light the primary importance of this relationship in HJ's life. Rayburn S. Moore in *Constance Fenimore Woolson* (NY, 1963), and again in 'The Strange Irregular Rhythm of Life: James's Late Tales and Constance Woolson', *South Atlantic Bulletin*, xli: 4 (Nov 1976), 87, maintained that there was 'insufficient evidence to establish with any certainty that Miss Woolson either conceived a passion for James or that she committed suicide as a result of unrequited love'.

F. W. Dupee: Henry James (NY: Dell, 1951, repr. NY: Delta, 1965).

Benedict: Five Generations, consisting of three volumes: i, *Voices out of the Past;* ii, *Constance Fenimore Woolson;* iii, *The Benedicts Abroad.* Privately printed, 1930.

5 *'preyed . . . upon living beings':* T. S. Eliot, 'Henry James: In Memory', first published in *Little Review* (Aug 1918), repr. *The Shock of Recognition: The Development of Literature in the United States Recorded by the Men Who Made It*, ed. Edmund Wilson (NY: Random House, 1943, repr. 1955), 856.

ten and a half thousand letters: According to Steven H. Jobe (who has made a complete 'Calendar' of HJ's letters) 'eight thousand or more' remain as yet unpublished. Article on the Adeline Tintner collection of James letters and memorabilia, recently acquired by the Berg. *Henry James Review* (1998).

pact to destroy their correspondence: Edel, iii, 329; *L(E)*, iii, 524: 'Miss Clare Benedict informed me of the agreement between her aunt and HJ to destroy each other's letters.' According to the late Clare Benedict, Miss Woolson's niece, the two destroyed each other's letters by mutual agreement, with HJ reclaiming such letters as remained in her rooms in the Semitecolo [her home in Venice at the time of her death]. It is possible the idea came from Fenimore, who had such a pact with her sister. According to Benedict, ii, 387, the sisters agreed to be 'safety valves' and promised each other to destroy letters as soon as answered. In one tender letter to

Morton Fullerton, HJ does ask him to destroy it, but it was not a reciprocal pact as with CFW, nor did Fullerton feel the necessity to obey.

6 *'interpretation ...* built into *the documents':* Alfred Habegger, 'New Light on William James and Minny Temple', *New England Quarterly*, lx: 1 (Mar 1987), 32–3.

'My dear sir ...'.: 'The Death of the Lion', *CS*, iv, 368.

'You see what I am': Maria Gostrey to Strether in *The Ambassadors*. See below, ch. 11.

7 *passion and 'hard' art:* HJ to A. C. Benson (26 Feb 1895), *Letters* op. cit. 7.

ineffectual men: Prufrock is from Eliot's 'The Love Song of J. Alfred Prufrock' (1911; first published 1915); Petroushka is a puppet, a sad clown, danced by Nijinsky, in the eponymous ballet, choreographed by Mikhail Fokine and produced for the Ballets Russes by Diaghilev. The little tramp is from the silent movies of Charlie Chaplin. Other ineffective men are the pierrots in Picasso's blue period, Gabriel Conroy in Joyce's 'The Dead', and Bloom in *Ulysses* (1922).

contemporary: Cynthia Ozick, *What the Jameses Knew and Other Essays on Writers* (London: Cape, 1993).

8 *'affronts her destiny':* Preface to *PL*, *E(CP)*, 1077.

'out-of-the-way-place': PL, ch. 4.

'The Private Life': CS, iv, 58–91.

Chapter 2 To the Frontier

10 *'noble flights': A*, ii, 283.

details of William Cooper: Conversation with his descendant Henry Cooper of Cooperstown, New York (July 1994); James Fenimore Cooper (grandson of the novelist), 'Reminiscences of Mid-Victorian Cooperstown and a Sketch of William Cooper' (1936; repr. Cooperstown, NY: Smithy-Pioneer Gallery Publications, 1986); William Cooper, *A Guide in the Wilderness; or, The History of the First Settlements in the Western Counties of New York* (Dublin, 1810), copy in NYHA; Alan Taylor, *William Cooper's Town: Power and Persuasion on the Frontier of the Early American Republic* (NY: Knopf, 1995; repr. Vintage, 1996).

1789: This date is 'unstable' according to Alfred Habegger, and could be 1793 or 1794. *The Father: A Life of Henry James, Sr* (NY: Farrar, Straus, 1994), 10.

the amount of Billy James's fortune: Ibid., 112. Habegger corrects earlier misconceptions about the size of the fortune. (An amount of three million is given in all previous biographies of the James family, as well as in a 1997 biography of HJ.) The Syracuse income would have propped up HJ so long as his father supported him in the first decade of his career; then HJ's portion was made over to AJ after HJSr's death, but after she died in 1892 it must have reverted to HJ since there are many references to his Syracuse income in letters to HJ from WJ.

11 *'not a morsel':* For William Cooper's version of the famine, see *Guide*, 15–16.

'original creation': 'The Haunted Lake', *Harper's*, xliv (Dec 1871), 20–30, repr. Benedict, i, 49–57. One of CFW's earliest publications.

Natty Bumppo: The details here are taken from the last chapters of *The Pioneers* (1823).

12 *'In 1785 . . .': Guide*, 13–14.

'He then feels himself . . .': Ibid., 11.

13 *'lightened his way':* William Cooper's appearance and manner recalled by JFC, Preface to ibid., xiii.

family wit: The supposition is made by the grandson of James Fenimore Cooper in 'Reminiscences', 44. The Queen Anne chair was eventually used by Cooper in the library of Otsego Hall, and survives in the house of his descendant Henry Cooper of Cooperstown.

14 *Elizabeth's messages:* Alan Taylor, *William Cooper's Town*, 150–4.

'You are the only English novelist . . .': HJ to WDH from Paris (Feb 1884), *L(E)*, i, 104–5.

15 *CFW's parody of Cooper:* Linn Cary Mehta, a descendant of Cooper, in conversation (15 June 1996) spoke of CFW 'clearing a space for herself'.

'St Clair Flats': Repr. in first volume of stories, *Castle Nowhere* (1875), repr. *WAWE*, 79–106.

16 *grief 'like a prisoner': WAWE*, 103.

de Tocqueville on resolute women: 'The Young Woman as Wife', *Democracy in America*, trans. George Lawrence, ed. J. P. Mayer (1966; repr. NY: Doubleday Anchor, 1969), 594.

17 *inscription for Hannah's grave:* Transcribed by Hannah Cooper Pomeroy in notebook (catalogued as 'Journal'), NYHA NM – 99.56.

future comfort: The Judge's verses to celebrate Hannah Pomeroy's birth, in which she consoles him for the loss of 'my Hannah'. Inventory of Pomeroy Place: 'Cooper', made early in the twentieth century by Clare Benedict. NYHA 237.1 NM – 58.63.

Indian legend: James Fenimore Cooper, 'Reminiscences'.

notebook: NYHA NM – 99.56.

Hannah's journal: 'Extracts from a Journal' in the 'Pomeroy Place' folder of the Inventory, op. cit., NYHA 237.1 NM – 58.63. This is a very incomplete typescript. Hannah Pomeroy spoke (in Jan 1878, a year before her death) of bequeathing a 'book' to her female descendants which consisted of extracts put together on 25 May 1871 at 131 St Clare Street, Cleveland, Ohio. What survives, here, are her granddaughter Clare Benedict's 'quotations' from her 'book', i.e. there were two stages of expurgation. The typing was done at Clare Benedict's instigation, and there is no knowing if she tampered with the text. She printed a version of the journal in Benedict, iii, 701–30. As a keeper of the shrine, she had no compunction about destroying papers or parts of them, and she had no notion of dating and sources. Since what passed through her hands and survived is unreliable, her records are to be avoided wherever possible. Unfortunately, as her aunt's heir, she controlled a lot of papers, including CFW's journal which has disappeared except for a few extracts (see below, ch. 10).

18 *the Glimmerglass: The Deerslayer*, ch. 2.

19 *furniture:* Inventory, op. cit. Extensive description of the artefacts of Pomeroy Place, where family memorabilia were gathered under the ownership of Clara and Clare Benedict when they bought the house. It was made into something of a museum, with each room assigned to the memory of a particular member of the family.

three identical graves: I am indebted to Sharon Dean for recent photographs.
20 One stone has fallen over.

'Forest-City': Hannah Woolson to her grandson, SM, who had described the industrial density of the Cleveland air (22 Aug 1878). WRHS MS 3735, container 24, folder 7.

*Woolson's houses in Cleveland, including 'Cheerful Corner':*Cornelia E. L. May, 'CFW', a three-page MS reminiscence in Constance Mather Bishop's Cuttings Book (a niece of CFW who lived in Cleveland), privately owned by Molly Mather Anderson.

'lovely, caressing ways': Benedict, iii, 699.

'flies buzzed': Ibid., 700.

photograph of the sisters: Reproduced by Cheryl B. Torsney, *Constance Fenimore Woolson: The Grief of Artistry* (Athens, Ga: Univ. of Georgia Press, 1989).

21 *observation:* Clara Benedict to Kate Mather (31 Dec 1909). WRHS MS 3735, container 24, folder 4.

'is that all . . .'. Clara Benedict to Kate Mather (26 July 1905) from Pitlochry, Scotland, where she was reading Scottish literature. WRHS MS 3735, container 24, folder 4.

'Europe': Ibid., and CFW to J. Bone, Cleveland journalist (16 Mar 1881), from Rome, cited in his obituary for CFW, *Cleveland Plain Dealer* (17 Feb 1894).

'I wish . . .': CFW to Flora Payne (later Mrs William Whitney). Benedict, ii, 16.

woman not logical: Clara Benedict to Will Mather. WRHS MS 3735, container 24, folder 3.

Eleanor H. Porter: Talk on the family history of the Woolsons, by Gary Woolson (Feb 1995). Rollins.

first cooking stove: A model is exhibited by the Claremont Historical Society, Claremont, NH.

22 *'Now you are just beginning . . .':* Clara Benedict to Kate Mather (9 Dec 1905) from Vienna. WRHS MS 3735, container 24, folder 4.

naming herself 'Fenimore': It was no more than a transient idea, but not unimportant in view of HJ's decision to call her that, at a time when no one else did, as though it were a pact of the private life. There is a letter from CFW (at 49 West 32nd Street) to an editor, Mary L. Booth (2 Feb 1871), thanking her for $50, as payment for an article. She adds, 'I would rather not have my name appear with the article, but if it is necessary, please give only "Constance Fenimore", as I have taken that for a nom de plume.' Princeton's Rare Books and Special Collections: General Manuscripts (Misc) CO140 Box WOODS–WOZ; folder: Woolson.

Obviously, she then chose to publish under her own name. On one occasion only, she used the pseudonym of Anne March for her children's book, *The Old Stone House* (1872). It is conceivable that she simply stressed 'Fenimore' to this one editor in order to certify herself, as it were, as a professional writer by placing herself under the aegis of her prolific great-uncle.

22 *'the girls'*: CFW to JH (9 Aug 1883). This correspondence at Brown University, Providence, Rhode Island has been ed. by Alice Hall Petry, ' "Always your Attached Friend": The Unpublished Letters of CFW to John and Clara Hay', *Books at Brown*, xxix–xxx (1982–3) 11–107. See below, ch. 8.

Cooperstown recipes: Recipe Book, NYHA, P771 FM – 19.59.

Pomeroy Place, the underground railroad, and Joseph Stewart's grave: Henry Cooper kindly showed me these places (July 1994) and relayed a history of the family.

23 *haunted by Cooper's scenes:* 'The Haunted Lake', op. cit.

Linda T. Guilford: Papers on microfilm at WRHS. For further details, I am indebted to Professor Gladys Haddad, a specialist in local history at Case Western Reserve. (In discussion, Cleveland, Aug 1994). Guilford published reminiscences in *The Story of a Cleveland School*. I'm indebted to Joan Weimer for her notes.

impact of Corinne: a lively and informed treatment in Ellen Moers, *Literary Women* (London: Women's Press, 1977), ch. 9.

Necker and Mme de Staël: James Fenimore Cooper, 'Reminiscences', 51.

24 *Mather family history:* Abundant records in WRHS.

Emma Carter in Aug 1851: Georgiana Mather to Hannah Woolson. WRHS.

Georgiana's birthday rhyme: WRHS MS 3735, container 1, folder 3.

25 *photograph at 15:* Benedict, ii, opposite p. 44. Reproduced by Torsney, *CFW: The Grief of Artistry.*

'The Lake of the Dismal Swamp': Poetical Works of Thomas Moore (Boston, 1857), 387–8. CFW underlined her copy (owned by the Claremont Historical Society, NH), and notes in the margin, 'Mackinac – August 1856'. This date suggests she got hold of the poem before she acquired the volume published the following year and bought by her in 1860.

roughs lose respect: 'The Lady of Little Fishing', *Castle Nowhere*, 351–86.

'The Daughters of Carolina': CFW to critic H. H. Boyesen (9 Aug. n.y.), about review of *Rodman the Keeper and Other Stories*, defending her

accuracy on Southern girls. From Lucerne. Barrett Library, Univ. of Virginia: 7331-a Barrett–Woolson.

26 *feet vs forehead:* Recalled in 'Extremities: The Feet', *Harper's Bazar* (18 Nov 1871).

proficient in French: Her multi-volume French translation of Turgenev and her Baedekers in French are at Rollins. The bulk of her French books – an impressive collction – is owned by Claremont Historical Society, Claremont, NH.

connection between refusing marriage and family tragedies: Weimer in *WAWE*, x.

CFW on marriage and spinsterhood: To Arabella Carter, afterwards Mrs Washburn. Benedict, ii, 18–19.

27 *'my lovely boy':* The bust by Horatio Greenough is in the Woolson Center, Rollins College.

'ugly': CFW to JH (26 Dec 1885). *Books at Brown*, op. cit.

men in stories: See 'Miss Vedder' (1879) and 'In Sloane Street' (1892). Discussed below, chs 7 and 9.

HJ a native of the James family: WJ to AJ (29 July 1889). Houghton. HJ, he said, was 'a native of the James family, and has no other country'.

28 *father's death:* CFW to JH (26 Dec 1885) *Books at Brown*.

'having been run away with': CFW to WWB (16 June 1892), from Venice. PML, Baldwin collection, RV 65E, Box 6. CFW's confidential letters to WWB are all in PML.

Chapter 3 'A Fighting Man'

29 *MT's letter (12 July 1862) to Helena de Kay:* This and all following quotations from MT's letters to Helena are from the privately owned Gilder Papers, TS by Rosamond Gilder, Helena's daughter, in a folder marked 'miscellaneous'. I did not find the originals amongst the Gilder Papers, but they could be there. A comparison of a Rosamond Gilder transcription and an original letter from a different correspondent suggests that the former could be inaccurate in small details. Habegger quotes from these letters in *Henry James and the 'Woman Business'*.

MT cut her hair: WJ to Kitty Temple (Sept 1861). Quoted from MS in Houghton. WJ, *Letters*, i (1920), 138, to be superseded by *CWJ*. Elly's arm was broken – it's unclear if this was connected with the 'affair of the wings', as the incident was called.

'a chronicle . . .': A, i, 10.

'nurseried and playroomed orphanage': Ibid.

30 *the downfall of John James:* Alfred Habegger, 'Dupine Tracks J. J.', *Southern Review*, xxvii (Oct 1991). This story of biographical detection should become a classic of biographical method. ('J.J.' was actually not John James but his unfortunate son, John Vanderburg James.)

30 *he vowed to outdo Hawthorne:* HJ to WJ (13 Feb 1870), *CWJ*, i, 146. He refers specifically to his regard for *The House of the Seven Gables*.

'couvé': HJ to MJ (17 Feb [1878]), *L(E)*, i, 156.

'My Bible . . .', etc.: A Landscape-Painter and Other Tales, ed. Robert Gard (Penguin, 1990), 64–98.

31 *'Shining Newport . . .': CWJ*, quoted in *A*, ii, 327.

32 *'invent a word':* Holmes's response to reading *A*, ii, in letter to Lewis Einstein (17 April 1914), *The Correspondence of Mr. Justice Holmes and Lewis Einstein, 1903–1935*, ed. James Bishop Peabody (London, 1964), 89–90.

'How in the world . . .': The Diary of AJ (12 Apr 1891), ed. Leon Edel (Penguin, 1987), 192–3. GWJ heard this discussion with George Bradford, a Newport schoolmaster, at Emerson's house (while GWJ was at Sanborn's school in Concord) and passed it on to AJ.

'life of God himself in human nature': Cited by Lewis, 42.

'no difference . . .': Ibid., 40.

HJ's attitude to father's writings: A, ii, 275.

flogging a dead horse: TSP, Autograph Memoir of HJ and WJ. Houghton. *L(L)*, i, 6–9.

physical appearance and talk of HJSr: Maud Howe Elliott, *This Was My Newport* (Cambridge, Mass., 1944), 85, quoted in Robert C. Le Clair, *Young Henry James 1843–1870* (NY: Bookman, 1955), 366, 373–4. Maud Howe Elliott was the daughter of Julia Ward Howe.

33 *possession, sin, Dr Curtis, and extermination:* Habegger, *The Father*, 4, 8, 310–11, shows certain of HJSr's beliefs to be 'injudicious', 'sometimes scandalous', and even 'monstrous'.

HJSr vs gamblers: Habegger, 'Dupine Tracks J.J.', 823.

bonding of James family in Europe: TSP, Memoir.

'into contact'; visit to Emerson: Linda Simon, *Genuine Reality: A Life of William James* (NY: Harcourt, 1998), 68.

34 *'Scant'; 'No one took . . .':* HJ to teenage niece, Margaret James (8 Nov 1906), *L(L)*, ii, 55.

voracious reader of novels, etc.: A, ii, 240 ff.

'waste and anguish': TS of fragments of early draft of *Notes of a Son and Brother*. Houghton bMS Eng 1213 (72).

HJ's secrecy about writing: TSP, Memoir.

35 *'long jump', etc.: A*, ii, 368.

36 *'For miles . . .':* 'Newport' (1870), *T(BA)*, 759–66.

'precarious tracks', etc.: HJ, *The American Scene*, *T (BA)* ch. 6.

George Bancroft in Newport: A, ii, 437.

37 'produced': *A*, ii, 520.

38 *MJ at the Carlyles':* Cited by Habegger, *The Father*, 215.

MJ's maternal availability: A, ii, 343.

AJ's straitjacket and rivalry: I owe this idea and image to Gila Bercovitch, founding editor-in-chief of The Library of America. In conversation (Saranac Lake, NY, summer 1988) and again (NYC, 2 June 1997).

39 *'Mrs Morte':* HJ to Ariana Curtis (25 Sept [1896]). Curtis Papers, Dartmouth College, Hanover, NH.

HJSr entertained AJ's proposal to kill him or herself: HJSr to RJ, privately owned by Vaux descendants of RJ, quoted in Introduction to *The Death and Letters of Alice James: Selected Correspondence with a Biographical Essay*, ed. Ruth Bernard Yeazell (Berkeley: Univ. of California Press, 1981), 15–16.

'immovable': AJ, *Diary* (26 Oct 1890), 149.

'Chérie charmante', etc.: A, ii, 328–9.

'Let Alice cultivate . . .': WJ to parents (22 Jan 1868), quoted by Strouse, 124.

40 *'The loveress of W.J.':* Howard Feinstein, *Becoming William James* (Ithaca, NY: Cornell Univ. Press, 1984), 284.

WJ's 'Song' to AJ: Enclosed in letter to HJSr. Houghton bMS Am 1092.9 (2495–2546).

'I hope your neuralgia . . .': A, ii, 320.

'lovely babe': WJ to family (early Nov 1861). Houghton.

what men say: title of Joan Smith's *What Men Say* (London: Chatto, 1994).

'desperately in love': Virginia Harlow, *Thomas Sergeant Perry: A Biography* (Durham, NC: Duke Univ. Press, 1950), 11.

41 *Miss Paige:* MT to Helena de Kay (12 July 1862). Gilder Papers.

Emerson's daughters: A, ii, 369. Observed during a visit to Emerson's house, when HJSr and MJ left their youngest sons at Sanborn's school.

'amateur priestess of rash speculation': A, ii, 283.

never again met anyone like MT: WJ to John Gray, quoted in *A*, ii, 504.

women disqualified from 'didactic dignity': Article on the Woman's Movement, *Putnam's Monthly* (Mar 1853), quoted in Lewis, 80.

Jane Austen's advice: Northanger Abbey, ch. 14.

Florence Nightingale on women: Cassandra (1859; repr. as Appendix to Ray Strachey, *The Cause: A Short History of the Women's Movement in Great Britain* (1928; repr. London: Virago, 1979), 395–418.

42 *'the low grey Newport sky':* AJ, *Diary* (21 Feb 1890), 95.

'absolutely afraid of nothing': A, ii, 282 ('audacity'), 283, 509.

slow of speech: TSP, Memoir.

MT's disgraced grandfather; 'THAT strain': HJ to WJ (12 Feb 1891), *CWJ*, ii, 172, details elaborated and corrected 173–4n6.

43 *Temple pedigree:* Good summary in *CWJ*, ii, 173–4n6.

44 *'prose unrelieved': A*, ii, 443.

'damage . . . by the professional pursuit of "art" ': HJSr to WJ, quoted by Tamara Follini, 'Pandora's Box: The Family Correspondence in *Notes of a Son and Brother*', a brilliant talk at the 1993 New York Henry James Sesquicentennial Conferences. *Cambridge Quarterly*, xxv:1 (Winter 1994), 26–40. Dr Follini notes that this letter is not included in *A*, and brings out HJ's ambivalence to his family.

44 *Mrs de Kay's letters:* (Feb–Mar 1863), Gilder Papers. Habegger quotes the warning against MT, *HJ and the 'Woman Business'*, 133. This published quotation came from Helena's daughter Rosamond Gilder's inaccurate transcription. The quotation here is from the original letter.

45 *details of Helena de Kay:* Rosamond Gilder, unpublished TS of 'Two Portraits', Gilder Papers; excerpts from the Reminiscences of Mary Hallock Foote, Gilder Papers; and Cecilia Beaux, *Background with Figures* (Boston, Mass.: Houghton Mifflin, 1930), 208–11. I am grateful to Mr Gilder Palmer, grandson of Helena de Kay, for alerting me to the last, and loaning his copy; for his copy of the letters of Richard Watson Gilder; and for a family tree of the de Kays.

46 *La Farge on Helena de Kay:* From Newport (21 Dec [n.y., but before her marriage in 1874]). Gilder Papers.

'Let me not . . .': Shakespeare, Sonnet 116.

'a passion': Helena de Kay to Mary Hallock Foote (1847–1938), whom she met at the Cooper Union art school in NY in 1866–7. Letter written in spring 1870 just after MT's death. Gilder Papers. Cited in Habegger, *HJ and the 'Woman Business'*, 255.

'dear, motherly *care':* MT to Helena de Kay (3 Apr 1863). Cited in Habegger, *HJ and the 'Woman Business'*.

WJ's walk with MT: WJ to AJ from Newport (5 Mar [1863]). Houghton.

47 *WJ and counterfeit:* MT to Helena de Kay (1 Jan 1863). Gilder Papers. At first I thought 'Willy' must be her brother, but her brother was with her at home, ill, when she received the letter at Christmas, replied a day or two later, and wrote the above comment on New Year's Day. Will Temple's illness dates from 13 December 1862, when he wrote in his diary: 'I feel so ill with intermittent fever that I can scarcely stand.' He must have been sent home soon after.

did not forgive: Habegger has done pioneering work on the antagonism to MT in the James household, so much so, he argues justly, that comments on her in letters the family exchanged do not need to be specified because they had been so frequently expressed (*HJ and the 'Woman Business'*, 139): 'Both tacitly and openly she challenged his [HJ's] father's opinions. Not only was she a sterling example of the earnest, restless young woman, a much publicized type in the early 1860s that the Jameses and many other Brahmins tended to frown on, but she denounced the philosopher's ideas to his face' (ibid., 11).

48 *'weak-minded' boys:* MT to Helena de Kay (1 Jan 1863). Gilder Papers.

'verity of character': A, ii, 509.

'the supreme case . . .': A, ii, 283.

'splendid shifting sensibility': A, ii, 283.

'psychologic': A, ii, 284.

'a marvellous production'; 'in our forgetting': MT to Helena de Kay (3 Apr 1863). Gilder Papers.

49 *AJ's memory of Bradford: Diary* (13 Feb 1890), 84.

49 *'obstinate questionings':* George Partridge Bradford to Helena de Kay Gilder (21 Nov 1875). Amongst a set of nostalgic letters. Gilder Papers.
'stoic visage': WJ to family (25 Dec [1863]). Houghton.
Daisy Miller: The novella (1878) which made HJ's name. See below, ch. 6.
'the pure Newport time': The American Scene, ch. 6.
50 *HJ drafted for the Union Army:* I am grateful for the fascinating, detailed research of Charles and Tess Hoffmann, 'HJ and the Civil War', *New England Quarterly* lxii:5 (1989), 529–52.
'more coercive': A, ii, 368.
'In our youth . . .': Cited by Thomas C. Gray, 'Bad Man From Olympus', *New York Review of Books* (13 July 1995), 4–7.
'a welt': HJ, *William Wetmore Story and His Friends*, ii, (Edinburgh: Blackwood, 1903), 30–1.
'drenched': HJ to Hendrik C. Andersen (4 May 1901), *L(E)*, iv, 188.
51 *'insuperable' eloquence: The American Scene*, ch. 7: iii.
'never to hold out . . .': A, ii, 276.
fire in Newport: Edel, i, 173f, suggests an alternative date, another fire on 28 October 1861, but HJ does say that the fire was in spring and coincided in his recollection with the outbreak of the war. *A*, ii, 414. His memory was more than excellent – it was a trained, exquisite instrument.
'obscure hurt': A, ii, 415.
'in the quietest of quiet ways': A, ii, 370–1.
HJSr's Independence Day oration: 'The Social Significance of Our Institutions' in a collection of his writings, ed. Giles Gunn (Chicago: American Library Association, 1974), 120.
52 *larger house:* Strouse, 60ff.
'highly disgusted': MT to Helena de Kay (30 Aug 1862). Gilder Papers.
'share': A, ii, 416.
'visit to wounded soldiers': A, ii, 424–5.
53 *'recruit', etc.: A*, ii, 417.
Lincoln's Preliminary Proclamation: American Primer, ed. Daniel J. Boorstin (1966; repr. NY: New American Library, 1968), 429.
54 *Readville: A*, ii, 456–7.
55 *state home guard:* Details from Charles and Tess Hoffmann, 'HJ and the Civil War'.
Temple's letters and actions: William W. Swan, 'William James Temple', in *Harvard Memorial Biographies*, ed. Thomas Wentworth Higginson, ii (Cambridge, Mass.: Sever and Francis, 1867), 334–47. (Swan drew on a journal found in Temple's blood-stained uniform, which he had carried on him into battle.) Copy in Harvard Law School Library.
56 *Temple's body and burial:* Charles and Tess Hoffmann, 'HJ and the Civil War', 547.
MT's grief, and exchange with Uncle Henry: MT to Helena de Kay (12 May 1863). Gilder Papers.
57 *'air of sacrifice': A*, ii, 457.

57 *'For the Union Dead':* Robert Lowell, *Selected Poems* (London: Faber, 1965; repr. 1973), 62–4.

58 *WJ's resentment of GWJ, and the cartoon:* WJ to AJ (5 Mar [1863]). Houghton.

59 *war record of Gus Barker:* Arthur Lincoln, 'Augustus Barker', in *Harvard Memorial Biographies*, ii, 357–62.

60 *HJ's memory of Gettysburg in the garden: A*, ii, 423.

Kitty depressed: WJ to Katharine James Prince (12 Sept [1863]). Houghton.

'ignobly safe': A, ii, 423.

'humiliating': A, ii, 460.

'arrested expression': A, ii, 384.

'stress of life': A, ii, 276.

exempted: Details from Charles and Tess Hoffmann, 'HJ and the Civil War'.

61 *HJSr's letter to Miss Peabody:* Daniel Aaron, *The Unwritten War: American Writers and the Civil War* (NY:OUP, 1973), 112.

'mite', 'smiting her children into line', etc.: GWJ, address to ex-servicemen, 'The Assault on Fort Wagner', published in the *Milwaukee Sentinal* (1883), quoted by Jane Maher, *A Biography of Broken Fortunes: Wilkie and Bob, Brothers of William, Henry and Alice James* (Hamden, Conn.: Archon Books, 1986), 25.

'we smiled . . .': A, ii, 458.

62 *'I cannot but adore . . .':* Quoted in Aaron, 110.

talk 'charged with natural life': A, ii, 459.

HJSr on manliness: Lewis, 149–50, drawing on Maher, brings together a telling collection of these statements.

seasoned warrior: RJ, undated reminiscent letter to WJ, clearly written much later in life. He describes a heroic act which remains to be verified (RJ was a drinker and mentally unstable). He claims that in the assault on Charleston, as a 'sassy first lieutenant', he took command of some thousand men, ignoring one or two generals who were in retreat, and turned two Rebel guns upon the enemy 'after I had captured their works'.

63 *'Can't H. come down . . .': A*, ii, 473

'smile of quiet contempt . . .': Mrs de Kay to son Charles, at school. Edel, i, 215.

64 *'scamps':* Lewis, 124.

no more robust: Aaron, 109.

'crass barbarism', etc.: 'Owen Wingrave', *CS*, iv, 256–90. The tale was turned into a one-act play, produced at the Little Theatre by Gertrude Kingston in 1911. Interesting that this anti-war drama should have appeared during the run-up to the Great War, i.e. a year before the Foreign Secretary Sir Edward Grey's famous warning that 'the lamps [were] going out all over Europe'.

'still so young': A, ii, 415.

65 *Yeats on the Irish hero:* 'An Irish Airman Foresees His Death', *Collected*

Poems (London: Macmillan, 1958), 152. Inspired by Major Robert Gregory, son of Lady Gregory.

65 *undated TS on turning point of his life:* 'The Turning Point of My Life', n.d. four TS pages. Houghton bMS Am 1237.9. Printed in *N*, 437–8. A date 1900–1 has been assigned by the editors without explanation. The piece was requested by WDH, as part of a series of articles for the *Atlantic.*

GWJ gaunt with agony: See sketch by WJ, Lewis opposite p. 234.

'Few spirits were as free . . .': A, ii, 504, drawn from WJ to JCG, thanking him for sending a letter from MT, n.d. Houghton.

66 *'affront':* Preface to *PL, E(CP)*, 1077.

'insistently romantic': A, ii, 482.

Chapter 4 A Girl of the Future

67 *rivalry:* Edel, i, 248–9.

'The Story of a Year': A Landscape-Painter and Other Tales 1864–1874, ed. Roger Gard (Penguin, 1990*), and CS*, i (a uniform edition of James's tales due from The Library of America).

HJ dates America's loss of innocence from the Civil War: Hawthorne (1879), repr. *E(AE)*, 315–457, and *The Shock of Recognition*, 425–565. I am grateful to Freddie Baveystock for pointing this out (letter, Sept 1995), and noting that HJ differs in this from his contemporary Henry Adams, in his *History of the Administrations of Jefferson and Madison*, which locates it at the beginning of the national period, during the War of 1812.

68 *'Now I am immortal':* HJ to TSP (25 Mar 1864), *L(E)*, i, 49. HJ was still in Newport. The family moved to Boston two months later. The story was accepted for publication in the *Atlantic* in Oct 1864.

Job and 'heaven-inspired': Unpublished letter HJ to TSP, n.d. but written from 13 Ashburton Place, Boston, i.e. probably between May 1864 and Mar 1865. James–Perry Papers, Colby College Library, Maine.

'agony of the spiritual life': T. S. Eliot, 'A Preface to Modern Literature', *Vanity Fair*, xxi (Nov 1923), 44, 118.

69 *genius of the place:* HJ to WJ (29 Mar 1870), *CWJ*, i, 154. HJ to MJ (26 Mar 1870), *L(E)*, i, 222.

Newport: The American Scene; *A*, ii; 'An International Episode'; and HJ, *William Wetmore Story and His Friends*, ii (1903), 177–8.

'conversing'; 'high art of peace': A, ii, 507.

70 *'slim and straight . . .': A*, ii, 538–9.

'ardently': Ibid.

MT's comments on what music meant to her: MT to JCG (30 Dec 1869). AHJ's transcript (with help of her daughter, Margaret James) of MT's 23 letters to JCG in 1869–70. Houghton bMS Am 1092.12. Originals destroyed by HJ.

'a grace of free mobility . . .': A, ii, 538.

70 *'eyes peeled', etc:* HJ to OWH (14 July 1865), *L(E)*, i, 60–1.
'If you don't mind it . . .' and 'snatch': HJ to OWH (24 July 1865). Microfilm of OWH Papers, Harvard Law Library (microfilm room in basement of Langdall Hall: drawer 383). The batch of letters from HJ to OWH is on reels 33–4. I quote always from the original source. See Mark De Wolfe Howe, 'The Letters of HJ to Mr. Justice Holmes', *Yale Review*, xxxviii (1948–9), 410–33.
North Conway in 1865: The American Scene and *A*, ii. 'Aunt Charlotte' is mentioned in a reminiscent letter from HJ to Henrietta Temple Pell-Clarke (5 May 1914), with memories of North Conway, 1865, in response to her letter about his chapter on MT in *A*, ii. Copy in Houghton. Quoted in full by S. P. Rosenbaum, 'Letters to the Pell-Clarkes from their "Old Cousin and Friend" Henry James', *American Literature*, xxxi (1959), 46–58.

71 *Gray in war: Dictionary of American Biography.*
Gray a bore: MT, remembering, to JCG (27 June 1869).
'hard-hearted': Postscript of MT to JCG (4 Oct 1869). From Newport.
'lovely': HJ to AJ (4 Jan 1867). Houghton.
wartime images of manliness: Letters (Oct 1861) from officers and doctors to Dr Oliver Wendell Holmes, Sr (the doctor-novelist) are on reel 16, microfilm of OWH Papers, Harvard Law Library.

72 *'kill – kill – kill':* on discarded envelope, ibid.
a desperate flirt: AJ, *Diary* (1 Dec 1889), 61.
'a perfect Voltaire in petticoats': HJ to Grace Norton (20 Sept 1880), *L(E)*, ii, 307.
'passionate breezes': OWH to WJ (19 Apr 1868). Houghton.
Wordsworthian lyricism: Cited by Thomas C. Gray, 'Bad Man from Olympus', *New York Review of Books* (13 July 1995), 4–7.
*'romantic eloquence', etc.:*HJ to OWH from Torquay, Devon (13 Oct 1895), reels 33–4, microfilm of OWH Papers, Harvard Law Library.
'swamped', etc.: *A*, ii, 488–9.

73 *'luxury' and 'painter':* *A*, ii, 508, 489.
'true connection' and 'such a heroine': *A*, ii, 508.
'one of the "irreconcilables" ': HJ to Grace Norton (1 Apr 1870), from Malvern, *L(E)*, i, 231–2.
'Hurrah for the new man and woman . . .': Helena de Kay to Mary Hallock Foote (1869). Gilder Papers.
'I loved her' and 'I never [loved] . . .': HJ to MJ and WJ (26 and 29 Mar 1870), *L(E)*, i, 219, 224; to WJ also in *CWJ*, i, 154.

74 *in the autumn of 1865:* Aziz, editor of *CT*, suggests a date in the last quarter of 1865, citing a letter of Dec 1865 from the mother of Steele MacKay, a Newport friend of WJ and HJ, who met HJSr and reports that 'Harry James has written a story for the Atlantic called "The Painter's Journal!" ' (*CT*, i, xxxiv). Presumably, then, it was already accepted for publication. It appeared in Feb 1866.

74 *'A Landscape-Painter': A Landscape-Painter and Other Tales*, 64–98. See *CT*, i, 57–87 for magazine version.

'I have only to let myself go!': (13 July 1891), *N(M)*, 106. See also 'a strange nervous fear of letting myself go' (23 Oct 1891), *N(M)*, 112.

attraction to young men: Sheldon M. Novick's *Henry James: The Young Master* (NY: Random House, 1996) tries unsuccessfully, it is widely agreed, to prove that HJ was an active homosexual from the mid-1860s, starting with OWH. This argument is not based on provable evidence but on a tissue of supposition. Quoted out of context, one of HJ's statements may sound suggestive of sexual initiation, but this deliberate use in his prose of what Philip Horne has called epistemological abysses, evades specificity. See Philip Horne's closely reasoned and sophisticated rebuttal of the way 'queer theory' has been applied to HJ, in 'Henry James: The Master and the "Queer Affair" of "The Pupil" ', *Critical Quarterly* (1995), and his review of Kaplan's biography, in the London *Guardian*, pointing out that, though Kaplan admits halfway through that HJ 'did not think of himself as a homosexual', his text is studded with buzz-words intended to support the story of 'the homoerotic sensibility', e.g. the young James is described as 'eager to come out of the closet of anonymity'. Kaplan's readings of literary work homoeroticises it to go with the biographic line. Kaplan plays up boys, as Horne points out, pinning HJ's description of a small boy at Torcello at the head of his text as an iconic moment, what Horne calls 'a pederastic-looking emblem' taken out of a context which looks less like an erotic ogle since HJ's emphasis really falls on Italian poverty.

No factual proof has so far come to light. There is a growing move amongst scholars to reach behind the biographical image HJ contrived for our credulity, but it seems a modish mistake, in his case, to plump for a simple answer. Informed scholars will know that he wrote in ardent tones also to women. We cannot safely demarcate his sexuality; those who try to do so have a predetermined political or critical agenda which, I believe, will soon date. John Bayley, discussing our vogue for honesty about homosexuality, an honesty we now take wholly for granted, cites the way HJ teased a friend who interrogated him about the significance of *The Turn of the Screw* by pointing out that '. . . An artist is wiser never to define just what he means when he presents an enigmatically fraught situation in that the truths of sexuality cast long shadows'. 'Fat and Fretful', *London Review of Books* (18 Apr 1996), 26.

76 *'Alice is busy trying to idle':* MJ to HJ (24 July 1869). Houghton.

RJ's history: Correspondence in Houghton. The fullest published account is Jane Maher, *A Biography of Broken Fortunes*. Maher has used this phrase from RJ, describing his life, as the apt title of her biography of the two younger James brothers. See also Lewis, 167.

77–8 *plans for the plantation and 'a great deal of good':* AJ to Frances (Fanny) Morse (4 Feb 1866). Houghton b MS Am 1094 (1496–1526).

78 *HJ's ridicule of RJ:* AJ to WJ (13 Oct 1867). Houghton b MS Am 1094 (1468–95).

'severe discipline': MJ to WJ (21 Nov [1867]). Houghton b MS Am 1093.1 (57–62).

'I am pretty lonely . . .' and 'mad': GWJ to HJSr (8 April 1868). Houghton.

'every year of this western life . . .': GWJ to JCG (20 Jan 1882). Houghton.

79 *'Inferno':* HJ to LB (24 Jan 1872). Houghton b MS Am 1094 (500–82).

'Bob's fits of madness': HJ to WJ and AHJ (28 May 1894), *L(E)*, iii, 478–9. HJ called him 'a madman'.

RJ as bladder: AJ to WJ (24 Apr 1887), *The Death and Letters of Alice James*, 127.

RJ in love 1869, and WJ's interference: WJ to RJ (14 Nov 1869). In possession of Mr and Mrs Vaux. Cited by Maher, 110. The name given in one letter is 'Kitty'. Maher infers that the only possible candidate was Catherine (Kitty) Barber Van Buren, daughter of Ellen King James, HJSr's sister, who married a son of President Van Buren. (Kitty Temple was married by then.)

'aged solemn owls': WJ to GWJ (20 May [1866]). Houghton. Cited by Lewis, 179.

Robert Temple's conviction: Lewis, 177

80 *'silent pluck':* WJ to HJ (2 Oct 1869), *CWJ*, i, 100: 'I cannot tell you my dear brother how my admiration of the years of silent pluck you exhibited during those long years has risen of late. . . . I give up like a baby in comparison.'

Swampscott: WJ to GWJ (20 May [1866]). Houghton b MS Am 1092.9 (2489–2994).

'bad little "sick" visit'; 'thrilled' by George Eliot: N, 239, or *N(M)*, 320.

George Eliot reviews: 'The Novels of George Eliot' and 'Felix Holt', *E(AE)*, 907–33.

'miserably stricken . . .': N, 239, or *N(M)*, 320.

'dismally alone', 'bad dreams': HJ to TSP (4 July 1866). Houghton.

'sick & disordered': HJs self-portrait in letter to WJ, excusing his failure in relation to MT, following her death (29 Mar 1870), *CWJ*, i, 154. HJ claims that MT never knew how 'sick & disordered' he was.

81 *'more active and masculine':* Ibid.

One of your friends: Mrs Holmes Sr to OWH Jr (21 May 1866), reel 33, Harvard Law Library.

'decidedly brighter': MJ to AJ ([Jan 1867]). Houghton b MS Am 1093.1 (20–31).

AJ's cure in NY: Lewis, 181.

'A hundred times a day . . .': HJ to AJ (4 Jan 1867). Houghton.

Holmes at the 'scene': OWH's diary: New Year's Day and 6 Jan 1867. Microfilm of OWH Papers, Harvard Law Library.

'quite disenchanted': MJ to AJ ([Jan 1867]). Houghton b MS Am 1093.1 (20–31).

'I lost my humanity . . .': The Holmes–Laski Letters, ed. Mark Howe (Cambridge, Mass.: Harvard Univ. Press, 1953), i, 769.

OWH's legal career: Useful summary in Gray, 'Bad Man from Olympus', op. cit. I am grateful for the views of Tony Honoré, who was Regius Professor of Civil Law, Oxford University, in conversation (26 Nov 1995).

82 *OWH's demeaning opinion of women:* OWH to WJ (Apr 1868). Houghton.
'Poor Richard': CT, 128–79. Since I look at the tales biographically, as a product of a period, it is sometimes useful to draw on the first published version: the periodical version. HJ revised this tale, as he revised most of his work, for book publication and for republication in later collections (Edel i, 237, says that 'Poor Richard' was written in 1866, without source note.)

83 *problems of 'the girls':* MJ to AJ (Apr 1867). Houghton b MS Am 1093.1 (20–31).

84 *'I have felt quite strong . . .':* HJ to WJ (10 May 1867), *CWJ*, i, 13–15.
HJ to Newport: Kaplan, 87. Novick claims the beard was grown 1862–3, perhaps on basis of a blotchy daguerrotype of that date where there is a shadow on the chin.
'I cared more to please . . .': HJ to WJ (29 Mar 1870), *CWJ*, i, 154.
Clover to Eleanor: (10 Jan 1870). Shattuck Papers, Massachusetts Historical Society.

84–5 *AJ's report on MT and the Van Buren engagement:* AJ to WJ (6 Aug [1867]), Houghton b MS Am 1094 (1468 95). Part quoted by Strouse, 115.

85 *'the dirtiest of little dirty children':* AJ to Fanny Morse (4 Feb 1866). Houghton b MS Am 1094 (1496–1526).
shaking head over career in medicine: AJ to Fanny Morse (3 Apr 1866). Houghton b MS Am 1094 (1496–1526).
'What pleases me . . .': WJ to AJ (23 June 1868), cited by Strouse, 124.
'a great blessing . . .' etc.: HJ to WJ (10 May 1867), *CWJ*, i, 13–14, 16, 19.
HJ's devotion to AJ: See Lewis, 181–2.

86 *'a perfect* furore': AJ (noting an observation by GWJ) to WJ, from Cambridge (6 Aug 1867), quoted by Strouse, 115.
reviewer of 'Poor Richard': Nation, iv (30 May 1867), 432, repr. *CT*, Appendix II, 513.
'question': HJ to Grace Norton (1 Apr 1870), *L(E)*, i, 232.
'as lively as the inner sepulchre'; 'ghastly simulacrum': HJ to WJ (22 Nov 1867), *CWJ*, i, 25.
'the poky banality . . .': Quoted by Edel in Introduction to *The Diary of AJ*, 5

87 *'extremely gifted':* WDH to ECS (5 Dec 1866), in *Life in Letters of William Dean Howells*, i, ed. Mildred Howells (Russell & Russell, 1928), 116. I am grateful to Polly Howells for the loan of her family copy.
'create his audience': WDH to Charles Eliot Norton (10 Aug 1867), ibid, 117–8. Also *CT*, i, xxxix.
'Would I cd think her sincere!': WJ to Edmund Tweedy (18 Dec 1867). Houghton.
WJ romancing Kitty after Montreal: WJ to Katherine Temple (3 Aug 1864). Houghton b MS Am 1092.9 (3815).
WJ drawn to Kitty, and slippers: WJ to AJ (18 Feb (1867]). Houghton.

88 *'ceased to improve'; 'It is plain . . .':* HJ to WJ (22 Nov 1867), *CWJ*, i, 25.
'Mason's eyes . . .': 'A Most Extraordinary Case', *CT*, 239.
'quite in her hands': Ibid., 236.

88 *inserted:* Ibid., 248.
revision: Stories Revived (1885).

89 *'mark of being drawn from experience':* WJ to HJ (13 Apr 1868), *CWJ*, i, 46–8.
WJ 'outraged': WJ to Katherine Temple (17 Aug 1868). Houghton.
racketing tavern and plan to go to Newport: HJ to OWH from Jefferson, NH (29 July 1868). OWH Papers, reels 33–4. Harvard Law Library.
letter of congratulation: HJ to Katherine Temple (28 July 1868). Houghton.
'disillusioning', etc.: Habegger, *The Father*, 289–90.

90 *MT's 'deep inscrutable soul':* HJ to Katherine Temple, (28 July 1868). Houghton.
Gabrielle: 'Gabrielle de Bergerac', serialised from July to Sept 1869, the only tale HJ published during this year abroad, and not reprinted in his lifetime. For details of Gabrielle's appearance and nature see *CT*, i, 373–4, 404. The name Bergerac was derived from that of a schoolfriend of HJ's in Bologne-sur-mer in 1857. MT wrote: 'My dearest Harry what a charming tale is Gabrielle de Bergerac. *Just* as pretty as ever it can be' (August 1869). Aziz gives convincing evidence that the tale was written nine months prior to publication, by Nov 1868 (*CT*, i, xli-xlii), 'before HJ's winter collapse'.
'Modern Women': Nation (Oct 1868), repr. *E(AE)*, 19–25.

91 *MT epitomises her sex and nation:* HJ to WJ (29 Mar 1870), *CWJ*, i, 154, 156.
MT fell ill: A, ii, notes that the illness began a few months before HJ's departure for Europe (in Feb 1869).
WJ on MT's illness: Undated letter from WJ to OWH. OWH Papers, reel 34, Harvard Law Library.
'not easily frightened': MT to JCG (27 Jan 1869). Houghton.

92 *'evil courses':* MT to HJ (3 June 1869). Houghton b MS Am 1092.9 (4387).
'coquette': In a letter to HJ, two years after MT's death, WJ mentions meeting one Miss Greene, who reminded him of MT except that she had nothing of the 'coquette' about her (27 Aug 1872), *CWJ*, i, 166. Even though WJ was reconciled to MT four months before her death, it is curious that this misjudgement prevailed, indicative of WJ's crude gender attitudes – similar to those that mark Winterbourne and society at large in HJ's *Daisy Miller* (1878). See below, ch. 6.
'abused': WJ recalled this in a letter to HJ (5 Dec 1869), *CWJ*, i, 129.
WJ's anti-Semitism: WJ to AJ (17 Oct 1867) and (17 Dec 1873). Houghton bMS Am .
'those stupid months': HJ to WJ (30 Nov 1869), from Rome, *CWJ*, i, 124.
'particularly': HJ to Grace Norton. Houghton bMS Am 1094 (0871).

93 *MT began correspondence with JCG:* On 20 May 1869 MT refers to the fact that they have been corresponding for a year.
cooling of friendship with Helena: Helena de Kay to Mary Hallock Foote (letter after MT's death, spring 1870). Kitty was only identified as the culprit many years later to the same correspondent. Gilder Papers. Cited by Habegger, *Henry James and the 'Woman Business'* 255.
'You must tell me . . .': MT to JCG (7 Jan 1869).
explored connections: A, ii, 527.

93 *'queer' and 'put an end':* MT to JCG (29 Aug 1869).
'usual inward question': MT to JCG (7 Jan 1869).

94 *'Pyramid' etc.:* MT quotes this back to JCG (7 Jan 1869). HJ omits this in extracts he made for the final chapter of *A*, ii, from this batch of letters.
'I can't stop them': MT to JCG (27 Jan 1869).
The Mill on the Floss: Vol ii, Book Third, end ch. 5 (p. 320 in Penguin edn).
'overpowering admiration ... for George Eliot': MT to JCG (4 Mar 1869), misquoted by HJ, *A*, ii, 513.
'a generous woman': MT to JCG (2 Apr 1869).
'as a pleasant': MT to JCG (27 Jan 1869).

95 *'no one':* The quotation in *A*, ii, 511, is not in the transcript for the letter of 3 Feb 1869, and my supposition is that AHJ suppressed it. Habegger suggests, alternatively, that HJ inserted a paragraph of his own invention, making MT appear more a victim of callous relatives than she really was. He argues (in a letter of 17 July 1996) that AHJ was a person of veracity, and that there is no other evidence of suppressions by her. I replied that this was a special instance when the family appears, with some justice, in a poor light, for no member of the family did bestir him- or herself to take MT into a healthy climate. My main argument is that the passage in question is written in MT's authentic voice – far different from the measured late style of HJ. There is no final answer, as yet. See Habegger, 'Henry James's Rewriting of MT's Letters', *American Literature*, lviii (May 1986), 166. Habegger prints MT's first four letters to JCG in parallel columns with HJ's shortened version of them, and discusses HJ's deletions, substitutions, and additions. The additions tend to bring MT's quicker, more informal voice into line with the more formal and measured rhythm of HJ's late style (see below, ch. 12). In other words, the additions are editorial, not inventive, and this is consistent with his idea of scrupulousness.
MT's February visit to Cambridge: Not mentioned in the transcript, memoir, or by any biographer. George P. Bradford in Newport to Helena de Kay in NY (14 Feb 1869). Gilder Papers. Bradford heard of Minny's visit, accompanied by Elly, from Mr Tweedy.

Chapter 5 Minny's Dream

96 *HJ's farewell visit:* *A*, ii, 514, and HJ to WJ (29 Mar 1870), *CWJ*, i, 155.

97 *laugh; mouth:* *A*, ii, 283, 514.
'give my love': Related by MT to JCG (4 Mar 1869).
'woodnote wild': *A*, ii, 519.
disagreement over David: MT to JCG (4 Mar 1869).
'wild excitement': Ibid.

98 *visit to Philadelphia:* MT to JCG (2 Apr 1869).
*JGG's opinion of Brooks and MT's reply: MT to JCG (*24 Apr 1869).

98 *HG's opinion of Brooks:* HJ to FB (23 Apr 1890 Houghton b MS Am 1094 (584–634).

99 *'mystery':* MT to JCG (24 Apr 1869).

'matchless lungs': MT, ironically, to JCG (4 Mar 1869).

confided: MT to HJ (3 June 1869). MT's four letters to HJ are in Houghton b MS Am 1092.9 (4387). Published by Robert Le Clair, 'HJ and MT', *American Literature*, xxi (Mar 1949), 35–48. Le Clair thinks MT writes 'petty' accounts of their circle and has 'meagre' convictions.

'quick affinity'; steeped: A, ii, 520–1.

100 *commas:* Edel thought this notable only 'for an abundance of misplaced commas'. Other misapprehensions were that MT wrote love-letters to JCG, and 'cousinly inconsequences' to HJ. Edel, i, 315, 317, 639.

MT to join Jameses in Pomfret: WJ to GH (12 June 1869), *CWJ*, i, 83.

100 *'unconscious'; 'if you could only fall in love' etc.:* MJ to HJ (24 July 1869).
–1 Houghton b MS Am 1093.1.

101 *'a great swell':* HJ to WDH (late 1876/ early 1877), *L(E)*, ii, 97. An early idea of *PL.*

MJ on Elly's match: MJ to HJ (21 Sept 1869). Houghton b MS Am 1093.1 (33).

102 *'a kind & devoted husband':* MT to JCG (29 Aug 1869).

July reply: A letter from MT to JCG on 7 July mentions receiving a letter from HJ the day before, i.e. 6 July. This letter must therefore have been written in late June.

'dearly beloved child': MJ to HJ (24 July 1869). Houghton.

103 *'one marvel':* HJ to HJSr (10 May [1869]), *L(E)*, i, 116.

104 *'noble flights' and 'drop': A*, ii, 283.

'What of . . .' and 'Is Minny . . .': HJ to MJ (Sept 1868). Cited by Edel, i, 313.

105 *'delightful', etc.: A*, ii, 526.

106 *'Mr Gray's office' in MT's letter of 27 June:* HJ altered this part of the letter in his memoir in order to eliminate Gray's name.

Gray's reply: The letter itself has not survived, but MT quotes two phrases from it in her next letter (7 July) to him.

'shook him up': MT to HJ (17 Nov 1869).

'I don't suppose . . .': MT to JCG (29 July 1869).

107 *'far off':* MT to JCG (30 Nov 1869).

'intellectually' unsympathetic: MT to JCG (12 Dec 1869).

'slowly but surely': MT to JCG (7 July 1869).

'You are a sensible man': MT to JCG (29 July 1869).

'priestess': A, ii, 283.

'Let us fearlessly trust . . .': MT to JCG (12 Dec 1869).

'a bit of compromise' and 'being true*':* Ibid.

declared the impossibility of marriage: MT to JCG (29 Aug 1869).

'eternal significance': MT to JCG (29 Aug 1869).

108 *Bishop Blougram:* Robert Browning, 'Bishop Blougram's Apology', from *Men and Women* (1855).

HJ's change to 'seriousness': A, ii, 528.

108 *appalled:* I infer this from a sentence (to JCG, 29 Aug) in which MT argues that, since Elly is not 'appalled', MT should accept the marriage.

Robert Temple's talk: WJ to father (n.d.) from Harvard in the early sixties. Houghton. He had bumped into Temple at the theatre.

Robert Temple begging from GWJ and HJSr: Reported in letters from WJ to HJ (25 Oct and 5 Dec 1869), *CWJ*, i, 114, 129.

'The world forgetting . . .': Alexander Pope, 'Eloisa to Abelard' (1717).

Robert Temple's letter about his sisters: To HJ (17 Sept 1869). Houghton.

109 *'I have written to Minny about her sisters':* HJ to WJ (25 Sept 1869), from Venice, *CWJ*, i, 99.

disturbance and bowel-trouble: Dupee (p. 38) suggests that it is 'logical to assume that James's invalidism, instead of preventing his courtship of Minny, was itself that symptom of some fear of, or scruple against, sexual love on his part . . .'. Dupee is good on remorse ('Did the suspicion that Minny had loved him contribute to his misgivings?'), and gives a more accurate interpretation of MT's letters to HJ than Edel, who does not perceive the depth of feeling conveyed by her light touch nor her fear to impose on James.

'none but the worst news . . .': HJ to WJ (7 Oct 1869), *CWJ*, i, 104–5.

110 *'I blush'; 'dorsal insanity':* WJ to HJ (12 June and 23 Oct 1869), ibid., 84, 82.

'born in Boston': HJ to WJ (25 Sept 1869), *CWJ*, i, 92.

'affliction': WJ to HJ (25 Oct [1869]). Ibid., 113.

'gondolas': MT refers to his comment (presumably, in his Sept letter, written from Venice) in this reply (17 Nov 1869).

111 *'friends':* MT to JCG (4 Oct 1869).

'might go far toward finishing me up': MT to HJ (15 Aug 1869). Houghton.

MT's and HJ's usages of 'sich is life': Ibid. (for MT) and HJ to LB (Apr 1871), *L(E)*, i, 255.

112 *MT's photo.* There are two photos of MT. The recent 'good' and 'melancholy' one was taken in the late summer of 1869, seated in a fringed chair. The other shows her in profile with her hair shorn in 1861 (see above, ch. 3). Both illustrated.

a great deal of living: MT to JCG (21 Nov 1869).

'epoch'; MT and Fanny Dixwell: Ibid.

113 *MT on AJ's snubs:* MT to Ellen Temple Emmet (19 Nov 1869), from Pelham. Houghton b MS Am 1092.9 (4387).

HJSr vs half-brother: This incident has been skilfully uncovered by Habegger in *The Father*, 4. HJSr himself related the incident to Julia Kellog.

HJSr's papers destroyed over three generations: Ibid., 6.

HJSr's letters burnt: KL to Henry (Harry) James III (eldest son of WJ) (n.d.). This happened after HJSr's death in Dec 1882, while AJ was ill in bed. KL tried to remonstrate in vain with Aunt Kate, and AJ was 'grieved'. Houghton b MS Am 1092.10 (113).

'I presume . . .': HJSr, *Harbinger*, vii, 37, cited by Habegger, *The Father*, 5.

114 *'lascivious memories':* Habegger, *The Father*, 7.

114 *'neither reasonable nor consoling':* MT recalled this scene for JCG (25 Jan 1870).

'discordance' and 'absence of intellectual *sympathies':* WJ to HJ (1 Nov 1869), *CWJ*, i, 120.

HJSr on Woman: 'Woman', Houghton bMS Am 1094.8 (72). This is a lecture HJSr devised for the newly formed New England Women's Club at the end of 1868, and which he repeated five times over the course of 1869. He also published a series of articles: 'Is Marriage Holy?' *Atlantic Monthly*, xxv (Mar 1869), 360–8; 'The Woman Thou Gavest Me', *Atlantic Monthly*, xxv (Jan 1870), 66–72; 'The Logic of Marriage and Murder', *Atlantic Monthly*, xxv (June 1870), 744–9. See also his essay 'Spiritual & Moral Freedom', Houghton bMS Am 1094.8 (29).

115 *'Father has been writing . . .':* WJ to HJ (19 Jan 1870), *CWJ*, i, 141.

'a life of the spirit': HJ to Grace Norton (1 Apr 1870), *L(E)*, i, 231–2.

WJ's review of Mill: North American Review, cix (Oct 1869), 556–65, repr. WJ, *Essays, Comments, and Reviews*, ed. I. K. Skrupskelis, as vol. 17 of *The Works of William James* (Cambridge, Mass.: Harvard Univ. Press, 1987), 246–56.

'M. Temple was here . . .': WJ to HJ (5 Dec 1869), *CWJ*, i, 129.

'I rejoice . . .': MH to WJ (27 [Dec 1869]), ibid., 139.

116 *bond:* Alfred Habegger makes a case for WJ's attraction to MT in 'New Light on William James and Minny Temple', *New England Quarterly*, lx:1 (Mar 1987), 28–53.

'sickening introspection . . .': MT to JCG (30 Nov 1869). MT does not mention any names but this is written soon after her visit to the Jameses. Habegger, 'New Light on WJ and MT', 36.

WJ's diary: Houghton bMS Am 1092.9 (4550).

'what if the good gentleman . . .': MT to JCG (25 Jan 1870).

'this Christianity': MT to WJ, n.d. Houghton bMS Am 1092.9 (4387a). Fragment on two sides, the second half of a letter. I deduce this is to WJ, from an empty envelope in the same hand which is postmarked 15 Jan 1870, and from the fact that the letter is in the same vein as that of the second letter written to WJ on 10 February. MT signs herself 'cousin'. In 1990, when I examined the fragment and wrote this source note, I did not know of Habegger's 'New Light on WJ and MT' (which he kindly sent me in 1996): he comes to the same conclusion, p. 40, with plausible speculations, in footnote 25, to the effect that since it is unlikely an empty envelope would have been kept, the missing first half of the letter could have been in the envelope and then destroyed after WJ's death by his wife or by his eldest son, Henry James III, who deposited the James Papers at Harvard.

117 *sent chloral:* Habegger, 'New Light on WJ and MT', has done fascinating detective work on the use of chloral hydrate at this point (Jan 1870) between its first announcement in Sept 1869 (in the *Proceedings of the American Pharmaceutical Association*), as an 'anaesthetic and hypnotic', a

possible substitute for morphine, and the first article on its toxic effects in Mar 1870, the very month of MT's death. Habegger cites J. R. Reynolds, 'The Poisonous Dose of Chloral', *The Practitioner*, iv (Mar 1870), 188–9. Also relevant is John Hughes Bennett, 'On Chloral in Phthisis', *The Practitioner*, iv (May 1870), 262–5.

117 *WJ sent Humboldt:* Simon, *Genuine Reality*, 117–8.

'What a real *person':* MT to JCG (25 Jan 1870).

'a proposal': MT to JCG (30 Nov 1869). Mrs Post is said (*CWJ*, i, 147) to be the daughter of Ellen King James, but this must be an error. Mrs Post's dates are here given as 1819–92. Ellen James's daughters were born in the 1840s.

'I don't remember . . .': MT to JCG (12 Dec 1869).

118 *report of letter from HJ:* MT to JCG (27 Jan 1870).

January decision not to wait in Europe: MJ to AJ on his decision to return home (Jan 1870). Houghton b MS Am 1093.1 (20–31).

'rather the most unpleasant night' and ' "pison" ': MT to JCG (27 Jan 1870).

'the brightest spot in history', etc.: MT to JCG (25 Jan 1870).

'Paganism': MT to JCG (27 Jan 1870).

118–19 *'Dearest Willy . . .':* Incomplete twelve-page letter MT to WJ (10 Feb 1870). Houghton.

120 *'Mrs. Post . . .':* HJ to WJ (13 Feb 1870), *CWJ*, i, 146.

MT, Dr Taylor, and Dr Metcalfe: MT to JCG (16 Feb 1870). (I've wondered if this could possibly be the Dr Taylor who imposed his stupid treatment on AJ in 1866–7. See above, ch. 4).

'open': HJ to WJ (30 Nov 1869), from Rome, *CWJ*, i, 123.

121 *'I'm glad . . .':* HJ to WJ (13 Feb 1870), from Malvern. *CWJ*, i, 146.

'as water unto wine': HJ to AJ (27 Feb 1870), from Malvern. Houghton.

'I was of course . . .': HJ to HJSr (19 Mar 1870), from Malvern, *L(E)*, i, 213.

urged his mother: HJ to MJ (26 Mar 1870), *L(E)*, i, 221. Mrs James's only surviving reply took four pages to discuss digestive ailments before she got to the subject of MT's death, but she had nothing to report beyond a brief and conventional statement of pity.

122 *' "so very nice" ', etc., and 'I revolt':* HJ to WJ (8 Mar 1870), *CWJ*, i, 149.

Chapter 6 'Pure Fellowship'

123 *'dear bright little Minny':* HJ quoted his mother's phrase back to her in a letter (26 Mar 1870), *L(E)*, i, 219, repeated 221. The point about HJ's inflation of this was made by Habegger, *HJ and the 'Woman Business'*, 139.

'absolute defiant' and 'breathing': HJ to MJ (26 Mar 1870), *L(E)*, i, 218, 221.

'promotion'; 'crystal walls': HJ to WJ (29 Mar 1870), *CWJ*, i, 155, 156.

124 'dead – *silent . . .':* HJ to MJ (26 Mar 1870), *L(E)*, i, 221.

'foundations': Ibid.

124 *'but one little dream . . .':* HJ to Grace Norton (1 Apr 1870), *L(E)*, i, 232.
'waking wider & wider . . .': HJ to WJ (29 Mar 1870), *CWJ*, i, 155.
'Twenty years hence . . .': HJ to MJ (26 Mar 1870), *L(E)*, i, 221.
'Twenty years hence . . .': HJ to WJ (29 Mar 1870), *CWJ*, i, 156–7.
'in the tomb', etc.: WJ's Diary (22 Mar 1870). Houghton b MS Am 1092.9 (4550).
HJ's night dream: HJ to MJ (26 Mar 1870), *L(E)*, i, 222: 'It was only the other day, however, that I dreamed of meeting her somewhere this summer with Mrs. Post.'
'In exchange . . .': HJ to WJ (29 Mar 1870), *CWJ*, i, 156.

125 *'what a secret . . .':* HJ to MJ (26 Mar 1870, *L(E)*, i, 221.
'I shall have her forever talking . . .': HJ to WJ, *CWJ*, i, 156.
'looked forward', etc.: HJ to WJ (29 Mar 1870), *CWJ*, i, 154.
'Travelling Companions': *CT*, ii, 1–41. Aziz, in the Introduction to this volume, gives convincing circumstantial evidence for dating this tale May–June 1870, though it was not published until the end of that year (by the *Atlantic*). Not repr. by HJ.

126 *'To have . . .'. HJ to WJ (30 Nov 1869), CWJ*, i, 125.
independence of Cooper: Freddie Baveystock, 'The Romance of Nationalism: Historical Authority in American Literary Culture 1809–1851' (Oxford thesis, 1995).
Edith Wharton's parents: EW, *A Backward Glance* (1936; repr. London: Century Hutchinson, 1987), 62. Travellers of her parents' generation were 'half-resentfully indifferent' to social opportunities abroad. 'It was thought vulgar and snobbish to try to make the acquaintance, in London, Paris or Rome, of people of the class corresponding to their own.'

127 Daisy Miller: HJ, *Selected Short Stories*, ed. Michael Swan (Penguin, 1963), 135–92. To come in *CS*.
Mrs Wister and MT: HJ to WJ (8 Jan [1873]), *CWJ*, i, 188.
'property': In cancelled fragment, p. 355, of *A*, ii. Houghton bMS Eng 1213 (72).
HJ on Middlemarch: *E(AE)*, 958–66. Originally published in *Galaxy* (Mar 1873).

128 *Eton Ascot, etc.: Hawthorne* (1879), repr. *E(AE)*, 315–457.
cool effrontery: Matched fifty years later by his imitator T. S. Eliot when he set out to dominate critical opinion in England.
'a city of shop-fronts': HJ to HJSr (18 Nov 1875), *L(E)*, ii, 6.
HJ's impression of the French: HJ to Katharine Bronson (16 Oct [1882]). MS Rucellai, transcribed by Leon Edel. Edel Papers, McGill. I am indebted to Steven Jobe for passing on his transcriptions of Edel's notes from James letters.
impressed by Turgenev's advice: HJ to WJ (8 Feb 1876), *CWJ*, i, 253.

129 *'wine unto water':* HJ to MJ (while writing *PL*), *The Selected Letters of Henry James*, ed. Leon Edel (NY: Farrar, Straus, 1955), i, 52. Cited by Elizabeth Marie Kennedy, 'Constance Fenimore Woolson and Henry James: Friendship and Reflections' (Yale dissertation, 1983), 127.

129 do: Preface to *PL* (1906). HJ's reminiscent prefaces were composed for the New York edition of his works, 1907–9, and collected as *The Art of the Novel*, ed. R. P. Blackmur, repr. *E(CP)*.

plot of PL *and* Daniel Deronda: Connection noted at once by CFW. See ch. 7 below. Discussed by F. R. Leavis, *The Great Tradition* (1948).

The question . . .': This question intrigued James repeatedly, from the mixed triumph of his Mme de Mauves, the American heroine of 'Mme de Mauves' (1874), to that of Maggie Verver, the American heroine of *The Golden Bowl* (1904).

HJ's responses to Deronda: HJ to AJ (22 Feb 1876), *L(E)*, ii, 29–30; Review, '*Daniel Deronda*: A Conversation', *Atlantic Monthly* (Dec 1876), repr. *E(AE)*, 974–92.

told AJ: (22 Feb 1876), *L(E)*, ii, 29–30.

'*never known a decent woman*': HJ to TSP (2 Nov [1879]). Houghton. Turgenev thought French literature, except for Zola, 'pitifully thin'.

Child: He was a graduate of Merton College, Oxford.

'*a lonely celibate*': HJ to TSP (12 Jan [1877]). Houghton.

130 *Huntington on HJ's changed looks*: Huntington to JH (17 Dec 1877). Brown University. Cited by George Monteiro *Henry James and John Hay: The Record of a Friendship* (Providence, RI: Brown Univ Press, 1965), 20

'*I positively* suck . . .': HJ to WJ (28 Feb 1877), *CWJ*, i, 281.

use of Mudie's: HJ to TSP (12 Jan [1877]). Houghton b MS Am 1094.5 (21).

131 '*fantastic immoralities*': HJ to AJ (25 Apr 1879) *L(E)*, ii, 288. He had been invited to Posilippo, near Naples, by a Russian aristocrat called Zhukovsky whom he had met through Turgenev.

'*with open-eyed desire*': 'Travelling Companions', *CT*, ii, 4.

'*She is very open to instruction*': Adams to Gaskell (26 Mar 1872), *Selected Letters of Henry Adams*, ed. Newton Arvin (NY: Farrar, Straus, 1951), 68.

132 '*superb*': HJ to AJ (17 Feb 1878), *L(E)*, ii, 158.

AJ's response to WJ's marriage; AJ and KL: Simon, 182.

133 *absence of intimacy:* In August 1877, he said he had formed 'no intimacies – not even any close acquaintances'. And again, 'I have made no intimate friends here at all, but have made a good many that are not intimate . . .', he told Charles Eliot Norton (17 Nov 1878), *L(E)*, ii, 197.

'*an outsider*': HJ to WJ (1 May 1878), *CWJ*, i, 300–1.

Emerson and HJ: HJ to Mrs Andrew (Habegger suggests that this could be the wife of the governor of Massachusetts) (19 Feb [1872]). Berg. He speaks of 'going down to Emerson to morrow [sic] to read my paper to his family, and I am too hoarse to do so'. HJSr said that Emerson was an admirer of Henry junior's letters from Europe during 1869 which the proud father pressed on his friend. Earlier, he had given Emerson some of the early tales to read, on which Emerson commented in that politely cordial tone of writers when they are compelled to read something they can't refuse.

134 '*the most enduring . . .*': Cited by Simon, 235.

134 *'a pious fiction':* HJ to MJ (18 Jan 1879), *L(E)*, ii, 212.
'hidden': WJ to AHJ (19 July 1889), cited by Simon, 224.
Miss Mary Peabody: Her proper identity has been recently discovered by Alfred Habegger, 'Mary Codman Peabody, Boston Conscientiousness, and "An International Episode"', *Henry James Review*, xiii (1992), 229–34. Until then she was believed to be Miss Elizabeth Palmer Peabody, the well-known Boston reformer who was a sister-in-law of Hawthorne and model for Miss Birdseye in *The Bostonians* (1886).
'quite in the Boston manner' and 'I know what I am about . . .': HJ to WJ (1 May 1878), *CWJ*, i, 300–1. HJ's pleasure in the 'native finesse and animation of the American female mind', exemplified by Miss Peabody and her five friends, may have contributed to the character of Bessie Alden in 'An International Episode', which he completed in July 1878. It was published in the *Cornhill* in Dec 1878–Jan 1879.
'London dinners . . .': 'The Death of the Lion' (1894), *CS*, iv, 356–92.
'tenderness' and 'moral portrait painter': HJ to Norton (17 Nov [1878]), *L(E)*, ii, 194.
'The great G.E. . . .': HJ to WJ (1 May 1878), *CWJ*, i, 301.

135 *'species of . . . invalids':* HJ to MJ (13 Oct 1869), from Florence, *L(E)*, i, 152.
'crepuscular' midwinter: HJ to Grace Norton (21 Dec 1879), *L(E)*, ii, 261.
'the shadow . . .': 'The Old Order' (1917), *Collected Essays* i, ed. Leonard Woolf (London: Hogarth, 1966), 270.
The Europeans*: Novels 1871–1880* (NY: The Library of America, 1983).

136 *Daisy's attachment to Winterbourne:* This reading of the novella, emphasising the implication of Winterbourne in Daisy's death, derives from a class I gave at Columbia University in the spring semester, 1976. HJ explained to the English novelist Eliza Lynn Linton in August 1880 (*L(E)*, ii, 303–4) that the 'keynote of her conduct is, of course, that she has a little sentiment about Winterbourne, that she believes to be quite unreciprocated – conscious as she was only of his protesting attitude'.
'The Pension Beaurepas': An International Episode and Other Stories, ed S. Gorley Putt (Harmondsworth: Penguin, 1985), 89–144.

137 *'Harry James . . .':* WDH to James Russell Lowell, (22 June 1879), *Life in Letters of WDH*, 271
price of failure: Ronald Bush, 'Changing His Mind About How to Do a Girl In: Poetry, Narrative, and Gender in the Revisions of HJ's Daisy Miller', *Letterature d'America: Revista Trimestrale*, xiv:5 (1994), 33–52.
slights of the James family: Ronald Bush has noted that Winterbourne was a native of the James family. He also links Winterbourne's voyeurism with that of Ralph Touchett in *PL*. Ibid.

138 *'You don't mind . . .':* MT to HJ (3 June 1869). Houghton b MS Am 1092.9 (4387).
'sense for what was English in life': *A*, ii, 520.
'Never': 'An International Episode', ch. 3, in *An International Episode and Other Stories*, 40.

139 *'irritable' intelligence; 'reckless' impatience:* Ibid., ch. 3; *A*, ii, 509.

139 *'divinely restless':* HJ told Grace Norton that MT was 'a divinely restless spirit' (1 Apr 1870), *L(E)*, i, 231.

Lambeth a trial-run for Warburton: Philip Horne, *Henry James and Revision* (Oxford: Clarendon, 1990), 199.

conceived PL*:* HJ's first mention of *PL* is in a letter to WDH (24 Oct 1876), *L(E)*, ii, 72.

'an aching fragment': HJ to WDH (17 June 1879), *L(E)*, ii, 244.

'I had [MT] in mind': HJ to Grace Norton (28 Dec 1880), *L(E)*, ii, 324.

'I am enclosing . . .': Helena de Kay Gilder to Mary Hallock Foote (11 Nov 1914). Gilder Papers.

140 *grasp of a single character:* HJ, Preface to *PL* See Alexis de Tocqueville, *Democracy in America*, trans. George Lawrence, ed. J. P. Mayer (1966; repr. NY: Doubleday Anchor 1969), 592–4, 602–3, for an American social context which fits HJ's idea of Isabel.

'a grande nature': HJ to WDH (2 Feb 1877), *L(E)*, ii, 97.

'that exquisite Bellosguardo': *N*, 219. Recalled in Boston (25 Nov 1881). I added '[and]' to the printed text because the Hotel he mentions was in town on the river.

'He wondered': *PL*, ch. 7.

'the door was fastened . . .': *PL*, ch. 7. This chapter has a long and highly original analysis of Isabel in terms of undefined womanhood.

what Isabel might become: Laura Miller, 'Henry James: Losing It at the Movies', Bookend, *New York Times Book Review* (Jan 1997), 31. A perceptive reader suggests that 'the driving force in James's novel isn't a character'. It is 'the idea of Isabel Archer: who she is, yes, but more important, who she might become . . .'.

141 *'I . . . I . . . I . . .':* *PL*, ch. 13.

'she liked his command': *PL*, ch. 3

Goodwood and Gray: Alfred Habegger, 'Henry James's Rewriting of Minny Temple's Letters', *American Literature*, lviii (1986), 166. Restated, stressing the wooden quality of both Gray and Goodwood, in 'The Fatherless Heroine and the Filial Son', *New Essays on 'The Portrait of a Lady'* (Cambridge Univ Press, 1990), 64.

revised version: For the New York edition of HJ's novels (1908). His autograph revisions to the 1881 edition are in Houghton S 1237.17.

'ladylike and patient': *PL*, ch. 14.

'Who was she . . .': *PL*, ch. 12.

'The liberty of falling in love . . .': *PL*, ch. 5.

'a sort of comfort': *PL*, ch. 33.

'he made her feel . . .': *PL*, ch. 42.

142 *'her conversation':* *PL*, ch. 7.

'prosaic', etc.: *PL*, ch. 15.

'a sort of vision': *PL*, ch. 34.

'adventure': Preface to *PL*.

'experiment of nature': HJ to WJ (29 Mar 1870), *CWJ*, i, 153.

143 *'larger qualities':* HJ's outline for the last long section (late Dec 1880–early Jan 1881), *N*, 14.

serpent: PL, ch. 42.

deathbed exchange: PL, ch. 54. Ralph's phrase, 'ground in the very mill of the conventional', appears in the outline, op. cit., *N*, 13.

ghostly visitation: PL, ch. 55.

145 *'You are too fond of your liberty': PL*, ch. 7.

final scene: PL, ch. 55.

'I don't know . . .': PL, ch. 19.

146 *ethos of the James family:* I'm grateful to Gila Bercovitch, editor in chief of the Library of America, who suggested this in discussion, Saranac Lake, NY (summer 1988).

'the integrity of the private mind': Ralph Waldo Emerson, 'Self-Reliance' (1841).

'The ladies will save us': PL, ch. 1.

serial: It ran in England in *Macmillan's magazine* (Oct 1880–Nov 1881) a month ahead of the *Atlantic* in America (Nov 1880–Dec 1881). Grace Norton was therefore responding to the first two instalments (the Dec one would have come out early) when she wrote to HJ, invoking a reply, in late Dec 1880.

147 *'completion':* HJ to Grace Norton (28 Dec 1880), *L(E)*, ii, 324. Horne, in *HJ and Revision*, does acknowledge that there is some 'evasion' but sees it in artistic rather than biographical terms: 'a pragmatic veering off from too big a statement' about the process of art. He rightly sees Isabel as 'a creative extension and continuation' of MT (p. 222) and gives as an example Isabel's vision of a 'very straight path' compared with HJ's impression of MT 'as of a child struggling with her ignorance in a sort of pathless desert of the genial and the casual' (*A*, ii, 514). Miranda Seymour, *A Ring of Conspirators: Henry James and His Literary Circle* 1895–1915 (London: Hodder, 1988), 170, comments similarly: through Isabel Archer, 'Minnie's life was extended'. Isabel was her 'surrogate' travelling to Europe. The creatively stimulating notion of the incompletion of MT appeared immediately on her death in HJ's letters of late March 1870.

made it public: Preface to *PL*, and again in *A*, ii, 522.

silver plate: PL, ch. 35.

Chapter 7 Meeting Miss Grief

148 *chapter title:* I owe this to Joan Weimer: a provisional title for her memoir involving CFW, *Back Talk: Teaching Lost Selves to Speak* (NY: Random House, 1994). She retained the title for ch. 14.

storm: CFW to brother-in-law Samuel Livingstone Mather (24 Nov 1879), Benedict, ii, 151–2.

'in its quietest part' etc.: PL, from last sentence of ch. 33.

148 *'end':* Recalled by CFW to HJ (30 Aug [1882]) Houghton b MS Am 1094 (496–498a). I quote here and below from the manuscript letters to HJ. The letters are from Sorrento (begun 12 Feb 1882), 19 pages; Dresden (30 Aug 1882), 12 pages; Venice (7 May 1883), 20 pages; and Venice (24 May 1883), 5 pages. Three of the four, therefore, are very long. There is a transcription (with a few inaccuracies) in an appendix to *L(E)*, iii, 253–61.

'desolate . . .': CFW to HJ (12 Feb 1882). The context is the death of HJ's mother.

depression: CFW to Edmund Clarence Stedman (23 July 1876), from Cooperstown. Stedman Papers, Manuscripts and Rare Books, Butler Library, Columbia University.

149 *Bone:* Constance Mather Bishop's Cuttings Book. Privately owned by Molly Mather Anderson.

soldier: Zeph Spaulding, who became a colonel in the Union Army, according to Moore, *CFW*, 23.

marked by the Civil War: CFW to the Mathers, from Egypt (c.1890).

biography of Lee: The author was an anonymous Virginian. *General Robert E. Lee: The Christian Soldier* (Philadelphia: Claxton, Remsen & Haffelfinger; Richmond: Woodhouse & Parham, 1873). Interestingly, the book appears to be a joint product of Northern and Southern publishing houses. CFW's copy, with its copious notes and dated in her hand 'Charleston. Nov 14th 1873', is in Rollins.

'I cannot even now . . .': CFW to ECS (1 Oct [1876]). Stedman Papers, Columbia.

CFW on the battlefields: CFW to 'Elizabeth' (Mrs Samuel Livingstone Mather of Cleveland, second wife following Georgiana Woolson's death) (4 Dec [1874]) from St Augustine, Florida. Rollins. Quoted from MS. Printed in Benedict, iii, 751–2, without date or address, and with the recipient wrongly identified as Mrs Mather's husband. Some crucial sentences are omitted, and there are some inaccuracies of transcription.

151 *'marching through Georgia':* Civil War song.

dancing crane: East Angels (1886), set in St Augustine.

'wild freedom', etc.: CFW to Mrs Washburn (n.d.), Benedict, iii, 740.

seeking snakes: CFW to SM (n.d.), Benedict, ii, 23.

152 *afraid of women:* CFW to ECS (28 Sept [1874]). Stedman Papers, Columbia. She met Stedman in St Augustine in the spring of 1874.

'same old grandiloquence': CFW to H. H. Boyesen (9 Aug, n.y.). Barrett Library, Univ. of Virginia: 7331-a Barrett-Woolson.

'Do you not think. . . ?': CFW to ECS (23 July 1876), from Cooperstown. Stedman Papers, Columbia.

153 *somewhat misleading:* Numerous critics have found it easy to denigrate her on the grounds of the minutiae of realism. One influential instance was in Edel, ii, 412, who speaks of her 'tiny brush-strokes' which showed her 'neatness, as well as her limitations'.

153 *'Up in the Blue Ridge': Rodman the Keeper: Southern Sketches*, repr. The American Short Story Series: 87 (NY: Garrett Press, 1969).

Charlotte Brontë and George Eliot: CFW to ECS (28 Sept 1874). Stedman Papers, Columbia. She also mentions the influence of George Sand.

Roxana: 'St Clair Flats'. See above, ch. 2.

Marion Manning: 'Bro' in *Rodman the Keeper.*

Miss 'Jonah': 'Ballast Island', *Appleton's Journal*, ix:223 (28 June 1873), 833–9. See Victoria Brehm, 'Island Fortress: The Landscape of the Imagination', *Critical Essays on CFW*, ed. Cheryl B. Torsney (NY: G.K. Hall, 1992), 172–86, and Sharon L. Dean, *CFW: Homeward Bound* (Knoxville, Tenn.: Univ. of Tennessee Press, 1995), 104.

154 *'Miss Vedder': Harper's Magazine* (Mar 1879). Uncollected.

'Miss Grief': WAWE, 248–69.

inner exile: Weimer points to this in the title of her selection.

'infesting': Cited by Dean, 217.

feared her publishers: Cheryl Torsney, talk on 'CFW and her Publishers', Conference on Mackinac Island (Oct 1996).

separate category from 'Local Color': CFW to Charles Scribner's Sons (2 Feb [1879–80]). Scribner's Archive: box 148 (folder on 'Stories by American Authors'). Special Collections, Princeton University Library. When an anthologist wished to collect 'Miss Grief', CFW wrote to say that 'Miss Vedder' could be an alternative, suggesting that to her mind these were stories of the same kind. It is possible that she hoped the anthologist might decide to print them together.

Miss Gardis: In 'Old Gardiston' (1876), *Rodman the Keeper* and *WAWE.*

156 *black grenadine; 'swell'; 'abashed'; fear; 'a very comfortable lot to be a Harper':* CFW to ECS (23 July 1876), from Cooperstown. Stedman Papers, Columbia.

'why did you find fault . . .': Ibid.

157 *'iron-men':* Ibid.

first collection: Castle Nowhere: Lake Country Sketches, repr. The American Short Story Series: 86 (New York: Garrett Press, 1969).

CFW's parodies of Cooper: Linn Cary Mehta, who is studying the women in the family. See above, ch. 2. In conversation in Oxford (15 June 1996).

'disappointed': CFW to ESC (23 July 1876). Stedman Papers, Columbia.

CFW's review of The Europeans: *Atlantic Monthly*, xliii (Jan 1879), 106–8, repr. *Critical Essays on CFW*, ed. Torsney, 70–3. Repr. *Henry James: The Critical Heritage*, ed. Roger Gard (London: Routledge, 1968), 66–9.

'Benvolio': Galaxy, repr. *CT*, iii, 23–59.

memento of Benvolio: CFW to HJ (7 May 1883).

'Nobody knows . . .': Ibid.

photo of HJ wearing tie pin: Edel, iii, 31.

158 *'the sanctuary . . .':* In her story of Miss 'Jonah', 'Ballast Island', op. cit.

'shadowed waters' and 'seldom . . .': 'The Flower in the Snow', *Galaxy*, xvii (Jan 1874), 76–85.

158 *'armor against suffering':* Appropriated from Miss Jonah.

159 *Leslie Pell-Clarke and Swanswick.* Le Clair, 294–5.

'a picture of blooming composure': CFW to HJ (30 Aug 1882).

HJ's appearance: CFW to Mrs Crowell (n.d.), Benedict, ii, 184–9.

'censorious and cynical': HJ's admission to Mrs Humphry Ward (9 Dec 1884), *L(E)*, iii, 59.

'shadowy': The word used by Edmund Gosse, one of the few who had visited HJ in his writing-room in his earlier years in London who were still alive after his death, in a perceptive piece in the *London Mercury*, i, (1920), 678–80, repr. *Henry James: Interviews and Recollections*, ed. Norman Page (London: Macmillan, 1984), 9. Gosse's memories suggest that the HJ of the early eighties was stranger and much quieter in manner than the facially exposed, voluble Master of the last years, most clearly remembered in the next generation.

'unpretending': CFW to Mrs Crowell (n.d.), Benedict, ii, 184–9.

HJ very English: CFW to nephew, SM (n.d.), ibid., ii, 192.

steel: CFW to Mrs Crowell (n.d.), ibid., ii, 184–9.

159–60 *CFW's appearance and manner:* 'CFW: Her Early Cleveland Days, her Home There and her Friends', *Cleveland Herald* (n.d.); Arthur Stedman, 'CFW', *The Book Buyer*, vi:9 (Oct 1889); ECS, 'CFW' (interview a day after her death) (28 Jan 1894). All in Constance Mather Bishop's Cuttings Book. Privately owned by Molly Mather Anderson.

'I cannot see . . .': CFW in Cooperstown to ECS in NY (1 Oct [1876]). Stedman Papers, Columbia.

paintings seen by CFW in Florence: Information derived from marginalia in her copy of a French *Catalogue de la R. Galerie de Florence* (Florence, 1878), dated March 1880 in CFW's hand on the title page, with another date 'Dec. 1880' added to mark a later visit. Rollins.

Giotto beyond her: CFW to Mrs Crowell (n.d.), Benedict, ii, 186.

'He has been so much in Italy . . .': CFW to SM (n.d.), quoted in ibid., ii, 192.

visits to the Duomo and the nudes: CFW to Mrs Crowell (n.d.), ibid., ii, 184–9.

161 *'that underworld . . .':* See ch. 7 (on HJ) in Mrs (Mary Augusta) Humphry Ward, *A Writer's Recollections*, ii (NY: Harper; London, 1918), 196–7, 201.

'intense': HJ to Catherine Walsh ('Aunti Kate'). Cited by Edel, ii, 418.

HJ's way of conveying learning: Mrs Humphry Ward, op. cit.

talk 'the most feminine of cities': HJ to HJSr (14 Jan 1870), *L(E)*, i, 188–9.

'radiant' spring: HJ to Charles Eliot Norton (31 Mar 1880), *L(E)*, ii, 279.

162 *'blissfully':* HJ to WJ (9 May 1880). Houghton.

'I am very impressionable' and 'I turn my head . . .' etc.: A mutilated letter (c.1882) in two fragments (bits of pp. 7 and 8), pasted into a book called *Florence* by Augustus J. C. Hare (London: Smith Elder, 1884). CFW's copy was bought from a Florentine bookseller. Rollins. (The mutilation is likely to have been the work of Clare Benedict, through whose hands a

large collection of CFW memorabilia passed to Rollins College. The second quote is printed in Benedict, ii, 31: a letter to G. Pomeroy Keese.)

162 *'to wander...'*: 'Henry Harland' (1898), *E(AE)*, 282–8.

a thirsty person: PL, ch. 31.

'make one's life a work of art': PL, ch. 29.

Buonarroti gallery, Riccardi palace, Bacchus by Michelangelo, and 'grotesque' fresco: Marginalia (including dates: 'May 1880') in French edition of Baedeker, *L'Italie Centrale*, 6th edn (1880), 359, 368, 373. Her Baedekers are crammed with quotations in every available space. Rollins.

Ruskin's ladders: CFW's notes on *The Stones of Venice*, in Benedict, ii, 88.

hate was enlivening: CFW to KL (Sept 1890) from Cheltenham. Beverly Historical Society.

'Bellosguardo': Benedict, ii, 181–2.

163 *'pretty well':* CFW to Mrs Crowell (n.d.), Benedict, ii, 184–9.

'I see no one...': HJ to AJ (25 Apr 1880), *L(E)*, ii, 288.

164 *'perfect lady':* HJ to Catherine Walsh (Aunt Kate) (3 May 1880). Cited by Edel, ii, 418.

'glamour' of Cooper: A, ii, 303–4.

'secret connections' and Cooper: 'A Letter to Mr Howells', *North American Review* (Apr 1912), repr. *E(AE)*, 510.

'Fenimore': Letter from CFW to HJ early in 1882 refers to his addressing her as 'Miss Woolson' (though privately he calls her 'Constance', at once, in the letter to AJ; he called her 'Fenimore' from 1886 in letters to the Bootts).

'We shall make a George Washington...': CFW to HJ (30 Aug 1882).

'Cleveland, Ohio': CFW quotes this back to HJ (7 May 1883).

'"inspirational" headland': CFW to HJ (12 Feb 1882).

'what I missed', etc.: A, ii, 460–1.

second volume: HJ comments on it in his 1887 essay 'Miss Woolson', *E(AE)*, 639–49. Also, *WAWE*, 270–9.

165 *'dry, still eyes':* 'In the Cotton Country', *WAWE*, 133–48. Discussed in Joan Weimer, 'Women Artists as Exiles in the Fiction of CFW', *Legacy* (1986), 5–6.

Maumee: CFW to HJ (12 Feb 1882).

adjusted to her deafness: HJ was to mention it in future only as a problem for her or for Boott meeting her.

rain, Bootts, and 'nothing': HJ to HJSr (14 May 1880) from Florence, and HJ to MJ (6 June 1880) from London. Houghton b MS Am 1094 (1751–1923).

166 *'divine':* CFW to HJ (12 Feb 1882).

'the deeper psychology': HJ, *Hawthorne*, ch. 3, repr. *The Shock of Recognition*, 476 and *E(AE)*, 368.

'the Unpardonable Sin': See Hawthorne's tales 'Ethan Brand', 'Young Goodman Brown', and 'The Minister's Black Veil'. It is the sin of Young Goodman Brown, who has a revelation of evil in the New England woods which shuts him off from all humanity including Faith his wife. And it is

the sin of a New England minister who lives and dies behind a veil that is a barrier between him and his congregation including the woman who is engaged to him. See also the portrait of Chillingworth in *The Scarlet Letter*.

166 *'the subject of a psychological experiment':* 'Ethan Brand'.

'a quiet, clever . . . man': PL, ch 26.

166 *'. . . How perfectly . . .', and everything below on* PL: CFW to HJ (12 Feb –7 1882).

168 *'Oh,* I *never copy':* This exchange and her feelings recollected in CFW to HJ (30 Aug 1882).

wrote every bit of PL *twice: N*, 220.

'master of [all the] situations': CFW to HJ (30 Aug 1882).

'cross' etc.: CFW to HJ (30 Aug 1882).

169 *'proud salmon of the pond':* CFW to HJ (12 Feb 1882).

'spoiled': CFWto HJ (7 May 1883).

'good': CFW to HJ (late Feb 1882).

'the atmosphere . . .': CFW to HJ (7 May 1883).

Anne: Serialised from Dec 1880. Book appeared in 1882.

'I am sorry . . .', etc.: CFW to HJ (30 Aug 1882).

170 *'incorruptible':* CFW to HJ (30 Aug 1882).

'no women': HJ to TSP (25 Mar 1864), *L(E)*, i, 49.

'Women aren't literary . . .': HJ to Edgar Fawcett (7 June 1891), brushing off an attempt to introduce him to a writer called Mrs Cruger. Princeton: Robert H. Taylor Collection (RTC 01), Box: File Cabinet; Folder: HJ.

'demoniac' and 'sweet Miss Hilliard': WJ scrawled on a letter from HJ (28 June 1877), *CWJ*, i, 291: 'Do you notice the demoniac way in which he speaks of the sweet Miss Hilliard?'

'the hen-sex': HJ to Charles Eliot Norton (31 Mar 1880), *L(E)*, ii, 280.

'. . . Virgin novelist': H to HJSr (25 Mar 1878), *L(E)*, ii, 159.

'I do not come in . . .': CFW to HJ (12 Feb 1882).

'elderly': CFW to HJ (7 May 1883), from Venice.

171 Moods: Reviewed *E(AE)*, 189–95.

'woman, after all . . .': CFW to HJ (12 Feb 1882).

'any woman': HJ to AJ (30 Jan 1881), *L(E)*, ii, 337.

'I'm Nobody!': The Complete Poems of Emily Dickinson (London: Faber, 1975), no. 288.

'sacrifice', etc.: CFW to HJ (24 Apr 1883), *Books at Brown*, 40–1.

172 *resolved not to marry:* HJ to Grace Norton (7 Nov 1880), *L(E)*, ii, 314. (HJ to WJ (29 May 1878), *CWJ*, i, 303 on the occasion of WJ's engagement, takes a more benign view as that occasion demanded.)

'the sweet young American wife', etc.: CFW to HJ (30 Aug 1882).

erudite women: HJ to WJ (26 July 1874), *CWJ*, i, 242.

'A Florentine Experiment': Dorothy and Other Italian Stories (1896; repr. 1899), 122–86. Copy in Rollins. The biographical bases noted by Edel, ch. entitled 'Fenimore' in *The Conquest of London*, and *L(E)*, ii, note on p.

289: meetings with HJ are recounted (in light disguise) in her tale 'A Florentine Experiment'.

174 *CFW at Coppet:* CFW to J. Bone, quoted in 'With and without Glasses', *Cleveland Plain Dealer* (17 Feb 1894), an obituary article collected in Constance Mather Bishop's Cuttings Book, privately owned by Molly Mather Anderson.

'At the Château of Corinne': Eventually published in *Harper's New Monthly Magazine* (Oct 1887), repr. *Dorothy and Other Italian Stories* (1896), repr. *WAWE*, 211–47. See Torsney for discussion of the importance of de Staël for women writers. She argues that as the nineteenth century identified de Staël with Corinne, so CFW identified with Winthrop. *CFW: The Grief of Artistry*, 87–107.

175 *'the American Corinne' in* PL: chs 26, 35, and 44.

Rome 'infested': HJ to MJ from Genoa (16 Mar 1881), *L(E)*, ii, 349.

176 *'sky-parlor':* CFW to HJ (7 May 1883).

'3 bright rooms' and 'obstinately refusing': CFW to WDH (4 May [1881]), from Rome. One of six letters to WDH. Houghton b MS Am 1784 (558).

'sputtering kettle': CFW to HJ (7 May 1883).

'Rest easy . . .': CFW to HJ (12 Feb 1882).

Vittoria Colonna: Marginalia in CFW's Baedeker, *L'Italie Centrale*, 148. Rollins. *PL*, ch. 24.

HJ's plans, as told to CFW in Rome (Apr 1882): CFW to HJ (7 May 83).

'The Figure in the Carpet': (1896), repr. *CS*, iv, 572–608.

177 *'I wonder if you will understand me . . .':* CFW to HJ (7 May 1883).

'resource': (25 Nov 1881), *N*, 222.

Campagna with Mrs V.R.: Ibid.

178 *'unimportant', 'terrible word', and 'limited':* CFW to HJ (12 Feb 1882).

'The Street of the Hyacinth': Repr. *The Front Yard and Other Italian Stories* (1895), repr. *WAWE*, 170–210. For the relation to HJ see Torsney, *CFW: The Grief of Artistry*, 108–26; Joanne Vickers, 'Woolson's Response to James: The Vindication of the American Heroine', *Women's Studies*, xviii (1990), 287–94; and Dean, *CFW: Homeward Bound*, 181–5. Joanne Skoller pointed out the naming of 'Faith' in a tradition of conquest, at a conference on CFW at Rollins College in February 1995.

180 *Mrs Bronson:* Michael Meredith (ed.) *More Than Friend: The Letters of Robert Browning to Katharine de Kay Bronson* (Winfield, Kansas: Wedgestone, 1985), xxxii. The Introduction provides a fascinating portrait of Mrs Bronson and her Venetian activities. I am indebted to Mr Gilder Palmer, grandson of Helena de Kay Gilder and a great-nephew of Katharine de Kay Bronson, for the loan of his copy.

rooms and view of the lagoon: HJ to ECS (20 Apr 1882). Berg. See also *N*, 221.

Curtises settling into the Palazzo Barbaro: HJ to Mrs Bronson (19 July 1881), *L(E)*, ii, 359. The Curtises did not buy the palazzo till 1885.

181 '"*amiable elements*"': CFW quoted this back to HJ (12 Feb 1882). This previous letter to HJ in America has not survived.

'Death is not terrible . . .': CFW to HJ (12 Feb 1882). The context is the recent death of MJ.

'It is under lock and key': CFW to HJ (30 Aug 1882).

182 *CFW's exertions in July–Aug 1882:* She was due to begin serialising her second novel, *For the Major* (published in book form in 1883).

CFW on Daisy Miller: CFW to HJ (30 Aug 1882). From Dresden, where CFW had gone to recuperate after her exertions.

'It was all for you . . .': Daisy Miller: A Comedy in Three Acts (Boston: Osgood, 1883), 185. Copy in Special Collections, Butler Library, Columbia University.

Winterbourne like a German stove: Ibid., 81.

183 *HJ's sympathetic reply:* This letter was of course destroyed, but something of its content is reflected in CFW's reply.

'Pray do me the favour . . .': CFW to HJ (30 Aug 1882). She recalls 'poor little Désirée' in *Fromont jeune et Risler aîné* (1874) by Alphonse Daudet, a novelist both CFW and HJ admired. HJ had recently published an article on Daudet in the *Atlantic Monthly* (June 1882). The published version has two errors. Firstly, the word 'favour' is printed in italics as though it were emphasised, which gives the wrong impression. In the actual letter CFW has used the American spelling 'favor,' then underlines his English usage – pointing to his affectation: 'fav*our*'. Secondly, the transcription does not indicate a break when CFW begins the letter anew from Cologne on 3 Sept: 'I have seen the Rhine . . .'.

memorabilia: NYHA at Cooperstown – see below, ch. 10.

184 *incident in NY harbour:* Cooper, *Gleanings in Europe: France*, 5–6, cited by David M. Kalstone, 'The Discovery of America: James Fenimore Cooper and Henry James as Critics' a *summa cum laude* thesis (1954). Harvard Archives, Pusey Library.

JH's poem: Harper's, viii (18 June 1864), 386. Set to music in 1917.

CFW and King: Patricia O'Toole, *The Five of Hearts: An Intimate Portrait of Henry Adams and His Friends 1880–1918* (NY: Clarkson Potter, 1990), 271–2. I am grateful to Dr Kathleen Reich for sending this to me.

'little tour': For travel book, *A Little Tour of France* (1884), repr. *T(C)*.

185 *'miserable':* AHJ to WJ (1 Jan 1883), correspondence, cited by Simon, 181.

verbal 'picture' and 'going': CFW quotes these words back to HJ (7 May 1883).

CFW's rooms in the Gritti: probably Suite 310 in the present Gritti Hotel.

186 *'involuted' hall:* Recalls the sexual imagery of the labyrinth in 'St Clair Flats'. See ch. 2 above. CFW to HJ (7 May 1883). Quoted from the original letter, which differs in minor details from the Edel transcription.

forgot 'troubles': CFW reminiscing to Mrs Howells (15 July [1884]). Houghton. The Howells family had been in Venice at the same time.

HJ, 'Venice': Written in the spring of 1881, when HJ was living in Venice while he completed *PL*. Published (Nov 1882), *Century*, repr. *T(C)*, 287–313.

186 *'I can't begin to tell you...', etc.*: CFW to HJ (7 May 1883).

187 *'If you will only care...'*: CFW to HJ (24 May 1883).

188 *'You could not possibly...'*: CFW to HJ (7 May 1883).

George Eliot and Turgenev dead: Eliot died in 1880, and Turgenev recently, in 1883.

'I mean to "quit"...': HJ to TSP (24 Jan 1881), *L(E)*, ii, 335.

'new era': HJ to Grace Norton (19 Jan 1884), *L(E)*, iii, 21.

189 *Balzac:* HJ to Grace Norton (4 Mar 1885), *L(E)*, iii, 76: 'Do like the Bostonians, dear Grace; it is something like Balzac!!!'

HJ denied using Miss Peabody: HJ to WJ (14 and 15 Feb 1885), *CWJ*, ii, 7–11.

three long novels of the 1880s: The Bostonians (1886), *The Princess Casamassima* (1886), and *The Tragic Muse* (1889).

'distinguished friend': HJ to John Hay (24 Dec 1886). *L(E)*, iii, 153.

Viola and Rosalind: Shakespeare's heroines in *Twelfth Night* and *As You Like It*.

190 *'And now of course...'*: CFW to HJ (12 Feb 1882).

'the riddle': CFW to HJ (7 May 1883).

'I do'nt know that you do...': CFW to HJ (30 Aug 1882).

'sin': CFW to HJ (7 May 1883).

'You may be what you please...': CFW to HJ (7 May 1883).

'my true country...': CFW to HJ (7 May 1883).

191 *co-creators:* The traditional view, stated by John D. Kern, *CFW: Literary Pioneer* (Philadelphia: Univ. of Pennsylvania Press, 1934) 178, is that CFW 'was more greatly indebted to [James] than he to her, even though there is no direct evidence of indebtedness on either side'.

Chapter 8 Unmarried Lives

192 *the usual conclusion:* Edel, iii.

'The Costanza': HJ to LB (14 Oct 1883 and 2 June 1884), *L(E)*, iii, 10, 44. Cited Edel, iii, 24.

'The Littératrice': HJ to LB (11 Dec 1883), *L(E)*, iii, 18. Edel, iii, 24.

even her: HJ to LB (11 Dec 1883), *L(E)*, iii, 18.

'the Rensellina' and 'The Realist': HJ to LB (11 Dec [1883]; [2 June] 1884), *L(E)*, iii, 18, 44. Edel speculates if 'The Realist' could be Vernon Lee, but two clues link her with 'the Rensellina', apart from the similarity in sound of the code names: one is that 'the Rensellina' is to settle in Half Moon Street (near James), and a few months later he is dismayed that 'The Realist' has moved yet closer than Half Moon Street into his own street. The other clue is his repeated relief that 'the Rensellina'/'The Realist' and CFW have not met.

'resource', 'infinite charity': see above, ch. 7.

193 *conquer or die:* HJ to Katharine Bronson (6 June [1886]), Edel's transcription from Ms Rucellai, Edel Papers, McGill University Library, Montreal. I am grateful to Steven H. Jobe for his transcriptions of certain HJ letters transcribed or noted by Edel, where the locations of the originals are at present unknown.

'the devouring sex' and 'the devoured': HJ to FB (15 Aug 1886), *L(E)*, iii, 131.

'perfect lady': see above, ch. 7, p. 164.

'conservative': HJ, 'Miss Woolson' (1887) repr. *Partial Portraits* (1888). *WAWE*, 270–9.

'worthy': CFW to KL (Aug/Sept 1890). Beverly Historical Society. Quoted in full, below, ch. 9, p. 237.

'I see her at discreet intervals': HJ to WDH (21 Feb 1884), *L(E)*, iii, 28. Cited Edel, iii, 31–2.

innovative essay on the art of fiction: 'The Art of Fiction', *Longman's Magazine* (1884), HJ's best essay on fiction as well as his clearest analysis of his contribution to the genre. HJ commented angrily in a letter to TSP (26 Sept 1884), cited in Harlow's biography, 53, on the lack of response to this essay, which he interpreted as a failure on the part of the English to take an interest in a theory of the novel.

194 *cause of Charley's death:* Torsney suggests he may have committed suicide.

took morphine: Discovered by Weimer. *Back Talk*, 260, cites a microfilm of letters concerning Charley Woolson which I was unable to find in WRHS in Aug 1994. The location she gives is Drawer 34.3: it was not there, and the librarians could not say where it now was. I am grateful to Joan Weimer for sending me a photocopy of her transcription.

'suffering so piteous . . .': CFW to SM (16 Jan 1884). WRHS MSS 3735: CFW letters 1882–89.

fifteen years: Weimer, *Back Talk*, 260.

'different air': Hannah Woolson to her grandson SM (25 July 1878). WRHS MS 3735, container 24, folder 7. CFW bathed at Narraganset, RI.

made her suffer: CFW to SM (16 Jan 1884). WRHS.

'an angel': HJ to LB (11 Dec 1883), *L(E)*, iii, 18. Cited Edel, iii, 24.

'Henry James comes to see me . . .': CFW to SM (16 Jan 1884). WRHS.

'confrère': Clare Benedict included this volume in her bequest of books to the Benedict Library, Protestant Cemetery, Rome, as she notes in *The In Memoriam Library* (Lucerne, 1960). Copy in Claremont Historical Society, Claremont, NH. Edel, iii, 140, 202, cites a volume of Shelley inscribed 'Constance Fenimore Woolson, from her friend and confrère Henry James, 1887'. Cited also by Weimer, *Back Talk*, 279.

'. . . I have asked Henry James . . .': CFW to Flora Mather (16 Jan 1884). WRHS.

194–5 *Flora Stone Mather and public service:* The authority on Mather family history, Professor Gladys Haddad, Dept of History, Case Western Reserve, has recorded the Mathers of Cleveland in documentary films.

195 *bovine:* Gladys Haddad called Clara 'passive' in contrast with Flora. In conversation, Cleveland (Aug 1994). HJ calls her 'vaccine' to Grace Norton when Hay brought his wife to London in 1882.

illness that 'hangs on . . .' and 'very unhappy', etc. to 'The effort . . .': CFW to JH (27 Jan 1884), *Books at Brown.*

196 *'I must bear my life . . .': East Angels,* 580. Copy of first edition in Bodleian Library, Oxford.

'a fullness . . .' Ibid., 100.

HJ's approval of East Angels: 'Miss Constance Fenimore Woolson', *Harper's Weekly*, xxxi (12 Feb 1887), 114–5, repr. (with excision) *Partial Portraits* (May 1888).

197 *'At Mentone': Harper's*, repr. *Mentone, Cairo, Corfu* (1896).

'not much entertained' to 'alas!': CFW to JH (27 Jan 1884), *Books at Brown.*

cubbyholes: Noted later by Edith Wharton. Cited by Edel in Introduction to *L(E)*, i, xx.

none of his London circle knew of CFW: Edel, iii, 25.

incident at the theatre: HJ in letter to AJ (29 Feb 1884), *L(E)*, iii, 35, mentioned that 'friends' were at the theatre for the opening night (*Othello*). CFW recalled Mrs Kemble's snub at the foot of HJ's essay on 'Frances Anne Kemble', in his gift to her of his *Essays in London* (1893), cited Edel, iii, 306. HJ regained possession of this volume and erased his inscription to CFW. Cited also (different wording) in Benedict, ii, 106.

198 *'a sort of festivity . . .':* HJ to AJ (3 May 1884). Houghton b MS Am 1094 (1550–1608).

leaving a dinner party: Recalled by W. Graham Robertson in *Time Was* (1931), repr. Page, 4.

displaced, etc.: Recalled by Edmund Gosse, *London Mercury* (1920), repr. as 'First Meeting' in Page, 7–10. This is a valuable piece as, after HJ's death, few could recall his early years in London. Most recollections in Page repeat the legend of the Master, an image of his later years.

'. . . The Costanza is handy . . .': HJ to LB (2 June 1884), *L(E)*, iii, 44.

199 *LB's painting:* HJ to WJ (9 Apr 1873), *CWJ*, i 201.

'But she is . . .': HJ to LB (2 June 1884), op. cit.

link of Mildred Theory and Milly Theale: Matthiessen's and Murdoch's note, *N(M)*, 61.

'. . . there is no one . . .': See above, ch. 4, p. 95. MT addressed JCG (3 Feb 1869) in Boston while HJ was still there during the last weeks before he sailed. It is not impossible that JCG would have relayed to HJ the latest word from MT, but it is a state of mind HJ could have inferred without being told.

'quite often': CFW to Mrs Howells (15 July [1884]), from Hampstead Heath. Houghton. She notes that she had had an apartment in London in June and mentions the photo from HJ and her wish for one of Howells.

'lodgings': Benedict, ii, 285.

visit to Stonehenge: Benedict, ii, 285.

200 The School for Scandal: By Richard Brinsley Sheridan (1777).

200 *'Miss Grief' in* Stories: Fourth vol. in Scribner's series (NY: Scribner's, 1884–5). Copy in Library of Congress PS 216.L5 1884. The James tale, 'A Light Man', was slight beside hers. Also included were stories by Elizabeth Stoddard ('Osgood's Predicament') and Frances H. Burnett ('A Story of the Latin Quarter').

photo of JH: CFW to JH (29 Apr 1885), from Vienna.

observations on photos: CFW to JH (26 Dec 1885).

AJ alone; 'a cruel and unnatural fate': Diary (16 Nov 1889), 57.

201 *AJ's moves:* Lewis, 396. In the autumn of 1885 AJ settles at 7 Bolton Row around the corner from HJ in Bolton Street; in Mar 1886, he moves to De Vere Gardens in Kensington, whereupon in Oct 1886 AJ moves close by again, to 8 Gloucester Road, Palace Gate.

CFW bought trunk: Benedict, ii. Cited Edel, iii, 131.

'troubles': CFW uses this word to Mrs Howells (15 July [1884?]). Houghton.

'the Katharine of another': HJ to AJ (5 Feb 1884). Houghton b MS Am 1094 (1550–1608).

'but I must tell you . . .': HJ to AJ (3 May 1884). Houghton.

202 *'on her':* HJ to WJ (10 Sept 1886), CWJ, ii, 48.

203 *six months later:* HJ to LB (17 Mar 1886). Houghton b MS Am 1094 (500–82). He expected to arrive in Sept.

'I wonder . . .': HJ to FB (25 May [1886]), *L(E)*, iii, 119–20.

204 *LB, FB and* The Golden Bowl: Linked by Edel, iii, 136.

'my cousin's memory': A, ii, 521.

Cooper in Italy: Van Wyck Brooks, *The Dream of Arcadia: American Writers and Artists in Italy 1760–1915* (NY: Dutton, 1958), 58–60. I'm grateful to Linn Cary Mehta for alerting me to this, and lending her copy.

'leaves behind . . .': James Fenimore Cooper, *Gleanings in Europe: Italy* (Albany: SUNY Press, 1981), 132. Cited by Freddie Baveystock, 'The Romance of Nationalism', Oxford thesis (July 1995).

205 *Castellani:* Some facts from Laura Wagnière-Huntington, *From Dawn to Dusk* (privately printed, c.1930), 127–9. Copy in the Bodleian Library. The Villa belonged to the author's mother's sister, and she inherited it, together with her brother, Henry. Eventually it belonged to a niece and nephew. By 1930, the name was changed to 'Villa Mercede'.

Huntingtons: CWJ, ii, 238 n2; 257 n3.

Lady Hobart and Pax: CFW to KL (16 Nov 1890). Beverly Historical Society.

'wonderfully well': CFW to WWB (30 June 1886), from 1 Via del Moro, Città. PML. First letter to WWB. PML: MA 3564, box 6.

WWB on royalty: CFW to WWB (16 June 1893) recalls these anecdotes. PML.

206 *Ibsen:* CFW recalls WWB lending her the plays, and rereading *A Doll's House* in letter to WWB (7 Oct [1889?]). PML.

reading Rousseau: CFW's copy in Claremont Historical Society, dated 'Geneva, Switzerland. 1886'.

CFW in Geneva: HJ to FB (15 Aug 1886), *L(E)*, iii, 130–1.

206 *'a large ancient structure' etc.:* CFW described the Castellani as the Villa Dorio in her story 'Dorothy', *Dorothy and Other Italian Stories*, 3.

207 *'the Ghost':* Benedict, ii, 296.

CFW godmother to LB's child: CFW to KL (19 Sept 1890), from Cheltenham. Beverly Historical Society.

'Francis': CFW uses this name in letter to JH (6 Aug 1887), *Books at Brown*, 98.

'almost intolerably . . .' etc.: HJ to FB (4 Nov 1886). Houghton b MS Am 1094 (584–634).

secret: HJ to FB (26 Nov [1886]), *L(E)*, iii, 138.

'I don't intend . . .': HJ to LB (18 Oct [1886]), *L(E)*, iii, 136.

208 *'devotion (to HJ!,)':* HJ to LB (18 Oct 1886), *L(E)*, iii, 135.

tea set: HJ to LB (18 Oct [1886]), *L(E)*, iii, 135. '(You mustn't apprehend upon this [his gratitude for their kindness to CFW] that you will have occasion to look up some article for a tea set for me!)'

inspected Brichieri: CFW to KL (9 Oct [1886]). Beverly Historical Society. (Misdated by the library 1887 – internal evidence points to 1886).

Aurora Leigh's villa: CFW to Mary Mapes Dodge (13 Sept [?]), the Donald and Robert M. Dodge Collection of Mary Mapes Dodge: Series 2: Correspondence. Princeton's Special Collections CO113, Box 3.

'writing-room': CFW to Mr Osgood, her publisher (30 Dec [1886]). The Huntington Library, San Marino, California.

'my landlady': HJ to FB (26 Nov [1886]), *L(E)*, iii, 139.

'whose devotion . . .': Ibid., *L(E)*, iii, 138.

209 *Duveneck's sketch of HJSr:* It is not possible to be certain when CFW acquired this or when she set it up on the easel, but she had a gift for hospitality, when she chose to exercise it, and this would have been an appropriate point of welcome at this time. The only reference to her possession of the sketch is in an unpublished letter from HJ to FB (26 July 1888), soon after FB and Duveneck had returned to America: HJ has asked for a loan of it, and writes to say it has arrived: 'Between the easel & my desire my indulgence doesn't hesitate – nor, I am sure, will Fenimore's own have done so, for an instant.' Houghton.

Ginori teacups, etc.: 'used by CFW at her Florentine villa' in Benedict's listings of CFW's possessions at NYHA.

The Bootts uneasy: Kaplan's plausible suggestion, 313.

'For what do you take me . . .': HJ to FB (26 Nov [1886]), *L(E)*, iii, 139.

'dine with her': HJ to JH (Christmas Eve [1886]), *L(E)*, iii, 153.

twenty tea roses: CFW to Osgood (30 Dec [1886]). Huntington Library, San Marino, Cal.

present of Turgenev and other books belonging to CFW: Rollins. Some books have disappeared since Clare Benedict's bequest of them in the 1930s, but an old list gives full details. Amongst the books she owned were Matthew Arnold *Essays in Criticism* (1887); Francis Bacon, *Essays* (1887); Gaston Boissier, *Mme de Sévigné* (Paris, 1887); William Cowper, *Poetical Works* (1886); Alphonse Daudet, *Adventures of Tartarin* (Paris, 1886); Ben

Jonson, *Dramatic Works and Lyrics* (London, 1886); Jules Lemaitre, *Les Contemporains* (Paris, 1888), said to be her favourite critic; James Russell Lowell, *My Study Windows* (repr. Cambridge, Mass., 1886 and inscribed 'Florence, 1887'); R. L. Stevenson, *Kidnapped* (1886).

210 *'Harry James':* CFW to the Mathers (Jan 1887). WRHS.

gift of The Bostonians: Edel, iii, 140.

'companions': CFW to Flora Mather, n.d. Benedict, ii, 52. *WAWE*, 219.

selection of Whitman: Leaves of Grass (London: Walter Scott, 1886). The book was bought in Florence.

211 *'a warm patriot':* CFW to WWB (7 Sept 1891). PML. The occasion was HJ's dramatisation of *The American*, which led the two to discuss American literature.

'This dust . . .': 'This Dust Was Once the Man', Walt Whitman, *Complete Poetry and Collected Prose* (NY: Library of America, 1982), 468. Transcribed (with 'cautious' omitted in the second line) at the foot of James Russell Lowell's essay on Lincoln in *My Study Windows* (1871, repr. 1886), 177. Inscribed by CFW 'Florence 1887'. Rollins.

'the plainness': CFW to JH (23 Feb [1887]), *Books at Brown*, 93.

'the great merit', 'brave thing', etc.: HJ to WJ and AHJ (23 Dec [1886]), *CWJ*, ii, 55.

'the gifted authoress': Ibid.

212 *Jeffrey Aspern and J. F. Cooper:* Edel, iii, 160, argues that the model for Aspern was James as he would have liked to be – a kind of Hawthorne figure liberated from the parochial and all puritan construction. The first part of this proposition is plausible. Van Wyck Brooks suggested Poe (*The Dream of Arcadia*, 175). Neither of these candidates fits the period, nor was their fame on the scale of Cooper.

'his own country . . .': The Aspern Papers, ch. 4 in *The Aspern Papers and Other Stories*, ed. Adrian Poole (Oxford: World's Classics, 1983).

letter 30 Dec: CFW to Osgood (30 Dec [1886]). Huntington Library, San Marino, Cal.

so run after: CFW to JH (10 Jan 1887), *Books at Brown*, 93–4.

'wretched little . . . smotherisation': HJ to LB (13 Nov 1887), referring to the previous winter in Florence. Houghton b MS Am 1094 (500–82).

213 *Silsbee:* HJ to Ellen (Bay) Emmet (26 Dec 1897), calls his cousin Bob Temple 'that terrible old wandering Jew of an unwashed Silsbee' who haunts 'according to his wont in such relations' civilised firesides. 'He has been to me, for thirty years, an apparition dimly – and yet distinctly! – recurrent at long intervals, and was here a couple of years ago, looming aesthetically and undesirably out of the winter fog. . . . I dread him as an ancient and soapless bore.' Houghton b MS Am 1094 (662–712).

'likes marriages': HJ added this criticism in *Partial Portraits.*

214 *deconstruction of femininity: For the Major*, in *For the Major and Selected Short Stories* ed. Rayburn S. Moore (New Haven, Conn.: College and University Press Services, 1967), 355, 356–7.

214 *'not so easy to die':* *East Angels*, 578.
erotic landscape: Ibid., 466. Ch. 28.

215 *'evil days':* HJ to WDH (2 Jan 1888), *L(E)*, iii, 209. A third commercial failure, *The Tragic Muse*, was to follow in 1889–90.
Jupiter Lights: I am indebted to Caroline Gebhard's striking analysis of domestic violence in a talk on 'Romantic Love and Battering in *JL*' at a CFW meeting at Mackinac Island, Mich. (5 Oct 1996).

216 *'Miss Grief' disappeared:* After its magazine publication in 1880, it was republished once in an 1885 collection of American stories, but otherwise remained uncollected amongst CFW's lesser works, though two further volumes of European stories were published posthumously in 1896 and 1899. Possibly, it was not given its due as one of her best stories because, written as it was before she left for Europe, the local colour is negligible. Rayburn S. Moore has the credit for recovering it in his selection, *For the Major and Selected Short Stories*, and it became the star story of the feminist selection by Weimer, *Women Artists, Women Exiles* (1988), which, together with the pioneering work of Cheryl Torsney, Sharon Dean, and a small group of American critics, mark the rise of renewed regard for CFW.
influential misreading: Reflected in most twentieth-century criticism that so much as remembers CFW. Rayburn S. Moore, for instance, in his 1967 introduction to *For the Major and Selected Short Stories*, perpetuates the opinion of Cowie in *The Rise of the American Novel* (1948) that CFW is a 'superior minor writer', 'worthy' and 'respectable', and that HJ was 'perceptive' in his critique of her work. Edel, iii, 141, calls CFW 'prosy', 'banal', 'a journeywoman of letters' without style, 'cluttered', 'magazinish', and worthy of no more than a 'footnote' to regional American fiction.
Soon after 'Miss Woolson': Came out on 12 Feb 1887. HJ arrived in Venice on 24 Feb, according to an unpublished letter to his Aunt Kate (26 Feb 1887). Houghton. (Edel incorrectly gives the date as 12 Feb.)
'much troubled . . .': HJ to Mme Wagnière-Huntington (Mar 1887), from Venice. Houghton b MS Am 1237.16.
'tell Fenimore': HJ to FB (15 Mar [1887]). Houghton b MS Am 1094 (584–634).

217 *not convinced:* HJ to WWB (8, 13 and 23 Mar 1887). PML. WWB, pressed for a diagnosis, suggested lumbago, which didn't please HJ.
'owing to mental depression': CFW to SM (10 Dec 1888). WRHS. She contrasts her present happiness with illness the previous winter, and quite matter-of-factly associates physical with mental illness.
12–14 April: Evidence conflicts as to the precise date. HJ said the fourteenth was his first day back in Florence in a letter to FB, writing from Venice on 13 April (Houghton). Yet on 12 April HJ wrote to Mrs Locker from Bellosguardo (Beinecke Library, Yale). This date would seem to be confirmed by a letter from HJ to Mrs Curtis (24 Apr [1887]), at Dartmouth College, NH, where HJ says he left Venice a fortnight before, i.e. about 10 April.

217 *'that house . . .'*: CFW to WWB (25 Jan 1891). After leaving the house, she recalls here one of her happiest memories.

'I sit here . . .': HJ to Gosse (24 Apr 1887), *Selected Letters of HJ to Edmund Gosse 1882–1915: A Literary Friendship* e.d Rayburn S. Moore (Baton Rouge: Louisiana State Univ. Press, 1988), 47. Edel, iii, 213, has noted that these letters breathe an air of calm and release and a sense of enchantment rarely to be found in HJ's correspondence.

happier: CFW to Mrs Sherman (1887), Benedict, ii, 298–9.

218 *'the most charmed . . .'*: HJ to Clara Benedict ([1912]), fragment only, Benedict, iii, 388.

'Florence . . . enchanting, etc.': HJ to Ariana Curtis (24 Apr [1887]). Curtis Papers, Special Collections, Dartmouth College Library, Hanover, NH.

'as personal . . .': Edel, iii, 152. Source given as Bronson (Rucellai) Papers (Monday [1887]). This must be one of two letters from HJ to Mrs Bronson (23 April and 3 May 1887) from Villa Brichiere, Bellosguardo, which survive (so far as known) only in Edel's notes at McGill. See Steven H. Jobe's privately produced 'Calendar of Correspondence'.

letter to Mrs Bronson: This line quoted, without source, by Edel, iii, 154. Ibid.

'There is nothing personal': HJ to Gosse (14 Apr 1887), *Selected Letters of Henry James to Edmund Gosse* 1882–1915, op. cit. 46.

It has been assumed that the narrator speaks for James: Edel aligns HJ with the narrator's realisation that he had 'unwittingly but none the less deplorably trifled'; his self-justification 'I had not given her cause – distinctly I had not' and his plea that he had been 'as kind as possible because I really liked her', followed by his unkind rhetorical question, 'since when had that become a crime where a woman of such an age and such an appearance was concerned?'; and the conclusion: 'At any rate, whether I had given her cause or not it went without saying that I could not pay the price.' Edel, iii, 225–6. Sharon L. Dean suggests that 'James as easily could have been rewriting Woolson's vision of "Miss Grief" ', *CFW: Homeward Bound*, 217.

219 *date of departure, plan for ten days, and return to Florence:* HJ to Mme Wagnière-Huntington (23 May [1887]). Houghton b MS Am 1237.16.

'a magnificent old palace': HJ to Catherine Walsh (16 June 1887).

'wonderful faded back rooms': Preface to *A London Life.*

dined in a gondola: HJ to KB (17 Sept 1887), Ms Rucellai, transcribed by Edel. Edel Papers, McGill. Transcribed by Steven H. Jobe.

'still-living' and 'do': 'The K.B. Case' (set out in Dec 1909–Jan 1910), *N*, 256–70. At this stage, HJ thought of calling the novel 'Mrs Max'. This material, reshaped, eventually went into a late, unfinished novel, *The Ivory Tower.*

220 *Mrs Bronson and the poor.* Michael Meredith, Introduction to *More Than Friend*, op. cit.

'squeezed': HJ to Mme Wagnière-Huntington (23 June 1907). Houghton. HJ used the phrase 'generations of incubi' to Mrs Curtis.

220 *'nursing mother':* HJ to Catherine Walsh (26 Feb 1887). Houghton.
'more than friend': Meredith, xxiii.
'jumped . . .': N(M), 76. Philip Horne has pointed out that it eerily prefigures Fenimore's end. Introduction to his edn of *A London Life and The Reverberator* (OUP, World's Classics, 1989), xiii. The above quotations come from this edition, chs 11 and 12 (pp. 116, 127, 130, 134).
'dreadfully corrupt', etc.: CFW to brother-in-law Samuel Livingstone Mather (23 Feb 1886), Benedict, ii, 289–93.
221 *'. . . if I could have a house . . .':* CFW to WWB (25 June 1887), from Brichieri. PML.
222 *'she ought . . .' and hope:* HJ to WWB (31 July [1887]). PML.
'Fenimore appears . . .': HJ to FB (29 Jan [1888?]). Houghton.
'The Lesson of the Master': The Figure in the Carpet and Other Stories, ed. Frank Kermode (Harmondsworth: Penguin, 1986), 113–88. First published in the *Universal Review*. HJ notes his first idea for this tale 5 Jan 1888, *N(M)*, 87, where it seems to arise out of a discussion on marriage with Theodore Child. Of course, one tends to discuss matters already on one's mind. I suggest a deeper, more hidden source in his literary debates with CFW.
225 *'all one's manhood . . .':* (11 Mar 1888), *N(M)*, 88.
226 *inscribed copy of* The Aspern Papers: HJ wrote her name and 'from the author, Geneva, October 16th, 1888' as reported by Edel, iii, 190.
Helena and heroine of The Tragic Muse: Helena de Kay Gilder to her lifelong friend Mary Hallock Foote (6 Oct 1914). Gilder Papers.
'the odd animal' etc.: The Tragic Muse, ch. 12.
'abjection' etc.: Jupiter Lights (1889; repr. NY: AMS Press, 1971), 163–5. I am indebted to Caroline Gebhard for drawing attention to this word.
'That excellent . . . woman . . .': HJ to FB (29 Oct [1888]) *L(E)*, iii, 246.
'About October 10th . . .': HJ to Catherine Walsh (30 Sept 1888). Houghton.
227 *'stale dingy London':* HJ to WJ (29 Oct 1888), *CWJ*, ii, 95.
excuse to Miss Reubell: HJ to Henrietta Reubell (29 Oct [1888]). Houghton.
'I have enjoyed . . .': HJ to FB (29 Oct [1888], *L(E)*, iii, 247.
'Nothing would be easier . . .': 'Louisa Pallant'. Edel makes this apt connection in *L(E)*, iii, 247.
228 *HJ's gifts to CFW and her own books:* Rollins.
Obiter Dicta: Augustine Birrell, *Obiter Dicta: Second Series* (London: Elliot Stock, 1887), 239. Inscribed 'From Henry James'. The link between CFW's dislike of Lamb's drinking and her brother, also the Branwellian aspect, was suggested by Joan Weimer, in conversation.
engraving of Shelley's grave: Ernest Dowden, *The Life of Percy Bysshe Shelley* (1886), vol. ii, opposite p. 536.
'buried in roses', etc.: 'The After-Season in Rome' (1870s), *T(C)*, 467–8.
'make one in love with death': 'From a Roman Note-book' (1873), *T(C)*, 471.
CFW's copies of Browne and Epictetus: Rollins. *Religio Medici and Other Essays*, with introduction by John Addington Symonds (1642; repr.

London: Walter Scott's Camelot Classics, 1886). Epictetus, *Teachings* (London, 1888). Both heavily annotated in CFW's hand. 'Another ugly word . . .' on p. viii, and 'He forgets . . .' on p. 66 in Browne.

229 *'the door is opened':* Epictetus, ch. 9 'On Solitude', 135. Stoicism was a system of thought which originated in Athens, but comes to us via the Romans where it flourished *c.*100 BC to AD 200. It was virtuous to follow Reason uncluttered by pain, desire, fear, emotions that belong to a lower level of existence. Stoicism therefore aspires to conquer the irrational self.

'What is death?': Epictetus, 57. I am indebted to Weimer, *Back Talk*, for the neat research on the cut pages.

'The phrase of the "open door" . . .': Epictetus, 200.

230 *HJ on Epictetus: E(AE)*, 9.

'of giving up her villa' and 'Fenimore's mind . . .': HJ to FB (18 Jan 1889), *L(E)*, iii, 249.

'I am grieved . . .': CFW to KL (9 Oct [1886]). Beverly Historical Society. Strouse, *Alice James*, 259.

231 *'You're not going to be married!'* AJ, *Diary* (4 Aug 1889), 51.

'flirting': AJ to WJ (4 Nov 1888), from 11 Hamilton Terrace, Leamington. *The Death and Letters of Alice James*, 149.

'porcupine fit': AJ's own phrase for this propensity: *Diary* (13 Feb 1890), 85.

'galavanting': AJ to WJ (first week of Dec 1888). Cited by Strouse, *Alice James*, 259, and Kaplan, 326.

232 *'mild':* Ibid.

'dear' and 'intimate friend': HJ to Rhoda Broughton [28 Jan 1894) *L(E)*, iii, 458 and to Ranee Margaret of Sarawak (28 Jan 1894), Columbia.

'There is no one here . . .': HJ to Henrietta Reubell (19 Nov 1888). Houghton.

HJ answered letter from Broughton: (6 Nov 1888), *L(E)*, iii, 247–8.

'quite scandalously well': On 10 Dec 1888 CFW began a letter spanning several weeks. Cited by Torsney, *CFW: The Grief of Artistry*, 16.

Chapter 9 A Message from Alice

233 *'Tell it not . . .':* HJ to R. L. Stevenson (5 Aug 1893), *L(L)*, i, 212.

'I am working . . .': Ibid.

234 *'loathed'; 'Bore':* HJ to FB (20 May 1889). Houghton b MS Am 1094 (584–634). Also HJ to FB (11 Jan 1890), *L(E)*, iii, 267.

tea, dancing, 'reception days': Invitation to WWB ([1889]) and letter to Mrs Baldwin (15 Apr [1889?]). PML.

'cheered': CFW to WWB (18 Jan 1890). PML.

334–5 *'float' and 'peace of mind':* CFW to WWB (13 July 1889), from Hotel Britannia, Canal Grande. PML.

235 *'I saw Henry James in London . . .':* CFW to WWB (7 Oct [1889?]). PML.

'. . . The rupture . . .': HJ to FB (11 Jan 1890), *L(E)*, iii, 267.

236 *'Grecian things . . .':* CFW to JH (20 Dec 1890), *Books at Brown*, 103.

236 *'the blessed Bellosguardo' and 'our modern Fenimore':* HJ to FB (23 Apr 1890). Houghton.
'I can expect nothing else': CFW to Flora Mather. Benedict, ii, 35.
'all ghosts': HJ to FB (19 July 1890). Houghton.
'without fail': HJ to FB (12 June 1890), *L(E)*, iii, 290.
'dingy': CFW to WWB (17 Aug 1890), sent c/o HJ. PML.
'refreshment': CFW to WWB (7 Sept 1890). PML.

237 *most lovely:* HJ to WWB (29 Sept 1890), transcribed by Edel. McGill. Transcribed by Steven H. Jobe.
'Henry James came . . .': CFW to WWB (5 Oct 1890). PML.
'Another': HJ to Rhoda Broughton (24 Sept [1890]). Chester Record Office.
'Do not suppose . . .'; asked Miss Loring: CFW to KL (19 Sept 1890). Beverly Historical Society.
'nothing good to say, etc.': HJ to FB (19 Dec 1890). Houghton.
'the ache': CFW to WWB (25 Jan 1891). PML.
told AJ to telegraph: HJ to AJ and KL (4 Jan 1891), *L(E)*, iii, 321.
'I paid . . .': HJ to WJ (8 Jan 1891), *CWJ*, ii, 164.

234 Mrs. Vibert: AJ, *Diary* (23 Apr 1891), 197. AJ notes that HJ wrote the play 'before Christmas' 1892. It was later renamed *Tenants.*
'very striking': CFW to WWB (25 Jan 1891). PML.
'depression . . . to the brother': Ibid.

238 *'blessing':* HJ to FB (19 Dec 1890). Houghton.
'inhuman': HJ to WJ (7 Nov 1890), *CWJ*, ii, 154.
'No one will fully know . . .': HJ to WWB (21 Mar 1892) immediately after AJ's death. Houghton b MS Am 1094.1.
powers of resistance: HJ to FB (19 Dec 1890). Houghton b MS Am 1094 (584–634).
'I am working away . . .': AJ to AHJ (26 Nov 1890), *The Death and Letters of AJ*, 185.
AJ and WWB: AJ to WJ (30 July [1891]). Houghton b MS Am 1094 (1468–99).
'inspiring': KL to WJ (30 July [1891]).
'grotesque obstructions': AJ to WJ (30 July 1891), *The Death and Letters of AJ*, 187.
empty pea pod: AJ, *Diary* (2 Feb 1892), 230. She was to die a month later.
'illusion': Ibid. (4 Aug 1889), 51–2.
'At the risk . . .': AJ to WJ and AHJ (20 Nov [1887?]), *The Death and Letters of AJ*, 137.
'tread mill': AJ, *Diary* (4 Aug 1889), 51.

239 *'white':* WJ to AHJ (29 July 1889), cited by Linda Simon, *Genuine Reality*, 223.
'born afresh' and 'bottled lightning': WJ to AJ (3 June 1888). Houghton b MS Am 1092.9 (1087–1159). AJ repeats 'bottled lighting', *Diary* (1 Dec 1889), 60.
'polished steel': WJ to AJ (27 Sept 1886). Houghton b MS Am 1092.9 (1087–1159).
'invincible and amazonian spirit': WJ to AJ (16 Oct 1887). Houghton.
'the hardest job': AJ, *Diary* (16 June 1891), 211.

'Arm yourself . . .': AJ to WJ (16 Mar 1890). Houghton b MS Am 1094 (1468–99).

239 *'concentrated essence':* AJ, *Diary* (12 Feb 1892), 230.

'moral discords': Ibid. (4 Mar 1892), 232.

'we had only to be . . .': A, ii, 371.

'shone . . .': KL to Frances (Fanny) Morse (7 Oct [1891]). This group of letters gives an interesting picture of AJ's dying and KL herself. Houghton b MS Am 1094 (1543–9).

240 *'potent': The Death and Letters of AJ* (10 Sept 1886), 116–17. WJ had written: 'You are visited in a way that few are ever called to bear, and I have no words of consolation that would not seem barren. Stifling slowly in a quagmire of disgust and pain and impotence! "Silence," as Carlyle would say, must cover the pity I feel' (8 July 1886). Though HJ was far more open to the potency of the private mind in women like his sister, he seems often, at least in his written comments on AJ, to subscribe to the pitying family view of her articulated by WJ. After her death, HJ writes to WWB (21 Mar 1892): 'She suffered much . . . & it was so painful to see her that the extinction of that daily helpless consciousness takes a burden from my spirit.' PML.

'fortitude': WJ to AJ (6 July 1891), *Death and Letters of AJ*, 185–6.

AJ's reply: Ibid., 185–8.

241 *'prostrated':* CFW to WWB (15 July 1891). PML.

'I should like . . .': Ibid.

'right & good': HJ to FB (20 July 1891), from Ireland. Houghton.

'a palace . . .' and 'Would that I . . .': CFW to WWB (25 Jan 1891). PML.

242 *'Through the Long Days':* FB set this poem by Hay to music in 1878.

242–3 *'Dorothy' and 'dizzy outer descent': Harper's New Monthly Magazine*, lxxxiv (Mar 1892); repr. *Dorothy, and Other Italian Stories* (1896). Parapet scene cited by Dean, *CFW: Homeward Bound*, 11.

243 Notable American Women: (1971), 671. Entry by Stella Gray, who wrote a thesis on CFW in the 1950s.

narrow cliff road: See ch. 7 above.

23 July: CFW to WWB (24 July 1891). PML.

British cooking: Ibid.

'the essence of old Oxford': CFW to WWB (7 Sept 1891). PML.

HJ visited: HJ to Gosse (26 Aug [1891]), *Selected Letters of HJ to Gosse*, 81–2. HJ says he has come in from a day in Oxford. Moore (ed.) suggests, plausibly, he may have been visiting CFW. See Benedict, ii, 369ff.

'very brilliantly': CFW to WWB (15 July 1991). PML.

opening night: CFW to Kate Mather (20 Oct 1891), Benedict, ii, 371–2.

244 *'a crowded and brilliant house':* CFW to WWB (16 Nov 1991), sent with the latest 'slips', i.e. extracts from reviews. PML.

collaborating: CFW to SM (29 Apr 1993): 'And perhaps we can write that play after all.' WRHS. Cited by Edel, iii, 255.

HJ's appearance in the 1890s: BBC 'Recollections of Henry James in his Later Years' (see above, ch. 1 ref. 1): interview with Ethel Sands, whose mother HJ used to visit in the mid-nineties.

244 *'delivered', etc.:* W. Graham Robertson, 'Remarkably Unremarkable', from *Time Was* (1931), repr. Page, 14.

245 *who passes for...:* Preface on similar artistic duality in *The Tragic Muse*, *E(CP)*, 1103–19.

landlady, Exeter College, etc.: Details from a mutilated letter in CFW's hand, a mere scrap, inserted in *Alden's Oxford Guide* (1912) belonging to Clare Benedict. Rollins.

force d'âme: HJ to WJ (31 July [1891]), *CWJ*, ii, 181.

'the moment of transition': AJ, *Diary* (2 Feb 1892), 230.

'Mystery': Ibid. (12 July 1889), 49.

'killing': Ibid. (21 Feb 1890), 95.

'justified': Ibid. (10 Feb 1890), 81.

'What a pity to hide it': Ibid. (5 Aug 1889), 52. The context is the suicide of Edmund Gurney, her exact contemporary. He was an English psychologist and friend of WJ.

246 *'infernal' pain:* CFW to WWB (5–6 Feb 1892). PML.

'neurotic': Ibid., and repeated CFW to SM (8 Feb 1892), quoted by Torsney, *CFW: The Grief of Artistry*, 18–19.

'If I do'nt...' and 'Illness is so depressing...': CFW to WWB (5–6 Feb 1892). PML.

'intense, stabbing pain' and 'The loss...' etc.: CFW to SM (8 Feb 1892). WRHS.

247 *'the cruel pavement': Horace Chase*, 278–80. Noted by Dean, *CFW: Homeward Bound*, 11.

'more or less from life': CFW to Kate Mather (2 July 1893), from Venice. WRHS.

'played out': Horace Chase, 284.

'just life': Ibid., 380.

'over-development': Ibid., 340.

a doll's house: CFW reread Ibsen's play *A Doll's House* at about the time she would have conceived *Horace Chase* in 1889. Letter to WWB (7 Oct [1889?]), from London, notes that the play was given there the preceding June; Ibsen was 'much talked of in London'.

'I almost asked...': AJ, *Diary* (4 Mar 1992), 232.

248 *'mortuary inclinations':* Ibid. (2 Feb 1892), 230.

'divine cessation': Ibid. (4 Mar 1892). AJ's last entry. She died two days later.

KL finished 'Dorothy': Ibid., 232–3. It is not quite clear whether this took place on the night of Thursday 3rd or that of Friday 4th (after the final entry was dictated) or on that of Saturday 5th (after AJ polished it). KL's phrasing allows for the possibility that the dictation of 4 March was rushing about in AJ's head the following day, and that she wasn't quiet until she had corrected it – this would place the reading of 'Dorothy' on the very last night of AJ's life. A letter to Fanny Morse (12 Mar 1892) says that she read the end of the story on the Thursday night. (Houghton). Ideally, we should choose the report closer in time to the event, but it is not so far known when KL added her final note to the diary – it may have been immediately after AJ's death; it may have been later, when she edited it for private printing.

248 *the context was HJ:* Strouse (pp. 312–3) suggested, plausibly, that the message itself had to do with HJ.

'You will see . . .': CFW to SM (29 Apr 1893). WRHS.

249 *'disappointment and depression': L(E)*, iii, p. xv. Weimer links this with CFW; see *Back Talk*, 243.

'griefs, or aches or disappointments': CFW to WWB (16 June [1893]). PML.

AHJ's 'fits of morbid low spirits': WJ to Elly (Temple) Hunter (18 Nov 1894). Houghton.

250 *'In Sloane Street': Harper's*, xxv (11 June 1892), 473–5.

the great white monsters of the lower waters: The Voyage Out (1915; repr. London: Hogarth Press; NY: Harcourt, 1991), ch. 1.

251 *'when I went down to the deep sea . . .':* AJ, *Diary* (2 Feb 1892), 230.

diary to be 'an absolute . . . secret': HJ to WJ [29 June 1894] *CWJ*, ii, 315.

'Greville Fane': Illustrated London News (Sept 1892), *CS*, iv, 217–33.

'evil days': HJ to WDH (2 Jan 1888), *L(E)*, iii, 209.

editors keeping back tales: Ibid.

found it hard to press on: HJ to WJ (29 Dec 1893), *CWJ*, ii, 296–7.

252 *'There was a general impression . . .':* Elizabeth Robins, *Theatre and Friendship* (NY: Putnam 1932), 168–9. Copy in Berg.

'The Middle Years': CS, iv, 335–55.

'had grief': CFW to WWB (16 June [1893]), from Venice, soon after her arrival there. PML.

'morbid depression': AHJ to WWB (1 Nov 1892). PML.

253 *'grim & desperate will':* CFW to WWB (16 June [1893]). PML.

WWB's depression: He had written in April, according to her reply (16 June [1893]). PML.

gout: HJ to Rhoda Broughton (18 Jan [1893]). Chester Record Office. The context is the death of Mrs Kemble.

lost facility, crushed, etc.: HJ to R. L. Stevenson (17 Feb 1893), *L(E)*, iii, 406.

Woolson assumed: She refers to this, briefly, in her 16 June letter to WWB. PML.

HJ promised: CFW to SM (29 Apr 1893). WRHS.

'prostrated': CFW to WWB (16 June [1893]). PML.

intercepted: There are two possible dates. One is that CFW pulled herself together and left at once for Paris, and was there from approximately 13 to 16 May. On 17 May HJ wrote to Mrs Bronson from Lucerne, mentioning a visit to Paris (Edel Papers, McGill). He was again in Paris on 22 May, for on that day he wrote two letters from the Grand Hotel, Paris, and was back in England from 27 May. So, the second possibility is that CFW was held up by flu and joined him between 22 and 26 May.

254 *better:* CFW to WWB (16 June [1893]). PML.

'I saw Henry James . . .': Ibid. I deciphered 'as wont' with the aid of a

magnifying glass, but the writing is too blotched to be sure. I think what is written over is less important than her worry over the possibility of indiscretion.

254 *'the* ingress': HJ to FB (14 July 1893). Houghton b MS Am 1094 (584–634).
secrets and characters: I owe this point to Eva Hoffman, in discussion (23 Aug 1996).

Chapter 10 The Death-House

255 'I should like to die . . .': CFW to JH (26 Dec [1885]) from Leamington, *Books at Brown*, 80. Elaine Showalter notes that female suicide was a trend in this generation, in *A Literature of their Own: British Women Novelists from Brontë to Lessing* (Princeton, 1977), 194.
suicide of Clover Adams: CFW to JH (26 Dec [1885]). On 6 December, when Adams went out for a walk, his wife killed herself by swallowing some of the chemicals she used to develop photos. Her sister, Ellen Gurney, upset by this death, followed by the death of her husband, threw herself under a train almost two years later.
cause of death: Persuasively argued by the most recent biographer, Eugenia Kaledin, *The Education of Mrs. Henry Adams* (Philadelphia: Temple Univ. Press, 1981).
'glad to go': CFW to HJ (12 Feb 1882).
'Life is not worth living . . .': CFW to WWB (15 July 1891). PML.
'depressed in spirits': CFW to Kate Mather (2 July 1893). WRHS.
'amazing wilderness of gloom': CFW to WWB (16 June [1893]). PML.
'Nothing . . .': CFW to WWB (15 July 1891).

256 *Biondetti:* Now, Sotoportego E Corte, Venier. dai Leoni. Kaplan says that CFW went to Venice and stayed at the Biondetti in 1892, and that her last meeting with HJ was early in 1893. In fact, the last meeting was later: in May, when they met in Paris. In 1892 HJ came to visit CFW in Oxford on 5 June : this doesn't fit the four days in Paris when CFW was en route to Venice, which must have taken place in May 1893 when he was in Lucerne with WJ and family.
reading The Law of Psychic Phenomena: (London: Putnam's; Chicago: McClurg, 1893). Copy in the Radcliffe Science Library, Oxford. CFW reports on this to WWB (20 July [1893]). PML. She is referring to ch. 20, 'Phantasms of the Dead', 300–5.
Dec 1890: CFW to HJ (20 Dec 1890), *Books at Brown*, 105.

257 *visit from KL:* CFW to KL (16 Nov 1890). Beverly Historical Society.
'I am so tired . . .': CFW to Kate Mather (2 July 1893). WRHS.
'actual domestication': HJ to FB (14 July 1893), *L(E)*, iii, 418.
'beautiful': CFW to Kate Mather (2 July 1893). WRHS.
assumed: Edel, iii, 288.
HJ to Ariana Curtis: (14 July 1893), *L(E)*, iii, 420–1.

259 *'A Florentine Experiment': Dorothy and Other Italian Stories* (1896; repr. 1899), 148. Copy in Rollins.

Casa Semitecolo: Known now as 187 Dossodura. I am indebted to a present occupant, Paola Martelli Penzo, who kindly allowed me to see some of the rooms which CFW would have occupied. Since her three servants were evidently on their 'own floor', I assume this would have been the top floor of the Casa, which would mean that CFW's rooms were on the floor below. This is still high up and would account of her reference to her 'long stair'.

'ablest Venetian artist...': In Baedeker under 'Padua', opposite p. 183. She goes on: 'His best efforts are those of 1367, at which date he executed an altar piece, now divided, in the library of the chapterhouse of the Duomo at Padua. – A masterpiece of the early Venetian school.' Rollins.

de Horsey: Benedict, ii, 381.

'...I am not': CFW to relative in Munich, Grace Carter (winter 1894). Quoted by Carter to SM (25 Feb 1894). WRHS 3735. Container 1; folder 5.

260 *'I shall do my best...':* HJ to Ariana Curtis (19 Sept 1893). Cited by Edel, iii, 288.

book on Colonna: By Alethea Lawley (London, 1889). Listed as one of CFW's books, now missing. Rollins.

'In this convent...': Baedeker on Rome, 148. Rollins.

'profoundly discouraged': One of several final letters quoted by Henry Mills Alden in an obituary article, 'Constance Fenimore Woolson', *Harper's Weekly*, xxxviii (3 Feb 94) 113–14. The recipients of these letters are not named, and I am guessing that she writes here to an editor. Constance Mather Bishop's Cuttings Book (a scrapbook of articles on CFW kept by the Cleveland family). Privately owned by Molly Mather Anderson. Cited in *WAWE*, 281.

'... by telepathy': Ibid. CFW had already showed enthusiasm for 'this new science of ... telepathy' to JH (20 Dec 1890), from Cheltenham.

a further existence as 'solution to the riddle': Quoted by Clare Benedict in *The In Memoriam Library* (a library for the Protestant Cemetery in Rome) (Lucerne, 1960). Copy in CFW collection, Claremont Historical Society, Claremont, NH.

'extremely exhausted': HJ to FB (21 Oct 1893). Houghton b MS Am 1094 (584–634).

261 *'I shall take Venetia by the way...':* Ibid.

'cozy': Edel, iii, 288.

CFW's 'things': Details from Clare Benedict's listings of the objects in the 'Fenimore' room at Pomeroy Place, Cooperstown. The old stone house was repossessed for the family by the Benedicts early in the twentieth century: they named each room for a member of the Cooper family, and filled it with more or less appropriate memorabilia. 'Fenimore' was arranged as far as possible like her 'library' at the Semitecolo, according to Clare Benedict. (CFW herself never refers to such a room, and I assume what is meant is her sitting-room.) The list of the contents of this room therefore gives us as exact record as could be had of her setting at the Semitecolo. NYHA, Cooperstown.

262 *expense of setting up house:* Torsney, ch. 1, stressed financial anxiety together with hereditary depression as chief cause of suicide.

asked SM: CFW to SM (20 Nov 1893). WRHS.

'superb palaces' and 'society of older persons': Ibid., and CFW to Kate Mather (12 Dec 1893). WRHS.

263 *Edith Bronson's research on Venice:* Letter to her aunt, Helena de Kay Gilder, in New York (1892). Gilder Papers.

'difficulty': CFW to SM (20 Nov 1893). WRHS.

silk cushion: Benedict, ii, 386.

began to look: CFW to WWB (17 Dec 1893). PML.

'far-away island': She went on 20 July 1893, according to a letter to WWB on the same day. PML.

notes: In pencil on pages that have been torn from a lined notebook. The pages are numbered 51–2 ('Lido' dated 18 Dec), 55–8 (on pp. 55 and 57 is 'Lido. St Niccolo' dated Christmas Eve). There is a note on 'Campalto' on unnumbered pages (reproduced in Benedict, ii, 408). Pages 56 and 58 are blank. In Clare Benedict's hand in ink a title has been added: 'Notes on the lagoons. These were among the last notes written by Miss Woolson'. Pages 53 and 54 are missing (was there something Clare Benedict did not wish posterity to see, as we surmise about the pages torn from CFW's copy of Epictetus?). Rollins.

'if I live . . .': Alden, op. cit.

264 *'I have taught . . .':* CFW to Mrs Washburn, Benedict, ii, 393. Edel, iii, 291–2, without source note.

'Mottoes, Maxims & Reflections': In blue notebook, unlined paper, pencil, n.d., each entry divided by wavy line. A commonplace book. Rollins. Edel found 'distressing banality', iii, 307.

265 *the Lido on Christmas Eve:* CFW to Kate Mather (25 Dec 1893), a continuation of the letter of 12 Dec. WRHS. (Cited Benedict, ii, 390–1.) See also 'Notes on the Lagoons', op. cit., 55, 57, and Benedict, ii, 409–11.

'immeasurable space . . .': 'Reflections' [Christmas Eve], in pencil on unlined scrap that matches neither the paper of her notes nor that of her mottoes and maxims. This is perhaps the last thing she wrote. Rollins. Benedict, ii, 411.

George Eliot: Cited Benedict, ii, 411, one of CFW's 'Reflections'.

266 *'think of those who are gone':* CFW to Kate Mather (25 Dec 1893), Benedict, ii, 390–1.

'Venetian spring': HJ to Daniel Curtis (27 Dec 1893). Curtis Papers. Dartmouth College, Hanover, NH.

very fond: HJ to Katharine Bronson (31 Dec 1893), Ms Rucellai. Edel's transcript. McGill. Transcribed by Steven Jobe.

266 *'that she hasn't . . .':* HJ to Daniel Curtis (27 Dec 1893). Curtis Papers. Dartmouth.

last letter from HJ to CFW: This could be the letter she received, about 17 Dec, which is the last she mentions (to WWB on 17 Dec), but of course he could well have written again, over the next month.

267 *the Holas testimony:* 'Miss Holas' account of Aunt Connie's last illness – '. A copy of the original. Privately owned by Molly Mather Anderson.

271 *flowerpots:* HJ to WJ (24 Mar [1894]), *CWJ*, ii, 304.

'fairly well documented': Alice Hall Petry in *Books at Brown*, 12.

gossip: Mrs Marie L. Thompson to SM (12 Feb 1894), from Florence. WRHS 3735. Container 1; folder 5.

273 *the Carter testimony:* Grace Carter to SM (27 Jan 1894) from Casa Semitecolo, San Gregorio. WRHS 3735. Container 1; folder 5. This is the first report for the Cleveland family, after the cables, and the first of two letters from Miss Carter to SM. The second was written on 25 Feb 1894 and is largely to report on her handling of finances and servants, with only a brief mention of the funeral in Rome, as she is aware there would have been immediate and full reports from John and Clara Hay.

not mangled, no bones broken, and facial expression: Reported orally by Grace Carter to Clara Hay during the funeral in Rome, and relayed by Clara to her sister, Flora Mather (31 Jan 1894). Letter from Rome. Privately owned by Molly Mather Anderson.

'A Florentine Experiment': Dorothy and Other Italian Stories (1896; repr. 1899), 136. Copy in Rollins.

274 *the dog that didn't bark in the night:* See 'Silver Blaze'.

275 *train from Munich to Venice:* As it turned out, Miss Carter did not make the night train, and took the next, arriving on Wednesday afternoon rather than in the morning. The morning, of course, would already have been too late.

276 *HJ decided against going:* HJ to Grace Carter (26 Jan 1894). 'Correspondence of HJ: Part V: Correspondence with Grace Carter'. 21 items, 106–26, C. W. Barrett Collection, Barrett Library, University of Virginia at Charlottesville. I am indebted to Doris Faber (who is writing a biography of CFW) for alerting me to these letters.

277 *'utterly in the dark . . .':* Ibid.

'MISS WOOLSON COMMITTED SUICIDE' and denial 'MISS WOOLSON NOT A SUICIDE': Newspaper cuttings (unidentified) in Constance Mather Bishop's Cuttings Book. Privately owned by Molly Mather Anderson.

'utterly sickened': HJ to Grace Carter (2 Feb 1894). C. W. Barrett Library, University of Virginia.

'exquisitely beautiful' and 'The ground is very crowded . . .': JH to SM and Flora Mather, his sister-in-law (31 Jan 1894), from Rome on the day of CFW's funeral. Privately owned by Molly Mather Anderson.

278 *'Yesterday I went to the Protestant cemetery . . .':* CFW to J. Bone, a

Cleveland journalist who had helped her at the outset of her career (17 Mar 1881). Quoted in the second of two obituary articles in his column, 'With and Without Glasses', *Cleveland Plain Dealer* (17 Feb 1894). In Constance Mather Bishop's Cuttings Book. Privately owned by Molly Mather Anderson.

278 *CFW and Daisy Miller:* Edel, iii, 300, suggests that CFW identified with Daisy Miller.

'trouble within trouble': 'The After-Season in Rome', *T(C)*, 467–8.

'the blest Roman cemetery . . .'; 'extremely honourable': HJ to JH (28 Jan 1894), *L(E)*, iii, 460.

278 – 9 *list of mourners and 'HJ had intended . . .':* Clara Hay to Flora Mather (31 Jan 1894), from Rome. Privately owned by Molly Mather Anderson.

279 *'utterly collapsed', etc.:* HJ to JH (28 Jan 1894), *L(E)*, iii, 459.

'gentlest and tenderest': HJ to 'Katrina' Bronson (2 Feb 1894), *L(E)*, iii, 465.

to Gosse: Selected Letters of HJ to Gosse.

deep student of the female heart: JH to HJ (5 June 1890), asking if he could explain the marriage of Dorothy Tennant to Stanley in 1890.

'extremely intimate': HJ to Ranee Margaret of Sarawak (28 Jan 1894). Columbia. HJ writes 'extremely infinite', crosses the second word out, and enters 'intimate' above.

'dementia': HJ to FB (31 Jan 1894), *L(E)*, iii, 463.

'Miss Woolson's sad death-house': HJ to FB (15 Dec 1894), *L(E)*, iii, 494.

HJ's letters following CFW's death: L(E), iii, 457–83, except for the letters to Grace Carter (Virginia), to Clara Benedict, and to the Ranee of Sarawak (Columbia). Weimer, *Back Talk*, 243, brings together HJ's most dubious statements. Patricia O'Toole has argued HJ's 'transforming her incomprehensible death into a private work of art' in *The Five of Hearts* (NY: Clarkson Potter, 1990), 271–2.

280 *'Your account . . .':* HJ to Grace Carter (2 Feb 1894). Univ. of Virginia.

281 *'insane':* HJ to WWB (2 Feb 1894), *L(E)*, iii, 464.

'greatly attached': HJ to the Ranee of Sarawak (28 Jan 1894). Columbia.

'unspeakably touching', etc.: HJ to WJ (24 Mar 1894), *CWJ*, ii, 304.

'insist': HJ to WWB (2 Feb 1894), *L(E)*, iii, 464.

282 *'quite baffling indisposition': N* (17 Apr 1894), 89. Written at the Casa Biondetti, Venice, about his state before he left London.

New York Herald: Cutting (n.d.) in Constance Mather Bishop's Cuttings Book. Privately owned by Molly Mather Anderson.

283 *asked Mrs Bronson:* ([20 Mar 1894]), *L(E)*, iii, 467–8.

284 *'I found . . .':* Edel, iii, 305. Written to Clare in Rome, before she and her mother reached Venice. After meeting their ship in Genoa, HJ awaited them in Venice while they went to Rome.

the dead 'capable', 'reaching', etc.: HJ contributed a fascinating chapter to a collection on the afterlife, entitled *In After Days* (1910), 214–32. Copies in Berg and in Library of Congress. He liked to think that the dead continued to exist 'as pure, individual spirits' somewhere 'in the mysterious infinite of the universe' (speaking of his parents and Wilky James to WJ on 24 Nov 1883, after Wilky's death), *L(E)*, iii, 15.

284 *'The Way It Came': CS*, iv, 609–34. HJ changed the title to 'The Friends of the Friends'.

285 *'deplorable':* HJ to Rhoda Broughton ([28 Jan 1894]), *L(E)*, iii, 458.

'in such a state': Clara Benedict to SM (2 May 1894). WRHS 3735. Container 24; folder 3.

two weeks: Over the subsequent three weeks, HJ did return to writing for a part of each day.

286 *'immensely accumulated effects':* HJ to FB (15 Dec 1894), *L(E)*, iii, 494.

'outcry': Her opportunity came with the publication of HJ's *The Outcry*. Clara made a comic story of this, but she was clearly put out that HJ would not willingly part with the painting. Clare Benedict's notes on the 'Fenimore' room, op. cit. NYHA. She bequeathed the Meacci to the National Trust, and it is now restored to Lamb House, where it hangs in the drawing-room, beside the French doors to the garden.

'never left us': Cited by Edel, iii, 367, who says Clara wrote this to a friend.

'Venice has been cold . . .': HJ to Grace Carter (11 May 1894). Univ. of Virginia.

'mad for her': HJ to FB (15 Dec 1894), *L(E)*, iii, 493–4.

287 *'surprising':* HJ to FB (28 Apr 1895). Houghton b MS Am 1094 (584–634).

ruses: The word isn't very legible. I am not certain of this reading.

'opposed': HJ to Grace Carter (11 May 1894). Univ. of Virginia. One sentence quoted by Kaplan, 386.

'worries': HJ to Henry Brewster, a Europeanised American (16 Apr 1894). C. W. Barrett Collection, University of Virginia. From the Biondetti. (Brewster lived in Palazzo Mattei in Rome, the supposed source for the Roman setting of *PL*.)

'an almost fatal job': HJ to WJ (25 May [1894]), from Ravenna. *CWJ*, ii, 307.

288 *persuaded the Benedicts:* Kaplan takes the view that HJ simply carried out the wishes of the Benedicts, but he does not take in the oppositional feeling cited in the letter to Grace Carter above.

Terminations: Volume of tales (1895).

'a strange story': Mercede Huntington, BBC 'Recollections of Henry James in Later Years'. Houghton. See ch. 1 ref. 1 above.

'mask': Clara Benedict to SM (2 May 1894). WRHS 3735. Container 24; folder 3. This word may not be correct.

'his quietus': HJ to Grace Carter (11 May 1894). His reference to this trouble corroborates the evidence of Clara Benedict.

289 *'poor, deluded . . . lady': The Aspern Papers*, ch. 9.

HJ at the grave: HJ to FB (28 Apr 1895). Houghton.

290 *nerves, 'horrid predicament', 'ferocious':* HJ to WJ and AHJ (25 May [1894], *CWJ*, ii, 307–8.

'cemetery of ghosts' and 'mournful eyes' of the Brichieri: HJ to FB (15 Dec 1894), *L(E)*, iii, 493–4.

290 *Miss Felton and Miss Norton still there:* HJ to WJ (29 June 1894). *CWJ*, ii, 314–15.

'demoralized and dematerialized': HJ to Morton Fullerton (30 June 1894), from Casa Biondetti. Houghton.

'vomitorium', Used twice. HJ to FB (15 Dec 1894), *L(E)*, iii, 493–4, and HJ to FB (28 Apr 1895). Houghton.

'fleeing the furies': HJ to Grace Norton (29 Mar 1894), *L(E)*, iii, 474. Cited by Edel, iii, 314 without date or source.

'the deadliest form of madness': HJ to WDH (22 Jan 1895), *L(E)*, iii, 513.

AJ on suicide: Diary (5 Aug 1889), 52.

291 *'dumbness':* HJ to Ariana Curtis (19 Aug [1894]). Dartmouth College, Hanover, NH.

HJ's visit to Norris: Norris to Rhoda Broughton (9 Sept 1894). Chester Record Office: microfilm DDB 79/2.

AJ's 'face-to-face': HJ to WJ (28 May 1894), from Rome, *CWJ*, ii, 311.

purpose in coming to Oxford: HJ's stated and immediate reason was to spend time with French friends the Bourgets, but they left after a few days, and HJ stayed on.

idea for 'The Altar of the Dead': (29 Sept 1894), *N*, 98–9. Kaplan, 390, notes MT's presence in the tale. First published in *Terminations* (1895).

292 *first outline for* WD: (3, 7 Nov 1894), *N*, 102–7.

'It is now . . .': (23 Jan 1895), *N*, 109.

Chapter 11 Posthumous Affairs

293 *'secret sorrow, trouble, fault':* *N*, 88.

'compunction' for 'wrong', etc.: *N*, 92. HJ's last tale, 'A Round of Visits' (1910), goes back to this idea in the wake of Woolson's death: the burden of guilt and the search for a recipient. In the end it was set in New York and coloured rather differently by HJ's return there in 1904–5.

'ugly' burden: *N*, 95.

294 *'face to face':* Ibid., repeated in 'The Way It Came' and 'The Beast in the Jungle'. See also 'face to face' in the notebook entry for the latter, *N*, 199.

'The Altar of the Dead': *CS*, iv, 450–85. First published in volume of tales entitled appropriately *Terminations* (1895).

295 *another incarnation of Miss Grief:* See discussion of *The Aspern Papers* in ch. 8 above.

quiet virtue: HJ's description of CFW in 1884. See ch. 8 above.

296 *'It's* full'*:* (14 Feb 1895), 115.

synopsis for WD: HJ mentions it in passing in a letter to H. G. Wells in the autumn of 1902; *N(M)*, 370, where HJ says he did away with it; and in four uncollected letters to William Meredith, son of the Victorian novelist George Meredith, and a director of Constable. *Desiderata* (2 Apr 1948), i: 14, 1–4.

296 *'represents to my memory . . .'*: Preface, *E(CP)*, 1287.

297 *purity:* John Pearson, in a lecture on HJ and CFW at Rollins College, Florida (Feb 1995), discussed the way 'The Altar of the Dead' transforms profane loss into the sacred.

'I see ghosts everywhere . . .': HJ to FB (11 Oct [1895]), *L(E)*, iv, 24. The context is his seeing the Benedicts (he declares Mrs Benedict 'is very considerably mad', extending his accusation of her sister CFW to her). He also refers to Kitty Emmet's death and the presumed ghostliness of Newport.

'It's the woman . . .': Outline for 'The Way It Came' (21 Dec 1895; expanded 10 Jan 1896), *N(M)*, 231.

298 *'the passionate things'*: *N* (24 Oct 1894), 99, on completing 'The Altar of the Dead'.

'I have . . . visions': *N*, 114.

'too late' *and 'the wasting of life'*: *N* (5 Feb 1895), 112.

Ellen ('Bay') Emmet: Her full name was Ellen Gertrude Emmet (1876–1941). As an artist she is known by her married name Ellen Emmet Rand. 'Bay' is in memory of Elizabeth Bay (1808–55), who married Augustus James (1807–66), the eldest son of Billy James and Catherine Barber, i.e. aunt to Henry James and the Temples. 21 letters, TS and MS, 1897–1915. Houghton b MS Am 1094 (662–712).

the Railroad King died in a railroad car: Bob Temple (writing with his usual insouciance from prison to WJ on 27 Feb [1887?]) points out the appropriateness. Houghton b MS Am 1095.2 (30a).

'back into the twilight of the past . . .': WJ to Elly (Temple) Hunter (13 July 1890). Houghton b MS Am 1092.9 (1066–86).

299 *'never loved before'*: AJ, *Diary* (28 Jan 1891).

HJ in the midst of three girls: HJ to Grace Carter (28 Dec 1896). Barrett Library, Univ. of Virginia.

Rosina: Her full name was Rosina Hubley Emmet (born 1873).

'the angel of Conversation': HJ to Gaillard Lapsley (16 Aug 1909). Houghton b MS Am 1094.4.

'She is so much the type of Minny': WJ to HJ (8 Apr 1895), *CWJ*, ii, 355–6.

WJ's attraction to Rosina: WJ to HJ (16 June 1895), *CWJ*, ii, 264.

Rosina's wish to publish: HJ to Rosina Emmet (2 Feb 1897; 28 Dec 1899). Transcribed by Edel. McGill. Transcribed by Steven Jobe.

300 *'brave Bay'*: HJ to Bay Emmet (16 Nov 1900 and 11 Oct 1903). Houghton. Some details of Bay from 1982 catalogue for exhibition of three women Emmets in the Berkshire Museum. I am grateful to Ellen Cohn for finding this.

Leslie: Her full name was Edith Leslie Emmet (born 1877). She was then 20.

WJ advised Rosina: WJ to Rosina Emmet (11 Aug 1897). Houghton.

'high pitch': HJ to WJ (11 Oct 1898), *CWJ*, iii, 46.

WJ and Rosina's truth: WJ to Rosina Emmet (9 Sept 1898). Houghton.

'completed': See ch. 6 above.

300 *'bounding, glowing juvenility':* HJ to Bay Emmet (26 Dec 1897). Houghton.
twenty-two letters: One not at Houghton transcribed by Edel at McGill.
301 *'time-stealing . . .':* HJ to Bay Emmet (addendum on 9 June to letter of 29 May 1903). Houghton.
'Suspect them . . .': HJ to Edward Holton James, Bob's son (15 Feb 1896), *L(E)*, iv, 30.
HJ letter to Grace Carter: (28 Dec 1896). Barrett Library, Univ. of Virginia. See also a letter to KL in 1897. Beverly Historical Society.
Lamb House: Clara Benedict to Kate Mather (8 Aug 1903). WRHS. The Benedicts went from Dover to Rye 'to see, at last, Mr. James' house. We spent a real old-fashioned "day" with him . . .'. Also HJ to AHJ (1 Dec 1897), *L(E)*, iv, 61–5.
'hermitage'; 'wave': HJ to OWH (10 Oct 1900). Reel 33, Microfilm of OWH papers, Harvard Law School.
the stimulus of other writers: See Miranda Seymour, *A Ring of Conspirators.*
'. . . how she . . . *would have liked* this *particular little corner of England':* HJ to Grace Carter from Lamb House (7 June 1900). Barrett Library, Univ. of Virginia at Charlottesville. Kaplan's date for this letter (1890) is incorrect. HJ did not know Miss Carter before 1894.
'mild': HJ to William Morton Fullerton (21 Sept 1900). Houghton b MS Am 1094.1.
'The Great Good Place': *CS*, v, 152–77.
302 *photo of MT in a drawer in Lamb House:* Violet Hunt, *I have this to say: The Flurried Years* (1925). Recounted by Miranda Seymour, who links the scene with HJ's request for the photo in 1870, *A Ring of Conspirators*, 169.
'I'm impatient . . .': HJ to Elly (Temple) Hunter (28 Aug 1898). Houghton.
'Do, do clutch . . .': HJ to Elly Temple Hunter [7 Sept 1899]. Houghton.
'as you see through the eye of a needle': HJ to Bay Emmet (7 Sept 1899). Houghton.
'wild fandango': HJ to Elly (Temple) Hunter (Mar 1902). Houghton.
'I applaud . . .': HJ to Bay Emmet (2 Oct 1901). Houghton.
'I stay in solitude . . .': HJ to Edmund Gosse (28 Aug 1896), *L(E)*, iv, 35.
303 *not great works:* There have been 'closet' readings of *The Aspern Papers*, 'The Pupil' , and 'The Beast in the Jungle', but Philip Horne has demolished scaffolds of supposition constructed without one firm fact. 'Henry James: The Master and the "Queer Affair" of "The Pupil" ', *Critical Quarterly*, xxxvii:3 (Autumn 1995) 75–92.
'I could wish . . .': HJ to Morton Fullerton (6 Aug 1901). Rare Books and Special Collections, Princeton University Libraries: CO140 General MSS [Misc]; box JA–JE, Folder James, Henry; sub-folders 2–3.
304 *'fire' = 'Light on your Life':* HJ to William Morton Fullerton (26 Sept 1900). Houghton b MS Am 1094.1.
'come': HJ from Rye to Bay Emmet at Dunwich, Suffolk (6 Sept 1899). McGill.
'possessed' of Lapsley: HJ to Gaillard Thomas Lapsley (27 Dec 1906), *L(L)*, ii, 64. See Houghton b MS Am 1094.4 for 77 letters, 1897–1915.

304 *date of Bay's arrival at Lamb House:* HJ to Grace Carter (27 June 1900). Univ. of Virginia. Says Bay to come next day.

305 *native rapids:* HJ to Bay Emmet (22 August 1900). Transcribed by Edel. McGill. Transcribed by Stephen Jobe.

'romantic summer': HJ to Bay Emmet (20 Oct 1901). Houghton.

'late afternoon stroke': HJ to Bay Emmet (11 Oct 1903). Houghton.

warmed his 'aged heart': HJ to Bay Emmet (16 Nov 1900). Houghton.

306 *'You remain . . .':* HJ to OWH (20 Feb 1901), Reel 34, Microfilm of OWH Papers, Harvard Law Library.

WJ's reply to JCG: No year given in the holograph in the Houghton Library. It is not known in what year the exchange took place. The letter is quoted by HJ in *A*, ii, 504. (HJ slightly alters one phrase.) See above, the end of ch. 3.

the Emmet sisters in NY: WJ to HJ (28 Nov 1901 and 31 Jan 1902), *CWJ*, iii, 189, 191–3.

307 *'a pure* painter': HJ to WJ (18 July 1900), *CWJ*, iii, 124.

'I feel your ghosts . . .' etc.: HJ to Bay Emmet (2 Oct 1901). Houghton.

308 *'She was alone . . .': WD*, Book Third: v.

'one of the finest . . . cases of American intensity': Ibid.

'the potential heiress of all the ages': Ibid.

'lineage of squalor': WJ to HJ (18 May 1907), *CWJ*, iii, 341.

suicide of John James: Habegger, 'Dupine Tracks J.J.', 803–25. See also paragraph on John James by Henry James III in Houghton b MS Am 1092.9 (4600), folder 14.

Howard James: Ibid., and WJ to RJ (29 Mar 1874). Houghton b MS Am 1092.9 (3133).

309 *outreach of evolution:* Virginia Llewellyn Smith, *Henry James and the Real Thing: A Modern Reader's Guide* (Macmillan, 1994), 226, notes the 'succession of flights and drops' which describes 'a bumpy but persistent evolutionary trajectory'.

'the dizzy edge': WD, Book Third: v.

'kingdoms': WJ to HJ (12, 14 July 1900), *CWJ*, iii, 122–3.

310 *'the face of a young woman . . .': WD*, Book Fifth: xi. Lucrezia Panciatichi lived from 1528 to 1572. The portrait is in the Uffizi in Florence. There is a supposed Bronzino in the English country house Mentmore, home of Lord and Lady Rosebery, which HJ frequented. The portrait hung in an octagonal library at that time.

WWB and Sir Luke Strett: Edel suggested a likeness between Sir Luke as WWB in *L(E)*, iii, 299–300, noting that when HJ stayed with WWB in July 1890 they had hiked to several Tuscan towns together with WWB's friend, an Italian named Taccini, the name used in *WD* for the doctor who takes charge of Milly when Sir Luke is in London.

311 *'one of the courts of heaven': WD*, Book Eighth: xxviii.

311 *'yet shall ye be as the wings of a dove'*: Psalm 68:13. See also Psalm 55.
'On the morning ...': Text published in *Harper's* (Sept 1902), 525–6. See set of Copley Color Cards in Houghton.
312 *'magnificently paid'*: Dr Bernard Richards set his students at Brasenose College, Oxford, an unidentified passage from *WD* where Densher reflects on the consummation of his love for Kate Croy. When the students were asked to place it, many thought it was by D. H. Lawrence.
'healing and uplifting passion': *WD*, Book Seventh: xxv.
'name': *WD*, Book Ninth: xxix.
'transcendent motions': Ibid.
313 *'might kill her'*: *WD*, Book Ninth: xxx.
'She has turned her face to the wall': Ibid. xxxi.
'If I begin to be indifferent ...': MT to JCG (16 Feb 1869). Houghton.
'Milly had held ...': *WD*, Book Tenth: xxxiv.
314 *'He kept it'*: Ibid.: xxxviii.
315 *'Her memory's your love'*: Ibid.
'single and faithful': *N(M)*, 173–4.
'We shall never ...': *WD*, Book Tenth: xxxviii.
'a woman ...': MT to JCG (24 Apr 1869). Context is her admiration for George Eliot.
'She was a case ...': HJ to WJ (29 Mar 1870), *CWJ*, i, 153.
'isolated': HJ to Ariana Curtis (21 Feb 1901). Tintner Collection, Berg. For Katharine Bronson's last years, including her 'many disillusions', see her four letters to WWB. PML. See also HJ to Edith Bronson, Contessa Rucellai (15 Feb 1901), *L(E)*, iv, 183.
CFW's eastern journey and HJ's initial settings for the novel: Edel, iii, 324: when he planned *WD*, 'the figure of Fenimore also stood beside him'.
316 *Mrs Humphry Ward on* WD: *A Writer's Recollections*, ii (NY: Harper; London, 1918), 206–7: she thought the cynical bargain of Kate and Densher improbable if Densher is the decent, humane person presented to us.
'The Jamesian Lie': In *A Future for Astyanax: Character and Desire in Literature* (Boston: Little, Brown, 1969; repr. 1976; London: Marion Boyars, 1978), 143–4: Milly's success in redeeming Densher is 'partly undermined by something unconvincing in his betrayal of her. It's as if Densher's prolonged deception of Milly were nothing more than the time-filling pretext which allows for his appreciation of her to mature. ... Her death seems hardly to matter when she has been treated for so long merely as an appeal of consciousness.' See, too, Virginia Llewellyn Smith, 179, who notes astutely that this novel terminates too much in the act of reading, which deflects us from the full weight of its moral content.
'love-story': HJ to William Meredith (18 Nov 1901), *Desiderata* (18 Apr 1948).

316 *'the Last of the Mohicans of my acquaintance':* HJ to Leslie Pell-Clarke (30 Dec 1903). Houghton b MS Am 1094 (1038–9).

'our romantic life together; 'designs': HJ to Eleanor Emmet (later, Lapsley) (19 Nov 1902). Houghton b MS Am 1094.1.

317 *'so solid & soothing', etc.:* HJ to WJ and AHJ (4 July 1902), *CWJ*, iii, 209–10.

'possessed' of Eleanor and 'use': HJ to Grenville Emmet (9 Jan 1904). Houghton b MS Am 1094.1.

aftermath: WD was published in August 1902 on both sides of the Atlantic.

'My autumn . . .' and 'a certain wild freedom': HJ to Eleanor Emmet (19 Nov 1902). Houghton.

318 *'. . . your ghost . . .':* HJ to Eleanor Emmet (30 June 1903). Houghton.

'a touch . . .': HJ to Bay Emmet (11 Oct 1903). Houghton.

'perfections': HJ to Gaillard Lapsley (17 Mar 1908). Houghton.

'poor words': W. B. Yeats, 'Words', in *The Green Helmet and Other Poems* (1910), *Collected Poems* (Macmillan, 1958), 100–1.

'Words alone are certain good': Yeats, 'The Song of the Happy Shepherd', in *Crossways* (1889), ibid., 7.

'get at', etc.: HJ to Elly (Temple) Hunter (22 Nov 1903). Houghton.

319 *the rest of the road:* HJ to Rosina Emmet (7 Dec 1903) at 2 East 15th Street, NY. Transcribed by Edel. McGill. Transcribed by Steven H. Jobe.

'celibate': HJ to WJ (6 May 1904), *CWJ*, iii, 271. He signs himself thus in the context of a rumour that he was to marry a Miss Grigsby, which he repudiates furiously.

The Ambassadors: The earliest *donnée* is a notebook entry on 5 Feb 1895 (*N*, 112) about 'the wasting of life', a realisation that comes to an older man 'too late'. Then, on 31 Oct 1895, HJ set out his first outline for a short work he called at this point *Les Vieux* (*N*, 140–2) about an ageing man who awakens to the fact that he hasn't 'lived'. HJ wrote a detailed outline for a full-scale novel (*N*, 541–76), dated 1 Sept 1900, and completed the work in June 1901.

velvet band: The Ambassadors, Book Second: i. See photos of CFW.

'our national consciousness', etc.: Ibid., Book First: i.

320 *'pirate's cave':* Ibid., Book Third: ii.

outline for The Ambassadors: 'Project of Novel by Henry James', typescript in PML: MA 3140. Most of the quotations below are transcribed from this typescript, pp. 12–13. See *N*, 541–76.

'vague resemblance': HJ to Jocelyn Persse (26 Oct 1903), *L(E)*, iv, 286.

'divination': See outline, quoted below, and *The Ambassadors*, Book Twelfth: iii.

321 *leaping from peak to peak:* outline.

allows Maria to see his hesitation: outline.

refusing 'life' in refusing Miss Gostrey: I am indebted to Dr Rachel Salmon of Bar-Ilan University, Tel-Aviv, for discussions in the late sixties at Columbia University, in which she shared her ideas about the ambiguity of

The Ambassadors, in particular the final scene between Strether and Maria Gostrey.

321 *'great ... at postponements': The Ambassadors*, Book Twelfth: iii.

322 *'one's life ...': N*, 543.

'expressive decency': Preface to *The Ambassadors.*

'convenience' and 'receptacle': outline.

'into requisition': The Ambassadors, Book Eleventh: iv.

'indulgence': Ibid., Book Twelfth: iii.

'... You've recognised me ...': Ibid., Book First: i. Cited by Weimer, 36.

323 *pistol point:* outline.

'right': The Ambassadors, Book Twelfth: v.

'The Beast in the Jungle': CS, v, 496–541. Same *donnée* on 'the wasting of life' (5 Feb 1895), *N*, 112–13. Outline (27 Aug 1901), *N*, 199. Written in 1902. Hard for HJ to place tale of this length, almost a novella, so not published until 1903, in next collection, *The Better Sort.*).

324 *'splendid moment'*: See above p. 286n. Benedict, ii, 144–5. Quoted by Edel, iii, 308.

turned back of May, linked with CFW: Noted by Torsney, *CFW*, 2.

high-toned idea: Eve Sedgwick in *The Epistemology of the Closet* puts forward a hypothesis about Marcher's 'male homosexual panic' and the damage it does to May Bartram. The argument turns on negations which she aligns with the love that has no name. Philip Horne, in 'The Master and the "Queer Affair" ', refutes the argument: 'only a few of the things unnamable in the public world are homosexual, after all'.

suggests the force of a recognition: Lifted from Ronald Bush 'Changing His Mind About How To Do a Girl In: Poetry, Narrative and Gender in the Revisions of HJ's *Daisy Miller*', op. cit.

Story's monument to his wife; his description, including 'utter abandonment', and HJ's impression: William Wetmore Story (1903), ii, 324–5.

325 *Katharine Fullerton:* She lived from 1879 to 1944. See HJ's letters to her (12 Jan 1905; 5 Dec 1907; and 23 Oct 1908) and a substantial number to Morton Fullerton (especially 30 Nov 1899; 18 Oct 1902; and 14 June 1903). Department of Rare Books and Special Collections, Princeton University Libraries: CO140 General MSS [Misc], box JA–JE: folder James, Henry; sub-folders 2–3.

'documents': HJ to Morton Fullerton (14 June 1903). Princeton.

'spoke': HJ to Morton Fullerton (30 Nov 1899). Princeton.

326 *HJ to Fullerton (18 Oct 1902):* Princeton. This important letter is transcribed from the manuscript in order to correct some inaccuracies in *L(E)*, iv, 243–5. Edel reads 'out, with every assistance' as 'not, with every assistance' (which doesn't make sense). For 'distinct & distinguished', he reads 'distinct and distinguishable'. Various underlinings by HJ have been omitted in the published text, and there are small errors of punctuation.

Chapter 12 The Figure in the Furnace

329 *'monster':* HJ to Henry Adams (21 Mar 1914), *L(E)*, iv, 706. The context is his cultivation of interest in the past for the purpose of art.

Dixon: Transcript of 'Recollections of HJ in his Later Years', BBC programme (1956). Houghton. See above, ch. 1. ref. 1.

'My dear fellow . . .': Ibid.: Mrs De Glehn.

330 *'furnace':* See below.

as though the bottom . . .: The American Scene, T(BA), ch. 7: i, 543–4.

'sacred grove': Ibid., ch. 1: iii, 379.

331 *'Remembrance':* EW, *A Backward Glance* (1934; repr. London: Century Hutchinson, 1987), 185.

ghosts of 'the Emmetry': Ibid., 193.

magazine instalments: North American Review (Jan–Dec 1903).

332 *'inward passion' etc.: N*, 238–9. Sheldon M. Novick, *Henry James: The Young Master* (NY: Random House, 1996) has supposed this to refer to active homosexuality with OWH: 'this passage seems impossible to misunderstand'. HJ, he concludes, 'performed his first acts of love' in 'a rooming house in Cambridge and in his own shuttered bedroom in Ashburton Place'. As Kenneth S. Lynn pointed out in a review (in the *Wall Street Journal*): 'It seems not to matter that this passage [in the notebooks] makes no mention of a rooming-house. Nor is [Novick] deterred by the fact that HJ was much given to expressing himself in powerfully emotive language that on occasion can make it all too easy to misunderstand him.' Lynn suggests that the subject on HJ's mind was what Shaw called 'the superior orgasm of creativity'. In short, the text is too non-specific for any certainty. The phrase 'inward passion' would seem to negate physical activity.

333 *'There was a voice . . .': The American Scene*, ch. 1: ii.

de Tocqueville: Democracy in America, trans. George Lawrence, ed. J. P. Mayer (1966; repr. NY: Doubleday Anchor, 1969), Part III, ch. 12, 'How the American Views the Equality of the Sexes', 603.

334 *the American girl and her vacant mate: The American Scene*, ch. 11: iii.

'The Jolly Corner': CS, v, 697–731.

'wounded myself': Robert Temple to HJSr (4 Jan 1877). Houghton b MS Am 1095.2(19).

'Harry has deserted me . . .': Robert Temple to WJ from Pendleton (prison) (27 Feb [1885]), Houghton. See also WJ to Kitty Prince (10 Mar 1885). Houghton.

335 *'pangs & pains':* HJ to Ariana Curtis (15 Aug 1908). Dartmouth College, Hanover, NH.

May Bartram's link with Miss Staverton: I am indebted to a fine essay by Amy Hing, from Singapore, during her first year at St Hilda's College, Oxford.

after third visit: A guess. The exact date of composition is not known. A link with CFW is suggested by the content of the tale, its connection with similar divinatory middle-aged women in other tales, and the dates of early *données*, the first on 5 Feb 1895, as part of the artistic ferment that followed CFW's death, and the second in May 1899 in Rome, the time of HJ's second visit to her grave. The strongest link seems to me the title: the similarity of the 'Jolly Corner' to CFW's childhood at 'Cheerful Corner' is unlikely to be a coincidence. 'Cheerful Corner' is recorded in Clare Benedict's listing of family possessions (the Cooper Room) in NYHA, Cooperstown, and is also recalled by Cornelia E. L. May, a three-page MS reminiscence, 'CFW', included in Constance Mather Bishop's Cuttings Book. See ch. 2 above for CFW's homes in Cleveland.

336 *'the most beautiful thing . . .':* HJ to Clare Benedict (13 Sept 1907), *L(E)*, iv, 460. Cited Edel, iii, 315.

'conversable': HJ to EW's sister-in-law, Mrs Cadwalader Jones (31 Dec 1903). Houghton.

'magic faculty': EW, *A Backward Glance*, 173.

'Nonsense, Henry . . .': Recalled by Gerard Hopkins, Transcript of 'Recollections of HJ in his Later Years', BBC (1956). Houghton. See above, ch. 1 ref. 1.

337 *'the little vanishing group . . .':* EW, *A Backward Glance*, 176.

brief fling: Shari Benstock, *Edith Wharton: No Gifts from Chance* (London: Hamish Hamilton, 1994). Benstock, drawing on letters unavailable to previous biographers, challenges their dating and interpretation of letters between EW and Fullerton, in which physical consummation of the affair was placed in spring 1908. Benstock claims that 'Edith's rhetoric of passion outdistances her actions' and suggests that she dithered until more than a year later.

338 *voyeurism:* suggestive review of the above by Joan Smith, 'Age of not so much innocence', *Independent on Sunday* (16 Oct 1994).

'The Letters': Tales of Men and Ghosts (1910), repr. *The Stories of Edith Wharton*, ed. Anita Brookner (NY and London: Simon and Schuster, 1988), 90–119.

Ellen Olenska: in EW, *The Age of Innocence* (1920).

339 *'Crapy Cornelia': CS*, v, 818–46.

HJ aligned with hero: 'You are not Cornelia, but I am much White-Mason', HJ wrote to Henrietta Reubell (19 Oct 1909), *L(L)*, ii, 145.

last drop of petrol: EW, *A Backward Glance*, 248.

341 *revision of* Daisy Miller: NY Edition, vol. xviii, 85–6. HJ was a lifelong reviser. See the full-scale treatment of this major subject by Philip Horne, *Henry James and Revision* (Oxford: Clarendon Press, 1990). Ch. 7 provides a detailed analysis of the revisions of *Daisy Miller*. I especially liked the idea that 'for Winterbourne being in love, with Daisy at any rate, involves what one might call a detective attitude to the loved one.' See, too, Viola R. Dunbar, 'The Revision of *Daisy Miller*', *Modern Language Notes*, lxv (1950), 311–17; Carol Ohmann, 'Daisy Miller: A Study of Changing

Intentions', *American Literature*, xxxvi (1964), 1–11; and Ronald Bush, 'Changing His Mind About How To Do A Girl In: Poetry, Narrative and Gender in the Revisions of HJ's *Daisy Miller*'. I am indebted to Bush for drawing attention to the quote from the 1909 version, and to Horne (p. 250) for the link with *WD*.

341 *revision of* PL: Copy in Houghton. See Horne, *HJ and Revision*, ch. 6.

342 *'there are times . . .':* Cited by Richard Davenport-Hines, *Auden* (London: Heinemann, 1995), 223.

fictions tell us more: In 1994 Fozia Bora made this unconventional point in her final year at St Hilda's College, when she did James as a special topic. John H. Pearson says 'James would create a monument to fix his identity as an author, yet he increasingly suspected the notion of a fixed identity.' Introduction, *The Prefaces of HJ* (Penn State Univ. Press, 1997), 8.

342–3 *imitations of HJ's fictions:* Leonard Woolf, *Sowing: An Autobiography of the Years 1880 to 1904* (London: Hogarth Press, 1960; repr. NY: Harcourt-Harvest 1975), 106–15.

343 *Sydney Waterlow's record:* Diary, dated Apr 1907 to Apr 1912. Berg. He proposed to Virginia Stephen in 1911 before he was divorced. She refused him kindly.

Waterlow to Virginia Stephen: Written from Cambridge in 1912. Berg. She married, and became Virginia Woolf later that year.

hideous trial: He dated the start of his breakdown precisely according to a letter to AHJ (17 Jan 1913), where he says it began 3 years and 18 days ago. Houghton.

thought of suicide: Henry James and Edith Wharton: Letters 1900–1915, ed. Lyall H. Powers (London: Weidenfeld, 1990), 139.

measure of relief: Afterwards, he told her that she gave him a permanent foothold towards recovery. HJ to AHJ (17 Jan 1913). Houghton.

'You can get better . . .': AHJ to HJ (13 Mar 1910). Houghton.

344 *Bad-Neuheim:* HJ to George Abbot James (29 July 1910). Houghton.

AHJ told HJ of RJ's death: HJ to AHJ (17 Jan 1913). Houghton.

'That moment . . .': Ibid.

'I sit here . . .': HJ to OWH from Chocorua, NH. Microfilm of OWH Papers, reel 34, Harvard Law Library.

'spoiling' . . . 'a couple of years': HJ to OWH (16 July 1911), from Nahant, Mass. Ibid.

'housemaid' and 'lost': HJ to Morton Fullerton (Oct 1897). Houghton.

'silent . . . victim', etc.: HJ to Morton Fullerton (2 Oct 1896). Houghton.

illness of his life: HJ to Elly Temple Hunter (25 June [1910]). Transcribed by Edel. McGill. Transcribed by Stephen Jobe.

'poisonous serpent': HJ to George Abbot James (29 July 1910). Houghton.

hell; loved Bay; clasp: HJ to Bay Emmet (26 June 1910). Transcribed by Edel. McGill. Transcribed by Steven Jobe.

345 *Freudian analysis:* Benstock, *No Gifts from Chance*, 250.

'accursed necessity': HJ to George Abbot James (May 1911). Houghton.

345 *'deep black hole', 'scrawl':* HJ to Elly (Temple) Hunter (10 May 1911). Houghton.

'speechless': HJ to Rhoda Broughton (25 Feb 1911), *L(L)*, ii, 186.

'emerge': HJ to Bay Emmet (6 Jan 1911). Houghton.

'I had to come . . .': HJ to Ariana Curtis (8 May 1911). Dartmouth College, Hanover, NH.

'prostrate . . .', etc.: HJ to KL (July 1911). Loring Papers, Beverly Historical Society.

'appalling summer': HJ to Bay Emmet (15 Aug 1911). Houghton. This confessional letter was written immediately after his return to Lamb House.

346 *'Paradise':* HJ to George Abbot James (16 May 1914). Houghton.

'waste of waters' and 'the same brassy sky': HJ to Bay Emmet (15 Aug 1911). Houghton.

'a good deal like her . . .': Ibid.

'the history of a mind', etc.: A, i, 105; ii, 305.

347 *recovery:* HJ to Elly Hunter (12 Jan 1912). Houghton.

'our cousins . . .' A, i, 10.

'My thoughts hang about you . . .': HJ to Elly Hunter (12 Jan 1912). Houghton.

348 *'a new plague':* HJ to Gaillard Lapsley (24 Oct 1912). Houghton.

'blisters', etc.: HJ to AHJ (29 Oct 1912). Houghton.

'down into hell': HJ to EW (4 Dec 1912), *L(E)*, iv, 643.

'howling': HJ to George Abbot James (16 Aug 1913). Houghton.

'full-blown' and 'sequel': HJ to AHJ (17 Jan 1913). Houghton.

'I have had blighted . . . weeks', 'inhuman', etc.: HJ to TSP (29 Nov 1912). Dictated typescript. Miller Library, Colby College, Maine.

349 *JCG's call on AHJ:* AHJ to HJ (17 May 1913). Houghton. Phrases from this letter have been cited by Habegger, *HJ and the 'Woman Business'*, 162.

351 *'infinitely pathetic . . . voice':* HJ to Peggy, WJ's daughter (later Mrs Porter), who had read the letters, since she helped her mother transcribe them (19 June 1913). Berkeley TS transcript, cited by Horne, 221–2.

MT 'speaking': A, ii, 520: HJ says her memory was 'most touching perhaps by so speaking'.

include 'dearest . . . M.T.': HJ to Helena de Kay Gilder (23 June 1913). Houghton b MS Am 1237.16.

completed NSB: HJ to AHJ (18 Oct 1913). Houghton b MS Am 1094 (1609–1750).

352 *'mistakes':* HJ to Caroline James (31 July 1913). Mr and Mrs Henry Vaux. Cited in 1986 by Maher, then by Kaplan, 550.

'the happy working . . .': Cited by Follini in 'Pandora's Box', a highly perceptive analysis of HJ's position on biographical record in relation to his memoir.

Henry senior and older brother; WJ's objection: See above, ch. 5.

'when she was still . . .': HJ to KL (2 Mar 1914). Vassar College.

'I daresay': HJ to Henry (Harry) James III, eldest son of WJ (15–18 Nov

1913) *L(E)*, iv, appendix. Follini makes a convincing case that this letter was not a record of unquestioned confidence but 'an anguished epistle of self-justification in which certainty coexists with doubt'.

352 *'What I have been able to do for* her . . .': HJ to AHJ (29 Mar 1914), *L(E)*, iv, 707.

353 *'ghostly image':* HJ to Lilla Cabot Perry (2 Aug 1914). Colby College, Maine. Mrs Perry sent HJ an enlarged copy of this photo which he said would replace his faded original: '. . . your enlarged copy has given it new life & reality, & I shall keep this before me instead of the other.'

MT's photograph before him: A, ii, 530.

at the back of his consciousness: HJ to Helena de Kay Gilder (2 Sept 1914), *L(L)*, ii, 416–18.

'the reach . . .': HJ to WJ (29 Mar 1870), *CWJ*, i, 153.

HJ rebukes Wells: HJ to H. G. Wells (21 Sept 1913), *L(L)*, ii, 348, and *L(E)*, iv, 688. He is considering the presentation of the heroine through the report of the hero in Wells's *The Passionate Friends.*

354 'abounding': AHJ to HJ (14 Mar 1914). Houghton.

Rosina reported: Ibid.

anger at MT's family: HJ to Helena de Kay Gilder (2 Sept 1914), *L(L)*, ii, 416–18.

'the third John Gray': AHJ to HJ (14 Mar 1914). Houghton b MS Am 1092.11 (27–55).

355 *'word of appreciation':* HJ to JCG (20 Apr 1914). Houghton b47 M-332 (73).

356 *'appear to have made . . .':* HJ to Henry (Harry) James III, son of WJ, HJ's literary executor (7 Apr 1914). Houghton b MS Am 1094 (1350–1425).

HJ's reply to Henrietta: (5 May 1914). Houghton. Quoted in full by S. P. Rosenbaum, 'Letters to the Pell-Clarkes from their "Old Cousin and Friend" Henry James', *American Literature*, xxxi (1959), 46–58.

357 *HJ's reply to Eleanor:* (24 June 1914). Houghton b MS Am 1094.1.

358 *emotional intensity:* Pamela Norris, in conversation, London (7 Sept 1995).

'they would say little . . .': HJ to WJ (29 Mar 1870), *CWJ*, i, 156.

359 *'there is little . . . to add': A*, ii, 544.

Chapter 13 All Manhood at One's Side

360 'outsiders': 'Americans Abroad' (1878), *T(BA)*, 787.

'our cause' and 'iron fist': 'Within the Rim' (1915), *T(BA)*, 329–40.

aligned with Civil War, 'the agitation', 'one swung off': Ibid.

361 *'change of consciousness', 'break with the past', 'interrogation points':* HJ to Alice Runnells James (wife of Billy, WJ's second son) (20 Aug 1914). PML: MA4640.

'too difficult to give verisimiltude': HJ to the romantic novelist Betham Edwards (5 Jan 1915). PML: MA4500.

'colossal convulsion': HJ to KL (13 Sept 1914). Vassar.

361 *HJ and the Grenadier guardsman:* HJ to Henry James III (31 Oct 1914). Houghton b MS Am 1094 (1609–1750).
march-past: HJ to AHJ (4 Dec 1914). Houghton b MS Am 1094 (1609–1750).
362 *'magnificently', etc.:* HJ's letters to AHJ (Feb–Mar 1915). Houghton.
'Nothing . . .': HJ's last letter to Bay (22 July 1915). Houghton.
letters to Eddie Marsh: 25 letters, mostly unpublished, including the one quoted, to Sir Edward Howard Marsh (3 July 1914–27 Nov 1915). Berg. Letter of 6 June 1915 in *L(L)*, ii, 489–90.
'howl': HJ to Marsh (14 June 1915). Berg.
to HJ from the Home Secretary: John Simon to HJ (19 July 1915). Berg.
363 *'Civis Britannicus sum':* HJ to Henry James III (28 July 1915). Houghton.
'You see . . .': HJ to Henry James III (6 Aug 1914). Houghton.
'manhood': (11 Mar 1888), *N(M)*, 88. See ch. 8 above, on 'The Lesson of the Master'.
desire of a different kind: Many critics take this view, including James Thurber, 'The Wings of Henry James', *Lanterns and Lances* (NY: Harper, 1961), endorsed by Philip Sicker, *Love and the Quest for Identity in the Fiction of HJ* (Princeton Univ. Press, 1980), xiv.
'corruption': see ch. 8 above, on 'The Lesson of the Master'.
'I snatch . . .': HJ to Elly (Temple) Hunter (Aug 1915). Houghton.
366 *Grace Norton ridiculed for her idea of MT:* HJ to TSP (13 Apr 1914), in Harlow, *TSP*, 345–7.
367 *'extreme pertinence':* Ibid.
HJ on Flaubert's letters: 'Correspondence de Gustave Flaubert' (1893), *E(CP)*, 296.
'the responsibility *of destruction':* *N*, 66: 26 Mar 1892.
'post-mortem exploiter': HJ to Henry James III (7 Apr 1914), *L(E)*, iv, appendix iv, 806.
'There are secrets . . .': 'She and He: Recent Documents', *Yellow Book* (Jan 1897), repr. as 'George Sand, 1897' in *Notes on Novelists* (1914), *E(CP)*, 742–3.
368 *'burn with fire':* HJ to WJ (28 May 1894), *CWJ*, ii, 311.
KL's letter on the diary: Copy of letter to Mrs (Margaret Mary James) Porter (6 June 1934). Princeton's Special Collections: Burr Family Papers, CO618, series VIII ('Papers of Others'), box 2, folder 16.
369 *KL asked to have letters to WJ destroyed:* KL to Ralph Barton Perry, who wrote a study of WJ (1935). Houghton.
portrait of KL in her later years: Letters in Beverly Historical Society; in the Schlesinger Library, Radcliffe College; and a more personal batch to a friend and author, Laura Elizabeth (Howe) Richards, written in her nineties (1934–43) from Pride's Crossing. Houghton *52M-301.
370 *KL's burning of letters:* Augustus P. Loring to Mary B. Parlee of the Radcliffe Institute (24 May 1973). Houghton.
'I kept . . .': HJ to Annie Fields (2 Jan 1910), *L(E)*, iv, 541 is inaccurate. The

quotation is taken from the original in the Huntington Library. Edel has it: 'save as to ... which *had* to survive.'

370 *an unread letter exerts a power stronger than fact:* I owe this point to Tamara Follini, 'Pandora's Box'.

documentary truth limited: Ian Hamilton rightly said that James deplores a biography which obliterates mystery. There is a cogent analysis of the biographical issues in HJ, in *Keepers of the Flame* (London: Pimlico, 1993), ch. 9, especially pp. 208–13.

'the whole Carlyle ... history': HJ to editor of Carlyle's correspondence, Charles Eliot Norton (25 Mar [1889]), *L(E)*, iii, 251.

HJ reviewed over fifteen volumes of letters: I owe this point to Sharon Dean in a talk on 'Woolson, Wharton and Class', Conference on CFW, Mackinac Island, Mich. (Oct 1996).

'exquisite'; 'indiscretion': William Wetmore Story, i, 14–15.

HJ and the Lovelace Papers: John Buchan, *Memory Hold-the-Door* (1940), 151–2, *N(M)*, 181–2, or *N*, 110–11. Cited by Hamilton, 219.

371 *'To Certain Biographers': Appleton's Journal*, v (Dec 1878), 376.

deathbed ramblings: Feb 1916. *L(E)*, iv, appendix v, 808–12.

'black cave', 'pushed down', 'necessity', 'I stayed ...': HJ to Henry James III (4 Nov 1915). Houghton b MS Am 1094 (1609–1750).

Select Bibliography

Primary Sources

MISSING PAPERS

Since this is a biography which tries not to lose sight of missing papers, it is appropriate to start with some of these items:

1. On 21 Dec 1869, HJ acknowledged his mother's letter of 23 Nov and Alice's letter of 28 Nov. These letters, following Minny Temple's last visit to the Jameses, don't survive; nor does any letter from WJ to HJ between 1 Nov and 5 Dec.

2. On 14 Jan 1870, HJ mentions the 'sermon' in his father's last letter supposedly dated 22 Dec 1869. All that survives is a fragment of a letter dated 26 Dec. Like all HJSr's extant letters, this fragment is silent about Minny Temple. No extant 1870 letters from HJSr to HJ.

3. Letters WJ and MJ wrote immediately after Minny's death don't survive.

4. The original letters Minny wrote to Helena de Kay in the 1860s may still turn up when the Gilder Papers are sifted more thoroughly, but apparently survive only in typed copies made by Helena's daughter, Rosamond Gilder.

5. Original letters from Minny Temple to John Chipman Gray were destroyed by HJ. (Holograph copies by Alice Howe James and Margaret Mary James are in the Houghton.)

6. HJ's 1869–70 letters to MT.

7. HJ's letters to CFW.

8. CFW's letters to HJ (except four sent to America which remained amidst William James's papers). CFW's letters to her sister.

9. A letter from William James to HJ in Nov 1869, presuming

that WJ would have reported to HJ his refusal to allow their youngest brother RJ to marry a cousin. Such a major family event would not have gone unmentioned.

10. All letters from the James family in response to *The Portrait of a Lady*. Since Grace Norton and Helena de Kay Gilder recognised Minny Temple as a source for Isabel Archer, it is possible that the family letters, too, commented on this.

11. Clare Benedict was committed to the idea of a Woolson House which would house memorabilia at Rollins College, Winter Park, Florida. She saw the house as a place for aspiring writers and for lecturers. This was duly built, and the memorabilia sent from Switzerland where Benedict eventually settled. Benedict then sent various requests for items to be sent back, for instance a pill-box given to CFW by Henry James. In 1985, when Dr Kathleen Reich (who supplied this information) was appointed curator of the archives, she discovered a lot was missing. She made an inventory which showed that of 229 items, 26 were returned to Benedict and 111 lost without trace.

12. CFW's journal. Extracts published by Clare Benedict, who inherited the papers of her aunt, and raided them for her unreliable compilation *Five Generations*. Her extracts, from her aunt's journal, letters, and notebook are fragmentary and undated, giving the impression that she suppressed material. This impression is reinforced by a letter in the Woolson collection at Rollins which she cut up in her misguided capacity as custodian. It was probably Clare Benedict who destroyed relevant pages, justifying suicide, from her aunt's copy of Epictetus. Certain scholars have speculated as to whether there could be a cache of papers which, so far, has remained restricted and which, hopefully, would one day be part of the family collection in the Western Reserve Historical Society. Early in the 1990s, Joan Weimer discovered there a microfilm of letters to do with the problems presented by CFW's scapegrace brother, Charley, and although I had the location number when I visited the library in 1994, these letters were not listed. Fortunately, Joan Weimer has transcripts, and kindly lent them.

13. Steven H. Jobe (see notes on LETTERS below) has noted that the provenance of many James letters is unknown beyond transcriptions, extracts, or notes by his authorised biographer, Leon Edel,

who for about forty years during the twentieth century was given exclusive access to the James Papers. These include letters to Helena de Kay Gilder, Katharine de Kay Bronson, Edith Bronson Rucellai, and the Emmet nieces. Edel's papers are at McGill University, Montreal.

LETTERS

I have drawn heavily on unpublished letters. Eight thousand out of ten and a half thousand letters by Henry James remain unpublished and scattered very widely in libraries across England and America. The four volumes (containing about two and a half thousand letters) edited by Leon Edel are increasingly recognised by scholars to be inadequate for several reasons: this is an under-edited selection for a writer of James's stature; there are inaccuracies; there is excessive emphasis on the 'twaddle' of high life; and Edel's obligation to the James family meant that he selected for propriety, instead of including, say, the distressed letters James wrote during his breakdown in 1911, or the tender letters to Gaillard Lapsley, or ardent letters to Minny Temple's young nieces.

Philip Horne has edited a selection of HJ's letters, *A Life in Letters* (Penguin, forthcoming) with more emphasis on his professional life.

There exist several one-volume collections of HJ's letters to a single correspondent such as Henry Adams, Edmund Gosse, and Edith Wharton (see below), or to a company (his dealings with the publishing house of Macmillan). These volumes reveal little or nothing of the private life.

HJ's letters to WJ are published accurately in full in the first three volumes of a complete edition of the correspondence of William James (see primary sources, below), which is a preferred source to Edel.

It is expected to take fifteen to twenty years for a centre at the University of Nebraska to bring out a complete edition of James's letters in 30 volumes, co-edited by Greg Zacharias. In the meantime, Steven H. Jobe of the Department of English, Hanover College, Hanover, Indiana, has made an invaluable, accurate listing of all known James letters and their scattered locations, 'A Calendar of Henry James Correspondence'. Professor Jobe has done an alphabetised listing according to correspondents as well as the chronological one.

Auden, W. H., Title poem of *Nones* (NY: Random House, 1951; London: Faber, 1952). Auden thought the insight of James into creative acts was unparalleled. He takes up the image of Clare Vawdrey in 'The Private Life': 'Our dreaming will', he wrote, escape

> ... to a room
> Lit by one weak bulb where our double sits
> Writing and does not look up
>
> That while we are thus away our wronged flesh
> May work undisturbed restoring
> The order we destroy, the rhythm
> We spoil out of spite.

— 'At the Grave of Henry James', *Complete Poems* (London: Faber, 1976).

— Sonnet (1940) ends with an image from 'The Jolly Corner', *New Year Letter* (London: Faber, 1941), published in NY as *The Double Man* (Random House, 1941).

— *The Dyer's Hand* (NY: Random House, 1962; London: Faber 1963).

Benedict, Clara, Letters (1884–1914). Western Reserve Historical Society, Cleveland, Ohio: 3735, container 24, folder 4.

Benedict, Clare (ed.), *Five Generations*, i–iii. See Abbreviations. A misguided protectiveness towards her aunt's memory led Benedict to tamper with her papers to such an extent – extracting, copying, possibly emending, destroying originals, obliterating sources and dates – that there is no knowing what is accurate and what is not. Where holographs are missing, the scholar is forced to use Benedict, but must do so with wariness.

Browning, Robert, *More Than Friend: The Letters of Robert Browning to Katharine de Kay Bronson*, ed. Michael Meredith, assisted by Rita S. Humphrey (Waco, Texas, and Winfield, Kansas: Armstrong Browning Library of Baylor University and Wedgestone Press, 1985). Meredith provides interesting detail on Mrs Bronson in his introduction.

Carter, Grace, Report on Woolson's death. WRHS.

Cooper, James Fenimore, *Leatherstocking Tales* (2 vols) (NY: The Library of America).
— *Notions of the Americans* (London and Philadelphia, 1828).
— *Gleanings in Europe*, ed. Robert E. Spiller and James F. Beard (Albany: State Univ. of NY Press, 1980).
— *Home as Found* (1838; repr. NY: Capricorn Books, 1961).
— *Letters and Journals*, 6 vols, ed. James Franklin Beard (Cambridge, Mass.: Harvard Univ., Belknap Press, 1968).
Cooper, James Fenimore (grandson of the novelist), 'Reminiscences of Mid-Victorian Cooperstown and a Sketch of William Cooper' (1936; repr. with introduction by Henry S. F. Cooper, Jr, Cooperstown, NY: Smithy-Pioneer Gallery Publications, 1986).
Cooper, Susan, *Rural Hours* (London: Richard Bentley, 1850; NY: Putnam, 1851; repr. with introduction by David Jones, Syracuse Univ. Press, 1968; repr. in paperback, 1995).
Cooper, William, *A Guide in the Wilderness; or, The History of the First Settlements in the Western Counties of New York* (Dublin: Gilbert and Hodges, 1810, repr. by Paul F. Cooper, Jr, Cooperstown, 1986). Copies available from the NY State Historical Association at Cooperstown.
de Kay, Helena, Letters to her mother, Janet Halleck Drake de Kay. Gilder Papers. Privately owned.
— Letters to Mary Hallock Foote. Gilder Papers.
— Diaries and photographs. Gilder Papers.
Eliot, T. S., 'Henry James I. In Memory'; 'II. The Hawthorne Aspect', *Little Review* (Aug 1918), repr. *The Shock of Recognition: The Development of Literature in the United States Recorded by the Men Who Made It*, ed. Edmund Wilson (NY: Random House, 1943, repr. 1955), 854–65. See also 'The Love Song of J. Alfred Prufrock', 'Portrait of a Lady', 'La Figlia che Piange', and Harry, Lord Monchensey in *The Family Reunion.*
Epictetus, *The Teaching of Epictetus*, trans. with introduction by T. W. Rolleston (London: Walter Scott, 1888).
Gerould, Katharine Fullerton, Letters to Morton Fullerton (1899–1910), Beinecke Library, Yale. Discussed sensitively by Cynthia Griffin Wolff (see below).
— *Vain Oblations* (NY: Scribner's, 1914); *The Great Tradition*

(NY: Scribner's, 1915); *Modes and Morals* (NY: Scribner's, 1920); *Valiant Dust* (NY: Scribner's, 1922).

Gilder, Richard Watson, *Letters*, ed. by his daughter, Rosamond Gilder (Boston and NY: Houghton Mifflin, Riverside, 1916). Copy owned by grandson, Gilder Palmer.

Gilder, Rosamond, unsifted papers, including materials for and drafts of unpublished biography of her mother, Helena de Kay. Gilder Papers.

Guilford, Linda T. (CFW's teacher in Cleveland), 'Reminiscences of CFW', in Torsney (ed.) *Critical Essays on CFW*, below.

Harvard Memorial Biographies, ed. Thomas Wentworth Higginson, ii (Cambridge, Mass., 1866), 35–62, 380, for lives of William Temple and Augustus Barker. Copy at Harvard.

Hastings, Katharine (Bagg), 'William James (1771–1832) of Albany NY and His Descendants', *New York Genealogical and Biographical Record*, lv (Apr, July, Oct 1924), 101–19, 222–36, 301–13.

Hay, John, *Letters and Extracts from Diary*, 3 vols (Washington, DC, 1908).

Holas, Marie, Letter to Samuel Mather on Woolson's last days. Privately owned by his grand-daughter, Molly Mather Anderson.

Howells, William Dean, *Life in Letters of WDH*, ed. Mildred Howells (Russell & Russell, 1928).

— *Selected Letters*, ed. George Arms, Richard Ballinger, Christopher Lohmann, and John K. Reeves (Boston: Twayne, 1979).

Hudson, Thomas Jay, *The Law of Psychic Phenomena* (London: Putnam's; Chicago: McClurg, 1893). Copy in Radcliffe Science Library, Oxford.

James, Alice, *Diary*, ed. Leon Edel (1964; repr. Penguin, 1987). The first, expurgated edition of 1934, *Alice James: Her Brothers, Her Journal*, was edited by Anna Robeson Burr.

— *The Death and Letters of Alice James: Selected Correspondence with a Biographical Essay*, ed. with introduction by Ruth Bernard Yeazell (Berkeley: Univ. of California Press, 1981). Selects about a third of her letters. A good number of unpublished letters to her brothers are in Houghton bMS Am 1094; others in the National Library of Scotland; Schlesinger

Library, Radcliffe; Colby College; and the (private) Vaux collection.
— *Her Life in Letters*, ed. Linda R. Anderson (Bristol: Thoemmes Press, 1996). Includes some unpublished letters, such as those to her friend Annie Ashburner.
— Twenty-seven letters to WJ (1867–92). Houghton bMS Am 1094 (1468–95).
James, Garth Wilkinson, Unpublished letters to parents. Houghton bMS Am 1095 (1–7).
— Unpublished letters to Alice James. Houghton bMS Am 1095 (10–15).
James, Henry, *Complete Notebooks*, ed. Leon Edel and Lyall H. Powers (NY and Oxford: OUP, 1987), and *The Notebooks of Henry James*, ed. F. O. Matthiessen and Kenneth Murdoch (1947; repr. NY: Galaxy, 1961; repr. Univ. of Chicago Press, Phoenix paperback, 1981). The latter is a selection, filled in by Jamesian notes. It is a product of a particular period in James studies which concerned itself with art rather than contexts. In its own terms it is a well-judged and continuously readable selection.
— *The Letters of Henry James*, ed. Percy Lubbock, 2 vols (London: Macmillan, 1920).
— *Letters*, ed. Leon Edel, 4 vols (Cambridge Mass.: Harvard Univ. Belknap Press, 1974–84).
— *A Life in Letters*, ed. Philip Horne (Penguin, due 1999).
— *Selected Letters of Henry James to Edmund Gosse 1882–1915: A Literary Friendship*, ed. Raymond S. Moore (Louisiana State University Press, 1988).
— *The Correspondence of Henry James and Henry Adams 1877–1914*, ed. George Monteiro (Louisiana State University Press, 1992).
— Letters to Henrietta Temple, printed in S. P. Rosenbaum, 'Letters to the Pell-Clarkes from their "Old Cousin and Friend" Henry James', *American Literature*, xxxi (Mar 1959), 46–58.
— 'The Letters of HJ to Mr. Justice Holmes', ed. Mark DeWolfe Howe, *Yale Review*, xxxvii (spring 1949), 410–33.
— Twenty-one unpublished letters to CFW's cousin, Grace

Carter, C. W. Barrett Library, Univ. of Virginia at Charlottesville.

— Fifty-eight letters to Alice James. Houghton bMS Am 1094 (1550–1608). HJ papers generally under bMS Am 1094.

— Twenty-four unpublished letters to Francis Boott, nearly all of which mention CFW. Houghton bMS Am 1094. There are numerous letters to Elizabeth Boott which are rather disappointing, far less interesting than those to her father.

— Twelve mostly unpublished letters to William Morton Fullerton (1899–1907) and to Katharine Fullerton (1905–8) at Princeton. General MSS (CO140) Box JA–JE, Folder: Henry James. A large batch of about seventy-seven mostly unpublished letters to Morton Fullerton at Houghton bMS Am 1094.1.

— Seventy-seven mostly unpublished letters to Gaillard Lapsley (1897–1915) which have been restricted. Houghton bMS Am 1094.4.

— Seventy-nine letters, almost all unpublished, to William Wilberforce Baldwin (1881–1900). Pierpont Morgan Library, NY. Three further letters to WWB at Houghton bMS Am 1094.1.

— Unpublished letters to Katharine Peabody Loring. Beverly Historical Society, Houghton, and Vassar.

— Important, mostly unpublished letters to Alice H. James, to do with breakdown, writing a memoir, and Mrs James's go-between role in the transmission of Minny's letters. Houghton bMS Am 1094 (1724–50).

— Eighteen largely unpublished letters to Henry James III. Houghton bMS Am 1094 (1408–25), discussed brilliantly by Follini (see below).

— Unpublished letters to Katharine and Grenville Emmet. Houghton bMS Am 1094.1.

— Twenty-one letters (1897–1915), almost all unpublished, to Ellen Gertrude (Bay) Emmet Rand. Houghton bMS Am 1094 (662–712).

— Mostly unpublished letters to Ellen Temple Emmet. Houghton bMS Am 1094.

— Unpublished letter to Helena de Kay Gilder (23 June 1913) Houghton, bMS Am 1237.16.

— Unpublished letters to Laura Wagnière. Houghton bMS Am 1237.16.
— Unpublished letters to George Abbot James. Houghton bMS Am 1094.1.
— Unpublished letters to John Chipman Gray (1914), about the memoir of Minny, and to Mrs Gray after the latter's death in 1915. Houghton b47M–332 (73–74).
— Sixty-six letters to Rhoda Broughton. Cheshire Record Office DDB/M/J/1/1–66.
— Vast batch of letters to Daniel and Ariana Curtis, Dartmouth College, Hanover, NH. MS194 Box 1. Ten letters to same, Tintner Collection, Berg, box 174, folders 8–10.
— Vast batch of letters to Thomas Sergeant Perry, and a few to his wife, Lilla Cabot Perry. Miller Library, Colby College, Maine. A number published in the Harlow biography below.
— *Theatre and Friendship: Some Henry James Letters with a Commentary by Elizabeth Robins* (NY: Putnam's, 1932). Copy in Berg.
— Twenty-five wartime letters, much unpublished, to Sir Edward (Eddie) Howard Marsh (3 July 1914–27 Nov 1915). Berg.
— Letters to Vernon Lee (Violet Paget) printed in Carl J. Weber and Burdett Gardner, 'Letters of James to Vernon Lee', *PMLA*, lxviii (Sept 1953), 672–95.
— *Letters from the Palazzo Barbaro*, ed. Rosella Zorzi (London: Pushkin Press, 1998).
— 'The Turning Point of My Life' (n.d.) four-page TS Houghton bMS Am 1237.9. Printed by Edel and Powers, *Complete Notebooks of HJ*.
— TS of *Notes of a Son and Brother*, with autograph corrections. Pierpont Morgan Library, NY: MA4500.
— *Autobiography*, ed. F. W. Dupee (1956; repr. Princeton Univ. Press, 1983), consisting of *A Small Boy and Others* (1913), *Notes of a Son and Brother* (1914), and *The Middle Years* (1917).
— *The Tales of Henry James*, ed. Maqbool Aziz, i–iii (Oxford: Clarendon Press 1973–1984). This is a scholarly edition of the earliest published version of the tales.
— *Complete Stories*, i–v (NY: The Library of America 1996–). Vol. iv (1892–1898) has notes by David Bromwich and John

Hollander; vol. v (1898–1910) has notes by Denis Donoghue. Vols i–iii to come.

— *Daisy Miller: a Comedy in Three Acts* (Boston: Osgood, 1883). Appendix iv to Aziz, iii (1984), 523–96.

— *Novels 1871–1880* (NY: The Library of America, 1983).

— *Novels 1881–1886* (NY: The Library of America, 1985).

— *Novels 1886–1890* (NY: The Library of America, 1989).

— *Literary Criticism*, vol. i: *Essays, American and English Writers*; vol. ii: *European Writers and The Prefaces* (NY: The Library of America, 1984).

— 'The Speech of American Women' and 'The Manners of American Women', *Harper's* (Nov 1906–July 1907).

— *William Wetmore Story and his friends*, i–ii (Edinburgh: Blackwood, 1903).

— *Collected Travel Writings: Great Britain and America*, with notes by Richard Howard (NY: The Library of America, 1993).

— *Collected Travel Writings: The Continent*, with notes by Richard Howard (NY: The Library of America, 1993).

— *Travelling in Italy with HJ*, ed. Fred Kaplan (London: Hodder, 1994): a collection of letters and travel writings usefully organised by place.

— Cheap, scholarly editions of novels and assorted tales in paperback by OUP: World's Classics.

— 'Is there life after death?', *In After Days: Thoughts on the Future Life*, with essays also by W. D. Howells, John Bigelow, and others (NY and London: Harper, 1910), 199–233, repr. by Matthiessen in *The James Family* (see below), 602–14.

James, Henry, III, Unpublished diary of visit to uncle. Houghton.

James, Mary, Twelve unpublished letters to Alice James. Houghton bMS Am 1093.1 (20–31).

— Thirteen unpublished letters to Henry James Jr. Houghton bMS Am 1093.1 (34–46).

James, Robertson, Letters to various members of the family. Houghton. (Other letters owned by his descendants in the Vaux family.) A few of his letters and those of GWJ are printed in Anna Burr's introduction on to her expurgated edition of AJ's diary in 1934.

James, William, *Writings 1878–1899* (NY: The Library of America, 1992).
— *Writings 1902–1910* (NY: The Library of America, 1987).
— *Correspondence*, i–iii, ed. Ignas K. Skrupskelis and Elizabeth M. Berkeley (Charlottesville: Univ. Press of Virginia, 1993–4).
— Seventy-three letters to Alice James (1861–91). Houghton bMS Am 1092.9 (1087–1159).
— Two letters to Kitty Temple (1864; 1868). Houghton.
— Letters to Kitty Prince. Houghton.
— Diary. Houghton bMS Am 1092.9 (4550).
Kemble, Fanny, *Further Records* (1891).
Loring, Katharine. She destroyed personal papers (see ch. 13). Her remaining papers, almost all to do with good works, are in the Schlesinger Library, Radcliffe College, Cambridge, Massachusetts, and in the Beverly Historical Society, Massachusetts. The latter has one interesting letter from HJ. A batch of letters to a friend in the Houghton Library gives a delightful picture of her in old age.
— Letters to HJ (1901–14). Vassar College.
— Letter to Margaret James Porter (1934) about AJ's diary. Princeton.
Mather family papers. Western Reserve Historical Society, Cleveland, Ohio: MS 3735.
Nightingale, Florence, *Cassandra*, written 1852, privately printed in revised form 1859, repr. as Appendix to Ray Strachey, *The Cause: A Short History of the Women's Movement in Great Britain* (1928; repr. London: Virago, 1979), 395–418.
Perry, Thomas Sergeant, MS memoir of Henry and William James. Houghton.
Pound, Ezra, *Instigations* (NY, 1920) 111–13, 122–8.
Temple, Minny, Four letters to Henry James (1869), Houghton. Printed in Robert C. Le Clair, 'Henry James and Minny Temple', *American Literature*, xxi (Mar 1949), 35–48, with some errors.
— Twenty-three letters to John Chipman Gray (1869–70). Transcript in Houghton bMS Am 1092.12.
— Fragments (one substantial: eight pages) of two philosophical letters to William James (1870). Houghton bMS Am 1092.9. (4387a) and Autograph file.

— Letter to Ellen Temple Emmet (19 Nov 1869). Houghton bMS An 1092.9 (4387).

— TS copies of eight letters to Helena de Kay. Gilder Papers. Privately owned.

Temple, Robert, Letter to HJSr (1877). Houghton bMS Am 1095.2 (19).

Wharton, Edith, *Novels* (NY: The Library of America, 1985).

— *Novellas and Other Writings* (NY: The Library of America, 1990).

— *The Stories of Edith Wharton*, ed. Anita Brookner (NY and London: Simon and Schuster, 1988).

— *Henry James and Edith Wharton, Letters 1900–1915*, ed. Lyall H. Powers (London: Weidenfeld & Nicolson, 1990).

Woolf, Virginia, 'Within the Rim' (1917), *Collected Essays*, ed. Leonard Woolf (London: Hogarth, 1966).

Woolson, Constance Fenimore, Four letters to Henry James, 1882–3. Houghton bMS Am 1094 (496–8a). Printed with a few inaccuracies as appendix to Edel's edition of letters, iii.

— Twenty-one letters to the Hays. John Hay Collection, Brown University, Providence, RI. Printed in Alice Hall Petry, ' "Always, your Attached Friend": The Unpublished Letters of CFW to John and Clara Hay', *Books at Brown*, xxix–xxx (1982–3), 11–107. Substantially annotated with rare information.

— Four letters to Elinor Gertrude (Mead) Howells (1882 and n.d.). Houghton. Also six letters to W. D. Howells (n.d.). Houghton bMS Am 1784 (558).

— Letters to Edmund Clarence Stedman (1876–83). Stedman Papers, Manuscript and Rare Book Collections, Butler Library, Columbia University.

— One letter of 18 June 1883 and fourteen letters to Paul Hamilton Hayne (1875–80). Duke Univ. Library. See Jay B. Hubbell, 'Some New Letters of CFW', *New England Quarterly*, xiv (Dec 1941), 715–35.

— Thirty-two letters and eight cards (1886–93) to William Wilberforce Baldwin. Pierpont Morgan Library, NY: Baldwin Collection: box 6. MA 3564. The most telling batch.

— Four letters to Miss Owen from 15 Beaumont Street, Oxford (Apr–May 1893). Miller Library, Colby College, Maine.

— Extracts from letters, journal, and notes in *Constance Fenimore Woolson*, vol. ii of Clare Benedict's three-volume compilation *Five Generations* (privately printed, London: Ellis, 1929–30; revised with additional material in 1932). The first volume is *Voices Out of the Past;* the third volume is *The Benedicts Abroad*. Copies in Bodleian Library, Oxford.

— Cuttings Book, originally belonging to Constance Mather Bishop, now privately owned by Molly Mather Anderson.

— Books owned by her are divided between Rollins College (about 30 remaining volumes) and Claremont Historical Society (about 100 volumes, the majority in French). Useful marginalia and dates.

— Furnishings and memorabilia in the Stone House built by William Cooper for his daughter Ann on her marriage in 1802 to George Pomeroy. The house was bought by the Benedicts early in the twentieth century, arranged as a museum, with rooms designated for each member of the Cooper family who distinguished him- or herself. A detailed, almost obsessive inventory by Clare Benedict. New York State Historical Association at Cooperstown.

— 'Ballast Island', *Appleton's Jnl*, ix (28 June 1873), 833–9.

— 'The Haunted Lake', *Harper's New Monthly*, xliv (Dec 1871), 20–30. Also in Benedict, i, 49–57.

— 'Miss Grief' in *WAWE*. First published in *Lippincott's Magazine*, xxv (May 1880), 574–85.

— 'The Greatest of All is Charity', *Harper's*, vi (8 Feb 1873), 90.

— 'To George Eliot', *The New Century for Women*, ii (20 May 1876), 1.

— 'To Certain Biographers', *Appleton's Jnl*, v (Dec 1878), 376.

— 'Miss Vedder', *Harper's New Monthly* (Mar 1879), 590–601.

— 'In Sloane Street', *Harper's* (11 June 1992), 473–8.

— *Two Women: 1862* (NY: Appleton, 1877).

— *Women Artists, Women Exiles: 'Miss Grief' and Other Stories*, ed. Joan Myers Weimer (New Brunswick, NJ: Rutgers Univ. Press, 1988). Well-chosen and only available collection. Paperback.

— *Castle Nowhere: Lake Country Sketches* (1875; repr. NY:

Manuscript Information Corporation's American Short Story Series, vol. 86, 1969).
— *Rodman the Keeper: Southern Sketches* (1880; repr. NY: Garrett Press: American Short Story Series, vol. 87, 1969).
— *Anne: A Novel* (NY: Harper, 1882; London: Sampson Low, Marston, Searle, & Rivington, 1883). Copy in the Bodleian Library.
— *East Angels: A Novel* (as above, 1886). The pages of Bodley's copy were still uncut when I opened it in 1996.
— *Jupiter Lights* (1889; repr. NY: AMS Press, 1971).
— *Horace Chase* (1894; repr. Upper Saddle River, NJ: Literature House/Gregg Press, 1970).
— *For the Major and Selected Short Stories*, ed. Rayburn S. Moore (New Haven, Conn.: College & Univ. Press Services, 1967).
— *The Front Yard and Other Italian Stories* (1895; repr. NY: Books for Libraries Press, 1969), including 'The Street of the Hyacinth'.
— *Dorothy and Other Italian Stories* (NY: Harper, 1896), including 'Dorothy', 'A Florentine Experiment', and 'At the Château of Corinne'.
— *Mentone, Cairo, and Corfu* (NY: Harper, 1896), comprising 'At Mentone' (1884); 'Cairo in 1890' (1891); and 'Corfu and the Ionian Sea' (1892).

ANTHOLOGIES:

Woolson has been anthologised from multiple points of view: as a Civil War writer ('Crowder's Cove') in *Civil War Women*, ed. Frank McSherry et al. (Little Rock, Ark.: August House, 1988), and in a two-volume collection of Civil War stories in the context of government amendments, *Where My Heart Is Turning*, from the Univ. of Georgia; as a regionalist ('The Lady of Little Fishing' and 'Wilhelmina') in *The Local Colorists: American Short Stories 1857–1900*, ed. Claude M. Simpson (NY: Harper, 1960), and in *Anthology of Western Reserve Literature*, ed. David R. Anderson and Gladys Haddad (Ohio: Kent State Univ. Press, 1992); and as a poet in *American Poetry: The Nineteenth Century*, ii (The Library of America, 1995) and in *American Women Poets of the Nineteenth Century: An Anthology* (New Brunswick, NJ: Rutgers Univ. Press, 1992).

Significantly, marking the extent of her eclipse, she was *not* included in an anthology of *Old Maids: Short Stories by Nineteenth Century U.S. Women Writers*, ed. Susan Koppelman (Boston: Routledge/Pandora, 1984). Most stories in this collection are undistinguished, while Woolson's stories of single women, the vein emphasised in this biography, are amongst her best works ('Miss Vedder', 'Miss Grief', 'In Sloane Street'). A sign of canonical revival is CFW's appearance in *Scribbling Women: Short Stories by 19th-Century American Women*, ed. Elaine Showalter (London: Dent, 1997). She selects, appropriately, 'Miss Grief' and 'At the Château of Corinne'.

Still needed are complete editions of Woolson's stories, travel writings, and letters (Cheryl Torsney's 'wish list' at the first meeting of a new generation of readers at Rollins College, Florida, in Feb 1995).

Woolson, Gary W., 'Woolson Family Genealogical Notes' (1984), 100 copies, one of which is at Rollins.

Woolson, Hannah Pomeroy, Diary of summer visit to Cooperstown, 1839. New York State Historical Association at Cooperstown.

— Memoirs, published (perhaps expurgated) by Clare Benedict in *Five Generations*. This is the only source; the original MS has not survived, though Hannah Woolson made a point of bequeathing it to her female descendants.

Secondary Sources

Aaron, Daniel, *The Unwritten War: American Writers and the Civil War* (NY: OUP, 1973).

Allen, Elizabeth, *A Woman's Place in the Novels of Henry James* (London: Macmillan, 1984).

Anesko, Michael, *'Friction with the Market': Henry James and the Profession of Authorship* (NY and Oxford: OUP, 1986).

Baveystock, Freddie, 'The Romance of Nationalism: Historical Authority in American Literary Culture 1809–1851' (Oxford thesis, 1995).

Bayley, John, *The Short Story: Henry James to Elizabeth Bowen* (Brighton: Harvester, 1988).
— *The Characters of Love: A Study in the Literature of Personality* (1960; repr. London: Chatto, 1968).
— 'Fat and Fretful', *London Review of Books* (26 Apr 1996), 26.
Baym, Nina, *Women's Fiction: A Guide to Novels by and about Women in America 1820–1870* (Ithaca, NY: Cornell Univ. Press).
Bell, Millicent, *Edith Wharton and Henry James: The Story of their Friendship* (London: Peter Owen, 1966).
— *Meaning in Henry James* (Cambridge, Mass.: Harvard Univ. Press, 1991).
Bennett, Arnold, *Things That Have Interested Me* (London: Chatto & Windus, 1921), 312–21.
Benstock, Shari, *No Gifts from Chance: A Biography of Edith Wharton* (London: Hamish Hamilton, 1994).
Bercovitch, Sacvan, '*Pierre* or the Ambiguities of Literary Assent', in *The Rites of Assent* (London: Routledge, 1993).
Bersani, Leo, *A Future for Astyanax: Character and Desire in Literature* (Boston: Little, Brown, 1969; London: Marion Boyars, 1978).
Bosanquet, Theodora, *Henry James at Work* (London: Hogarth Press, 1924).
Bradbury, Nicola, *Henry James: the Later Novels* (Oxford: Clarendon Press, 1979).
Bradley, John R., 'Henry James's Permanent Adolescence', *Essays in Criticism*, clvii (Oct 1997), 287–314.
Brodhead, Richard H., *The School of Hawthorne* (NY and Oxford: OUP, 1986).
Bronfen, Elisabeth, *Over Her Dead Body: Death, Femininity and the Aesthetic* (Manchester Univ. Press, 1992).
Brooks, Van Wyck, *The Dream of Arcadia: American Writers and Artists in Italy 1760–1915* (NY: Dutton, 1958).
Buelens, Gert (ed.), *Enacting History in Henry James: Narrative, power, and ethics* (Cambridge University Press, 1997).
Bush, Ronald, 'Changing His Mind About How to Do a Girl In: Poetry, Narrative, and Gender in the Revisions of Henry James's

Daisy Miller', *Letterature d'America: Rivista Trimestrale*, xiv: 5 (1994), 33–52.

Cagidimetrio, Alide, 'Sceltadi Città: Venezia, Black Balloons and White Doves', in *Henry James e Venezia*, ed. Sergio Perosa (1987), 54–5.

Cott, Nancy F., *The Bonds of Womanhood* (New Haven, Conn.: Yale Univ. Press, 1977).

Davenport-Hines, Richard, *Auden* (London: Heineman, 1995). Shows substantial influence of HJ.

Dean, Sharon L., *Constance Fenimore Woolson: Homeward Bound* (Knoxville, Tenn.: Univ. of Tennessee Press, 1995).

— 'CFW and HJ: The Literary Relationship', *Massachusetts Studies in English*, vii:3 (1980), 1–9.

Donadio, Stephen, *Nietzsche, Henry James and the Artistic Will* (NY: OUP, 1978). Discusses the homelessness of HJ.

Douglas, Ann, *The Feminization of American Culture* (NY: Knopf, 1977).

Dupee, F. W., *Henry James* (NY: Dell, 1951; repr. NY: Delta, 1965).

Eakin, Paul John, 'Henry James and the Autobiographical Act', in *Fictions in Autobiography: Studies in the Art of Self-Invention* (Princeton Univ. Press, 1985).

Edel, Leon, *The Life of Henry James*, i–v (Philadelphia: J. B. Lippincott, 1953–72); revised and abridged edn, 1 vol (NY: Harper and Row, 1985; London, 1987).

Feinstein, Howard M., *Becoming William James* (Ithica, NY: Cornell Univ. Press, 1984).

Fogel, Daniel Mark, *Daisy Miller: A Dark Comedy of Manners* (NY: Twayne, 1993).

Follini, Tamara, 'Pandora's Box: The Family Correspondence in *Notes on a Son and Brother*', *Cambridge Quarterly*, xxv:1 (Winter 1994), 26–40.

Fowler, Virginia C., *Henry James's American Girl: The Embroidery on the Canvas* (Madison: Univ. of Wisconsin Press, 1984).

Freud, Sigmund, *Das 'Unheimliche'*, trans. for James Strachey's Hogarth Press edn, repr. in *The Pelican Freud Library*, xiv: *Art and Literature*, ed. Albert Dickson (London: Penguin, 1985).

Gebhard, Caroline, 'Constance Fenimore Woolson Rewrites Bret Hart: The Sexual Politics of Intertextuality'. In *Critical Essays*, ed. Torsney, 217–33.

Geismar, Maxwell, *Henry James and His Cult* (London: Chatto, 1964).

Giorcelli, Cristina, *Henry James e l'Italia* (Roma, 1968).

Gittings, Robert, and Manton, Jo, *Claire Clairmont and the Shelleys 1798–1879* (OUP, 1992).

Goode, John (ed.), *The Air of Reality: New Essays on Henry James* (London: Methuen, 1972).

Graham, Kenneth, *Henry James, The Drama of Fulfilment: An Approach to the Novels* (Oxford: Clarendon Press, 1975). An extended reading of *The Wings of the Dove*.

Gray, Thomas C., 'Bad Man from Olympus' [on OWH], *New York Review of Books* (13 July 1995), 4–7.

Gunn, Peter, *Vernon Lee, Violet Paget, 1856–1935* (London: OUP, 1964);.

Gunter, Susan, *Dear Munificent Friends* (forthcoming: on HJ's relations with four women).

Habegger, Alfred, 'Henry James's Rewriting of Minny Temple's Letters', *American Literature*, lviii (May 1986), 159–80.

— 'New Light on William James and Minny Temple', *New England Quarterly*, lx:1 (Mar 1987), 28–53.

— *Henry James and the 'Woman Business'* (CUP, 1989).

— 'The Fatherless Heroine and the Filial Son', *New Essays on 'The Portrait of a Lady'*, ed. Joel Porte (CUP, 1990), 49–93.

— 'Dupine Tracks J.J.', *Southern Review*, xxvii (Oct 1991), 803–25.

— 'Mary Codman Peabody, Boston Conscientiousness, and "An International Episode"', *Henry James Review*, xiii (1992), 229–34.

— *The Father: A Life of Henry James, Senior* (NY: Farrar, Straus, 1994).

Hamilton, Ian, *Keepers of the Flame: Literary Estates and the Rise of Biography* (1992; repr. London: Pimlico, 1993).

Hampshire, Stuart, 'What the Jameses Knew', *New York Review of Books* (10 Oct 1991).

Hardy, Barbara, *Henry James: The Later Writing* (Plymouth:

Northcote House, in association with The British Council, 1996).
— 'Henry James: Reflexive Passions', in *Forms of Feeling in Victorian Fiction* (London: Peter Owen, 1985), 191–215.
Harlow, Virginia, *Thomas Sergeant Perry: A Biography and Letters to Perry from William, Henry and Garth Wilkinson James* (Durham, NC: Duke Univ. Press, 1950).
— 'Thomas Sergeant Perry and Henry James', *Boston Public Library Quarterly* (July 1949), 43–60.
Hayes, Kevin J. (ed.), *Henry James: The Contemporary Reviews* (Cambridge Univ. Press, 1996).
Henry James: The Critical Heritage (collected reviews), ed. Roger Gard (London: Routledge, 1968; repr. 1976, 1986).
The Henry James Review, published by Johns Hopkins University Press.
A Henry James Encyclopedia, ed. Robert L. Gale (Westport, Conn.: Greenwood Press, 1989).
Hoffmann, Charles and Tess, 'HJ and the Civil War', *New England Quarterly*, lxii:4 (1989), 529–52. Meticulous factual research brings to light this unexplored area in HJ's life.
Honour, Hugh, and Fleming, John, *The Venetian Hours of Henry James, Whistler and Sargent* (Boston: Little Brown/Bulfinch; London: Walker, 1991).
Horne, Philip, *Henry James and Revision* (Oxford: Clarendon Press, 1990).
— 'Henry James: The Master and the "Queer Affair" of "The Pupil" ', *Critical Quarterly* xxxvii:3 (Autumn 1995). 75–92. Argues against narrowed readings of HJ to fit a predetermined agenda, as represented by Sedgwick below.
— review of Kaplan's biography of Henry James, *Guardian* (15 Dec 1992), repr. Peter Rawlings (ed.), *Critical Essays on Henry James* (Critical Thought Series: 5) (Aldershot: Scolar Press, 1993), 342–3.
Hyde, Harfort Montgomery, *The Story of Lamb House, Rye, the Home of Henry James* (Rye, Sussex: Adams of Rye, 1966). Copy in Berg.
Iser, Wolfgang, *The Act of Reading: A Theory of Aesthetic*

Response (Baltimore: Johns Hopkins Univ. Press, 1978). Uses 'The Figure in the Carpet' as a model text.

Jones, Susan, *Conrad and Women* (Oxford: OUP, forthcoming).

Kaledin, Eugenia, *The Education of Mrs. Henry Adams* (Philadelphia: Temple Univ. Press, 1981).

Kalstone, David M., 'The Discovery of America: James Fenimore Cooper and Henry James as Critics' (summa cum laude honors essay, 1954). Harvard Archives, Pusey Library.

Kaplan, Fred, *Henry James: The Imagination of Genius: A Biography* (NY: Morrow; London: Hodder, 1992).

Kappeler, Susan, *Writing and Reading in Henry James* (NY: Columbia Univ. Press, 1980).

Kern, John D., *Constance Fenimore Woolson: Literary Pioneer* (Philadelphia: Univ. of Pennsylvania Press, 1934).

Khan, Coppélia, and Greene, Gayle, *Changing Subjects: The Making of Feminist Literary Criticism* (London: Routledge, 1993).

Kelly, Cannon, *Henry James and Masculinity: The Man at the Margins* (London: Macmillan, 1995).

Kennedy, Elizabeth Marie, 'Constance Fenimore Woolson and Henry James: Friendship and Reflections' (Yale thesis, 1983).

Kitterman, Mary P. Edwards, 'HJ and the Artist-Heroine in the Tales of CFW' in *Nineteenth-Century Women Writers of the English-Speaking World* (Westport, Conn.: Greenwood Press, 1986), 45–59.

Krook, Dorothea, *The Ordeal of Consciousness in Henry James* (Cambridge UP, 1962).

Le Clair, Robert C., *Young Henry James 1843–1870* (NY: Bookman, 1955).

Lee, Vernon (Violet Paget), 'Lady Tal', in *Vanitas: Polite Stories* (London, Heinemann, 1892).

Lewis, R. W. B., *Edith Wharton: A Biography* (NY: Harper & Row, 1975).

— *The Jameses: A Family Narrative* (NY: Farrar, Straus, 1991; repr. Doubleday/Anchor, 1993; London: Deutsch, 1991).

Lustig, T. J., *Henry James and the Ghostly* (CUP, 1995).

Maher, Jane, *A Biography of Broken Fortunes: Wilkie and Bob,*

Brothers of William, Henry, and Alice James (Hamden, Conn.: Archon Books, 1986).
Matthiessen, F. O., *The James Family* (NY: Knopf, 1948).
— *Henry James: The Major Phase* (London: OUP, 1946).
Miller, Laura, 'Henry James: Losing It at the Movies', *New York Times Book Review* (Jan 1997), 31. Perceptive piece on why James speaks to us now, with insights into 'The Jolly Corner' and *Portrait*.
Millgate, Michael, *Testamentary Acts: Browning, Tennyson, James, Hardy* (OUP, 1992), especially pp. 93, 96.
Moers, Ellen, *Literary Women* (London: Women's Press, 1977).
Monteiro, George, *Henry James and John Hay: The Record of a Friendship.* (Providence, RI: Brown Univ. Press, 1965).
Moore, Rayburn S., 'The Strange Irregular Rhythm of Life: James's Late Tales and Constance Woolson', *South Atlantic Bulletin*, xli:4 (Nov 1976), 86–93.
— *Constance Fenimore Woolson* (New Haven, Conn.: Twayne, 1963).
Notable American Women 1607–1950: A Biographical Dictionary (Cambridge, Mass.: Harvard Univ. Press, Belknap Press, 1971).
Novick, Sheldon M., *Henry James: The Young Master* (NY: Random House, 1996).
Nussbaum, Martha C., *Love's Knowledge: Essays on Philosophy and Literature* (NY: OUP, c.1990).
Ozick, Cynthia, *What the Jameses Knew and Other Essays on Writers* (London: Cape, 1993).
Page, Norman (ed.), *Henry James: Interviews and Recollections* (London: Macmillan, 1984).
Pattee, Fred, 'CFW and the South', *South Atlantic Quarterly*, xxxviii (Apr 1939), 130–41.
Pearson, John H., *The Prefaces of HJ* (Penn State Univ. Press, 1997).
Perry, Ralph Barton, *The Thought and Character of William James* (Boston, Mass., 1935).
Poirier, Richard, *The Comic Sense of Henry James* (London: Chatto, 1960).
Poole, Adrian, *Henry James* (Hemel Hempstead: Harvester, 1991).

Porte, Joel (ed.), *New Essays on the Portrait of a Lady* (CUP, 1990).

Postnock, Ross, *The Trial of Curiosity: Henry James, William James and the Challenge of Modernity* (NY: OUP, 1991).

Putt, S. Gorley, *The Fiction of Henry James* (Harmondsworth: Penguin, 1968).

Rahv, Philip, 'The Heiress of all the Ages', *Literature and the Sixth Sense* (London: Faber, 1970), 104–25.

Rawlings, Peter (ed.), *Critical Essays on Henry James* (Aldershot, England, and Brookfield, Vt: Scolar Press, 1993).

Reynolds, David S., *Beneath the American Renaissance: The Subversive Imagination in the Age of Emerson and Melville* (NY: Knopf, 1988).

Richardson, Lyon N., 'Constance Fenimore Woolson, "Novelist Laureate" of America', *South Atlantic Quarterly*, xxix:1 (Jan 1940), 18–36.

Rimmon, Schlomith, *The Concept of Ambiguity: The Example of James* (Chicago Univ. Press, 1977).

Saxton, Martha, *Louisa May Alcott* (Boston: Houghton Mifflin, 1977; repr. NY: Farrar, Strauss, 1995).

Sedgwick, Eve Kosovsky, *Tendencies* (London: Routledge, 1994). Includes 'Is the Rectum Straight?: Identification and Identity in *The Wings of the Dove*'.

— *The Epistemology of the Closet* (Berkeley & Los Angeles: Univ. of California Press, 1990; Hemel Hempstead: Harvester, 1991). Includes 'The Beast in the Closet: James and the Writing of Homosexual Panic'.

Seymour, Miranda, *A Ring of Conspirators: Henry James and his Literary Circle 1895–1915* (London: Hodder, 1988).

Simon, Linda, *Genuine Reality: A Life of William James* (NY: Harcourt, 1998).

Smith, Joan, *Different for Girls* (London: Chatto, 1997).

Smith-Rosenberg, Caroll, *Disorderly Conduct: Visions of Gender in Victorian America* (NY: OUP, 1986).

Springer, Mary Doyle, *A Rhetoric of Literary Character: Some Women of Henry James* (Univ. of Chicago Press, 1978).

Strouse, Jean, 'Semiprivate Lives', *Studies in Biography. Harvard*

English Studies 8, ed. Daniel Aaron (Cambridge, Mass.: Harvard Univ. Press, 1978).

— *Alice James: A Biography* (Boston: Houghton Mifflin, 1980; London: Cape, 1981).

Taylor, Alan, *William Cooper's Town: Power and Persuasion on the Frontier of the Early American Republic* (NY: Knopf, 1995).

Thayer, William Roscoe, *Life of John Hay* (Boston: Houghton Mifflin, 1915).

Tintner, Adeline R., *The Museum World of Henry James* (Ann Arbor: Univ. of Michigan Research Press, 1986).

— 'Autobiography as Fiction: "The Usurping Consciousness" as Hero of Henry James's Memoirs', *Twentieth Century Literature*, xxiii (May 1977), 239–60.

Torsney, Cheryl B., *Constance Fenimore Woolson: The Grief of Artistry* (Athens, Ga: Univ. of Georgia Press, 1989).

— 'The Strange Case of the Disappearing Woolson Memorabilia', *Legacy*, ii:2 (1994), 143–51.

— (ed.) *Critical Essays on Constance Fenimore Woolson* (NY: G. K. Hall, 1992). Includes Torsney's 'The Traditions of Gender: Constance Fenimore Woolson and Henry James', 152–71.

Townsend, Kim, *Manhood at Harvard: William James and Others* (NY: Norton, 1996).

Uglow, Jenny, *George Eliot* (London: Virago, 1987).

VanBergen, Carolyn, 'Constance Fenimore Woolson and the Next Country', *Western Reserve Studies*, iii (1988), 86–92.

Vickers, Joanne F., 'Woolson's Response to James: The Vindication of the American Heroine', *Women's Studies*, xviii (1990), 287–94.

Walker, Cheryl, *The Nightingale's Burden: Women Poets and American Culture before 1900* (Bloomington: Indiana Univ. Press, 1982).

Walton, Priscilla L., *The Disruption of the Feminine in Henry James* (Univ. of Toronto Press, 1992).

Weimer, Joan, *Back Talk: Teaching Lost Selves to Speak* (NY: Random House, 1994). A memoir in which the author develops a restorative relationship to CFW. Weimer has taken a leading part in the new revisionist interest in CFW, and her book blends her exploratory scholarship with its more intimate vein.

— 'The "Admiring Aunt" and the "Proud Salmon of the Pond": CFW's struggle with Henry James' in *Critical Essays*, ed. Torsney, 203–16.

— 'Women Artists as Exiles in the Fiction of CFW', *Legacy*, ii:2 (Fall 1986), 2–15.

Welter, Barbara, 'The Cult of True Womanhood: 1820–1860', in *Dimity Convictions: The American Woman in the Nineteenth Century* (Athens, Ohio: Ohio Univ. Press, 1976).

White, Allon, *The Uses of Obscurity: The Fiction of Early Modernism* (London: Routledge, 1981).

Wolff, Cynthia Griffin, *A Feast of Words: The Triumph of Edith Wharton* (NY: OUP, 1977; repr. Radcliffe Biography Series, 1995).

Wood, Michael, *The Magician's Doubts* (London: Pimlico, 1995). The opening chapter offers a sophisticated consideration of the challenges of critical biography.

Yeazell, Ruth Bernard, *Language and Knowledge in the Late Novels of Henry James* (Univ. of Chicago Press, 1976).

BIBLIOGRAPHIES

A Bibliography of Henry James, ed. Leon Edel and Dan H. Laurence, with James Rambeau, 3rd edn (Oxford: Clarendon Press, 1982).

For secondary criticism see Nicola Bradbury, *An Annotated Critical Bibliography of Henry James* (Brighton: Harvester, 1987); K. P. McColgan, *Henry James, 1917–1959: A Reference Guide*, and Dorothy M. Scura, *Henry James, 1960–1974:* A Reference Guide (Boston: G. K. Hall, 1979); Judith E. Funston, *Henry James, 1975–1987: A Reference Guide* (Boston: G. K. Hall, 1991).

A complete bibliography of the works of Constance Fenimore Woolson is an appendix to John D. Kern, *Constance Fenimore Woolson: Literary Pioneer* (Philadelphia: Univ. of Pennsylvania Press, 1934), 180–94. A brief bibliography from a current point of view – an excellent basis for an introduction to her writings – is to be found in Joan Weimer's selection of her stories, *Women Artists, Women Exiles* (New Brunswick, NY: Rutgers Univ. Press, 1988), xliv–xlvii.

Acknowledgements

Anyone writing on James must be indebted to previous biographers, Leon Edel, Fred Kaplan, and R. W. B. Lewis. Their accumulations of detail are so abundant that it would have been redundant to attempt a similar book. Thanks, then, to the existence of full-scale chronological studies, I was free to focus on a buried story, emphasising the woman's point of view central to James. This book has been written with respect and appreciation for what scholars have discovered or clarified.

It is dedicated to Linn Cary Mehta who came to St Hilda's College, Oxford, in 1976 when we became friends. A gifted descendant of James Fenimore Cooper, she has a particular interest in the women in her family, including, of course, Constance Fenimore Woolson. Linn's uncle, Henry S. F. Cooper, great-great-grandson of the novelist, kindly showed me around Cooperstown in upstate New York, relating as we went a well-phrased history of the Cooper family. His sister, Mrs Cary, had us to stay in her home, with its lovely old things, where we felt transported into an earlier America at its most civilised. Linn also arranged a visit to Gilder Palmer who has the Gilder Papers in his farmhouse, amongst which are Minny Temple's letters to his grandmother, Helena de Kay. Linn's farmhouse in the Berkshires, its extraordinary library of nineteenth-century books, and the Gilder farmhouse with its portrait of the distinguished New York editor, Richard Watson Gilder, its great piano, and Italian garden, will always be with me as part of coming to know people of the past as I wrote this book.

Vital to the story was the eye-witness record of Woolson's last days and hours, which has remained in family hands. I am therefore deeply grateful to Molly Mather Anderson for allowing me to quote it in its entirety, and for bringing out various other precious items, the letters of 1894 and the contemporary 'Cuttings Book'.

Joan Weimer, together with Cheryl Torsney, Sharon Dean, and others, has led the revisionist interest in Woolson over the last twelve years. With her infectious enthusiasm for her subject, Joan Weimer has been immensely generous with information – to the extent of sending shoals of material across the Atlantic, including her research for a book. (It became a memoir, *Back Talk*, in which she recreates her own past through the mirror of Woolson's ordeals.) At the first meetings of the newly-formed Woolson Society in Florida and Michigan, I benefitted from excellent papers, including John Pearson on Woolson and James, 'Woolson and Her Publishers' by Cheryl Torsney, 'Language and Gender in Woolson's Short Fiction' by Trinna Frever, 'Woolson's Travel Writing' by Carolyn VanBergen-Rylander, and a lively presentation from the Purdue Nineteenth-Century Reading Group. The historian, Gladys Haddad, talked to me about the Mathers in Cleveland, and showed her documentary movie about Flora Stone Mather. There was a remarkable atmosphere of support, not least from Dr Kathleen J. Reich, the archivist of the Woolson papers and memorabilia at Rollins College. A special thanks to her for undertaking a journey to St Augustine, Florida, where (with advice from Jean Parker Waterbury of the St Augustine Historical Society) we followed Woolson's trail to her boarding house and along the wall of the fort. And I must thank her also for making me buy a thick pair of socks in view of a blizzard in New York. Gertrude F. Laframboise helped to make the archives at Rollins a welcoming place to work.

At the time I planned this book, in the summer of 1988, Gila Bercovitch came to stay at Saranac Lake in the Adirondacks. As the founding editor-in-chief of the Library of America, Gila was at that time seeing certain James volumes through the press, shaping every detail with her grasp – deep, individual, meticulous – of American writing. Her views of James family ideals, and of Alice James in particular, are part of this book. Even when Gila was very ill, in June 1997, she talked of Alice and 'Fenimore' with characteristic verve and conviction. Faith Williams another old friend from the 'wild' Columbia of the late sixties, gave me her witty poem on Henry James, diving for her heart of the matter with the bold simplicity of Emily Dickinson. Mark Bostridge, the biographer of Vera Brittain, sent two articles I had missed, and we continued to mull over the problems and possibilities of Lives. I am always stimulated by discussions on the nature of women with crime novelist Joan Smith and poet Carole Satyamurti. The novelist and critic, Stevie Davies, has written letters that speak with 'unbridled spirit' about the pacifist and feminist beliefs we share, while other writers, Eva Hoffman and Pamela Norris, offered influential opinions as readers of James. In Venice, my American aunt, Victoria de Luria Press, took me with her to the fabulous Palazzo Barbaro. Paola Martelli Penzo kindly invited me into her lovely home in what was once the Casa Semitecolo, and Cristina Giorcelli, head of American Studies at the University of Rome, who wrote the first full-length study of James and Italy, met for an animated exchange in October 1996.

Professor Steven H. Jobe of Hanover College, Indiana, sent his most recent print-out of his invaluable 'Calendar of Correspondence', a complete record of all known letters of Henry James. He also shared his transcriptions of Edel's notes on a multitude of James letters whose provenance was then unknown. In Cambridge, Massachusetts and again in Oxford, it was helpful to talk to Alfred Habegger, a born detective who has published new findings on James and Minny Temple, as well as his biography of Henry James senior. He kindly sent me relevant notes and his 1974 correspondence with Rosamond Gilder, the daughter of Helena de Kay.

Cambridge University has produced outstanding James scholars, notably Philip Horne (with his work on James and revision) and Tamara Follini (with her work on the *Autobiography*). It was Dr Follini who, at the outset, directed attention to the Civil War – this conversation, as it turned out, gave a central thread to the book, with the help of Charles and Tess Hoffmann's exploratory research.

Over the years at St Hilda's, I discussed James with many students, especially Dr Susan Jones who did an innovative thesis on Conrad and his understanding of the unknown aspect of women. There were fertile talks with Fozia Bora, Sushila Dhall, Theresa

Garnett, Amy Hing, Penelope Jowett, Jennifer Noon, and Alison Shell; and also, occasionally, with Dr Bernard Richards of Brasenose College, who gave the James lectures during his long stint at Oxford. I learnt much from Freddie Baveystock who included Cooper in his doctoral thesis on 'The Romance of Nationalism' in early nineteenth-century America.

With libraries, my main debt of course is to the Houghton Library at Harvard, the main repository for the James papers. Their William Dean Howells Visiting Fellowship for 1996–7 helped to make a lot of this work possible. Polly Howells, great-granddaughter of the novelist, came all the way from New York for a delightful day's visit. As always, the Reference Librarian, Susan Halpert, prompt and knowledgable, made the Houghton reading room an effective workplace, ably assisted by Melanie Wisner, Denison Beach, Thomas Ford, Jennie Rathbun, Emily Walhout, and Joseph Zajac, the stacks supervisor.

Thanks are also due to the following librarians: Mimi Bowling, Curator of Manuscripts in the New York Public Library, and John Stinson, Melanie Yolles, and Valerie Wingfield, Manuscripts Specialists; Philip N. Cronenwett, Curator of Manuscripts and Chief of Special Collections at Dartmouth College Library who photocopied a huge number of Curtis Papers; David de Lorenzo, Curator of Manuscripts and Archives in Harvard's Law School library, and Mary Person, the reading room supervisor; Patrice J. Donoghue and Brian A. Sullivan in Harvard Archives, Pusey Library; Anne Engelhart, Associate Curator of Manuscripts at the Schlesinger Library on the History of Women in America, Radcliffe College; Cathy Henderson, Research Librarian at the Harry Ransom Humanities Research Center of the University of Texas at Austin; Sara S. Hodson, Curator of Literary Manuscripts, the Huntington Library, California; James H. Hudson, chief of the Manuscript Division of the Library of Congress who took the trouble to do searches on the internet, and Robert R. Shields, Reference Specialist in the Rare Book Division; G. T. Johnson of Special Collections, C. W. Barrett Library of the University of Virginia at Charlottesville; Nancy S. MacKechnie, Curator of Rare Books and Manuscripts, Vassar College Libraries, and Elaine S.

Pike, Assistant; Robert E. Parks, Curator of Autograph Manuscripts, The Pierpont Morgan Library, New York who kindly made a microfilm of the Henry James letters on deposit, and Ms Du Pont in the reading room; Rodney Phillips, Curator at the Berg Collection in the New York Public Library, and once again, Philip Milito; Kermit J. Pike, Director of the Western Reserve Historical Society, who faxed an enlarged image of a letter I had been unable to decipher, Ann Sindelar, the Reference Supervisor, and Barbara Billings, a terrific Reference Assistant; Katherine E. Pinkham, ex-Curator of Beverly Historical Society; Henry Rowan in Rare Books and Manuscripts in Butler Library, Columbia University; Colin Sanborn, President of the Claremont, NH, Historical Society; Margaret M. Sherry, Archivist, Rare Books and Special Collections, Princeton; Wayne Wright, Associate Director, Research Library of the New York State Historical Association at Cooperstown who found the photo of Henrietta Pell-Clarke, and the librarian, Amy Barnum; and finally, Valerie Mitchell of the Miller Library, Colby College, Maine, for photocopies of Perry papers. Ellen Cohn helped with Bay Emmet.

In 1990 in Cambridge, Massachusetts, George Abbot White allowed me to stay in the Matthiessen Room in Eliot House, Harvard, while I was working at the Houghton Library. In Cape Town, Barbara and Jeff Fisher let me use their sunny flat as a workplace in July-August 1996. In Oxford, Danuta Garton Ash advised on the first chapter, and Laurence Turley did final printouts, while Christine Holt gave practical help. In St Augustine, Eugenie Wedyck sent a photo of the Fatio House; and in Newport, RI, George Perry had photos made of nineteenth-century landscapes in his collection.

It is fortunate for a biographer to be edited by so admirable a biographer as Jenny Uglow: her gently persuasive and well-judged comments were appreciated, as was the incisive editing of Alane Mason in New York: both understood what I was trying to do, and provoked a transforming revision. Neither of course is responsible for what flaws remain. At Chatto, Eugenie Boyd took the book through its schedules with easy efficiency.

This book has been the favourite of my husband, Siamon Gordon. For some reason, he liked this one from the start, and since I trust his honesty, his encouragement helped me to go on. He read every draft, and my gratitude for his assurance is, to steal a James word, 'unspeakable'.

Index